H. G. Adler

H. G. Adler

A Life in Many Worlds

PETER FILKINS

OXFORD
UNIVERSITY PRESS

OXFORD
UNIVERSITY PRESS

Oxford University Press is a department of the University of Oxford. It furthers the University's objective of excellence in research, scholarship, and education by publishing worldwide. Oxford is a registered trademark of Oxford University Press in the UK and certain other countries.

Published in the United States of America by Oxford University Press
198 Madison Avenue, New York, NY 10016, United States of America.

Library of Congress Cataloging-in-Publication Data
Names: Filkins, Peter, author.
Title: H. G. Adler : a life in many worlds / Peter Filkins.
Description: New York City : Oxford University Press, [2018] |
Includes bibliographical references and index.
Identifiers: LCCN 2018018276 (print) | LCCN 2018022226 (ebook) |
ISBN 9780190222390 (updf) | ISBN 9780190222406 (epub) |
ISBN 9780190222383 (alk. paper)
Subjects: LCSH: Adler, H. G. | Authors, German—20th century—Biography.
Classification: LCC PT2601.D614 (ebook) |
LCC PT2601.D614 Z54 2018 (print) | DDC 833/.914 [B]—dc23
LC record available at https://lccn.loc.gov/2018018276

1 3 5 7 9 8 6 4 2

Printed by Sheridan Books, Inc., United States of America

to Paul Taunton
who saw it all
&
to Susan, Malina, and Isabel
who saw it through

CONTENTS

ACKNOWLEDGMENTS

First and foremost, I wish to thank Jeremy Adler for his patient counsel, many questions and suggestions, guidance on and permission to use archival materials, detailed response to each chapter, and many hours of interviews and conversation. The world owes him a great debt of gratitude for keeping his father's memory and work alive. I also wish to thank his wife, Eva, for her kind welcome in their home on several occasions.

My thanks to the Deutsches Literaturarchiv—Marbach (DLA) for permission to quote and reprint from Adler's archive, as well as to its excellent staff, especially Heidrun Fink, Thomas Kemme, Hildegard Dieke, and Rosemarie Kutschis, for their kind and professional service. In addition, I am grateful to the director of the DLA, Ulrich Raulff, as well as Ulrich von Bülow and Marcel Lepper, for their support, and for several Marbach Fellowships that helped fund my stay and research.

I am also grateful to Bard College at Simon's Rock and Bard College for a sabbatical and leave from teaching, as well as several Faculty Development Awards. I am deeply thankful for a fellowship year spent at the Leon Levy Center for Biography at the CUNY Graduate Center, as well as to the National Endowment for the Humanities for a Fellowship to complete the first draft. Further critical funding also came from a DAAD Faculty Research Grant, as well as a grant from the Österreichische Gesellschaft für Literatur to support my translation of Adler's poems.

For interviews in which they shared reminiscences and expertise about H. G. Adler, I wish to thank the following: Yehuda Bacon, Ivan Ivanji, Otto Dov Kulka, Peter Demetz, Manfred and Gudrun Sundermann, Werner and Christiane Sundermann, Wolfgang Schwarzhaupt, Carlo Caratsch, Fred Kurer, Gian Nogler, Derek Bolton, Sylvia Finzi, Henry Shapiro, Friedrich Danielis, Susan Salm, and Ursula Oppens. I also must thank Peter Demetz for the gift of several books on Prague. I am indebted to Ulrich van Loyen for a discussion of Adler and the life and work of Franz Baermann Steiner, to Ellen Fauser for a tour of Langenstein-Zwieberge, to Wolfgang Grosse for a tour of Niederorschel, to Peter Brod for a tour of Prague, and to Peter Carpenter for a tour of Merthyr Tydfil and South Wales.

For further archival help I wish to thank Tomáš Federovič at the Ghetto Museum at Terezín; Magda Veselská, Michal Frankl, and Martin Jelínek at the Jewish Museum in Prague; Lenka Matušíková, Vlasta Měšťánková, and Marie Malá at the Prague National Archives; Jan Skoda and Jan Cihak of the Prague City Archives; Tereza Pošvec Matyášová at the Prague City Registry; Eva Wichsová at the Jewish Community of Prague; Alfons Adam at the Institüt Theresienstädter Initiativ for his discussion of and expertise on the Prague Urania; Sabine Wolf and Helga Neumann at the Akademie der Künste in Berlin; Galia Weisman and Alice Baron at the Israel State Archives; Diana Manipud and Adam Cox at the Kings College London Archives; Marieke Zoodsma at the Institute for War, Holocaust, and Genocide Studies (NIOD) in Amsterdam; and Karin Fleisch at the Literaturhaus Vienna, Petra Witting at the Archive of the *Westdeutscher* Rundfunk, and Tobias Fasora at the Sudwestrundfunk.

I have also benefited greatly from ongoing discussion of Adler's work with many colleagues whose writing and thinking on Adler has informed this book, including Marcel Atze, Belinda Cooper, Julia Creet, Helen Finch, Franz Hocheneder, Sara R. Horowitz, Katrin Kohl, Sven Kramer, Amy Loewenhaar-Blauweiss, Jürgen Serke, Ruth Vogel-Klein, and Lynn L. Wolff. For their reading and commentary on several chapters, I thank Gary Giddins, Bernie Rodgers, Lawrence L. Langer, Thomas Ort, Thomas Kohut, and especially Michael Gately for his careful editing of the entire manuscript. For the transcription of handwritten letters I am also grateful to Dorothee Callanan and Ingrid MacGillis, and I wish to thank my colleagues Chris Callanan and Laurence Wallach for their conversation and insight over many years.

Sarah Whittier provided a wonderful home away from home during my fellowship at the CUNY Graduate Center; Werner, Christiane, Manfred, and Gudrun Sundermann were kind enough to host me in Cologne and Münster; and Gary Smith arranged for me to stay at the American Academy in Berlin while doing research at the Akademie der Künste.

Lastly, I wish to thank all of the editors I have had the pleasure to work with on Adler over the years: Paul Taunton, Lindsey Schwoeri, and Sam Nicholson at Random House, and Brendan O'Neill and Norman Hirschy at Oxford.

ABBREVIATIONS

Published Works by H. G. Adler

AW	*Andere Wege: Gesammelte Gedichte*, ed. Katrin Kohl and Franz Hocheneder, with Jeremy Adler (Klagenfurt: Drava, 2010)
AZB	*Auschwitz: Zeugnisse und Berichte*, ed. H. G. Adler, Hermann Langbein, and Ella Lingens-Reiner (Frankfurt: Europäische Verlagsanstalt, 1962)
DPS	*Die Dichtung der Prager Schule* (Wuppertal: Coll'Arco, 2010)
FM	*Die Freiheit des Menschens* (Tübingen: J.C.B. Mohr, 1976).
FS	*Der Fürst des Segens. Parabeln—Betrachtungen—Gleichnisse* (Bonn: Bibliotheca Christiana, 1964)
J	*The Journey*, trans. Peter Filkins (New York: Random, 2008)
KV	*Kontraste und Variationen* (Würzburg: Echter, 1969)
NB	*Nach der Befreiung: Ausgewählte Essays zur Geschichte und Soziologie*, ed. Peter Filkins, with Jeremy Adler (Paderborn: Konstanz UP, 2013)
OH	*Orthodoxie des Herzens: Ausgewählte Essays zur Literatur, Judentum und Politik*, ed. Peter Filkins, with Jeremy Adler (Paderborn: Konstanz UP, 2014)
P	*Panorama*, trans. Peter Filkins (New York: Random House, 2011)
SU	*Sodoms Untergang* (Bonn: Bibliotheca Christiana, 1965)
T	*Theresienstatdt 1941–1945: Das Antlitz einer Zwangsgemeinschaft*, reprint of 2nd ed., 1960 (Göttingen: Wallstein, 2005). All quotes and citations are from *Theresienstadt 1941–1945: The Face of a Coerced Community*, trans. Belinda Cooper (New York: Cambridge UP, 2017)
UG	*Unser Georg und andere Geschichten* (Vienna: Bergland, 1961)
VM	*Der verwaltete Mensch: Studien zur Deportation der Juden aus Deutschland* (Tübingen: J.C.B. Mohr, 1974)

W *The Wall*, trans. Peter Filkins (New York: Random House, 2014)
WV *Der Wahrheit verpflichtet: Interviews, Gedichte, Essays*, ed. Jeremy Adler (Geringen: Bleicher Verlag, 1998)

Adler's Chief Correspondents

LB Letter to Bettina Gross, or later Bettina Adler
LFBS Letter to Franz Baermann Steiner
LFK Letter to Franz Kobler
LFW Letter to Franz Wurm
LG Letter to Gertrud Klepetar
LHL Letter to Hermann Langbein
LHS Letter to Hans Siebeck
LKE Letter to Knut Erichson
LLW Letter to Luzzi Wolgensinger
LTWA Letter to Theodor W. Adorno
LWB Letter to Wolfgang Burghart, October 17, 1947
LWU Letter to Wilhelm Unger, May 10, 1950
LYB Letter to Yehuda Bacon

In return, *LHGA* signifies a letter written to H. G. Adler, the author of which is named in the body of the text or in the endnote.

Other Abbreviations

BB Jeremy Adler, *Das bittere Brot: H. G. Adler, Elias Canetti und Franz Baermann Steiner im Londoner Exil* (Göttingen: Wallstein, 2015)
BF *H. G. Adler: Buch der Freunde*, ed. Willehad Eckart and Wilhelm Unger (Cologne: Wienand Verlag, 1975)
HBHGA "Hermann Broch and H. G. Adler: The Correspondence of Two Writers in Exile," trans. Ronald Speirs, ed. John J. White and Ronald Speirs, in *Comparative Criticism* 21 (London: Cambridge UP, 1999)
OB Marcel Atze, *"Ortlose Botschaft": Der Freundeskreis H. G. Adler, Elias Canetti, und Franz Baermann Steiner im englischen Exil, Marbacher Magazin* 84 (Marbach: Deutsche Schillergesellschaft, 1998)
PFS Franz Hocheneder, *H. G. Adler (1910–1988), Privatgelehrter und freier Schriftsteller* (Vienna: Böhlau, 2009)

S Jürgen Serke, "H. G. Adler: Der versteinerte Jüngling, der ein weiser Mann wurde," in Jürgen Serke, *Böhmische Dörfer: Wanderungen durch eine verlassene literarische Landschaft* (Vienna: Zsolnay, 1987), 327–343

ZE *Zu Hause im Exil: Zu Werk und Person H. G. Adlers*, ed. Heinrich Hubmann and Alfred O. Lanz (Stuttgart: Franz Steiner Verlag Wiesbaden, 1987)

ZV *Zeugen der Vergangenheit: H. G. Adler—Franz Baermann Steiner Briefwechsel 1936–1952*, ed. Carol Tully (Munich: Iudicium, 2011)

NOTE ON SOURCES

DLA—This designates a manuscript, document, or letter located in the H. G. Adler Archive, Deutsches Literaturarchiv, Marbach-am-Neckar, Germany. Any material not so designated, and without archival designation, can also be found there. Smaller but important Adler archives exist at the Institute for War, Holocaust, and Genocide Studies (NIOD) in Amsterdam, the Kings College London Archives, and the Beinecke Library at Yale University. Other archives consulted are listed in the acknowledgments.

I have read, admired, and learned from the four main biographical works to appear on Adler to date: Jürgen Serke's 1987 profile in his book, *Böhmische Dörfer: Wanderungen durch eine verlassene literarische Landschaft*, Marcel Atze's 1998 *"Ortlose Botschaft": Der Freundeskreis H. G. Adler, Elias Canetti, und Franz Baermann Steiner im englischen Exil*, Franz Hocheneder's *H. G. Adler (1910–1988), Privatgelehrter und freier Schriftsteller*, published in 2009, and Jeremy Adler's *Das bittere Brot: H. G. Adler, Elias Canetti und Franz Baermann Steiner im Londoner Exil* of 2015. Unless otherwise noted, all accounts, facts, and quotes cited I have researched and verified on my own.

All letters, poems, excerpts from Adler's fiction and essays, reviews of his work, and critical comments on it have been translated by me from German, except for quotes from Belinda Cooper's English translation of *Theresienstadt 1941–1945* and those spoken, written, or published in English, as noted. Titles of works are initially given in German, followed by an English translation in parentheses, after which the text utilizes the English translation of the title. In regards to the poems, rather than a translation aimed at conveying formal meter and rhyme, I have sought more literal renderings that convey the content of the poem while also trying to be sensitive to expressive nuance.

H. G. Adler

1

The Lecture

The note is small. A thin piece of paper, brown with age, of obviously poor quality, though the words typed on it remain firm, black, and clear:

TEREZÍN

Franz KAFKA
60 Jahre.Wer ist K? Dichter,Denker,Träumer.Der religiöse u.philosophische Mensch.Die Entwicklung,das Milieu.Vorbilder u.Vergleiche,der Stil,die Einmaligkeit,die romantische Tragödie.K und seine Zeit - sein Gegensatz zu aller Mode.Nicht Phantast,nicht"interessant".Besprechung des Prozess.Die Wirkungen und Nachwirkungen.Das Zeitlose:K als Symbol des leidenden Menschen dieser Zeit für den es einen Ausweg nicht gibt. Die Versöhnung durch den Tod.

der Erzählungen

Adler's lecture note on Kafka in Theresienstadt. Credit: The Estate of H. G. Adler 2019, Deutsches Literaturarchiv Marbach.

<u>Franz KAFKA</u>
60 years. Who is K? Writer, thinker, dreamer. The religious and the philosophical person. His development, the milieu. Influences and comparisons, the style, the uniqueness, the tragic romance. K. and his times – his resistance to all fashion. Not fantastic, not "interesting". Discussion of [the stories] The Trial. Their effects and aftermath. The

timeless: K. as symbol of the suffering human of these times for whom no way out exists. Atonement through death.

Then the notation. Upper left corner, written in pencil, likely many years later: TEREZÍN. The Czech name for Theresienstadt, the enforced ghetto set up by the Nazis, who promised lifelong care and safety to Jews who signed over their apartments and worldly goods to them. Soon Theresienstadt would also become a center for deportations to the death camps of the East. Of the 141,000 who arrived on transports before April 20, 1945, less than one-sixth survived the war, while of the roughly 88,000 deported from Theresienstadt before November 1, 1944 (when the deportations ended), only 3,500 survived. Hans Günther Adler was one of them.[1]

It was here of all places that Adler, who had just turned thirty-three the previous day, stood to give a lecture on July 3, 1943, in honor of what would have been Kafka's sixtieth birthday to about one hundred people in "Barracks B V," known as the "Magdeburg Barracks." Among the audience was Kafka's younger (and favorite) sister Ottla, known affectionately as Ottilie, who at the conclusion of the lecture said to Adler, "I thank you on behalf of our family," no doubt still missing the brother she had lost to tuberculosis in 1924.[2] Since the Nazis had banned and burned his books, it is likely one of the few lectures, if not the only one, delivered on Kafka in the German-occupied countries of the time.

The lecture proved so successful Adler repeated it ten days later to a smaller group in the "House of the Fire Brigade, L 502," though then without being introduced by Emil Utitz, the Prague academic, schoolmate of Kafka, and co-founder, with Rabbi Leo Baeck, of the "Office for Leisure Time Activities" in Theresienstadt. A month later Adler wrote to Utitz that he would be prepared to give lectures on Jean Paul, Friedrich Hölderlin, Heinrich von Kleist, Christian Dietrich Grabbe, Georg Büchner, and Kafka, as well as to talk on art and literature. Utitz took him up on his offer to give lectures on "The Baroque and the Modern," "Literature in the Present Age," "Jews in German Literature," "The Modern in Art," and "Idealism, Naturalism and Realism in Art."[3] Along with the Kafka talk, six lectures survive in manuscript, three typed as essays, the other three existing as notes.

Yet it is the note for the Kafka lecture, no doubt held by Adler during the talk, which still attracts one's attention. In Adler's archive it is in a small envelope marked "Original note with key words for the lecture delivered twice by HGA in the summer of 1943 in honor of Kafka's 60th birthday." "HGA" is of course Hans Günther Adler, born in Prague in 1910. Because of one of many twists of fate that ruled Adler's life, he would only use "H. G. Adler" as his pen name.

The thought of perpetuating the name of Hans Günther, head of the Central Office for Jewish Emigration in Bohemia and Moravia, and just seven weeks younger was too much to bear, for *that* Günther, who reported directly to Adolf Eichmann, had deported Adler to Theresienstadt on February 8, 1942. After surviving thirty-two months there, as well as six months divided between Auschwitz, a neighboring camp of Buchenwald called Niederorschel, and two months in an underground factory for airplane parts called Langenstein, Adler chose to erase "Hans Günther" from his public name for the rest of his life.

Though the note on Kafka reveals little of what Adler said about each of his points, one page marked "KAFKA-NOTES" and two more headed "Kafka" provide some quotes from his work and fleeting comments, such as "One must wait for the right moment to understand Kafka, one must feel the same as he does inside, and be in the same place as he is." Was Theresienstadt such a place? Undoubtedly. Adler said of it:

> In Auschwitz, there was only pure despair or an inexorable awareness of the game. Even if a spark of indestructible vitality remained, even if the soul fled, through some transformative magic, into sweeter self-deception (*holder Trug*), still reality had to be seen; no one could really fool themselves. It was different in Theresienstadt, where illusion proliferated and hope, only slightly subdued by feelings of fear, outshone everything else, which was concealed beneath an impenetrable fog. In no other camp had the true face of the times retreated to such a remote distance from the inmates. . . . The truth only occasionally arose out of the darkness, touched people, and then, after a moment of terror, allowed them to fall back into their masked existence.[4]

Yet reality had a way of reminding the inmates just where they were, often in a cruel manner. After eighteen months in Theresienstadt, Adler felt the precariousness of each day. The notion of the "timeless" or the idea of "K. as symbol of the suffering human of these times for whom no way out exists" must have moved his audience in ways we cannot understand. As for "Atonement through death," Ottilie soon came to know herself whether it was to be. Three months later she volunteered as one of 53 caretakers for the 1,260 children who arrived in Theresienstadt from the Bialystok ghetto in August 1943.[5] Writing joyfully to her ex-husband, Joseph David, an "Aryan" whom she was forced to divorce in order to protect their two daughters from deportation, she thought she and the Bialystok children were headed to Sweden or Denmark.[6] Only after their departure by train on October 5, 1943, did they learn their destination was Auschwitz.

Peter Kien: Portrait of Dr. H. G. Adler. Credit: PT 9887, Terezín Memorial.

As Adler noted to his audience on that July day just three months before Ottilie's deportation, the painter Titorelli reminds Josef K. in *The Trial*:

> In an actual acquittal, the files relating to the case are completely discarded, they disappear totally from the proceedings, not only the charge, but the trial and even the acquittal are destroyed, everything is destroyed. An apparent acquittal is handled differently. There is no further change in the files except for adding to them the certification of innocence, the acquittal, and the grounds for the acquittal. Otherwise they remain in circulation; following the law court's normal routine they are passed on to the higher courts, come back to the lower ones, swinging back and forth with larger or smaller oscillations, longer or shorter interruptions. . . . One day—quite unexpectedly—some judge or other takes a closer look at the file, realizes that the case is still active, and orders an immediate arrest.[7]

To this K. asks incredulously, "And the trial begins all over again?"[8] It in fact did for Adler. Almost a year to the day of Ottilie's departure, Adler and his wife, Gertrud Klepetar, were deported to Auschwitz along with her mother on October 12, 1944. Arriving two days later, Gertrud decided to join her mother on "the bad side" when she was selected, the thought of her mother dying alone being simply too much to bear. Adler, however, was not selected and made it through. Gertrud and her mother perished.

"Atonement through death"? Perhaps. Yet what about the living? One need only read the dedication to Adler's book on Theresienstadt to consider how much the loss of Gertrud, whom he called "Geraldine," haunted him:

FOR GERALDINE, AS A MEMORIAL.
GERALDINE, DR. GERTRUD ADLER-KLEPETAR, BORN ON DECEMBER 9, 1905, IN PRAGUE, MURDERED BY GASSING AND INCINERATED ON OCTOBER 14, 1944, IN AUSCHWITZ-BIRKENAU,
ALONG WITH HER MOTHER.

FOR THIRTY-TWO MONTHS AND AT THE LIMITS OF HER ENORMOUS STRENGTH, SHE GAVE HER ALL IN THERESIENSTADT FOR HER FAMILY, FOR MANY FRIENDS, AND FOR COUNTLESS AFFLICTED.

TIRELESSLY, SHE SACRIFICED HERSELF. IT IS FOR HER MOTHER THAT SHE WENT TO HER DEATH.
IN HER, HUMAN DIGNITY DAILY CELEBRATED THE VICTORY OF HUMILITY OVER THE THREATS FROM IGNOMINY.[9]

As if carving the memorial on a tombstone, Adler resolved that the shame of Gertrud's horrible end would outlive her. It would take over a decade for the book to see the light of day.

After surviving Auschwitz, Niederorschel, and Langenstein, Adler returned to Prague in June 1945, barely alive. There he wrote to his boyhood friend Franz Baermann Steiner, a poet and anthropologist who had escaped to England, saying, "I am the only one of my family and my wife's family to have survived this terrible dream." He then informed him that Steiner's parents were deported to certain death in Treblinka in October 1942.[10] A few weeks later Adler returned to Theresienstadt to retrieve from Leo Baeck the black briefcase full of documents he had collected on the camp, many of them passed on by Gertrud through her position as head of the infirmary and then hidden in her lab.[11] With these were over one hundred poems he wrote there, as well as the manuscript for an experimental theology he had started as early as 1938, the first draft of a novel, and notes to his lectures. From this material would come the next forty years of his writing and thinking.

Adler took all of it with him eighteen months later when he left for England in February 1947. There he was met by Bettina Gross, a childhood friend who had left Prague at his urging in 1938. Her mother remained behind, was imprisoned in Theresienstadt, and gassed in Auschwitz after being deported there three days before Adler and Gertrud on October 9, 1944. As with Steiner, Adler felt compelled to find Bettina and write to her to report her mother's death and to find out if she was still single. Ironically, after seven years of separation their first letters to one another crossed in the mail in November 1945, Bettina having heard through a friend that Adler was alive and in Prague. Soon they were writing to one another each day, sometimes twice a day. Adler eventually told Bettina of his own ordeal and admitted, "I am like someone who, despite all expectations, has risen from his deathbed and feels strong once again, even if he still stumbles around in a daze. Would it not be better for me to say nothing at all?"[12]

But speak he did, pouring himself into letter after letter before proposing marriage to Bettina by mail two months later. She accepted immediately, yet it took another year to arrange a visa for him. At last Adler flew to London on February 11, 1947. Five days later he and Bettina were married in Merthyr Tydfil, South Wales, where during the war Bettina had worked as a designer in a button factory. Soon they moved to London, where Adler reunited with Steiner and Elias Canetti, whom he had met when Canetti visited Prague in 1937, as well as joining a circle of postwar German exiles that included Erich Fried and George Rapp. Work was hard to come by, and further income was needed when that fall his son Jeremy was born, but Adler refused to take any kind of menial job, choosing instead to work feverishly on the Theresienstadt study. Over the next nine years, he spent long hours of research in London's Wiener Library while also writing six novels, dozens of short stories and parables, and some two hundred poems.

Yet had Adler indeed left Theresienstadt and the camps, or did they remain forever with him? The answer might lie in Kafka's brief story "The Next Village," which Adler read in its entirety as part of the Theresienstadt lecture:

> My grandfather was fond of saying: "Life is so very short. Looking back on it now, I find it all blurs together so in memory that I can hardly comprehend, for instance, how a young man can ride over to the next village without being afraid that—terrible mishaps notwithstanding—even the span of a normal happy life is not nearly long enough for such a journey."

A meditation on life's uncanny and perilous journey, the story reflects how Adler's trajectory seems as fated as it was chosen. The only way forward was indeed the way back, and it was at that crossroads that Adler remained—the survivor, the scholar, the writer, the husband and father who, penniless, hungry, and without a job wrote across a page of his pocket calendar on February 9, 1952, a single question: "Was ist geistige Arbeit?" ("What is intellectual work?"). Three days later the daily entries ceased. Only after the publication of the Theresienstadt book brought him a glimmer of fame and modest security do they begin again in 1956, and continue until his death in 1988.

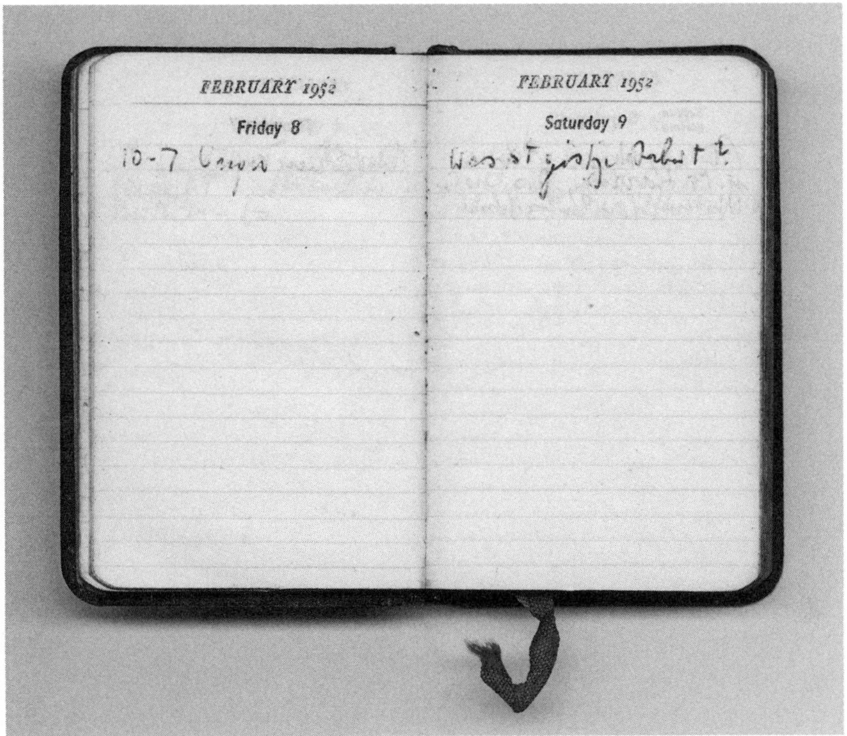

Adler's pocket calendar for February 8 and 9, 1952. Credit: The Estate of H. G. Adler 2019, Deutsches Literaturarchiv Marbach.

What could Adler have meant by the question? Was he wondering why he had spent the previous day sorting and cataloging books for the German Library in London for Wilhelm Unger, as he had once sorted libraries stolen from Jews by the Nazis and deposited with the Jewish Community of Prague, where Kafka's own library passed through his fingers? Was he asking himself what the work of the intellect really consists of? Was he wondering whether scholarship or literature was the proper way to convey what he had been through? Was he wondering about the worth of his own work, or the worth of any such work to anyone? Or was he wondering whether any of it was worth the price he had to pay?

The answer is impossible to know. Given that the previous day, February 8, 1952, marked the tenth anniversary of his deportation to Theresienstadt, the question takes on more gravity, especially when he observes on February 10, "5 years in England. No success at all the entire time!" Then, on February 12, Adler attends a performance of the Ralph Vaughan Williams opera "The Pilgrim's Progress" with Elias and Veza Canetti. The burden of his own journey shows in the fact that the calendar ends there, even though his fifth wedding anniversary followed on the 16th. Without a publisher and feeling himself a failure, bereft of a career and with no prospects, the silence that ensued testifies to a life and mind held in the clutches of "Terezín."

2

The Exile

Toward the end of his life, nearly forty years after leaving Prague for London, H. G. Adler observed that he was "at home in exile, and exile is my home." Despite the duress of war and the penury of postwar life in England, he added that "emotionally, I had already experienced the feeling of exile even in my childhood."[1] Like all exiles, Adler never completely left his native city, for it remained the "spiritual foundation" of his life, but the foundation that nurtured and informed his work was built from the start on shifting sands.

Invited to contribute a "Living Obituary" to a 1970 anthology, Adler wrote that he grew up in a Jewish household but that "hardly anything to do with Judaism was present in the house"; the home was infused more with a "mildly progressive humanism" than any religion.[2] Curiously, he mentions by name neither his father, Emil, nor his mother, Alice Fraenkel, as though even in birth he stands alone, cut off from them by channels of time. Instead, he notes that by seven he began to write stories and poems, only later appreciating writing as a means to "urgently, continually speak." For Adler, to "write" was to "indite" in the old sense of the word—to set down on paper what happened—rather than the legal term for a formal accusation.[3] Writing set Adler's life in motion as much as his upbringing did, and in his own obituary Adler stands at an oblique angle to his life to observe its scope, its essence, and between the lines to invoke the spirit that allowed him to endure what he had and make of it what he could.

In the opening lines Adler sets down the essential elements of his life:

> H. G. Adler was born in 1910 in Prague in the last years of the Habsburg Empire as Franz Kafka began to forge his unique art. "H. G." stands for "Hans Günther," these being the names of two of his mother's brothers who died young. However, without wishing to betray his mother or her brothers, he never used these names officially, for Hans Günther was the name of Adolf Eichmann's deputy in the "Protectorate of Bohemia and Moravia" from 1939 to 1945.[4]

Literary roots stretching back to Kafka. A family tragedy that generated the names he would bear. And history's black veil obliterating the names themselves, so that, like Kafka's "K.", he would be known to the world by his initials, though close friends and family called him "Günther." As an adult, he found it meaningful that his July 2 birthday fell one day before Kafka's and was the same as Friedrich Klopstock's, the eighteenth-century poet on whom he wrote his dissertation. But Adler was thirty-one when he entered Theresienstadt in 1942, and the fact that he says he "never" used his forenames in public almost erases his life prior to Theresienstadt, as if his later fear that he had become known as "Theresienstadt Adler" was not only true but inevitable.

On his father's side Adler was descended from generations of Jews who lived in the Bohemian countryside. His grandfather David was a restless man who worked as a stationer, printer, and publisher of the theater newspaper *Theater-Zwischen-Acts-Zeitung* and was a calligrapher granted the title of "Professor" by Emperor Franz Joseph in recognition of his skill as a teacher in the schools. After leaving the countryside for Prague, he became a fan of opera and befriended the impresario Angelo Neumann, who staged celebrated productions of Wagner operas, helped bring Gustav Mahler to Prague as a guest conductor, and championed the city as a cultural hub of German-speaking Europe.[5] As a father, however, David was quick-tempered and impatient and loved only the eldest daughter, ignoring his five other children from two marriages, including Adler's father, Emil, born in 1882, a year before Kafka, with whom he attended elementary school. Emil followed in his father's footsteps, taking over the family stationery and bookbinding business in Prague, run primarily by Adler's grandmother Paula Gröger after David Adler's early death in 1896. She was the only grandparent Adler knew, as his maternal grandmother died before he was born, and his maternal grandfather died in 1911 from injuries in a traffic accident. Adler remembered Paula as a small, brave, tough, and hardworking woman, who before her senile old age possessed a love of truth so deep that it could descend into rudeness. She was unafraid to speak her mind, a trait inherited by Adler that he would recognize as his boon and bane.[6]

Adler's lineage is more complicated on his mother's side. While his father's family came from Bohemia, family legend had it that the Fraenkels were descended from a great-great-grandfather who was a Russian aristocrat, but not Jewish; his name does not survive, nor does that of the great-great-grandmother. Exiled to Siberia, he apparently left behind his only son, adopted by a Jewish cobbler named Fraenkel, who moved to Prussia and from whom the orphaned son adopted the family name and religion. He worked as a tailor and had several children, including a son, Isidor Fraenkel, who started a printing business in Sorau (Żary, Poland). There Isidor married Martha Harmuth, who was Christian, although she converted to Judaism before marriage, a common practice in the nineteenth century. The couple moved to Berlin, and Isidor fought in the Franco-Prussian War of 1870–1871 before turning to journalism. He covered the railroads and their burgeoning growth, and he eventually represented the Federation of Railroads, the only attorney without a law degree allowed to argue before Germany's supreme court. He continued to write and publish in newspapers and was elected to a highly esteemed society of writers, for which he traveled throughout Europe. Substantial wealth and respect garnered over a long career, however, could not prevent the tragedy of losing his sons, Hans and Günther, who died in childhood. In addition to daughter Alice, two other sons reached adulthood. His son Herbert, who married Emil Adler's sister Ada long before Emil and Alice met, was a successful journalist, as well as an amateur poet and dramatist, and H. G. Adler took pride in the fact that both sides of his family demonstrated literary talent.

Adler's religious lineage is less clear than his literary lineage. He described Alice's mother as "nicht jüdisch," though he later said that she had converted before marriage.[7] Alice herself received only Protestant religious instruction at school, and after her marriage to Emil attended Catholic services with Günther in tow if only because of her deep love of organ music. At twelve Günther was baptized as a Protestant with his father, a common practice, although the Catholic Church held a far greater majority in the Habsburg Empire.[8] In 1925, Alice wrote to her son from Berlin, urging him to study for his confirmation with Pastor Zilcher, who had baptized him, and whom she had known for sixteen years. In another note she applauds Günther's "enthusiasm for lovely 'Jesu,' which I share entirely." However, given that after 1920 Alice was under constant care and frequent institutionalization for bipolar disorder, it is hard to know if the son's "enthusiasm" was to cheer his ill mother, or a real legacy from her. Emil felt compelled to write to his son in 1922 that "there is no need for grandmother to know about" the baptism, so one can surmise that it was not embraced by the Jewish side of the family.[9]

Both Hanukkah and Christmas were celebrated in the Adler household, young Günther receiving half his gifts on each. Adler nevertheless felt that religion played no role at home and that "as a spiritual essence or as an important system of values for my upbringing Judaism did not exist as such in either my parents' house, my extended family, or the compass of my childhood."[10] He recalled shock and amusement when his first-grade religion instructor asked, "Christian or Jew?", and he had no idea what to answer. Because of his family name and appearance, he was deemed a Jew. The haggadic legends fueled his young imagination, and though he claimed to his religion teacher that the story of Adam and Eve was a fiction ("Aunt Gisa told me so!"), he demanded to be taken to temple. A change in religion teachers in the third grade ended his early education in Judaism. Adler later noted cryptically that there was "no one around who could prevent the quick decline of that first feeble flowering, in fact quite the opposite . . ."

Interweavings of religion and ethnicity were not unique in turn-of-the-century Prague, which along with the overwhelming Catholic majority contained cadres of Protestants, German-speaking Jews, ethnic Germans, Czechs, and Czech-speaking Jews, all of whom sought upward mobility amid shifting grounds of national, religious, and class identity and the social tensions that came with them. Heightened by competition amid a burgeoning economy and the longing for an independent Czech state after World War I, distrust and resentment deepened between the Germans and the Czechs. The Germans felt they were the inheritors of the high culture of the Habsburgs, which they brought to the uneducated Slavs, whereas the Czechs thought of themselves as the champions of democracy and a pluralistic society.[11] Jews were caught somewhere in between. The overwhelming majority identified with German language and culture, and the Czechs initially did not blame them for doing so, even though it set the Jews on the side of their German adversaries. The Germans, however, resented the Jews for not supporting vigorously their own urge to maintain a strong hand in governance, leading many Jews to become more chauvinistic in valuing all things German. Czechs often saw Jews as rivals, many Germans did not consider them to be fully German, and the Jews were left to fend for themselves.[12]

Adler recalled, "Those better off—and amongst them especially the educated—were often only Jewish in name and saw themselves even more than in Kafka's youth as liberal, sometimes even social-democrat Germans, which is how they were perceived for the most part by the German Christians in Prague. The Jews could take heart from this, for anti-Semitism was very rare amongst the Germans in Prague, whilst in wider Czech circles, Jews and Germans were simply seen as one and the same, and the more anti-German they were, then the more anti-Semitic too."[13] Such prejudice erupted into attacks upon Jews and their businesses and sensational trials involving accusations of blood libel murder, lacing the cultural air with an anxiety breathed by all.[14] For Czechs, and even Czech-speaking Jews, many of whom chose to speak Czech as fellow patriots in the hope of fostering Czech independence, the German-speaking Jews of Bohemia and Prague represented the greatest affront to their evolving Czech identity. A classmate of Kafka who attended a primary school near Prague's meat market with Emil Adler remembered walking "past the hanging pieces of meat, and on the left, opposite the butchers' shops, we passed a Czech Volksschule, at the entrance of which there was a quotation from Comenius: 'A Czech child belongs in a Czech school,' and then on the right there was our school."[15] Over two decades later, Adler would experience such antagonism firsthand

"It was inevitable," he wrote, "that both German-speaking and Czech-speaking students encountered each other on the way to school, the Czechs by far being in the majority. The Czech boys, especially the older ones, ambushed the German youths who already walked in groups as a precautionary measure, throwing stones and rotten vegetables at them, hitting them and pricking them with needles, and causing serious wounds. The victims, who were showered with epithets such as 'Stinking Jew! Stinking German!,' could only attempt to flee, for they were hardly in the position to fend off their attackers."[16]

Nor were such attacks the product of mere childhood rivalries, for at their heart was the poisonous valuation of "blood" over "culture" that would set in motion Europe's great cataclysm.[17] In one skirmish Kafka's friend Oskar Baum was blinded as a boy, and Kafka later observed the paradox that "The Jew Oskar Baum lost his sight as a German. As something which in fact he never was, and which he was never accepted as being."[18] On the other hand, Czechoslovakia may have been where such tensions had the best chance of being worked out peacefully. Prague was a German-Jewish "island" amid the receding tide of German-liberal hegemony that upheld the cultural values of the Habsburg Empire, and a Czech populace that had begun to advocate for independence during World War I, then seized it through negotiations with the Allied Powers at Paris in 1919. This established the most prosperous, progressive, and democratic state in Central Europe, but one challenged by a contradiction between its commitment to democracy in the equal rights of all citizens and minorities and its invocation of a specifically Czechoslovak national culture. The first led to an array of parties spanning the political spectrum that remained committed to a constitutional parliamentary system, while the second threatened the country with a split into ethnic territories or the expulsion of minorities, both of which occurred with Germany's takeover in 1938–1939 and the engulfment of its Jewish populace by the ghettos, camps, and crematoria.[19]

Günther Adler, like Kafka, learned Czech early, having had private lessons from his beloved first- and second-grade teacher Fräulein Hurich.[20] As an adult, he could write letters in Czech and read and speak it, which proved advantageous to his postwar research. Adler always felt, however, that he had grown up immersed in the "insular world of the Prague Germans." But such insularity did not provide him automatic or clear identifications with nationality and religion amid what Johannes Urzidil sardonically coined the "*hinter*national mosaic" of Prague.[21] Adler said that "the German language was never completely natural to me. I had to continually fight to maintain it in Prague, in Theresienstadt, in London."[22] The multinationality of the Habsburg Empire complicated an ambivalent sense of belonging, as well as the fin-de-siècle anxiety spawned by modernity. The Czech nationalist song that became the republic's national anthem asks, "Where Is My Home?" Though the answer implied is Bohemia, like many of his Czech, German, and Jewish compatriots, Adler recalled that between the racial and nationalist tensions of the country, as well as "the helpless condition in which I was raised, . . . the very ground that one so casually refers to as one's 'homeland' sank away beneath my feet."[23]

This feeling of instability was deepened by other difficulties in the Adler home, primarily his mother's struggle with depression. Born in Berlin in 1885, Adela Alice Fraenkel had studied dance and wanted to become a doctor, a profession then barred to women, so instead she trained as a nurse, masseuse, and gymnastics instructor. In 1899 she met Emil Alfred Adler at the wedding of a mutual cousin, and at the respective ages of fourteen and seventeen they fell in love. The courtship, however, lasted a decade. Alice's bouts with depression caused her mother to make her son Walter swear on her deathbed in 1908 that he would never permit his sister to marry Emil Adler, for she could never make a suitable wife. Even a marriage offer from Rudolf Herzog, a bestselling novelist who would become an early and ardent supporter of Hitler as well as his first biographer, could not alter Alice's mind or Emil's determination. In 1909 Emil traveled to Berlin to ask Isidor Fraenkel for his daughter Alice's hand in marriage, which he was granted despite Walter's protests. A few months later they married and moved to Prague, where Emil took over the family bookbinding and stationery business.

Adela "Alice" Fraenkel Adler, 1921. Credit: National Archives, Prague.

Adler always remembered his mother Alice as "a very good, though a strict, by-the-rules woman who loved to recite fairytales and sing lovely songs" and "the most wonderful person when she was healthy."[24] In reality, though, he had little chance to know her, for soon after his birth she became mentally unstable and was forced to seek medical care for the disorder shared by her grandfather, August Harmuth. This led to long absences, during which Günther was cared for by relatives and servants, until Alice was institutionalized permanently in 1920 when Günther was only ten. Several aunts on his father's side tried to supply the love and attention he needed. Ada introduced him to music through her playing of the cello, and his favorite aunt, Ottla, introduced him to poetry through poems that she wrote and instructed him to recite by heart. Yet the boy showed the effects of his unhappy home life, suffering from anemia, boils, and skin infections. His father, Emil, who left school at fourteen to apprentice as a bookbinder in Leipzig, although Adler never remembered him reading a book, and was incapable of raising him on his own, sending his only son to be raised by others, initially with a family in the Bohemian countryside and then as a

Emil Alfred Adler, 1919. Credit: National Archives, Prague.

boarding student in Dresden. Working at the bindery until ten at night and on Sundays, never taking a vacation, and inattentive to his son's interests or education, Emil was ill equipped for single parenthood. Even when, after five years away from home, his son begged to be allowed to return, it was only with the help of his Aunt Gisa that Günther convinced his father to take him in. Emil loved his son and frequently wrote to him, dreaming of the day when, "in 10 or 15 years, Günther will be a big help to me," but early on Adler realized that he was largely on his own.

The opening chapter of *Panorama,* the first novel Adler completed after the war in 1948, poignantly echoes the strains in his childhood. Set against World War I and the fall of the Habsburg Empire, it portrays Josef Kramer's upbringing in a family whose father works all the time and whose mother is busy tending to wounded veterans as a nurse and physical therapist. While aunts and servants hover around Josef, his mother and father are largely absent. Josef feels overwhelmed by the adults and wants only to be left alone:

> But it doesn't help that he likes to be on his own, that's not allowed, even if he's allowed to go to school on his own and doesn't have to be picked up, that's not the same thing, or if he's allowed to play on his own, that's also not the same, because no one ever seriously believes that he can be completely free and on his own. It's obvious to him that he's not at all allowed to do what he wants, for someone is always watching and the day is totally arranged for him, and there's nothing Josef can do about it.[25]

Adler captures a willful desire for freedom that many young children experience and depicts a sense of confinement and control worthy of the sufferings of Kafka's "Josef K." Readers have connected Josef Kramer to the protagonist of *The Trial,* but Adler claimed that he thought more of the biblical Josef, the son of Jacob.[26] Ironically, Josef Kramer was also the name of the commandant of Bergen-Belsen, a fact that could not have been lost on Adler the historian, although he might not have known it in 1948.[27] Allusions aside, *Panorama* tells the life of the young, innocent Josef in ten "scenes" roughly between the ages of five and thirty-five with no account of the time in between each scene present in the narrative. The reader has no idea that the child's struggles to "be on his own" will later resonate with his conscription to help build a railroad or his imprisonment in the Langenstein concentration camp, both of which Adler experienced firsthand. Unlike the typical *Bildungsroman,* the reader is left to wonder what happens to Josef in the years between chapters or what events took him from scene to scene. When in the second chapter we find him at age ten living with a family in the countryside, the explanation given is that "Josef has become too anxious, his parents not knowing what to do with him."[28] Something is wrong in

Josef's life, but we do not really know what, as he instead seems to be on a fated path that he can experience but not see. Adler made clear that it was "soaked in autobiography, but was in no way an autobiography," a novel and not a memoir, and that while it expressed "the truth," it was not his "private truth."[29] Much like James Joyce, whose Stephen Dedalus is a portrait of his own life, Adler the artist shapes material from his lived experience, distancing himself by somewhat idealizing it. Although the parents are largely absent in the first chapter and Josef lives with another family in the second, the mother is never described as ill, nor is the father helpless and neglectful. Josef bravely ventures into the world, wanting to embrace it and "be on his own" while attempting to maintain equilibrium and dignity when circumstances conspire against him.

Hans Günther Adler, 1914. Credit: The Estate of H. G. Adler 2019, Deutsches Literaturarchiv Marbach.

For Adler, the five years following Alice's institutionalization in 1920 were in many ways his first exile. Fortunately, the first year was a happy one. In Deutsch Beneschau (Benešov nad Černou), on the Czech border with Austria, he lived with a Jewish family named Frischmann that ran a dry goods business and a farm, later portrayed in the second chapter of *Panorama*. Adler recalled that in Deutsch Beneschau he spent more time herding goats and cows than he did going to school, but it was "the only happy time of my childhood. . . . It was a time when, more than any other, life's dreaminess was most closely bound to a healthy and real situation."[30] Attending school in the village, however, he was forced to switch from writing with his left hand to his right, a common practice then that prevented him from ever writing legibly, which family members complained about in letters to him. As an adult, he wrote almost exclusively on the typewriter, although he trained himself in calligraphy like his grandfather David. In Deutsch Beneschau, Adler began to read from a literature anthology given him by his mother that contained ballads by Ludwig Uhland and Friedrich Schiller that he would later think ridiculous but that piqued his interest in language and poetry. Together with the love of nature cultivated among the fields and hills of the Bohemian Forest, these became the sustaining forces in his life.

Such an idyll was not to last. Returning to his father for the summer holidays, the eleven-year-old Günther was sent in fall 1921 to the Freemasons Institute of Dresden, a boarding school for boys founded in 1772. Thirty years later, Adler described it as "besides Auschwitz—the two most horrible years of my life. . . . It was a breeding ground of anti-Semitism, militarism, nationalism of the worst kind, and the most spurious philistinism imaginable."[31] As late as 1985, at the end of his life Adler would say that the two years in Dresden "had actually helped me survive World War II, for in many ways [the institute] was my first concentration camp."[32] Not even his 1922 baptism at the beginning of his second year in Dresden relieved such persecution. He had been used to being ambushed by Czech boys and called a "Stinking Jew! Stinking German!" in Prague, but in Dresden he was hounded as a "Czech pig!" If he dared to yell back "German pig!" more dire consequences ensued, for the director of the institute would beat him himself, and the boys who started it would pay no price at all.[33]

In Adler's *Panorama*, life in "The Box," as Josef calls the building that still sits at Eisenacherstrasse 21 in Dresden, pitted ten- to seventeen-year-old boys against one another amid a dreary regimen of marching exercises, sports, classes, and the cold comfort of open sleeping quarters shared by the entire school in one large room. Wolfgang Burghart, a fellow student, describes their shared misery in a 1947 letter to Adler: "The washroom, Inspector Müller, various mischief, and then one time pouring water carefully over the head of the Czech, another time it being poured over me, the pig with glasses, the Austrian. I thought of revenge or howled. You did something else. You looked at the tormentor with sadness and compassion. To me you didn't say a single word. But once you said to me: You mustn't pay it any attention; I simply don't let it bother me at all. . . ."[34]

Whether because of the difficulties of his home life or having to fend for himself away from home, stoic compassion remained central to Adler's personality. It was a quality that helped him to survive the camps. In "Nach der Befreiung" ("After the Liberation"), one of the first essays he wrote after returning to Prague in 1945, Adler observes, "The soul can stand anything, so long as the soul does not give in, even when the body is abused." For Adler, the sustenance of the soul lay within one's power to maintain dignity, for when this was lost so was all else. "In the camps one saw people who for no clear reason, or without having suffered particularly brutal treatment, would suddenly give up and then quickly go to pieces. An experienced eye could see with almost total certainty that such a person would not make it, that in a week or even less he would be gone."[35] Given the loss of Alice to mental illness and Emil's retreat into work, it is unsurprising that Adler later observed that "there was hardly anything horrible and sad that could possibly burden and harm a sensitive child that I didn't experience myself."

Adler spent two years in Dresden and as an adult marveled that it had not destroyed him intellectually, spiritually, morally, or even physically. In the summer of 1923, however, the thirteen-year-old was so worn out and distraught that Aunt Gisa whisked him off to an Austrian spa to recuperate, promising that they would not return to Prague until she secured her brother Emil's promise that he would not have to return to Dresden. They visited the Alps and Vienna, a city Adler would not see again until his late forties. Finally the father agreed and Günther was sent to collect his things from Dresden and return to Prague. At the station Emil repeated that he preferred that his son stay in Dresden, but the boy was not afraid to demand that he return home. For years he had nightmares about his treatment and the anxiety it had caused. Nevertheless, it was in Dresden that he first read and was inspired by the poems of Nikolaus Lenau and Christian Friedrich Hebbel and the stories of Heinrich von Kleist. While he recalled no aspirations to become a writer, he began to write poems, "all of them childish," but some of which he could recite as an adult, although he rarely did.

Although his son was relieved to have escaped the Freemasons Institute, Emil remained unable to care for him. He kept his promise not to send him back to Dresden, but he found another family to care for him in Mährisch Trübau (Moravská Třebová), a small town in the Moravian countryside and the largest German-speaking enclave in Czechoslovakia. Günther boarded with the family of a lawyer named Dr. Busch in a house where music was played and he was encouraged to appreciate art, if only in books. Forced to repeat a year of school because of poor Latin grades, he read widely on his own, venturing into Eastern mysticism and the Buddhist teachings of the Brahmins at age thirteen. Dr. Busch tried to inspire him to try his hand at verse dramas, as he had at his age, but Günther stuck to poetry before turning to philosophy, politics, botany, and biology. At fourteen he was a confirmed atheist and a budding socialist. Consuming all of Darwin and studying vocabulary lists and grammatical inflections in Sanskrit, Greek, Latin, French, Italian, German, and Czech, he invented a language of his own that had ten cases and a host of conjugations. He made few friends in Mährisch Trübau, but he was content on his own, taking long walks through the countryside and attending concerts, lectures, and poetry readings.

Most important was his discovery of Adalbert Stifter's 1857 novel *Der Nachsommer* (*Indian Summer*), a classic of nineteenth-century Austrian literature whose emphasis on nature and self-reliance he valued throughout his life. Adler read it again and again, and it remained a lifelong passion also shared by Bettina Gross and her family. Heinrich, the protagonist, is a boy raised in Vienna by a merchant father who, regardless of his deep love for his family, remains immersed in his business or in his library contemplating his books and art. The mother cares deeply for her son but is hardly present, leaving the moral guidance of the son and daughter to the father, who works so hard in part because he hopes to allow Heinrich to be financially independent so that he can become a "General Scientist"[36] who understands the complexity and beauty of the world.

Part novel, moral treatise, and scientific tract, Stifter's *Indian Summer* is an epic pursuit of a profound if fleeting sense of balance between nature and art, self and world, God and man, city and country, or truth and reality. "[E]verything had become different; I was seeking and grasping for some sort of inward thing," laments Heinrich at a low point, while eventually he comes to enjoy "a mood of consecration and reverence for the infinite."[37] To a young Adler in search of his own inner balance, these were heady words, particularly when combined with the notion that "Our times need the family, more than Art, science, transportation, commerce, prosperity, or anything else that seems desirable."[38] Much of Adler's formative childhood was not "beautiful," nor had there been much of a "family" to sustain him. But *Indian Summer* articulated what he sought: his own family in his native Prague.

After two years in Mährisch Trübau, Adler convinced his father to let him come home for good in 1925. Yet it is doubtful that Palackého 72 (now Křižkova 76) in the Prague suburb of Karlín, where Adler was born and his father lived until 1933, offered much of a home. The three-room apartment shared by Günther, his father, and a maidservant had been neglected for years, becoming decrepit. Emil was rarely there. His fifteen-year-old son was granted free run of the city, and often he visited friends rather than invite them home. He appreciated the liberty that his father gave him, but even he thought that it demonstrated abandonment more than trust. Nevertheless, having spent five years in exile from Prague and navigating various social dangers, Günther could take care of himself.

Prague had changed since Adler's early childhood. On October 28, 1918, the first Czechoslovak Republic was founded, buoying Czech pride. Adler was only eight, but he remembered the day vividly. Walking with his mother, they were confronted by a Czech man holding out a piece of gilded plaster broken off from a double-headed eagle, the symbol of the Habsburg Empire, yanked off a public building. "Adler" means "eagle" in German, and an unimperial carved eagle still adorns the entrance to Palackého 72. The man thrust it at them, yelling, "Nix deitsch mehr, jetzt böhmisch!" ("No longer German, now Czech!"). Soon after Adler recalled that his sailor hat, with "Viribis Unitis," the first Austro-Hungarian battleship and Emperor Franz Joseph's motto, stitched on the front, was ripped from his head by a Czech boy, and he no longer felt safe wearing it.[39]

Adler retained a deep affection for Prague and Bohemia, and he valued the complexity of his roots. In later years, when asked where he was from, he said that he was "born into the German language, of Jewish extraction, as well as Czech and Bohemian, and eventually a British citizen who identified with the culture of the Habsburg Empire."[40] The empire and the new republic led by the philosopher Tomáš Garrigue Masaryk bookended Adler's later worldview. On one hand was the thousand-year reign of the House of Habsburg and the rich, multicultural world of Vienna, Budapest, and Prague that had given birth to so many artists, musicians, scientists, and writers. On the other, Masaryk worked to create a modern democratic republic that repudiated both the Habsburg and ancient Bohemian monarchies in pursuit of a government based on social justice and the principle "that the state and political work has to have regard for *all the needs of all classes* and of course those of the biggest class of *the people*."[41] This framework lies at the heart of Adler's later sociological and political views. It also made Czechoslovakia the most democratic state in Central Europe. Its Declaration of Independence proclaimed that the new state would "guarantee complete freedom of conscience, religion and science, literature and art, speech and press, and the right of assembly and petition. The Church will be separated from the State. . . . The rights of minorities shall be safeguarded by proportional representation. National minorities shall enjoy equal rights."[42] Even Jews were allowed to identify as such as citizens, the only group to claim nationality on the basis of religion, supported in part with the hope that it would deplete the number of Germans and Magyars.[43]

Prague was a natural locale for the cross-pollination that produces great culture, as the capital of a country bordering Germany, Austria, and Hungary. The "Prager Deutsch" that had developed there since the sixteenth century was rich enough in verb formulations and vocabulary to create a literature distinct from that produced by classical High German. German intellectuals generally looked down upon it as an impoverished dialect, but Prague German and German-Jewish writers used it to foster their own subversive creativity amid a "dilemma of identity, language, and territory."[44] Events such as the Edvard Munch exhibition of 1905, a show of Cézanne, Gauguin, and Van Gogh in 1907, and one of Bonnard, Braque, Maillol, Matisse, Vlaminck, Redon, and Derain in 1910 also drew immense crowds and inspired a generation of Czech painters to forge their own artistic vision.[45] Visits by the Art Theater of Moscow, productions of Shakespeare by Max Reinhardt, and Italian operas directed by Angelo Neumann at the Deutsches Landestheater stimulated the imaginations of poets, artists, and thinkers in the last days of the Habsburg Empire.[46] When the monarchy ended in 1918, a distinct notion of Czech art and literature that was more than parochial patriotism meant that Prague was once more a capital city.[47]

Johannes Urzidil (1896–1970), a writer and critic who was a friend of Kafka and Adler, characterized the Prague that fifteen-year-old Günther encountered after returning from the countryside as a "tremendous intellectual dynamo" possessed by "a sort of electrical high tension."[48] Adler also thought Prague "something special, indeed unique, almost every one of its proponents feeling that it embodied something mysterious, tragic, and sacred."[49] Central to Prague's "mystery" was a polarity between the irrational and the rational evident in Kafka's distrust of bureaucratic control and its effect on the human psyche and Gustav Meyrink's depiction of the supernatural come to earth in *The Golem.* Karel Čapek and Franz Werfel, both born in 1890, also employed, respectively, rationalist and irrationalist approaches, and sought to reimagine the role of the individual within the modern world. For Werfel, a sense of alienation brought on by the coldness of mechanization led to an expressionism meant to inspire the spiritual revival of humanity.[50] Čapek, whose work Adler admired and whose 1920 play *R.U.R. (Rossum's Universal Robots)* introduced the word "robot," also rejected mechanistic models of human behavior in order to embrace a relativism, pluralism, pragmatism, and humanism bent on supporting the democratic values of the new republic led by his friend Masaryk.[51] In the 1920s and 1930s both writers were more famous than Kafka, their novels and plays published and performed throughout Europe and America. Werfel, who wrote in German and moved to Vienna after serving in World War I, and Čapek, who wrote in Czech and remained in Prague, also epitomize the language "frontier" running through the heart of Prague culture. On one side were the Germans, who used culture to sustain a fading hegemony, and on the other the Czechs, who used it to bolster a predominantly Czech-controlled "nation state" versus the more multicultural "state of nations" that existed in the streets.[52] The collapse of the Habsburg Empire liberated the Czechs especially. Unlike the writers and artists of fin-de-siècle Vienna who explored the psychology of individuals amid a fraying social fabric, those of Prague thought themselves part of a new nation whose prospects were on the rise.[53] Only the Jews may have felt surrounded by currents of competing nationalisms, with no stable culture or politics to which to attach themselves.[54]

Adler, however, did not remain trapped, for his early years in the countryside and in Dresden forced him to bridge cultural and ethnic divides. His ability as an adult to embark on serious scholarship and ambitious literary undertakings reflects the commitment of Josef Čapek (brother of Karel) to "The feeling of revelation and at the same time the feeling of truth and existence" in the quotidian.[55] Adler felt the dynamism of Czechoslovak democracy in the 1920s and the humanist idealism that accompanied it rather than the alienation of Kafka and Werfel. At fifteen Günther not only enjoyed the autonomy and tolerance necessary to nurture his intellect but also benefitted from the confrontation between rational pragmatism and universalist idealism present throughout Europe.

Prague was a rich realm to explore during Adler's long walks through its cobblestoned streets, across its statue-lined bridge over the Vltava, or attending the concerts, plays, opera, talks, and readings on offer for both its German-Jewish and Czech-speaking citizens. Despite being around 5 percent of the city's population by 1921, German-speaking Jews joined German-speaking Christians to regularly fill two magnificent theaters, two large concert halls, two universities, five high schools, and four vocational schools.[56] They enjoyed two daily newspapers with morning and evening editions, large clubhouses, and a lively social life. Some Czechs benefitted from and participated in these cultural offerings, and a few Germans, such as Kafka and Max Brod, visited the Czech National Theater and National Opera. For the most part the communities otherwise remained separate, but Adler was able to maneuver the city's complicated cultural frontiers with ease, recalling, "I was lucky that hardly anything, except for a few minor mishaps, ever really happened to me up until the time of Hitler's rise, though my inner development experienced several significant crises."[57]

One crisis occurred after Adler's enrollment in Prague's German State Realgymnasium or high school in 1925. Older than most students, and emboldened by the hardships of the previous five years, Adler approached the world around him with a biting irony and arrogance that was laced with a deep sense of insecurity. The school in Dresden had stripped him of his innocence and geniality, and he was determined not to be taken advantage of again, choosing to act superior and above the fray. At the same time, he forged an important friendship with a fellow student only to have it fall apart over a strong disagreement in May 1926, details of which remain unknown. Günther was so distraught that he contemplated leaping from a bridge into the Vltava, writing a rambling statement with a diatribe about how children should be raised and cared for and how his own parents had failed him.

Adler was of course not the first child to lash out against his upbringing. One cannot help but be reminded of Kafka's indictment in the now-famous "Letter to His Father" written in 1919 but never sent. In it Kafka describes himself as "a Löwy [his mother's family] with a certain Kafka core that is simply not driven by the Kafka will to live, prosper and conquer, but by a Löwy-like force that moves more secretly, more timidly, in a different direction, and which often breaks down completely."[58] Similarly, Adler tended toward dreaminess, fantasy, and solitary preoccupations derived from his mother's love of stories and music, and he was overwhelmed as well by his father's driven nature. Günther was an anxious child, but also stubborn and disobedient, as evidenced by his willful self-education and pronounced demands to return home. His relationship with his own father was no doubt tied to Alice's illness and institutionalization and Emil's retreat from parenthood. This left father and son in a helpless, ultimately blameless, yet mutually debilitating stalemate. While Kafka protested to his father that "I could never escape you,"[59] Adler did escape, even as his father all but abandoned him. The result was that Adler did not feel suffocated and oppressed but bereft of his father, which forced him to liberate himself and achieve the hard-won self-reliance that guided him later.

Adler did not leap into the Vltava, but like many adolescents, he longed to understand who he was, torn between struggles at home and the tension-filled "dynamo" that was Prague. Although Alder claimed that "religion played no role" in his family life, it could not help but be a part of the cultural struggle around him, as well as contributing to the difficulty of understanding who he was and to what, or whom, he belonged. Zionism was also in the air, and in Prague its evolution mirrored the broader debate on the rational and irrational in human existence. Kafka's classmate Hugo Bergmann (1883–1975) helped to shape this debate as the head of Bar Kochba, a student organization devoted to the cultural renewal of Judaism within Czechoslovakia rather than the political aim of restoring a homeland in Palestine. This entailed a spiritual effort at "self-liberation" through a turn inward to reflect on what it meant to be a Jew, as well as reeducating oneself in neglected customs and beliefs, and learning Hebrew and Yiddish. Bergman felt such cultural work would "fulfill the Jewish community with real life" rather than succumb passively to assimilation.[60] Such sentiments were cemented by Martin Buber, who addressed the members of Bar Kochba in lectures over the course of 1909–1910, later collected as *Three Addresses on Judaism*. Buber argued, "What matters for the Jew is not his credo, nor his declared adherence to an idea or a movement, but that he absorb his own truth, that he live it, that he purify himself from the dross of foreign rule, that he find his way from division to unity, that he redeem himself."[61] For Buber, one's subjective connection to the Jewish nation superseded any need to adhere to an objective political reality.[62]

The Zionism that Adler came to know after World War I took a different course. The violence, suffering, and death unleashed over the war caused Bergmann to realize the power of modernity's uncontrollable machinations and the need for more collective support of Jewish historical tradition and continuity.[63] During formulation of the new republic, this led to greater demands for Jewish schools and the teaching of Hebrew and Czechoslovak citizenship that sanctioned Jewish nationality.[64] Czech nationalists and many Czech-speaking Jews fought against such separatism, while German-speaking Jews remained torn between their German cultural roots and their religious and civic identities.[65] Stripped of the inner spiritual renewal avowed by Bergmann and Buber, Czechoslovak Zionism only had room for an "objective" valuation of individuals based on bloodlines and nationhood rather than the integrity of the soul, which young Günther longed to sustain in its own right.

Looking back at a life of exile since age ten, Adler captures the array of competing forces when he sums up the trajectory of his childhood in "Zu Hause im Exil":

> [I]t would be an exaggeration to claim that such harmful experiences [e.g., at the Freemasons Institute in Dresden] and the impossibility of a healthy family life were the only things that turned me into an emigrant or someone without a home, especially given that the decade after the five years from ten to fifteen was a relatively good one; yet the wounds that occur early never quite heal, even though the pain from them lessens. Nevertheless, my early literary efforts, which I took up in earnest at age fifteen, were entirely German and indeed looked to the great models and traditions of the past from Germany itself that shaped my entire life, even though that life would not be considered German for much longer, especially when I became deeply enamored of the ancient Jewish teachings, though I was not at all interested in modern Zionism, and certainly not in any enforced or voluntary ghetto. . . . I felt inwardly pulled toward Judaism more and more, but I had no idea how to launch any kind of life. And so I escaped—not with complete blindness, but also not in any clear-sighted manner—into a world of lovely illusions.[66]

Such was Adler's difficulty in navigating his way to a sense of himself. Yet in his late teens he did manage to find a path, one that opened up to him in the Bohemian Forest of his youth and that he and his generation would follow for good and for ill.

3

The Wanderers

Adler returned home to Prague in 1925, but in another way, the fifteen-year-old soon left again. He found an outlet for his restless spirit in the Jugendbewegung ("German Youth Movement"), the hiking and scouting clubs that grew loosely on their own in the late nineteenth century before being organized in 1901 in Berlin as the Wandervogel ("Wayfarers" or "Wanderers"). By the time Adler joined the Neupfadfinder ("New Scouts"), which was similar to the Boy Scouts, the movement had gone through several transformations. In 1913 it became the Freideutsche Jugend ("Free German Youth"); then in 1923 a loose federation of competing groups was dubbed the Bündische Jugend before being absorbed into and corrupted by the Hitler Jugend in 1933. To say that the Jugendbewegung led directly to the Hitler Youth would be a mistake.[1] Instead, the movement was a microcosm, and almost every German political, intellectual, and military leader born between 1890 and 1920 was once a member, including Willy Brandt, Walter Benjamin, Paul Tillich, Hermann Hesse, Werner Heisenberg, Ernst Jünger, even Rudolf Höss, the commandant of Auschwitz.[2] Given its influence on the youth of Germany at the start of the twentieth century and its fitful evolution over four decades, it is important to understand the movement's history and values to appreciate its abiding effect on Adler.

"It is difficult to describe such an experience," Adler recalled, "especially when it is part of a spirit shared intimately by young, irrepressible souls caught up in a communal adventure, indeed one that could only occur in a full and unadulterated manner among small, freely formed groups of very young people."[3] The Wandervogel was initially more an outgrowth of disillusion with the status quo than it was a movement. Arising out of a middle class suspicious of industrialization, parliamentary democracy, and the social constraints imposed by German bourgeois society, the Wandervogel resonated with a World War I generation that distrusted the values of their parents and longed to establish its independence and vision for German education, culture, and politics. In its early years, the movement was innocently idealistic. Rejecting any political association, it consisted of clubs organized solely for hiking and camping amid the untainted beauty of nature while instilling in young people the importance of human relations over material needs.

Hans Taussig, Günther Adler, and Hilde and Emil Vogel, 1929 or 1930. Credit: The Estate of H. G. Adler 2019, Deutsches Literaturarchiv Marbach.

From the moment he joined in 1925, Günther was swept up in the Neupfadfinder. Though his troop did not wear uniforms and was mildly Social-Liberal in its political outlook, weekly meetings held at club headquarters provided the camaraderie he longed for, and weekend and summer expeditions to the Bohemian Forest reanimated the love of nature he experienced in Deutsch Beneschau. The movement's disdain of bourgeois values and the conviction that contemporary society was corrupt resonated with him, and the fact that "there was one German for every four Jews" freed the group from the broader nationalistic tensions of Prague.[4] From age ten, Adler's life lacked consistent parental guidance and structure, and formal schooling had not provided him with models by which to shape his character and thinking.[5] Instead, the values gleaned in his late teens from the youth movement—selflessness, honor, discipline, loyalty, simplicity, and truthfulness—defined the core of how he lived his life and how he thought life should be lived.[6] Even the pledge recited at troop meetings contained a commitment to decency that he carried with him into adulthood: "We wish to remain young and happy and be responsible to ourselves. We wish only to advise and act in such a way as to achieve good and just ends. We wish to lead each other by bestowing trust and valuing loyalty in one another."[7] Despite what may seem like cloying good will, forty years later Adler maintained, "For anyone deeply affected by the movement, the experience, no matter how preposterous or immature it seemed later on, also formed them as human beings, transforming them and providing them with something that was ever-lasting."[8]

The Wandervogel was entirely led by young people to achieve complete self-governance in the retreat from the self-interest and rationalism of modern industrial society (Gesellschaft) by modeling a rural-agrarian community (Gemeinschaft) based on inner feeling, spontaneity, and friendship.[9] In *Panorama* such values cause a scout named Hans, a name Adler later shed, to conclude that the youth movement "will be the first sensible generation to exist once they grow up," even though Alfred, the troop's leader, reminds him with a smile that "there have always been philistines" who do not share the same ideals.[10] Alfred is a stand-in for Emil Vogel, a student of medicine and a musician several years older than Adler,[11] who remained a mentor and friend for the rest of his life. In Alfred's gentle reminder about the persistence of "philistines" (the term echoes Goethe and E.T.A. Hoffmann) we see the kind of spontaneous education that allowed younger boys to remain skeptical of the previous generation and optimistic for their own. The Wandervogel was an organization interested not only in pastoral hikes but in allowing young people to create a world of their own apart from modernity, rooted in intellectual inquiry, spirited debate, and camaraderie.[12]

The Wandervogel members were long on idealism but short on organization. Claiming "Our lack of purpose is our strength,"[13] they sought to remain free of political and social ties, but they permitted groups to split off and rename themselves and allowed liberal and conservative views about Germany's future to define a vacuous idealism that sought purity, truth, and love.[14] The movement's branches became so numerous and varied that troop leaders held a summit on October 10, 1913, on the Burg Hanstein, a mountain outside of Kassel, followed by two days of speeches and proclamations on the heights of the Hohe Meissner nearby. Some three thousand members, including Max Weber, attended.[15] After many speeches and much wrangling, the factions agreed on the name

"Freideutsche Jugend" (Free German Youth) and issued a statement later known as the Meissner Formula:

> Free German Youth, on their own initiative, under their own responsibility, and with deep sincerity, are determined to independently shape their own lives. For the sake of this inner freedom, they will take united action under any and all circumstances. All meetings of the Free German Youth are free of alcohol and smoking.

Determination to "take united action under any and all circumstances" indicates how seriously the movement believed that the youth of Germany represented a separate, autonomous social entity ready to take responsibility for shaping Germany's future.

The statement set off conflicts between the movement's conservative and revolutionary elements, as well as scathing attacks from centrist politicians who perceived a threat to parental, school, and political authority. This forced an addendum the following year: "We wish to add to the store of values which our elders have acquired and transmitted to us by developing our own powers under our own responsibility and with deep sincerity." Notwithstanding this seeming capitulation, the genie was out of the bottle. The Free German Youth acceded to the elder generation, but the urge for self-determination at its heart for nearly two decades continued to drive members to seek the "united action" necessary to shape a new Germany.

After the First World War decimated their hopes and their ranks, one may have thought the movement would fade, but with the November Revolution of 1918 in Germany and replacement of the monarchy with the Weimar Republic, the semblance of order offered by the Wandervogel provided a respite amid economic and political instability. In the 1920s some 400,000 young people were connected to the movement, and by 1933 the government-sanctioned groups overseen by the Reich Committee of German Youth Groups had nearly 5 million members.[16]

The Neupfadfinder that Adler joined in Prague in 1924 represented an important, if not curious, mediation of the vexed issues of nationalism, tensions between liberal and conservative factions, and racial identity at the core of the movement. Organized in 1921 by Martin Voelkel and Franz Ludwig Habbel, the group gave rise to the elite "Weiße Ritter" ("White Knights"), later a leading force in the movement's progressive wing.[17] Although they sought a return to the autonomous idealism of the Wandervogel, Voelkel and his cohort stoked the quasi-nationalist fervor for "The Holy, divine Reich of the German vision, which is everywhere and nowhere."[18] Invoking Goethe's *Faust*, Walter Laqueur summarizes their confused spiritualist brew: "If an outsider enquired about the meaning of all this, he would be told that if he did not feel it he would never understand it."[19]

Adler describes the spirit of the Neupfadfinder as "a pseudo-Christian circle of knights in pursuit of a Holy Grail while disposed toward mystical-religious infatuation combined with a hedonistic, nationalistic nature cult and an overarching affinity for universal brotherhood at times invoked in heavy-handed fashion, and at others only fleetingly alluded to."[20] In *Panorama* he provides a sympathetic portrait of the White Knights and their nostalgia for medieval heraldry and rituals as they consider whether younger "knaves" are fit to join the upper echelons. The scouts gather for a *bal paré,* at which a humble meal is laid out on a large table in the woods before the ceremony:

> The Great Commander opens the *bal paré* with words by saying loudly that the knights will soon get the festivities under way and that they should add to their old heroic ventures, in order that the Landstein Castle Camp do honor to its predecessors and set an illustrious example for the heroes to come in later generations, while in his capacity as Great Commander he also tenderly acknowledges the young but brave knaves, who most certainly should meet with no opposition in being accepted today into the circle of knights, though first the Great Commander has to make sure that the knaves have memorized the sacred rules and mores of the aforementioned circle of knights and taken them to heart, to which purpose he then passes the tankard round the circle.[21]

Such formality, quasi-feudalism, and militaristic overtones might seem to presage the rise of the Hitler Youth, but Adler defuses this by saying that, at least in this troop,

> No one wants to know much about other organizations, on the one hand because they are too much like the military and practice battle charges, and on the other because they are too middle-class and seek out the approval of the adults, some also being too nationalistic, others too internationalist, others belonging to some church, still others being appendages of political parties that are always yelling out some party slogan, real Wanderers meanwhile not wanting to have anything to do with politics.[22]

Given that the tankard is full of hot chocolate and the younger knaves have trouble drinking from it without spilling, Adler undercuts the formality of the rite by allowing the boys their endearing innocence. Nor is the challenge of fulfilling "heroic adventures" so tough as to undermine the boys' confidence or cause them anxiety, for the task that one knave takes on amounts to getting lost in the woods at night, while another is commended for the "scrumptious food . . . magically coaxed from our meager kettles" when the meal is barely edible at best.[23] Poignantly, Adler's description of the romantic, lengthy train journey the knights take to set up camp at Landstein Castle cannot help but remind the reader that in little more than a decade these boys will again find themselves on trains, be it as guards or prisoners, and to fortresses equally remote but vastly more formidable.

Adler's own journey took him from Landstein Castle to the Langenstein concentration camp, and his version of the Wandervogel foreshadows later history. Laqueur may rightly conclude that, with the White Knights, "Never before or since has German youth been led to remove itself so far from realities,"[24] but the Jugendbewegung as a whole provided many young people with opportunities for self-reliance and discipline unavailable at home or at school. Adler also came to see the misguided and blinkered nature of the movement's elitism. In his 1963 essay on the fiftieth anniversary of the Hohe Meissner gathering, he observes, "As sincere in their belief as many members were, they were equally misguided in preparing the way for their own doom."[25]

With its unwillingness to engage with politics or middle-class values, the movement may have failed to provide its members with broader socialization beyond the small-group mentality that dominated the "Horde" ("hordes"). Even the role of "the fire" in the everyday workings of the camp underscored such psychological control. A Pfadfinder from before World War I recalled, "The outing and the fire, these are what we sought in the night, they being the powerful symbols of our endless longing and the fellowship to which we had sworn allegiance. . . . To us life was at all times so formless and frenzied that we could not have wished for happier hours than those we had during our idyll."[26]

Hunger for physical and spiritual wandering lessened for many members as they got older, and yet in 1959, a former scout recalled, "Remembering back, we know what we were given: the archetype of what it meant to be a man, the model of a dignified, disciplined expression of that which already stirred within us. We were young, we were friends, we embraced life whole-heartedly, but we knew the difference between that which was noble and that which was vulgar, between the genuine and the meaningless."[27] This is the state of mind Adler brought to Theresienstadt and the camps. As early as his "first concentration camp" at the Freemasons Institute in Dresden, he had eagerly joined hikes and outings in the countryside, which set in motion habits and stamina that helped him survive later. But though the Jugendbewegung taught many anxious and solitary adolescents to tap the restorative powers of nature, the importance of loyalty to friends, and the strength found in maintaining one's ideals, it did not serve all similarly. Quoting Robert Oelbermann, an enthusiastic young scout who felt that "within the German Youth Movement belief in the value of giving orders and following them loyally is still alive," Adler suggests that the movement's antidemocratic "leadership principle" ("Führerprinzip") led the Germans to submit their collective will to one leader in pursuit of a harmonious national collective. As if to underscore the disastrous consequences of militaristic idealism that he could foresee when he left the Neupfadfinder in 1929, Adler, despite himself having risen to the rank of group leader, adds grimly, "Robert Oelbermann died in a German concentration camp."[28]

Several Pfadfinder members remained lifelong friends of Adler, but the most important was Franz Baermann Steiner. Adler had known him since their childhood in the Prague neighborhood of Karlín, where they played in the parks and walked together to primary school through the low-lying neighborhood of factories, metalworks, and workshops that produced leather, printed fabric, shoes, and gloves. A year older, Steiner became Adler's closest friend, and he was the first person Adler wrote to on his return to Prague in 1945. Steiner dropped out of the Pfadfinder in 1926 to join the "Roter Studentenbund" ("Red Student League"), a Marxist organization, but both maintained a love of hiking and camping. The following summer they spent three weeks hiking the Bohemian Forest, and in 1928 they hiked together in Austria and Yugoslavia. Later that fall, they began sharing their early literary works, Steiner surprising Adler with a poem he had written and wanted him to hear, although previously Steiner had been more interested in science than in literature. By the following year Steiner had committed to poetry to such an extent that he joined Wolf Salus, Paul Leppin Jr., and Friedrich S. Ost to form the "Freien Gruppe Prag," which gave a public reading in December 1929.[29]

Steiner's ancestors on his father's side, like Adler's, were Jews from western Bohemia, while his mother grew up in Prague. His father was also a businessman who ran a small shop that sold waxed cloth, leather goods, and linoleum. Religion was not practiced in the Steiner home either, but Franz did receive religious instruction at school. Steiner and Adler attended the German State Realgymnasium in 1925 after Adler returned to Prague, although Adler withdrew in 1927, having convinced Emil to allow him to study whatever he wished, if he passed the comprehensive exam, or "Matura," required to attend university. Over the next three years Adler became an autodidact in literature, music, philosophy, and history who only needed tutoring in geometry and math to pass the exam in 1930. Although Steiner and Adler ceased being classmates as early as 1920, the Wandervogel allowed them to maintain a bond through adolescence outside of the social institutions of family and education that would have normally defined it.

Their three-week hike through the Bohemian Forest in the summer of 1927 occurred at a crossroads in their lives and came close to ending their friendship. Steiner was deeply immersed in Marxism and so fanatical in his desire to live a "natural life" that he spurned manufactured goods and wrote on birch bark rather than paper. Günther, however, had become interested in spiritual matters and mysticism after reading the *Bhagavad Gita* the year before, and he was passionate about literature and the arts. But if Günther equated the beauty of nature with anything in art, Steiner was quick to say that had nothing to do with natural history, or that Günther's fondness for rustic dwellings ignored the economic disparity that fomented them. As boys, they had built a massive shared collection of fauna, insects, rocks, and lichens, but now their interests and sensibilities seemed incompatible. Steiner had become extreme in his socialist ideals, whereas Adler was a dreamy spiritualist who gave his friend a copy of the *Bhagavad Gita* in a hand-bound leather binding probably done by Emil Adler. By the end of the trip the divide was so deep that they saw little of each other for most of the next year, their only contact when Adler came to tutor Steiner in history for his own "Matura," which Franz passed in the spring of 1928.

Günther Adler, 1928. Credit: The Estate of H. G. Adler 2019, Deutsches Literaturarchiv Marbach.

That autumn Adler again opened up about his increasingly mystical beliefs and immersion into Eastern mysticism, but this time Steiner was willing to listen and was moved. Under Adler's tutelage, he immersed himself in the German mystics, Jakob Böhme, Angelus, Silisius, Lao Tzu, Lieh-tzu, Chuang Tzu, and Indian holy writings, especially Adler's beloved *Bhagavad Gita,* which soon became Steiner's favorite book too. Steiner enrolled at the German University of Prague, where he studied and wrote a dissertation on Semitic languages, although he also took courses in ethnology and anthropology at the Czech-speaking Charles University. Two years later Adler also enrolled at the German University to study musicology, literature, psychology, and philosophy. Divergent interests can cause close friends to lose touch, but Steiner's literary interests blossomed with Adler's. Steiner stepped away from Marxism when he severed his ties with the Prague Communists in 1930, immersing himself in another series of extended hikes through the forest.[30] In spite of his own flirtation with Marxism in the late 1920s, Adler lost interest in it, and their joint rejection of Communism deepened their lifelong bond.[31]

Franz Baermann Steiner, 1932. Credit: The Estate of H. G. Adler 2019, Deutsches Literaturarchiv Marbach.

"Wandering," however, is what most united them. Their spirit of independence and hunger for travel superseded differences in their views of literature, religion, or politics. As a boy, Steiner's keen interest in botany had drawn him to the wider world to add to his collections, and his love of travel writing fueled his interest in other peoples and civilizations.[32] In 1930–1931, Steiner traveled further afield to the Hebrew University of Jerusalem, where he studied Arabic at the School of Oriental Studies and boarded with Hugo Bergmann. It was life-changing, for Steiner returned to Prague a Zionist. Even though he refrained from attending synagogue, he thought himself an "Oriental" forced to live within Western values, a view of Judaism shared by Martin Buber and popular at the time.[33] Unlike Buber, his was a deeply traditional Judaism, and Steiner was skeptical of any Western influence or involvement with Palestine, hoping instead that Oriental and North African immigrants would shape its future. He and Adler took another five years to complete their degrees, and then Steiner traveled to Vienna in 1935 to study ethnology before arriving in London in 1936 to study anthropology under Bronisław Malinowski. In the summer of 1937 he did fieldwork in Subcarpathian Ruthenia, and in 1938 he was back in England, where he did a second doctorate at Oxford under Alfred Radcliffe-Brown and E.E. Evans-Pritchard, then the most prominent anthropologists in Britain.

Following hiking trips in Austria, Yugoslavia, and Italy during the late 1920s, Adler visited the Dalmatian Coast with Steiner in 1933 and with his Aunt Pepa in 1934.[34] He also traveled to Berlin in 1933 to do research for his dissertation, "Klopstock und die Musik" ("Klopstock and Music"), earning his doctorate in 1935. He spent six months in Milan in 1938 in the hopes of securing an exit visa to Brazil to work as a salesman of industrial abrasives, only to return to Prague and face forced expulsion. Like many of their generation, both led a peripatetic existence in search of a foothold amid dramatic circumstances beyond their control.

The idealism and quasi-spiritualism of the Wandervogel kindled their interests in the metaphysical, and the "metaphysical madhouse"[35] that was Prague fired their quest for answers to the deepest questions. In Adler this manifested itself in his early passion for mysticism and Eastern religious writing. For Steiner such interests involved what it meant to be a Marxist and a Jew. What united their investigations was a desire to find a "new synthesis of the rational and non-rational" beyond the Enlightenment's valuation of reason.[36] This was a natural extension of the debate among Prague's writers and artists since the turn of the century. It was marked by both the celebration of expressionist and spiritualist freedom by writers like Franz Werfel and Paul Kornfeld and the investigation of modern social and psychological repression by Kafka and Paul Leppin. Rather than side with either the rational or the nonrational in pursuit of truth, they wished to fuse them. This led to Steiner's valuation of myth as a means to understand human essence, whereas Adler advocated the power of "intuition" in grasping it.[37]

As successors to what Max Brod dubbed the "Prague Circle," Steiner and Adler wished to set themselves apart from their predecessors, but their legacy also inspired them. Adler had shared a school bench with Felix Hermann, a nephew of Kafka, before he had read the latter's work, and his own father had attended the same school as Kafka. Steiner and Adler were close friends with Wolf Salus, son of the poet Hugo Salus, whom Brod dubbed a "literary pope" who espoused aesthetic and cultural loyalty to Vienna and the Habsburgs in mentoring Werfel and Rainer Maria Rilke.[38] Steiner's close affinity for Leppin meant that he was also connected to writers interested in breaking away from conservative German cultural traditions in order to embrace their Slavic and Jewish roots. Prague did not foster just one "circle" but generated many.[39] Its strands of surrealism, expressionism, Cubism, rationalism, Zionism, and mysticism were intertwined with religious, cultural, and national identities to form a sturdy nest in which the hungry intellect was nurtured and fed.

Adler and Steiner were shaped by Prague's literary and artistic heritage yet eager to claim their own turf within it. Like his grandfather David, Adler took up cultural journalism, reviewing Bernard Reder's solo exhibition at the Manes Gallery in 1935 for *Der Tag* and reviewing Alfred Mombert's poetry collection *Sfaira der Alte* for *Zeit und Bild* in 1937.[40] In 1933, with the poet Helmut Spiesmayr and the musician and composer Peter Brömse, Adler and Steiner formed a circle of writers "in opposition to what we considered to be the public literature business" carried out by luminaries such as Werfel and Brod. Adler later said of it:

> This league of friends, which others joined loosely, was set up according to the principles which the composer [Anton] Webern had established years earlier for a similar group: to fight for good and against evil in life and in art, unstinting mutual openness, especially in relation to the evaluation of each other's artistic efforts, bold intervention on behalf of that acknowledged as good and right, and the fight against all types of protectionist economy in cultural and artistic matters, in particular the views put forward by a corrupt press.[41]

The testament reads like a credo of the Wandervogel, with its revolt against the press and the "protectionist economy" of the literary elites or the commitment to defend what is "good and right," while the fact that Spiesmayr and Brömse were Christians reflects Prague's tangled social strata. Adler's insistence that the group was not "an esoteric society but instead good friends with a liking for bold humor and grotesque pranks" resembles his depiction of the scouts in

Panorama. Similar to the ominous portent of young men riding on trains, Adler admits, "Perhaps this was the only form which a group of young intellectual people could take, as yet unburdened by the terrible events of the time," which later led to the disappearance of Spiesmayr in East Prussia at the end of the war and to Brömse joining the Nazi Party in 1938, the year the group disbanded.

Forging a new relation between the rational and the nonrational also lies at the nexus of the three paths posited by the *Bhagavad Gita*, the disciplines of action, of knowledge, and of devotion.[42] Despite their belief in adhering to and uniting these into a single path through life, a clear and consistent way to do this evaded Adler and Steiner. The Wandervogel provided an outlet for action, but largely cut off from social institutions. Steiner's early love of the natural sciences shaped his passion for knowledge, but his inability to use a microscope because of poor eyesight scuttled his hope of becoming a biologist. Their shared hunger for knowledge made them passionate learners, but often lacking focus. Adler's love of literature held steady, but even that was often taken over by his absorption in mysticism.

This began as early as 1926 when, in the middle of the school day, he was transported by what he described as "a moment of rapture."[43] By the summer of 1926, Adler was so immersed in Eastern mysticism that, walking through the Bohemian Forest, he experienced visions and felt he could sense the Earth's rotation. Thinking back to these moments of spiritual transport, Adler recalled, "What for most people might be brought on by their first experience of love was for me something that clearly took full possession of me and, along with my gradual and simultaneous growing aversion to Christianity (I never had anything to do with the Church), eventually freed me, a development that would occur in 1932, and which took some three years to happen even then."[44] Adler's "crass atheism" developed into a "tentative pantheism" fed by his immersion in the Bible and the *Bhagavad Gita*.[45] What eluded him was a system of inquiry to unite these passions and cultivate them as a writer and intellectual.

Enter the Czech photographer František Drtikol. Born in 1883, the same year as Kafka, Drtikol was one of a bevy of photographers, sculptors, and artists who forged Czech modernism in the early twentieth century. Gaining fame with the Art Deco movement, he made his mark through photographs of old Prague neighborhoods such as Josefov, home of the Jewish Quarter demolished entirely by 1913 by city planners eager for modernization. Soon he became interested in Buddhism, and in the middle 1920s he founded a circle for the study of religious texts and spiritual discussions, which Adler joined in 1928. He rarely mentions Drtikol in later letters, interviews, or essays, but Adler remained involved with the circle until 1935, and it is prominent in *Panorama*. Josef Kramer visits a gathering led by Johannes Tvrdil at the invitation of his friend Thomas.

Josef is skeptical of it and concludes "that each person must find his own way, and that only on your own is it possible to do so, therefore no one can tell you what to do, it will quickly lead to misunderstandings, and there is nothing more important than to maintain your independence."[46] Nevertheless, revelation is at hand when Josef realizes:

> Truth can be found only through a spiritual life like the one Josef now embraces. Certain voices said that he must withdraw from the world if he wanted to attain understanding, as nothing is as it appears, for everything evolves amid the continual depths in the midst of life, one having to be very still, for then the onslaught occurs, colored beams pressing down upon humankind from the firmament to the sounds of sacred music, slowly progressing toward the body that will be bathed with pureness, the beams then pressing their blessing into the body until they strike the heart, at which thunderous sound is released, you experience a freedom never felt before, you feel light, and you are released from the world and know that you are accountable only to yourself, everything else is immaterial and leads only to painful confusion, the inner realm the only thing that continues, each having to go his own way, though he must not be forced by anyone, for that is not allowed.[47]

Such a powerful spiritual experience seems to have consumed Drtikol. By 1935 he had taken his last photograph, choosing to devote himself entirely to paintings that depicted the "aura" of ecstatic emotion, meditation, and Buddhist study. He died in 1961 nearly forgotten, his artistic contribution erased by Czech Communism and only rehabilitated after a 1972 retrospective of his work at the Museum of Decorative Arts in Prague.[48]

Notwithstanding Josef's skepticism in *Panorama*, Drtikol's circle was an important influence on Adler. Part of the appeal was involvement in a group of like-minded people, especially for a young man who had enjoyed little consistency in his early social circles. More important was the presence of Drtikol himself, an accomplished artist at the height of his talent and fame. During these years Adler also befriended the Romanian sculptor Bernard Reder and the writer and musician Hermann Grab, role models for both life and art. Drtikol no doubt had a profound effect on Adler's spiritual growth, but his ideas on art may have carried equal weight, as Drtikol's circle met each week in his studio, where Adler would have seen his photographs on the walls.

Drtikol's chief contribution to Czech photography was, along with Jaromír Funke, to declare that it was "changing into an instrument suitable for individual expression" and that the camera was "what a brush is to a painter or a pen to a poet."[49] He was known for his portraits of prominent politicians, artists, and thinkers, including Czechoslovak President Tomáš Garrigue Masaryk, Foreign Minister and later President Edvard Beneš, the composer Leoš Janáček, the writer Josef Čapek, and international figures such as Paul Valéry and Rabindranath Tagore. Drtikol mounted a catalog of nudes comparable in their artistry and renown to that of Robert Demachy and Edward Steichen.[50] Widely contrasting work in public portraiture and expressionistic nudes may seem surprising, but art historians find that his work forms a single, unified whole.[51]

Drtikol's mysticism held that "the center of the universe is everywhere."[52] The studio in Vodičkova Street was suffused with this spirit, its walls adorned with masterful expressions of the photographer's two great themes: character made manifest in formal portraiture and the sublime as expressed through the female body.[53] Drtikol was not a fanatical Buddhist and approached religion as an instrument for higher learning.[54] In the hatha yoga he practiced, Drtikol's creed is similar to that of the Wandervogel: "A good person enhances the material world with each action he takes." Elsewhere he remarks, "[A]ll these teachings of the truth were written by a single person at one and the same time. And this is because they all start from truth—the one true reality—from Nirvana, from the void that stands above time and space."[55] Like the art that Drtikol transformed into the "borderland between photographic reality and painterly illusion,"[56] the circle's effort to square the quotidian with the ideal spoke to Adler's urge to find a way to act within the world guided by a higher calling.

Adler's poetic pursuits during these years joined with Drtikol's search for "the one true reality," especially through the influence of the neoromantic, mystical poet Alfred Mombert (1872–1942).[57] Adler discovered Mombert's poetry in 1929, and through Steiner's friendship with the poet Emmanuel Leschehrad, who translated Mombert into Czech, he learned everything he could about Mombert's work and life. That year Adler sent him a poetic cycle called *Das Volk* (*The People*), with a heartfelt letter of praise confessing that the elder writer's poems had "touched upon something kindred to the soul, but which existed on a far higher plane."[58] It seems likely that Mombert helped him in 1931 to publish his first book, the verse drama *Meer und Gebirge* (*Sea and Mountains*). In any case, given that Adler responded in 1937 to Mombert's magnum opus *Sfaira den Alten* (*Sfaira the Ancient*) with a poem titled "An Sfaira den Alten" ("To Sfaira the Ancient)," Mombert's effect remained deep and long-lasting.

Belying its titular naturalism, Adler's *Sea and Mountains* is a mystical verse-drama set in a mountaintop tower above the sea. The creation story is told by Taumarchias, who long ago helped form the world through his marriage to Airysia, goddess of the sea. It unfolds with the ebb and flow of chaos, beauty, fire, earth, sea, and silence amid "a drama of churning worlds" within which ancient writings make clear to humankind,

You are witness, behold the meaning!
Explorer, on you the light is dawning!
Strength, will, and act must radiate in quiescence!
Be silent, then you will know and behold all essence![59]

Toward the end, Taiga, spirit of the spring, arrives to embrace Taumarchias as her son, but he demurs, saying, "Too long you have fed my dreams, / I will remain loyal to you in memory," before asking that she forget him and die, in order to be reborn.[60] One might be tempted to see a reference in this to Adler's pain and loss at the absence of his own mother, an uncharacteristic biographical reference, yet he later notes, "Mombert's mysticism . . . also taps timely images as a vehicle for his experience."[61] "I have lived in many worlds," says the title character of Mombert's 1911 verse-drama *Aeon*.[62] Adler would later disown *Sea and Mountains* as juvenilia, but Mombert's influence is evident in "Anders bin ich" ("I Am Different"), a poem from 1934 whose first line he often quoted in letters to friends and loved ones as the essence of his attitude toward life:

I live in many worlds.
Considering this, right away
One must add the following:
Within a vast network, back and forth
Among the measureless multitude
Of multifarious heavenly bodies
I can be everywhere
Close to the spirit.
Here and there
So much is allowed,
And every ocean wave
May remain poised eternally,
So that I may know with assurance,
In solace and in each deed,
The glowing current of my connection
Never ending among these celestial paths.
Nevertheless, eternally remote,
Withdrawn into my deepest self,
I take in the endless network
And smile through falling tears
About the multiplicity of knowledge,
How, sated and hungry at once,
It devours me and rejects me.

And yet there is something else: It's true
That I live in many worlds,
But this is only a saying,
A permissible image,
And a useful record;
It is also—what many
Pursue—the meaning
Of all pursuits or
(Should this be heard)
The pursuit of all interpreted meaning,
And thus this is life.
And yet that is something aside, fallen
As well, and collected
In countless mirrors.
Yet I am not that:
I do not know myself in life,
I know nothing of it
And never did know,
Yet what I know is life
And what I knew are worlds.
This is knowledge, this is vision,
This is not me. I am different.
I am different, different.[63]

Adler's claim to difference taps the figure of the outsider in German literature stretching from Goethe's Young Werther through Thomas Mann's *Tonio Kröger* and W. G. Sebald's melancholic narrators wandering memory and the haunts of war beneath the surface of daily life. All arrive at a truer sense of self by leaving society behind, knowledge that comes with the price of knowing oneself to be different and extraneous to the quotidian. Converting the past tense of Mombert's "I have lived in many worlds" to the present of "I live in many worlds," Adler straddles three phases of German poetry demarcated by Jethro Bithell in 1939: the "Ichgehalt" or interest in the self, the "Weltgehalt" or "the contemplation of the divine," and the "Zeitgehalt" or the "lyric creed of those who would reform the institutions of temporal earth."[64] Bithell places Mombert in the second category, but Adler's speaker struggles to know himself in this world while remaining everywhere "close to the spirit." That he is "different" cannot help but counter his concerns to those of the everyday, but one senses that for Adler, as well as Mombert, history is not merely "a mechanical sequence of events but a vital interaction between the creative forces within the world and man's imagination."[65] Action, knowledge, and devotional faith—the three paths to fulfillment in the *Bhagavad Gita*—were what he sought as an individual wandering in search of sure footing.

Adler later said of Steiner:

> He owed a debt to mysticism and religion for his personal relationship to all phenomena, their imaginative comprehension and study, the true essence of his artistic creativity, which he always wanted to be understood as a religious achievement, even when dealing with what were actually non-religious approaches. The more mature Franz became, the more these elements fused together and were combined in his most successful creations.[66]

This also serves as a précis of Adler's own development from 1925 to 1935, as well as the spirit he carried into the coming darkness. In turning down a manuscript of Adler's poems submitted to S. Fischer Verlag in 1933, Peter Suhrkamp commented generously, "I find within them a person who has a pure and open relation to things, which also confesses perhaps a writerly relation."[67] Both Adler and Steiner sought to say what it meant to be human amid the systems and restrictions imposed by society, of religious and cultural identity, or physical and class barriers that threatened to wipe out identity altogether. Soon this effort became more about survival than intellectual and spiritual development. Having left behind the Wandervogel and Drtikol's mystical circle, Adler had no choice but to forge a viable "universal matrix" of his own when, as a Jew, he was denied even the intimation of a soul and was seen as "different" to an insidious extreme.

4

The Cataclysm

Legend has it that the Old-New Synagogue in the Jewish Quarter of the Josefov neighborhood of Prague was built from stones flown from Jerusalem by angels after the destruction of the Second Temple in AD 70 with the understanding that the building must never, on penalty of death, be altered.[1] Yet twentieth-century Prague was replete with metamorphoses. The "magic capital of Europe" was not only a "breeding ground for phantoms, an arena of sorcery, a source of *Zauberei*, or *kouzelnictví* (in Czech), or *kishef* (in Yiddish)," but also a bridge between the old and the new, tradition and innovation, mind and spirit, reason and imagination, stasis and change.[2] The Old-New Synagogue remains intact, but from the turn of the century onward everything around it was in flux.

The city in which Adler and Steiner came of age during the late 1920s and early 1930s could not have been more dynamic. The razing of the poverty-stricken Jewish Quarter during the century's first decade provided an open canvas for architects and planners, and the optimism unleashed with the founding of the republic inspired an urge to fashion a capital of the first order. The Art Nouveau movement that grew out of the Vienna Secession gave way to Prague's blend of "Cubo-Expressionism" before the onset of World War I and the functionalist avant-garde of the 1920s. Inspired by the Cubism of Paris, the Prague version had at its center an art that sought "to conquer and spiritualize matter," leading to its more psychological and philosophical bent. "The artistic consideration counts more for us than does the utilitarian aspect," the architect Pavel Janák wrote. This prevented enslavement to fixed ideals, for Czech Cubism was "above all a vehicle for a personal style, imbued with poetry."[3]

In 1895 the manifesto of Czech Modernism proclaimed, "We want individuality. . . . We want artists, not echoes of someone else's tones, not eclectics, not dilettantes. . . . We want individuality swelling with, and creating, life above all."[4] This desire for uniqueness was spurred in part by the desire to found a culture independent of the Habsburg Empire, for Czech artists and writers "acknowledged no contradiction between modern life and national life or between cosmopolitanism and patriotism."[5] These polarities played out across the spectrum of Prague's art world in exhibitions at the Mánes Union of Fine Arts, the Municipal House, the newly built National Gallery, and the Weinart Art and Auction Hall, as well as talks, shows, and readings by Man Ray, Le Corbusier, F. T. Marinetti, Hannah Höch, and Alexander Archipenko.[6] With the flowering of Czech Surrealism in the 1930s, Prague's art scene broadened further with the participation of Jean Arp, Salvador Dali, Max Ernst, Alberto Giacometti, and Joan Miró in the *Poesie 1932* show at the Mánes Union, followed by the arrival of André Breton in Prague for several important lectures the following year.[7]

At the heart of the city's cultural and architectural development lay a tension between innovation and tradition. By 1900, electrification, public water systems, and city trams allowed for rapid improvement in living conditions. The population soon doubled in size, reaching nearly one million by 1930. The first Czech feature film was shown in 1898, and by 1910 the city boasted fifteen movie houses. The first auto factory opened in 1907, and by the start of World War I three new bridges spanned the Vltava to carry the growing traffic.[8] The nightlife of Wenceslas Square pulsated with jazz and electrified advertisements for department stores, clubs, and cinemas, as trams and automobiles raced by, increasing the speed and rhythm of city life.[9] With "machines, concrete, steel," modernity "blew in from all sides," wrote Karel Čapek, "even to our provincial backwater."[10]

And yet throughout Europe there was anxiety beneath the gleam of remade cities. Modernization brought with it alienation and upheaval, spawning social and spiritual instability. Artists turned to archetypal, primitive, and spiritual investigations for their inspiration, much as Drtikol had with Eastern mysticism. Painters František Kupka, Emil Filla, and Vojtěch Preissig used abstraction to project "cosmic unity" onto contemporary fragmentation in search of what Filla called "the direct expression of the artist's inner state."[11] They were followed in the 1910s by Bohumil Kubišta, Jan Zrzavý, and Josef Čapek, whose "Cubo-Expressionism" celebrated the "magic" in everyday objects. This fostered a tension between rationalism and irrationalism in the competing strains of Functionalism and Surrealism in the late 1920s and early 1930s. Whereas modernization led to alienation and retreat in Vienna and Budapest, in Prague there was "an acceptance of the impossibility of overcoming the fragmentation and differentiation of modern life," which inspired the celebration of everyday life.[12] Behind this lay a deep optimism about and identification with Czech culture.[13] Karel Čapek was even denounced as not embracing Czech art fully enough, and while he campaigned for Czech art to assimilate foreign influences, amid fierce disagreements and competing factions the feeling was that "real national art was modern art, and to be Czech was to embrace the present."[14]

Though Czech-speaking Jewish and German artists were welcome to contribute to this artistic blossoming, such expansive optimism did not generally extend to German-speaking Jews of Kafka's generation. Despite having abandoned their own cultural practices and beliefs through assimilation, they could not think of themselves entirely as Czech, nor did some Czechs think of them that way. But by the time Adler and Steiner came of age, the antipositivist leanings of Čapek's generation were ingrained, while the collectivist turn of the 1920s avant-garde sought "wholeness" in a different way through "the rational, utilitarian, and efficient rule of the machine."[15] Adler's studies under Drtikol and his esteem for Mombert aligned him more with the first generation of the Czech avant-garde, which valued individualism and the spirit, versus the socialist functionalism of the second.[16] But his pursuit of a unifying theory of mind and spirit through mysticism, as well as Steiner's deep commitment to Marxism, meant they also held affinity with the 1920s avant-garde. Both drew the line at submitting themselves to systematic thinking, however, and in this they harkened back to the Čapek generation. Rather than the post–World War I generation's "social faith" in the proletariat or in the ability of art to achieve social justice, Čapek's cohort chose "a path in which each person, individually, had to sort the good from the bad, to discover his or her own values on the basis of experience and observation alone."[17]

Entering the German University of Prague in 1930, Adler was hard at work discerning his own values in a city and culture that André Breton described then as "leading out of yesterday into always."[18] Like many in his generation, Adler sought permanence amid flux after being weaned on modern mechanical progress in a city that contained "everything shady, abnormal, weird, murky, mystical, ambiguous, multilayered, as well as grotesque, . . . all of it woven together by a singular shade of gray."[19] Little did he know that his real education over the next five years, and his country's efforts to maintain its autonomy over the next eight, would consist of a life-and-death struggle between the multiethnic liberalism of Czechoslovakia's democracy and Germany's dive into totalitarianism. With Germany's annexation of the Sudetenland in 1938 and its takeover of the remaining rump state in 1939, the struggle for Czech independence was finished before it had hardly begun. Adler's own struggle for survival, however, was just starting.

Adler was intensely interested in an array of subjects. He took classes in musicology, literature, and art history, as well as psychology and philosophy. Although just twenty, he held the daily life of students at a far remove, preferring instead to visit lectures while keeping his own company. He lived at home, but his own mother found him sometimes a bit standoffish, reminding him even before he completed his Matura to be careful not to seem arrogant since his tall height, glasses, and lush head of sable hair already made him striking enough. "You're much too serious for someone your age and not cheerful enough: in short, too self-involved," she warned. "You think of writers whom highly educated people value a great deal as 'incompetents.' That doesn't please me very much."[20] Dashing, erudite, and passionate for literature, music, and art, the young Adler could be a dandy while dazzling friends with his wordplay and wit. Wolfgang Burghart, his only close friend from Dresden days, found him to be "not exactly over-modest," especially about his own poems, though when Burghart visited him in Prague, Adler attended to him generously and introduced him to his circle of friends.[21]

At the German University of Prague his most important teacher was the musicologist Gustav Becking (1894–1945), who developed what became known as "Becking curves." Analyzing the beat patterns of a range of composers, nations, and historical periods, these revealed a culture's attitudes and philosophy of life and showed that music composed by different cultures, periods, and peoples required different approaches to conducting.[22] Becking was a pioneer in ethnomusicology, tracing the impact culture has upon individual artistic style, which helped to develop a more informed ethnology honoring the uniqueness of musical cultures rather than valuing one against another.[23] Adler at first declined when Becking suggested he write a dissertation in musicology, saying that he was not a good musicologist. Becking suggested that Adler work with his colleague Herbert Cysarz, a German literature professor turned political extremist who avidly supported the "return" of the Sudetenland to Germany. Adler refused, saying he could not work with him.[24] Becking then simply announced that he would serve as the dissertation advisor and Adler's subject would be "Klopstock und die Musik," which is what Adler wrote on.

Becking would join the Nazi Party in 1939, but he was less extreme than Cysarz, nor did he allow his scholarship to be corrupted by politics. He took Adler under his wing, serving also as dissertation advisor to Peter Brömse, as well as Kurt and Edith Oppens, both of whom fled Prague in 1938 but remained lifelong friends to Adler.[25] A year after he completed his degree Becking attended a poetry reading Adler gave in October 1936, after which he sent warm congratulations praising Adler's ability "to relentlessly strip away anything that might impair the essential core" of a poem.[26] In 1945, Becking was drafted into the Volkssturm, the ragtag band of old men and boys ordered up by Hitler as a last-ditch effort to defend the Reich. Adler expressed sympathy for Becking's rather gruesome death, for when the Czechs arrested him in a bunker the day after the war ended and asked if he was enlisted in the Volkssturm, Becking replied that he was, believing he would be treated as a regular army enlistee.[27] Instead the Czechs asserted that he was fighting against the Prague Uprising, and they shot him and forty other German collaborators on the spot.[28] "The man whom they shot," Adler lamented later, "had prevented the Germans during the Occupation from absconding with the Strahov Library, the most valuable collection in the entire land."[29]

Becking remained an important figure in Adler's education. The dissertation proved a catalyst to Adler's intellectual development, especially in the late fall of 1932, when he traveled to Berlin for research on Klopstock in the Prussian State Library. During his several months' stay with his aunt Ada, he was introduced by his cousin Ernst Fraenkel to the philosophy of Erich Unger (1887–1950), and Adler participated for several weeks in a circle led by Unger at the Urania House of Berlin. Many writers and academics from literature, mathematics, psychology, religion, and politics took part over time, including Bertolt Brecht, Alfred Döblin, Robert Musil, Gottfried Salomon, and Walter Benjamin, who enthusiastically wrote to Gershom Scholem about Unger's work.[30] As with Drtikol, what attracted Adler to Unger was the philosopher's interest in revelation as a means to understand the true essence of reality.

Unger was influenced by his Berlin schoolmate Oskar Goldberg, a devout orthodox Jew who believed in the possibility of achieving a reentry of the Shekhinah, or Divine Presence, into the modern world and in his ability to channel it himself.[31] Rather than succumb to Goldberg's messianism, Unger believed humans were capable of evolving to a point at which they could experience a renewed appreciation of the divine within themselves.[32] Unger valued the imagination in tandem with reason as a means to pursue philosophically the known, the temporarily unknown, and the eternally unknown, which together he considered the "All of Reality." Whereas Immanuel Kant had argued that knowledge consisted of "intuition and thinking," Unger privileged intuition and concluded, "[I]f ordinary intuition provides the sensuous element for the knowledge of understanding, imagination is the sensuous element of reason as the organ of thought for ultimate reality. Without imagination, indeed, reasoning is 'empty.'"[33]

Adler was deeply attracted to the spiritual role of the imagination, which made possible the "cosmic unity" sought by painters like Emil Filla. In his 1960 essay "Erinnerungen an den Philosophen Erich Unger" ("Memories of the Philosopher Erich Unger"), Adler admires Unger's conception of reality as a single entity versus the division into the modern disciplines of religion, mysticism, philosophy, science, and art.[34] Adler concludes that the quintessence of Unger's thinking lies in the notion "that the next world and beyond can be found in the real and ideal meeting point of the here and now. This meeting point lies at the center of each human being, thus making his spirit an organ of thought whose insights give birth to his essential being."[35] Unger's philosophy was more "practical" than the *Bhagavad Gita* in its ability to account for the presence and worth of the divine through the "confrontation with the conditions of the world." It allowed the mystical "unknown" to remain a valid means of understanding the moral consequences of actions in the real world rather than relying on "static dogma" to decide consequences or dismiss perception of the divine as a "psychological illusion."[36] For Unger and Adler the pursuit of the "unknown" comprised the "experiment" of philosophy itself.[37]

While Adler worked to reach beyond "static dogma," the world around him seemed all too pleased to settle for it. As a child, his mother had often taken Günther to Berlin to visit relatives, and he had vivid memories of seeing Kaiser Wilhelm II pass by on a tall horse and of visiting the city during the 1919 workers' uprising at Alexanderplatz led by Karl Liebknecht and Rosa Luxemburg.[38] The Berlin of the Weimar Republic he visited in 1932–1933 was another matter. The tumult unleashed with the burning of the Reichstag on February 27, 1933, spread rapidly. Accusing a Dutch Communist of setting the fire, the Nazis stirred fear among the public that a Communist putsch was imminent, allowing Chancellor Hitler to force President Paul von Hindenburg to sign a decree suspending most civil liberties in Germany. The elections that followed on March 5 saw the Nazis gain a 52 percent majority in the Reichstag. Nevertheless, Adler remained in Berlin until mid-April 1933, experiencing these dramatic and frightening events firsthand. Though he felt fairly safe in having a Czechoslovak passport, he was astonished to hear young Nazis chanting "Everything for the damned Nazis!" In the heart of Friedrichstrasse, he watched a man stamp the windows of closed Jewish businesses with anti-Semitic slogans and swastikas as if conducting a civic duty. When he told a Nazi collecting donations for the Party, "I'm a Jew, I'm not giving anything," Adler was astonished to hear him respond, "That doesn't matter. Even if you are a Jew, you can still give something."[39]

Returning to Prague later in April 1933, he settled down to complete his dissertation. But after experiencing the frenzied pitch of Berlin politics, he could see that difficult times lay ahead for Germany, if not all of Europe. Indeed, Unger and Goldberg also fled to Prague that same year. Unger stayed a few months and saw Adler occasionally before moving on to Paris and eventually London. Goldberg settled in the United States for the duration of the war. Adler would fondly recall Unger's ability to lead lively discussions in Berlin in which ideas were debated among fifty or sixty people with great vigor but without ever descending into bitter quarrels, even though much of German politics was awash in derision.

Yet by 1933 the Berlin circle was finished. Adler again relied on his involvement with Drtikol for stimulation and visited a salon held at the house of Bertha and Dr. Emanuel Gross, a prominent gynecologist, just north of Wenceslas Square. Starting in 1918, the Gross family had hosted gatherings for artists and friends attended by Emil Filla (1882–1953) and Alfred Justitz (1879–1934), pioneers of Czech Cubism, and the Expressionist painter and sculptor Willi Nowak (1886–1977), who painted Max Brod's portrait and whose studio Kafka visited. Nowak and Filla were members of the influential pre–World War I Czech and German artist group called Osma (The Eight), itself a vestige of multinational Habsburg unity in Prague. A later generation of visitors included the Surrealist painter Endre Nemeš (1909–1985) and Jakub Bauernfreund (1904–1976), a student of Nowak's at the Academy of Fine Arts in Prague, and the Romanian-born sculptor Bernard Reder (1897–1963), who had his first solo exhibition at the Mánes Union of Fine Arts in 1935. Reder became a close family friend and a teacher to Bettina Gross, Bertha and Emanuel's daughter. Reder and his wife, Gutza, suggested that Günther Adler and Bettina Gross would make a lovely couple. Both were embarrassed by the idea at the time, but they remained close friends.[40]

Emanuel and Bertha Gross, 1930s. Credit: The Estate of H. G. Adler 2019, Deutsches Literaturarchiv Marbach.

Left to right: Bettina Gross, H. G. Adler, Gutza Reder, Helmut Spiesmayr, Bertha Gross, Gina Wurm, Maria Gross, Emanuel Gross, and Bernard Reder in Roztoky near Prague, 1930s. Credit: The Estate of H. G. Adler 2019, courtesy of Jeremy Adler.

Adler later admitted, "I did not worry my head very much" over the Nazis, though he expected "nothing good from them." The contrast between the mounting menace of Nazism and the deceptively peaceful reality of Prague meant a deep divide between the inner life of a young intellectual such as Adler and the society around him. At the German University he witnessed the "general indoctrination of people older than me who were a lot smarter than me."[41] Czechoslovakia lagged behind Germany in barring Jews from professional positions, and its government did much to protect them, but anti-Semitism was evident among the medical faculty of the German University, where Jewish professors were so harassed that Dr. Josef Gach took his life in 1935, and Jews were barred from most student clubs.[42] After the Nazis took over, several prominent professors at both the German and Charles University were stripped of their titles. Among them were Emil Utitz, who as head of the "Office for Leisure Time Activities" later invited Adler to give his lecture on Kafka in Theresienstadt, and Oskar Kraus, a prominent philosopher and jurist. Kraus's wife, the actress Midia Pines, would start a salon in postwar London at which she gave the first public reading from Adler's second novel, *The Journey*, in 1951.[43] Adler's life and world were soon to be undone, but relations and connections were set in place that he would draw on in the future.

Along with Unger's philosophy, Adler brought back from Berlin a love of Kafka's writing after his aunt loaned him the unfinished novel *Der Verschollene*, later translated as *Amerika—The Man Who Disappeared*. At first he was disturbed by its alienation and nightmarish vision and debated whether he could continue reading Kafka at all. Eventually, however, Kafka became the single most important influence on him as a writer. During the mid-1930s he also read Dostoevsky, Jean Paul, Laurence Sterne, Cervantes, Kleist, and more of Stifter. Another Prague writer who grabbed his attention was Jaroslav Hašek (1883–1923), the author of the satirical antiwar novel *The Good Soldier Švejk*, published in Czech in 1923 and in German translation in 1926. Its protagonist, Josef Švejk, is a hapless dealer in stolen dogs whose effort to volunteer for the Austrian Army in World War I is so avid that officials cannot decide if he is an idiot or a traitor. Adler's attraction to the novel's absurdist humor and subversive politics complemented his love of Stifter's high-minded classicism and Kafka's dark evocations of the uncanny. All three writers cast a cold eye on the workings of the state and the prospects for modern civilization, and all posit the good will of unwitting, seemingly well-meaning individuals against people and forces that undermine them. The picaresque informs the adventures of each protagonist, for all are wayward characters who must navigate the perils of the corrupt societies they inhabit. Stifter's Heinrich does this most easily, leaving society for the innocence of nature. Švejk and Josef K. fend for themselves amid the treachery of the world, much as Adler had learned to do living away from home as a child and navigating Prague's multinational culture as a student.

While completing his dissertation Adler began to write a great deal of prose, although he described it in hindsight as "quite wild and ragged." One piece used a "mixture of Kafka and Jean Paul" to tell of a young art historian who forgets where his home is and accidentally enters an apartment where he had previously lived.[44] A highly cultivated family mistakes him for their son's tutor, who, they assume, only wished to come by to introduce himself, and an ensuing dinner scene unfolds complex exchanges and comic misunderstandings. This anticipates the sixth chapter of *Panorama*, in which Josef Kramer works as a private tutor for a bourgeois family anxious about the Depression and the demise of society around them, and the sense of returning to a home that has since become unrecognizable resonates with what was left of Adler's own home in Prague. By 1933, despite what Günther described as Emil's "touching naiveté . . . in thinking that his love could make his spouse healthy," Adler's father finally divorced Alice and married Zdenka Pisinger, nine years his junior. Adler claimed that the union drew out his father's "lesser qualities," the marriage soon proving a disappointment to both spouses. Günther did not get along with his stepmother and claimed derisively that "an entire novel could have been written about her." The most immediate impact on Adler was the dissolution of his childhood home when Emil moved with his second wife from Palackého 72 to Poděbradova 8, a few blocks away, right after the wedding.[45] At twenty-three Günther was a fully independent and mature young adult, but he moved there as well. Since his only surviving grandparent, Paula Gröger, had died in 1931, his father's new marriage and apartment marked a final break with whatever secure and recognizable childhood he knew.

Adler's unsettled home life mirrored the increasing disarray in Czechoslovak politics. After the founding of the First Republic in 1918, tensions between Czechs and Germans persisted throughout the 1920s, taking their most disastrous shape with the founding of the Sudeten German Homeland Front (Sudetendeutsche Heimatfront) by Konrad Henlein in October 1933. This developed into the Sudeten German Party (Sudetendeutsche Partei), which captured 67.4 percent of the votes of those who identified as German in the national elections in the spring of 1935 and an astounding 86 percent by 1938.[46] It would assist the Nazi annexation of the Sudetenland that year, but like the German Youth Movement, it did not begin as a Nazi organization. Instead, it resulted from the fact that for almost two decades there had been no third party to mediate between the Czechs, who controlled the state, and the Germans, who felt they had little power within it.[47] No matter his determination to rise above infighting, Masaryk declared famously in his first address to the National Assembly in December 1918 that the Germans "had originally come to the country as immigrants and colonists," a comment that salted German wounds for the next two decades.[48]

Destabilization was compounded by economic duress, the first upheaval occurring after the First World War and the second with the Great Depression. When independence was declared in 1918, three-fifths of heavy industry in the Austrian Empire was in Czechoslovakia, which made the economic calamity that followed the Armistice particularly grim. By 1925 the country was back on its feet, but the crash of 1929 crippled it again with nearly a million people out of work, around half remaining unemployed until 1937.[49] Hard times, however, were good for the Communists, who received 10 to 13 percent of the national vote throughout the 1920s and 1930s. The Social Democrats sided increasingly with the Czech nationalists to assemble a governing coalition under Masaryk, which forced the conservative German movement to vie for power with the

Communists.[50] The two groups held competing May Day rallies each year, at which the Czechs would demonstrate in support of the state and the democracy they cherished.[51] By 1938 such confrontations became so heated that the sight of traditional German dress could send Czech demonstrators into a frenzy, leading some to strip German nationalists of their white stockings and lederhosen in broad daylight. The Communists meanwhile complained that their traditional celebration of the proletariat had been coopted by both.[52]

Czechoslovakia's culture also suffered as a result of economic and political strife. Despite the renaissance in Czech painting, photography, and architecture of the 1920s, young German-speaking writers and intellectuals took editorial and teaching jobs in Leipzig, Vienna, Munich, and Berlin. Among writers the excesses of Czech nationalism drove out Werfel, the playwright Paul Kornfeld, and the novelist Ernst Weiss.[53] Only a handful of the Prague Circle stayed until the Nazis invaded in 1939, among them Johannes Urzidil and Max Brod. When Brod left on the last train out of Prague for Poland on March 15, 1939, he carried with him the Prague phone directory for 1938. It is said that it still lay on his desk when he died thirty years later in Tel Aviv.[54]

This allowed room for the next generation of Prague writers to flourish, including Adler and Steiner, as well as Hermann Grab, Helmut Spiesmayr, H. W. Kolben, Georg Kafka (a distant relative of Franz), Peter Kien, and Franz Wurm.[55] Besides publishing *Sea and Mountains* in 1931, Adler wrote some 120 poems between 1927 and 1936 that survived the war, as well as working on two novels that were lost. One of the novels was written entirely in the conversational voice of the female head of a bourgeois household afraid of the advent of Communism, and the other portrayed the music staff of a radio station, anticipating the sixth and seventh chapters of *Panorama*. Adler wrote the lengthy essay "Zur Bestimmung der Lyrik" ("On the Nature of Poetry)," which survives with several drafts he worked on before delivering it as a lecture to the Bayerische Akademie der Schönen Künste in 1956.[56] Cultural hindsight may tell us that, for the most part, the tensions of the country's *Realpolitik* swallowed whole the world of Kafka, but amid such dissolution Adler found a way to create and evolve as a writer in his own right.

After earning his doctorate in musicology in June 1935, in December of that year Adler, at twenty-five, stepped into the thick of Prague and Czech nationalist politics, taking a job as secretary of the Prague Urania House. A cultural center that presented lectures, films, language classes, and readings, the Prague Urania House was modeled on the one founded in Berlin in 1888 to educate the public about science, and it still exists. The Urania was predominantly a Jewish cultural organization, but as the biggest and most important German cultural center in Prague it also mounted programs by speakers and politicians sympathetic to Henlein and the Sudeten German Party. Thus, Adler experienced firsthand the difficulty of serving such vastly different constituencies as the third in command under the director, Oskar Frankl, and the assistant director, Heinrich Fischer. The house factotum, Adler taught German-language courses for Czechs at the center's "Masaryk-Volkshochschule" and recorded talks of his own and by others for Prague German Radio. He gave lectures at the center and organized public readings, including one by Thomas Mann, who fled Germany in 1936 and briefly held Czechoslovak citizenship before leaving for the United States in 1939. Regardless of Mann's fame as a writer, Adler was put off when the Nobel Laureate simply handed him his suitcase upon arrival at the train station and walked on without saying a word.[57]

VOLKSBILDUNGSHAUS URANIA

Prag II. Klimentská 4

EINLADUNG

ELIAS CANETTI.

der Wiener Dichter

LIEST

aus seinem Roman

DIE BLENDUNG

und aus seinem Drama

DIE HOCHZEIT

Einleitende Worte: Günther Adler

Freitag, am 21. Mai 1937 • 20 Uhr

Karten: Urania

Invitation to Elias Canetti's Reading at the Prague Urania, May 21, 1937. Credit: The Estate of H. G. Adler 2019, Deutsches Literaturarchiv Marbach.

On May 21, 1937, Adler took greater delight in organizing and introducing a reading by Elias Canetti, whose novel *Auto-da-Fé* had appeared in 1935. The event was a success, and Adler spent a week showing Canetti around Prague. Friendship and correspondence ensued, and the following year Adler was invited to join Canetti and his wife, Veza, for a week at the Salzburg Festival. At Adler's urging Canetti met Steiner in Vienna, their friendship later proving an oasis amid their shared exile in England. Canetti's masterful study of violence and political transgression, *Masse und Macht* (*Crowds and Power*), owes much to the thinking of Steiner as well as many conversations with Adler once he got to London. Canetti's 1937 reading at the Urania set in motion an intense friendship and rivalry among the three of them for years to come. Both Canetti and Steiner would eventually be thanked by Adler for their advice and loan of materials in the first edition of his Theresienstadt book, and it was they whom Adler would turn to when trying to escape the coming cataclysm. However, as with many a friendship between powerful minds and spirits, there were rocky patches, particularly with Canetti, whose habit of not answering letters angered Adler. By 1966 Adler would declare, "I have not seen him for over two years and also don't want anything more to do with him. I've personally invested more of myself in him than in any other person, and more than I ever received back." Nevertheless, Canetti continued to visit Adler in London in the 1970s, and Adler saw him in Zurich and in Germany.[58]

In Chapter 7 of *Panorama,* the tensions that consumed Prague are pointedly on display when Josef Kramer is interviewed by the beleaguered Professor Kamill Rumpler, the director of the cultural center, who complains that he is

> . . . constantly pulled to and fro, everyone wanting to put his two cents in, because he knows everything about the matter, though of course no one knows anything. What you think doesn't mean a thing, nor is it a question of taste, but you have to take precautions in order to defend democracy and freedom when they're threatened. But freedom, what is that? Goethe knew the answer, that's clear, but he didn't have to live in our times and take social and political precautions that I have to keep an eye on. You see, you have to make compromises if you want to balance the swastika with the Socialists. You also have to know the government's plans exactly and what it wants, in order to be careful. If I speak to someone on the left, then they scream that Rumpler is a Red, and then if I briefly talk to someone on the right, then the lefties start screaming that Rumpler is a Nazi. My friend, people begrudge Rumpler, but it's easy for people to run off at the mouth. Who today

> appreciates humanity and democracy? They don't mean anything, you might say, but you have no idea of the difficulties.[59]

Anxious as Rumpler sounds, Adler satirizes the cultural center as a kind of ongoing calamity ("Rumpler" means "noise bag" in German). One customer who wishes to buy a ticket for the cinema waits forever for change from the business office, only to have Rumpler invite him to do a radio talk on raising canaries, the man's hobby. Meanwhile the guest lecturer for the evening is upset there is no projector available, the projectionist having called in sick. A crazy woman demands of Professor "Rapp" (i.e., Rumpler) that she be allowed to read stories about animals on the radio, and she has proposed to the ministry of the interior a statute that "establishes a society for mixed marriages between enemy nations, religions, and races." This she is sure will bring an end to hate and war, since "Czechs would marry Germans and Jews would marry Christians."[60] The only seemingly serious proposal is from a Herr Kummerhackl ("misery pick"), who wants to give a talk on his book, *The Solution to the Social Question: A Practical Plan for the People of Europe*. Rumpler has ignored the man for three months and does not book him now. Rumpler may think that "Everyone is diligent and does his work" in his "Reich,"[61] but the underlying message is clear: the workings of the cultural center are an administrative travesty at best and a reflection of the chaos in the culture that surrounds it at worst.

Not merely a mocking pastiche of a poorly run institution the author once worked at, the chapter is a searing cultural critique that uses humor to mask the tragedy below its surface. One reads it without knowing whether to think it sad, if it were not so funny, or funny, if it were not so sad. At the end of the day Josef can only stand

> . . . under the blue neon lights that spell out CULTURAL CENTER in large letters, everything exuding the feel of culture, a place of Goethean calm and the pure human spirit, but all of it destroyed through stamped tickets, . . . radio talks trilled by canaries, . . . while others make epochal discoveries, Frau Michalik having selected beautiful passages from new writers about mixed marriages between red shirts and brown, . . . the conflicts of the time resolved through the love of animals.[62]

Walking home, Josef finds that he "long ago lost any sense of where he lives."[63] The statement resonates on multiple levels, again echoing the poignant question posed by the Czechoslovak national anthem, "Where Is My Home?", which Adler asked himself as he watched the city and the culture he loved rapidly fall apart.

The tragedy of the destruction of Czechoslovakia's democratic republic in the 1930s, and the eradication of its Jewish population, is not only that it occurred, but that there was no internal reason for it. From inception the country's social balance was indeed precarious. The Czechs made up a bare majority of 51 percent, and deep ethnic, linguistic, economic, and educational divides existed between and within its four provinces—Bohemia, Moravia, Slovakia, and Subcarpathian Ruthenia. Bohemia and Moravia were modern in both culture and industry, Slovakia was predominantly agrarian and less educated, while the Ruthenians were poor and barely literate.[64] Cultural tensions had also festered for centuries among the Counter-Reformation Catholicism of the Habsburgs; the Protestant, mostly Czech underclass; the mostly Catholic Germans; and the Jews. Yet for over a decade it worked, and for the most part well. Ruled by a coalition of five parties held together by Masaryk's calm and reasoned guidance, it was the most pluralistic and tolerant state in Europe. Although it suffered severe economic struggle following World War I and further duress in the Great Depression, it had inherited 70 to 80 percent of the empire's heavy, light, and consumer industries, allowing it to weather economic downturns better than most.[65] With separation between church and state, parliamentary participation, legalized intermarriage, and census laws that, though flawed, allowed citizens to choose their legal identity through language, religion, and nationality, Czechoslovakia contained enough room for its competing factions to not only coexist, but also to ascribe to democratic statehood as central to the idea of being "Czechoslovakian," even amid the growing recalcitrance of its German-speaking population. Masaryk reflected at the end of the 1920s, "Thirty more years of peaceful, rational, efficient progress and the country will be secure."[66] But it was not to be.

So what happened, and why could the country's eventual demise not be stopped?[67] First, uneven distribution of economic struggles between ethnicities sowed seeds of resentment when, beginning in 1930, the three million Germans who made up nearly a quarter of the population felt they bore a disproportionate share of job losses brought on by the Depression, particularly because Czechs controlled so much of the bureaucracy. Resentment was fomented by Hitler's rise in neighboring Germany and his vow to protect ethnic Germans everywhere. In Czechoslovakia, this led to the birth of the German National Socialist Party, or Nazi Party, which doubled in size between 1930 and 1932. Czechoslovak authorities prepared to ban the Nazi Party within its borders in the fall of 1933, but the party dissolved itself and several of its leaders fled to Germany. Konrad Henlein, who helped turn the gymnastic association he led into a pro-Sudeten movement, formed the Sudeten German Homeland Front, whose immediate and meteoric popularity among the German population made it a vehicle for antiliberal and anti-Semitic fulminations that radicalized the Bohemian Germans as a whole.

By 1935 the Sudeten German Homeland Front changed its name to the Sudeten German Party. Funded covertly by the Nazi Party of Germany, it saw tremendous success in the elections, which allowed it to claim to speak for the entire German population, eliminating more liberal "activist" organizations, such as the German Social Democrats, whose right to call themselves "German" was publicly questioned.[68] Soon Hitler overcame his hesitancy to get involved in Bohemian German politics, and his rhetoric about the need to "protect" the rights and dignity of Germans everywhere increased with each broadcast and rally. The Nuremberg Laws in September of that year sealed the Nazi ideology upon Germany and set off a wave of Jewish refugees and antifascist Germans fleeing to Prague, including prominent writers and intellectuals. Thomas Mann and his brother Heinrich arrived, and Bertolt Brecht landed there for a few days before going to Switzerland. Erich Maria Remarque, author of *All Quiet on the Western Front*, wrote a novel about his stay in Prague called *Liebe deinen Nächsten* (translated as *Flotsam* in 1941). The young poet Stefan Heym was also a resident, and from Austria came the painter Oskar Kokoschka, who stayed in the hotel room next to Canetti when he had visited. The future playwright Peter Weiss lived in Prague for four years while studying at the Academy of Fine Arts before fleeing to Sweden.[69] For nearly four decades Prague had been an intellectual crossroads of Europe by choice, but now it was out of necessity.

Henlein and his party rose to great popularity in the Bohemian countryside, but Czechoslovakia as a whole remained tolerant toward the Jews and vigilant of their needs. As early as June 1933, Edvard Beneš, the foreign minister and Masaryk's eventual successor, stated, "No one, and naturally no Jew, declaring himself a member of the German nation—and I underline that—could in our country be persecuted because of this, as long as his allegiance to our state remains beyond doubt." A Jewish Committee for Aid to Refugees from Germany was established in Prague in 1934, and in 1935 the Parliament and the minister of the interior assured petitioners that residency permits would be quickly granted to Jewish refugees whose political conduct was "irreproachable." Funding for these efforts, and numerous other committees set up by sectarian and nonsectarian organizations, was mostly organized by wealthy Czech citizens, but it also came from England, the United States, and even the Soviet Union, which had become a haven for religious and political refugees alike.[70]

Adler witnessed both the attacks on Jews and the support of them and other refugees. He saw the outburst of hostilities between Czechs and Germans at Prague's two universities, the Czech-speaking Charles University and the German University. In 1934, Czech nationalist students at Charles University demanded the enforcement of a 1920 law that called for the transfer of ancient insignia held by the German University to the Charles University. Seemingly minor, it incensed the Germans. Both sides marched through the streets, smashing windows and singing patriotic songs, causing Karel Čapek to lament, "It would seem that our republic indeed has a spiritual and ideological affinity with the Third Reich. . . . A peculiar type of Czech anti-Semitism."[71]

Soon antiliberal pressure forced curtailment of rights and support granted to refugees, and borders were tightened. Despite appeals by the National Coordinating Committee that governed all refugee organizations, some 3,600 Jews were transferred to other countries in 1936–1937.[72] Given that Prague had hosted an important Zionist Congress as late as 1933 and the fact that Masaryk himself had visited Palestine in 1927, the political tensions suffered by Professor Rumpler in *Panorama* were clearly true for the country as a whole, and no doubt for Adler as secretary of the Urania. "Czechoslovakian democracy was dying and nearly in shambles," Adler later recalled. "I didn't like the job at all and actually wanted to leave Europe altogether. Although I could see what was happening, for some strange reason I didn't leave, even though I made some attempts to do so in 1938 and 1939. In any case, my position at the Urania allowed me a peek into a culture that in truth had nothing more to do with culture, but only its mendacious and half-destroyed semblance."[73]

Nevertheless, Adler continued to grow as an intellectual. His engagement with Eastern mysticism and Drtikol's circle ended in 1935, but his theological interests persisted as he turned to "the long-term goal of a messianism, in the Jewish sense, that could engage with the world." The world about him, however, was fast closing down, a fact evidenced by the thousands of refugees who had fled Germany. Among them was the poet Alfred Wolfenstein (1888–1945), who persuaded Adler to give a reading at the Urania on October 7, 1936. "It was the only poetry reading I gave before the war, and it was warmly received, though it was also the last time that my many German, Jewish, and Czech friends were together as one." Both Gustav Becking and the composer Viktor Ullmann attended, as well as Max Brod, who reviewed the event for the *Prager Tagblatt*, praising Adler's "idyllic verse," which reminded him of Joseph von Eichendorff and "along with powerfully realistic passages was the highpoint of the evening." But for Adler and others, such moments of celebration were laced with sadness, since almost anyone from Prague "could not help but perceive a heightened sense of fleeting melancholy, whether in regards to all of creation, his own life, or the city of Prague—this 'beautiful stony corpse,' as a writer of the times said."[74]

EINLADUNG

GÜNTHER ADLER
lädt höflich zu seiner
VORLESUNG aus
EIGENEN DICHTUNGEN ein.

ZEIT: MITTWOCH, den 7. OKTOBER 8 h.
ORT: URANIA, Prag II., Klimentská 4, KLEINER SAAL.

Regiebeitrag Kč 6·-, Studenten Kč 4·-.
Karten: Urania, Wetzler und Abendkassa.

Invitation to Günther Adler's Reading at the Prague Urania, October 7, 1936. Credit: The Estate of H. G. Adler 2019, Deutsches Literaturarchiv Marbach.

The situation for both Adler and Prague was untenable, but worse days lay ahead. In September 1937, Masaryk died at 87. Having handed over the presidency to Edvard Beneš in December 1935 because of failing health, he remained the founding father of the nation, and his death was an ominous blow in uncertain times. Hitler was determined to grab the Sudetenland, and on November 5, 1937, the Führer told his military staff to prepare to invade Austria and Czechoslovakia "to make secure and to preserve the racial community [of Germany] and enlarge it," to stem the decline of Germandom and, more strategically, secure enough farmland to feed Germany. This would require the expulsion of two million people from Czechoslovakia and one million from Austria and the annexation of the Sudetenland. In the long term, it also meant the destruction of Czechoslovakia.[75]

Hitler's support of the Sudeten German Party enabled Henlein to pressure the Czech government to grant more consideration to German interests, as well as material aid, government contracts, and jobs. With Germany's annexation of Austria on March 12, 1938, Czechoslovak officials hoped to appease Hitler by granting more power to the German minority, but they did not know what he told Henlein in secret: "We must always demand so much [of the Czechs] that we can never be satisfied."[76] The annexation of the Sudetenland was not just a threat, but an inevitability. France and Britain paved the way at the Munich conference in September 1938, demanding that Czechoslovakia turn over the Sudetenland or have its alliance with France dissolved. Prime Minister Neville

Chamberlain betrayed Britain's ambivalence when he admitted, "How horrible, fantastic, incredible it is that we should be digging trenches and trying on gas masks here because of a quarrel in a faraway country between people of whom we know nothing."[77]

September 30, 1938, marked the founding of the Second Republic, whose name changed from the Republic of Czechoslovakia to Czecho-Slovakia.[78] Rarely has a hyphen signified more, the name foreshadowing the political struggle between what was left of Bohemia and Moravia to the west and Slovakia to the east. Hitler hoped to capitalize upon this, and within days Sudeten Germans rode a wave of euphoria as its paramilitary Freikorps arrested over 10,000 "enemies of the Reich" and sent them to Dachau. In Germany, Jews and their businesses were attacked, the widespread violence reaching its apex with the "Kristallnacht" pogrom of November 9–10. In the weeks following, some 20,000 to 30,000 Jews fled the Sudetenland for the interior of Bohemia and Prague, and another 160,000 Czechs and German liberals joined them.

Adler's 1938 poem "Stadtplatz im November" ("City Square in November") captures the anxious, eerie mood the refugees found among a populace half in denial of what was happening, half asleep before the trouble ahead:

> Cold, threatening clouds roll in
> Above a tense evening in the city.
> Beneath the trees dark steps shuffle
> Aimlessly through the swirling winds.
>
> Shrilly sounds the hawker's cry:
> The latest headlines—on sale here!
> Weary with arrogance, gold and silver shine
> Behind a glass pane in velvet-lined cases.
>
> Strange bronze faces loom proudly
> Above the square, the menacing granite.
> Sharp lights shimmer errant and forsaken,
> Passing heedless, mouldering in fog.[79]

Inside the vibrant city a light switched off when Britain, France, and the world turned their backs to Prague in Munich. Adler and his fellow citizens could only stand by as the fog rolled in.

On March 15, 1939, the Germans invaded, Hitler dined on Czech ham and beer in the Hradčany Castle, and Czechoslovakia disappeared as a state.[80] A rickety "Third Republic" existed briefly after the war, before the Communist putsch of 1948, but it would take another sixty years for democracy to return in earnest with the Velvet Revolution of 1989, a year after Adler's death.

Unfortunately, the Second Republic of 1939 was not as hospitable to refugees as the first. Ruled by the fascist National Unity Party that refused membership to Jews, Poles, Germans, and Magyars, the government dismissed its Jewish employees, drove out Jewish professors from the universities, and shut down Jewish newspapers, theaters, and cultural organizations. In no time at all, over twenty thousand Jews were forced into another exile. Even more restrictive laws were proposed, and when Czech officials dismissed several Slovak leaders in March 1939, Hitler urged Slovakia to declare independence. When it did, he was free to march into what was left of Bohemia and Moravia and declare an autonomous "Protectorate" as Poland sliced off Silesia for itself and Hungary took over Subcarpathian Ruthenia and parts of Slovakia.

The most immediate consequences for Adler were twofold. Realizing that he would soon be forced out, in June 1938 he resigned his position at the Urania. Emil Franzel, successor to Oskar Frankl as director, awarded him a month's severance, extended his work papers until September, and wrote him a glowing recommendation. In spite of being registered as a Protestant who held German nationhood through his mother tongue in the 1930 census, his Jewish birth certificate meant that his rights as a citizen of what was left of Czecho-Slovakia were curtailed even more. The Protectorate in 1939 was followed by official adoption of the Nuremberg Laws, denying citizenship even to Jews who, like Adler, were identified officially as "German."

Given Adler's "flawed" German citizenship, Canetti's memory of their first meeting in 1937 is poignant: "He was intensely idealistic and seemed out of place in the damnable times to which he was soon to fall victim. Even in Germany it would have been hard to find a man more dominated by German literary tradition. But he was here in Prague. He spoke and read Czech with ease, respected Czech literature and music, and explained everything I did not understand in a way that made it attractive to me."[81] Regardless of such poise, Adler as a Jew was condemned to a political and economic limbo. "I could see that Czechoslovakia's days were numbered, and that any Jew who was at all free of encumbrances had best leave the German sphere of power as fast as possible."[82] In the summer of 1938, Adler attempted exactly that.

5

The Flight

Adler claimed that in the early 1930s he did not worry much about the Nazis, but by the time Germany invaded Austria in March 1938, he appreciated the danger he and others faced. In early April, Steiner's mother, Martha, wrote to her son in London, "They say things here are 'tense.' The situation, about which nothing can be done, can't help but make one feel fatalistic. What good does it do to be nervous and anxious? . . . The most anxious of all is Günther, who is already thinking of going to Palestine in July."[1] Written that June, Adler's "Flight Song" reveals his fatalistic turn of mind only weeks before his twenty-eighth birthday:

> What is left you but continual flight
> From one battle to another,
> What is it you seek from these times
> But yet more time itself?
>
> Anxieties accompany you
> On the wild hunt from bay to bay,
> Toppling you into the abyss
> Between a moment and eternity.
>
> The real world seems a dream,
> And dreaming, you grasp the real,
> Barely grasping how either realm
>
> Palpably prepares your fate:
> In seeking what fortune is left you,
> You fall into time's sure flight.[2]

Thinking about what increasingly seemed inevitable, Adler elevates the historical necessity of flight in the immediate moment to the flight of time itself, recalling, too, the biblical flight into Egypt. His sonnet speaks on three levels: the individual caught in dire circumstances, the participant-observer standing outside circumstances to see a larger context, and a modern Jew seeing within the quotidian a mytho-poetic fate that spans millennia. Adler may have indeed been "the most nervous of all," but "Flight Song" reveals the way that writing served as the compass charting his journey.

In addition to Palestine, Adler considered fleeing to Paris, where Bernard Reder had moved in 1937. A letter to Steiner in May also mentions Milan. No matter the destination, Adler felt compelled to disperse the essentials of his life in Prague for safekeeping—namely, his library and his manuscripts. Trusting several hundred books to Hans Rosenkranz, a close friend who had emigrated to Jerusalem, he also sent copies of the two novels he had started, his diaries, and several manuscripts to Reder in Paris. Unfortunately, Rosenkranz sold Adler's library to a book dealer in Jerusalem named Meyer, and Reder left Adler's writings behind when he was forced to flee Paris in 1940. While Adler could forgive Reder, he never forgave Rosenkranz and mourned the loss of his library ever after.

By July 1938, the question of where Adler would land after leaving Prague seemed settled. After giving two weeks' notice at the Urania in June, he left for Milan, where he took a training course to sell industrial abrasives in South America for a company with headquarters in Prague. By mid-July he wrote to Steiner from Italy that he had dismantled his "Lebensraum" in Prague but felt "well fitted out" and prepared for whatever might come. "And that means a great deal," he continued. "I managed it all with an inner calm that, now in retrospect, almost astounds me."[3]

Adler's reference to "Lebensraum" reveals a sly undermining of Hitler's fantasy that without more "living space," Germany could not feed itself and attain its full promise. In speech after ranting speech it had become shorthand for rabid expansionism, which had swallowed Austria and within a year would claim Czechoslovakia and Poland. Convinced that "foreign policy is the art of securing for a people the necessary quantity and quality of Lebensraum," Hitler vowed it would dominate his "entire being" as long as he lived.[4] For Adler the reference encompasses his personal possessions and property, as well as the household and community he had long inhabited. In household after household across Prague, however, the individual's existence was precisely what was obliterated to serve the needs of the "Volk." Adler's effort to coopt a sullied collective term demonstrates his awareness of what was at stake. Sending off his books and papers and selling whatever remained, Adler traded one "Lebensraum" for another, but seizing the word as his own term was a form of resistance anticipating his later listing of over six hundred Nazi terms and euphemisms in his monograph on Theresienstadt.

Adler brought only a few manuscripts, books, and papers with him to Milan. A single contact from a female singer in Prague helped him to rent a pleasant room with a balcony overlooking a garden at Via Lanzone 5. He also met some of the locals, who quickly revealed that Italy promised little respite from fascism.

Some of the Italians he met were "complete partisan fanatics," although they "tolerated the candor of the 'ebraico' [Jew] quite well."[5]

By September, anti-Semitism was everywhere in Italy, its newspapers and periodicals flooded with stereotypical depictions of hooked noses and shady characters familiar from Nazi publications. In a lengthy letter to Steiner he parses the more subtle depictions in the *Corriere della Sera,* Milan's mainstream newspaper, and the overt antagonism of rags like *Il Giornalissimo* (*The Daily Journal*) and *La difesa de la razza* (*The Defender of the Race*). They served up a "barely disguised hatred of the Jews," but unlike the violence and chaos he had experienced in Germany in 1933, Adler noted that on the street it "is completely quiet and there is nothing at all to see. . . . The people are neither interested in nor against the Jews. In private my fascist friends approve of the measures being taken, while at the same time they could not have more sympathy for me or offer to help more. I'm smart enough to make sure not to distance myself from them, but also to make sure to keep my head down."[6]

Adler's ability to live within the culture at hand while maintaining distance from it was influenced by Bronisław Malinowski's "participant-observer" approach as an anthropologist, whereby a researcher must be both part of the culture studied and stand apart from it as a detached observer. Adler read Malinowski's classic 1922 *Argonauts of the Western Pacific* when Steiner loaned it to him in the early 1930s, and its influence is clear when, after describing to Steiner his cautious relations with his Italian cohort, Adler shares a "debate" he has with "one of the nicest" of the locals:

ME: So what's so different today from yesterday?

HE: We used to be tolerant; we wanted to give the Jews every chance to prove themselves good fascist Italians. Even if yesterday someone was my friend, if today he is not friendly toward me, then now he cannot be my friend.

ME: Why do you need to make such generalizations?

HE: It's not about atoning for their guilt; I agree that's awful.

ME: What then does "racism" mean to you?

HE: Nothing, but the Jews have brought it upon themselves, because they always think of themselves as a people apart. It almost always is the case: first a Jew, then an Italian. But here the demarcations need to be totally clear. If one wants as a Jew to be a Jew, and will leave the country, then I have no problem with that. It's just not possible to reap the benefits of Italian citizenship, and do so with *riservatio* [reservation].

This continues in the same vein for two pages. Adler cuts to the heart of the politics that surround him, maintaining the scholarly calm necessary for a convincing yet damning portrait. Adler exclaims, "[Y]ou stand before such thick clouds of ignorance, and it is nothing short of hair-raising," but within the exchange the tides of hate and distrust hardly seem to affect him.

Adler was not ignorant of the threat of what he was witnessing, nor did he appreciate any less the dangers that could arise from it. At the end of a 1936 letter to Steiner from a tense Prague, he admitted, "I find myself in a situation that I realize marks a time of great decisions, one could even call it a crisis, if my nature were so disposed. Nonetheless, it's a time whose developments I am living through intensely." In the next sentence Adler tells Steiner he's borrowing books on ethnology from Steiner's library at his parents' house in order to learn "something more about ethnological practice than what is received through general knowledge."[7] Anticipating the crisis ahead, the scholar prepares. Meanwhile, the skills he developed helped him keep his head.

Adler readied himself for emigration by studying Italian as well as Spanish, Portuguese, English, and Hebrew. His plan to emigrate to Brazil was contingent on getting a visa, and he hoped to get to Paris and Reder by Christmas or the New Year or find a way to get to England. " 'Who knows what the next week will bring?' " he comments jauntily to Steiner in early September, but follows with the plaintive hope that he and Steiner can meet again, although "it will likely be a couple years" before that can occur.[8] A month later, hard on the heels of the Munich agreement, Adler tells Steiner of his visit to Lugano and wishes they could enjoy the beauty of the countryside there together, longing to return to the peace and easy exchange they had known hiking the forests of Bohemia. Planning to emigrate to South America, Adler dreamed of returning to Czechoslovakia. He hoped to be able to "commute between Palestine and Europe, spending most of my time in the Middle East," but he knew the chances were slim.

The clear-eyed realist lived hand in hand with the wistful dreamer, especially after Munich. "I am not afraid," Adler writes a week after the loss of the Sudetenland. "I never was afraid, yet my stomach kept turning over. I know well, and can see for the moment that it will not come to war, but only for the time being. The entire celebration in the West was unjustified, and peace will not be assured through this shameful agreement—not in any way! That I don't believe. England just didn't want to do anything—that's all; so they sold out the Republic." One could have heard the same opinion on any street in Prague. Despite claiming that "politics always felt unfamiliar and repulsive," his prediction of what is to come is remarkably accurate:

> In short, the Republic will have to depend on the good graces of its neighbors as archangels. No international guarantee, no matter from whom, can save it by any practical or moral means. The game that our

> English and French friends have set into motion can only be labeled as repulsive. At last Germany has a clear path all the way to the Romanian border, and their concerns will likely be met with a great deal of sympathy in the Republic of Romania. It is easy to imagine that Mr. Preiss and Mr. Beran and Mr. Tiso . . . and the rest of the Republic will stand entirely under German influence.[9] Once again the truth conquers all! Germany will take over the legions of the Czech minority, the streets of Prague will be overrun with Jews, more oppression will occur (by the so-called original grassroots movement). Once again there will be a slew of refugees headed for God knows where, since they won't be able to go to Palestine, while some English bishop will pray for them, France will have lost its last moral and geographic footing in Europe, and England hopes that through its courageous diplomacy it has prevented a new version of the Thirty Years War breaking out after yet another battle for the White Mountain.[10]

In October 1938, Beran and Tiso had yet to assume their respective positions as prime minister of Czecho-Slovakia and president of Slovakia that would turn them into Nazi pawns, but Adler could see the writing on the wall, and he shared it with his Italian colleagues only to be met with disbelieving smiles.[11] His analysis betrays his anxiety about the lack of political options, although a few lines later he comments astutely, "I can only think that whoever wishes to have peace must not fear war." Adler sent numerous drafts of poetry and prose to Steiner for safekeeping, ominously reminding him, "In your hands you have everything which, in its present and albeit unfinished and unsatisfactory state, I think matters."[12] Four months earlier he sent Steiner a copy of his will.[13]

Adler's time in Milan, however, was not entirely wasted, for as he often proved, extreme duress stirred his creative energies. During his six months there he worked on poems and prose and thought deeply about religion, philosophy, and politics. Only a few poems stem from this time, but a dozen prose pieces survive. After the war he collected them with other stories as *Gegenüber der Wirklichkeit* (*In the Face of Reality*), which he tried unsuccessfully to publish, although they eventually made up the bulk of his 1964 collection, *Der Fürst des Segens: Parabeln—Betrachtungen—Gleichnisse* (*The Prince of Blessings: Parables, Observations, Analogies*). Of its twenty-seven pieces, twelve were written in 1938 and nine in 1940, the first of his mature fictional work, although "fictional" is a somewhat misleading term, for only a few are fictionalizations of daily events. Most are pithy "observations" on the plight of a society coming undone, or parables that seem straight out of Kafka, but really are slightly mythologized renderings of the absurdity he found every day in Germany, Czecho-Slovakia, and Italy.

The title piece observes that "in the face of reality the individual is powerless and defenseless" and that "courage and the readiness to act" are nothing more than "tokens that always can be ridiculed by accepted public opinion." Adler concludes that "any such behavior is in the face of reality only a duty, but one promising no fulfillment."[14] As grim as this is, it would be a mistake to take it as defeatist. There is a way in which such statements carry the tone of the propaganda and edicts issued by the powers that be. Whether warning, realization, or pronouncement, it is up to the reader to decide; Adler presents the reality at hand rather than offering pat solutions.

Thus he gives the tale of a newspaper that refuses to acknowledge the "calamity" rumored to be afoot, while even the brief dismissal of such rumor is ignored by its readers. Or the parable of a mayor who employs an inmate from the local insane asylum to preside over a macabre farce in which citizens to whom the inmate gives red cards are sent away immediately, while those who receive white cards are allowed to consult the officials they seek. Or the parable of a people who love their duke and are willing to forgive slight "mistakes" and "injustices" as they have received "assurances" that they are not the duke's fault but the fault of "negligent civil servants who will be relieved of their positions and soon meet with just sentences."[15] Or the trial in which the judge despises the defendant so much that he insists that he speak for him rather than allowing him to testify in his own defense. Despite the judge's well-known history of corruption, when he hands down a sentence of twenty years, all agree the trial has been handled impeccably.

And all of this in 1938, a year before the start of the war and six months before the invasion of Czecho-Slovakia. Be it the tax collector who asks a merchant cryptically to "forsake your immediate presence" ("von Ihrer Vorhandenheit ablassen"), which beyond his befuddlement leads the merchant to eventually take his own life, or "The Magician Joan Filipescu" whose rousing speeches seduce a fawning public, or the persecuted man named "Feindfreund" ("enemy-friend") who "sees the world as *the* calamity, while it seemed to him the world saw him as the *calamity*," Adler's observations and parables extract the absurdities and terrors of the time with precision.[16] Although they raise the specter that there is "no justice for the individual, at least not in this life," Adler maintains that "the question of justice is only an attempt at grasping perfection." Anyone caught up in similar circumstances may ask, "What should he undertake, when he knows that he cannot escape the injustice of the times, and at the same time knows that 'simultaneously' he will be expelled by them, and yet after all he has to do something?" For Adler, asking this leads one toward "a Redeemer genuinely believed in or which one may hope to find," as well as the ultimate question, "Will the impossible make itself perhaps for once possible within the possible, and the possible become the really real?"[17]

Adler also brought such questions with him to Milan in the draft of an essay he began in 1936, "Von zweierlei Arten der Wirkung" ("On Two Types of

Actuality"), the ideas for which had appeared in his poetry since 1932. With the aim of exploring "the most vital aspects of my world view in an impersonal manner," Adler wanted "to come to terms with a number of conceptions through the exploration of messianic aims posed in abstract form." Drawing on Erich Unger's project of the "known" in dialogue with the "eternally unknown," Adler hoped to expand his conception of reality beyond the empirical in order to tap a messianic engagement with the divine that he felt had been lost.[18] From Milan he complained to Steiner that he was not writing or reading much or that he was just working on a few "shreds of theology," but he continued to make progress on spiritual matters that had long occupied him.[19]

Bettina Gross, summer 1938. Credit: The Estate of H. G. Adler 2019, Deutsches Literaturarchiv Marbach.

As ever, Adler wrote numerous letters to friends and family. His letters to Steiner refer to correspondence with his father, Reder, Brömse, Spiesmayr, and a host of other Prague acquaintances, among them Bettina Gross, with whom he carried on serious discussions about his ideas on reality. She destroyed his correspondence after leaving Prague for England in December, but she kept his November 8, 1938, letter to her from Milan. What he would soon refer to as his "Traktat" (Treatise) consisted of twenty-eight single-spaced pages, totaling over sixteen thousand words and spelling out his beliefs about reality, the role of religion and politics in shaping human behavior, and the importance of "intuition" as a means for perceiving the true nature of reality beneath life's surface. At the same time that Hitler was arranging for the fulfillment of the Munich "Diktat" (Decree) that culminated in the betrayal of Czecho-Slovakia and set it on a path to destruction, Adler composed a "Traktat" that explored human history and its potential for engagement with the divine. Faced with a world quickly going to hell, Adler chose to write on what transcended it.

The "Traktat" represented over a decade of thought and study, and by March 1939 he had enough confidence to number it among the works he had made significant progress on in Milan, sharing its title, "Über die Wirklichkeit—ein theologischer Versuch" ("On Reality—A Theological Approach") with Steiner.[20] He wrote another draft titled "Über Wirklichkeit und Sein" ("On Reality and Being") in 1941, and at the end of his life he mined it for his final book, *Vorschule für eine Experimentaltheologie: Betrachtungen über Wirklichkeit und Sein* (*Draft of an Experimental Theology: Observations on Reality and Being*), published in 1987. Discounting *Sea and Mountains*, the 1931 poetry collection that he later disowned as juvenilia, the "Traktat" in many ways was his first and last book, a "life book." Its central tenet, that Being was larger than reality, and its mantra, "know what you can do, and what you do," were cornerstones of what carried him through the camps.

After his six months of training in Milan, Adler's plans to emigrate soon came to nothing. When he returned to Prague in December, he learned from the Brazilian embassy that he would have to purchase a roundtrip voyage in order to receive a visa. "I remained quite calm, but of course I could not afford it," he wrote to Steiner just ten days before the Nazis invaded Prague. When he tried to secure a bank loan, he was turned down, as no financier was confident of repayment. He describes the bleak mood descending on Czecho-Slovakia, saying, "It's all so miserable and disgusting. The nation for all intents and purposes keeps up a good face. A betrayed people full of suppressed rage and despair."[21] Steiner could see what was obvious; the entry for April 14, 1939, in his diary simply states, "Günther in despair."[22]

When the Germans invaded and the country was dissolved, despair turned into panic. Adler tried desperately but unsuccessfully to secure a visa for

France. England was his best and last chance of escape, for Steiner and Canetti were there and had connections. Writing on April 11, 1939, Adler pressed Steiner for some concrete plan: "What are you all thinking of? Some kind of invitation? Or a student visa? Or something else? Scholarly work? Work in some kind of continuing education center? Radio? As a writer? Graphology? Italian? As an expert in the abrasives industry? Literature, music, art history? What have any of you tried? What kind of connections do you have? Any among the English? Are there costs that I won't be able to cover? What kind of information or documentation do you need?" Adler assures Steiner that his passport is good until 1942, that he is a Czech citizen, and that he has evidence of his doctorate and a record of his baptism as a Protestant.[23] On the 24th he tells Steiner, "For me it's important to know whether you or Elias can guarantee anything, or scrape up anything. At least let me know! . . . How can one leave somebody in the dark so? It would almost be better not to do anything at all!" If such neglect were not enough, dredging up his baptism is painful, admitting, "You know how I can't stand the whole baptism thing . . . But since I have this scrap of paper, I might as well perpetuate the charade and get whatever use out of it I can. If I amount to something someday, I can decide for myself what I want to be, and this won't matter in the least, no matter how much I'm disgusted by it."[24]

Given the speed and force of German oppression, such panic was not only warranted but sensible. When on March 16, 1939, Hitler signed a decree inside the Hradčany Castle establishing the "Reich Protectorate of Bohemia and Moravia," only patriotic Germans of the former Czecho-Slovakia could have believed that the nation would enjoy "the fullest autonomy," as he had promised President Emil Hácha two days before in Berlin. In the same decree Hitler reminded all that the Nuremburg Laws stated that Jews could not be citizens of Germany. During the first week of occupation alone, a thousand refugees and Communists were arrested, and within weeks 4,639 were behind bars.[25] Two days into the occupation Hácha's government imposed severe restrictions excluding Jews from participation in public life, and three days later the German Military Authority made it illegal for Jews to serve in the administration of any enterprise they owned in whole or in part.[26] On March 20 the Old-New Synagogue in Prague was set on fire, and in May the "viceroy" of the Protectorate, Konstantin von Neurath, decreed that Jews were banned from civil service, the courts, working in the stock market, and as teachers in schools. It took until July for Adolf Eichmann to set up the Central Office for Jewish Emigration in Bohemia and Moravia, which all Jewish congregations in the Protectorate had to answer to, but before then nearly nine thousand Jews fled the country, while another ten thousand left before the end of the year.[27]

Adler was not among them, for neither Steiner nor Canetti did much to save him. After the war, Steiner admitted to Rudolf Hartung, "My incompetence and impracticality prevented me from getting him out before the war"—but in fairness, it was not easy.[28] A sum of fifty pounds had to be paid to the Home Office as a guarantee, although Britain also sharply curtailed the number of visas.[29] Canetti's silence, however, disturbed Adler, who complained to Steiner, "I find it very strange that at such a time Elias does not answer any of your questions. These are really not the kind of pleasant times in which one can let letters go unanswered."[30]

Years later, in the novel *Die unsichtbare Wand* (*The Wall*), the first draft of which Adler completed in 1956, Arthur Landau questions the motives of Oswald Bergmann, a stand-in for Canetti, and why he ignored pleas to help Arthur emigrate, even though Bergmann acknowledges that " 'an unanswered letter can result in a murder' " in times of crisis. Arthur realizes "Oswald was not a murderer, . . . but his neglecting to answer my letter felt as if he were."[31] Adler continued to feel wounded by the unwillingness of his friends to help him get out. At the time Adler knew that he was making demands, and he apologizes for any duress he has caused them. "I perhaps am writing in impatience," he writes to Steiner on April 24, "and sharing with you every last detail of the very real situation here with the false assumption that doing so might provide some possible way out of it. But don't think I am at all uneasy. Whoever sees clearly can quite easily tamp down all such distress. I am really quite fine." And yet he was not. Time was running out; something had to happen soon.

Something did happen: Günther fell in love. Returning to Prague in late December 1938, Adler met Gertrud Klepetar on New Year's Eve. Five years older, she posed a striking presence that took him aback. "She was tall, blond, very elegant, yet a troubled person, radiant one moment, dejected the next, possessed of the manliest kind of intelligence and yet the most feminine of sensitivities, incisive analytical powers and a superstitious shyness. One would take her for a Scandinavian or someone from northern Germany with a shot of Red Indian blood in her."[32] She was a woman of significant depth and accomplishments. A 1930 graduate of the German University with a degree in medicine, she was a trained physician (something Adler's mother had longed to become) and an expert in hematology, bacteriology, and internal medicine. She was also an accomplished marksman who won prizes in shooting competitions, an engaging letter writer, well versed in ancient mythology, handy at arts and crafts, and adept at bridge. Although initially he found Gertrud too much to handle, in July 1939 they began to see each other regularly and by the end of September they were in love.

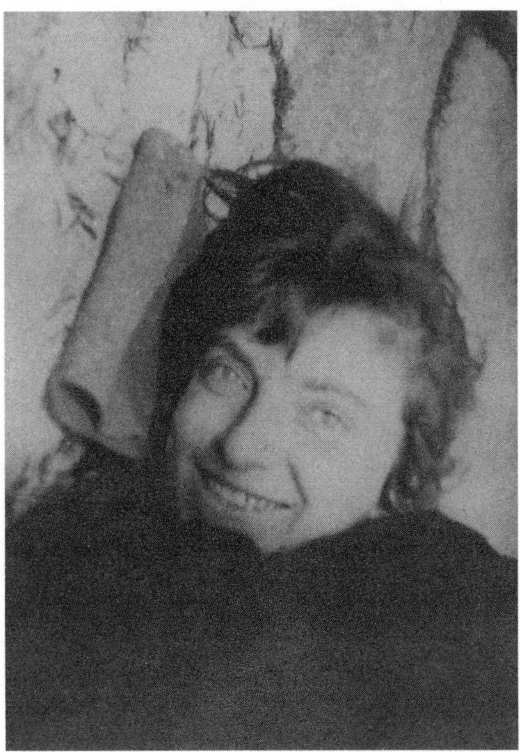

Gertrud Klepetar, ca. 1938. Credit: The Estate of H. G. Adler 2019, Deutsches Literaturarchiv Marbach.

It might seem astounding that love could blossom amid such dire circumstances, but as bad as things were, no one foresaw the horrors that were to come. With the collapse of Czecho-Slovakia in March and the outbreak of war in September, prospects were grim. Writing to Gertrud two weeks after the invasion of Poland, Adler declares, "I love you" in English in the top right corner, and a few lines down admits, "I'm no worse off than usual, but clearly and plainly, today I feel unspeakably sad over the unspeakable beastliness which a pack of thieves is allowed to carry out, and even might get away with, while the rest of the world is already so pathetic that they say nothing or impassively give in to such violation, or simply have to. It's a real tragedy to be a human and even a European, though we are not just cattle."[33] With storms approaching, Gertrud's letters proved "a little island of peace in the sea of loneliness"[34] in which Adler felt adrift.

Although the two lovers lived just two tram stops away in Karlín, they wrote to each other frequently, often twice a day. The exchange helped them maintain equilibrium, as well as providing a respite from the drudgery of daily life.

There is little mention of the pending crisis in their correspondence. Adler uses the letters to work through the tenets of his "Traktat": the human desire for perfection and the failure to attain it through "distractions" like art, politics, religion, science, philosophy, love, and work; the incompleteness of understanding in its adherence to reason; the need to supplement rational thinking with nonrational "intuition"; the sanctity of the individual versus the collective amid attempts by politics or the state to perfect human behavior; and the need for theology to become a "permanent experiment" that tests the nature of reality rather than offering dogmatic propositions. More than a meditation on good and evil or the nature of God, Adler's theology is a radical inquiry that suggests transforming the classical aim to "Know thyself" into the open-ended imperative "Know what you can do, and what you do."

"Existence consists of real and non-real existence," he explains to Gertrud. "Non-real existence is not worth striving for, as it cannot be attained, except as a fiction. But the realization of a preliminary and not-yet-real existence is conceivable under certain modalities and informs the provisionally real nature of what we call possibility. Possibility augurs reality, which at least theoretically can be seized hold of in some capacity. That is the task of a creative theology whose conclusions and propositions must be tested and realized in the face of practical theology and teachings handed down from the past." He claims that the need for such critical inquiry stems from very real problems in the world, namely the positivist errors "of politics, of religion, of art, and of philosophy. And also the error of science." That error was most centrally rooted in the "limits" imposed upon nonrational, intuitive modes of understanding by a slavish adherence to empiricism. "I want to be a person who respects limits," Adler writes, adding, "But I'd prefer to die at an advanced outpost rather than just savor the bliss of our predecessors."[35] He is convinced that "a new mode of knowledge must be developed, which would render accessible hitherto unrealized aspects of Being" through "intuition."[36]

Gertrud was not just a sounding board for these ideas but contributed her views as well. "There is no kind of 'good' that can easily be determined," she asserts at the start of one letter, continuing a discussion from their trip to the countryside the day before. "'Good' is not kitsch," she adds, and in another letter she asserts that "ethics is more important than art," demonstrating that she approached such questions with equal seriousness.[37] "I'm afraid that I'm exceptionally hard-headed," she tells him, and that for her "there is only one principle above all others, and that is the need to always be decent and ethical," a statement that Adler could have uttered himself at any point in his life, especially after the war. Her forthrightness was invaluable, allowing him to test his ideas with someone unafraid to say, "No sentence, no theory which one simply *knows* is worth anything at all if it cannot be confirmed through our experience."[38] Even their love for each other was worthy of objective consideration, as she states, "Love is *not* blind; being in love is. . . . Being in love always leads to those recurring accusations about failings or unintended failings, which are ever present, but which the blind simply erase from the picture."[39]

Gertrud may sound somewhat cold and heartless, but her caution was built from past hurt and disappointment and an open-eyed view of the world, which dovetailed with Adler's vow to "know what you can do, and what you do." Gertrud echoes his valuation of the need to understand one's present when she confirms, "A decent person has no past, he only has a present and perhaps a future." She echoes his sense of the role of fate in human events, stating, "We willingly embrace our fate as much as that is in fact what we call 'Fate.'"[40] She even hints at the cool demeanor required of the participant-observer when she writes, "We both are the kind of person who, despite having plenty enough capacity for fantasy and imagination, despite whatever may be gained through speculation, in part through reading and in part even through knowledge acquired practically, still know the terrible things that go on, yet without ever really being affected by them."[41]

"I had to wait for someone who was ready to accept me as I am," Adler tells her, while she needed to be able to trust someone enough to risk again a "human relationship."[42] Each needed the other and complemented the other, so much so that when Günther was ready to venture a new draft of his "Traktat" in late 1939 and into 1940, he asked her for the letters he had written her the previous August.[43] Within their intellectual partnership, however, there is a marked difference in their mien. Günter remains optimistic and committed to the future; Gertrud is more pessimistic. Having suffered through several disappointing relationships, she is ready to "shed the past," convinced that "One cannot do anything to make a bad past good; one can only try to be good in the present or in the future, and even that can turn out badly."[44] She confesses to a darker side, claiming, "I fear only one thing, and that is that I fear nothing, since nothing more can happen to me that has not already happened to me, nor can anything more terrible ever happen to a person like me."[45]

What was so terrible remains veiled within their letters, but the residue of a deep disappointment in human nature pervades her passion for her new love.[46] In letters to the sociologist Ludwig Heyde (1888–1961), written in 1933 and 1937, Gertrud speaks of having been infatuated with a prominent leader of the Wandervogel twenty years her senior in Prague during the 1920s. Whether the relationship was sexual is unclear, but his influence was strong enough that for eight years she followed his "program" of no drinking or dancing and accepted that, for "racial reasons," he could not introduce her to his friends. Toward the end of her university studies, her romantic life with a number of younger men became so intense and complicated that it led to a breakdown. Another relationship with a young German caused a second breakdown in the early 1930s, after which she threw herself into her work as a doctor and chemist, which led to exhaustion and depression in 1936. "Other people have their stories of love," she confided to Heyde in February 1933. "However, I am capable of experiencing with any person the most ghastly of things. I am a master at that. Because I never have the courage to simply feel indifferent to someone else. For I either really like someone or not at all."

"It pleases me that there is you," she writes Adler in 1939, "and it pleases me that you are there and that I can write to you, and that you are the only one to whom my letters speak. All of it is wonderful and seemingly perfect. But the idea that one can in any way rely on other people for help, I no longer share such a view, and I will likely struggle to ever believe in it again."[47] Adler replies, "You certainly are judging people very harshly. . . . One has to judge people for the possibility they hold. One cannot expect too much."[48] In the end, all they can do is take care of each other as best they can. "There is such a beautiful, clear spirit, so much soul in the two of us, that we must overcome our frailties," she reminds him. "You the physical setbacks (at the moment) of weariness and listlessness, and I the accompanying effects of pity, fear, and loathing."[49]

Undoubtedly the stress of life in Prague augmented such moods. Although Adler found himself downhearted about their prospects, rarely does he despair. "It's indeed true that today we are shattered and subdued, and the best part of our strength is taxed. . . . It seems to me that we are mired within a pause between this life and the life to come. We are stretched between two realms, but our efforts seem to me enough for us not to be ripped apart in the middle, to not lose the link to the past, and to carry its resources into the realm to come."[50] Clearly, they were in it together, for as early as September 23, he told her that he no longer wanted to leave Prague without her and that "only with my dear friend Reder have I ever felt . . . so certain and secure."[51] "Above all," he reminds her, "we must escape. Somehow (and this time the imprecision of this word is adequate to express the state of one's soul) it has to happen, and we will have to think quite intensely about it." As they waited to figure out just how to escape, there was only one option: "Work: whenever you can and are able to, keep in your heart the hope that I will be able to complete my Traktat."[52]

After returning from Milan, Adler worked for the industrial abrasives firm that sent him to Italy, but when the prospects of a visa for Brazil fell through in March, he had no choice but to spend each day at his father's book bindery and stationery store, where he often wrote to Gertrud between serving customers. Less than a year earlier he had been arranging cultural events and radio broadcasts at the Urania. Now, with the creation of the Second Republic, at twenty-nine he was unemployable in any public capacity as a Jew, while the writers, thinkers, and artists he admired most and felt closest to—Canetti, Reder, Steiner, Erich

Unger, Hermann Grab, and Alfred Wolfenstein—had fled to safety. He hoped to join them and in early 1939 made every effort, but once the Protectorate was established, that became unlikely. Meeting Gertrud, falling in love, and having someone to whom he could pour out his thoughts and feelings, and console in return, was an oasis. Even Bettina Gross, to whom Adler had sent his first "Traktat" from Milan, was gone. She had taken Adler's advice and followed her brother and sister to England in late 1938, her mother choosing to stay in Prague and take care of family, her father having died six months earlier. Absent those dear to him, Gertrud became his polestar.

"People today are hemmed in by a combination of madness and criminality," he tells her days after the start of the war, and he sees no way to escape it. Nevertheless, he hopes to continue "treatising" ("traktieren") after reassuring her that "the strength of my good attitude and my sustained hopes remain unbowed" and that his "theology" is equal to the times.[53] He was convinced that one must "remain true to oneself under any conditions. The times can be overpowering, but I must remain more powerful than the times. . . . Only within yourself can you remain truly at home."[54] Such stoicism takes on metaphysical consequences when Adler responds to Gertrud's claim that "God is, will be, should be, must be, and will always be the one true authority." Although in essence he agrees with her, as a "theologian" he cannot say so, for he rejects dogma. "If for just one moment I were entirely satisfied, if I were ever content enough to be satisfied and say 'yes, that is the way it is and it can be no different for others,' then I would cringe, and life would no longer be worth living."

Such words, however, are not the voice of despair, for within his determination Adler finds solace:

> But even in taking such a stand I feel quite good and feel an unusual strength within me, something that allows me to enjoy in a fundamental and practical way the sweetness of life even more intensely than any sensualist or epicurean. Instead I immerse myself in a protective loneliness as I plunge with feverish vigor into ever-unfolding possibilities and continually realized "dreams," all of which I find very healthy and which I don't wish to cease. I wouldn't say that fate is a blessing when doom leads me into its darkness, nor do I wish to be reckless in any recognizable way. And as for the danger itself, which I don't think is all that grave, I will use any means to lessen it and escape it. The very last thing that one can give should not be squandered away; it needs to be conserved and the inner fire tended and kept at the ready.[55]

High-minded yet guarded, rapt yet with feet on the ground, Adler's approach functions as both a pragmatic strategy and a moral credo, while underneath it also serves to console an anxious Gertrud. "It's not that I don't worry," he tells her, "but I don't fear that we will survive these difficult, profound days and suffer anything more than surface agitation, even though sometimes really hard moments might threaten one's courage. Our bond means something, for through it we help each other in body and soul. We will and we must endure."

Two days later, on October 20, Adler expounds on the importance of religion and language to him and in troubled times. Insisting that, notwithstanding all his effort to learn other languages, "I am deeply tied to the German language and especially its lyric possibilities, which I could never find in any other language," Adler also states that he does not consider himself a member of the German people and that he holds "no national sentiments whatsoever." He writes, "I am a Jew by lot, I speak German by coincidence, and I am the person who I am according to my own free will, . . . though indeed there is a certain Jewish aspect to who I am which is probably more spiritually prominent than any German aspect in me."

Adler outlines his conception of Judaism as a whole when he tells Gertrud, "The Jewish people, or better yet the fate of its people, is the gauge by which to measure the condition and well-being of all other peoples around it. Wherever things go badly for the Jews, they also go badly for others, and vice versa." According to Adler, however, the Jews are the "most anti-political" people, for whenever they get mixed up in "the politics of others or even their own, disaster follows more quickly for them than for those born into a 'stable' state." This leads to the sufferings of Jews through the intolerance or hatred by non-Jews, as well as what Adler calls "the ideality of the Jewish people." He adds:

> Judaism is a possibility, and I love the possibility of this people of possibilities. And I myself have a responsibility as a Jew to live and to fulfill that responsibility, so long as it is clearly reconcilable with my humanity and my responsibilities as a human being. That's why I can calmly carry on speaking German, nor do I have to attach myself to the Jewish nation, nor even practice the Jewish religion. The swings of the pendulum between Germandom and Ziondom, both of which doubtless remain always open to me, these I have brought into perfect balance. And there is no reason to reproach myself for having adopted a bland, featureless personality. Nor am I saying that what I have chosen for myself is the only choice to make or even that it is for everyone. But it is what I have chosen, though for the greater part of the German-speaking Jews it does not seem to be what they have chosen or will choose in the future. Instead I will calmly take on the responsibility of what it means to be the last Jew to write in German.[56]

The sweep of Adler's claims is fascinating in the context of Prague's long-standing multiethnic, multilingual, and multireligious culture amid the chokehold of anti-Semitic policies and laws within the Protectorate. Adler implies the "possibility" of Judaism as more a state of consciousness than a religion and argues that Judaism is a "gauge" for the general state of humanity, raising the stakes of the fulfillment of its "possibility" for all. Rather than a Zionist pursuit of separate nationhood, Adler balances Germandom and what he calls "Ziondom" (Ziontum) within himself, maintaining each as a refuge he can choose at will. He makes clear that his self is shaped "according to my own free will," yet what he chooses is to take on the burden of being "the last Jew to write in German." A Jew who is not a practicing Jew, a German who does not feel German, he instead aspires to the "possibility" of each and the hope of affirming the highest possibility of humanity. Despite such "ideality," Adler admits, "The Jewish problem (a complex of various problems) is therefore unsolvable, simply because it is the problem of humanity and tolerance, only minor aspects of which have been thought about, and ultimately not at all." The only real hope is the individual himself: "Only the individual is today capable of the good, rather than the collective. . . . Only the individual respects his neighbor, if only because he recognizes him as his neighbor and not just 'a part of the mob.' "[57]

Adler's theology is a synthesis of sociology, messianism, and a strategy for personal survival through its antifascist and anti-Communist stance. The more one can rise above the collective, the better chance one has of being true to oneself and thereby remaining true to others. As a Jew, it means being true to the "possibility" of what it means to be a Jew, without stipulating that one must practice as a Jew. Paradoxical as this may seem, it makes his "experimental theology" pertinent, for he tells Gertrud the crux of the issue is that "[t]he individual's sensibility can only be grasped and explained through that of the whole, and the sensibility of the whole only through that of the individual."[58]

By mid-November 1939, self-knowledge and respect for oneself as an individual were the only respite, for after creation of the Central Office for Jewish Emigration in Bohemia and Moravia almost the entirety of Jewish life in the Protectorate fell under the control of the Nazis. Overseen by Eichmann, the actual head was an SS officer named Hans Günther, whose name led Hans Günther Adler later to refuse to ever again use his full name in print. Yet the dangers were greater than nomenclature. Beginning in July, Jews were banned from walking in public parks and in some cities were not allowed on the sidewalks. They were barred from cinemas, theaters, museums, and libraries, and all were subject to a curfew of 8:00 p.m. Travel by rail required written permission from the Gestapo; even if granted, Jews had to ride on the back platform of the last car. Jews were required to register with the police, their ration books were stamped "J," and their food and clothing rations were less than those of Czechs and Germans.[59]

In *The Journey*, a novel that he completed in 1951 but was not published until 1962, Adler writes, "Life was reduced to force, and the natural consequence was fear, which was bound up with constant danger in order to rule life through terror." Then he introduces a litany of the forbidden:

> Highways and byways were forbidden, the days were shortened and the nights lengthened, not to mention that the night was forbidden as well. Shops were forbidden, doctors, hospitals, vehicles, and resting places, forbidden, all forbidden. Laundries were forbidden, libraries were forbidden. Music was forbidden, dancing forbidden. Shoes forbidden. Baths forbidden. And as long as there was still money it was forbidden. What was and what could be were forbidden. It was announced: "What you can buy is forbidden, and you can't buy anything." Since people could no longer buy anything, they wanted to sell what they had, for they hoped to eke out a living from what they made off their belongings. Yet they were told: "What you can sell is forbidden, and you are forbidden to sell anything." Thus everything became sadder and they mourned their very lives, but they didn't want to take their lives, because that was forbidden.[60]

Adler captures the sweeping, absurd restrictions and deftly rises above them in his musical scoring of "the forbidden." Doctors, hospitals, vehicles, and resting places were off-limits to Jews, but the banning of shoes and baths, or even the day and night, reflects the obsessive extremes of the perpetrators more than the effect on the victims. That they refuse to take their lives, "because that was forbidden," speaks to their continuing to observe a moral law higher than the ridiculous laws to which they are subjected. Although they will later be killed in body, they must not and do not kill themselves, a seizure of the moral high ground that allows Adler to mockingly recall such menacing tactics.[61]

Such bans were designed to break the spirit of the Jews and to foment resentment among Germans and Czechs. The most sweeping consequences, however, were those created by the decree requiring Jews to register their businesses and turn them over to German "trustees." It is estimated that before the war nearly one-third of the industrial and banking capital of Czechoslovakia was controlled by Jews and that the total property confiscated was worth 17 billion crowns.[62] The invasion of Czecho-Slovakia was not merely to protect Germans, but to systematically raid its economy. Munitions factories, ironworks, timber mills, and coal mines were incorporated into the Hermann Göring Works, and huge sums of gold and foreign currency were transferred from the Czech National Bank to Berlin. Half a million German nationals moved from the Reich to the Protectorate to take over Jewish factories and businesses, and 120,000 of them took over Jewish homes and apartments. Of the "trustees" appointed to run Jewish businesses, only 8 percent were Czechs, the other 92 percent making it clear that the takeover of government, economy, and everyday life was to serve the Germans themselves.[63]

Soon after the invasion both Sudeten Germans and those who identified themselves as Germans in the former Czecho-Slovakia began to resent the Nazi regime and actively opposed plans to "Aryanize" the country.[64] Czechs could not become German citizens without receiving special approval, so there was little reason to stop acting "Czech." What it meant to be a "good Czech," rather than a democrat, Communist, or antifascist, superseded any civic duty to the Protectorate itself.[65] This nurtured active and public Czech resistance. On September 28, 1939, four weeks after the war started, ten thousand people lined the streets to see religious leaders carry the remains of St. Wenceslas, medieval king and patron saint of Bohemia, from St. Vitus Cathedral. When the crowd sang the national anthem at Wenceslas Square, arrests were made. On September 30 there was a massive boycott of public transportation, and thousands walked to work gleefully watching empty trams pass by.[66] A month later demonstrators again filled the streets to celebrate Czecho-Slovakia's Independence Day, although the country no longer existed. When things turned ugly, the police moved in and a young Czech named Jan Opeltal was killed. On November 15, students flooded the streets for his funeral. After the car of state secretary Karl Hermann Frank was overturned and his chauffeur injured, Hitler ordered the Gestapo to arrest some 1,200 students. Nine were shot at dawn the next day and the rest sent to Dachau. All institutions of higher learning were closed for good and intellectuals were attacked throughout the country. Whatever "autonomy" had been promised to Hácha's government was no more, and by the spring of 1940 the Nazis ran everything.[67]

This was the hothouse in which Gertrud and Günther's love blossomed between the summer of 1939 and the spring of 1940, when it became clear that the Nazis were in control. "I kept hearing a voice that said 'get out, get out,' but even though it was counter to what I understood and counter to what I foresaw happening, inside I was at peace and so I stayed," Adler explained to Wilhelm Unger. What lay ahead for the Jews, however, seemed clear: "Steadily increasing confinement and cruelty, more and more unbearable, more and more inhumane. Kindness, but also corruption, and the corruption of countless Czech flunkies, as well as the moral failing and inhumanity of the Germans. Only a few friends on either side remained true."[68]

Günther and Gertrud became inseparable. Adler spent almost all of his free time with her and her parents at Palačkého 3, down the street from his childhood home. During the days he worked at his father's side, but the crackdowns and restrictions took their toll. On his son's advice, Emil let all of his employees go except for a young Jewish woman. Günther and his father were determined to dissolve the business before the Nazis got hold of it, so they worked day and night, emptying the shelves so that the "trustee" appointed to take over was met with nothing but a gutted storefront. Emil made sure to send away personal goods and valuables, including his prized collection of stamps. Part of it he mailed to a distant cousin in England and another he hid in the elevator of his apartment building. Because of his father's extreme secrecy and the contrariness of Emil's second wife, Zdenka, Adler did not learn where the stamps were until after the war.[69]

In the summer of 1940 the Gestapo "visited" the business and the apartment, turning both upside down. In October a German "trustee" was appointed to run the business, and by November it was shut for good. Without a job and short on food, Adler resorted to occasional tutoring to be found, as well as selling books, antiques, and carpets under the threat of arrest. Not all of the books were sold, for Adler kept a small collection of philosophy, psychology, law, and literature while completing the first full draft of his treatise. The only relief from the increasing isolation of the Jews into a virtual ghetto was "to travel for days and nights on end through almost every province of the mind" with "Geraldine," the nickname that Günther had given her. That and "to prepare one's soul for the disaster to come."[70]

6

The Railroad

There are two clocks on the Old Jewish Town Hall in Prague. The top one has Roman numerals on its face and the hands run clockwise, whereas the numbers on the bottom clock are in Hebrew and the hands run in the opposite direction. Given the rapid devolution in the lives of Jews under the Nazis, many must have had the sense of time running backward to the pogroms of centuries past. 1867 brought full enfranchisement, but after barely more than seventy years, the biblical measure of a human lifetime, it was gone in a flash.[1]

The Jewish Quarter was leveled and replaced with modern apartment buildings at the turn of the century, but a new Jewish ghetto had been created in the files of Eichmann's Central Office for Jewish Emigration in Bohemia and Moravia. In it were the addresses of every Jew in the country as well as their racial lineage across generations. The deportation lists for Theresienstadt and the East were developed from these files, the hands of time jerking suddenly forward with the advent of an entirely new kind of pogrom. In 1940 no one may have foreseen the death camps and the rising smokestacks of the crematoria, but with the fall of France in June a pall was cast across Europe as the Nazi grip on the Jews tightened. Time slowed down and time sped up. Without the daily rituals of jobs, school, civic life, or even a stroll in the park, people languished amid hours and days filled with hunger and anxiety. And yet, as curfews were announced and each day brought another restriction or a further advance of Germany's shadow, time moved faster and faster, unstoppable as a train piercing the horizon.

Wickedness and terror, however, move faster than time or trains. After the murder and arrest of students and the closing of institutions of higher learning in late 1939, Nazi persecution intensified.[2] Jews were forced to sell their valuables to the government and to deposit stocks and other assets in a centralized foreign currency bank, with all proceeds going to the Emigration Fund for Bohemia and Moravia, which eventually subsidized Theresienstadt.[3] Jews were barred from owning businesses in different industries, including film, textiles, shoes, insurance companies, banks, and even cafés, and by March 1941, all businesses assigned a "trustee" had been closed.[4] In the interim, any payments made to Jews, such as rent, had to be made to blocked accounts from which only limited amounts could be withdrawn.

After the start of the war in September 1939, a curfew of 8:00 p.m. was imposed and entrance was barred to parks, swimming pools, sporting events, forests, and eventually even the main streets, while cemeteries became the only open-air space left in which to meet or stroll. Trolleys, buses, and trains were off-limits, and by September 1940, Jews could not rent apartments but could only sublet from other Jews. Housing that became vacant fell under the control of the Central Office, and in October 1940, a decree disallowed any change in residence or temporary absence from the city. Telephones were banned, as well as radios, and only one post office was kept to serve some forty thousand Jews. In August 1940 the hours in which Jews could shop were 11:00 a.m. to 1:00 p.m. and 3:00 to 4:30 p.m.; six months later the hours were reduced to 3:00 to 5:00 p.m., provided one could find a store that did not forbid entrance. Laundries and libraries banned Jews, as well as hairdressers and pharmacies, and ambulances refused to transport the sick or the injured. Eventually all fresh goods or produce were banned, as was tobacco and even the playing of music. No part of life went unregulated or unrestricted, which naturally led to almost everyone breaking some law. Fearing consequences if caught, many were worn down physically and psychologically long before deportations began.[5]

"During this time," Adler recalled, "I used to dream repeatedly that I was walking around Prague with Hitler while trying to talk him out of his hatred of the Jews."[6] In the meantime a mix of Czech capitulation and silence borne of necessity accompanied the increase in anti-Semitic laws and theft of Jewish property. When the Protectorate's state secretary Karl Hermann Frank threatened to execute 1,200 Czech university students sent to concentration camps after the protests of 1939, President Hácha was forced to raise a *Sieg Heil* to Hitler in spring 1940 and sign an oath of allegiance. Less publicly, some 730,000 Czech workers continued to man the heavy industry and munitions plants crucial to the war effort, while their wages and rations remained higher than those of Czechs in other professions.[7] Ironically, silence itself was a means of subversion. The editor of a weekly paper wrote, "The nation is fighting the manly fight; and its silence is a powerful weapon as explosive as a large grenade."[8] Lost on him was the double meaning of his words. Adler, however, turned a spotlight on such betrayal of public duty by a newspaper in his story "Das Unglück" ("The Debacle"), although it took another twenty-five years for it to see print.

Czechs and Germans remained locked in a stranglehold of interdependence from which neither could free themselves. The Czech propensity to remain silent while dutifully fulfilling the Protectorate's bidding mixed collaboration and resistance.[9] "Švejkism" was adopted by many Czechs, whereby repression by the occupier spurred opportunism among the working class eager for higher wages and greater security through compliance.[10] George F. Kennan, then American ambassador to Prague, ascribed to the Czech government a "boggling willingness to comply with any and all demands and an equally baffling ability to execute them in such a way that the effect is quite different from that contemplated by those who did the commanding."[11]

The challenge in Prague was to navigate the increasingly repressive measures imposed by the state, yet also find some solid footing amid ever-changing circumstances. Forced to shovel snow off the runways at the airport for no pay throughout the severe winter of 1940–1941, Adler maintained his equilibrium by devoting himself to Gertrud.[12] Starting in 1940, he practically lived with her in her parents' apartment at Palačkého 3, just blocks from where he was born. He also worked continually on a first draft of his "Traktat" and helped his father in his business, although his sinking spirits soon mirrored Emil's own, watching what his father had worked for slip through his hands rather than having to hand it over to a "trustee." Martha Steiner, writing to Franz in England in April, saw the toll it took on Günther: "He never eats at home and doesn't look good at all. He stands around the entire day at his father's shop. He can't keep on this way for much longer."[13] Adler kept at his "Traktat." He finished a first draft of 318 pages by June 1941, the version he would return to years later. Europe was almost entirely under Nazi control, Germany having overrun France, Denmark, Norway, the Netherlands, Belgium, and Luxembourg in less than two years. The fall of France in 1940 closed the door on the continent's western shore, and although the British managed to escape from Dunkirk, they settled into a prolonged air campaign as Hitler turned his gaze to the East.

Adler's family was also in disarray. Ottla's husband, Curt Beihoff, who worked for Emil as a salesman, had died in 1933, forcing her to move to an apartment owned by Emil at Havličkova 6, next to his stationery store. She initially joined her sister Gisa, married to František Wagner, a Roman Catholic who claimed German nationality. Wagner divorced Gisa in July 1940, however, and she and František moved to separate addresses. No mention is made of it, but racial laws requiring Jewish registration likely caused the split, just as between Ottilie Kafka and her Catholic husband, Joseph David, when Ottilie proposed divorcing him to protect their children from deportation. Günther's mother, Alice, listed Gisa's address as her home after Emil divorced her in 1932, although she remained hospitalized for the rest of the decade. Emil's marriage to Zdenka Pisinger in 1934 saw the newlyweds move to the apartment at Poděbradova 8, but even Emil's baptism as a Protestant with Günther in 1922 could not prevent him from being registered as a full Jew in 1940. That Zdenka claimed to be both Jewish and Czech sealed their fate.

Emil Adler, 1938. Credit: National Archives, Prague.

Gisa's former husband, František Wagner, survived the war in Prague but ironically was deported from Czechoslovakia as a German national in March 1946. Adler's family was a microcosm of the cultural, political, and religious complexities of families all over Prague. A father who in the 1921 census had listed himself patriotically as Czech and Jewish was by the 1930 census listed as German and Protestant, as was his son, while the mother remained designated as German, Jewish, and institutionalized. The father's second wife remained Czech and Jewish. Of the two aunts closest to Adler, one claimed to be atheist and German, the other Jewish and German, married to a Roman Catholic. Günther complicated his official identity when in 1933 or 1934 he renounced his Protestant denomination before a magistrate and listed himself as "konfessionslos," or unaffiliated with any religion.[14] Such tangled identities could lead to permanent ruptures in any family, and for František and Gisa they likely did, although Günther remained close to his father and his aunts.

Living nearly full time with Gertrud and her parents provided some respite, but Adler also experienced firsthand the rising anxiety of the Klepetars. A German friend tried to help them navigate the increasing array of bans

Zdenka Pisinger, 1938. Credit: National Archives, Prague.

and regulations, but already Jewish apartments were seized, food supplies dwindled, and there was no work to be found. Since the spring of 1940 Jews also had to register with their local congregations. The forced registration of those who, like Adler, considered themselves fully assimilated citizens of the former Czechoslovakia caused consternation and resentment, particularly among those for whom the designation of nationality by mother tongue, or religion for the Jews, had been the norm for two decades. Now, however, each person's identity was shaped by factors almost entirely outside of his or her control, and emigration became increasingly hopeless. With the war's start in September 1939, 1,500 travel permits granted to the British Empire became invalid, and the low quota of visas (only 2,700) granted by the United States to those wishing to flee the Protectorate further dimmed prospects. The Palestine Office in Prague was closed in May 1941, and although 26,000 of the roughly 118,000 Jews in the Protectorate managed to emigrate after 1939, some 88,000 remained trapped in June 1941.[15] For Jews in the Protectorate life was made more circumscribed and precarious by the fact that behind any request or imposition made by the Jewish Community stood the force of the Gestapo.[16]

Germany's invasion of the Soviet Union at the end of that month set off events in Prague and the Protectorate that led to the next escalation in the catastrophe. Early victories swelled the bloated egos of the Nazis, although this gave the Czechs fresh hope that America would soon join the war and help defeat Germany. The Communists took it as inspiration to rally the world against fascist aggression and to call for acts of sabotage by their former Czech comrades. Railcars were set on fire, brake lines severed, tracks destroyed, and the industrial output of the Protectorate dropped by a third in the early summer months.[17] General strikes and boycotts were called. The threat of one caused Göring's sister-in-law to flee to Switzerland in a specially protected railcar, while even the presence of anti-Hitler graffiti led authorities to shut Czech cinemas and sporting facilities.[18] The situation under Reich protector Neurath was getting out of hand and questions about his leadership were raised in Berlin.

Intensifying this scrutiny was Hitler's call on July 16 for a "Garden of Eden" to be established in the East and the employment of "all necessary measures—shootings, resettlements, etc."[19] to accomplish it. "Lebensraum" opened up with the conquest of Poland, and initial victories against the Soviet Union not only created the opportunity for Germany to think about how it would resettle the East with Aryan blood but also forced the Nazis to consider what they were going to do about the millions of Slavs, Jews, and Gypsies taken into its fold. That civic unrest had returned to their own backyard in the Protectorate complicated issues of control and depopulation writ large in the East. Strong measures were needed closer to home to meet stronger demands further afield. Hearing from friends and relations about deportations from Vienna and Luxembourg to Poland, the Jews of Prague worried that they would be next. As Adler later noted, "In late summer 1941, everyone felt that the situation was hopeless and was seized by panic. . . . From then on, 'transport' remained the most terrifying word for every Jew."[20]

Fears multiplied with the arrival of Reinhard Heydrich in Prague. The former director of the Reich Security Office, which held sway over the Intelligence Service, the criminal police, and the justice system, Heydrich was named deputy Reich protector on September 27, 1941. Neurath was put on "leave" and recalled to Berlin after handing all power over to Heydrich, who now reported directly to Hitler and maintained a close working relationship with Heinrich Himmler, the head of the SS. The epitome of the Nazi Übermensch—intelligent, a slave to ideology, an avid athlete, and a relentless solver of "problems"—Heydrich was ruthless to the core. On July 30, he had received from Göring the authorization to make "all necessary preparations" for "bringing about a complete solution of the Jewish question within the German sphere of influence." The end of that memo called for a "final solution" ("Endlösung") to the "Jewish question," the first use of the term, and Heydrich's task was to find the most efficient and thorough means to accomplish it. After two weeks as Reich protector, he announced at an October 10 meeting that Hitler demanded "all Jews be removed from this German space by the end of the year." The next day Heydrich added that he had "decided to go through these stages also in the Protectorate as quickly as possible."[21] A September 1 decree forced all Jews to wear the yellow star, and on October 1 Eichmann demanded the Jewish congregation of Prague register anew every Jew in the Protectorate.

If nothing else, Heydrich was a man of his word, for the first deportation to the Polish ghetto of Łódź left Prague on October 16 with roughly 1,000 Jews. Four more transports followed over the next weeks, the last on November 4. The Nazis had rounded up political prisoners and sent them to Dachau as early as 1933, and they had killed physically and mentally handicapped people as early as 1939, not to mention Soviet prisoners in Auschwitz in the late summer of 1941, as well as 500,000 to 800,000 Jews in the occupied East.[22] The use of railcars to transport Jews to Łódź that October, however, commenced the systematized, bureaucratic death that distinguishes the Holocaust from other mass killings. Eventually the deportations claimed the lives of 77,297 of the 88,686 Protectorate Jews counted by the Nazis in the summer of 1941 and killed by April 1945.[23] With the closing of railcar doors in Vienna, Prague, and Luxembourg in mid-October, the Final Solution had begun.

As often occurred, Adler was both absent and present for the occasion. Required under Eichmann's decree to register with the Jewish congregation in June, he was conscripted by its Labor Office that summer to help construct a new trestle for a rail line running from Brno to Prague being built by the Hermann Göring Works. On August 17, five weeks before Heydrich's arrival in Prague, he was transported to a forced labor camp in Sázawa-Velká Losenice, a tiny village located on the high windswept plains that extend east from Prague to the border of Bohemia and Moravia. "It was very hard work digging earth and rock," he later recalled, and living conditions were tough.[24] His letters to Gertrud are full of pleas for her to send extra ration cards, as well as his complaints about poor housing and food. Although it was the first hard labor he had done in his life, many years of hiking and wandering the Bohemian Forest helped provide the needed stamina. Compared to the conditions he later experienced in Theresienstadt, life in the camp was relatively tolerable. Its population consisted of 170 Jews and his work unit numbered eighteen. As room leader, he oversaw six younger workers who treated him with respect, referring to him in Czech as "Pan Doktor!"[25] Rather than doing dangerous excavation work in the mountains, he was a day laborer who helped load and unload materials, or he worked digging on the railroad line itself. Still, the work was hard and involved up to sixty hours a week, plus ten hours on some Saturdays.[26] He was paid roughly 850 crowns per month, around $500 today, but almost everything he earned went to buying extra food and clothing from the camp canteen and the village shops.[27]

Adler was helped by the good will of the camp wardens and his fellow laborers. "I got along well with the people there and I was generally respected and liked by both Jews and Czechs alike. We had most Saturday afternoons and every Sunday free, and we were hardly even supervised. In the evenings I cooked for my entire group, or at least what there was to get hold of in the area, if only to avoid the terrible and insufficient food from the canteen. I spent the free days on my own or with another inmate in the lovely woods that stretched out endlessly over the hills in which pleasant little lakes were hidden away."[28]

Much harder to bear than the physical duress of work on the railroad was anxiety about what was happening in Prague, for with Heydrich's arrival the danger of deportation escalated. "Things are coming more and more to a head," his father wrote to him on September 9, "life is completely unbearable." Ten days later Emil worried that he and Zdenka would soon be forced out of their apartment, while by October 6, Ottla reported, "Everyone is depressed and anxious about the days ahead. Even father has lost his sense of humor, which is saying a lot." Adler recalled, "I was nervous because of Geraldine, because of my father. Yet I could not leave. And with good reason I did not opt for an illegal journey to Prague. . . . But the times were very serious. The Jews from the Protectorate were registered, the deportations soon followed. Heydrich arrived and imposed martial law, the Jewish star, an extremely hard regime. Ever more stringent surveillance of us and regular visits by the Gestapo from Iglau."[29]

Wanting to remain together no matter what, Gertrud and Günther knew that they had to do something, and so he proposed marriage. "As soon as we are married, you will be protected to the extent that I am as a worker. Then I won't be afraid of registering as much as I am now. The firm here needs workers. I'm not all that valuable, but I am reliable and liked because of my manner, and I am fairly confident that since the firm is German . . . they will continue to need us as long as we are not slackers."[30] Although they planned to marry around November 1, this was easier said than done. Adler recalled, "It took super-human effort on her part to allow me to receive permission to travel to Prague for a couple of days where she managed through her amazing talents to arrange for us to get married . . . in order that we might end up together on the *same* Gestapo list."[31] "Gertrud is running her legs off, trying to take care of everything so that you can get married," Ottla reassured him, but until the wedding occurred, nothing was certain.[32] Travel documents had to be applied for, forms filled out, all of it through the mail amid increasing anxiety about when the transports would begin and who would be on them. "Just today," Adler writes to Gertrud on October 12, "a boy in my room received an express letter which said that his pregnant sister, her almost blind husband, and his mother must leave as soon as Monday. All he could do was howl. Some here want to know whether it is to Poland, or if it will be to a camp somewhere in the Protectorate (Milovice, etc.). Which is it? Who is sending people off or having them sent off? Who is registering them?"

If such news was hard to take while stuck in the barracks of a work camp, even worse was no news at all. On October 13 Adler pleads, "Please, don't leave me without any word from you in these crazy times. I'll just die of worry if I don't know how you are . . . I've gotten no mail today at all. And I'm worried about Father and whether he has thoughts of suicide." The next day Adler says, "I'm indeed worried but not particularly upset over the fact that my father and his wife are registered or even that I might be registered with them," and a second letter sent on October 14 betrays the rumors he had heard as he asks, "Tell me, is it true that really *everyone* has to leave Prague all of a sudden? Those poor, poor people!"

Adler's letters to Gertrud alternate between a cool awareness of the need to engage with the bureaucracy and desperate fears about what the authorities have planned. As if reminding her of an errand, he writes on October 15, "Sweetheart, can you make sure that we are together if the deportations start off at a maddening pace? Someone can help you out. Are you not yet registered? I heard by the way that Dr. Reiser and Dr. Synek had or will have to go on the first transport *without* having been registered. It's all topsy-turvy." On October 16 he can only think of the "horrible notion of my finally getting to Prague and I won't be able to see you or Father," while three days later he returns to instructing her that "if anyone wants to register you before we get married, then you have to try to tell them that it must be postponed in consideration of the marriage notice we have posted and our impending marriage. Also your future husband must work and is not yet registered."

A second letter that day, however, returns to worry in asking, "Tell me, dear, is there any kind of new ban that will endanger my taking the train the short distance it is from me to you?" The following day Adler laments, "My goodness, what kind of hell you all must be suffering in that damned city." Despite such fears, on October 21 he tells her, "I really don't have any kind of bad feeling, even though I am very down and very worried." Even after receiving a telegram from Gertrud telling him that his father and stepmother were due to be transported four days later, he can only say, "I am not afraid of the future, not afraid for us, and not at all afraid for my father. I am indeed anxious, apprehensive, sad, and worried, but I feel no fear at all. Not because I am cowardly (O cowardice is so pathetic!), but also because fear is *not at all* appropriate, especially if we are together, remain together, and together manage to do what we can do in this obviously terrible time."[33]

As for Gertrud, her letters show her constantly exhausted and unable to sleep, Günther scolding her for not eating. Early on she is pleased to be able to do research in the laboratory and see patients, but with the arrival of Heydrich, her distress mounts, even though there is no mention of him or any of the authorities. "I keep to myself and keep the horribleness at a distance," she tells Adler on August 22, but by early September she admits, "Life is nearly impossible. I weigh less than 55 kilos and hardly sleep. It's terrible of me to write you that, rather than be more considerate, but I am tired, tired, tired, and what's more, tired, and cannot lie."[34] Five days later she says that she has slept but remains "dead tired" and says, "it won't last long; in fact it would be better if they just killed us now." She found the strength to continue to send Günther packages of food and clothing, as well as those assembled for him by friends and family. She is distressed to hear of his hunger, but by October admits she and her parents are also short of food. Ten days after Heydrich took control of the Protectorate and a week after Eichmann ordered that all Jews be registered, she writes, "I am on the brink of despair and want only to sleep in order to not have to know anything else. . . . I still feel that I have faith, but I my head is spinning and I hardly know what to think."[35] After Emil and Zdenka are forced to register, Gertrud makes sure that Günther's things are moved to her apartment. Like him, she could only hope that they could remain "together," even though when she consoles Günther about Emil's pending departure she observes, "It is often harder to remain alive than it is to die, something that no one knows as well as I do."[36]

Adler shared Gertrud's foreboding about a total liquidation of Protectorate Jews, and such fears were shared by many as news trickled in about deportations from Vienna and Germany and what was happening to Jews in Poland. "A dull weight lay upon each day and feared morrow. Everyone felt that things could not go on like this; people suspected what was coming: the transport. With a bleak sense of expectancy, they felt themselves at the mercy of its horrors."[37] The full weight of this struck home when he learned from Gertrud that Emil and Zdenka left Prague on Transport C to Łódź on October 26. Although they managed to survive the winter in the wretched conditions of the Łódź ghetto, in May 1942 they were sent to Chełmno, where some of the earliest and crudest forms of systematized extermination were practiced: as prototypes of the later gas chambers, mobile trucks were adapted to gas prisoners with carbon monoxide.[38] In mid-December, after hearing nothing from Emil, Adler requested information about his whereabouts from the authorities. Not until after the war did he learn his father's fate, and Adler lamented for the rest of his life having no photograph by which to remember him.

Four days after Transport C left for Łódź, Günther and Gertrud exchanged vows in the municipal district office of the Prague neighborhood of Střešovice. On the marriage certificate she is listed as "Gertrud Sara" and noted as unaffiliated, and he is "Hanus Israel" and Jewish, their false middle names a label forced upon all Jews in the Protectorate. Emil Vogel, Adler's Pfadfinder troop leader, served as best man, and both of Gertrud's parents were present, as were Ottla and Gisa. After the ceremony Gertrud and Günther appear in photos with yellow stars sewn onto their coats, as do the other guests. In the photos Gertrud and her mother are beaming, while Günther appears attentive to and deeply moved by his bride. Gertrud's father, David, appears gaunt, the look of trepidation felt by all despite the joyous occasion. Adler believed that married status protected them from being deported separately, but no one could know what the future held. Nor was there the chance to spend a few days with his new wife. Allowed no more than three days away from the labor camp, Adler reported back to Sázawa-Velká Losenice the next day. As a married man, he could visit Gertrud every other weekend, and he did so regularly over the next weeks. Tensions continued to run high, however, Gertrud complaining that "you don't at all see what it's like for me here when you say that I am *only* being nervous."[39] To this Adler could only reply in late November, "I'd rather die than to go through all this misery alone. That is indeed the sacred meaning of our marriage in these times. . . . We have been beset with a devilish fate unleashing a gloominess worthy of Kafka against which the falsely vaunted free will can do nothing."[40]

Gertrud Klepetar and H. G. Adler at their wedding, October 30, 1941. Credit: The Estate of H. G. Adler 2019, Deutsches Literaturarchiv Marbach.

Three days earlier the first construction crews had arrived in Theresienstadt. Their marriage and Gertrud's persistence helped to win permission for Adler to return to Prague, as they hoped, after which he was assigned to work for the cultural wing of the Jewish Community of Prague. Since 1906 it had collected and preserved objects and documents related to the history of Jews in Prague and Czech lands. The Museum Association had been dissolved by the Nazis in the spring of 1940, but the collection remained open and under the control of the Jewish Community of Prague with the approval of the Central Office for Jewish Emigration in Bohemia and Moravia led by Hans Günther, Eichmann's deputy. During the winter of 1941 the museum was closed for renovations, followed by a struggle within the Nazi administration for control over Jewish artifacts gathered across the former republic. In 1942, SS-Sturmbannführer Günther agreed to a plan to mount exhibitions using materials confiscated from Jews throughout Bohemia and Moravia. These were installed by museum staff, and though only private tours for Nazi officials were permitted, the staff preserved a trove of books and religious and cultural artifacts. The Jewish Community of Prague managed the museum, and towns from the countryside sent their moveable assets in an effort to save whatever they could.[41]

Adler was, to say the least, ambivalent about such work. "I turned up, almost against my will, in the Jewish religious community, which soon turned into a center for the liquidation of possessions stolen from Jewish apartments, etc.,

Elisabeth and David Klepetar at the wedding of Gertrud Klepetar and H. G. Adler. Credit: The Estate of H. G. Adler 2019, Deutsches Literaturarchiv Marbach.

and which was completely run by Jews. The synagogues were desecrated and turned into storage facilities for textiles, furniture, musical instruments, electronic devices, and who knows what, all of which now was collectively taken and therefore stolen for good. Nevertheless it all had to be inventoried, cleaned, and arranged so that valiant Germans could buy such treasures and plunder from the Gestapo. I sorted textiles for a couple of days, which was gruesome. Then someone had the idea to have me work in the book repository, where I was the supposed 'expert' on old editions. It was a terrible task. I still recall that Kafka's library (taken from his sister's apartment) passed through my hands. Within it were books that he would have loved to have, with his precious signature, with dedications to him from Brod and other Prague authors, as well as the first English edition of *The Castle* that had been given to his sister. I managed to set aside and save these and many other books until the catastrophe that had seized hold of us a couple of times already, but which—above all through my improbable efforts—had let us go, finally befell us and would not let go."[42]

Adler's stint at the museum only lasted until February 1942, but he returned to work there immediately after the war. His distaste for the work of sorting through possessions stolen from the Jews magnified with time, for those possessions became a haunted vestige of the many who were exterminated. While the idea that the Nazis would create a "museum of an extinct race" may be largely apocryphal, goods were stolen from people who, minimally, were to be deported and in all likelihood were fated to die.[43] Adding to the gruesomeness of the work was knowledge that his and Gertrud's own stolen possessions, as well as those of her parents and her mother's sister, were likely in the heaps of books, prayer shawls, and religious artifacts surrounding Adler in the book repository set up in a defunct synagogue.

There were other reminders of their plight. Emil and Zdenka were gone, shipped off to the East. Gisa and František had divorced, and the first transports had left for Theresienstadt. Soon after he started work in the book depository, Gisa herself was sent there on December 17. On the same train was Bertha Gross, the mother of Bettina, to whom he had sent his "Traktat" from Milan, and who herself had left for England three years earlier. Whether Adler knew about Bertha's deportation then is unclear, although later he would visit her regularly in Terezín. There is no mention of Gisa's departure. As a result of the divorce, she left the apartment Emil owned at Havlíčkova 6 and moved to another part of the city. Given the curfews and the restrictions on travel, he may not have known about it, especially with the absence of Emil as intermediary.

Soon, however, the "devilish fate" they had tried to avoid swept up Günther, Gertrud, and her parents:

> I thought I had saved Geraldine and myself, as well as her parents and her aunt from being transported when, on the night of February 6 and 7, 1942, the official henchmen of the Jewish community surprised us and gathered us together, taking us just as we were to the internment station in Prague from where the transports were dispatched. Thankfully we had already packed all of our personal items, so it didn't take much effort to gather up our things. I was very cold, but unspeakably tired and sad when I realized how helpless I was while looking on at my 75-year-old father-in-law who understood very little of what was going on as he put on his hat and packed his umbrella, as well as articles on medicine which the dear man clung to with touching and solemn dedication. Then we marched through the Prague night. It was bitter cold, perhaps 5 degrees Fahrenheit, or even colder. As we left the building there were numerous lists to fill out, the concierge arriving like a vulture to steal what she could, the Jewish transport itself run by bandits who stole whatever they could get their hands on. The macabre collapse of a society in its death throes. At the entrance to the holding center Geraldine, who had till then held herself together, completely collapsed. She had to be dragged off. I kept pressing for them to set us free, but to no avail. The desperate efforts I had made, the many sleepless nights, the anxiety of weeks and months, all of it had taken such a toll on body and soul that, once I had to confront the hopelessness of my struggle, I could

> not keep from sobbing heavily myself. We remained for many hours in the ghostly confines of the holding center. On February 8, we were taken late at night to a little nearby rail station. I was given the transport number W 982, which would remain mine for the next thirty-two months. The train left early the next morning and soon arrived at the station in Bohušovice. Then we arrived in Theresienstadt.[44]

One would be hard pressed to describe such a scene more directly or more wrenchingly, but comparing it to the deportation of the Lustig family in *The Journey*, Adler's artistry again reveals his urge to transform such duress. Günther, Gertrud, and her family were brought to the holding center across the street from the Museum of Technical Arts in Prague (which serves now as the Museum for Contemporary Art), but in the novel everyone is detained inside the Technology Museum. Adler believed that the roots of the Holocaust were in the technological state that treats humans as objects rather than persons, which is underscored by his description of the detainees and one of their captors:

> Those formerly known as human beings now appeared made of wax, but they were still alive. As the morning dawned its gray, they sat upon their bundles and rocked their upper bodies to and fro, though they did not pray. They had no future, nor was the past recognizable within them any longer. "Here you can't remember anything." The cross-eyed youth walked back and forth among the cowering people. He was almost completely dressed in leather. It was forbidden to those whose lives had been snuffed out to wear anything upon their heads inside the halls, but Cross-Eyes wore a leather cap. In his right hand he swung a leather whip with which he could strike whenever it pleased him. And yet he didn't harm anyone, silent threats being enough to satisfy him.[45]

Written a decade after the exhausting hours spent in the holding center, the passage captures the withering of human relations caused by the wielding of absolute power over them. Referred to officiously as "Those formerly known as human beings," a phrase as likely to come from the mouth of the oppressor as to occur to the author looking back, the victims are "made of wax," as if figures in a museum, or analogous to the bizarre mannequins installed in the Prague Jewish Museum to depict the daily life and religious rituals of "an exterminated race." These are people without a past or a future, condemned to a present they cannot choose or experience on their own terms. For them time has stopped and their everyday lives have been "snuffed out," although bodily they remain present and sitting on their bundles, swaying back and forth in misery, unable to pray. The only distinct person is "Cross-Eyes" with his leather whip. But given his supreme power, he need not even lift it. He, too, is objectified, his name suggesting a malformation or handicap so often ridiculed by the Nazis, as well as a reminder of the hook-nosed and leering caricatures that had long fueled anti-Semitism in newspapers and periodicals. The whip defines him, for with it rests the only power he has, himself a pawn in the deportation of nameless victims.

Adler's account of "one Prague transport" in his scholarly study of Theresienstadt provides a closer glimpse of what his own experience must have been like:

> The "call up" for a transport and for the "reserve" was often delivered by an employee of the JKG [Jewish Religious Community], very often at night. Usually—but by no means in every case—, an entire family was affected. On pain of unnamed "measures," they were ordered to arrive at the JKG at a given time to receive new orders. . . . As soon as someone's lot had come up, feverish activity began, even if he had long been prepared for this moment.[46]

Here we find the resonance of lived experience rather than just a historical account, in the "feverish activity" that must have ensued with each "call up." Yet only in a footnote does Adler address his own experience directly, the reality of what he lived through appearing between the lines and in expressive asides. In the book's third chapter, his note that one could have "the 'transport number' W 982 or AA1 475 or Cv 13" does not mention that W 982 was in fact his own transport number, or that transport AA1 brought both his mother and Ottla to Theresienstadt on July 2, 1942, his thirty-second birthday.[47] Adler is again absent and present, using numbers that were of great significance to him to inscribe himself into the history he felt compelled to write for the sake of the many others who did not survive.

Adler's account of the deportation from Prague provides the semblance of the moment itself by including the actual "Explanation of the Official Summons" rather than a summary of it.[48] Couched in the officious language of Nazi bureaucracy, the document explains who is to appear and when; how many and what kinds of items can be brought; what forms must be filled out ahead of time; what kinds of documents the deportees must present; what properties, jewelry, and cash are to be forfeited; and what items must be left behind. Only after including the entire document does Adler describe what is likely firsthand experience:

> The transfer of property was often nasty, as Fidler [Hauptscharführer Johannes Fidler (a.k.a. Hans Fiedler) from the "Central Office"] was not satisfied with the process, and he tried especially hard to find

> money, valuables, and tobacco. The "Transport Department" was responsible for "smooth execution"; its infamous leader, Robert Mandler, along with his assistants, was a true Jewish scoundrel. Even the Czech police trembled before Mandler, with whom the SS could be satisfied; he forced them by threats to address him only in German. With his riding boots and his leather jacket, Mandler even looked like an SS man.[49]

Adler again is a "participant-observer." Naming the officials and departments establishes objective facts and events, while observing what was stolen, as well as the dress, character, and demeanor of the officials, confesses to more immediate firsthand knowledge. Adler's tone, capturing what it was like to board the trains from the Trade Fair Hall (the Technology Museum in *The Journey*), seems that of a novelist more than a scholar, especially in ending the chapter on the deportations to Theresienstadt with a simple vignette:

> Then, in the early hours of the morning, they marched, escorted by German and Czech police, to a nearby suburban train station. Before that, they were forced to spend many hours standing in the courtyard of the property of the trade fair, in all weather, with no consideration for age or illness. Those who collapsed were laid on stretchers, along with those who could not walk or were recognized as "seriously ill." During the march, they were subject to harassment by the SS and their Jewish lackeys. Abuse was a constant accompaniment to all deportations in Hitler's Reich. The equipment and private "additional luggage" accompanying the transport was loaded onto separate freight cars. Fifty to sixty people, always sorted according to "transport numbers," were loaded into each passenger or freight car, along with their "hand luggage." A transport of 1000 people took not quite four hours to load. After the escort of German policemen had boarded, the train departed. In two to three hours, it arrived at the station of Theresienstadt, in Bohušovice.[50]

Adler's quotation marks around "seriously ill" or "additional luggage" harkens back to the terms laid out in the "Explanation of the Official Summons" and his explanation that such terms were a hoax, as no real care was given to the ill and extra luggage was confiscated on arrival. A good historian could render the same passage with equal veracity, but Adler the writer lets the moment speak for itself, as the prisoners march "in the early hours of the morning," "in all weather," with "[f]ifty to sixty people" in each "passenger or freight car," it taking "not quite four hours" to load the train before its journey of "two to three hours" to the Bohušovice train station.

In the frigid early morning hours of February 9, 1942, Adler could not have had any idea what lay ahead for Gertrud and himself as they arrived in Theresienstadt. He entered the ghetto a mature man of thirty-one, a trained scholar with a doctoral degree, with three years of administrative experience in dealing directly with the Jewish cultural community and Nazi officials, and with a wife who, like her father, was a highly skilled medical doctor.[51] He carried with him his continuing ambitions as a novelist, short-story writer, and poet who had laid out his deepest convictions about the human condition in his "Traktat." His was in many ways the ideal profile for not only facing the bizarre, dysfunctional, and crippling system administered by the Nazis, but also for surviving and detailing it as a scholar and artist. Whether or not he could endure was an open question. But what he promised himself he would do if he did survive was decided soon after his arrival in Theresienstadt.

7

The Ghetto

To understand Theresienstadt, one needs to understand what it was and what it was not.[1]

It was not considered the worst place to be. Most of the Protectorate Jews deported to Theresienstadt were relieved to hear they would be sent there, as they would be near Prague rather than shipped to "the East," a realm as foreign and terrifying to assimilated Czech and German Jews as it was mythologized by their captors as their desired "Lebensraum." Most Nazi guards and officials were happy to work in the secure confines of a fortress town where they could prosper off of what they stole from prominent Jews rather than work amid the destitution of the death camps or serve on the front. That said, although Heydrich had asked the Prague Jewish Community to suggest a suitable location for a ghetto, it was only a ploy, for he had already chosen Theresienstadt at a secret conference of deportation officials (including Eichmann and Hans Günther) at the Hradčany Castle on October 10, 1941, less than two weeks after being named acting Reich protector.[2] Calculating that internment and enforced labor in support of the Nazi war machine were preferable to expulsion to the East, the Jewish Council of Elders appointed on December 4, 1941, soon were forced to take responsibility for administering the day-to-day operations of the labor camp and later composed lists of names for deportation. Unsurprisingly, this created immense distrust and hatred of the Council of Elders among those they should have felt bound to protect. It led the Elders themselves to succumb to a moral duplicity that caused those who were "not originally bad themselves" to become "bad as a result of circumstances."[3]

Theresienstadt was also not a ghetto. Although the Nazis euphemistically called it an *Altersghetto* (old-age ghetto), a *Prominentenghetto* (ghetto for the privileged), a *Musterghetto* (model ghetto), and eventually a *Judenstaat* (Jewish state), its purpose was spelled out at the October 10 conference when Heydrich decreed that the number of Jews in the Protectorate must be substantially reduced. This required evacuation to the East. At the Wannsee Conference three months later, however, Heydrich distinguished "evacuation" (*Evakuierung*) from "transfer" (*Überstellung*) to an "old-age ghetto." Theresienstadt was the only "old-age ghetto" created by the Nazis, and its initial function was to provide a state of arrest for Protectorate Jews rather than immediate extermination. There were no deportations from Germany and Austria to it in the five months following the Wannsee Conference. And yet between November 1941 and April 1945 no less than 470 transports arrived in Theresienstadt and 63 left. The last of the deportations to the East occurred in October 1944, and most often the transports going out were much larger than those coming in. Over the three-and-a-half years of its existence 141,162 people entered and 88,196 left for the East, where the vast majority met their death. Adding this last figure to the 35,088 who died in Theresienstadt itself, one can appreciate why less than 12 percent of those who set foot within the "ghetto for the privileged" lived to tell about it. Of the 15,000 children who entered Theresienstadt, only 100 survived, and of the 88,000 deported to the East in total, only 3,500 survived.[4] Of them, 2,971 were among 75,828 Protectorate Jews who entered the town during the war, meaning a survival rate of less than 4 percent for those brought to the supposed "haven" for them in their native land.[5]

Third, it was not a concentration camp. Unlike Dachau or Sachsenhausen, it was not set up principally to imprison and torture political opponents, though the Small Fortress located across the Eder River from Theresienstadt was used for this purpose for both Jews and prisoners brought in from the outside. Soon after workers arrived to set up the camp in November 1941, "social evenings" were held at which songs and poems were recited. Later, operas, concerts, lectures, readings, and cabarets were held as part of the *Freizeitgestaltung* (Office for Leisure Time Activities) headed by the philosopher Emil Utitz. Indeed, among those first workers were the musicians Gideon Klein, Rafael Schächter, and Karel Švenk, all of whom were allowed to bring in instruments. Because of such liberties, life in Theresienstadt provided for a certain measure of "decency," or as an inmate named Leo Strauss dubbed it in a poem, a life lived "als ob" ("as if"). As part of what became known as "The University Over the Abyss" within the Office for Leisure Time Activities, no less than 2,430 lectures on art, science, music, literature, medicine, economics, history, and Jewish topics were delivered by 520 different individuals, among them Adler himself.[6] It had a library eventually of 130,000 books, most on Jewish history and religion confiscated from prisoners entering the ghetto, but later available for use by them.[7] Operas, songs, and chamber music were composed, thousands of poems were written, plays and satirical sketches were performed, and artists rendered their day-to-day experience in hundreds of drawings and paintings that have survived.

In Theresienstadt a fake money economy, bank, and post office were established, and by May 1943 its own "currency" and "postage" were in circulation. Fourteen "shops" sold groceries, men's and ladies' wear, lingerie, shoes, household items, notions and perfumery, and perhaps saddest of all, suitcases. Most of the goods displayed were taken from prisoners arriving in the camp. One had to pay exorbitant prices to buy back one's own clothes, while the rest of the goods were often only for display and were not for sale at any price. Adding to such mockery was a café established in 1942, where inmates could sign up to spend a few hours, and a small orchestra played during the day. For Adler, "[t]hese reforms alleviated the situation somewhat, but they lent the 'Ghetto' an increasingly eerie character."[8]

All of this happened in a town that, because of overcrowding, Adler describes as resembling "a city hit by a natural disaster."[9] Its footprint measured only 1,200 × 920 meters and covered 411 hectares (roughly 1,000 acres or 1.5 square miles) and from its normal capacity of 3,500 soldiers and 3,700 civilians in 1940 it swelled to nearly 60,000 in September 1942. The segment of the town allotted to the inmates measured only 700 × 500 meters, which meant no more than 1.6 square meters per person in which to live, work, eat, and sleep. Daily life took place amid double- and triple-tiered bunks; overheated or frigid attics with only bare wooden or concrete floors to sleep on; lice-infested bedding and clothes; outbreaks of typhus, enteritis, and scarlet fever; extreme shortages of medical supplies; constant hunger; the threat of arrest and torture; humiliation at the hands of Czech gendarmes and Nazi officials; corruption and theft among the inmates themselves; and always the constant worry of deportation.

And yet it was not a death camp. Unlike Bełżec, Sobibór, and Treblinka, it was not built for extermination, nor did it have a gas chamber.[10] In fact, Theresienstadt is the only internment facility in which the deceased, at least in the first months of its operation, were buried in coffins and in which both Jewish and Christian religious services were allowed for funerals. After a crematorium was built in September 1942, the ashes of the deceased were held in a columbarium or memorial hall, although in 1944 the ashes of some twenty thousand victims were removed from it and dumped into the Eder River in an effort to cover up the number who had died in the camp.[11] Jews from Germany "agreed" to go to Theresienstadt after the Nazis fooled them into signing over their homes and life savings as part of a "home purchase contract" (*Heimeinkaufsvertrag*); they did not think they were brought to Theresienstadt to die but were enticed into thinking it the best chance to live. Its function was as a holding space in which to extract wealth, labor, and camouflage for the extermination camps that it fed. This deception was not lost upon the Jewish Council of Elders, who were in the uncomfortable position of acting as both doomed saviors and helpless collaborators.

Containing eleven barracks and 219 buildings, most of them two-story apartment houses, the walled garrison town of Theresienstadt was built in 1780 by Emperor Josef II, the same Habsburg ruler who first extended religious tolerance to the Jews and granted them access to all professions. Succeeding to the throne after the death of his mother, Maria Theresa, Josef II named the fortress after her. Ironically it was she who expelled the Jews from Bohemia in 1744, allowing them back four years later after imposing a "toleration tax" of 300,000 gold pieces on the community.[12] Sixty kilometers northwest of Prague on an open plain abutting a ridge of mountains that separates it from Lower Saxony, the fortress was built to guard against Prussian invasions, although it never faced serious attack and was abandoned in 1882. It was converted into a prison housing many thousands of prisoners over the years, the most famous of which was Gavrilo Princip, who lit the fuse of World War I when he assassinated Franz Ferdinand, Archduke of Austria, in Sarajevo in 1914. Princip died of tuberculosis in Theresienstadt in 1918. After the breakup of the Austro-Hungarian Empire it became a garrison town for the Czech army. With the annexation of the Sudetenland it came under German control in 1938.

By the early fall of 1941 the road to the Final Solution ran through Theresienstadt. Heydrich declared martial law as soon as he was appointed acting Reich protector in September 1941. President Hácha had tried to allow a thousand prominent figures to be designated as "non-Jews," and for Jews to be registered by religion rather than race, protecting assimilated nonbelievers and those who had converted to Christianity. Heydrich denied those efforts and declared on October 4, 1941, that "in principle no one could be exempted."[13] On October 10 he held a private conference in Prague attended by Adolf Eichmann, Hans Günther, and other officials to discuss removing fifty thousand Jews from Germany and the Protectorate to Łódź, Riga, and Minsk. By the end of October five thousand Jews were deported to Łódź from Prague alone, among them Emil Adler. At that conference Theresienstadt was designated as a "temporary collection camp" for Jews destined for Łódź and other sites in conquered Poland. Heydrich announced the next day that the "final aim" was not only to exclude Jews from social and economic life but to "resettle them outside of Europe . . . as quickly as possible."[14]

On November 24 the first detail of 340 Jewish workers was sent to turn Theresienstadt into an "old-age ghetto" for Jews over sixty-five, decorated Jewish heroes from World War I, wounded Jewish war veterans, and at least initially "Mischlinge," or Jewish spouses of non-Jews and their children. Just six days later a transport of one thousand women, children, and elderly people arrived from Prague, followed by another one thousand from Brno on December 2. Little had been done to prepare for their arrival, so they were forced to sleep on bare concrete floors in damp, unheated rooms. Only on December 4 did another one thousand workers arrive, but despite increased manpower, a shortage of lumber and supplies made construction and renovation extremely difficult. Adler's family knew these conditions first-hand, for his aunt Gisa was deported from Prague on December 17 along with Bertha Gross, Bettina's mother.

Heydrich realized the difficulty of coordinating transports and agencies across the Reich necessary to carry out his mission and on November 29 planned a conference at the Reichssicherheitshauptamt (Reich Main Security Office or RSHA) offices in the Berlin suburb of Wannsee, originally scheduled for December 9. It was postponed because of America's entry into the war after Japan's attack on Pearl Harbor on December 7 and was eventually held on January 20, 1942. Eichmann toured Theresienstadt the day before giving his approval to the bunks that at last were being built for the prisoners.[15] Officials from every major ministry in the Reich except Finance and Transport, already fully cooperating in the deportations, were present in Wannsee, and everyone enjoyed lunch before getting down to the business of murder.[16]

Time slowed down and time sped up. The Endlösung did not occur at once but evolved over time and unfolding circumstances. As Christopher Browning argues, "Hitler's words and Himmler's and Heydrich's actions at the center set in motion waves of political signals that radiated outward. Like expanding concentric circles, they encompassed more and more people who, reading these signals, became aware that something new was expected of them."[17] In important ways, Theresienstadt stood at the center, for it came to serve the systemized expulsion to slave labor and death in the East and represented the betrayal by the Germans of Jews who had long considered themselves assimilated.[18] It held sixty thousand prisoners at its height in September 1942, but the vast majority of them had arrived only that summer, leaving little time or preparation for handling immense overcrowding in sweltering heat.

Otto Zucker, the engineer selected to serve as assistant to Jacob Edelstein, the first Head of the Council of Elders, gives an account of the conditions that awaited each arrival:

> Accommodations of the masses arriving in close succession was a truly insoluble task. The barracks were already fully occupied in July [1942] and the buildings were crammed to capacity by August. . . . The only alternative was to make use of the rooms considered hitherto unfit for habitation. Next came attics in a state of total neglect [covered with decades' worth of dust and soot] with no insulation against cold or heat, no wiring for lights, no plumbing, and no lavatories. In the heat of the summer the prevailing temperatures made living there exceptionally hard. In addition many of the feeble and sick were [physically] unable to use the stairs in order to take refuge from the rooftop quarters

> during the peak of heat. More than 6,000 persons were put up under the rafters.[19]

In July, 32 people died each day, 75 per day in August, and a staggering 131 per day in September, whose monthly death total hit 3,941.[20] The speed with which the town was transformed from a crude, if not cruel, form of sanctuary into a grotesque community of disease and death was astounding. As early as January 9, 1942, the first deportation of 2,000 Jews to the East and to Riga revealed as well its covert function in the Final Solution. When Adler arrived a month later, the bureaucratic machine that would soon feed the crematoria of Auschwitz was in full operation.

Theresienstadt, ultimately, was too many different things at once, part ghetto, part old-age home, part death sentence, part cultural oasis, part depot for transports, and part alibi for atrocities in the East. What Adler would have become without his having spent thirty-two months there is impossible to know. If one were to draw a circle with a radius of roughly 550 kilometers around Theresienstadt, the key sites of his life—Terezín, the later camps he was in, the camps that several of his relatives were in, the places of his childhood, where he did his postwar research—would all fall within it. Only Milan and London stand outside, Milan a temporary respite in which Adler first set down ideas about spirit, intuition, and human existence that preoccupied him throughout his life, and London the foothold of a postwar exile from whose perch he constantly looked back to bear witness to Theresienstadt and the camps. How he was shaped by it is the story of his life.

Early in his imprisonment there, Adler made perhaps his most crucial decision about how to make use of whatever time was left him. It did not come easily or immediately. The disorientation and despair he experienced upon arrival was profound and lasted several weeks. In the early stages of the ghetto prisoners got off the train in Bohušovice and were forced to march 3 km to Theresienstadt through bitter cold, carrying the 50 kg of luggage they were allowed to bring with them. Inside the fortress new arrivals were taken to the "Schleuse" ("sluice"), a barracks set aside to fleece them of any "contraband" (i.e., money, postage stamps, and valuables), including items they had been told they could bring with them, such as flashlights and batteries, shaving equipment, toilet paper, writing paper, cookers, and candles. The "sluice" functioned as a temporary quarantine for preventing the spread of infectious diseases the Nazis were terrified of catching themselves. Men were given a crewcut and women were forced to wear their hair short. Until July 1942 men and women were housed separately. Even when they were allowed to share barracks they had to sleep in separate rooms, although they were allowed to be together during the day.

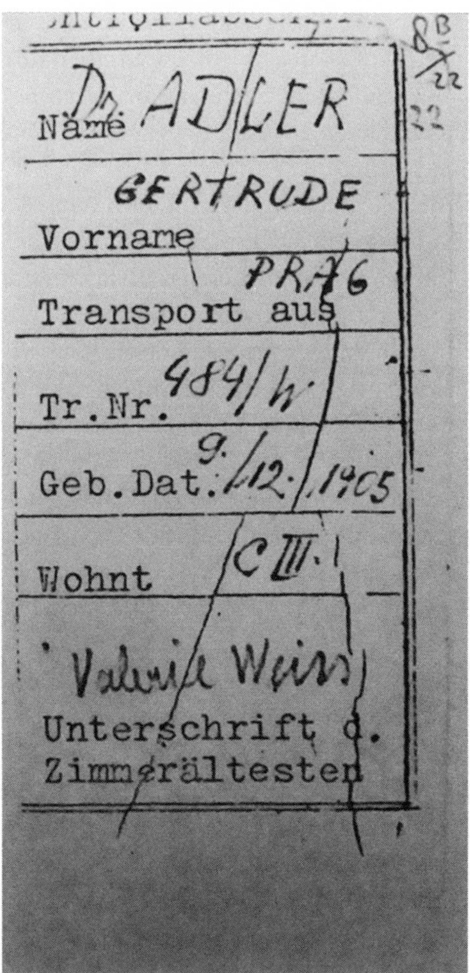

Name Dr. ADLER

GERTRUDE
Vorname

Transport aus PRAG

Tr.Nr. 484/W

Geb.Dat. 9./12./1905

Wohnt C III.1

Valerie Weiss
Unterschrift d.
Zimmerältesten

Gertrud Klepetar's registration paper, Theresienstadt. Credit: H. G. Adler Archive, NIOD, Amsterdam.

Upon arrival, Gertrud was taken to live with other women in the Hamburg Barracks, while Günther was housed with other able-bodied workers in the Sudeten Barracks. Nearly empty of furniture and with hardly any working toilets, the Sudeten Barracks soon housed over five thousand inmates. Most lived in seven large rooms and slept on straw-covered concrete floors huddled around makeshift iron stoves that provided little heat. Initially, there was only one three-hundred-liter pot available to cook for thousands of people, and because it constantly sat on the heat, it was soon badly damaged. Eventually larger facilities were set up, but food portions continued to be meager and represented half the amount necessary to feed the prisoners, as any increased quantity was offset by the rapid rise of the population. The food quality was also miserable, consisting of rotten potatoes and beets, some thin soup, a pound of bread every two days, and a watery sausage now and then.

Because of the strict separation between men and women, Adler could only see Gertrud when he was granted the rare "Transit Pass" or was willing to risk arrest by visiting. The Hamburg and Sudeten Barracks stood within a couple of hundred yards of each other, but after only three months of marriage the couple were forced to communicate mostly through letters and notes passed among inmates. This was somewhat easier for them to manage than it was for others. Gertrud's position as head of the central laboratory in the Hohenelber Barracks on the northeastern side of Theresienstadt meant that she walked along the dusty and decaying streets and encountered numerous other inmates whom she could entrust with notes rather than remaining stuck in a workshop in her barracks. Günther also was granted a fair amount of mobility, assigned to one of the work details (*Hundertschaften*) that consisted of a hundred men charged with setting up and making the camp somewhat habitable in the early days. Nevertheless, parts of the ghetto remained off-limits. The streets they could traverse were a maze that ran between high wooden fences separating the prisoners from their captors. Mail remained strictly controlled. In January 1942, it could be delivered from barrack to barrack, and one postcard per month of thirty words to the outside world was allowed, although none were actually delivered. Any violation of this system was serious: early that month nine men had been hanged for "defaming the German Reich" when it was discovered that they had sent letters home through some of the Czech civilians who still lived in the town.

As Adler walked about the ghetto trying to fathom its nature and his purpose within it, he was overcome with depression and anxiety. The conditions he encountered in the living quarters assigned to him in the Sudeten Barracks made the first weeks in Theresienstadt almost unbearable. "For me this place was the worst of all; nowhere else did my soul suffer as much as it did here. Nowhere else did I encounter such abysmal horror. For the few who managed to live through it, Theresienstadt held a grip on their lives forever. It amounted to the most genuinely diabolical span of falsehood stretching over the terrible abyss that existed. It was the most hellish ritual mask that death ever wore."[21] Writing to Gertrud, he laments, "If only I could break the curse of these times. We are both sick with these times, the evil afoot in the two lowest levels of existence, material conditions and the state (can't you see the Traktat at work in all this?) wants to break us, but since to us this can't happen entirely, it just keeps eating away at us, though that won't work, either." Regardless of such avowals, he cannot help but confess to feeling a "loneliness among the sacrificial mounds of disgusting, reeking bodies."[22]

Yet he was compelled to work, for anyone between sixteen and sixty-five had to report for work each day. Throughout his thirty-two months in the ghetto Adler never held any position in the Jewish administration, even though his experience at the Urania in Prague and his work sorting books for the Liquidation Office of the Prague Jewish Community qualified him to take on the more privileged position of an administrator if he had wanted it. He also aligned himself with neither the Zionists nor the Communists, the two largest political organizations in the camp, wishing to remain politically and spiritually independent. It amounted to a risky choice, as such ties often meant the difference between being included in a transport list or not. Instead, for the first two months, he was assigned to a Hundertschaften. From April 1942 until the spring of 1943 he served as a room orderly and handyman in the barracks. He then returned briefly to the Hundertschaften before working as a typist in the office of the Ghetto Police that summer. He then joined the builders unit and worked as a bricklayer until the summer of 1944, when he became an assistant librarian in the ghetto library founded by Emil Utitz. Adler would later muse about how much of his "terrible work" as a bricklayer could still be found in Theresienstadt.[23] Although his skills were better suited to administration, and he delivered lectures and talks as part of the "Leisure Time Activities" program, he chose manual labor jobs in order not to involve himself with what he had come to see as a corrupt and doomed leadership. Ironically, his utility as a laborer would eventually save him.

Adler found his footing in March when he said to himself, "I will not survive this. But if I survive, then I will describe it, and through two different means: I will research it in a scholarly manner and in such form leave myself completely out of it, and I will also describe it in poetic manner."[24] This was the decision that enabled him to survive Theresienstadt, and it set in motion the closely interlinked aims of his work as a scholar and writer. As a bricklayer and manual laborer, he could roam the town and observe many aspects of the skewed yet orderly oppression within it while planning to write a scholarly study of it. "A strange sort of double existence of a reflexive nature," he describes to Gertrud. "To live as a participant and to live as an observer. It's really like they are two different people."[25] Later he recalled, "Strangely, this decision granted me a salutary strength. It indeed was some months before I regained my inner balance, yet the vague plan for a book that would serve as a memorial to this time did a great deal of good for my anxious spirits. . . . I trained myself to observe things around me from a cool distance . . ., but this coolness had to be regularly conquered anew, for I had to let the fire, the blaze, and the glow of the horrible events constantly sweep over me in order to be tested, hardened, and ultimately . . . able to muster the will to perceive the entire truth."[26]

Adler, however, did not use his regained composure to sustain just himself. Walking by a horse stable one day that same month, he heard Beethoven's violin concerto being played inside a locked stall. It was bad enough that someone had smuggled in an instrument, but playing it was more dangerous yet. When the player finally unbolted the stall, Adler found sixteen-year-old Tommy Mandl and his father. Adler took a particular interest in the young man and for the rest of their time in the ghetto discussed philosophy, literature, art, and music with him.[27] Mandl later survived Auschwitz, where his father perished, but Adler remained a surrogate father to him after he escaped Czechoslovakia in 1961. Through Adler's help, Mandl became Heinrich Böll's private secretary in Cologne, yet meeting him there one day Adler could not help but observe, "Unfortunately, he still needs help disentangling himself from the past. In this way we (myself included) are always thrust back into the world of persecution and the pain of others, the horrors never letting go, threading their way through the fabric of the world in diverse ways."[28]

Despite his plan for a scholarly study of the ghetto, poetry was the first genre Adler turned to once he had gathered his wits. Its concision was central to restoring his focus in those first months. Adler wrote 108 poems in Theresienstadt and gathered them into six "collections," some of which are structured as numbered cycles. That none is arranged chronologically according to the date of each poem's completion underscores how Adler used poetry as a means not just to give expression to his experience but also to shape and cohere it. Writing to Steiner after the war he calls the poems "testimonies generated from a crossroads of the soul, some of them attempting here and there, and some throughout to achieve the full lyric expression of such a state in order to grant it lasting form."[29] He acknowledged that they stemmed from "subjective" reactions to what he had seen and lived through, but he consciously avoided naturalism. He aimed for a "coherence" that would allow his experience to rise above the "private sphere" and achieve the condition of poetry.

The first poem he wrote is dated March 23, 1942, just seven weeks after his arrival. It commences a cycle of twenty-five numbered poems sardonically titled "Theresienstadt Bilderbogen" ("Theresienstadt Picture Book") completed between March and December that year. The cycle is headed by an epigraph, "Arrogance is punished — / It is brought down and condemned," and the opening poem sets that urge in motion:

> THE DEATH MILL
> Scorched suffering curdles in the death mill,
> Bowed bodies sweat, grotesquely writhing heaps
> Of chaos lie contorted and smeared in the terrible chill,
> As dusty smoke from the fire swells above them,
>
> And the mad cries and rampant distress
> Rip through the sharply flecked day, crippled
> Hands clasping together outside the prison bars,
> As hunger crackles in a tear-soaked cloth.
>
> Dazed, dull, and broken glances falter,
> The veil of pale fears flares across mouth and brow,
> The throats of miserable fates rattle.
> A stifled, extinguished cry chokes to death.[30]

The formal control of the tightly rhymed and metered quatrains in the German provides a jarring contrast to the poem's grotesque imagery. The German is also awash in the consonance of "sh" and double "ss" sounds broken up by hard "k" and "g" gutturals. The effect is something like the hiss and strike of a poisonous snake, and the images possess a powerful expressionism beneath which bristles both horror and outrage.[31] And yet the first full rhyme of "Totenmühle/Kühle" (death mill/chill) speaks to the same newfound "Kühl" (coolness) that Adler employed observing daily life around him. Poetic distancing appears in how the victims are depicted as suffering objects rather than sentient beings. Suffering "curdles" in the death mill as disembodied "mad cries" fill the air, "glances falter," and the "throats of miserable fates rattle." One has the feeling of human suffering, but unattached to any recognizable individual, nor suffered directly by the speaker. Given that in the spring of 1942 the gas chambers and crematoria of the East were just starting to be used, it is unlikely that Adler would have known of them. His evocation of a furnace burning human bodies is eerily prescient.

Surprisingly missing are the perpetrators, nowhere to be seen, nor granted any command or control of what occurs. This might seem to distance the suffering of the victims or even to deny culpability to their tormentors, but the suffering is displaced from both victims and perpetrators as a force in itself. This denies the perpetrators any "volition" in their actions, as they remain hidden cogs in the machinery of the "death mill," mirroring the Nazis' relationship to their victims, for in their blind following of a mad ideology many chose not to see the suffering they caused, a byproduct of the force they felt compelled to employ to serve their larger plans. The more they inflicted such suffering, the less human their victims came to seem, freeing them of feelings of remorse or responsibility.[32] Adler's reduction of the victims to body parts and grimaces echoes the stereotypes of anti-Jewish propaganda that had been employed for centuries, which fed the indifference of others when Jews began to be deported. Adler opens a direct view onto the reality of suffering, but through the scrim of indifference that kept it hidden and even enabled it. It has been said, "the road to Auschwitz was built by hatred, but paved with indifference."[33] Adler saw this well before Auschwitz was in full operation. "The Death Mill," written within the sealed anonymity of Theresienstadt, captures a crucible of suffering fired by "the blaze" of events that had hardened its author enough to allow him to render its essence in poetic form.

The observing scholar in Adler appears in his poetry, and his poetry served his scholarship. As he began to gather materials and make notes that he would use later in his two books on Theresienstadt, the poems provided a constant and more readily realizable means for recording actual events and subjective experience. Ruth Vogel-Klein adds to these points in noting that collectively the poems "convey iterative aspects of life in the camps through the spectrum of violence, oppression, and humiliation inflicted on people."[34] As the title implies, like a chain of postcards brought back from an awful tourist destination, Adler's "Picture Book" presents the principal sites and moments of terror: "At the Station," "Prisoners," "The Hangman Helps," "Hunger," "The Sick Room," "The Funeral," and "Deportation." Bookending these is the shocking imagery and wrenched syntax of "The Death Mill" and "Dance of Death," which underscore the otherworldly nightmare of the cycle. Katrin Kohl observes that Adler's poems supply the "intellectual-psychological space that, even in the midst of the most demeaning of imprisonments, offered the possibility of realizing his indestructible desire for freedom."[35] This becomes the driving force behind his scholarship, and the combination encompasses the "entire truth" he hoped to convey.

Adler's second poem, written the very next day, makes this even more apparent, for it speaks to the way "cool" observance fed his lyric imagination in stepping away from the extreme expressionism of "The Death Mill" to render a more commonplace event in the ghetto. Eventually it becomes the fifth poem in the cycle:

> SEARCH
> The eye socket peers through rotting dust.
> A finger threatens. Fear falls silent.
> A bald knob of flesh surrounded by gray.
> The gold tooth shines, gnashing at theft.
>
> A whistle sounds. The hall is sealed off.
> Expectation hardens a hollow face.
> Frozen light grows ashamed
> Of silence. Only a small boy whimpers.
>
> The guard enters looking morose,
> Plunging cold-heartedly and cross into household goods,
> Stealing a beggar's meal, snatching up a shirt.
> A cry is choked back and swallowed down.
>
> The step clanks off. A storm breaks loose.
> The iron bar slides through the door with might.
> The shadows cower. Then comes night.
> An old man listens, sniggering in his gut.[36]

Adler introduces human figures, although reduced to references to body parts, such as the "bald knob of flesh" circled by the gray of a Nazi uniform, the "hollow face" of the prisoner, or the "gold tooth" gnashing its lips for the theft to come, which eerily anticipates the theft of gold teeth that did take place in the death camps, although again Adler could not have known that then. The perpetrator is defined as a "guard," but in appearing "cold-hearted and cross" while stealing a beggar's food, he is dehumanized and transformed into the "step" that clanks in the last stanza as the iron bar slides shut on the prisoners. Only in the middle of the poem are we told "a small boy whimpers." It is as if that "boy" represents the spirit of the old man being searched and fleeced of his food and clothing. Once darkness falls, the old man sniggers in his gut because of his disdain for the guard. The boy's "whimper" remains the clearest and most pure expression of emotion in the poem, all else seeming a collision of forces within the "search" purportedly for contraband, but in fact for booty to be carted off by the guard.

DURCHSUCHUNG

Die hoffnung schielt aus schmutz und staub.
Ein finger droht. die furcht verstummt.
Schief bleckt ein fleischwulst grau vermummt.
Ein goldzahn blitzt und giert nach raub.

Ein pfiff – die höhle ist versperrt,
Erwartung strafft ein hohl gesicht,
Es schleicht verstohlen trüb das licht
Ins schweigen, nur ein Knabe plärrt.

Verdrossen bricht die wache ein,
Stößt in den haushalt wild und fremd,
Nimmt dürre nahrung, packt ein hemd –
Ein schrei erstickt in jähem schein.

Der schritt verhallt. – ein sturm wird groß
Der eisarm schlägt durchs tor mit macht.
Die schatten fallen. es wird nacht.
Ein greis lauscht seufzend hoffnungslos.

24. 3. 42.

Häschen, ich habe jetzt mit dem Kommen Pech; gestern in Hamburg ohne Dich nur eine 1/4 Stunde. Wer weiß, was morgen wird? Heute hoffte ich auf Dich, leider … Lustig die 7. Woche ohne Beschäftigung; alles ein Pack. Nun macht nichts, und ich weiß meine Zeit so halbwegs zu nutzen für hiesige Verhältnisse. Wie findest Du die „Durchsuchung"? Bitte, gib mir über diese Sachen strengen Bescheid, es ist unter all den waltenden Umständen so schwer, objektiv und verläßlich selbstkritisch zu sein. Gewiß ist die Vermeidung des Naturalismus und eine bestimmte formale Gestaltung gelungen. Aber ob hier mehr ist, Kindchen, sollst Du mir sagen. Liebste, wie gefällt Dir der Tag? [illegible]. Ich will sehen, wie ich mit der Schreiberei weiter zu liegen komme. Ich habe auch schon 3 Gedanken notiert. Darf ich sie aufschreiben? Bitte:

Adler's poem "Durchsuchung" ("Search") and his letter to Gertrud, March 24, 1942. Credit: The Estate of H. G. Adler 2019, Deutsches Literaturarchiv Marbach.

The speed with which Adler captured in verse the "search" he and Gertrud had suffered weeks before is impressive, but the use of an expressionistic style banned by the Nazis shows the degree to which these are poems of protest written to speak to the moment. A draft Adler sent with a letter to Gertrud the day it was written reveals how quickly he could arrive at a complex lyric expression in spite of shifting conditions around him. There is no record of when he revised it, but the final version that appears in his collected poems differs only superficially from the initial one, something true of most of Adler's poems. The note to Gertrud that accompanies the poem reveals Adler's anxious state of mind, his distressed circumstances, and his determination to rise above them:

> Sweetheart, I had bad luck with coming to see you. Yesterday I was in the Hamburg Barracks with you, but only for a quarter hour of bliss. Who knows what tomorrow will bring? I hoped to see you today, but unfortunately it didn't happen. How funny to have nothing to do for seven weeks; such a *crowd*. Well, it doesn't matter; at least I know how to use the time to sort out the lay of the land. What do you think of "Search"? Please tell me what you really think of it, for under such extreme conditions it's so hard to be objective and reliably self-critical. Certainly I managed to avoid naturalism and there is a definite formal cohesion to it. But whether or not there is anything more, sweetheart, you need to tell me.[37]

The letter provides a window into Adler's thought and living conditions. There is the reference to the quick fifteen-minute meeting in Gertrud's barracks, most likely illegal, while circumstances the next day do not allow such a risk. Then the mention of seven weeks with no real occupation speaks to Adler's sense of alienation and displacement upon entering the ghetto, although he makes use of the time to build relations and get to know "the lay of the land." Most important for securing a sound foothold is to find a way to move ahead with his writing. Having finished the poem, he includes it in the letter to ask Gertrud her true opinion, for the crowded, miserable conditions make it difficult to judge his own work.

The need to rise above such circumstances as a writer was essential to his survival. "For me the most important question was: How can a person protect his inner life from what happens to that life? So amid the cries in the concentration camps, when people began to complain, I always tried to bring them to their senses. I would say, 'Look at the sun, or look at that beetle there.' I always tried

Otto Ungar: Sketch of Gertrud Adler-Klepetar, Theresienstadt, 1943. Credit: The Estate of H. G. Adler 2019, Deutsches Literaturarchiv Marbach.

to buck up others and give them hope in the middle of such inhumanity. Again and again I said to them, 'These are tests of us.' "[38] Such an attitude runs the risk of sounding naively stoic, except when one considers the real tests Adler faced day to day. Not only was the separation from Gertrud painful, but having family members in the ghetto carried with it the fear that they could be taken away at any time on one of the transports.

This was all too apparent just weeks after he entered the ghetto when his dear aunt Gisa, whose arrival in Theresienstadt preceded his by nearly two months, was deported on April 1, 1942, to Piaski, a village outside of Lublin that had a concentration camp from which two thousand Jews were transported to their death by gas in Bełżec on April 11. Gisa was most likely among them, unless she was shot on arrival.[39] Adler could not have known for sure of Gisa's fate at the time, but the abruptness of her parting amid the arriving throngs of deportees could only have reminded him of the loss of his father five months earlier and the threat of losing Gertrud or her parents at any moment.

Just four months later an even more wrenching loss occurred. On July 2, 1942, Adler's thirty-second birthday, his mother and his aunt Ottla arrived in

Theresienstadt on transport AA1 from Prague. Being reunited with family was normally cause for joy, but because Alice had been taken from a mental hospital in Prague, Adler felt that visiting her risked his also being branded "geistgestört" ("mentally ill"), endangering Gertrud and her parents as well. While the Nazis generally did not brand relatives of the mentally ill as genetically flawed and therefore dispensable, such a fear was plausible. Racial condemnation through marriage and ancestry was part of legal statute and mentally handicapped people had been "euthanized" in Poland in 1939, followed by the gassing of seventy thousand mentally ill Germans over the next two years. Public unease about such practices grew so broad that by late 1941 the SS shut down the program, although a staff of trained killers would soon set up much larger and more sophisticated gas chambers.[40] Having last seen his mother at the end of 1940 in the "Jewish ward" of the central hospital in Prague, where the mentally ill had been separated into "Aryan" and "Jewish," Adler could only conclude that his mother was doomed and that association spelled danger to himself and others.

He would later reflect, "Matters had become unbelievably wicked, the last vestige of humanity having been torn asunder. Barbarity and wickedness showed here their twin sinister grimaces."[41] In Theresienstadt Alice was housed with other mental patients at the Central Hospital, but only for seven weeks. On August 25 she was among 1,000 inmates sent to Maly Trostenets, a small village outside Minsk. She was most likely taken to the forest and shot upon arrival or gassed in one of the portable gas wagons, as Emil and Zdenka had been in Chełmno. Adler never saw her again. Ottla stayed in Theresienstadt for a few more months until she was selected for the first transport sent from the ghetto to Auschwitz. Of the 1,866 Jews who left on October 26, only 215 men and 32 women were admitted to the camp; the other 1,619 were taken immediately to the gas chamber. A few months shy of her sixty-fourth birthday, most likely deemed too old to be of use as a laborer, Ottla would have been one of them.

Günther and Gertrud's first year in Theresienstadt was full of upheavals, for the daily arrivals and departures of the thousands of people who passed through and the arbitrary conditions handed down by the Nazis guaranteed a constant state of flux and panic. By the end of 1942 they had witnessed the arrival of 227 transports that brought 95,000 people into the fortress while 33 deportations saw 41,000 people leave, never to return. Another 16,000 died in the ghetto, while in August alone there were over 176,000 visits to the infirmary. In less than six months they saw the population rise from 13,000 to 53,000, with all of the expected outbreaks of sickness and disease that challenged Gertrud and her colleagues in the Health Service. Numbers alone cannot capture how difficult it was to live through constantly worsening conditions, for the nature of the real horror of Theresienstadt was the whipsaw change in conditions endured week by week and month by month.

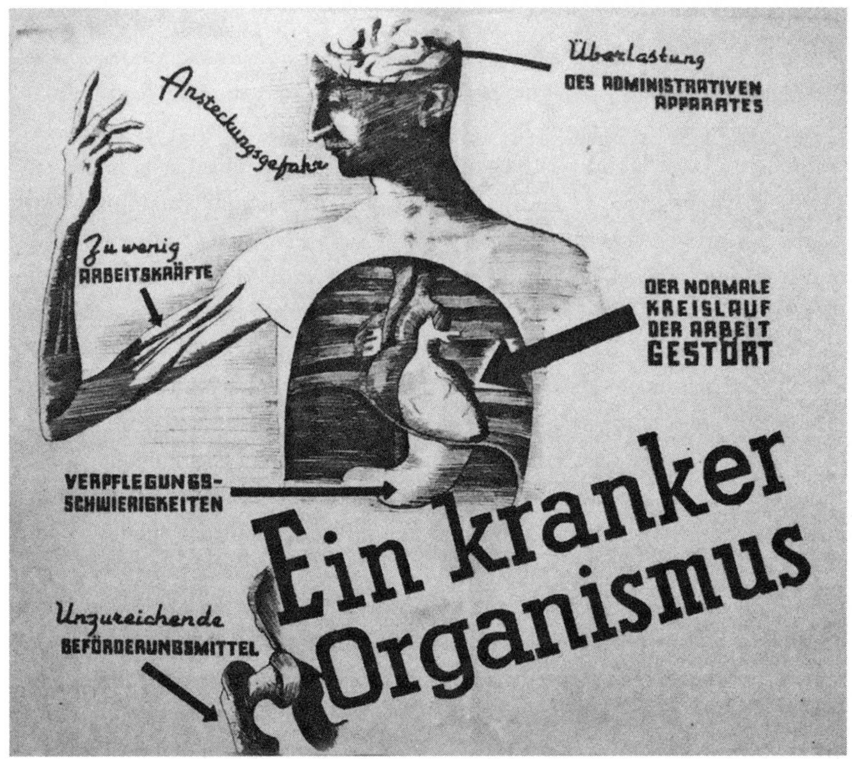

Medical Poster, Theresienstadt. Credit: H. G. Adler Archive, NIOD, Amsterdam.

The same months that saw the deportation of forty-one thousand prisoners also brought a more "civilized" state of affairs to the running of the town. In March 1942 the wives and families of Jacob Edelstein and his colleagues arrived and were installed in more tolerable living quarters of their own. While this created a hierarchy and set off the Council of Elders from the plight of the inmates, it was a first step in allowing the Jews an increased amount of self-governance and control. In April, however, prisoner access to the storage facilities containing luggage confiscated in the "sluice" was cut off, allowing the Czech gendarmes and the Nazis to rummage through it and steal whatever valuables they could find. May saw an improvement in the food when spring crops replaced rotten winter vegetables, but it also brought the construction of the crematorium whose tall smokestack beyond the fortress walls reminded all of their tentative hold on life. The opening of the Central Bath that month, however, allowed for better personal hygiene, and the digging of wells and laying of water and sewer pipes by Jewish workers substantially improved day-to-day life. A fire in the Central Disinfection Station in August, however, forced it to be shut down. It was then ominously replaced with a hydrogen cyanide facility to disinfect clothing inside small gas chambers in the ongoing war against lice. Best of all was that men and women were at last allowed to visit each other at will and for as many hours as they wished before curfew, although they still could not live together in the same room. This was at the beginning of July, when daily administration of the ghetto was turned over to Edelstein and the Council of Elders. For the first time inmates were allowed to roam freely in their part of the ghetto. At the same time such liberties were announced in early July, however, the names of streets and barracks were replaced by numbers and letters, emphasizing to the prisoners that they lived in an unnatural, forced community in which they were jailed.

The influx of arrivals in the summer included a surge in transports from Berlin, Munich, Cologne, and Vienna, which drastically altered the cultural makeup of Theresienstadt. Until then it had been, for better or worse, a fairly homogenous community of Bohemian and Moravian Jews with a shared history and culture, with months of experience maneuvering the demands of ghetto life together. By August, however, Germans and Austrians exceeded the number of Czechoslovak citizens, who despised them for taking away their country. "The Jewish Czech does not love us. He sees us only as Germans," noted the Berliner Philipp Manes in his Theresienstadt diary,[42] and another prisoner from Berlin recalled, "The Czechs hated us just as we hated Hitler, and they held us partly responsible for the misfortune they had met with. They did not see in us fellow sufferers, but only Germans whom they hated."[43]

Tensions ran so high that by October a change in the Council of Elders was necessary. Six of the thirteen Czech-speaking Jews on the Council were forced to step down, replaced by four Reich Jews and two from Vienna. A few months later the leadership was altered again. Edelstein served as first deputy to Paul Eppstein, the new Council head from Berlin, and Benjamin Murmelstein of Vienna was appointed second deputy. Competition and power struggles broke out among the triumvirate, as distrust and envy plagued relations among the inmates. The Council had its hands full trying to fill the transports demanded by the Nazis, as well as the daily operations of the teeming ghetto, and cultural and political tensions forced them to square off against one another.

"Between these fronts," Adler observed, "the frail administration found itself with its back to the wall: hounded by the SS, pressured by the prisoners, ambivalent itself, and driven by its own desire for self-preservation." Adler also saw such chaos as symptomatic of the real "chaos" that plagued Theresienstadt:

> Everything was anticipated, everything provided for—the only thing missing was life. The monstrosity and absurdity of this structure could hardly be surpassed, as responsibilities were hopelessly entangled and overlapping; a superstructure like this, in which each inmate and object was repeatedly registered and categorized, was ultimately unable

> to register anything. It was a deceptive ordering of chaos—a spectral order that was embellished with powerful-sounding terms but that in fact had no power over itself. It could not be cohesive and immediately would have dissolved into the nothingness that it really was had not a mixture of active insanity and passive obsession held it together under the pressure exerted by the SS.[44]

Such was the dynamic of Theresienstadt, as it was and was not. It was a ghetto that was not a ghetto, and a town that was not a town, and where, as Philipp Manes observed in his diary, "Since our first days here, we cling to the words *if* and *when*."[45] Although in July the Czech gendarmes were withdrawn and replaced by an Order Guard of Jews, this meant an increased hierarchy of power and control within the community. Opportunities for abuse and corruption among their own increased. Nor did the handover of power diminish the severity of conditions on the ground. In the same month the use of coffins was abandoned to speed up funerals by burial in mass graves. New deportees arriving in August saw even their hand luggage confiscated in the "sluice," and construction was soon begun on a rail line from Bohušovice directly into the fortress. While this made it easier for inmates to arrive in the ghetto, it sped up the transports and reminded everyone that the one way out was to the dreaded East.

Notwithstanding poor living conditions, a thriving industry was built up in Theresienstadt. Jews manufactured women's clothing, produced fur sheared from rabbits for insulating coats, split mica for industrial production, sewed leather galoshes, and produced an array of handicrafts, all for export to the Reich. Curfews were moved as late as 10:00 p.m., and inmates were allowed to sleep in open courtyards during the summer heat. By fall, however, the curfew returned to 8:00 p.m., and movement throughout the city was again restricted when the Nazis feared a revolt led by the Order Guard. Things got better, things got worse. Time sped up and time slowed down. Stores opened in the fall, and by December the first ersatz coffee was served in the new coffeehouse. October, however, saw the first transport leave for Auschwitz, and singing and whistling were officially banned. Doubt and anxiety reigned in Theresienstadt as Adler looked on from the margins and saw a pattern. "The SS technique was always the same: unclear information, deception, lies. . . . But every improvement in the difficult living conditions at the same time contributed to the prisoners' deception and self-deception."[46]

Harsh conditions in Theresienstadt tended to be exacerbated when the SS suspected betrayal or rebellion on the part of the Jews or when outside events inspired them to use the ghetto to satisfy their own sadistic sense of revenge, most intensely in June 1942 when Heydrich was assassinated outside of Prague by the Czech underground. Hitler immediately ordered the killing of ten thousand

Czech prisoners, although Heydrich's replacement Karl Hermann Frank talked him out of it, citing the danger of a general uprising. Nevertheless, because a bicycle and a suitcase were found where a bomb had exploded beneath Heydrich's car, all twenty thousand prisoners in Theresienstadt had to line up, view pictures of the items, and sign an oath that they knew nothing about them, although they had been imprisoned throughout the entire event.

Elsewhere the Germans raided 5,000 towns in the Protectorate, arrested over 3,000 people, and handed out death sentences to 1,300.[47] This was not enough to satisfy Hitler's rage. When the Gestapo suspected the Horák family in Lidice of ties to Heydrich's assassination, Hitler ordered the village of 500 inhabitants burned to the ground, all of its men shot, the women and children deported. On June 9, 1942, ten trucks filled with security police surrounded the village. Mattresses were attached to the side of the Horák family barn, and all 173 men of the village were lined up in groups of five or ten and shot. Fifty-two women were killed and over 200 were sent to the Ravensbrück concentration camp; only a handful survived. Of the village's 105 children, 88 were transported to Łódź, though seven were selected to live with SS families after being judged suitable to be "Germanized." On July 2, 1942, all of the 81 remaining children were taken to Chełmno on Eichmann's order and gassed in the same trucks that had consumed Emil and Zdenka Adler.

Lidice itself was erased. The day of the executions the Nazis burned it to the ground and brought in bulldozers to level it entirely. Along with its roads, even the stream passing through it was rerouted. Pets were killed, farm animals were carted off for slaughter, and the graveyard was dug up to loot the dead of gold and jewelry. On June 11 a detail of thirty workers arrived from Theresienstadt. They were forced at gunpoint to bury the bodies outside the village's smoldering ruins over the next thirty-six hours. Told not to say anything about the mission once they returned to Theresienstadt, word nonetheless spread that the Nazis had leveled Lidice, inspiring deep fears of further reprisals. After the Nazis announced with pride what they had done, however, the world took up the cause of Lidice. Movies were made in the United States and Britain, towns in several countries renamed themselves Lidice, Edna St. Vincent Millay wrote a book-length poem about it, and the rallying cry "Lidice Shall Live!" became shorthand for early awareness of the Nazi potential for atrocity. Such protests, however, did little to check the escalation following Heydrich's death. That summer "Aktion Reinhard" led to the completion, upgrading, and full operation of the six major death camps—Treblinka, Sobibór, Auschwitz-Birkenau, Chełmno, Bełżec, and Majdenek. Before Heydrich's death roughly one million Jews met their death primarily by a gunshot to the neck; after his death a staggering five million died over the next twenty-four months, the majority of them in the gas chambers.

The Order of the Day issued by the Council of Elders on November 24, 1942, the one-year anniversary of the founding of the ghetto, betrays no foreboding about the future or regret over what the community had suffered already. It strikes an upbeat tone on what had been accomplished and what more could be done to improve life in Theresienstadt. Adler quotes it:

> In the past months, we have experienced difficulties; it was necessary to bring together thousands of Jews from various social circles, who introduced various worldviews and were used to completely different manners and customs [*sic*], for only in that way was it possible to bring forth the creative forces, totally dedicate them, and overcome difficulties.
>
> The Council of Elders . . . addresses to all ghetto inmates the admonition to continue to persevere in discipline and loyalty. Branches of our work can point to successes, . . . thus the assumption is permissible that . . . cooperation would ensure the further success . . . of our work.

The need for leaders to maintain hope in challenging times is understandable, but given thousands of deaths and deportations in a mere twelve months, Adler found such sentiments intolerable. Not recorded until after the war with the completion of his book on Theresienstadt, his insertion of "[*sic*]" betrays his indignation at the use of a phrase like " 'completely different manners and customs' when contrasting life in freedom and Theresienstadt," for he remained convinced that such "awkward words are influenced by Nazi thinking and are frightening."[48] Having lost in less than thirteen months both his father and mother and the two beloved aunts who had looked after him as a boy, he was hardly willing to let euphemism gloss over searing loss. All he could do was look on in outrage and dismay, gather documents ("Many people stole bread, I stole documents!"), write, and take care of Gertrud and her parents while knowing that "the running bitter joke was that Theresienstadt was a concentration camp made *worse* by its self-administration."[49] "Words cannot suffice to portray this improbable and dreamlike chaos," Adler wrote of his first year in the ghetto, although he added, "Nevertheless, this was the period of greatest vitality in the camp."[50] Somewhere between these observations lies the madhouse of distortion and deception that Theresienstadt had become. That it could devolve further hardly seemed imaginable, but it was precisely the "civilizing" that took place next that transformed it from a holding facility and transit camp into what Adler called "the most gruesome ghost dance in the history of Hitler's persecution of the Jews."[51] It was no small measure of solace that he and Gertrud were able to survive it together, as well as manage to have worthwhile work that did not implicate them in the wrenching decisions made in drawing up names for the transports. That they were forced to look on as social relations within Theresienstadt turned into a menacing charade while the world turned a blind eye to the persecution of the Jews became the challenge of the increasingly darkening days of their next twenty months there.

8

The Resistance

With the deportation of Rabbi Leo Baeck from Berlin to Theresienstadt on January 28, 1943, the fate of German Jewry suffered a mortal blow. And yet for the prisoners of Theresienstadt his arrival was a godsend. Deeply respected as the spiritual leader of Germany's Jews, Baeck tirelessly affirmed the vitality of faith in the face of persecution while tending to the needs of his people amid their suffering. At the founding of the Representative Body of Jews in Germany (Reichsvertretung der Juden in Deutschland), in response to Hitler's rise in 1933, Baeck famously stated, "The thousand-year history of German Jewry is at an end."[1] What was not at an end, however, was the Jewish faith, for Baeck saw the rise of repression in Germany as an opportunity for assimilated German Jews to reconnect with their religion, and for many to learn its teachings for the first time. Following a twin commitment in the 1930s to convince as many German Jews to emigrate as possible and to nurture the spiritual life of those who remained, Baeck had his feet on the ground and his eyes peeled for danger.

On the eve of the war, Baeck refused numerous offers for safe passage out of Germany. His somewhat late arrival in Theresienstadt can be attributed to his desire to watch over the Jews of Berlin for as long as possible. Even though he was the most prominent Jewish leader in Germany and generally respected by the Gestapo, in the ghetto he was expected to work until he turned seventy in May 1943. Like Leopold Lustig in *The Journey*, he was assigned to work the garbage detail that pulled converted funeral wagons by hand through the streets and beyond the walls of Theresienstadt, where the refuse was dumped in open fields. He was offered a position on the Council of Elders but turned it down, preferring to serve as an honorary advisor, which enabled him to focus on tending to the sick and officiating at funerals. His independence and the respect he commanded allowed him to lobby the Council to demand that the SS provide better living conditions for all prisoners. On one occasion, after his pleas had been ignored, he burst into a Council meeting, grabbed a member by the collar, and hauled him up the stairs of a barracks to force him to see the miserable conditions for himself. Improvements were made the next day.[2]

Leo Baeck with the Council of Elders in Theresienstadt. Credit: The Jewish Museum in Prague.

Like Adler, Baeck used his time to work on what became his central work, *This People Israel: The Meaning of Jewish Existence* (*Dieses Volk Israel: Jüdische Existenz*), the first volume of which was published in 1955 (the same year as Adler's Theresienstadt book), followed by the second in 1957, a year after Baeck's death at age eighty-three. In Theresienstadt he contributed lectures on religion, philosophy, and history to the "University Over the Abyss," among them "Survival," an address he delivered on June 15, 1944, to several hundred detainees in the Community House. In it he made clear what was necessary for survival:

> An equal emphasis is placed upon "life" and upon "continuity." Taking "life" first: this does not merely imply an aimless vegetating, a state of random movement swinging vaguely to and fro at the will of external impulses, but an existence that has become aware of itself, conscious of its yesterdays and tomorrows, of the paths leading up to and those leading away from it, conscious of what has gone before and what is still to come, conscious of its course and destiny.[3]

As Baeck had outlined years before, any existence "aware of itself" must also understand that "There are two experiences of the human soul in which the meaning of his life takes on for a man a vital significance: the experience of mystery and the experience of commandment; or as we may also put it, the knowledge of what is real and the knowledge of what is to be realized."[4] This is the "polarity" of living between the "here" and the "beyond," between what is and what ought to be.

This approach to knowledge aligns with Adler's "Traktat," to "know what you can do, and know what you do." Baeck also deeply believed in the power of the irrational to inform wisdom. "The freedom of *man* . . . is based on what man experiences in himself as being beyond all men and all events," he wrote to a German friend in 1933. "It is not as the freedom I described before, something rational; but it means something irrational. It consists in the knowing about that which is real, and that is the connection with the godly."[5] Albert H. Friedlander explains, "Baeck saw the entrance of the Jew into the modern world as that of *homo mysticus* whom the world of the Enlightenment would only admit as *homo rationalis*."[6] Where these two essences have the chance to coexist is the moral sphere, where man can act as *homo creator* when "Individuality, in its genius, creates what is individual, whether in the formation of knowledge, in the works of art, or in the moral action. Something individual is here created, i.e., something unique and inexplicable."[7]

Adler had yet to fully embrace his Judaism, but in the 1930s his thinking had in many ways become Judaic. "I became ever more diametrically opposed to Christianity," he recalled, "and the process started in 1932 and was completed by 1934,"[8] a period that coincides with his having renounced Protestantism and declared himself unaffiliated with any denomination. Several tenets of Judaism now occupied his worldview, most of them aligned with the thinking of Baeck. Early in his career, Baeck "understood Judaism to be pure religion and therefore [that it required] opposition to, or at least abstention from those concerns, involvements, and tasks which Palestine as a natural and cultural center of the Jewish people presented," a position echoed by Adler's opposition to Zionism.[9] Baeck maintained that Judaism was a religion free of dogma and that its center lay within individual responsibility. Similarly, Adler made plain that "to do good and follow the teachings of the Torah, which teaches us what it means to do good, is what, according to the Talmudic sages, Judaism adheres to."[10]

Baeck thought that as a minority Jews could not help but be seen as different. "We have always been the few," he wrote. "We have never had the calmness that comes from the knowledge that our views are those of the men in power, and we have never found the proof of our convictions in that the people around us think and believe as we." Baeck cited a reason for this in his inaugural lecture at the Jüdische Hochschule of Berlin in 1913, when he said, "The Torah is thus opposed to the Gnosis, the knowledge derived through sacraments." For Baeck, as for Adler, knowledge could only involve "constant searching, which one knows can never reach its end."[11] Adler wrote, "Judaism involves discussion, a lifelong discussion, and specifically a discussion of the Bible and the Torah. . . . But in no way is this discussion religious. . . . No, Judaism involves practical life lessons that speak to all men. . . . Judaism deals with reality, dwells upon it and offers no ideal that is unattainable or beyond the human."[12]

The lack of certainty inherent to constant questioning and the need for Jewish thinking to remain ever "realistic, experimental, empirical" was what, according to Adler, turned Judaism into the hated enemy. In an unpublished essay from 1946 he states, "[T]he deep undercurrent within 'the fear of the Jew' [is that] the Jew takes away one's comfortable position, contentment, and the deceptive semblance of a 'certainty' that in the face of reality is doubtful and falls to pieces." This is so for those who want religious, philosophical, scientific, or political certainty, and thus power. Hence, Jews deceive themselves in thinking they can ever assimilate entirely, since Judaism "seeks a transformation of empirical reality, and thus a change within human beings of a kind not at all sought seriously or even claimed by Christianity or other religions and philosophies, and which politics can in no way bring about." What it means to be a Jew is undermined, he writes, when the "theological inclination of Judaism is altered the moment it is merely practiced, 'organized,' and not entirely and anxiously preserved, or when amid rigid dogma real life can no longer be perceived." Only when Judaism is "really pursued and tested, when it evolves from theory through experiment to a realistic theology," can Judaism survive in its true form.[13] The new direction Adler felt Judaism could embrace was to "not only to powerfully maintain an old traditional religion, but also to develop a new one which through confrontation, self-criticism, and clearly articulated conditions will at last see the Emancipation achieve its proper end."[14]

In his 1956 eulogy Adler said, "Leo Baeck wanted nothing more, but also nothing less, than to be a human being. He taught us what was essential; he showed us what is essential and endures."[15] Much of Baeck's teaching, if one ignores all references to religion, is echoed in Adler's "Traktat": dogma precludes knowing; knowledge is unfinished and must remain experimental; the restrictive rationalism of religion, philosophy, science, and politics from the Enlightenment onward has failed to account for the power of irrationality to access a fuller awareness of reality. Adler identified with Baeck's rectitude as "the middle point of a moral resistance," which Baeck "practiced and taught, as well as modelled through his determination to remain at all times and in the most challenging conditions a human being: kind, truthful, and always ready to help."[16] In his care of Gertrud and her parents, the attention he paid to Bertha Gross, his loyal attendance to the needs of Steiner's parents, the youth he took in and watched over in the camps and after the war, Adler followed Baeck's example and the Talmud teaching that observes, "And whoever saves a life, it is considered as if he saved an entire world." To accomplish this the primary step was to respect the individuality of each human being, for as Baeck had written years earlier, "If a person is a child of God, then each soul has its own eternal meaning; there are no masses, there are only human beings."[17]

Adler's thinking takes a more radical turn in his ideas about the fate of the Jews. Given their history of persecution, he argued after the war, "The state of the Jews among Gentiles, at least to the extent they are allowed to live and act as they choose, as well as the degree to which they suffer under Gentiles, can also reveal the state of humankind."[18] Since it was impossible for Jews to assimilate without abandoning their faith, tensions were inevitable, and persecution lay waiting to extend its shadow across history. "Judaism *must* suffer, that *is* its fate, but the moment it suffers, and what and how it suffers, this is also suffered by humankind, for then humankind *must* suffer, and that *is* its fate."[19] Jews must suffer not, in his view, because they were Jews but because the majority of humans were not Jews, and fear of the "other" inevitably gives rise to persecution. The only resolution to this rests in the messianic hope that humanity's desire for oneness with God will be fulfilled for all when "the goal of humankind and the goal of the Jews is seen as a common goal." For Adler this would come about when, as Baeck believed, all human beings embraced the essence of Judaism, the command to "love one's neighbor as oneself" (Leviticus 19:18) while acknowledging God's pronouncement to Moses, "I am that I am" (Exodus 3:14).[20]

According to Adler, one's fate is one's own and that of one's people:

> Free will and the freedom to act sometimes result in a denial of, but rarely a conquering of fate, which can frequently result in shunning it. But if one denies it, then fate works all the more strongly than freedom and one will be doomed to fate. Here "doomed" means "that which must be yielded to," accepted, but not always a catastrophe. . . . Only he who reaches the end of life can say that he has not been touched by the fate met by his people. Such an individual fate would mean that he is no longer counted among the Jews and is therefore relieved of their common fate as a people. He will, however, be touched by it the moment even a shadow of its consequence is cast upon him.[21]

Adler's fate is that of the Wandering Jew in search of a return to the homeland. He does not pose this as an argument for Zionism but as a reminder that Jews cannot help but remain in exile, that they must be ready to commence another exile at a moment's notice, and that they must embrace "readiness." In Adler's view, until humanity is as one, such a fate remains a foregone conclusion, but even at the end of his life after years of exile in England, he would still maintain, "Homelessness to me means freedom."[22]

Adler addresses the fate of the wanderer in "Hassimangu," a story written in Theresienstadt, later collected in *The Prince of Blessings*. The titular character, whose name breaks down to "Hate I Man," enjoys the privilege of knowing that "the creation of his own thoughts is profoundly singular." He also recognizes that "individual fates do not differ from one another." When he dies of starvation after writing down his singular thoughts, there is pathos in the fact that "his thoughts, their form, their bulk, their achieved depth" will disappear, since the "unfavorable conditions surrounding Hassimangu mean that his papers will be scattered to distant lands which his few friends will not be allowed to enter for some time."[23] Such was Adler's fear, especially for the "Traktat" draft he had left behind in Prague, the works he sent to Reder in Paris and to Steiner in Oxford, or the poems and stories he wrote and kept in Theresienstadt. That fate, like Hassimangu's, was one not divorced from those around him, and only in facing his communal fate could Adler grasp his own.

In Theresienstadt, Adler also drew on Friedrich Nietzsche's thinking in order to embrace his fate as an individual and as a Jew. Studying Nietzsche's writing on the will to power and the concept of *amor fati* (love of fate), he delivered a lecture in Theresienstadt titled "Drei Denkformen: Schelling-Spinoza-Nietzsche" ("Three Forms of Thinking: Schelling-Spinoza-Nietzsche") in 1944. Josef Kramer in *Panorama* quotes lines of a Nietzsche poem from memory, and an essay that Adler later published surveys the central tenets and problems he saw in Nietzsche's thinking. He observes, "Nietzsche is the most powerful Nay-sayer produced by all, or at least in recent philosophy. . . . In [his] metaphysics . . . there is certainly strength, a sense of becoming, of acceptance and of life, but nothing incarnate, no sense of Being and no finality, nor anything of God."[24] Adler sees limitations in this for the social and political foundation of everyday life, and his essay notes Nietzsche's disdain for democracy, socialism, Christianity and Judeo-Christian teachings, traditional values, morality, and compassion, as well as his embrace of power, destruction, and war as forces, at least metaphorically, necessary to advance a "revaluation of all values" and affirm the individual against the masses. Adler, however, only notes these drawbacks in relation to the workings of society and politics. Philosophically, he understands that Nietzsche "demands that one must move beyond nihilism in order to see the necessity of the revaluation [of values] in order to arrive at new values."[25] The problem for Adler is that for Nietzsche "there is no beholding of a new future full of value other than one which involves the devaluation or inversion of the highest values that have come before. . . . [Nietzsche] almost always ends up the reckless destroyer of values, which in turn plunges one into a desolate sense of horror."[26]

In Adler's critique we also see what he valued in Nietzsche and how it served his own thinking in Theresienstadt. "It is not justice that rules here," he quotes from Nietzsche, "it is even less so mercy that forms any judgment: instead it is life itself, its dark, driving, insatiable and self-propelling power."[27] For Nietzsche this is an underlying condition of human existence, but in the ghetto Adler experienced life as self-propelling insatiable power in both the negative and positive sense, be it the Nazi will to subjugate human beings to achieve their ends or the will of the prisoners to survive at all costs. Add to this Nietzsche's valuation of the individual above the "herd instinct," and we see how his works deeply affected Adler. "Where people are dominated, there exist masses," writes Nietzsche. "Where there are masses, there is a need for slavery. Where there is slavery, there are very few individuals, and they have to battle the herd instinct and their own conscience."[28]

Such words were not an idle matter of philosophy for Adler in Theresienstadt. He lays bare what it was like to live there:

> No individual could remove himself from the intricacies of the camp apparatus as long as he remained within the camp, except through death. Even those who participated in nothing, neither good nor bad—those who seemed merely to be victims—suffered inescapably and, before they knew it, were actively involved a hundred times over. Thus the camp was in fact a coerced community. Never before, perhaps not even in a strict concentration camp, had everything been so broadly immersed in a bottomless abyss of coercion as in Theresienstadt. There, freedom concretely meant death.[29]

Tension between "necessity" and "freedom" lies at the heart of what Nietzsche saw as a perpetual state of Becoming, and Nietzsche's ideas on the need to embrace, even love, one's fate speak to Adler's understanding of life in Theresienstadt and the camps as a series of "tests" to be endured, matters not just of physical survival, but of one's soul.

Even when life there settled into some semblance of a routine, as in the first half of 1943, arbitrary power could disrupt it at any time. In January, Paul Eppstein's appointment as the Head of the Council of Elders, sharing governance with Jacob Edelstein and Benjamin Murmelstein, shook the balance of power between Czech-speaking and German-speaking leadership within the ghetto, a tension exacerbated by an influx of Jews from both groups totaling 14,000 over the next six months. But in that time there were no transports to the East, making it the most extended period of relative calm. The total population hovered at around

45,000 throughout the spring amid extremely overcrowded conditions in which vermin and disease thrived. With improvements in the town's water system, food production, and medical services, the death rate dropped, but the health clinic struggled to meet the demand of over 100,000 visits each month. Add to this the thirty-day suspension of "Leisure Time Activities" and implementation of a lights-out curfew after an escape attempt in April; the reduction in May of the number of postcards that purportedly could be sent to the outside world to one every three months; plus a two-week "grace period" in June in which inmates could hand in illegal goods without penalty, and it is easy to appreciate the "totally immanent, perpetually transitory" world that Theresienstadt posed, even in the so-called "best" of times.[30] In July, Adler experienced this firsthand when he and 5,000 inmates had to evacuate the Sudeten Barracks in less than twenty-four hours. Fearing destruction of concentration camp records in the bombing of Berlin, the RHSA commandeered the barracks as a warehouse, forcing the prisoners to scramble for housing elsewhere.[31] Adler landed in the Cavalier Barracks on the north side of the ghetto, where he remained for the rest of his time in Theresienstadt. As for the camp records, they were burned by the SS in April 1945, their ashes a grim metonym for the many listed on them who had disappeared as well.

Despite his study of philosophy and Jewish thinkers, as well as the fact that he was lucky enough to have an electric light that allowed him to read late at night, Adler did not work on his "Traktat" in Theresienstadt. This does not mean its concerns were no longer important to him. Just six weeks after being deported there, he wrote to Gertrud, "The belief in our eternal existence stems only from the idea of activity. If I work on incessantly until my death, nature is bound to give me another existence when the present one can no longer sustain my spirit." He quickly adds, "That's not me, dearest, though I'd be proud if it were, but rather Goethe writing to Eckermann on February 4, 1829. An amazing postulation of immortality which in its audacity touches upon Nietzsche and even me, for you can sense the Traktat in it."[32] Musings on death and immortality might seem ironic or poignant, but the letter shows that amid dire conditions Adler was determined to push on with his work as a writer and intellectual.

Much of 1943 was spent doing that. Amid the daily grind of manual labor and poor living conditions, Adler carried a copy of Alexander Pope's translation of Homer, dipping into it whenever he could steal away time for himself, particularly while serving as a roving handyman in the barracks.[33] How fitting the description of the warriors in Book XVII of *The Iliad* must have seemed when Homer describes them as "O'erlabour'd now, with dust, and sweat, and gore, / Their knees, their legs, their feet, are covered o'er," or even Zeus's sorrowful condemnation of man when asking, "What is there of inferior birth, / That breathes or creeps upon the dust of earth; / What wretched creature of what wretched kind, / Than man more weak, calamitous, and blind?" Adler even tried his hand at translating Percy Bysshe Shelley's "Ode to the West Wind" and its "dirge / Of the dying year, to which this closing night / Will be the dome of a vast sepulchre," the only salvation being that "A heavy weight of hours has chain'd and bow'd / One too like thee: tameless, and swift, and proud."[34]

Adler continued to be enormously productive as a poet, writing some sixty poems, versus the forty or so of the previous year. In June and July, he began his second novel, *Raoul Feuerstein,* his first having been lost with the papers left behind by Reder in Paris, although Adler did not know it then. Based on the ruminations of a narrator who asks, "Can there be a more agonizing name than Raoul Feuerstein?," the novel takes up the concerns of the "Traktat" in fictional form. The narrator turns out not to be named Raoul Feuerstein at all, but Bruno Güter (close to "Günther"), although we do not learn this until a third of the way through. Güter (literally "goods," and also suggestive of the "good man") remains obsessed with the name Raoul Feuerstein, which he stumbles upon amid correspondence with an American branch of the accounting firm where he works. Unable to forget or explain why the name causes him such agony, his consciousness is divided between who he truly is and what he cannot help but be obsessed by. "I only wish to be at one with myself, something which I never tried to do before I fell into this agonizing state." The effort to reach his innermost agony feels like stripping away the layers of an onion, only to discover that once they are all shed, there still exists an "unconquerable agony" whose source cannot be found. The effort to find it, however, is still worthwhile, for in seeking its true essence, Güter "is gripped by unknown realms, comes closer to the unknown, which at least through one's own agony, which can strike any of us and props up everyday appearances, can also reveal itself to us and for once finally let us know it."

Few are willing to go to such lengths, particularly in "the Age of Forgetting" when "eccentric monarchs" cause people to forget what it means "to be a human being." The result is that "We are at an end," a conclusion Adler also arrives at in his "Traktat." The paradox, however, is that this final "end" also provides an opportunity to transcend the limits of language and "names." "Only he who understands the secret nature of names and from whence they spring is capable of betraying neither ideas nor names, for he alone understands them and knows how to use them." Who or what "Raoul Feuerstein" signifies Güter does not know, but in recognizing this, he is far ahead of the masses that take language at face value and submit to it entirely. For it is then that we "transform the power of life into the power of death" when "the living word still floats above the deaf ears of human beings as the dead words from the loudspeaker deafeningly croak on, rattling their bones, and not just at the annual fair providing the spectacle of its hellish fun, but also within the sacred institutions of scholarship and art where the word is no less squandered." Invoking here the burning of books by the Nazis and the frenzy of mass political rallies, as well as the vacuity of modern entertainments, Güter portends that despite "all the holy words, syllables, and sounds, only their resounding renunciation leaps up from the horrible caustic flames." Ominously, such ignorance cannot help but lead to the day when those who are intoxicated by the power of empty words "force the damned with shoves and pushes—whether old people or children, sick people and women—naked into hermetically sealed chambers in order to kill them."[35]

Language not only shapes reality, according to Güter, but the quality of its employment can lead to menacing results. In revising the manuscript after the war, Adler benefitted from hindsight in positing such dire consequences, but Karl Kraus, whom he deeply respected, had made the same warnings decades earlier. With its early drafts subtitled "Eine Betrachtung" ("A Meditation"), the discursive nature of *Raoul Feuerstein* echoes the philosophical investigations of Ludwig Wittgenstein, whose work Adler admired, Ferdinand de Saussure's semiotics, and the writings of Walter Benjamin. It also presages W. G. Sebald's blurring of the line between fiction and nonfiction while tracing his meditations on language, history, and literature. But as the monologue of a twentieth-century Underground Man teasing out the consequences of language and hermeneutics, *Raoul Feuerstein* anticipates more so the tragicomic exploration of human consciousness by Samuel Beckett in *Malloy, Malone Dies,* and *The Unnamable.* Although not as funny, lyrical, or poignantly tragic as Beckett's trilogy, Adler's novel renders the warp and woof of consciousness itself while exercising our own.

After Adler's lecture in Theresienstadt commemorating Kafka's sixtieth birthday on July 3, his private work became more public. In June he had already written Philipp Manes to propose lectures he later gave on art, contemporary German literature, and German-Jewish writers for the Orientation Service Lecture Series.[36] Writing to Emil Utitz in August, he offered to contribute to the "Leisure Time Activities" by lecturing on topics related to his "Traktat" and the crisis in modern consciousness. He suggested lectures on poetry tied to ideas from his 1937 essay "The Purpose of Poetry" and talks on Jewish writers in German literature, eighteenth-century German writers, Hölderlin, Jean Paul, Kleist, Christian Dietrich Grabbe, Georg Büchner, and Kafka. He also proposed reading from his own poems.[37] On October 18, 1943, Adler recited twenty-two poems before an audience, some of which were written in the days leading up to the event, including "Aufklang" ("Beginning"), later retitled "Zueignung" ("Dedication") and placed at the front of the manuscript for his collected poems.[38]

A song, a new song begins,
And flows forth to unknown hours:
The venture begins. Will it succeed?
Here I stand and this I have felt.

A heart astounded by what emerges,
Such that its new tune encompasses
A fate which now consumes it:
A true paradigm for life's journey.

Who knows whether from the song,
Amid the tumult of wildly tossing waves,
A destination will be reached or lost?
Or even if anyone will hear its call?

The song begins. What a strange sound
Appears to me at first as strength and comfort;
Now the song of the world will be confided
And its unspoken wishes shall be served.[39]

Adler's reading occurred during the festival commemorating the Jews' forty years of wandering in the desert, and like the sound of a shofar blown during Sukkot, the poem invokes the fate the poet saw unfolding for himself and his audience. He wished to evoke a "true paradigm for life's journey," for the singer singing, for those to whom it was sung, and for the poetic journey Adler set off on in Theresienstadt, but like Odysseus launching out on "wildly tossing waves," he does not know if he will reach his destination.

"The lack of outer freedom was replaced through an inner, albeit imaginary freedom," Adler said of the role of art in Theresienstadt. "Where the inmates at least temporarily sought to protect themselves from the worst, where the reach of the murderous hand remained invisible or the inmates were constantly under the oppressive threat of deportation into the unknown, among the often described human efforts to survive there was also a cultural effort."[40] Poetry supplied this function for Adler, and his poems offer a broader and more subtle range of emotions than those rhymes about the "dread" of not having any "bread" written by most inmates. His turn toward love or nature or God creates a dynamic by which the darkness lurking behind whatever light is affirmed still manifests itself like a photographic negative.

In *Questions* (*Fragen*), the collection that follows the grotesque imagery of *Theresienstadt Picture Book,* Adler regards his plight from a higher plane, as in the first stanza of "Before Eternity":

> What are the things of this our world?
> What are its goods?
> Alas, what passions they so painfully kindle,
> For useless stuff that goes to pieces!
> Who would think to paint a pretty picture?
> What have we done
> When so little pleasure combines with so much suffering
> And we only awaken as the dead?[41]

Although this touches upon suffering, no concrete evidence indicates the lines are spoken in a ghetto or concentration camp. Yet to "only awaken as the dead" strikes a desperate note, as does the conclusion reached at the end of "Dialogue" ("Zwiesprache"):

> Who here is guilty: I know
> Not at all. I only know that I am in pain, that an intense
> Pressure suffocates me, that I know through tears,
> Though of course silent tears, my fate will end.
> I only know that, in solitude, I am null and void,
> I only know: I can only learn how to live on
> Through time and after death. That I know.
> And I know much else. Deep within I turn
> Into myself, sinking within, wrapped in mystery.
> Thus I am: the miserable sleeper—me: the animal.[42]

Amid the urge to "learn how to live on," Adler's abasement in the ghetto threatens his humanity, leaving him nothing more than an "animal." From such dejection he must find a way to rise.

Adler's third collection, dedicated to "Geraldine," offers a possible way out by invoking the *Assurance* (*Zuversicht*) that only a loved one can supply. Such affirmation is often expressed in the face of impending peril alluded to, as in the last three stanzas of "Die Liebe kommt" ("Love Arrives"):

If I have to leave you, or you leave me:
Then lovers' dreams will sadly suffer
Until we embrace each other once again
In the child-like ways we know.
The flag lifts and the journey cheerfully commences.

At evening, bright horizons shine;
Thoughts of home may beckon
And within twilight's soft, playful colors,
Sink us entirely into each other.
Soon the night greets us, swallowing us inside.

Forgotten, no, yet hearts at rest,
Love allows us its devout pleasure
And grants us its blessе́d ease,
Through which we accommodate our days.
The lark rises, and we must plow the field.[43]

Having seen by March 1942 transports to and from Theresienstadt, the flag used to signal the start of those journeys is all that is needed to allude to a future as uncertain as it is potentially dark. And yet the poem's last stanza asserts that "Love allows us its devout pleasure / And grants us its blessе́d ease." "The lark" rising symbolizes the poet's lyric affirmation in the face of the night "swallowing us inside," while nature remains a source of "gracious wonder" out of which love "arrives" amid the possibility of sudden departure.

Einsam in Banden (*Alone in Chains*) returns to the starker emotional distress of the *Theresienstadt Picture Book* and as a "cycle" is more formally complex than others. "I consciously opted for technical complexity and traditional forms," Adler later wrote, "in order to distance myself as far as possible from the adverse circumstances."[44] Each of the cycle's ten poems consists of eleven stanzas of *terza rima*, the three-line stanza of alternating triple rhymes invented by Dante for his journey through Hell, Purgatory, and Paradise. As in *The Divine Comedy*, each "canto" rolls on in seemingly unstoppable fashion to fulfill the expectation of its final rhyme. In "Despair," the cycle's eighth poem, Adler counters that expectation with repeated midline full stops and closed stanzas that vie with occasional enjambment:

Ripped to shreds by claws,
On this unbearable and loveless day,
Trapped in misery—a misery unceasing.

> I'm so desolate I can hardly comprehend a thing;
> The horror of murder wants to howl from within!
> Oh, that I even exist! Every hour's strike
>
> Torments me. If I could only hide my face!
> Only by forgetting could I feel any better.
> The burden I carry. If only I could crumple
>
> Together the shreds of feeling when everything
> Is hollow and void as my wishes,
> My existence no longer controlled by the pole
>
> Around which guilt turns with force and gravity:
> Then there would still be hope! All I have
> Would blindly disperse to the unconscious void.[45]

Less saturated with the imagery found in *Theresienstadt Picture Book,* the poem is emotionally raw and directly spoken by the poet himself. But because of the alternating triple rhyme scheme of ABA/BCB/CDC, etc., in the German, its expression of pain is highly ordered and controlled. It mirrors the walled-in conditions under which it was written, while the virtuosity of its expression reminds us that a consciousness seeks to rise above those conditions.[46] Adler's turn away from the depiction of bodily suffering in his poems toward a more spiritual plane distinguishes his work from most poets writing in the camps and signifies a "metaphysical, if not real liberation of the victim from his chains, and thus no longer presents him as an object forged by the actions of others, but instead as a free-acting—if not physically so—conscious entity, and thus: a human being."[47] The link between accurate historical depiction and the desire to evoke a higher spiritual plane through language holds true throughout his writing. "Whenever he nears the mystery of life," observes Rüdiger Görner, "his word images take on a pastel-like character, a forceful subtlety and stillness. Even when he speaks of the relentless facts of the machinery of extermination, he still demonstrates a feel for words."[48]

The use of form as a means to battle against the chaos of Theresienstadt was employed by other artists, especially the composer Viktor Ullmann. In "Goethe und Ghetto," an essay he wrote in Theresienstadt, Ullmann states:

> Thus Goethe's maxim "Live in the moment, live in eternity" seemed to me entirely to reveal the mysterious meaning of art. Theresienstadt was and is for me the school of form. . . . Here, where one must overcome material through form in everyday life, where anything artistic stands in complete contradiction to its environment—here is the true master

> craftsman's school. . . . It simply should be stressed that in my musical work I was encouraged, and not limited, by Theresienstadt; that we did not merely sit lamenting by the waters of Babylon, and that our will to create was equal to our will to live. And I am thoroughly convinced that all those who have striven, in art as in life, to wrest from form resistance to material conditions, will say that I am right.[49]

Robin Freeman notes, "The only way Terezín could have been fruitful for the lives of these composers was if they had survived it," but he concedes that Ullmann's testimony that " 'our will to create was equal to our will to live' . . . represent[s] the triumph of German idealism over German barbarity, then as now."[50] Adler's devotion to form as a means "to maintain my dignity through a devotion to timeless values" echoes this aspiration.[51]

Peter Kien: Sketch of Viktor Ullmann in Theresienstadt. Credit: The Jewish Museum in Prague.

Having known each other in Prague before the war, Ullmann and Adler shared deep agreement on the vital role that the engagement with form played in their work and in their lives. A student of Arnold Schönberg and Alexander von Zemlinsky, Ullmann had befriended Adler when the latter helped arrange several performances of his works at the Urania Cultural Center in 1936–37.[52] A prominent composer and conductor, Ullmann formed a circle of musicians and composers upon arrival in Theresienstadt in September 1942 that included Gideon Klein, Pavel Haas, Hans Krása, and Rafael Schächter. They remained devoted to their craft and extremely productive during their time in the ghetto, but all were sent to Auschwitz, all of them perishing. When Ullmann was deported there on October 16, 1944, four days after Adler's own departure, he left behind twenty-six reviews of musical performances in Theresienstadt, plus "Goethe und Ghetto," song cycles, three piano sonatas, and his Third String Quartet, as well as a short opera, *The Emperor of Atlantis, or the Refusal of Death*, a biting satire of Hitler and Nazi tyranny. In it an emperor mounts a universal war and puts Death in charge of his troops, at which Death balks and ceases to end the suffering of the emperor's wounded soldiers. The emperor has no choice but to strike a bargain by allowing Death to return to the empire and make the emperor its first victim.

Emil Utitz, director of the "Leisure Time Activities," handed all of Ullmann's manuscripts to Adler for safekeeping after the war.[53] The opera was rehearsed in Theresienstadt in September 1944 but never performed there. Only in 1975 was it finally premiered by the Netherlands Opera in Amsterdam. Adler preserved the score during the intervening decades, as well as Peter Kien's libretto, also written in the ghetto by the young, gifted artist and poet who left behind sketches of both Adler and Ullmann. The Amsterdam production, which Adler attended and wrote the program notes for, was a resounding success, and the opera is now performed throughout the world. With Krása's opera *Brundibár*, written before the war and performed by children in Theresienstadt, it is now a classic example of art employed as moral resistance.[54]

In Theresienstadt, Ullmann set two of Adler's poems to music as a two-part cantata and asked him to write a series of haiku to set to music. For the two-part cantata Ullmann used Adler's poems "Immer inmitten" ("Ever in the Midst") and "Vor der Ewigkeit" ("Before Eternity"). They were sung in Theresienstadt by mezzo-soprano Hedda Grab-Kenmayr with Ullmann at the piano on October 30, 1943, Günther and Gertrud's second wedding anniversary.[55] Ullmann asked Adler that same year to write twelve haiku on the theme *Der Mensch und Sein Tag* (*The Mensch and His Day*).[56] Adler did not feel the form was suited to poetry written in the West, so he asked Ullmann if he could adapt it by extending the classic five–seven–five syllables per line to a consistent eight-syllable line.[57] In doing so he taps the Zen-like evocation of the fleeting and transcendent at the heart of the haiku but maintains the plaintive, stoic lyricism that characterizes the Theresienstadt poems. The first of them, "Break of Day," begins, "Eyes open. Hands shielding brows. / And maternal light. The meadows. / A stem. A step. The blossom's dew glowing." The cycle then touches on themes of nature, love, and God taken up by many of the Theresienstadt poems before culminating in a moment of "tranquility," the speaker "at peace. In contemplation. / In God's own hands while sleeping."[58] This marks a conclusion of the journey through catastrophe, the need for love, the solace of nature, the pain of alienation, and the reconciliation with one's fate constructed over the six collections Adler composed in Theresienstadt. *The Mensch and His Day* was the final of these, the cycle capping the twenty poems within it (only his *Theresienstadt Picture Book* has more).

In "Ever in the Midst," the fourth poem of the cycle *The Mensch and His Day* and the title poem of the two that Ullmann set as a cantata, Adler embraces his fate, which in turn allows him to be in the world and within himself, providing him with a twin means of living

> Ever in the midst, ever in the midst,
> Traversing every wondrous region,
> Far from home and yet nearer the source,
> What has the soul not suffered,
> Soon stretched out on bare moss, soon pierced by the thorn
> Ever in the midst, ever in the midst.
>
> Ever in the midst, ever in the midst,
> Twixt despair and fervent pleas
> A person finds himself in a house that harbors him,
> Slowly forgetting what he's traversed,
> A ghostly rattle one day ending,
> Ever in the midst, ever in the midst.
>
> Ever in the midst, ever in the midst,
> Death rides sleepily into life,
> Cup and pitcher breaking, the shards clanging,
> Wailing and cheers at a stroke erupting,
> No one can say what tomorrow will bring,
> Ever in the midst, ever in the midst.[59]

Written on May 31, 1943, more than five months before the nadir of "Despair" found in *Alone in Chains*, the poem taps a question repeated in letters between Günther and Gertrud going back to their first days together: "who knows what tomorrow will bring?" Here it is spoken neither out of anxiety nor fatalism but from a stoic mien able to still appreciate "every wondrous region" despite "despair and fervent pleas." Adler's placement of "Ever in the Midst" after "Despair," despite having written it months earlier, argues that the poems are not meant to be read as chronology. They seek to engage the reader in a transformative journey of the soul similar to Baeck's urge to embrace the world as it is and as it can be.

Throughout his thirty-two months in the ghetto, Adler remained skeptical of many of the activities to entertain the inmates through theater, recitals, and cabaret, for he felt they "benumbed oneself, denied the present and, worst of all, unsuspectingly carried out willingly the wishes of the SS. The intended deception of [outside] visitors became the self-deception of the prisoners."[60] In writing poetry and fiction privately and delivering public lectures and poetry readings, however, he also sought solace as an individual alone on his own terms before a crowd, rather than feeling that he was participating in a cynical delusion. Gertrud also contributed talks on hematology and the research she carried out in her laboratory, and both attended lectures and concerts, although Adler eschewed lighter entertainments such as cabaret or sporting events. "It is difficult to distinguish between forced participation in a wicked game and the positive face that one puts on it," Adler later observed. Culture and its making was for him a form of resistance, but to sit in cafes, attend open-air concerts, and put on "Herzl" sporting events or bicycle races using bicycles loaned by the SS amounted to "an intoxication, an empty complacency."[61] Nevertheless, from the gritty reality of the "here," Adler and Ullmann were joined in trying to speak to the "beyond." Only one of them lived to see it.

The absurdity and extremity of conditions in Theresienstadt was enough to expose cracks in any set of beliefs. Each day provided a test of physical endurance, resilience being more than just an adopted attitude, at times the only buffer between life and death. Reading Homer's *Iliad* while working as a handyman and bricklayer, working on *Raoul Feuerstein*, writing poems whose intricacy belied the barbed wire that encircled their maker, or reading Nietzsche, Schelling, Spinoza, and the Jewish thinkers, Adler saw each day as more than a test of physical survival. Larger events, however, could not but keep intruding, especially when Gertrud's prominence among the medical staff exposed her to the mounting toll of illness, death, and psychological pressures throughout the ghetto.

One such event was the arrival in early August 1943 of a special transport of 1,260 children dressed in rags from the Bialystok ghetto in northeastern Poland. In 1941 the Germans began murdering Jews from the ghetto, some 1,300 of them burned alive in a synagogue and another 4,000 shot outside of town. In February 1943 another 11,000 Jews were killed and 12,000 more carted off to Treblinka. In August the ghetto revolted and the Nazis murdered everyone within it except for children between the ages of six and fifteen who had lived through it all. Upon arrival in Theresienstadt, none smiled and most walked around semicatatonic. When they were sent to the delousing station and saw signs warning "Danger, Gas," they broke out into weeping panic, having seen their parents sent to their death in the "Baths" of Bialystok.

The medical orderlies were able to calm them and the children were taken to a special camp under strict guard outside of Theresienstadt. They were well cared for and the sick nursed back to health over the next six weeks. Those with contagious diseases were killed in the Small Fortress, while the bodies of those who died were cremated. Eventually fifty-three caregivers from Bohemia and Moravia, among them Kafka's sister Ottilie, volunteered to take care of the children. Suddenly on October 6 the children and their nurses were loaded onto trucks and taken away as quickly and mysteriously as they had arrived, never to be heard from again, rumored to have been taken to Switzerland in exchange for German prisoners. Where they ended up was Auschwitz, nurses and children alike led to the gas chambers on arrival.[62]

That same week, Günther and Gertrud were devastated by a loss even closer to home. On October 2 Gertrud's seventy-seven-year-old father died, an event that Adler later captured in *The Journey* in the demise of Leopold Lustig:

> The color empties from Leopold's face, the rattle in his throat is quieter and less frequent, his breathing is weaker and more superficial, his breast barely rises and sinks. The fattened fleas creep around and out from under the blanket and gather on the wall like a band of troops. In Ruhenthal that's a sure sign of the arrival of death.[63]

Vivid and wrenching, there is no mention of Adler having been present for his father-in-law's death. That is not to say that the depiction is not true, but Adler chose to render its "truth" in fiction, turning David Klepetar's death into an emblem of the thousands who died amid the misery and deprivation of the old people's infirmary in the Engineer Barracks, where even his daughter had to apply for special permission to visit him.

A month after the deportation of the children from Bialystok, Adler witnessed perhaps the largest demonstration of the arbitrary abuse of power that kept life in the ghetto teetering on the brink of collapse. On November 9, 1943, the SS ordered the arrest and deportation of the Head of the Council of Elders Jacob Edelstein and his family to Auschwitz after they discovered he had failed to report fifty-five people missing from the first old people's transport sent to Auschwitz on October 26, the same transport that carried Adler's aunt Ottla to her death. Obsessed with total control over the forty-five thousand inmates crammed into the ghetto, everyone except the bedridden was ordered to rise at 5:00 a.m., gather in the courtyards of their buildings between 5:30 and 9:30 a.m., then march five abreast through early morning frost to a drill ground outside the fortress walls.

They stood for hours without shelter or anything to eat as a cold drizzle fell from a low gray sky. At last the SS arrived around 3:00 p.m. and proceeded to count every last person by having the Jewish gendarmes organize them in groups of one hundred. As expected, the tallies of various SS officers and their assistants failed to agree, forcing them to repeat the process three times as the cold drizzle turned into a pouring rain.

By 5:00 p.m., extreme panic and distress broke out among the soaked and frozen prisoners, many of them elderly and frail. Worse, the SS disappeared, leaving no orders. By 9 p.m. rebellion erupted and thousands tried to return to the ghetto, sometimes trampling others along the way. By ten o'clock the gendarmes restored some order to the retreat, but it was not until midnight that all reached their barracks after having spent nearly eighteen hours in such conditions. The SS had debated whether to keep them in the field and for some reason the order to return them was never conveyed to the gendarmes. Two to three hundred prisoners died as a result of the census. Some two weeks later the Nazis were able to determine the real population of the camp by counting the registration cards they already had on file.[64]

The most absurd and disturbing example of the ghetto's sham "reality" began in June 1944 as the SS prepared for a visit by the International Committee of the Red Cross. Pressured by the Danish Red Cross to determine the well-being of 450 Danish Jews transported to Theresienstadt in October 1943, Eichmann agreed to a visit by the ICRC and representatives from the Danish government, but only if it occurred in the summer of 1944. This allowed the SS to start a vigorous "beautification program." Streets were cleaned, flowers were planted, benches and a music pavilion were installed in the main square. A children's playground and a soccer pitch were built, and a café and phony shops meant to serve as a bakery, pharmacy, bank, perfumery, and grocery store in the newly dubbed "Jewish Settlement" of Theresienstadt. Streets known by single letters like "L" or "J" were given names like "Rathausgasse" and "Seegasse" ("Town Hall Street" and "Lake Street"). Concerts and sporting events were held each day in the open air and attended by hundreds of cheering inmates. Life returned to some form of "normal," and most prisoners played along in their assigned roles, happy for the slightest reprieve from their usual grim routine.

Yet as Adler looked on from his lowly position as a bricklayer, he knew the price of turning Theresienstadt into a "paradise ghetto" was high. In the six months before the Red Cross visit no less than 17,500 people, roughly two-fifths of the population, were deported to Auschwitz. While some were no doubt deluded into thinking a permanent change had taken place, such delusions made matters worse, for after the Red Cross visit many of the inmates thought that the worst of their troubles were behind them, even though 7,500 people were deported as the beautification program got under way in May 1944.

Adler was distressed that the "prisoners succumbed to the magic and the bewitchment: they listened to spa music while their downfall was already prepared."[65] It was the commission that visited on June 23 that was entirely fooled, however, for they came away thinking Theresienstadt superior to the ghettos of Poland. This was enough to discourage many, for when they saw how easily the commission had been fooled, they felt there was little chance that news about the real state of things would ever reach the outside world. "The [members of the delegation] appeared to be completely taken in by the false front put up for their benefit," Baeck recalled later. "Perhaps they knew the real conditions—but it looked as if they did not want to know the truth. The effect on our morale was devastating. We felt forgotten and forsaken."[66]

In September 1944, the transports resumed, with over four thousand prisoners deported to Auschwitz. More perverse was a second push at "beautification" in anticipation of another Red Cross visit that never occurred. Instead the SS ordered the making of a propaganda film. Directed by the Berlin cabaret artist Kurt Gerron, assisted by the Dutch illustrator Joe Spier and the Prague stage designer František Zelenka, the film was a fabrication depicting the "paradise ghetto" where the Jews lounged in cafés, attended concerts, worked pleasantly in gardens, and gleefully attended soccer games. It was never publicly released, although a segment appeared in a German newsreel in the fall of 1944. By the time it had been dubbed with music in the spring of 1945 before being shown to foreign visitors, the directors, writers, and crew who had made it had all met their death in the gas chambers.

The sinister care of children and their nurses earmarked for death while likely believing they had gained their freedom; the sadism of counting prisoners dying in a frigid rain; the "beautification" of a town in which thirty thousand prisoners had already died and twice that many had been deported to their deaths; and the making of a film to disguise all these atrocities, as well as prepare a case against accusations of war crimes—such was the immanent, maddening, transitory nature of day-to-day life in Theresienstadt. As Adler summed up:

> [E]verything skewed, dangerous, foolish, and mean that proliferates in humans and human institutions, often in secret and ornamented with aesthetic conventions, emerged in Theresienstadt so uncannily and in such unmerciful nakedness that no one who did not turn his eyes away in fearful flight was spared insight into the prevailing situation. . . . [I]n Theresienstadt there was no evasion, at least not for the courageous. One could protest that the dark side of life is truly not all there is, and that wallowing in sadness, suffering, and misery, when all this is over, is not worthwhile, for we should pay more attention to all the good and noble things and, seeing as we have referred to history, all

> the luminous role models and impressive examples. This is probably true—one should not sink into endless grief—but, if one is honest and hopes to avoid lying to oneself, this can succeed only if, in the grace of the sublime, one also recognizes oneself in the curse of guilt, if one grasps and understands the evil, and if one knows that one is entwined in its mechanisms as both perpetrator and witness.[67]

Like Leopold Lustig staring at the rubbish heap of life in Ruhenthal, Adler remained firm in his conviction that "when everything appears to be over, when the past means nothing at all, what should have been will again be known by those who come after."[68] Somehow he had to make sure that happened.

9

One Thousand Paces

Writing may have helped Adler maintain a sense of dignity amid the chaos and menace of Theresienstadt, but that could not stop the inevitable. In September 1944 the deportations began again, and October proved to be the worst month. Desperate for able-bodied workers to use as slave laborers in the armaments industry, and knowing they could not maintain the population of the ghetto at its current levels, the Nazis transported over twenty-two thousand prisoners to Auschwitz. The majority were gassed upon arrival. Only a small percentage of able-bodied workers was selected and sent to labor camps set up to support the war effort.

Adler knew his time had come, so he gathered all of the documents he had collected on the administration and workings of Theresienstadt, the beginnings of *Raoul Feuerstein*, several short stories and essays, and the poems he had written during his thirty-two months there. Placing all of these in a black leather attaché, he left them with Leo Baeck for safekeeping, telling him that he would return for them after the war, although he had no idea if he would, or if Baeck would not be deported as well. The indefatigable rabbi not only survived but saw his people through the typhus epidemic that kept the prisoners of Theresienstadt locked up under quarantine until June 1945, a month after Soviet troops had liberated it.

Adler was deported with Gertrud and her mother on October 12, 1944. Three days earlier Bertha Gross and her sister had left on a transport of 1,600 inmates to Auschwitz. Both women likely were gassed upon arrival, and only 22 people from the entire group survived the war.[1] Beyond instinctively knowing that deportation to the East meant something bad, neither Günther nor Gertrud knew what awaited them on arrival.[2] Although Baeck had learned about the gas chambers from an escapee as early as August 1943, he decided to tell no one in the ghetto. "No one should know," Baeck insisted. "If the Council of Elders were informed, the whole camp would know within a few hours. Living in the

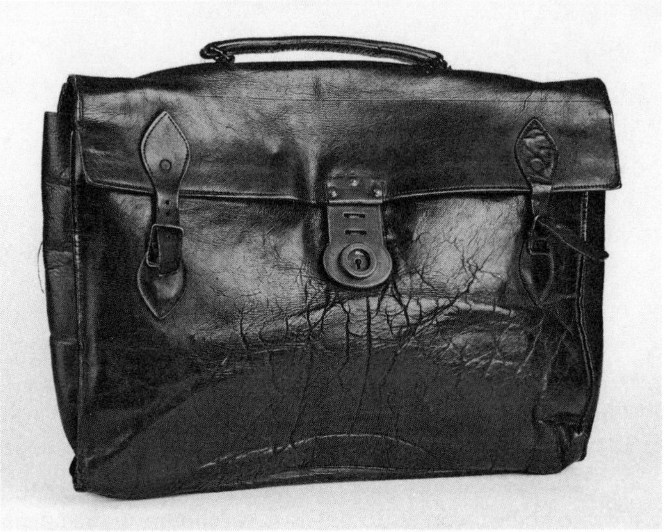

The black attaché Adler left with Leo Baeck. Credit: The Estate of H. G. Adler 2019, Deutsches Literaturarchiv Marbach.

expectation of death by gassing would only be the harder. . . . So came the grave decision to tell no one."[3] The mass upheaval of the deportations, and the fact that they consisted mostly of young and able workers, and the ghetto's leadership, was enough to cause alarm. Gertrud knew the suffering that would follow in the ghetto once the medical staff was gone, and Günther had firsthand knowledge of the labor it took to keep the infrastructure from collapsing. After Paul Eppstein was shot by the SS just before the mass deportations started in September, even the Jewish administration was reduced to a shell under the merciless and inept leadership of Benjamin Murmelstein, who replaced Eppstein as head of the Council of Elders. All signs indeed pointed to this being the end.

Auschwitz is just over three hundred miles northeast of Theresienstadt, but the journey there in a sealed cattle car crammed with up to 150 people lasted two days. Heat, hunger, lack of sleep, and parching thirst claimed a number of lives along the way. After the train pulled in through the archway that opens onto the ramp built to receive the prisoners in the Auschwitz II camp known as Birkenau, the doors opened with a rush of fresh cold air striking the press of anxious prisoners wondering where they were. Adler stepped from the freight car adjacent to the one containing Gertrud and her sixty-four-year-old mother, Elisabeth. It was the first time the three of them had seen each other since leaving Theresienstadt.

Men and women were separated immediately by SS guards shouting orders for everyone to leave their luggage in the cars, line up, and proceed ahead as guard dogs barked and snapped, keeping them in line. A "Kommando" of specially assigned prisoners wearing the worn and filthy zebra-striped uniforms of the concentration camp rushed the train, shouting at the new arrivals in an array of languages reduced to guttural commands. A van with the insignia of the Red Cross painted on it as camouflage drove back and forth beside the ramp, carrying inside it the cans of Zyklon B gas pellets used to kill most of deportees. The "Kommando" tossed the luggage and possessions left in the cars onto the platform before loading them onto trucks that hauled them to the camp storage depots, known as "Canada," where everything was sorted and looted.[4] The whole process took no more than thirty minutes. The old, the sick, and those unfit for work were selected by physicians, among them the notorious Josef Mengele, who simply pointed to the left or the right. Elisabeth was ordered into the larger group that was immediately directed to the left, which meant the gas chamber, and without hesitating Gertrud joined her. Günther and Gertrud exchanged a last look as she cast him a stoic smile, took hold of her mother's arm, and marched on. Where she thought she and her mother were headed is anyone's guess. It takes a mere one thousand paces to walk from the arched entry point of Birkenau's train ramp to the gas chambers of Crematoria II and III, and in October 1944 both facilities belched out smoke around the clock.

After seeing Gertrud walk away, Adler was ordered to march in the opposite direction toward the quarantine barracks of BIIa near the entrance to the camp. Although only a short distance separated him at any time from Gertrud, her mother, and their swift demise, they might as well have been living in parallel universes. Before Günther had to strip naked, have his head shaved, take a cold shower, be sprayed with disinfectant, and have a Buchenwald number, 95714, stamped on his chest like "slaughtered cattle," Gertrud and her mother arrived at the crematorium and descended stairs leading to the "dressing room" in the basement. At the entrance signs in German, French, Greek, and Hungarian pointed "To the Baths" and "To Disinfection."[5] Entering a room made purposefully spacious in order to allow the victims to calmly undress in relatively uncramped conditions, they found wooden benches along the walls and numbered hooks on which to hang their clothes. The Jewish Sonderkommando (Special Detail) forced to work in the gas chambers and crematoria told them to remember the numbers in order to retrieve their things after their shower. They were sometimes issued a piece of soap and a towel before passing through a short passage to the anteroom containing a door to the "showers." Once inside, the doors were bolted and sealed behind them. Zyklon B pellets were poured down the vents of the induction shafts descending from the floor above the perforated plates designed to mimic shower heads. The heated air of the facility dissolved the pellets, producing a fog of hydrogen cyanide, which when inhaled, paralyzed their respiratory system. Within twenty minutes, Gertrud, her mother, and the roughly 1,500 other victims who had joined them on Transport "Eq" were dead. Even those selected for entrance into the camp fared little better: only seventy-four of them lived to see the end of the war.[6]

Rudolf Höss, the commandant and chief architect of the death camp at Auschwitz-Birkenau, personally observed many gassings, and gave this description at his trial in 1946: "It could be observed through the peephole in the door that those who were standing nearest to the induction vents were killed at once. It can be said that about one-third died straightaway. The remainder staggered about and began to scream and struggle for air. The screaming, however, soon changed to the death rattle and in a few minutes all lay still."[7] When the Sonderkommando opened the chamber an hour later, after the gas had been extracted, the bodies lay stacked in a pyramid, victims having climbed upon each other to seek the last gulps of air available at the top of the chamber. Most often the children and elderly were crushed underneath.[8] After the Sonderkommando extracted gold fillings, crowns, and bridges, an elevator adjacent to the anteroom lifted the bodies up to the crematorium and the furnaces above.

Josef Kramer also breaches the invisible abyss of the gas chamber in *Panorama*:

> Josef imagines all of this and sees as well the chimneys smoking before him, hearing the screams of those choking on the gas, breaking into praise, as amid the moment of death they say the name of the One who is the only One. Josef's thoughts must wrap themselves around the death rattles, as he sees how the blood runs from the eyes, from the nose, from the mouth, he sees how body after body writhes and stretches and rears up and screams, screams, screams, as long as they can scream, and how their screams seethe, how they sink together, the Zyklon gas having already exterminated them.[9]

The bridge between the reader's gaze and that of the actual victim is Joseph's imagination, which also implicates us within the scene. Regardless of the anonymous ones lost to the killing machine, we are compelled to witness their horrible death as best we can.[10]

The official capacity of Crematoria II and III allowed for 1,400 bodies to be incinerated in a twenty-four-hour period but often around 2,500 were actually cremated. By sundown of the next day anyone from Transport "Eq" selected for death had been gassed and cremated, their ashes ground down by wooden mortars and dumped into pits outside the crematoria before being carted off to the Vistula River, used as fertilizer on the camp farms outside Birkenau's electrified fence, or spread upon the icy paths and roads of the camp in winter. This last activity was performed by fourteen-year-old Yehuda Bacon that year.

He worked for a "Rollwagenkommando," a special detail of twenty children who pulled a wagon loaded with blankets, clothes, papers, wood, or ashes. The one benefit was that on the coldest days the "Aryan" Kapo in charge of the crematorium, Jozef Ilczuk, would let the children warm themselves inside the gas chamber before they spread their dismal loads. Some days, however, he had to turn them away, as the chambers were already occupied.[11]

About 20,000 bodies per day were incinerated in the summer of 1944, but on October 30, Gertrud and Günther's third wedding anniversary, and only two weeks after Gertrud's gassing, a final transport from Theresienstadt underwent selection for the gas chamber. By November 3, all new arrivals were placed in the camp as prisoners. With the approach of the Soviet Army and increasing bombardments by the Allies, the Nazis were anxious to cover up evidence of their atrocities. Heinrich Himmler went so far as to order the destruction of the gas chambers and crematoria on November 25.[12] They were dynamited just prior to the camp's liberation on January 27, 1945, but there was not enough time to obliterate them. Like toppled sentry posts to the gates of Hell, they lie dormant upon the grounds of the camp to this day.

By October 1944, Auschwitz had claimed over one million lives and was a world on the brink of collapse. The nerves of the guards, civilians, and prisoners alike were extremely frayed. In the quarantine camp Adler heard veiled references to "the chimney" and its hold on everyone's future. Over the three days he spent there, the prevailing west wind drove the stench of the crematorium toward him. Enough killing had gone on by the fall of 1944 that it was as if a black cloud hung over all who entered the camp, and the flames from the crematoria could be seen for miles. Only a week earlier a revolt had occurred during which the Sonderkommando of Crematorium IV set fire to the building, damaging it so badly that it had to be torn down. Three SS men were killed, but the rebellion was suppressed and the Sonderkommando executed, while four Jewish women who smuggled explosives from an arms factory where they worked were hanged in front of prisoners gathered for roll call a week before the camp's liberation.[13]

"[E]verything was incalculable and nothing impossible," writes Hermann Langbein in summing up the enormity of the camp's misery and horror, and the tenuous and arbitrary line between life and death.[14] Adler may have been in shock at the loss of Gertrud and the puzzlement of his new surroundings, but he had his own challenge ahead. The main purpose of the quarantine barracks was to test the stamina of inmates to see if they were worthy of being kept in Auschwitz as able-bodied workers or sent to one of the auxiliary camps.[15] Given the brutality of the circumstances, "quarantine" is a misleading term implying observant caution. But many prisoners died after arriving in the camp. Since many intended to be shipped as workers to satellite camps were never registered, how many passed through is unknown.[16] Prisoners were forced to squat or hop about for hours on end to the laughter and derision of the drunken SS, or driven toward the barbed wire where they were shot as would-be escapees. Allied bombings of the camp in 1944 sent the SS into a panicked rage they took out on inmates with wild beatings that killed many. Even grabbing at a cigarette butt in the gravel or talking to a female prisoner through the barbed wire of the neighboring camp could lead to brutal attacks or shootings. Nor were the food and living conditions any better than in the labor sectors of the larger camp. Many new prisoners lost their strength quite quickly, leading to weekly selections in which the weakest were carted off and gassed. In October alone, 185 prisoners were deemed too weak to work and were killed.[17]

No less threatening was the treatment at the hands of the Kapos and Block Elders throughout Birkenau, most of whom were hardened career criminals selected by the SS for their sadistic bent. Equating "collaborators" with "rats" in their work for the SS "conspirators," who in turn served "the Conqueror," Adler gives a vivid, archetypal view in *Panorama* of what it meant to be transformed into an inmate:

> The rats swing truncheons with which they whale away at the naked, and the rats bellow out that this is no sanatorium, threatening to punish anyone who has hidden anything, for everything will be found, and punished, anyone who has hidden something in his mouth or in the folds of his body, it will be punished, all of it a crime, it will be punished, every possession is a crime. . . .
>
> The naked now stand in a cold hall, the bodies still damp from the showers, but there are no towels, the naked having to form rows as, without a care for shape or size, ragged shirts are tossed to them, dirty trousers and jackets often damaged and ripped, trousers and jackets with blue patches and made of gray striped material. In clothes made of the same material the collaborators run about in "zebra stripes," though for ages there have been none available to the naked, the Conqueror's weavers incapable of fulfilling the endless demand, though from the repositories of the death factories the worst rags have been selected from a limitless supply of clothes that once belonged to the hecatombs of nameless murdered people, miserable trash still able to be utilized for the Conqueror's marvelous deeds and relief work, as now the mottled zebras fitted out with the plunder of the murdered victims, after which a brush is dipped in rust-red varnish and circles and crosses are smeared on the trousers and jackets. . . . The naked barely finish dressing before being driven out of the hall under the threat of blows, as they stand in the dreary October cold of the year

> 1944, realizing at last that they are lost, though there is no time to reflect on this as they are bellowed at by angry voices that want to bring order to the misshapen heap, though it is not done with screams but rather with clubs and whips.[18]

Such a passage captures the humiliation of being transformed from a person to a nameless object, and the motley mixture of "zebra stripe" material and civilian clothes garnered from the "dressing rooms" of the crematoria after the gassings reveals the further irony that Adler had to don the clothes of "nameless murdered people" at the moment Gertrud's, her mother's, and his own clothes were being grimly repurposed elsewhere. By the autumn of 1944, full "zebra stripes" were in such short supply that guards simply threw "whatever they happened to pick up from the pile" at the prisoners.[19] Much to his luck, Adler was handed the clothes of a Czech Communist, with a red triangle badge rather than the yellow triangle of the Jews. "I never wore yellow," Adler said to Jürgen Serke in 1987 while showing him the red badge marked with a "T" for "Tscheche" or "Czech." "Certainly that helped my standing."[20] Leaving the hall with the red stripes and circles painted on the garments of dead civilians, and the red badge of a Czech political prisoner, Adler was literally a "marked" man: part prisoner, part civilian, part slave laborer, but not a Jew. These were the clothes he wore for the rest of the war. In the meantime, all that remained was to avoid joining the largest constituency of Birkenau—the dead.

Now thirty-four and with two-and-a-half years of mostly working as a bricklayer behind him, Adler passed muster and was moved to BIIe, better known as the Gypsy Camp. At the time it held over 18,000 prisoners living in wooden barracks designed to hold fifty horses, now crammed with 400 men each.[21] On average, the 105,000 prisoners housed in Auschwitz-Birkenau each had eleven square feet in which to sleep, sit, and store their belongings, amounting to a volume of fifty-three cubic feet, or roughly the size of a shallow grave.[22] Auschwitz is located at the confluence of the Sola and Vistula Rivers, so the water table of its lowlands is very high and there were often floods transforming the grounds into a morass of mud and sewage. During the rainy seasons of fall and spring, the prisoners' wooden clogs would be sucked off their feet while walking. With the sewage of 100,000 people and a lack of proper systems with which to process it, it is easy to imagine the filth, stench, and bone-chilling damp that suffused every step outside the barracks. Nor did the spongy clay of the earthen floors inside the wooden huts provide any relief.

The Gypsy Camp in which Adler was housed was one of the worst. The Roma were deemed racially inferior and thus largely neglected by the camp administration until their eventual extermination in August 1944, thousands having already died of dysentery, malnutrition, and typhus. Within the Gypsy

Camp, Adler stayed in the Auschwitz II Transit Camp set up to house prisoners awaiting transit as slave laborers to munitions factories and camps serving the war industry.[23] Located next to the notorious "hospital" of Josef Mengele, who served as the camp's doctor, he was now three-quarters of the way closer to the gas chamber. And yet his value as a potential laborer relieved him from serving on the work detail in Auschwitz, nor was he permanently tattooed. Instead, he spent his days, as Langbein describes, "on ice" awaiting orders as to where he would be sent next.[24]

Although Adler could not have heard the cries of the Jews invoking "the One who is the only One" at their death in the gas chambers, as does Josef Kramer in *Panorama,* it was in Auschwitz-Birkenau that he discovered the essence of his own faith as a Jew. In the Gypsy Camp, he was housed with a number of Orthodox Jews from Slovakia with whom he soon found himself in lengthy discussions about faith, his knowledge of Czech allowing him to communicate with them in Slovakian. One of them, the forty-four-year-old rabbi Max Schiff, saw something in Adler that, at the time, he did not see in himself. Asked if he prayed, Günther said that he considered himself to be a "marginal Jew" at best. Schiff responded, "Still, it is there within you, you do not have to learn it."[25]

Adler did not know how to respond, for he felt unable to affirm or dispute it. He engaged Schiff and the other Talmudists in the Gypsy Camp in what he described as "the kind of discussion of first things that one only risks during puberty," as he had done with Steiner as a young adolescent. In response to thoughts he had on religion, Schiff and the other rabbis responded that the gist of what he said could already be found in the Talmud, and the famed commentary written by Rashi in the eleventh century.[26] As Josef remarks in *Panorama,* so too for Adler the brief time in Auschwitz represented "both the darkest and the lightest time in his life," for Schiff and his cohort provided a credo by which to remain "defiant and strong before the final end."[27] Mordechai, Schiff's stand-in within the novel, says this harkens back to the *Pirkei Avot* (*Sayings of the Fathers*) in the Talmud:

> Observe three things, and you will not fall into sin: know from where did you come, where you are headed, and before whom you will lay yourself one day in order to give your account and be judged. And from just where did you come? From a miserable drop of nothing. Where are you headed? To a place full of dust, mold, and worms. Before whom will you lay down to account for yourself and be judged? Before the King of Kings, before the Holy One, may He be blessed![28]

Mordechai reminds Josef that "such consummation is possible, . . . and even if it is done silently, one can still lift oneself in prayer." Given the circumstances in which they found themselves, however, for the older Jew and Josef ("ten years younger," roughly the same difference in age as between Schiff and Adler) "there is mercy in their being able to come to the huts . . . and talk and exchange ideas, none of that is pointless, even if they don't survive the test."

We do not know what Adler and Schiff talked about standing in the mud and misery of the Gypsy Camp, but it is possible to speculate about the spirit of their discussions. Adler's lack of experience with formal worship as a "marginal Jew" was what prepared him to find in Judaism what he later called an "orthodoxy of the heart." As he reasoned, the benefits of Enlightenment emancipation carried with them the danger that religion became a private matter rather than a culture binding individuals in a community. This was truer for Judaism because of its lack of sacraments. Jews were forced to choose between the practices of a centuries-old religion and the liberalization that saw those practices as antiquated follies. Adler saw opportunity amid such dilemma and argued, "For such a Jew, if he was not simply a free thinker who in eclectic fashion wished to put together a private religion based on all teachings of the East and West, there is the possibility of an orthodoxy of the heart, a stronger and more solid faith (which in any case is much more important than any intellectual conviction, no matter how strongly it is held)."[29]

Adler by then was in many ways a free thinker who had studied the world's religions to form his inner life, although the teachings of Judaism had become more central to his ethos, especially the *Pirkei Avot*. Talking with Schiff in Auschwitz, they may have debated such passages as 3:19, which states, "Everything is foreseen, yet freedom of choice is granted; in mercy is the world judged; and everything is according to the preponderance of works," or Hillel's mysterious question in 1:14, "If not I for myself, who then? And being for myself, what am I? And if not now, when?"[30] He was also in a position to realize what Buber advocated in his "Renewal of Judaism," the third of the three lectures he delivered to the Bar Kochba student organization in Prague between 1909 and 1911. "At the time of one's most naive relation to God," Buber wrote, "urgent matters can result in a secret, magical connection to Him." The loss of Gertrud and her mother, as well as conditions in Auschwitz, without question provided the most urgent circumstances Adler had ever encountered. Add to this his belief, perhaps from Schiff, that the story of Judaism rested on three central events—exodus, wandering, and the return to the Holy Land, all allegories for the fate that has replayed itself in Jewish lives throughout time—and it is easy to see how the extreme exodus and suffering as a wanderer longing to return home were made real to Adler within sight of the crematoria.[31]

"I had already reflected on such deep matters in Theresienstadt," Adler later wrote, "but here I attempted to come as close to the absolute as anyone can possibly be allowed to come. I never doubted for a moment, despite all that I saw and understood, that I would not survive the catastrophe. I went through it all with open eyes and with the certainty of a sleepwalker. Most likely this is also the place where I came to feel that I did not regret the experience of these horrible years, or at least so far as it concerned *only* my own person. I was unhappy, even sad, but never completely hopeless, never in complete despair. It was a spiritual Dresden [referring back to the misery of the Freemasons Institute], but I was a man in Theresienstadt, while above all in Auschwitz I became a complete person."[32]

Max Schiff helped to save Adler's life by enabling him to find something larger to believe in and a people with whom to believe it. Both were crucial coping mechanisms for survival. A "stable pairing" meant that you would look out for another person who in turn looked out for you, allowing for a semblance of trust and support in a more manageable microcosm than that of the camp as a whole.[33] Attachment to a cohesive group and to a value system provided a larger cause by which to live. In Gertrud he had had both, but within hours of her death he had been cast into what David Rousset called "the universe apart, totally cut off, the weird kingdom of an unlikely fatality."[34] Schiff and the other Talmudists in the Gypsy Camp provided an oasis of debate and conversation and comfort that served as a lifeline, one that in spite of the stench and muck in which all were mired helped form the man that Adler would become. He never became a practicing Jew, observed the high holy days, attended a synagogue, or joined a congregation, but his identification as a Jew from this point forward remained unshakeable. Having lost his parents, his wife, and her family, he entered the camps a secular man interested in matters of the spirit; he left confirmed in his religious identity and hoping to serve God and his people through whatever means remained available to him.

Adler's stay in Auschwitz lasted just two weeks. The Allies had been heavily bombing armaments facilities throughout Germany since the start of 1944, and the SS Office for Industry set in motion a plan to locate a number of *Außenkommandos*, or external detachments of prisoners in smaller camps neighboring larger concentration camps, such as Buchenwald. German manufacturers whose plants and factories lay in ruins worked with the SS to outfit workshops and small factories to produce armaments and materiel as fast as possible. Tallying nearly 1,200 across Germany, these camps were kept small and secret, some hidden in tunnels and mines underground. In fact, although the number of prisoners in concentration camps more than doubled between 1943 and 1944, from 224,000 to 524,000, half to three-quarters of the population of each was now assigned to subcamps.[35]

Before the war ended 136 of these facilities were set up by prisoners from Buchenwald, seventy-six of them built in the last six months of 1944 alone.[36]

While conditions in the manufacturing sectors tended to be slightly better, those in the underground facilities were quite brutal. Because of the dramatic increase in the number of prisoners and extreme conditions in underground camps such as Dora and Langenstein-Zwieberge, in the first quarter of 1944, as many prisoners died in Buchenwald and its surrounding camps as had perished between 1937 and 1940.[37] The system set up by the SS Security Office to exterminate the Jews was transformed by the SS Office of Industry into a conscious means of "Extermination by Work" ("Vernichtung durch Arbeit"). This returned to the central camps 4 Reichsmarks per day for laborers and 6 to 8 Reichsmarks per day for skilled craftsmen.[38] The secrecy shrouding each location and the small size of most of the camps both prevented the Allies from easily bombing them and allowed the SS to justify returning a large population of Jews as slave laborers to a supposedly "Judenfrei" Germany.

With heavy bombing of airplane production plants by the Allies in February 1944, relocating and rebuilding the aviation industry was a top priority.[39] By October the workforce dedicated to it totaled 900,000, half of them civilian forced laborers and half concentration camp prisoners.[40] Junkers, a manufacturer of airplanes and engines, erected thirteen production sites and sent engineers to Auschwitz in search of able-bodied and skilled workers to build and staff each facility. Located at the southern foot of the Harz Mountains, the Niederorschel concentration camp was erected by slave laborers purchased from Buchenwald by Junkers in September 1944 to build airplane wings and fit out landing gear for the newly designed D-9 series of Focke-Wulff Fw 190 single-engine fighters.[41] When three engineers from the company arrived in Auschwitz in search of metal workers, Adler and others jumped at the chance to be chosen, claiming expertise and readiness for such work, even when they possessed none. Adler ended up working as a metal cutter, a skilled craftsman worth 6 to 8 Reichsmarks per day to the coffers of Buchenwald.[42] The engineers struck some of the prisoners as humane, despite working for the Nazis, so the 283 chosen were pleased to climb into cattle cars marked "Danger! Political Prisoners" in groups of 50 on the cold, clear evening of October 28. If nothing else, it meant they had escaped the gas chamber for now.[43]

Since each was given a loaf of bread, and fairly large portions of honey, sausage, and margarine, they knew they were headed far away from Auschwitz. Such a reprieve was welcome, but especially lucky were the large number of young men, some of them thirteen and fourteen years old, chosen by Franz Schaumann, the head engineer. Of the 734 inmates from fifteen nations brought to Niederorschel in the fall of 1944, 20 percent were under twenty years of age. Among them was sixteen-year-old Ivan Ivanji, a future novelist and theater director from Yugoslavia whom Adler befriended and watched over.[44]

The 465-mile journey took three nights and two days. If the prisoners felt hopeful at the calm demeanor of the civilian engineers, the large number of youth selected, or the rations handed out, they were soon disabused of any hope of better treatment.[45] While the two SS guards assigned to each car drank, smoked, and ate the whole day long, the prisoners suffered terrible thirst and cramped conditions, as well as enduring the Nazis' idiotic roll calls inside the locked wagons. On the second day, a doctor from Slovakia named Jacob Heimann lost his nerve and attacked an SS officer in Adler's car, grabbing him by the throat and wounding him badly before being shot dead. Down to 282, the transport arrived on the third day. Hard as the trip had been, the inmates were relieved to be free of the cattle cars, and to see no crematorium. Instead, the first snow of what would prove a bitterly cold winter fell as they marched in rows of five toward the camp circled by barbed wire a few hundred yards from the station.

As if waking in a dream, the prisoners were astonished when greeted by the head Kapo, Otto Herrmann, who stood before tables laid with bowls of hot, thick soup and aluminum spoons resting next to them, a luxury rarely seen in Auschwitz. Such comforts soon ceased. After their first night in the barracks, they were assigned to one of two grueling twelve-hour shifts, each of which was expected to produce three wings a session inside an unheated workshop set up in a former plywood factory. The noise of power riveters was deafening and aluminum particles and dust filled the air. Conditions outside the workshop were not much better, as eight prisoners had to split a loaf of bread each day while trying to subsist on a lunch of thin gruel and potato peels mixed with a bit of horsemeat. Barracks set up in a former weaving mill across from the main workshop contained the standard three-tiered wooden bunks in which prisoners were crammed two and three apiece and slept in shifts. With fifteen different countries represented in the camp, a cacophony of competing languages filled the air. A camp language comprising slang, crude neologisms, grunts, and mute gestures served as the rudimentary communication necessary to carry out the barked orders of the roughly forty SS guards and officials.

In relative terms Niederorschel provided a respite after the misery of Birkenau. The prisoners were housed within a few paces of their work stations, so they did not have to walk through the winter cold for miles each morning and night, and toiling in the workshops sheltered them from the elements. The entire camp measured just over an acre and included the main workshop, where airplane wings were riveted together, and a weaving mill that doubled as a barracks and a workshop for making moveable flaps to conceal landing gear.[46] The same cook who prepared meals for the SS was in charge of the prisoner's canteen, which meant that the food was of a slightly higher standard, and the bread for the camp was provided by a local baker in the village.[47] In the later war years there was a shortage of SS officials to serve as guards in the ballooning number of concentration camps, so half of their corps were made up of middle-aged men drafted from the army rank and file, who tended to be less sadistic and murderous.[48]

Niederorschel, however, was no sanitarium. Adler in fact ran afoul of the commandant, Hans Masorsky, a pedantic brutal man prone to outbursts of temper at the slightest violation of protocol or any awkward exchange, especially when he was drunk. Likely it was he who was ready to give Adler a beating for some minor infraction, although before he started Adler asked, "Could you wait a moment, please, I just want to take off my glasses." The beating proceeded, but Masorsky did pause to allow him to remove his glasses, and Adler felt he was beaten less severely as a result, although it still proceeded.[49]

If the constant threat of violence was not enough, there was the maddening plague of lice infiltrating the straw of the bunks and biting the prisoners incessantly. There was a constant lack of food, and in addition to the threat of pleurisy, dysentery, phlegmon, and typhus, there was mounting pressure to increase production. One might add the psychological torment of being forced to produce airplane parts for the Nazis, an irony not lost on Himmler, pleased that "this race of subhumans produces weapons for the war" while working twice as hard as foreign workers. In truth the great majority of factories that used slave labor attained only half of the production sought from them. As Nikolaus Wachsmann notes, "[The] main output was not fuel or planes or guns, but the misery of its prisoners."[50]

Even in Niederorschel, which managed a consistently high output, the prisoners could take solace in the fact that, because of problems in distribution and rail service, not a single airplane wing assembled by them lifted a German fighter into the sky. They were stacked several high in a field to the west of the camp and ended up buried in snow.[51] Prisoners also made sure to misassemble the flaps for the landing gear, cut cables in the wings, and undermine assemblage with poor-quality work whenever possible.[52] There was little quality control or oversight beyond the civilian foremen who supervised them, many of whom empathized with their plight and looked the other way when mistakes were made.

Adler had a knack for finding or forming an oasis wherever he was. In Niederorschel this continued through the good fortune that Max Schiff traveled with him on the same transport from Auschwitz via Buchenwald.[53] In the barracks Schiff and other Jews from Bratislava gathered for prayer and ate together at the "religious table."[54] Adler did not join them in worship and sat at either the "intellectual table" or the "free table" for nonbelievers, but no doubt he and Schiff continued their discussions on Judaism.[55] Also of help to Adler and the other prisoners was the former owner of the plywood factory, Hermann Becher, who handed out clandestine batches of wood glue made from potato starch, which prisoners ate by the fistful and later claimed saved their lives. People from the surrounding villages managed to slip food to the prisoners, who then manufactured rough-hewn utensils and containers from scrap pieces of aluminum sheet metal, straw, and plywood as thank-you gifts.

Perhaps most extraordinary were the efforts of Johannes Drössler, a civilian fitter who worked in the weaving mill where Adler and Ivanji assisted in the fabrication of the moveable flaps.[56] Besides passing on food, chocolate, and cigarettes to the prisoners, in February 1945 he began to hide prisoners in the barn behind his house down the road from the camp. Drawing a map that showed them how to make their way through the fields, he took in twelve in all, feeding them with the assistance of his wife and daughter until the camp was liberated in April. Such bravery and kindness was not lost to the annals of the war, for numerous survivors and townspeople recalled and admired Drössler's feat. Adler was moved to write him from Prague after the war and later tried to send him food and medicine when he heard that Drössler was ill with liver cancer. The package did not make it in time, and all Adler could do was write to his widow in 1947 to praise Drössler as "one of those absolutely good and simple people who, during a time when one might rightfully lose faith in the good of humankind, was a gracious figure who nevertheless could not let himself give up hope that things would one day be better."[57]

The aluminum box in which Adler hid his poems. Credit: The Estate of H. G. Adler 2019, Deutsches Literaturarchiv Marbach.

Adler also benefitted from the clandestine work of the inmates who turned out cigarette cases, metal containers, and utensils. A co-worker fabricated for him an aluminum box the size of a standard sheet of A4 paper folded twice over, as well as a knife with a wooden handle. In the box he stored the poems he wrote in Niederorschel, smuggling it out when he was transferred to Langenstein and taking it back to Prague and then London. To the end of his life both it and the knife sat upon his desk, the box a symbol of the need to protect and nurture the inner life his poems represented and the risk involved in such an act. If discovered, either the box or the knife could have been deemed sabotage and cost him his life on the spot.[58]

Besides Schiff, the two men who had the most profound effect on Adler's survival were the head Kapo of the camp, Otto Herrmann, a German Communist from Halle, and Charles Odic, a medical doctor from France who had fought in the Resistance and ran the infirmary. The help extended by Herrmann was more general. He managed to convince the Nazis that it was in their interest not to mistreat the prisoners or kill them, as their skilled labor was needed for the war effort, and to retrain new workers wasted valuable time and productivity. Between October 27, 1944, and February 19, 1945, only nineteen prisoners died, a remarkably low number considering the severe cold that winter and the dire living conditions. Herrmann's courageous and shrewd leadership was so instrumental in the lives of the prisoners that he was eventually included among the "Righteous Among the Nations" at Yad Vashem, a rare distinction for a Kapo.

Adler benefitted more directly from Odic's presence, as the two became fast friends. When Adler entered the infirmary one day, Odic declared, "Voilà, un homme!", the words with which Goethe was greeted by Napoleon.[59] As a result, another "stable pairing" was formed in addition to those made with Schiff and Ivanji. Given his position as the chief medical officer, Odic would have had plenty to talk about with Adler regarding Gertrud's work in Theresienstadt. Odic's aspirations as a writer of fiction served as another connection. Born in

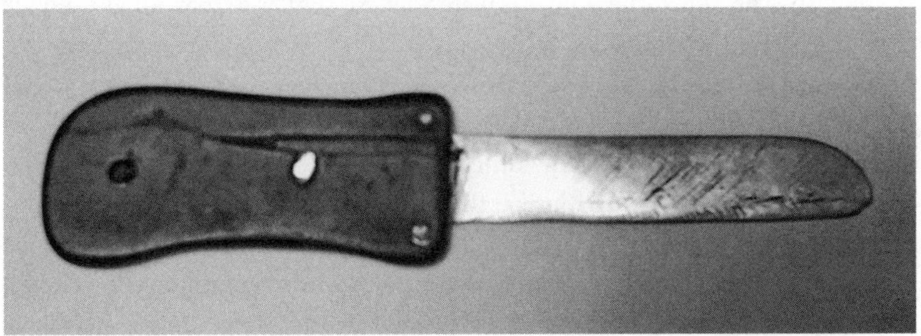

Adler's knife. Credit: The Estate of H. G. Adler 2019, Deutsches Literaturarchiv Marbach.

1894, he was sixteen years older than the thirty-four-year-old Günther, which made him slightly closer in age to Adler's father, Emil, than was Schiff, and therefore just old enough to provide needed counsel and support, especially after the loss of Gertrud.

Within a few months after arriving in Niederorschel, Adler dedicated a poem to his new friend. Written in the intricate *terza rima* that he had taken up in the later poems composed in Theresienstadt, "An Odic" ("To Odic") is the second poem in a brief cycle later titled *Grüsse* (*Greetings*). In its last three stanzas Adler makes clear the solace he took from their friendship.

> My dear friend, how we would have loved to escape
> These difficult hardships full of afflictions,
> Preferring instead to conjure warmth and wine—
>
> But no one asked us to; though what we imagine
> And wish for deep inside can still exist
> Somehow in quiet signs, silent gestures.
>
> We found each other. Blesséd be the hour.
> Since we are brothers, nothing can harm us.
> Amid such strife our bond is made more real.[60]

The urge to "conjure warmth and wine" alludes to the creative spirit able to imbue meaning through "quiet signs, silent gestures." The poem does the same amid the "hardships full of afflictions" in which the two writers formed their bond. What is striking about the handful of poems written in Niederorschel is that half of them are written "to" another, be it Odic, another doctor named Franz Bass, or an abstract "distant loved one," undoubtedly Gertrud. Such efforts to extend "Greetings" to others betrays the poet's sense of entrapment. Unfortunately, the essence of the "Reply" received by the lover who asks the distant loved one, "Do I hear your voice, my dear? / I sense you are there, but cannot reach you," is final and certain: "Your reply?—There is never any reply."[61]

The paper on which these poems were written, similar to that Adler used for his Kafka lecture, was most likely provided by Schiff, which underscores the importance of trusted connections in Auschwitz or in Niederorschel. Upon arrival in the camp, the Orthodox Jew had been so bold as to say that he had worked as a secretary before the war. Such admissions to previous experience other than manual labor were fraught with risk; they could paint a prisoner as useless, unproductive, and fit for extermination. Remarkably, Schiff was granted an office job with no night shift, a position that kept him warm and relatively well fed, while providing a means for other prisoners to have access to a few spare sheets of paper on which to write out the *Haggadah* for a clandestine Passover, or Adler his poems.[62] The only other possibility would have been bits of paper handed out by the SS on which, once a month, prisoners were allowed to send a letter home.[63] Given that he had not a single family member or friend left in Prague to whom he could write, such an opportunity was of no use to Adler, making "Greetings" he sent to those near and impossibly far all the more poignant.

Adler left Niederorschel on February 18, 1945, on a transport of 135 workers sent to Langenstein-Zwieberge, most of whom were no longer deemed able-bodied.[64] With raw materials in shorter supply, the Niederorschel workshops shut down almost entirely, and the mines of Langenstein-Zwieberge had a greater need for bodies to toil inside them.[65] The distance was fifty miles, but the journey traveled was from relatively tolerable conditions to the worst Günther had experienced thus far. With 5,000 prisoners from thirty-eight nations, Langenstein had also been set up by Junkers in October 1944.[66] Rather than taking over a plywood factory or a textile mill, however, the plan was to use slave labor to carve out an underground facility of forty thousand to sixty thousand cubic meters in a mine three kilometers from the base camp. No special skills or training were necessary to work twelve-hour shifts swinging a pickaxe in the damp frigid caverns, so the SS had no reason to be more lenient on the prisoners. Conditions in the mine made it easy to fulfill the Nazi aim of "Extermination Through Work." Official records list 1,800 deaths between October 1944 and April 1945. One in three inmates perished over these five months, although given the sudden dismantling of the camp in April when American soldiers liberated it, the exact toll is likely higher.

Most of the five thousand prisoners were housed in the mines outside Halberstadt, beneath the twin peaks of Zwieberge on the northern side of the Harz Mountains, where Goethe sets the Witch's Sabbath on Walpurgis Night in *Faust*. Adler's contingent, however, was housed in the small "Junkers camp" near SS administrative offices some three kilometers away.[67] Those working in the mines were fed once a day, and many died from accidents and falling stones, or malnutrition and the effects of the bone-chilling cold. Because of a shortage of overalls and zebra stripes, workers were forced to wear civilian clothing, which wore out quickly and provided little protection from the rain and cold on the lengthy hike back and forth from the barracks, often in total darkness. The barracks of the "Junkers camp" had no heat or running water, and the prisoners were forced to bathe quickly at a series of cold taps in a large brick-walled lavatory. Parasites were rampant, as were the usual cases of enteritis and malnutrition. This forced an expansion of the infirmary, which in reality served as a death ward.

Worse than the conditions was the sense of menace with which the camp was run. Any sign of weakness or resistance from the prisoners was dealt with swiftly and violently, and there was one officer, SS Oberscharführer Paul Tscheu, whose sole job was to oversee hangings from a tall oak tree atop a small rise at the far end of the Junkers camp. Whether produced by the dangerous and exhausting work of the mines, the starvation and illness incurred in the camp, or the hangman's rope, each day bodies were hauled away on a horse-drawn cart owned by a local farmer quietly puffing on a clay pipe as he headed to the state crematorium in the nearby town of Quedlinburg, the birthplace of Klopstock, the poet on whom Günther had written his dissertation.[68] When the crematorium broke down from overuse in the spring of 1945, prisoners were forced to dig mass graves in which they buried their comrades. And whereas the townspeople of Niederorschel gave assistance to the prisoners by providing food and clothing, in Langenstein civilians were extensively employed as guards and servants, which also led to a lack of direct oversight. This allowed some to pass food to the inmates, but others zealously employed the sadism of their superiors. The head Kapo, Otto Kutscher, was deeply feared, for unlike the wise and crafty Otto Hartmann of Niederorschel, he would murder prisoners for slight transgressions on a moment's notice.

Perhaps taking a cue from Schiff's boldness in Niederorschel, when asked upon arrival in Langenstein-Zwieberge what his occupation was, Adler felt compelled to say, "I am a doctor of philosophy."[69] Although the admission may have sent him packing on the next transport to Buchenwald, the SS officer instead asked if that meant he could type. When Adler said yes, he was assigned the position of Lagerschreiber (Camp Clerk). He was spared the grueling and dangerous work of digging in the mines and for the first time since leaving Theresienstadt, he had access to a typewriter and paper, allowing him on the sly to type the poems he had written in Niederorschel and smuggled into Langenstein in the aluminum box.

Adler's "Schreiber" armband. Credit: The Estate of H. G. Adler 2019, Deutsches Literaturarchiv Marbach.

One day an SS Blockführer (Block Leader) searched him and found the box. Adler knew this meant at best a severe beating; likely he would be hanged. The officer indeed shouted at him and rained down threats of punishment before demanding that Adler appear before him that evening in the camp's main office. As he entered, he was sure that he was about to die, and yet after a severe dressing down the poems were returned to him with the warning to "make sure that you are never caught with them again!" To his astonishment, he was dismissed. Shortly thereafter Adler learned he had been made a "Hallenschreiber" (Factory Clerk), moving him higher up in the camp's hierarchy, which meant he could remain in the relative comfort of the Junkers camp and help other prisoners by keeping them off of the wrong lists.[70] Not only did this spare his life, it allowed him to continue to type up the poems he later carried out of the camp in the makeshift box on April 12, when the SS abandoned the camp, fleeing the approach of American troops.[71]

Why the official let him go with no more than a warning is not clear. Some factors likely contributed to it. Although officially a member of the SS, the "Blockführer" was probably a recent recruit from the army or a local civilian, less ideological and sadistic. Soon after entering the camp, Adler also became the "Hofdichter" ("Court Poet") to a "powerful" Kapo (perhaps Otto Kutscher) who asked him to write love poems he could pass off as his own to his sweetheart in town.[72] Between discovering the cache of poems and Adler showing up that evening at his office, the "Blockführer" may have learned this after consulting the Kapo. Adler's later claim to Wilhelm Unger that "my poetry saved my life" was factual. Without having boldly declared himself an intellectual, he would not have been made a "Schreiber," and without serving as a "Court Poet" to the Kapo, he might not have been spared. And without poetry to occupy him, he might not have preserved his mind and spirit amid such conditions.

The first stanza of one of the very last poems Adler wrote in Langenstein reads:

> This is the end;
> I sense it clearly,
> Thrown upon the serrating teeth:
> This is Death, the Über-Death,
> The Death of all Deaths,
> Never dying and never dying out,
> Frozen within the eternity
> Of ancient blue ice,
> Buried beneath
> The layers of ultimate forgetting.[73]

Written on March 21, 1945, just three weeks before the camp was liberated, the poem depicts Adler at the end of his own endurance. Later he claimed that he would not have lasted another three weeks in the camp. Nor is his feeling of being buried and forgotten entirely metaphorical, for toward the end rumors flew that the Nazis planned to herd the nearly 5,000 prisoners still left into mines, blow up the entrance, and bury them alive.[74] The constant drone and thunder of air-raid alarms and Allied bombing sorties raised hopes that the war would soon end and the prisoners would be freed, but even these were crushed when on April 9 the SS ordered 3,000 inmates to set off north on a death march that lasted nearly three weeks and three hundred kilometers. There are no precise figures of the number of dead, but it is estimated that nearly 2,500 perished or were shot along the way.[75]

Adler knew that he could not survive such a march, and that if he held out for a while longer the Allies would arrive. He and Ivanji hid in the camp, joining the 1,700 sick and dying prisoners (34 percent of the population) left behind in the infirmary and recovery wards.[76] Once the SS left, there was no food left to feed them, and over a hundred died of hunger in the next few days. Covered with feces because of the enteritis that had sunk its teeth into the population, the bodies were stacked so high and thick in the infirmary that the corridors became impassable.[77] Nights were illuminated by the thunder and lightning of the Allied bombing, although when that ceased on the 11th the prisoners were able to poke their heads out of the barrack windows and see that the watchtowers were empty, the last SS having fled.

Not knowing how long before the camp would be liberated and with no food to be found, Adler, Ivanji, and another young Czech named Alphen set out on foot for Halberstadt on the morning of the 12th.[78] Once they reached the bombed-out city, they pleaded with an American officer to send troops to help the inmates left behind, but the officer had no power to do that. Receiving chocolate from the soldiers, the next day they returned to the camp to see what they could do, only to find German civilians tending to the sick and the dead, not out of altruism, but because the Americans had arrived and ordered it.[79]

Soon the one thousand patients who had survived were transferred to a temporary infirmary in an abandoned army barracks in Halberstadt. The three companions, fearing quarantine for weeks on end, avoided the facility and the Americans. Instead, they roamed the city's rubble, living on provisions found among the ruins. Ivanji and the young Czech were eager to head home and soon left Halberstadt. It took Ivanji until September to reach his native Serbia, while the Czech was never heard from again. Adler was suffering from a severe inflammation of the nerves in his left leg brought on by twenty-five blows from a lead cable inflicted by an SS officer two weeks earlier on Easter Monday and had to stay behind.[80] He lived at first in an abandoned military barracks on the edge of town, and American forces let him rifle through a German military warehouse. He ditched his motley prison garb and donned, of all things, the uniform of a German storm trooper after cutting off its insignia. "The moment I put the uniform on I felt triumphant," Adler recalled. "There I was, the scum of the earth, and wearing their clothes!"[81] Still, without a job and no family to return to, there was nothing to do but try to recuperate. "I read by the hour and ate by even more hours," he later told Bettina Gross. "Books, food and drink came from God knows where, most of it from what I was able to steal from the ruins or with other former inmates I hooked up with. We combed through half-destroyed buildings and took what we thought could be of use."[82]

When the barracks were reoccupied by German prisoners of war, Adler moved in with a German family named Harmuth, which was the maiden name of his grandmother on his mother's side.[83] One day he thought he heard Gertrud's name on the radio among the thousands of names that were shared daily by relatives seeking one another in the war's chaotic aftermath.[84] Could she be alive? Was she back in Prague? There was only one way to find out. His leg healed, he set out with two Czechs, traveling three hundred kilometers to Prague via Halle, Leipzig, Plauen, through the Bohemian countryside, passing through Eger (Cheb) and Pilsen. Arriving in Prague on June 22, he discovered she was not there: it had been another Gertrud he heard on the radio, if he had in fact heard the right name at all.

And yet he was alive, having survived what so many had not. Schiff, Odic, Drössler, Ivanji, and many others had managed to come through it as well, but none of them could replace Gertrud or his family, and each had traveled on in search of his own home and healing. What way forward lay open to him he could not know, although he soon realized that "Prague and all of Czechoslovakia is, after the death of my loved ones, worse than a graveyard," and there was no way he could live there.[85] All that he could do was what had stood by him since childhood and throughout the camps. And so, sitting down at a typewriter, he began to write.

10

The Letter Writers

Writing to Steiner on June 24, 1945, two days after returning to Prague exhausted, destitute, but taken in by his childhood friend Susie Tieze at Brněnská 126, Adler wasted no time in painting a stark picture of what he had survived, what it had cost him, and what he had gained:

> I am the only one of my or my wife's family to survive this terrible nightmare, which also claimed my wife as a victim. The day before yesterday I returned from Germany, where I was in a number of different concentration camps. I have not changed; my principles have remained the same, and have only grown more firm, more committed, and perhaps more mature. I have experienced horrible things, but the fact that I have experienced them causes me no regret, nor do I wish that I had not experienced them. Only a few came through, and among them fewer yet remained true to themselves. One catastrophe after another. And yet over the years I also had the chance to work, and I worked a great deal. I stood always on the margin, always at the outer limits. I am somewhat down and out, and yet I have come through relatively unscathed, my health is intact and not seriously harmed. But enough about me. . . .

In the next paragraph he turns to what so many first letters written to those who escaped the war report: news of the dead.

> Your steadfast parents were together with me in Theresienstadt from July to October of 1942. Neither my wife nor I were able to save them from the transport. I made every effort in the short time we had together to be a good son to your loved ones, as I and my wife tried as hard as possible to help them and to ease their bitter suffering, and I checked on them each day (which in this type of camp was quite hard to do).[1]

Adler could not have known that Steiner had received news of his parents' death by telegram just a week earlier, but it would not have mattered. His letter follows the formula one may expect: news that the writer is alive, then news about those who have died. Steiner, however, could have felt a silent rebuke hearing of their death again, having survived safely in England after Adler's boyhood friend Wolfgang Burghart urged him to leave Czechoslovakia as early as 1936.[2]

Adler's next letter to Steiner, on July 9, references a telegram from him that is now lost, suggesting that Steiner had heard that Adler was alive and had tried to reach him. Writing now two weeks after returning to Prague, Adler reports that in August he will begin working in Štiřín, a small town outside of Prague where the Christian pacifist Přemsyl Pitter set up a rehabilitation center in the former palace of a German aristocrat to care for children orphaned by the war. Most were Jews who had lost their parents to the camps, but there were Czechs and Germans as well, unusual for the time and a demonstration of Pitter's expansive humanism. Emil Vogel, leader of Adler's Pfadfinder troop and still a revered and close friend, was the doctor for the four camps Pitter set up in the region, and through him Adler was hired to help the older students prepare for high school entrance exams. "They really have nothing going for them," he writes Steiner, speculating that it will be useful to tap Jewish teachings to help them find their way. Nevertheless, Adler is unafraid to face whatever may come, "for why should I be afraid when nothing could possibly be any worse than the horrors I've been through."[3]

Yehuda Bacon: Portrait of H. G. Adler, 1945. Credit: The Estate of H. G. Adler 2019, Deutsches Literaturarchiv Marbach.

By this point, however, Adler's stoicism had begun to strain, for in his next sentence he laments the true state of affairs: "Ruins, everywhere ruins, no matter where one looks." Prague came through the war largely unscathed, so it's doubtful that Adler is referring to conditions there, and indeed the rest of the paragraph reveals him to be speaking more generally:

> A world destroyed and hardly any hope that people will find a way out of their moral demise any time soon. Unfortunately it becomes more and more clear to me that Nazism is not an illness that has been cured, and that Nazism is an illness that stems from neither recent years nor the present, but instead is a symptom that perhaps was successfully eradicated, yet the illness itself gnaws at the foundations of human coexistence. I don't know how things look in England. But wherever Hitler ruled is now sad and laid low. The question is, just how will we define our own role within it?

This was a vexed question for Adler. Besides losing his entire family and having no immediate prospects of a steady income, at thirty-five he was eager to get on with his life. It was natural for him to reach out to Steiner for help and advice, but both the geographic distance and the gulf separating their experiences of the war were impediments. Likely realizing the limits of not only what his friend could do for him but his own ability to say what happened, Adler addresses this directly:

> I would love to see you, but I don't know if that will be possible anytime soon. I think that seeing each other in person would bring us close together again. Of course our experiences were different enough that there is bound to be some awkwardness, but I am convinced that we would eventually understand one another. I often ask myself what you would make of how things are here. Last night I had a dream about you. We were together in Italy. If only that were a premonition! No one can understand entirely the core of what happened to us, but there's no reason for you to feel pity. I'm just happy that you were not here, even if you had been able, like me, to miraculously survive. Neither Dante nor Dostoevsky could have dreamed up such an unreal Hell, though Kafka could, for he has become a prophet, a realistic prophet of these horrors.

The matrix of relations in this passage is fascinating. Adler longs to see his friend again and dreams of returning to their idyllic years of wandering the European countryside together. But he knows that there is no way that he can explain the horror of his experience, nor any way that Steiner can understand it. Given Steiner's own mourning for the loss of his parents, and the guilt he would have felt having survived while ensconced in Oxford, one can almost feel him wince with shame reading Günther's letter. That Adler "miraculously survived" seems a bit of one-upmanship and a reminder that "you were not here," although such resentment likely remained unconscious, Adler feeling abandoned by Steiner before the war and referring to Italy, from which he had hoped to escape. Meanwhile, his question "just how will we define our role" speaks to the dilemma of representing his suffering. As an anthropologist writing a dissertation on slavery in response to the barbarism of the age, Steiner had found a way to respond; Adler now had to do the same.

Adler's first two letters to Steiner were wrenching, his third letter even more so, for he laments that he has heard nothing back beyond a brief telegram, although five weeks have passed since he first wrote. As if to underscore the pain of Steiner's neglect, he reminds him, "I have been through a lot and still don't feel like my old self." Then, assuming that his previous letters have gone missing for good, he again gives a synopsis of the camps and the fate of Steiner's parents:

> I have survived almost four years in several different concentration camps. I spent a long time in Theresienstadt, where your parents were from the beginning of July '42 until almost the middle of October of that same year. Your father endured it all patiently, but your mother was in terrible shape. I visited them every day and tried as best I could, as far as it was possible under such conditions, to ease their miserable state and take on the role of a son. I am so sorry that it came to such a bad end, but it was not within my power to prevent the terrible fate that most likely awaited them in Auschwitz. No one came back from those transports, and it is highly likely that they were killed immediately in the gas chambers. That which they could not escape was also the fate of my own family. No one survived, not even my wife—for only three years I was married to an unbelievably lovely, cultivated, and highly educated woman, who was gassed last October. I was liberated by the Americans near Halberstadt and finally returned to Prague on June 22 after having recovered from an illness.

That Adler has to retell the entire story is painful, but that he feels compelled to give more graphic detail speaks to the pressure to make real what he has survived. "I am healthy," he adds,

> . . . but my nerves, my nerves—I feel empty and unbelievably sad. People feel so distant, and I am afraid to be alone, yet I also don't like being in the company of others. All of you who had the luck not to have to live through any of it, you cannot imagine what we in fact went

> through. The misery, the hunger, the filth, the hatred, sickness, horror, every kind of pain imaginable—and yet all of that is nothing compared to what one suffered on the inside and which cannot be put into words. Even what Dostoevsky writes in *The House of the Dead*—nothing, really nothing is comparable![4]

As in the second letter, Adler makes a literary allusion to help Steiner imagine what he is talking about, although he negates it by writing that "nothing is comparable" to his experience. As if not wanting to show himself as too vulnerable, in the next sentence he says, "And yet the healthy attitude of my view of life was able to stand it all, for I am the same H. G. A. as before—just a little older and sadder." He reports on his work on his "Traktat" and his poems, and how he avidly read philosophy despite the daily grind of intense physical work with a shovel and pickaxe. Plaintively asking, "What prospects might there be for me in England?" Adler imagines there are likely none, although he urges Steiner to reach out to his friends there, "if I still have any! Or have you all forgotten me?" Shuttling between feelings of despair, desperation, stoic pride, and abandonment, Adler's letter is a message in a bottle, tossed into the silence between himself and his oldest friend.

Steiner sent a telegram the next day acknowledging receipt of a letter, but it took yet another week for Steiner to write his first full letter in return. His own ambivalence at having survived the war in England appears front and center. After noting that a package is on the way and Canetti also promises to write, Steiner explains:

> I don't wish to say anything about what you've been through. Our suffering and anxiety here, when compared to yours, is so small that one can't say anything. But I have to admit that it makes me very happy that you can see things the way you say you do in your letter. Certainly the memory of such horrors is your most valuable possession. But somehow all of this must be shared, and it will need to be taken in by the broader collective. How, when, where? Who knows?[5]

It is hard to imagine a more ambivalent response, or to know how Adler would have taken it. Defensively, Steiner "can't say anything," although almost dismissively he announces, "I don't wish to say anything." Neither intention feels true. Wishing to acknowledge his own inability to know of or speak to the suffering and death of his parents, Steiner can only own up to his failure by choosing silence. More curious is that "the memory of such horrors is your most valuable possession," which will have to be shared with and by "the broader collective." He acknowledges that Adler possesses an experience through memory that Steiner cannot experience, but he casts the suffering attached to it as a commodity to be shared with a larger audience through writing. Given that Steiner himself *is* that audience as the first to hear of Adler's trials in written form, his declaration that "one can't say anything" calls into question the degree to which Adler's experience can be understood, even if he were to give full expression to it.

Steiner could not have known it at the time, but he outlines the dilemma that Adler would find himself in for the rest of his career as both a scholar and writer. In asking "How? When? Where? Who knows?" he highlights the problem of finding an audience for such material. Even if Adler found an audience, the question would remain what Adler hoped to accomplish through his writing. "There is no such thing as coming to terms with the past," Adler declared time and again, although he felt the importance of bearing witness to "the lost." Yet if such testimony were to fall on deaf ears, what would be the point and how was he to live? Consciously or not, Steiner had outlined the extraordinary challenge that lay ahead, one that would vex Adler professionally, psychologically, and artistically for the next four decades.

Yet not all letters are in vain, for when received by the right party, the response can be a genuine embrace. In the summer of 1945, Adler moved to Koněvová 126, where he shared the former apartment of a Gestapo agent with Wolf Salus, a high school friend he had last seen in Auschwitz, as well as another camp survivor, Jiříček Šubert.[6] That fall he finally learned the address of Bettina Gross in Wales and sent his first letter to her on October 29.

> Dear Bettina!
> After extended efforts I finally got hold of your address and am happy to be able to write to you at last. I say that I'm happy—and yet it is very difficult for me to write and I have to struggle for every word. Too much has happened in between and it's been too long since we've heard anything from one another! What can we still possibly mean to one another and can we even know each other anymore? One can't help but ask. And yet I have often thought of you. And those aren't just empty words, for I have *really* thought about you and about Maria [Bettina's sister] as well. But what can that possibly mean? First one has to figure out if further contact makes any sense. I hope so. I do hope so, though often I have the feeling that all ties with the acquaintances and friends I knew before '39 have been severed. We, the ones who stayed behind, are the ones who in some ways are now stuck in the past, as if some kind of slip-up is the reason why we are still here. People remember us, but *really* it's like we shouldn't exist at all, that it is indecent that we do. And if we indeed do exist, then we are at best museum pieces, no longer individuals, but something impersonal, abstract.

Most of Günther's first letter reports on the fate of Bettina's mother, but to begin with an open acknowledgment of his own frail state of mind is striking. He suffers from survivor's guilt in feeling it "indecent" that he even exists, or that all ties with former friends have been severed for good. But unlike the first letter to Steiner, there is little here aimed at reminding the recipient that she, too, escaped the worst, or that the writer holds some knowledge that the recipient will never grasp. Instead he lays bare his vulnerability and speaks more to the trust he places in her, a woman he had not seen for over seven years.

Adler goes on to say that he feels very "cut off from all of you out there," a feeling that has increased since only Steiner has ever written back. He returns to "the fact that I survived is a miracle." What he's been through was "really grisly, so grisly," and those on the outside cannot possibly understand, but he is quick to say that the only reason it bothers him at all is because of the loss of his dear wife, whom he reminds Bettina she knew through a mutual friend. In the rest of the letter Günther gives a detailed picture of the courage and dignity of Bettina's mother, and how close he remained to her after Bettina's departure from Prague in December 1938. Adler devotes nearly half the letter to portraying Bettina's mother in a manner that could have only moved and comforted the woman he hoped to connect with again. Only at the end does he return to his own state: "Today I am totally alone. Not only did I lose all of my relatives and my wife, but almost all of my old friends and my new ones are gone. I am stuck here. Though I'd love to get out of here, obviously."

Bettina not only answered Günther's letter immediately, she had searched out his address before receiving it, after hearing from Steiner's cousin Lise Seligmann that Günther had been inquiring for her address. In fact, her letter of October 21 and his letter of October 29 crossed in the mail, each receiving the first news of the other in seven-and-a-half years almost simultaneously, an event central to their later bond. Bettina's first letter to Günther is a polite and well-meaning inquiry as to how he is and how glad she is to hear that he is alive, but her response to his letter, written November 7, shows how deeply moved she was to hear from him. "Since getting your letter first thing this morning, I could think about nothing else. I had no idea my heart was capable of feeling such joy. Your words feel warm and close, no matter the distance, and there is something within them that only brings to mind the word 'resurrection.'" She thanks him for telling her about her mother. Although she had heard the news already, the details he related make it all the more believable and finally end her brother Josef's hopes of seeing their mother again. Calm and accepting of a fate she cannot change, she can only look at her own life in South Wales and begin to question its meaning.

> Günther, I am sitting in a lovely little room with pictures of my parents, as well as a figure of justice on the wall, and I feel warm, Joseph and

> his young wife having just been here, during which time we laughed and joked and were happy. But is there any way to escape the weight of the guilt that I feel? Don't answer if you don't feel you can. But when you write that you have to find a way to live again—I know what you mean, for in the last weeks I have thought to myself: I am not alive, not fully and not entirely, for guilt has wounded me and almost crushed me. Can you forgive me? Is there anything that can take away the guilt I feel? And as an answer there arrives only the feeling of something—big and warm and with outstretched hands, yet I don't dare approach it. Günther, you have been through terrible things which I do want to hear about and understand, but I have battled so against loneliness, against isolation, against feelings of despair and self-reproach, and I need your strong, clever words, your understanding, your friendship. Is it friendship? Only you can say, for we have remained here safe and warm, and perhaps my joy over your letter is only as deep as my longing to be understood. But grant me the joy of being able to help you, and write to me about how you manage to get by, and what you are working on.

Her lines broke like a warm wave over the cold paralysis Adler found himself frozen in since returning to Prague. She cannot help but confront the guilt she feels, yet in giving voice to it she is able to reach out to her friend all the more, while her own vulnerability and need creates an opportunity to offer herself genuinely and selflessly through her urge to help in any way she can.

Adler could hardly contain his excitement after hearing from Bettina. Even before she responds to his first letter so movingly, he jumps at the chance to answer the polite, concerned query posed in her first letter by writing back on November 4 to say, "I am so immensely alone that the wonderful regards ostensibly offered by just the sight of your handwriting are enough to bring me real joy."[7] If this were not enough to show his hand, he adds, "I have hardly anyone left in the wide world to whom my heart still belongs; you belong to the very few that still mean something, if not a great deal to me. And certainly after having received these dear lines!" He remarks on how her handwriting has matured, although it still contains the "loving tenderness" he had known, while he apologizes for typing his letters since his handwriting is so bad. Even before receiving Bettina's confession of her own feelings of guilt, he offers up his feelings of shame, saying,

> I'm healthy—for the most part through and through, though sometimes I get tired, but less and less, and with time it will go away. Yet I feel ashamed more often than not whenever I find myself feeling "in a good mood." I am often completely overcome with a feeling of deep

> shame about everything that has happened, and this shame almost always leads to feelings of despair when I realize that the world does not want to hear about all of the horrors it is guilty of. I don't mean the sensation of the horrors themselves, but rather the deep spiritual problems that have resulted from them, the solution for which is not being sought for at all, for I further realize that there really is nothing to prevent such atrocities from happening again soon through war, and that further hate killings in perhaps even greater numbers could be repeated—or in fact will be. But for what then did we suffer?

On display is the shame expressed by many survivors over what has happened to them, and guilt in having any feelings of normalcy or well-being, for the fear is that such feelings are undeserved or dishonor those who died. But instead of remaining trapped by his suffering, Adler also despairs at the world's negligence in not working to prevent it from happening again. This mirrors Bettina's wish to be forgiven for the guilt she feels (although he does not know of it yet), which inspires her to offer any help that she can give. It is as if symbiotically, and albeit at this point unknowingly, their needs dovetail with one another: she the one who has survived in the safety of exile while dear ones perished, he the survivor who came through the worst, only to have no loved ones to return to.[8]

As in his letter to Steiner, after treading on the brink of despair Adler reports that he continues to write, and that he wrote throughout his time in the camps, as if what relieves his shame is the ability to remain cogent and dedicated to doing what he knows best how to do. This is also meant to resonate with Bettina, for he is pleased to report that the "Traktat" that he sent her from Milan ("do you still have it?") remains alive and substantially expanded, and that he also worked on a novel and many poems in Theresienstadt. The intensity of his letters and his need to connect cause him to veer from one topic to another, and as if he does not know where to start or to turn, he suddenly takes up the one plaintive question Bettina asked in her otherwise discreet first letter: "was the price too high" in having left Prague and her mother for Wales? [9]

> After many years you are asking the question closest to your heart: whether you did the right thing in leaving. Yes, my dear friend, yes, and again yes! I say yes from my own conscience and with thoughts of your mother. Knowing that her children had gotten out was the thing that without a doubt made her most happy. Her sheer selflessness would have never been freed of self-reproach if one of her children had not made it to safety. This I promise you! My mother-in-law was not so selfless; she held onto and chained down her one dear child, and therefore swept her away with her into an early death.

Adler's bitterness at the loss of Gertrud is evident. Although it risks causing Bettina to feel further guilt at having survived, his tone remains a cri de coeur more than a stab at blame. He emphasizes how selflessly Gertrud had served as a doctor and head of the laboratory in Theresienstadt and how many she had helped. The intensity of his admiration for his wife betrays his own ravaged sense of loss. As the deep guilt expressed in Bettina's soon-to-arrive second letter helped seal their emotional bond, Günther's pain over Gertrud's death, which he believed occurred to save her mother, must have touched a tender nerve in Bettina, whose mother had sacrificed her own life for hers.

At risk in their exchange is the breaking of a taboo through the sprouting of affection, even love, in the wake of the deaths of Gertrud and Bertha in Auschwitz, and the many others who perished as well. After such an intense exchange, it is not surprising that a pause ensues, as if each had to step back and consider the consequences of their outpourings. Bettina writes three more letters on the 8th and 9th, but although she again expresses how grateful she is to be in touch again and be able to unburden herself in writing, for the most part these contain cheery descriptions of her life and work, the Welsh countryside, what has become of her siblings, and ideas on publishers for his work in Switzerland and England. She goes so far as to express eager interest in hearing about "what it was like" in Theresienstadt, and whom he knew there. Like the rest of the world, and despite Günther's statements about it having been "horrible," she has no idea of the brutal conditions.

As if recovering from a catharsis, Adler does not write again until November 20, more than two weeks after his effusive second letter to Bettina, and only after receiving her three cheery, concerned, practical-minded, yet blamelessly naive letters. This time, however, what he writes is not just an effort to take up with and be heard by an old, dear friend but to engage with the full-bore nightmare that has brought him to this point. Insisting that they use the familiar form of "Du" with one another, and begging forgiveness if this should insult her, Adler goes on about the need to speak freely and directly, saying how helpless he is in taking such a risk, even when he knows very little about her life these days. Caveats aside, he then lets go:

> When I returned in June and succumbed to the terrible feeling of emptiness that I in fact could not even sense completely in the camps or even in the first two months of "freedom" in Germany, and when I could not help but slide into that understandable state of mind in which I could only regret having survived, having irretrievably lost that magnificent, ever bright, and kind creature who had given of herself to me, that is when I realized truly for the first time that I was wounded. Oh Bettina, I was covered under by more ice than there exists in the world—again

> and again having to see that last glance, the one she gave me on the death ramp at Auschwitz, looking straight at me, courageously and with what deep knowledge, and then calmly walking away at her mother's side and smiling; this I will never entirely get over nor do I wish to.[10]

Again an entreaty, but this one deeper yet, placing Bettina directly on the ramp in Auschwitz with him and Gertrud. It is from this point, and only from this point, that he can go forward with her. As much as he is grateful for having found Bettina again, and for the depth and warmth of her response, he must confront it with the worst that he has seen so that she truly may see what he has become, proclaiming from the most reduced of states:

> I don't know what you can offer me—I don't know what I can offer you. Does it mean being abandoned to the loneliness of a saint? Shall it mean friendship and a deep resolution to be there for one another? Shall it mean the urge to serve and sacrifice and lift each other up? Or more than all of this? I don't dare think about it. I don't dare think at all at the moment. I am agitated in a way that I have sensed has been building for some months, and which I have actually tried to silence or didn't wish to acknowledge. What's the matter with me and who am I to be so presumptuous? A poor man laid low, a castaway? Indeed! But still a fire burns within me! I am still me.

Needing to convince Bettina of just who he is, Adler's four-page single-spaced letter rides alternate waves of pride in his having remained true to himself and the painful remembrance and adoration of Gertrud. As he had to place Bettina with him on the ramp at Auschwitz, he also feels the need to fully explain his love for his wife and give Bettina a clear window into their relation.

Nor is it an idealized or sentimental portrait. He admits that, enigmatically, Gertrud had said to him, "I will be with you during this terrible time, but once things are better again, I will likely be gone" and that she really meant it. On the other hand, she also acknowledged, "You are the only one who really understands me" and that "it is so lovely to have you in my life." She could also be stern ("Betrayal is the worst thing of all. I would never forgive you if you betrayed me") as well as demanding ("One always has to keep to the high road with me"). For although she was "admired and loved like a genuine angel," she also had a way about her that "intensively felt, thought, and lived, which another man would have found hard to bear. . . . And really everything with her not only meant taking the high road but also following it to the very end, whether it be her exuberant spirits or her crippling depression. She was everything to me."

H. G. Adler, 1945. Credit: The Estate of H. G. Adler 2019, Deutsches Literaturarchiv Marbach.

If Bettina had any idea of replacing her, she had her work cut out, but Adler also makes clear that he often spoke of her to "Geraldine," who was well aware of his fondness for Bettina and why he felt the need to watch over her mother. "I don't see her in you and I don't see you in her," Adler is careful to note, nor is he "chasing her blesséd shadow." Instead, he wonders if there is anything "good" left in him, and whether or not Bettina might find him "tactless" in sharing so many intimacies, especially when he confesses that Gertrud had tried to convince him that they should both take sleeping pills and kill themselves rather than be deported to the East, although Adler refused. He feels that because of what he has suffered he has a right to speak openly with Bettina, although he hopes he has not cloaked himself in sorrow, ignoring her own loss or seeing it as anything less. "I know that all of you suffered," he says compassionately. "I felt your agony through six hard years of duress and uncertainty—every day, every hour, every second—even in the most unprepossessing and thus most tender of times." Adler closes the circle that his letter began by placing Bettina on the ramp with him, for wherever he happened to be, he was also mentally with her and the others who had escaped, and that he felt sorry for what they endured as well. Rather than "tactless," it is a masterly and moving demonstration of empathetic imagination, offering a reciprocal means by which each can claim validity for the pain still felt while acknowledging the need to embrace what the other felt as well.

Perhaps the most impressive thing about Adler's letter, and for that matter his entire correspondence, is that there is hardly a visible mark on the four typed pages beyond the single-spaced, typed text. Instead, the ebb and flow of his consciousness appears directly on the page, now swinging toward remorse, now surging toward remembrance, now pouring out its heartfelt sorrow, now expressing trepidation at how the reader might be taking it all in. This effect is heightened by his composition of the four pages as one single and uninterrupted body of text, a habit that took years for Adler to abandon, the need to conserve paper and make use of every inch of every page having been spawned in Theresienstadt. More to the point, however, is the tidal power of his letters and the remarkably pure manner by which that power is delivered to the page. Bettina had asked to hear what Günther was thinking and feeling and just what life had been like in Theresienstadt. Little did she know that he would describe it entirely, seamlessly, and with his full consciousness alive upon the page.

Adler worked on his letter of November 20, the opening day of the Nürnberg trials of former Nazi leaders, until nearly three in the morning, and he was back at it the next day, unable to stop his outpouring of angst, regret, and tenderness. Two days later, however, he worries that he had come on too strong and with too much, too soon. Reverting to the formal address of "Sie," he begs Bettina's forgiveness and understanding and goes on for several pages to calmly tell her about how, after being liberated from Langenstein, he recovered from a severe inflammation of the nerves in his left leg in Halberstadt. He describes his journey back to Prague and the vain hope of finding Gertrud waiting there, followed by his work in Štiřín and at the Jewish Museum, adding a few pages of speculation about whether he might emigrate to America or England, what work he might find, and who might help him. Only at the end does he again approach the question at the heart of the twelve pages of letters he has written over the last three days when he observes,

> We both stand before the graves of the souls of an endless number of murdered loved ones which we cannot nor may not tend with any kind of reverence anywhere in the world. What a responsibility! Must we not then seize hold of the fact that we are here and can begin again and do all that we can? And where and under what signs might we reach out a hand to one another? Or should we not at all? Would it amount to blasphemy? I don't think so at all. I think that if we can do good we not only have a duty to do so in this world, but also the right to do so in this life.[11]

The real question, however, was how would she react? After delicately noting that she has only felt the same once before for another man when she was very young, Bettina declares a week later on the same day his letters arrived:

> Günther, my heart and soul go out to you. My longing, battered by deep loneliness, was only waiting to be fulfilled by the wonder of real companionship. And the fear that this longing might lead us down a wrong road is still there. But I don't want to be afraid. I place my hands together and give thanks very quietly and reverently that I have been granted the chance to read these words—your words, and to hear "Du" once again in my life. Once again this blessing, this miracle, this incredible word "Du."
>
> I don't know what it is you wish to offer me. I know only that I hope to have the spirit and the heart to go forward from all this horror without bitterness and hate. I have come to know my own strength. I no longer am afraid of life. I only wish to live.[12]

As sincere and welcome as this must have read to Adler, a subtle caution runs through it. Bettina knows that he is caught up in intense and ever-shifting emotions, just as she is herself. And so she carefully balances gratitude and warmth with sobriety and calm. Her next paragraphs even turn to practical matters, such as not wishing to bother asking Steiner for copies of Günther's poems and that his typing his letters does not bother her. Cautious, grounded, even shrewd, her real answer to his pleas is to see matters as they stand and to face them. This was the grounded awareness and courage that Adler valued and felt had kept him intact through it all. Yes, her warmth and acceptance counted most, but her savvy, spirited awareness struck a deep chord.

And yet Bettina, too, had her doubts. Two days later, she notes how through the years she has learned strength in taking care of herself and others, holding a job and making friends, and that it was that strength that led her to write to him in the first place one month earlier. Nevertheless, she realizes:

> All that has now disappeared, at least on the inside. I no longer know anything of the many little ordinary things of my daily life. There is nothing but the thoughts and dreams that circle around your words. Yet that is not what you need. If I am to be anything at all for you, then I need to be strong, brave, and cheerful—all the things that I thought I had become, but which now, at least for the moment, have disappeared altogether. . . . My friend, I thought I was strong, but now I feel small and unsure and anxious.

> Hold me, if just for a moment, until my heart calms down, until we both can find our way forward again. Forgive me, O forgive me, if I am disturbing you. I only want to be a whole person.[13]

Were these the words of lovelorn adolescents, it would be easy to dismiss them as melodramatic. But they are adults, Bettina having turned thirty-two in September and Günther already thirty-five. Neither had work that fulfilled them nor was close to what they aspired to. Both had lost family, and both were exiles from their life and past—Bettina literally so, and Günther essentially so, since the culture he had grown up in had disappeared altogether. Not caught in the swoon of their first declarations, these are two people who cannot help but feel the weight of the choices that stand before them, and what it will mean to take on those choices, and perhaps more important, what it will mean if they do not.

The pressure that Bettina felt taking on such a burden appears in the letters she writes on December 1 and 4, both of which show her tempering her emotions and reverting to the more formal "Sie" form of address. Like Günther, she felt she had gone too far and said too much, that writing with such passion could only lead to trouble. She remains clear and steadfast in wanting to help him. The reason why speaks to the pact on which their relationship would be built:

> My motives in wanting to help you are quite simple. My pride simply cannot be satisfied with the complete betrayal of my mother. I will do anything I can to help you. Your last letters helped me appreciate the strength and depth of your soul. That a personal note has entered into our letters is what gives me the strength to do what I have to do. That I thought to ask you about matters of "guilt" may seem strange, but it's true, for I know your acuity and integrity, and have so for years.
>
> That I want to help you is no reason for either of us to feel responsible to the other. I believe indeed that seeing each other again would lead to the kind of calm and steady friendship we used to have.
>
> Should it be more, should our lives be fulfilled by one another, then we are not the kind of people to turn our backs on such a thing. On the other hand, we are also not ones to live out a lie. . . .
>
> Forgive me. Perhaps when we see each other we will know that we want nothing to do with one another. But that our paths have brought us together, and that still we can make our way together for a little while and work toward the same ends, who knows how long it will last! For we are both lonely and perhaps will find each other again sometime soon—so let me for this brief moment be with you, quiet and still, if only to tell you that life here is cheerful and good.[14]

Balancing calm and strength, Bettina's acknowledgment of the need to address her own guilt by doing what she can is a means by which to assert her own stakes in whatever might unfold. The power of Günther's letters and the extremity of his circumstances had overwhelmed her, but she recovers her footing and lays out the ground rules of how they are to move ahead. Yet by the end she has reverted to the informal "Du" form, making clear that she is not turning her back but trying to keep her head amid dizzying emotions. In the two letters she sends on December 4 and 7, she settles for good on the familiar form, even though both letters are concerned most with business matters such as writing to Steiner and Baeck. She says, "I could also use 'Sie,' but I'd much prefer a certain closeness between us if I'm going to do all these things."[15]

If Bettina expected that Günther's passions would cool or that he would have second thoughts about emigrating, the letters he wrote while waiting to receive hers made clear that his longing and excitement were not passing phases but a reinvigoration of the fondness he felt for her as long ago as Milan or in her parents' salon in Prague amid their friendship with Bernard and Gutza Reder. He feels cheerful for the first time in years, and he assures her it is because of her, as she will not stand between him and the memory of Gertrud, nor will she stand in the way of her. "You have asked a very deep question: What can I offer you?", and he answers for his own part as honestly and passionately as he can.[16] He admits he has weaknesses and that he does not know what will become of him, yet he is certain that "love is what I can offer you," and out of that they can build a life together.[17] "It has been 7 1/2 years since I've seen you. And yet for me it is as if no time has passed at all. So much has happened in between. I climbed toward the heights and I fell. And now all at once you are more present to me than ever before. Because it is love. Love that exists between us. I know it. So how can I hide it?"[18]

Many a lover has been taken in by such words, but in the circumstances out of which they are spoken and the cavernous void of time, loss, and history they have crossed, one must appreciate the weight they carried. Adler turns the cause of convincing Bettina into a quest, but one rooted in the idealism he possessed before the war, even as a young man in the Wandervogel. Bettina's open declaration that she is entering the relation to try to pay homage to her mother confesses to its own inverse idealism. Not only is the course of their lives at stake, but the fleeting potential to make something out of the lives lost that they carried within them, whereby "a pursuit of happiness *despite* the Shoah . . . also binds them together.[19] Their correspondence over the next fifteen months offers a rare glimpse into what it means for individuals to take on such burdens in the aftermath of a great catastrophe. But once they both committed to moving ahead together, there was no stopping them. Between October 1945 and February 1947, when Adler at last made it to England, they wrote over 250 letters to the other, many of them pages and pages long, sometimes twice a day. The exchange became so frequent that they started to number their letters to keep track of what letter each was responding to. Nor was the subject only the sorrows of the past or the practical concerns that occupied them. As in Günther's exchange with Gertrud in 1939–40, his correspondence with Bettina ranges across expressions of love, regret, hope, and musings about the meaning of their lives and the project they must advance. But foremost it is their tenderness toward each other that is evident, growing with every page they wrote. By December, Adler could write in a poem titled simply "An Bettina" ("To Bettina"):

> Here on life's path, passion sprouts,
> Many traces of it glowing in these familiar fields.
> Rising familiarly from the blossoming glow,
> The future awakens, auguring true awakening.
> "Accept it!" The heart will be freed
> With summer's blessing, joyfully delivered to it.[20]

As a childhood friend, as a fellow poet, writer, and intellectual, and as a Prague Jew equally bent on living up to their shared ideals, Steiner represented all that Adler had left of the past and everything that had been taken away. As a long-admired friend, a confidant, a survivor desperate for a way to honor the dead, and most important a woman he now loved, Bettina represented the future and all that it could become. "[Y]ou cannot expect that a response will ever come," writes Arthur Landau at the end of "The Letter Writers," the parable that he sits down to write in *The Wall*. "But this doesn't keep cold humanity from waiting with determination and concentrated patience for the great miracle to occur."[21] Steiner would remain a great and trusted friend, but the "miracle" had not occurred with him. With Bettina it did. Now the task was to find a way for the miraculous to become the real.

11

The Escape

"I said to myself, if I can find this woman and she will have anything to do with me, then I can go on."[1] That Adler did find her was the first good fortune he had experienced in years. He was lucky to be alive and to have made it back to Prague, unlike so many others. But there was nothing there for him—neither family nor home. And he was soon exhausted after walking any distance, could barely climb a flight of stairs, and suffered from hypersensitivity, especially to music, a recording of Beethoven's "Eroica" Symphony reducing him to tears.[2] By the time he and Bettina reconnected in early November 1945, Adler had gained weight and strength, but his health remained fragile for years, suffering from bronchitis and a complete loss of smell due to the chronic catarrh and sinusitis he had contracted in the camps.[3]

Bettina, too, had suffered, but in understated ways she did not reveal to Günther at first. The daughter of a highly respected gynecologist in Prague, she had been raised as a young child on a country estate run by her mother's family in Kočvar, just south of the city. After starting school in the capital in 1918, she frequently returned to Kočvar for holidays and summer breaks. There she and her younger brother and sister enjoyed a warm upbringing with marvelous feasts and festivities, a stream of visiting families and friends, rides through the forest in an open wagon, and an expansive orchard with fruit trees, flowers, and beautiful views of the hills and countryside. Bettina's interest in art was eagerly supported by her parents, and the salon they began holding in 1918 at their apartment near the bustle of Wenceslas Square exposed her early to prominent artists such as Willi Nowak, Endre Nemeš, Emil Filla, Jakub Bauerfreund, and Bernard Reder. In 1934, Reder became her teacher and remained a friend until his 1963 death in New York, where he had found success as a sculptor, including a 1961 solo exhibition at the Whitney Museum, the first time the museum devoted its entire space to one artist. Encouraged by Reder, Bettina spent a year at the School for Applied Arts in Vienna. There she fell deeply in love with a young man she wished to marry, but her parents forbade it, forcing her to return home to Prague a gifted yet broken-hearted young artist. After her father's death in 1936 and a journey to Sicily in 1937, Reder arranged for her to study at the École des Beaux Arts in Paris, where she worked with Moissej Kogan and visited the studio of Aristide Maillol. This too was cut short by the need to return to Prague amid the coming cataclysm. The days of impassioned study, travel, and the rich cultural interests of her parents ended when she was the first of her siblings to leave for South Wales in December 1938.

Although three years younger than her brother Joseph, Bettina was made responsible for their care and well-being. Her mother could not bring herself to abandon her sister Ella in Prague, and they were eventually deported to Theresienstadt and death in Auschwitz. Family connections landed Bettina a job as a designer at a Welsh button factory set up by Rudolf and Janne Adler (no relation to Günther) in the Dowlais neighborhood of the coal-mining town of Merthyr Tydfil. For a person with artistic ambitions, it was demeaning work that paid one pound per week to start. Over the eight years she worked there, not only did her meager salary have to cover her expenses while lodging with a Welsh schoolteacher named Mary Davies, but she also had to pay for her sister Maria's training in midwifery and her brother Joseph's second doctorate in law, as his Czechoslovak degree did not qualify him to practice in the United Kingdom. Her pride, and the burden of knowing that her mother and aunt were likely lost, kept Bettina from complaining about her reduced circumstances. By 1945 she was an independent woman who had made her way almost entirely on her own. She no longer enjoyed the comfortable and lively circle in which she had been raised but remained an acknowledged beauty, whose poise and grace belied the hurt and ill fortune she had endured.[4]

Bettina Adler at the Welsh button factory, 1946. Credit: The Estate of H. G. Adler 2019, Deutsches Literaturarchiv Marbach.

It is easy to see not only why Günther remembered her and thought of her while in the camps, but how finding her revived his spirits and his writing life. Letters to her allowed him to work through his thinking on the past and carry it into the future more directly than he could with Steiner, and writing was equally cathartic for Bettina. The sheer volume speaks to how much they felt compelled to write to each other, for both were fully occupied with work and daily life. In August 1945, Adler had begun working full time at Přemsyl Pitter's center in Štiřín. By October he was also employed as a full-time cataloger and curator at the Jewish Museum in Prague, although he continued to travel out to Štiřín on weekends throughout that winter, finding the work rewarding. "There is nothing more lovely than to be able to help these children from the concentration camps and to prepare them for a life of freedom," he tells Steiner on October 3. "No one who has not experienced the horrors of the camps for himself could know so well just what these children need."[5]

Although Adler felt a special kinship with the Jewish children, both Czech and Polish children were taken in, as well as orphans from Sudeten German families and even former Hitler youth.[6] Some 150 children arrived from Theresienstadt in July 1945, and by the winter of 1946 the facilities housed over 300 children ranging between ages two and sixteen in five small chateaus.[7] Many suffered psychologically and found it hard to trust their caretakers, despite being well fed and cared for. "As experienced concentration camp inmates," remembered one resident, "before we went to sleep we'd stick a piece of bread in our pocket or under our pillow, for one never knew what the next day would bring."[8] Others had to be taught to lower their voices while having a conversation after living for years in overcrowded rooms where they had to scream to be heard.[9] Even sweeping the floor and carrying out daily chores proved a vital life lesson. Work had previously been something one was forced to do to survive in the camps. In Štiřín, however, Pitter and the teachers instilled the dignity of work, preparing the children for the hard years ahead.[10]

Adler worked mostly with the older boys around sixteen years of age, helping them to prepare for their school entrance exams, although he felt he was able to nurture their character as well. One pupil especially affected by his teaching was Yehuda Bacon, who also had been at Auschwitz. Born in the Czechoslovakian land of Moravia in 1929, Bacon was deported to Theresienstadt at thirteen in September 1942 with his parents and two older sisters. Twelve months later he was transported to Auschwitz, where his father was gassed, and from which his mother and eldest sister were sent to Stutthof, where they died of spotted fever. Bacon managed to survive and was assigned to the Rollwagenkommando, which delivered wood and documents on small wagons drawn by children through the camp. Following the liquidation of Auschwitz in January 1945, Bacon lived through a seventy-kilometer death march to a neighboring camp before being shipped to Mauthausen and nearby Gunskirchen. Liberated from a neighboring camp in May 1945, he arrived at Pitter's facility in Štiřín as a sixteen-year-old orphan passionately interested in art.[11]

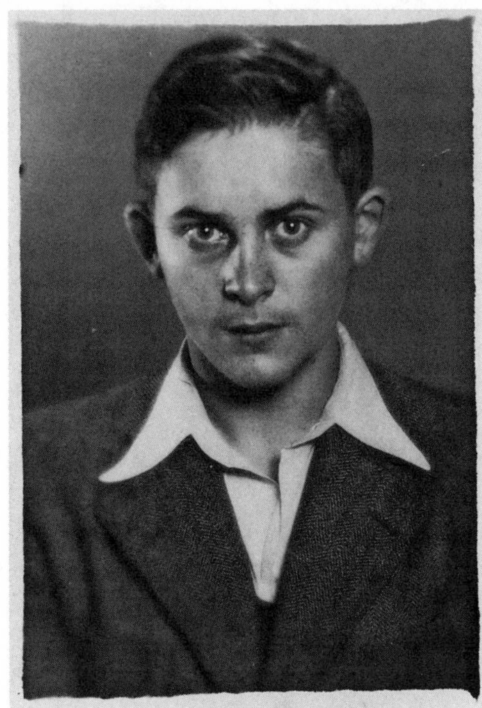

Yehuda Bacon, 1945. Credit: The Estate of H. G. Adler 2019, Deutsches Literaturarchiv Marbach.

Adler noticed his talent for drawing and began talking to Bacon about painting and how to learn from great art. "He was my salvation," Yehuda recalls. "He devoted time to me and introduced me to Prague. He took me to a museum and made me stop as I rushed past the paintings. 'Stand in front of a painting and look at it for a minimum of fifteen minutes!' he told me, and I remember doing that with El Greco's 'Head of Christ'. He also took me to meet and take free lessons with Willi Nowak, the Secretary of the Academy of Art, and he later wrote to Max Brod and Hugo Bergmann in Israel on my behalf." Bacon also recalled a lunch in Štiřín at which a devout Jewish boy named Wolfgang Sinai Adler (no relation) was reprimanded by Pitter for not removing his hat while eating. "It was Günther who quietly took Pitter aside and explained that, as the son of a rabbi, he was only observing Jewish custom by covering his head, for he had no yarmulke. Twenty-five years later, when Pitter visited Israel he happened to meet Wolfi Adler, recognized him, and asked his forgiveness."[12]

Bacon emigrated to Palestine in 1946, but he and Adler remained lifelong friends in much the same way that Günther had been befriended by Emil Vogel in the Pfadfinder.[13] Vogel served as the head physician for all five of the refugee centers and was a childhood friend of Pitter as well. Deported by the Nazis to Łódź in 1941, he was one of the few who survived the ghetto, and like Adler he had returned to Prague a near skeleton, his wife having died in the firebombing of Dresden.[14] Štiřín was as much a restorative sanctuary for those who worked there as it was for the children they tended. The work reminded them what it meant to be a human being and to care for others, especially at a time when few in Czechoslovakia were ready to extend compassion to German nationals, Jewish or not. "To love your enemy" was the credo at the center of Pitter's consciousness. After being persecuted by the Communists and fleeing Czechoslovakia for Germany in 1951, he continued to uphold this deep sense of charity. For the next ten years he tirelessly ran a camp near Nürnberg for refugees from Communist countries that at its height held four thousand people living in terrible conditions.[15] Many were touched by his selfless idealism, and by that of Olga Fierz, his partner in running the centers in Czechoslovakia and Germany. Both were later named by Yad Vashem as among the "Righteous Among Nations."[16]

With his modest salary at Štiřín and additional income at the Jewish Museum starting in October, Günther could at least tell Bettina in November that his immediate material needs were met. For the first time in years he could count on a certain amount of food, warmth, and decent clothing. This did not mean life was free and easy. Holding two jobs kept him occupied completely, as did the demands of setting up day-to-day life again, with no end of government offices to visit and forms to fill out to reestablish residency and try to claim whatever was left of his father's estate. Steiner had also asked him to help recover whatever remained of his own inheritance, so during lunch breaks or after work at the museum, Günther was busy.[17] This did not stop him from starting on his scholarly study of Theresienstadt or writing essays, poetry, and fiction. With Helmut Spiesmayr having died in the war and Peter Brömse in Germany, his former literary circle was gone, but he formed a new one with the poet Peter Demetz, the painter Oswald Stein, and a nephew of his old boss at the Urania, Otto Fischer. Meeting at Suse Tieze's apartment, they read their work to each other, as well as the English poets Stephen Spender, Wilfred Owen, and T. S. Eliot. Stein, who had met Steiner in Oxford, also shared with the group the latter's poems, and the response was so strong that Suse Tieze sent them on to her husband Willi Sattler in Munich in the hopes that he might get them published in the *Neue Zeitung*, where he worked.[18]

Beyond the vital correspondence with Bettina and Steiner, there was also no end of letters to write in trying to find or reconnect with friends and colleagues, to track down what had happened with his library in Palestine, and to figure out what had become of his father's stamp collection and what it was worth. With his library, Adler was soon disappointed, but in late November he learned that the stamps held by a second cousin in London were worth £350 (well over £10,000 today). Those that traveled to America with his Aunt Pepa would fetch him $100 (around $1,300 now).[19] Both were substantial sums and meant that, if Adler could make it to England or the States, he would have something to live on while trying to secure a livelihood. The demands of postwar life in Prague, however, rather than trepidation or second thoughts, sometimes caused him delays in answering Bettina's letters. That his letters tended to run to several pages and often thousands of words meant that sitting down to write to her meant more than jotting off a simple note about the weather or matters at work. To win her interest and affection from afar, he thought the task required a rendering of his soul.

Adler's work at the Jewish Museum during the day was both interesting and taxing. Initially given the task of sorting mounds of books left behind by those who had died, he was in some ways back where he was before being deported, working in the book repository of the Jewish Community of Prague. The bizarre mission for the Jewish Museum agreed to by Eichmann's subaltern Hans Günther meant that the macabre dioramas with life-size mannequins depicting religious rites and scenes of Jewish family life were still on display in the Klausen Synagogue, even though the community had been essentially wiped out.[20] For many years the assumption was that the Nazis had taken over the Jewish Museum in 1941 in order to found a "Museum of an Exterminated Race," although no documentation has surfaced to support this. No matter the motive, control of the museum under Hans Günther between 1941 and 1945 was superseded by the careful work of a different Hans Günther (Adler) who, along with others, was dedicated to saving all that could be saved and telling the story of all that had been lost, no matter how disturbing it was to live among the vestiges of the dead.

The director of the museum, Hana Volavková, was the force behind the project, for she saw that if the Jewish community was ever to rebuild itself, it would be on the roots of its culture and its past. Adler augmented this vision in a crucial way by proposing that the museum collect and catalog documents and materials from Theresienstadt. Zeev Shek, a survivor of Theresienstadt and Auschwitz, and later Israeli ambassador to London, had collected and hidden documents already in Theresienstadt. After the war, he headed the Documentation Commission of the Czech Jewish Agency that tried to rescue as many records as possible once the ghetto was liberated. Some copies of this material were deposited in the museum in Prague, but most of the material ended up in Yad Vashem after Shek emigrated to Palestine in 1946. Adler saw the value in what had been left behind and in the host of other documents, objects, and materials amassed through liquidation and personally processed and cataloged over ten thousand documents that illustrated the social workings and history of the ghetto. In proposing to Volavková that these materials be preserved, he created the foundation of the ghetto's archive that is now housed in both Prague and Theresienstadt.[21]

After Shek's emigration, Adler insisted that the collection be expanded beyond Shek's interest in Zionist resistance and good works in the face of oppression. On several trips to Theresienstadt he gathered more items and urged the museum to preserve the work of the artists imprisoned there, helping to organize a show of Otto Ungar's paintings and drawings in 1946. In November 1946, in consultation with Emil Utitz, Adler drew up a questionnaire in Czech and German that asked survivors at home and abroad about their experience. Although it was never sent out, it testifies to his plan to garner as full a history as possible.[22] The urge that had led him to amass his own set of documents and notes in Theresienstadt, stored in the suitcase he entrusted to Leo Baeck, and to write a book from them, inspired Adler to help set up a catalog of an exterminated race, but for reasons entirely different than the obsessions of his Nazi namesake.

Adler never lost sight of the circumstances that generated these materials or the millions of lost lives attached to them. Writing to Bettina in December, he described feeling like "a miner digging amid the books that have been stowed in our cellar, as if deposited there, and which I hope to now save and put into some kind of order. I like doing this, for I feel an inner bond with all these mishandled objects whose rightful owners were for the most part murdered, while a smaller number ended up scattered across the planet. It's like a bittersweet epilogue to all that's come before. And there amid the isolation and inadequate light of the cellar it feels like a kind of promise. And a sense of deep devotion comes over me."[23]

Arthur Landau, the protagonist of Adler's 1956 novel *The Wall*, sums up the burden he feels cataloguing paintings and prayer books in his work at a postwar museum that is a stand-in for the Jewish Museum in Prague. Reprimanded for thinking of the portraits of the dead as "patients," he says to his colleagues:

> We are remnant survivors, who are there for all who are not. That's true in general; the living are there for the dead, for their predecessors, and thus we also represent the history of the dead. How difficult it is, then, to exist as oneself when we are history, so much history! You know what I mean, those of whom not a trace . . . We are the history of the exterminated, the history of the shadow that consumed them. And we collect what was stolen from them, what we can store up of their remains. But that is indeed alive and really not history. It amounts to neither memory or keepsakes; it is commemoration.[24]

Much like Landau, Adler was both a preservationist and a mortician handling the objects of the dead, embracing this work for the purposes of life and the future.

Still, Adler's singular goal was to find a way to get out of Prague and begin a career elsewhere. His work at the museum could have provided a launching pad, for he was good at it and he received a raise after just over a year.[25] But Adler saw early on that Prague was no longer a city in which he could live and that

Czechoslovakia was headed for trouble. Most disturbing was the vengeance the Czechoslovakians unleashed against their own countrymen, for anyone who had any connection to German language, culture, or ancestry was suspect. On May 14, 1945, soon after the liberation of Prague, Prime Minister Zdeněk Fierlinger had called for "cleansing" the country of Germans, and three days later the National Social Party (*not* the Nazi Party) demanded that all Germans be sent "Heim ins Reich" (home to the Reich).[26] The Germans were helpless amid the backlash as bands of Czechoslovak partisans and vigilantes shot former Nazis on sight and brutalized German nationals.

Law soon supported them. President Edvard Beneš decreed on May 19 that the property of Germans, Hungarians, traitors, and collaborators would be taken by the state. June brought the expropriation of land, even if owned and lived on by families long before the war, and Czechs and Slovaks gained ownership of it in July. Germans and Hungarians living in Czechoslovakia were stripped of their citizenship in August and forced to hand over all moveable goods to the state in October, the same month in which all German institutions of higher education, including the German University of Prague, Adler's alma mater, were closed. In December 1946, Foreign Minister Jan Masaryk reported that 2,256,000 Germans had been expelled or murdered since August 1945, a figure that does not include the estimated 600,000 who had been pushed out by vigilantes.[27] While the Nazi invasion and takeover of 1938–1939 had severed the complex yet enriching Czechoslovak–German relations that had fed a vibrant culture for over three hundred years, retaliatory measures by the Czechoslovakians in 1945–1946 wiped out that culture for good.

"Oh the de-Germanization that's happening here!" Adler wrote to Steiner in January 1946. "It's a full blast of mean-spiritedness that can only be seen as strangely comic."[28] He knew the forced deportation of three million German nationals, and the murder of many others, was no laughing matter, and there was a disturbing irony in the fact that František Wagner, the ex-husband of Gisa, was loaded onto a train in March 1946 and shipped to Germany empty-handed.[29] Despite suing Wagner to recover some of the furniture left behind by his father and Gisa, Adler got none of it. The only solace was that it would have mattered little, for his sights were set on leaving Prague as fast as possible.

Bettina was his best hope, for her capable and supportive nature was better suited to the task than was Steiner's. Canetti, meanwhile, did not respond at all, which hurt Adler deeply. "Canetti and his wife (though I still treasure them both) are not true friends," he complained to Steiner. "If after many years I learned that my friend had come through the Nazi slaughterhouse, I wouldn't hesitate for a second to help him."[30] The Canettis, however, were not in central London, but in Amersham, north of the city. Elias Canetti was consumed by the research and writing for his 1960 study *Masse und Macht* (*Crowds and Power*), and his wife,

Veza, was most often the one to correspond on his behalf, adding a further remove. Both Steiner and Canetti were in a position to provide more engaged assistance to their friend, and Steiner did correspond at length with Adler, but it was easier to stick to the discussion of poems and stories, evolving thoughts on Judaism, news of friends and colleagues still turning up after the war, and steps necessary to navigate bureaucratic hurdles while trying to lay claim to whatever family property and savings they could.

Adler, however, knew he was in real danger, for as early as August 1945 he foresaw the impending Communist coup.[31] The Russians had liberated the country and it remained in their sphere after the Yalta Agreement ironed out by Stalin, Churchill, and Roosevelt, and the Czechs themselves were overwhelmingly pro-Communist. Adler warned of the eventuality of such a takeover and he knew himself to be in danger as a camp survivor, for many ended up going from the camps to the Communist prisons. The poet known as "Sonka" (Hugo Sonnenschein) was a case in point. Although having spent two years in Auschwitz, he was accused of having collaborated with the state police during the war and was sentenced to twenty years in prison, where he died in 1953.

Besides being a potential source of emotional support if he were to emigrate, Bettina stood for life itself. "I am alive again," he tells her in one letter, "I am alive not only in terms of the spirit that I never let be extinguished in the hardest of times, I am once again alive within the world and am 'no longer lost to the world.'"[32] A week later he proclaims, "I am no longer an object, not just a bloodless thought who at best could be reduced to a crystal, but instead . . . I am present in that magically blessed and sun-drenched mixture of pain and joy in which a person becomes a person."[33] Nor was her ability to listen to him and to care the only thing he sought:

> Through your letters, your endlessly valuable encouragement, I can slowly begin to bridge the terrible gulf that separates me from this other world that I would love to experience so much of, and from which I have been separated so horribly and what seems at times almost irrevocably. But believe me, my dear, that is not all that you mean to me. No, such an idea wouldn't even occur to me. You mean much, much more to me! And it is only a special bit of grace that in this case the two are bound up with one another. It feels to me as if you came along and extinguished my past and then immersed it in a warm forgiving light. For this feeling alone I want you to know how grateful I am, even if I were to do wrong and no longer meant anything to you.[34]

Adler was well aware of the burden he was placing on Bettina, and he made clear that she should feel free to turn away and live whatever life she wished on her own terms, that she owed him nothing. Defending his need to declare his passion, he does not want her to feel trapped by it:

> I really have the ability to pass by like a silent pilgrim who only once takes a chance and says something—and he must take that chance—before disappearing into thin air. . . . I have taken a hard look at myself and asked myself if I am simply being impulsive, if I have simply succumbed to an almost timeless despair. Yet that is not the case at all . . . [H]ow easy it is for people to deceive themselves, but I don't believe I am doing that at all. The feeling runs too deep, is too immediate. But I have it under control, and completely within my power. For how can I behave recklessly? I indeed have a responsibility to my past, as well as to the mission that almost certainly awaits me. And in those matters I am cool and calculating.

Stoic, willing to go it alone, Adler reminds Bettina of his passion for her and his commitment to serve those who had died. Speculating whether he might be so fortunate as to become the "husband and brother, lover and friend" of a certain "touching woman," no matter how "solicitous" it might seem to pose such an "imposition," makes clear his mounting intentions and how much rested on her response.[35]

Knowingly or unknowingly, in a two-page letter to Bettina dated December 12, Adler raises the intensity when he explains at length the existential conditions of the camps and what it took to survive them:

> The soul can withstand anything as long as the soul does not give up, even when the body is abused and in fact experiences the very limits of the physiological-biological conditions needed to sustain life without actually being killed. Short of these limits one can appreciate the soul's capacity to endure the worst kinds of suffering and deprivation, however limitless, especially when it is singularly determined to protect itself. One saw in the camps people who for no visible reason, and without having been severely abused nor sick nor suffering great deprivation, suddenly collapsed and fell to the ground before suddenly slipping away. In such circumstances without fail an experienced eye could see: he will not make it, in a week or less he will be gone.

Changing hardly a word, on the same day Adler retyped this letter as an essay titled "Nach der Befreiung—ein Wort an die Mitwelt" ("After the Liberation—A Message to the World"). Part torch song, part manifesto, and what no doubt felt like a gauntlet thrown down to Bettina, the letter and the essay function as foundational documents outlining what Adler hoped to accomplish as a writer and scholar. Bettina's desire to understand what Günther had survived had served as a catalyst for him to explain the essence of his experience to those who had not been through it. At the end of the essay Adler speaks for the survivors:

> Not what we have suffered, but what we have come to understand must be heard and understood, for here lies the problem and indeed the gain to be had for us, the world, and also much more. It does not lie with us alone as to whether our task will be taken up and appreciated. What matters is to show the world that our time in the inferno of the camps was not in vain and did not hinder the advancement of humankind, that something can be formed out of this last darkness that may indeed become light. What this requires is that we have to say what happened to us, though not through sentimental portrayals aimed at making others feel sorry for us, even if we do have to serve it up ourselves. But from the world we expect that it will also be willing to listen to us and grant our words and acts the attention and regard which we do not necessarily want for our sufferings, but rather for the experiences born out of this calamity and the works dedicated to conveying it.[36]

After a matter of weeks, the relationship with Bettina represented the possibility of his own salvation, and what he could do to seek justice for those who had been lost, by saying what had indeed happened to them.

In a note that accompanied his essay-like letter from December 12, Adler tells Bettina:

> What I am sending to you today was in fact written first and foremost as a letter to you, but in the course of writing it I also began to realize that it might be useful for others to know about as well. Hence I would not only be willing for you to show it to others, but I would even welcome it, if you were so inclined, nor would I have anything against it being published in translation or in the original. I'll leave it to your discretion and wisdom. One could title it "Concentration Camps and Character—A Message to the World."

That the title is slightly different than the version he typed as an essay argues that most likely the essay indeed began as a letter, showing again that Bettina helped him regain his footing in the world as a writer and intellectual. "I feel you more strongly and more genuinely than ever. You fill me with such joy. You dear creature!" ends the card. This same buoyant warmth had spurred him to take confidence in his observations about what it took to survive and the need to write them down, which meant that he had indeed survived in the most important way of all.

Sending the essay to Bettina and granting permission for her to send it to others or have it published marked an important turn in their relationship. As he had needed to place Bettina on the ramp with him watching Gertrud walk away with her mother in Auschwitz, he now needed her to join him in acknowledging "what we have come to understand must be heard" by taking in his letter and helping to disseminate it as an essay. Whether she knew it or not, this made her a partner in his project from the start, which made their relationship more than a romance and more than an arrangement to help him emigrate. They would "pursue their emerging love without repressing the inheritance of the Shoah," making their correspondence almost unique in the vast literature of the Holocaust.[37] Sending her the essay, he writes, "I believe you, Bettina, and perhaps you believe me as well. How lovely it would be to be together. And perhaps you not only believe me and in me, but also what can become of others through me, and in my future, which must and should be about more than my miserable little self, which in my view has been given a task that must be upheld and fulfilled, because it involves entirely a duty and a sacrifice."[38]

If Bettina had any doubts about what she was being asked to take on, she no longer did. Günther began to describe life in the camps in more specific terms, something that she increasingly was interested in learning about. Until this point he had remained cautious, not wanting to overwhelm her with the horrors, no doubt also not wanting her to see him as irreparably damaged. He also wished to describe it without falling into "sentimental portrayals" or trying to gain sympathy for himself. "[A]ny mere report alone says little," he tells her, "and seems to me a desecration of that which only through conscious shaping can gain the dignity which alone can spare me the shame of having survived such disgrace and degradation, especially since such distress might not only cause me pain, but also because I must try to formulate finely-tuned insights into it all."[39] He had a deep sense of the ethical difficulties that needed to be navigated in venturing any account of what he had survived, but he also knew that only a careful rendering of his experience in literature and scholarship would do it justice. Yet a few lines later he launches into a detailed account of the horrors of Auschwitz and Langenstein that culminates in asking her again to stand in his shoes, writing,

> Just imagine, you are yourself half-starved, crawling with lice and filthy, tired and feeling faint, and all around you can be heard the cries of the most pathetic misery as each day masses of people die over whose bodies you trip, as you notice how they have been literally beaten and also desecrated, as well as robbed, and how they have been forced to do deadly work that even a healthy and well-fed person could not stand to do, while you have to look on and can do nothing at all.

Few writers have produced in one sentence as powerful a depiction of what it was like for body and soul to live through it all; the effect on Bettina's must have been overwhelming.

As if needing to expound such horrors in all their rawness, Adler ends two pages of graphic details of the camps with two larger insights. The first is personal, as he admits, "Bettina, when I actually think about what I survived and had to watch in Auschwitz and Langenstein, then sometimes I am better able to deal with the thought that Geraldine and many others who were not cut out for such things at least disappeared before having to witness this last phase of Hell." The second, however, is more far-reaching and historical, if not more "finely-tuned," as he states, "The torments under Hitler were a constant crescendo, in which for a moment a diminuendo occurred, followed immediately again by a sforzando, after which the crescendo rose again." Reaching back to his work in musicology, Adler elevates his report to a sweeping observation. But whereas the earlier account was too grotesque to be scholarly, and the gratitude for Geraldine and others not having to suffer the worst was too personal, the extended metaphor of this last observation provides an operatic view of Hitler's rise to power that, although supported by historians decades later, was a first for its time.[40] By writing his way through Bettina to the past, Adler expunges the raw material of his suffering, as well as granting it the moral shape and acumen needed for a broader historical audience. Formulating a description of what had happened to him individually, he captures what had happened in Germany and Europe collectively, but through the kind of perspective whose development normally requires decades of scholarly study and reflection.

Adler's very next letter to her, written four days later, consists of a six-page account of the day-to-day privation and persecution imposed on the Jews of Prague by the Nazis between 1939 and 1941, the bulk of which later becomes the first chapter of his monograph on Theresienstadt. In his letters to Bettina he is "drafting" all the time, and her role as interlocutor and audience was as important as his own ability to provide her a means of witnessing what she had not witnessed but nevertheless was haunted by each day.[41] Nurtured by love, founded on tragedy, their partnership was ideally suited to ensure that "What happened *must not* be forgotten; the harvest must be brought home."[42] This in turn deepened the bond between them, as Adler admitted, "I see the horrors of Auschwitz and experience the awful memory of it—and yet feel all the closer to you."[43] To this Bettina responds, "It is awful, and yet somehow relieving. . . . It is as if indeed such an intricately detailed portrait can only be formulated somewhere between our own escape and the suffering you all experienced, and only through hearing such unspeakable suffering can we understand the greatness of those who suffered."[44] Although the burden to tell what had happened rested on Günther, Bettina's empathy from afar helped to coax it into print.

H. G. Adler, 1946. Credit: The Estate of H. G. Adler 2019, Deutsches Literaturarchiv Marbach.

Still, there was one crucial impediment to the realization of their reciprocal relation, and Bettina above all appreciated it. "How can we size up one another and know what each is about without being physically near one another?"[45] Given what Günther was implying about the potential bond between them, the distance and the difficulty of crossing it was a catalyst for doubt. Bettina agreed in early December to visit Prague as soon as possible, but both knew it would take several months to arrange for a visa and transportation, nor could she easily leave her job at the button factory. "The day snuffs out my feelings, reality destroys my dreams," laments Bettina, and she remains concerned that, despite wanting to be there for him, she will disappoint him or they will find that they have nothing in common. Adler encourages her to take confidence, but often in the early letters his passion and optimism are met by her trepidation and worry. "You know little of my shortcomings, and I know little of your virtues," she writes. "I was strong when I first wrote to you. Then your wild words made me weak . . . What if they are only words and feelings, which only give rise to words and feelings without taking into account the hardness, the disparity, and the brunt force of reality?"[46] Adler answers, "I have courage and am not afraid of reality. For what are we? We shape reality, we form it. What do I have to be afraid of?" Brazen words, perhaps, from someone whom external forces had tried to brutally shape and control for the last seven years. And yet that first essay, "After the Liberation," written just six months after returning to Prague, states his case. He will not simply give in and collapse, nor is there any need for her to either. All he can do is to convince her that "perhaps I can show you a way out, a path that you can take, but which you certainly must not feel forced to take. It stands open before you."[47]

"Günther, what have you done? You say that we are engaged—yet you haven't even asked me, but just assumed it as self-evident and thus have touched upon my innermost thoughts. I have not been myself since yesterday evening. You have unleashed a subterranean current that has carried me away entirely. I know these depths, the full surrender of myself—it's that which has made me so anxious, as you have seen—no matter the many miles between us. And now I am yours entirely."[48]

Ten weeks was all that it took for Günther to realize that he and Bettina belonged together and that it only made sense for them to marry. But as she states with a mixture of shock and delight, he had not asked her. He had hinted at the question for weeks, and so had she. Writing to him the day before New Year's Eve, she responded to a batch of his poems and his hopes of getting them published by wondering whether "it might not be easier to tackle it all as two" rather than as one.[49] What she probably did not remember, or Günther may not have appreciated, was that seven years before on New Year's Eve he had first met Gertrud. It must have been a reflective time for him, and the fact that he spent the New Year helping to entertain the children in Štiřín reminded him where he had been and where he needed to go. Looking out at the snow-covered countryside and writing to Bettina at the same time she was writing to him about things going better for two, he notes, "I feel so strange. Deep and stirring thoughts move about inside me. If I were to step out into the dark I would be surrounded by an incredible stillness. . . . And yet I cannot suppress a certain excitement within me. . . . I long for complete peace, but I know that it cannot exist. Such a wish is selfish and must remain hidden. And so it is all swallowed in with one great breath that contains our secret."[50]

What that "secret" is he does not explain. One week later, having returned from Štiřín the day before, he writes her an eight-page letter that cuts to the heart of the matter: "Do you wish to live with me in England, or the USA, or somewhere else?"[51] Posed as a question of logistics, rather than a marriage proposal, his tone is more an assumption, for he admits, "I should have written all this from the heart. You'll have to forgive me if it comes off as so hasty and urgent, but the situation requires it." A letter he had received from the Reders in which they said how much they and the Oppens wanted to help him get to the United States forced the question of where they might live and what plans they needed to set in motion. "Do you, my dear, have it within you to say a happy and joyful yes if I were to ask if you, God willing and to the extent He will bless our hopes and aspirations, to stand by my side and walk with me as my wife into the future?" That he poses this as a query if she would say yes, rather than directly asking if she will marry him, suggests that the question did not need to be asked, but that he could not risk an answer either. Asking Bettina to marry him carried the chance that she might say no, and that would have been too much to take, since his life and work depended on their being together. Fortunately, she felt the same, adding, "My only love! I will give myself over to your protection, and embrace the spirit these new depths will release within me."[52]

There remained much to do to make it happen. The next day Bettina wrote to a friend in London to ask what was needed to arrange for a visa for Günther. She wrote to Reder and his wife in America to follow up on the help they had offered, although she remained convinced that the best first step would be for Günther to come to England so that they could marry. It was clear to Adler that "the continent and especially Central Europe are simply no place for us. Here the culture, or at least what we recognized as such, is no more."[53] Another possibility was Palestine, but Adler felt that "no matter our Jewish sympathies and the possible appeal and employment of what we might have to offer, it's not for me." Writing to Yehuda Bacon, Adler made clear that "I'm greatly worried about the future of Palestine. We [the Jews] should not follow the lead of others and do bad things, but instead think of our great past in order to maintain the spirit of Judaism."[54] What Adler feared in the founding of Israel was the grip of Zionist ideology. "Our people should have no ideology, for ideology kills people. We saw it with the Germans and with many other nations, and now we see it with the Communists."[55] For him, the departure of the British would provide "no solution and no improvement for the Jewish situation in Palestine or the world" and would cause "many people to die miserably, while Jewish nationalism, which is no better than any other and had made the same mistakes as fascism and socialism, and repeated them as well, can bring neither peace nor a healthy foundation on which to build."[56] At the heart of such views lay Adler's conviction that "the home of the Jews should be the world" and that "a Jew [should never] really feel at home except in the hand of God and within himself."[57] This meant that "wherever I am, I am at home," although put another way, Adler also felt "someone like me indeed belongs nowhere."[58]

But somewhere it had to be, and the best options were England or America. Bettina spoke of how friendly, fair, and open she found the culture of England and South Wales, but Günther was still suspicious of the British government having turned away so many Jews before the war, and he worried that the country had suffered too much deprivation. America was far richer, but he was convinced that the United States was the next place where anti-Semitism would rear its head, since so many Jews had emigrated there. No matter where they might land, he knew one thing: "We must live for one another, and these days that's a great deal in itself."[59]

Their letters over the next weeks and months increasingly concern themselves with plans for getting Günther out of Prague and finalizing plans for Bettina to visit in June 1946. Having moved in January to Havličkova 38, just down the street from his father's former business, Adler continued to share details of his camp experience, even sending a yellow star, an example of Theresienstadt "money," and several ghetto documents he had collected.[60] His work in the Jewish Museum allowed him access to many documents, drawings, paintings, and photographs left behind, and he shared his wonder and despair at such archival material, making vivid to Bettina the experience of the camps. It took time to arrange her visit to Prague, so their correspondence allowed them to further get to know each other as Adler ranged over thoughts on Judaism, the rise of the Communists in Czechoslovakia, what it meant to have survived, his hopes for publication, his curiosity and reservations about life in England, and his continued attraction to starting anew in America. Throughout all of this Adler maintained a balance between telling her of all he had been through and reassuring her that he was at last free of it. "Don't worry," he says. "I will not drown in the past, no matter how much I will always know it and now and then research and attest to it with nothing less than scholarly diligence. . . . But I can only live for today, and that means with you, my dear friend."[61]

"Geraldine," however, remains an ominous and unspoken presence. She never quite leaves the letters. Thinking about the difficulties of survival or the camps themselves, Adler alludes to her by recalling something she said or did, or noting that he will always seek to preserve her memory. He had plans to publish a book containing her letters, testimonials from her friends, and drawings of the dried leaves she loved to include in letters, which he wished to title *Geraldine—A Life in Letters and Leaves*.[62] Bettina maintains her equanimity, understanding how Gertrud was not only the love of his earlier life but in many ways the symbol of what he had lost. Her handling of Gertrud evolves over time. "I don't dare speak of your wife," she tells him early on,[63] but after reading some of his poems from Theresienstadt she admits "they contain a charm that seems completely unfathomable, and which I think I am right to guess has to do with Geraldine. How you loved her so!"[64] Acknowledging their engagement, Bettina is confident enough in their relation to say that she could never mind hearing of her, for it reassures her of his "great loyalty and love—and why should I wish that only for myself and not begrudge it to another?"[65]

But Geraldine is always present, even in Adler's eight-page letter suggesting marriage. A few lines after telling Bettina that "now the waiting is over, I will take you in and offer a home for your soul, a refuge for distress, and an anchor for your hopes," he confesses:

> Geraldine's death was such a great loss. I was perhaps immature, for she was certainly much more mature and also richer than me, but her vital essence was already broken when we first grew close to one another. She knew it, I felt it, and both suffered continually because of it in a number of different ways. The poor thing always said to me: "Things will never be lovely again!" But I am alive, and I bless the ever precious and sacred thought of her, for she was the most decent person I indeed ever met in my life, though she was also perhaps the most difficult character I ever encountered, her ethical standards being higher than a host of extraordinary people I have known.[66]

Adler's further jubilation, "I am alive: IT IS WONDERFUL!" is a way of saying that Geraldine is truly gone and that he has found new life in Bettina, but his first wife's presence casts a long shadow. Gertrud embodied all that could not be retrieved for either of them, and for Adler to entirely let her go would have meant a betrayal he could not face. For Bettina to ask him to do so would have meant both a betrayal of Günther and his project, as well as betraying her mother and the memory she wished to honor through their partnership. Gertrud represented both all that they were and all that they could never be.

Bettina's visit to Prague in June 1946 was a step forward. It was crucial that they begin the bureaucratic process necessary to secure a visa but most important was the chance to see each other face to face. "It's a different journey than in the gloomy days of December 20, 1938," he tells her in a note just before her return to Prague on June 14. "I will smile at you in such a way that you won't even recognize me, neither the old Günther nor the H. G. A. of the letters. It will be a different, a 'new' man."[67] In "Der Besuch" ("The Visit"), a barely fictional account of Bettina's arrival and his own anxiety about it, Adler wonders, "Will I only represent the past to her? An awful and tragic past that she believed she had escaped, even if I was the one who urged her to flee, and even ordered her to? Will she approve of me? And will she be able to accept my past. What do I have to offer her? And what will she offer me?" Although Adler chronicled the three-week visit in detail as an outline for a longer story, it breaks off after the arrival of "Clarissa," who like Bettina, brings with her a baby whose refugee parents had died and whom she had arranged to return to its family in Prague. Symbolic of a life reborn, Bettina handed the infant over to the weeping relatives, then turned to kiss Günther and accept the roses he had brought.[68]

The itinerary Günther set carefully charted landmarks of the past, as well as giving them time alone to shape their future. Bettina spent a few days visiting her family's former housekeeper, seeing her cousin Peter Slotty, and visiting the painter Willi Nowak, which powerfully recalled her childhood, her family, and her aspirations as an artist. Not wanting to dwell on the past, Adler whisked her off to visit his friend Stephan Zaplethal in Leitmeritz, where they had their first chance to be alone. After two days there they visited her uncle in Reichenberg, then three days with her friend Gertrud Hönig in Choceň. Back in Prague she met Suse Tieze, who remained a friend of both Bettina and Günther after emigrating to England in 1949. A day-trip to Štiřín and visits to the Jewish Museum filled out Adler's current life, while three days walking in the Bohemian Forest returned them to a landscape they both loved and grew up in, the place also that Günther identified most with Gertrud.

On long hikes over three days through the forests and mountains surrounding Dörrstein, Spitzberg, and Eisenstein—some of the most beautiful countryside in Europe—the couple were at last able to be together in the present. Their wanderings also deeply reconnected them to the past. For Bettina that meant the love of nature and the landscape her parents had known in their own early days together, which she grew up in as a child and had sketched as a young artist. For Adler these were the hills and valleys he loved to read about in Adalbert Stifter's novels and stories, close to Bettina's heart as well. He had crisscrossed this countryside with Steiner, Emil Vogel, and the other Pfadfinder during his formative years, and of course with Gertrud before the war. And yet the trip allowed them to fuse their separate pasts into a shared present. "I am yours only," Adler had written in "Zur Begrüssung" ("Greeting"), a poem that he sent to Bettina before she left England. "And as you rest / with me in loving devotion / You are mine. And what you do / And what I do with you amounts to *one* life."[69] Bridging the past and future, Bettina's trip to Prague accomplished this for them both.

Which is why Adler was stunned when, in a letter to him in early September 1946, Bettina suddenly called into question their entire relationship. "I took my ring off my finger early this morning," she announced. "Nothing, nothing in your words indicates that you are at all emotionally ready to face the demands of a new life."[70] She accuses him of refusing to learn English, relying too much on her to work out the logistics of getting him out of Czechoslovakia, and not working hard enough "to free your prose from the clutches of irony and make it more plain and readable." It is not only the burden she carries that bothers her; she also finds him too "cold and hard," despite her efforts to warm his heart through tenderness. "I still know the sweetness of your lips and the softness of your hands. But I still do not know the complete absorption in one another that we both craved. For you are still hard and inflexible. And without a trace of mildness." Needing him to understand that she has a life as well, she explains that she is ready to be with him but that "you will never subdue my soul." A line had been drawn in the sand, but what had given rise to it was lost on Adler. A letter from her a week earlier lamented, "It is hard to be free with you when at the same time you keep pursuing your goals without considering my feelings," but it was nothing like this outburst.[71] "Why did you do this?" was all he could ask, although he conceded that "the question is pointless, for you don't know the answer yourself."[72]

Bettina knew all too well what had brought it on. Tommy Mandl and Steiner had paid her a visit in South Wales days before. Mandl had brought along greetings from Czechoslovakia and a cache of letters between Gertrud and Adler from before the war. Unable to rein in her curiosity, she read one of them. The power and depth of feeling it expressed sent her into a fit of jealous insecurity, and she sat down and wrote a four-page indictment of Günther's failings and posted it immediately.[73] The next day she regretted having sent it and wrote to beg his forgiveness, but the damage was done. Adler was deeply hurt and deeply confused, for he saw that, no matter what had prompted her, "this was not just criticism, nor was it just an angry outburst." "This was something that has much deeper roots," he told her, "and I neither recognize nor understand the ground that has nurtured them. . . . It has robbed me of the uninhibitedness and naiveté with which I accepted everything essential from you as welcome salvation, and about which I had no illusions. You have killed something inside me which I am now struggling to reawaken."[74]

Bettina conceded that seeing the letters to and from Gertrud was only a trigger for her ire, for underneath it lay the pressure of all that she was taking on in devoting herself to him. "It was a dread arising from this new trust, this new closeness, and the awareness of my own deep dependency on this feeling," she acknowledges.[75] Two days later she provides a deeper, more mortified, and more complicated analysis:

> Günther. I have bungled my life thus far. I know it doesn't look that way from the outside. But inside, where we are the most honest with ourselves, I know I have only tried and failed. Again and again so tough; again and again I cave in at the last moment. My art—if I had kept at it, perhaps God would have found a way to take care of my siblings. And Mother—I need not say a thing.[76]

Lovers quarrel, nor is it uncommon for someone to feel trepidation about an approaching marriage. But there is more going on here. Bettina feels she has "bungled" her life, as if every important choice she has made has been wrong, despite having behaved so responsibly for years in following her mother's wish that she emigrate to safety and watch over her grown siblings, and in having taken up Günther's cause so quickly and passionately. Not even having left her mother behind entirely explains this, nor her own self-doubt. What is at work is her feeling of having failed, of not having lived up to the ideal of the artist stretching back to Goethe and the Romantics, of having been forced to abandon artistic aspirations that she recognized as still within her.

Adler's response speaks to this when, in a letter suggesting they either stand by each other or part in peace, he asks:

> What shall I do? Can you feel the darkness that surrounds us everywhere, and how difficult it is to carry one's own lit torch through this night? It is a struggle. How hard it is to continue it. How unrelentingly our fate hangs over us, the desolate, and which we cannot escape. Because of this we should not make it hard on ourselves. We have to try to maintain peace within our inner selves in order to at least affirm one another. I'm not talking about what happened to me, or what happened to millions of others, nor even what happened to you. I'm talking about something much more powerful. About the forlorn fate of this generation from which no one has been able to free himself, since it is more powerful than the ability of the strongest human to oppose it. If we don't want to lay down our arms—and I certainly don't wish to—then we should not harm one another. Then we should not allow each other to act out of smallness and pettiness, which would prematurely render these weapons dull and ineffective before we have achieved the least thing and won, which would not mean having achieved what we need to, but rather to keep seeking, which in itself would allow us to maintain an edge. We must rise above the unworthy sentiments of our vanity, vulnerability, and low self-worth in order to not test our mutual trust in dangerous and hard-to-bear ways that will only exhaust us and grind us up. That's why you have to decide—yes or no.[77]

Adler proposes here an "either/or" on which depends the course of both their lives. Behind that, however, lies a grim exhaustion tied to the "fate [that] hangs over us, the desperate, and which we cannot escape." That fate is much larger than their own, and the battle they face will be one fought for a generation. And yet, because of such stakes, they must not harm each other, for only human care and tenderness can carry them, even if on separate courses.

Given the stark choice posed by Adler, one can sympathize with the pressure Bettina felt at the prospect of taking on such a mentality. In response she musters the hope that perhaps "we could forge a partnership in which one time one of us, and then another time the other takes over responsibility, leadership, and the work to be done" rather than one single-minded purpose.[78] And yet she felt, "You have not woken an easy joy with easy means. With total sincerity you have prepared a blessedness whose fulfillment I await with devotion."[79] Shuttling between the need to remain "always independent" and feeling "gratitude for the chance to help you,"[80] her willingness to commit to what she knew would be a demanding and complicated partnership was neither blind love nor submission but a clear-eyed choice to embrace a man for whom she felt great love and tenderness, whose project she knew was theirs together—his for the way it would return him to life, hers for the chance to redeem what she had lost after having escaped. "You need me next to you. Not under you," she wrote.[81] He responds, "Nothing is certain with me. This I have never hid, never glossed over. I know so myself, and you know it well enough as well. I am a person in danger and a dangerous person."[82]

As painful as the episode was, it enabled both to articulate what was at stake for each other in facing the future, and the challenges inherent to their relationship. It was Bettina, however, who had to make the biggest leap of faith, and her willingness to look past differences in their temperaments that carried the day, for she was in the better position to refuse it all and turn away. She found a balance and concluded, "It took the awful shock of these last days to show me: I do trust you . . . A trust forged by our common roots, people and things we both know. Yet different in almost every other relation. Franz and Tommy's visit again made that clear. And to make a home with you is what I still desire."[83]

Nor did it hurt that he had sent flowers. Returning to Prague from a weekend visit to Stephan Zaplethal in Leitmeritz after asking her to make up her mind, yes or no, Adler ordered a bouquet of roses and carnations that were brought to her in South Wales from London.[84] In the same charmed way that the two of them had somehow reached out to each other nearly a year before, her letters asking forgiveness crossed his, while in the interim each came to recognize that there was no turning back and that their love for one another meant everything.

If they needed any reminder of the practical concerns underlying their negotiations, one arrived on Adler's doorstep as a summons from the police to question him about his Jewish and German heritage, his experience in the war, and his plans for staying in Czechoslovakia.[85] They were trying to determine whether he should be classified as a former German national and whether he should be expelled like the rest. For the moment he could answer their concerns. His position at the Jewish Museum helped his claim of Jewish identity, although he knew that with the rise of the Communists his Jewish roots soon would be as suspect as his German ones. He was eager to emigrate and felt no regret in having to seek exile. Surveying the oppression of German nationals by the Czechoslovakians, the disappearance of the dynamic culture he had grown up in, and the continued persecution he saw as inevitable, he concluded, "I am completely done with this misery. I know it won't be easy for me and I will have to continually do battle, because I want to leave, and I must leave if I am not to perish. There is simply nothing more for me here. This I know inside. . . . Prague means my spiritual death, a living tomb."[86]

Without citizenship, however, he lacked standing to apply for foreign visas, and the Czechoslovakians would not grant him a passport. The Jewish Community of Prague was of little help, for they were powerless to perform a wedding for a noncitizen, suggesting only that he and Bettina marry in England.[87] To smooth over their relations after the near split in September, and to see if progress could be made securing a visa for Günther, Bettina returned in December, arriving on the 19th. With the support of Hana Volavková at the Jewish Museum, Adler had applied for a visa to England on the premise of needing to do research in the Wiener Library and to report on the collection of Theresienstadt materials he had archived in Prague.[88] Before Bettina arrived for her second visit he heard that he might be issued a Czechoslovakian passport good for six weeks in late January or early February.[89] Bettina stayed until January 6, but not until two weeks later did he write with the exciting news from the British Consulate that he had been granted a four-week visa and could fly to England as soon as he had settled his affairs in Prague and bought a ticket.[90] Knowing that he likely would never see Prague again, there were many goodbyes to say and the need to gather together as much as he could take with him. Ironically, it was the Jewish Museum, and what it embodied as a vestige of the many who had died, that made it possible for him to escape.

February 8, 1947, marked the fifth anniversary of his deportation to Theresienstadt, and Adler could not resist returning with Stephan Zaplethal on February 4 for a final visit to a place that had shaped his past but that he hoped to command through his work on it in the future. "The atmosphere still powerfully affected him [Stephan], while I looked on with cool interest at it all, as if it were Pompeii. I wanted above all to have a look at the place after it had in part been resettled as a town—one last time, in case I should in fact write about it. Indeed, my stay in that locale had also become its own allegory."[91] In his last real letter to Bettina before leaving for England, his cool bravado in returning to Theresienstadt marks his need to state that he had overcome his imprisonment and to reassure her that he would arrive in London free of the place. Both knew, however, that his life and writing would be consumed by it and that what he was really leaving was the isolation of Prague and the dead end it had become. "An important time in my life, April '45 until February '47," he reflected. "From death to a new life. Life with you."[92]

A week later, that new life began in earnest when at age thirty-six he boarded an airplane for the first time and flew, nervous and hopeful at once, to London and Bettina.

12

The Survivor

When Adler landed in London on February 11, 1947, he was met at Croydon Airport in a driving snowstorm by Bettina, Steiner, and Canetti.[1] Rather than being allowed to spend his first night with his fiancée, he was whisked off to dinner, hungry and exhausted, by Canetti and Steiner, who were eager to speak to him firsthand about Theresienstadt and the camps. He finally got some sleep in the apartment of Marie-Louise von Motesiczky, an exiled Austrian painter who was Canetti's lover, which accounts for his wife, Veza, not being there regardless of her and Adler's fondness for one another.[2] Canetti and Steiner had been in contact with Adler by letter for well over a year, yet seeing him came as a shock, as neither had expected he would survive. Heading off to a Chinese restaurant, their talk turned to their work. Canetti was in the thick of research and writing for his 1960 study *Crowds and Power*, and Steiner devoted himself to *A Comparative Study of the Forms of Slavery*, his dissertation at Oxford, which he completed in 1949, despite having lost all his notes and early drafts in a suitcase inadvertently switched for someone else's on the train between London and Oxford in 1942. Though Canetti and Steiner started their separate projects in 1939, Adler had with him the nearly finished first draft of *Theresienstadt 1941–1945*, which set him ahead of them in the completion of a major scholarly response to the Nazi cataclysm, Adler the only one of them to have experienced it directly.[3]

The gathering marked the first time Adler, Canetti, and Steiner were all together. Restoring their shared ties to a Central European intellectual tradition marked by debate and a deep sense of moral purpose, it also brought together scholarly and literary talents that were deeply interconnected. Canetti and Adler were novelists who had turned to sociological studies of political power gone awry. Canetti and Steiner wrote of their respective travels and cultural observations, while Adler and Steiner worked seriously as poets.[4] All three forged a "Gesamtkunstwerk" ("A Single Unified Work of Art"), a term coined by Richard Wagner and used by Jürgen Serke to describe Adler's accomplishment across several genres.[5] Moreover, their friendship fueled and shaped their intellects in important ways. Even before Adler arrived in England, he exchanged poems and vigorous commentary with Steiner. During the war Canetti and Steiner were close, Steiner's thinking on ethnology and myth becoming so influential that some think Canetti's *Crowds and Power* could not have been written without it.[6] Adler and Canetti would see each other often in London, and although Adler was five years younger, Canetti shared his private thoughts to such an extent that he would later say, somewhat self-servingly, that it was "a sign of my sympathy for him that I had to rein myself in and not tell him everything."[7] Looked at another way, however, it was Adler who told him "everything." Signing a 1962 first English edition of *Crowds and Power*, Canetti wrote: "To H. G. Adler who lived what I only thought."[8]

The ability to see and talk with each other helped alleviate the loss of the world they had left behind. Their rigorous and often volatile debates helped to differentiate their views and enriched their intellectual life beyond the reduced circumstances of their daily existence. Together they tapped anthropological approaches in new ways to reflect on the workings of power and composed literary works of the highest order, a rare combination. As Marcel Atze points out, Canetti and Steiner shared a "thoroughly problematic relationship with their own society," which resulted in their interest in different ethnic groups and ethnology. Adler was cast in an even more "problematic relationship" through imprisonment and enslavement but also employed anthropological practices to study and survive it.[9] Writers such as T. S. Eliot, Virginia Woolf, and W. H. Auden wrote essays and criticism, but none conducted the extended research and scholarship that Adler, Canetti, and Steiner did over decades while developing (or in Canetti's case resurrecting) their literary powers.

All three criticized what they saw as an imbalance within modern science and scholarship, its propensity for positivist, scientific rationalism that too often leads to a rejection of myth, magic, and imagination.[10] Born out of a Prague that embraced the uncanny and produced both *The Golem* and Kafka's otherworldly quotidian and saw Čapek's coining of the word "robot," Adler and Steiner were steeped in religion and myth and looked beyond historical events for deeper currents of thought and feeling. This filled a void for Canetti, whose distrust of the overly rationalist constructs of modern philosophy and psychology spurred him to understand the mythmaking at the heart of modern political power and its hold over the masses. Whereas Adler's prescription for battling the dehumanizing nature of the "masses" tapped a "radical Enlightenment" that replaced the crowd with "the ideal of 'humanity,' the idea of the 'Mensch,'" Canetti left behind past concepts in order to "re-work the whole tradition of crowd theory." Meanwhile, Adler cited Steiner's definition of slavery as "the exploitation of man by man with no contractual relationship" in his book on Theresienstadt.[11] Together the three not only worked out new ways of thinking about slavery, political power, and the Holocaust, but the cross-fertilization in their literary/scholarly enterprise introduced new approaches. What remained was to find a way to bring their work to the public.

Yet one cannot live on ideas alone. With the extreme loneliness he had felt in Prague and the difficulty he still had conveying his sufferings to Canetti and Steiner, Adler knew where his real future lay. The next day he headed for Merthyr Tydfil, and he and Bettina were married there on February 16 in the oldest purpose-built synagogue in Wales, the rabbi performing the wedding despite the banns not having been fully read, as he knew the need for haste so that Günther would be allowed to remain in the United Kingdom.[12] A grimy, soot-laden town of former coal and iron workers struggling on the dole, Merthyr Tydfil was at the center of a bevy of coal, iron, zinc, copper, nickel, steel, and tin-plating operations once matched only by the industrial powers of the United States and Germany's Ruhr Valley. At one time the region produced a third of the world's coal, but after World War I the coalfields swiftly declined and the Depression saw their output reduced by half. In 1934 126,000 workers in South Wales were still employed by the coal trade, but nearly 400,000 had been forced to search for work elsewhere.[13] During World War II there was an uptick in mining, steel production, and tin-plating, but it was light industry such as Rudi Adler's button factory that sprang up when former ironworks and slag heaps were converted into industrial parks.[14] Amid such conditions and in a synagogue whose congregation was in decline, Bettina and Günther were married, Adler having written Steiner from Prague saying that he was "the only person . . . who can serve as a witness to my past as well as stand in for my family."[15]

What the surrounding area had going for it was the beauty of the countryside. Within walking distance of the Cefn-Coed neighborhood where Bettina shared an apartment with the schoolteacher Mary Davies, rugged hills and steep valleys follow the descent of swift-running streams and brooks, while to the north lie the windswept, bare rocky slopes of the Brecon Beacons, their highest peaks capped with snow even in summer. Leaving behind the Neo-Gothic sprawl of the city, one is swept up in the wild paradisal beauty of the region, and the peacefulness of the villages and slate-roofed houses that spring up at crossroads bear witness to a culture largely unchanged for hundreds of years. More open and less covered by forests, the romantic beauty of the landscape surely reminded Adler of the Bohemia he had left behind, reassuring him that other landscapes awaited. Unsurprisingly, in *The Wall* the region is the setting for Arthur and Johanna's commitment to one another when he gives her the pearls of his first wife, Franziska, who like Gertrud died in the camps, saying that they share a "duty to begin again . . . like the first human couple," a duty that carries the extra responsibility of honoring and maintaining the memory of those lost to the past.[16]

Bettina's friends from work, and her brother Joseph and his wife, Rhoda, provided Adler with the first vestige of family life in nearly a decade. Not since 1938 had he lived in an unoccupied country, and 1941 was the only year he lived in a settled and stable household, with Gertrud and her parents. In fact, given the turmoil of his early childhood, the absence of his mother in his early adolescence, and the years spent away at school or living with other families, Adler's arrival in Wales marked his first entry into a close-knit and stable family free of political and religious persecution. But he knew it could not last; to have any kind of a life as a writer and intellectual he would have to be in London. South Wales provided their new life with a temporary refuge, and it had given Bettina a secure if meager livelihood and pleasant social life for eight-and-a-half years, even though she had put her artistic ambitions on hold. Yet Adler was keen to build a career as a writer and intellectual, and that meant moving to the city.

Bettina and Günther Adler, May 1947. Credit: The Estate of H. G. Adler 2019, Deutsches Literaturarchiv Marbach.

Without a job or an apartment, it was difficult for them to pick up house and settle there, so after a week with Bettina in the countryside, Adler left for London, taking a room at the Hotel Arosfa at 77 Gower Street, the home of University College London and down the block from where Bettina's sister, Maria Gross, was completing her nurse training at University College Hospital. Bettina continued working in the button factory, hers their only income. Navigating a strange city mostly alone, Adler began to look for an affordable apartment, and he saw Steiner and Canetti more frequently and expanded his contacts among the exile community. Adler soon gained a foothold within a talented and ambitious circle that had remained, despite the war having ended nearly two years earlier. Steiner helped by introducing him to other writers, and they joined a group led by Erich Fried that included the young poets George Rapp, Hans Werner Cohn, and Hans Eichner.[17] They generally met at Fried's house off Finchley Road in South Hampstead, a shared admiration of Steiner's poetry bringing them together. All six were German-Jewish exiles who did not wish to return home or, as was true for Steiner and Adler, soon could not because of the February 1948 Communist putsch in Czechoslovakia. Their meetings between 1947 and 1950 led to a small anthology of their work edited by Erich Fried in 1949 that was never published. With Eichner's emigration to Canada in 1950, the group lost cohesion and was defunct by 1952.[18]

Though Fried argued in a 1949 letter to the Hamburg publisher Eugen Claasen that the group should be published because it was "free of certain German ills," it did have a survivor of the camps in Adler, and his poems unsurprisingly reveal a direct confrontation with the Holocaust as well as its aftermath, such as in "Nichts" ("Nothing"):

At last it is behind us—and yet what has happened?
Nothing. The ugly sickness seeps through the blood.
Nothing has happened. Nothing. Evil's black spawn
Forfeits only time. And time can surely just pass by,

Otherwise nothing. There remains the tide of darkness
Washing thick and heavy in the depths, and what we see
Is unredeemed and stands like an obscure question.
Nothing has happened. Alas, nothing. Yet always courage

Is greater than misery and will not just pass by.
Our ship runs aground on misery. How are we to endure
When we are so lonely in the furnace of our hearts,

When we are bereft of any benign protection
And know nothing? Nothing. And nothing is our realm.
And nothing—And nothing even comes close to atonement.[19]

Written in July 1945, just a month after Adler arrived back in Prague, the poem speaks to the gulf between the catastrophe that had occurred and the normalcy of life that has superseded it. The "nothing" that he inhabits is still real, and he and fellow survivors search for atonement as time passes by the "black spawn" of the many dead produced by evil. Nevertheless, the world moves on, uncaring or unaware that survivors like Adler continue to "run aground on misery." And yet, although having known such despair, for Adler "courage / Is greater than misery and will not just pass by," an unyielding stoicism rare in postwar poetry.

Hans Eichner's "The Days of Seth," which appeared in Fried's anthology, also invokes "our accursed places," but his are looked on from afar as he invokes the Bible in the poem's middle stanzas:

> And no prayer helps us,
> Nor any star from the East
> Amid our accursed places
> In the days of Seth,
>
> And as the flood rises,
> Instead of stars,
> It is the burning flames
> Of fallen cities that shine.

At the end of "In Extremis," Fried confesses to the helplessness of the refugee forced to look on at the catastrophe from a distance:

> At night I have drawn near to my fears,
> which have now become my closest of friends.
> The horrible becomes my own horror,
> hate becomes my home and fortification,
> and war a pitcher carried to the fountain of life.

Even Steiner, then the more gifted and mature poet, speaks of his grief for his parents through a rendering of the story of "Leda," the end of which reads:

> As Leda limped toward home stunned,
> Dripping green water on good and bad stones,
> Her sobs sucked from her wounded lip
> The iron taste of the bright blood.
>
> With grayer barrenness the world bristled,
> Her parents there, looming at the gate:
> "Wherever you were, you should've taken better care,
> You filthy child, you, the gods' white splendor!"

> To which she replied bitterly: "It was dark . . . I
> Got hurt in the dark. O, wipe off the mud,
> I couldn't see, it won't happen again.
> Please, please, make me clean again!"[20]

Whereas the other five poets write from the exile they had lived through for over a decade, Adler remains caught in a different exile, distancing him from the past as well as the present. Like Arthur Landau in *The Wall,* he finds himself where "there are no more hours, the realms of past and future are shattered, not to be recovered or put back together."[21] The loss experienced by his fellow poets entraps them in a valley of sorrow, cut off from their native lands. But to have seen the ravages close up, and to feel alienated from both the past and the present, embodies a "nothing" that, while "behind us," is cruelly "nothing" in the eyes of those who cannot know it, cannot experience it, and, in some cases, wish to do neither.

This sense of demarcation kept Adler somewhat on the margins of the writing group, for in letters among them he is referred to formally as "Dr. Adler," and he was the group's second-most-frequent absentee, behind Rapp.[22] The feeling of being different or being treated differently carried over into his vexed relations with the exile community, for returning survivors were met with an almost phobic reaction from those who hid out during the war or escaped the atrocities by emigrating before it began. Even Steiner admitted, "The experience [captured in Adler's poems] does not appeal to me, for I have never entirely conquered the despair that I felt during the war in regards to the suffering and death of my people while I was safe abroad. Such guilt is real, and I have to admit that it makes a normal judgment of my friend's poems impossible."[23] In *The Wall,* Arthur Landau faces such guilt disguised as disdain when he is invited to a party hosted by wealthy refugees whose villa is full of furniture brought with them from their native country, he having recently arrived with only a suitcase. Initially they are interested in talking to Landau, yet he soon feels like some "exotic mythical beast." "I didn't mean anything to them," he observes, "for they just stared at my mouth as it spewed out surprising news that they wanted to listen to, only to go on making light conversation, the stinging accounts about the horrors endured pleasing the spoiled ladies and gentlemen."

Within minutes, the "allure of the stranger" dissipates for Arthur, "everyone having heard enough of my plans, all fondness for me dissolving," his isolation now "fatally set in motion."[24] Even the famous Professor Kratzenstein, a caricature of Theodor W. Adorno, with whom Adler corresponded from London before beginning *The Wall,* warns against Arthur undertaking his sociology of the oppressed, since "[a]nything subjective is dangerous," and as a survivor he is too close to his material to be objective.[25] Cultivated yet quickly dropped like a fad, dismissed intellectually, finally having to beg for support for his writing only to receive offers of menial jobs, Arthur is told, "You are not the center of the universe just because you suffered."[26] Viewed as a pariah of unsatisfiable need and a wallower in past suffering, Arthur must "exist by clinging," having no choice but to remain "ensconced . . . within nothingness."[27]

"No one, neither committees nor individuals," recalled Grete Fischer, "helped those who came out of the concentration camps or who were banished. A survivor was supposed to just be content that he had survived the horror, that he escaped, but had to find his own way otherwise."[28] Anthony Grenville adds, "The revelation of the extermination of family, friends and entire Jewish communities was a fresh trauma, with which many refugees could only cope by treating it as a taboo subject never to be discussed."[29] This led to "scapegoating the survivors" and shunning them as "spiritually unclean."[30] Steiner's personification of his guilt through Leda's shame at her own violation echoes this, for Leda beseeches her parents to make her "clean again." This can be read as Steiner asking his parents to forgive him, but on another level, it casts blame on the victim for returning with the unclean mud of her own violation upon her. Steiner's reluctance to speak of what had happened to Adler after receiving his letter that he had survived amounted to a passive rejection bound up with his inability to know how to respond and a turning away from the unclean shame of the violation itself, as if telling Adler that he should "have taken better care" to prevent what had happened to him. Veza Canetti even shouted at Adler on the phone, "You should have died in Auschwitz! You should have never survived!"[31] This was not a wish on her part but an outburst of shame and guilt driving her to turn away from a friend's wound that she did not want to be confronted by and that she could not heal.[32]

Spiritually and psychologically, these tensions taxed exiles and survivors alike, but the most immediate effect was in a lack of paid employment. Regardless of contacts as powerful and respected as Canetti, Steiner, and Baeck, Adler found that earning even the most meager living was exceedingly difficult. In part England's economy after the war remained in bad shape. Hundreds of thousands of people relied on government support, and the rationing of food and many material goods remained in effect for years. Little work was to be found in journalism, publishing, or the universities, and competition remained stiff among exiled intellectuals, particularly second-generation refugees. Friends often concealed from each other work they learned of to capitalize on it themselves. Such rivalry was all the more difficult for Adler to navigate, the new arrival among the ninety thousand refugees who had landed in Britain since 1933, half of whom chose to stay in Britain after the war rather than return to cities reduced to rubble.[33]

In May 1947, Adler proudly told Yehuda Bacon that he had earned his first money in England and spoken on the radio for the first time, reviewing *Der Totenwald* (*Forest of the Dead*), Ernst Wiechert's barely fictionalized account of his four-month imprisonment in Buchenwald. A year earlier, Adler had written to Wiechert, praising his *Rede an die deutsche Jugen* (*Address to the German Youth*), which Wiechert delivered in Munich in November 1945 as a diatribe against Nazi crimes and a call for Germans to return to their traditional humanistic values. Adler told Wiechert he was the first German he had approached since 1938 and that "the harrowing aftermath [of the horror] makes me wary of the Germans, a barrier having been erected that can never really be lifted, but which I hope to cross and will cross," since Wiechert's speech had "finally once again recalled the warmth of this language, and had nothing to do with the 'move it! move it! You scumbag!' " he had become accustomed to.[34]

Reading *Forest of the Dead* in March 1947, Adler wrote to Wiechert again, praising the novel but protesting deeply his latent anti-Semitism in referring to Jews as "more guilty than other peoples," although Wiechert made clear that the Nazis were far guiltier still.[35] In his review for the BBC that May, Adler ignores the remark, instead linking Wiechert to the moral tradition of Klopstock, Lessing, Goethe, Schiller, Jean Paul, Hölderlin, Eichendorf, and Stifter, the writers Adler valued most highly. Adler praises Wiechert's ability to "not just depict" the horrors he experienced but to allow the reader "to experience them in detail through the refined consciousness that reflects on them." Wiechert narrates the novel through a character named Johannes, perhaps inspiring Adler's choice to filter the sufferings in *Panorama* through Josef Kramer's consciousness. Adler's conclusion to the review belies the project that he wished to set in motion himself. "Follow the writer through the horror," he writes, "in order that it will be made manifest to you, not that you must helplessly succumb to it, but so that you initiate the kind of reflection that will allow in future the Germans to rise again, not out of hateful extravagance, but rather to rise in pursuit of a truer, freer humanity!"[36]

A high-minded aim, but there was still a living to be made, and Adler only managed to record for the BBC's Third Program on a few occasions during his first years in London.[37] Since Erich Fried also worked for the Third Program, arranged for the broadcast of a poem by Steiner in 1947, and was in a poetry group with Adler, one might expect a helping hand, especially for a refugee of the camps who had no means of support or secure footing. But this did not occur.[38] To Adler such neglect felt particularly cold-hearted, since he had suffered the worst of the war, while many like Fried had escaped. It was as if, standing before them, he was invisible. All they could see was their own need to find some way through the matrix of jealousies, politics, and competing interests among the exiles, not to mention the difficulty of securing a viable home among the British.

If the difficulty of making a living in postwar England was not enough pressure already, Bettina called from Wales in early March to say she was pregnant.[39] Günther was taken aback by the news, although both had suspicions. They also knew the challenge it meant for them. Bettina would be forced to give up her job, their only steady income. It also threatened their visa status, as Bettina was on a work visa tied to the Welsh button factory and Günther was still trying to secure permission to stay and work in England. Learning less than a month after his arrival from Prague that he was about to be a father was daunting, but Günther took his newfound responsibilities in stride, seeing it as an outgrowth of their love and a blessing they must rise to.

> One never knows how a child will turn out, what fate and what path it is destined to travel, and how it will one day make use of the only thing it truly has, namely life itself. But it will be a child of love. Its parents loved each other dearly at the time it was conceived, even if they had no idea of its creation at the time. They love each other now and will continue to love one another. And their love will protect that same child and guide it through the years in which it will be ours to care for. We can and will care for it without pampering it unnecessarily. Our love for it should not be blind, but rather knowing. And its upbringing not hard but rather cheerful. We want to show it how to determine the good from the bad. That means we want to help the child judge for itself.[40]

Parents often want a better life for their children than that which they had themselves, and given the difficulty of Günther's childhood and the wretchedness of the war years, one might expect loftier hopes than what he expressed, a simple yet genuine commitment to love, decency, good cheer, and guidance. Yet these seemingly modest aspirations are rooted in a determination to do the best they could under the circumstances and to give the child the greatest gift they could think of, the ability to think and judge for itself. Bringing a child into the world without a secure job or even a place to live must have been terrifying. But all that they could do was what they had done for the last decade: live on and care for themselves and others as best as they could while maintaining a discerning if not wary eye and enough good cheer to arm them against the worst.

Money and some employment were needed more than ever, but finances remained dire. It took until June 1948 for Adler to be granted permanent residency, which carried with it permission for salaried work. For the next seven years, Adler had no stable income whatsoever, and what he managed to take in through lectures and reviews was sporadic and minimal. Fortunately in March 1947 he was able to retrieve his father's stamp collection from Hans Jelinek, a nephew of his Aunt Pepa who lived in Birmingham, and it was worth even more than he thought.[41] He brought it to a broker named Eckstein, who agreed to sell the stamps on commission, which provided Adler with some steady revenue.[42] Once this began to roll in on a monthly basis he was at last able to rent an apartment at 96 Dalgarno Gardens in North Kensington after a friend shared an ad in *The Daily Worker* placed by the landlord, Mr. Blackmore, a Communist whose ideals were matched by the fair rent he charged. There he and Bettina first set up house together on July 14, 1947, five months after being married and just twenty-one months after their first letters to each other after the war.

Bettina, Günther, and Jeremy Adler outside 96 Dalgarno Gardens, 1948. Credit: The Estate of H. G. Adler 2019, Deutsches Literaturarchiv Marbach.

The lower half of a duplex, the one-bedroom apartment was laid out in railroad-like fashion with Günther's study taking up the front room that looked out onto a rundown apartment complex across the street, behind which rose the Ladbrooke Grove gasworks. Frankie Harris, who restored typewriters, lived upstairs with his wife and son. Next door was Rhoda Poole, a widow, with her son Bill and his wife, Edna. When Bettina and Günther moved in, it was Rhoda who unwittingly commented on the "dirty Jews" of the neighborhood who had moved there from the East End in the late nineteenth century, to which Bettina shot back, "My mother was a Jew, and she was the cleanest person I ever knew." This put an end to such comments, and the two families became lasting friends. The Adlers also befriended the Gilbert family down the street toward the Little Wormwood Scrubs, where the neighborhood's children played. Churchgoing folk, they were the first to rent rooms to law students from Africa, although the neighborhood still took a dim view of strangers, and even Jews who had lived there for decades granted little truck to the Adlers.[43] And yet, at last, at thirty-seven, Adler could live independently with his wife under the same roof. With stacked orange crates for Günther's bookshelves, Bettina crammed the drafty, leak-ridden apartment with the dark wooden cabinets, tables, and furniture her mother had sent with her from Prague, a vestige of the past amid a working-class slum.

Between rent, food, clothing, transportation, and postage, expenses tallied some £350 a year. They lived on £3 per week, when the postwar average wage for a married couple was more than £4.[44] Bettina took in roughly £70 a year through freelance sewing and the decorative painting of lampshades and placemats, and Günther was able to raise £100 to £125 at best. Another £150 or more of annual expenses had to be covered by the gradual sale of the stamps and money Bettina had set aside back in Wales. The stamps brought in £425 between 1947 and 1950, leaving another £500 worth to last them the following five years, which were just as tough. More than a matter of making ends meet, it was really about finding ends at all. When the German writer and editor Hans Hennecke, who when visiting slept on the couch in Günther's study, never returned £5 he borrowed, it was a calamitous loss.[45]

Giving talks and recording on the radio, Adler returned to what he had done for three years at the Urania in Prague, but none of it provided him with adequate income. Despite a private loan of £200 from Elias Canetti and a gift of £25 from Steiner, Adler could not pay the annual fees for National Insurance between 1948 and 1955.[46] No form of assistance was available from either the British or the Czech governments, even though organizations such as the Jewish Refugee Committee and the Czech Refugee Trust Fund were created to help those fleeing the Nazis since 1933. Bettina had come on an official work permit arranged by Rudi Adler, owner of the Welsh button factory, so she did not qualify for assistance. By the time Günther arrived in Britain the focus of the Czech Refugee Trust Fund had shifted to supporting those who had fled the Communist putsch rather than survivors of the camps. Since he was deemed to be a Czech victim of the camps, not a German, he was disqualified from reparations or assistance from Germany, while Czechoslovakia did not recognize him as a citizen, since he had registered as a German in the 1930 census. With so little to help those who actually survived the war and the camps, they were, in essence, persons who had disappeared, treated by friends and government as the walking dead.

Unable to provide connections that might lead to a job as a librarian or academic, Leo Baeck did reach out to Adler and help him with advice and contacts, and even deposited some of his own speaking fees into Adler's account.[47] Just a week after moving to London, Adler spoke at a meeting of the Jewish World Congress about the sociology of life in Theresienstadt, and in early March he prepared a talk for the Jewish Historical Society of England at the West London Synagogue on the problem of the preservation of Continental Jewish treasures and delivered a lecture on the history of the Prague Jewish Museum to the Leo Baeck Lodge of B'nai B'rith, where like an oracle he announced, "The world stands shattered and still without a true measure or understanding of what Jews know all too well as the results of a 'modern' barbarism carried out with scientific thoroughness, though for 12 years Nazi Germany remained practically untouched by it."[48] During these first weeks he met Alfred Wiener, who had provided the raison d'être for the four-week visa issued to Adler to do Holocaust research in London for the Jewish Museum in Prague. At the time the Wiener Library he headed in London housed the oldest collection on the Holocaust and genocide in the world, dating to 1933, when Wiener fled Germany for Amsterdam before moving to London following the pogroms of November 1938. Opening as the Jewish Central Information Office on September 1, 1939, the day Germany invaded Poland, the collection became known as "Dr. Wiener's Library"; it was later named for its founder and remained a nexus for Jewish intellectual life in London after the war.[49]

Wiener proved an invaluable connection. The library was the principal resource for Adler's research while revising his monograph on Theresienstadt and provided sporadic income when Eva Reichmann hired him to conduct survivor interviews she archived. Wiener wrote letters of recommendation and published Adler's first article since leaving Prague in the spring 1947 issue of *The Wiener Library Bulletin*. In fewer than five hundred words "Concentration Camps to be Investigated by Social Science" lays out in English the need for a sociological analysis of the camp experience, concluding:

> What is needed, therefore, is this: to describe the internal life of a ghetto or concentration camp in such a way as to expand and enrich the field of social science. Again and again the question must be asked: what happens as a result of each order and prohibition? How do community and individual behave in the face of increased oppression? How much scope remains, within the steadily narrowing confines of existence, for any self-chosen activity? More important than what happens is the way it happens. The procedure of a "normal society" will have to be referred to for comparison with this highly abnormal society; the dwelling of an ordinary citizen, for example, as compared with the accommodation in a camp. Only by confrontations of this kind will it be possible to arrive at something like a psychology of the camps, in which terrible destinies were fulfilled under often unfathomable circumstances—destinies from which have sprung impulses that will reverberate through the story of this age.[50]

This is what Adler had set out to accomplish in the first draft of his study of Theresienstadt, which he started in Prague and completed in London in early 1948. Much scholarship has been devoted to the camps in the decades since, but at the time, as Adler notes, "The sociological character of the camps . . . is for all intents and purposes, especially for the purposes of social science, a *terra incognita*." Only a few studies of the camps had appeared, most notably Eugen Kogon's *Der SS-Staat: Das System der deutschen Konzentrationslager* in 1946 and David Rousset's *The Other Kingdom* in 1947. Adler drew on what Kogon and several firsthand accounts documented, but he sought a deeper understanding of not only the camps and ghettos, but of their meaning within society as a whole—hence the need to compare and connect an "abnormal society" and the "ordinary citizen," arriving at an analysis that would "reverberate through the story of this age." In calling not for a history of the camps but an analysis of how they came to shape history in general, his was a much larger and more theoretically grounded project than that of Kogon or Rousset and formed the basis of what would become known as Holocaust Studies.

Adler's rejection of "literary" approaches in that article seems to contradict his desire to capture his experience through poetry and fiction, but really he warns against the conflation of memory and fact in valuing firsthand accounts above primary research and scholarly analysis. Such "slipshod 'impressions' are bound to run the risk of presenting a corrupted picture. Many features will appear overdrawn, others badly blurred," he warns, noting that "these stories can hope to find a mature artistic form only after many years of collection, reflection and conscientious research." Adler already saw as a problem the unreliability of testimonials and memory itself, later taken up at length by many Holocaust scholars. Lawrence Langer argues, "Every narrative about the death camps includes an encounter between fact and memory, persuasive horror and the will to disbelieve. . . . The internal vision invariably sacrifices some of its truth as it struggles to find an idiom that will make the events of atrocity seem veracious to the outsider."[51] Adler understood this already in Theresienstadt, for by collecting materials and making notes just weeks after arriving in the ghetto he was substantiating his own experience with verifiable research. In writing over 130 poems, a novel, and several essays during those years, he commenced the "many years of collection, reflection and conscientious research" that would allow his own story to find its "mature artistic form" in time. Gathering documents, he had validated memory; writing poems and fiction, he hoped for his research to shape his art. In many ways this anticipates Saul Friedlander's "middle ground" between memory and historiography, whereby "historical consciousness" is between the "public-collective memory . . . at one pole, and the 'dispassionate' historical inquiries at the other pole," a method he develops to great effect in *Nazi Germany and the Jews*.[52]

Somewhat shunned by the refugee community because of the discomfort he posed as a survivor, Adler was also met by silence and a lack of understanding by publishers. Grete Fischer recalled,

> [M]uch worse than the indifference toward his situation was the misunderstanding with which his work was greeted. Initially it was rejected on thematic grounds. There appeared numerous reports from the camps and coverage of them, but one could ignore them as individual expressions or take them in with reservations. Statistics were only data, one need not read them or attest to their far-reaching implications. Adler's book, however, was comprehensive, shot through with historical authenticity, undeniably true. This truth then hit home all the harder, since behind the objectivity of a judge there stood the expressive power of a writer. Therefore publishers did not like *Theresienstadt*. But they were even less willing to risk taking on its poetic narrative approach, which amid such events was able to express feeling and thought.[53]

This tension between feeling and fact is what makes Adler's monograph so compelling. Its title—*Theresienstadt 1941–1945: Das Antlitz einer Zwangsgemeinschaft* (*Theresienstadt 1941–1945: The Face of a Coerced Community*)—bears witness to this through the historical name and dates, and an imagined "face" of a "coerced community," which fuses one visage with the whole. Nazi ideology employs similar algebra, whereby each Jew is defined by their link with an entire race, whose eradication is the end sought in killing each individual.[54] Adler's intent is to tell the story of the whole by drawing attention to the plight of individuals amid the suffering of many, allowing numbers and facts to remain attached to people, rather than human beings reduced to racial statistics as quantifiable victims.

Adler uses tables and statistics about how the ghetto was run, the numbers brought there and deported, and its social and political makeup, yet his fact-collecting is often countered by a subjective tone. Discussing the increase in deportations to Theresienstadt, he ends one paragraph with precise statistics: "On November 1, 45,312 were counted, but on December 24, there were again 50,006 people. If, however, the total numbers at the beginning of November are compared to those at the end of this phase, the number remains unchanged, as 45,635 prisoners were counted on September 1, 1943." In the next paragraph, Adler augments his findings with commentary that culminates in emotional release: "By the end of September, the worst turbulence of those wild months was now over, but what does this word 'worst' mean in view of the misery concealed behind the numbers for November 1942 and September 1943! How many people came to Theresienstadt within these ten months! How many fates were sealed in a cruel death!"[55] Adler switches back to factual reporting on the increase in deportations and inhabitants, but his interjection underscores the horror represented by the numbers, a practice Adler employs to prevent the reader from forgetting that numbers refer to living beings.[56] Adler's description of the event thus links to his severe critique of any language that ignores or covers up suffering, something he felt tantamount to a crime itself.[57]

Adler's handling of the arrival of the children from Bialystok and their deportation and murder illustrates his roles as observer, theoretician, witness, and historical siren.[58] Describing the arrival of "1260 neglected children" shipped from the Bialystok ghetto to Theresienstadt on August 24, 1943, Adler begins with a moving observation on their condition: "They were shy and seemed mute; many were barefoot; all wore pitiful rags and were half-starved. In their hands they clutched small packets or prayer books, if they had any 'luggage' at all."[59] He quotes a long passage from a Czech account of hygiene in Theresienstadt published in 1948 describing their fear of being gassed when taken to the showers for delousing. The children's severe anxiety provided one of the first indications of gas chambers in the East. Adler notes, however, that the people in Theresienstadt did not believe these accounts. He quotes Leo Baeck writing after the war, who learned of what was going on in Auschwitz as early as 1941 but decided that sharing such knowledge could do no good. Positioning himself as a seeming eyewitness to the arrival of the Bialystok children and reflecting on the psychological consequences of knowledge of the gas chambers, Adler serves as both observer and historian. His facility with Czech, German, and English allows him to move through sources with ease before concluding that a "general ignorance of the probable fate of all who were deported from Theresienstadt to the East led most of those in the camp into a thoughtlessness and self-deception that often bordered on an alteration of consciousness."[60]

Adler probably knew little about Auschwitz and the gas chambers at the time, but the narrative skills he employs make it seem as if he did, and references to documents add to his apparent omnipresence. This is germane to good historical writing, but it is the introduction of Adler's own anguish that breaks the "fourth wall" of his account, while the thoroughness of the scholarship sets the stage for it.[61] Alternating between factuality and outrage is one of the most striking features of the book. In his discussion of the Bialystok children he quotes the Daily Order of the Council of Elders for September 29, 1943, just a week after the children were deported, which blithely observed, "On the occasion of the New Year, the Council of Elders thanks everyone for the work accomplished in the past year and expects that in the future everyone will remain aware of their responsibility for the community." After then citing the Daily Order for November 24, the second anniversary of the ghetto's founding, which blandly congratulates the community for its sense of civic responsibility, Adler erupts: "The appeal continues in this way, after [Jacob] Edelstein's arrest, after the deportation of nearly 56,000 people! . . . [The] words meant nothing real; they no longer expressed a reality. . . . Husks and shells of a former reality led a shadowy existence, . . . they wandered like ghosts in this real world of broken stammering."[62]

Adler is not content to leave it at this but reaches for a broader conclusion: "Only someone able to empathize a bit with this improbable world can grasp the events to come and understand the extent to which this 'ghetto' was more uncanny than any of the other camps." Acknowledging that "Mass murder—a machinery set in motion to devour thousands daily and hundreds and millions of people in the course of two years—is certainly far more terrible than 'harmless,' 'civil' Theresienstadt," Adler compares the ghetto with the worst of the concentration camps:

> In Theresienstadt, however, the game functioned in an endlessly varied, individual form; everything private and personal contributed to the game, in a ghastly carnival of which almost no one was entirely conscious. In Auschwitz, there was only pure despair or an inexorable awareness of the game. Even if a spark of indestructible vitality remained, even if the soul fled, through some transformative magic, into sweet self-deception [*holder Trug*], still reality had to be seen; no one could really fool themselves. It was different in Theresienstadt, where illusion proliferated and hope, only slightly subdued by feelings of fear, outshone everything else, which was concealed beneath impenetrable fog. In no other camp had the true face of the times retreated to such remote distance from the inmates of a camp as in Theresienstadt; this condition was even more pronounced than in the Jewish transit camps in Western Europe, especially once "normalization" blinded the prisoners with "city beautification." The truth only occasionally arose out of the darkness, touched people, and then, after a moment of terror, allowed them to fall back into their masked existence.[63]

Adler's four-page analysis moves from the desperate plight of the children from Bialystok, to what was known about Auschwitz and its effect on the psychology of the Theresienstadt inmates, to the hollowness of administrative pronouncements, and finally to a piercing analysis of the unique "masked existence" that defined the ghetto. What holds it together is himself, writing from within and outside his own experience. His work is "deeply suffused" with Theresienstadt, and as a "participant-observer" he is there and not there, both immersed and distant.

Adler's willingness to address the culpability of *both* the SS and the Jewish administration in the corrupt workings of the camp also distinguishes the book. Some still find his judgments about individuals and the collective to be controversial, misguided, and even unfairly harsh. Miroslav Kárný, who was also interred in Theresienstadt, finds Adler's account to be "for the most part completely reliable," but he strongly disagrees with Adler's assertion of an "internal, illegal coalition of Zionists, Communists, and Czech-assimilated Jews" who were responsible for corruption within the ghetto administration. Ruth Bondy sums up Adler as "a bitter man who collected a massive array of documents which he only used to play God." Livia Rothkirchen musters an array of documents questioning Adler's contention that Paul Eppstein, the second head Elder, was in denial about the impending Final Solution. More recently, Wolfgang Benz dismisses as "unjust" Adler's view of the Jewish Community of Prague as heavy-handed in organizing deportations to the ghetto and finds it wrong of him to apply the "morals of a free individual to life within a coerced community." Even at the time, besides feeling the book to be a "tremendous success," Salomon Adler-Rudel worried that Adler's judgment of Jacob Edelstein showed "how little you like him and how difficult it is for you to separate him from everything he represented." To Franz Wurm's admission that he found the book "too upsetting" to read, Adler stated firmly, "I believe whoever makes the effort to work through this book methodically . . . will also be set free and gain useful victory over many dark powers that only threaten us more the more we avoid them and close our eyes."[64] Indeed, what such critiques often miss, however corrective or thorough they may be, is Adler's larger aim, as he wrote in that first article for the *Wiener Library Bulletin,* to capture "destinies from which have sprung impulses that will reverberate through the story of this age." His subject is not the guilt of individuals alone but the forces that set in motion the awful if not impossible choices they faced, the consequences that led them and their people to such a tragic end, and that such "dark powers" remain afoot to this day.

Adler's many misgivings about Jewish leaders can be summarized in two areas of concern: first, how the menacing employment of Nazi power caused Jewish leaders to fail at thwarting it, leading to the corruption of leadership and individuals alike; and second, what such failings teach about the relationship between abuses of power and the need to defy it in order to sustain one's humanity. Such an analysis of coercion experienced under Nazi control would seem acceptable, even innocuous. However, when Adler casts specific blame on the Jewish leadership itself and argues, however disproportionally, both Jews and Nazis were guilty, that's when criticism of his views occurs.

In his foreword to the second edition, Adler writes, "The issues, which I raise in all seriousness, are not meant to incriminate or exonerate anyone; they are only intended to deepen our insight into the tragedy that befell those who were in charge—a tragedy for which they remain blameless—and our understanding of their failures, for which they might be blamed."[65] In the second chapter Adler acknowledges that from the start there were two possible responses to Nazi oppression: either dissolve all Jewish communities and refuse to cooperate, even at the cost of many lives, or try to navigate the policies, delay their deadly outcomes, or negotiate their terms over time. That the Jewish Community of Prague opted for the second was, in his view, a tragic mistake, although he repeats that those "responsible should not be blindly condemned."[66]

Yet condemn he does, even if reluctantly when observing of Jacob Edelstein, the ghetto's first Jewish Elder, that it is "extremely difficult to draw the line between feigned servility toward the SS in order to save lives and spineless collaboration."[67] Adler observes a further undermining of the validity of the leadership when they moved into separate, more comfortable accommodations in March 1942, which opened up a gulf between them and other prisoners.[68] Edelstein's successors are met with more withering assessments, for while conceding that Edelstein's "tragic downfall ennobles him," Adler dismisses Paul Eppstein, who replaced Edelstein in January 1943, as a cowardly "show-off, theatrical, soft, and vain" and inclined to womanizing. Benjamin Murmelstein, who replaced Eppstein in December 1944, is described as "ice-cold and self-assured" while seeming "indifferent to the Jews for whom he was responsible" and "well armed against compassion."[69] Beyond their individual flaws, Adler asserts it is their collective failings as well as those of their followers that "made it much easier to control the camp than would have been the case if the camp representatives had confronted the SS with a united will."[70]

Adler attacks the culpability of leaders "who opened themselves up to attack for ideals that they dragged down with them into ossification and decay, even though they may have originally had a pure belief in their ideals and even though they believed they still represented these ideals—ideals that they could no longer represent, and that, in the affliction that was the camp, could no longer even be represented."[71] Even the effort to save prominent Jews represented, in his view, a doomed strategy, for saving one led to the deportation or killing of another, and the survivor became "tragically entangled in [the] guilt" that also ensnared all.[72] For Adler, "the immorality of the accused Germans cannot excuse the immorality of the imprisoned Jews," but as he explained to Gershom Scholem, "Besides the tragedy to which one falls victim to in the worst of times, misdeeds can occur that may tie to that same tragedy, but which nevertheless are not the same as the tragedy itself, but still remain wrong"[73] The system with which those individuals consciously, even at times courageously, engaged had undermined them from the start, nullifying their individual will and character and guaranteeing that they would succumb to the same abuse of power inflicted upon them. This led to a systematic malaise in which "people fell almost irretrievably into a struggle of all against all, in which only people with deeply anchored morality could keep from sacrificing their souls."[74]

The book's section on the sociology of the ghetto underscores the sinister effect upon the Jewish administration of Theresienstadt by revealing how its institutions "no longer were subject to the standards associated with healthy existence. In fact, they nearly were torn out of existence itself, while at the same time their function was inflated, as if to demonstrate the madness of a super-administration emptied of life, resembling a gigantic factory, created to deal with a 'faceless mass'—to categorize it a hundred times over, record its statistics, nourish it with calories—but entirely removed from anything human."[75] During the two-and-a-half years he spent there, Adler turned Theresienstadt's mechanized bureaucratic systemization against itself by collecting the documents with which he would provide an almost day-by-day, department-by-department unraveling of the ghetto's pseudo-governance, "a spectral order, embellished with powerful-sounding terms, but that in fact had no power over itself."[76]

Running to over six hundred pages, the first two sections, on the history and sociology of Theresienstadt, provide an encyclopedic rendering of the ghetto's structure, workings, and, most important, the madness built into both. The last section's fifty pages on the psychology that dominated the ghetto reveal what Adler saw as the philosophical implications of Theresienstadt for history, for the Jews, and for the modern world. There he offers some of his most provocative assertions, but accusations about his judgments on the prisoners and administration unfairly miss the mark, and even undershoot it, for his concerns are with modernity itself, a position he later made clear in asserting, "The problems of National Socialism pose nothing other than an extreme—albeit a maddeningly extreme—case of the conditions or even the possibilities that at a minimum are latent, though more often manifest in modern societies found across the entire planet."[77]

Adler's conviction is that "the history of the camp is defined by the surrounding history as the power that becomes destiny; in other words, one history is the object of another."[78] By "destiny" he means the powerlessness when a human being "recognizes his limitations as a created, transitory individual."[79] Normally such a confrontation remains distant from everyday life and is often ascribed to the provenance of the divine. In Theresienstadt "[p]ower reduced life's rationally indescribable richness . . . to the object of an inorganic experiment in which all history was unconsciously negated and driven almost to dissolution." Instead "of serving to create order in life, administration imperiously [became] an end in itself."[80] This meant "most victims were treated as commodities" while "some individuals were chosen to play the role of dogs in a herd of sheep." More expansively, Adler sees a warped sense of Greek tragedy at work, whereby "Power played the role of fate. Powerlessness was humanity, degraded to a commodity, which was sorted, numbered, and through the magic of statistics, turned into the object of a perverse mysticism."[81]

As in *The Journey*, what is notable is the lack of specific reference to Nazis, Jews, or prisoners. Adler intends his anthropological analysis of the camp's psychology to speak to a broader malaise than Theresienstadt or the Holocaust. He addresses the essence of Nazism in founding a "coerced community" (or

Zwangsgemeinschaft, a neologism he coined to describe it) through the employment of "mechanical materialism," a concept dating to Descartes' contention that an entity remains unchanged until acted upon externally, later applied by materialist philosophers to people and societies, and still later the "dialectical materialism" of Marxism where inner social conflicts are the engine driving outward change. Marx and Engels dismissed "mechanical materialism" as a bankrupt way of thinking about the social dynamic, but Adler redeploys the term to describe how Nazism resorted to "a way of thinking that is devoid of ideas, colorless and coarsely sensual, and that exists in poor, rigidly rational forms that are unable to see or accept the potential of life."[82] Adler's critique of "mechanical materialism" is not Marxist, but it carries with it the valuation of that which it consumes, the ineffable nature of Being itself and the essence of any individual.

Words like "life," "destiny," "fate," "magic," and "mysticism" may seem striking in a discussion of Nazi ideology and the oppression of Jews, but in the last section of the book Adler elevates his concerns to a religious plane.[83] That the regime "turned everything good into bad and everything bad into good" gives rise to the conclusion that those "who were not bad to start with inevitably were corrupted through entanglement in guilt,"[84] leading people to make "common cause with the source of all evil" such that "[t]ormentors and tormented suffered from the same social disease."[85] Adler admonishes that "Humaneness is the only party that can offer moral fulfillment in the face of immorality," and he underscores its religious roots by insisting that there is "but only *one* morality,"[86] the violation of which leads inevitably to a biblical fall from grace:

> Guilt is the sum of history in a country or a camp, a manifold guilt that no one has escaped, for humanity is a community of guilt. . . . The guilt of humanity in the confused state that it was in even before Hitler's rise to power; the guilt of inhumanity that, if one wishes, can also be considered godlessness; the guilt of an unkind era in which order is transformed into schematics, the organic into mechanics, life into masses, the human being into a commodity, the soul into complexes, the mind into ideology; the guilt of the misconception or devaluation of values and the confusion of concepts that led to decay; the guilt of a dull species so blinded in this transformation by foolishness, hate, self-interest, and lies that it could not see the disaster that was conjured up and would inevitably follow, as mechanical materialism and its destructive, all-consuming outgrowth in the form of National Socialism overtook the world; and finally, the greatest guilt, which we call the inability to experience guilt, because humanity that has become "masses" can no longer conceive of or accept any kind of guilt.[87]

Adler arrives at an indictment of not only the Nazis and the evil carried out under them but the whole of modernity.[88] His conclusion that "Guilt was finally transformed into punishment" which "has an effect . . . into the third and fourth generation" carries the consequences of such moral collapse into the future. Adler anticipates the protests of those born later by saying that "the question of whether one may justifiably assert one's innocence becomes unnecessary—the punishment that has come to pass has already given the answer."[89]

According to Adler, there is no room for escape, neither for the tormentor nor tormented, nor humanity at large, nor even the Jews. This last is the argument that riles critics, as Adler expected it would, admitting to Franz Kobler that his "book will be in many respects a damned hard morsel for Germans as well as for Jews and other readers."[90] As daunting as his religious arguments can seem, behind them is a desire to cleanse, not accuse. In his preface to the second edition, where he tries to answer protests, Adler turns to scripture for defense when he argues, "Keeping guilt hidden exacerbates it and has a corroding effect, but revealing and investigating guilt has a cleansing effect and promotes the inscrutable mysterious workings of grace, which stir up the healing powers of the conscience and which cleanse the conscience of guilt unto the end of days, when the great promises made to humanity will be fulfilled and 'though all the peoples walk each in the name of its gods, we will walk in the name of the Lord, our God, forever and ever' (Micah 4:5)."[91]

Adler's mission is religious but devoid of zealotry. "I am neither pro nor contra Jews or non-Jews," he later declared. "I recognize only one humanity composed of two different groups, people who are good in various ways and people who are less good in various ways."[92] His defense against critics is that "the spiritual underpinnings for the opinions" he expresses are bound up with "the concept of goodness in the name of the Eternal that we have been taught about ourselves—most forcefully through the commandment to love one's neighbor as oneself—together with a view of the everlasting determined [by] my understanding of Judaism." Revealing to the world and to the Jews the tragedy of the hopeless choices foisted upon them, Adler mourns not only those lost but also what has been missed, "the opportunity for a human catharsis or for the rediscovery of a Judaism that most only knew superficially," since "[h]ardly anyone found his way back to Judaism as a result of being in Theresienstadt." In the second edition his only concession was to change "most" to "very many" and "hardly anyone" to "few."[93]

Who did find his way back to Judaism among the camps was of course Adler himself. Yet his relation to it remained private, for he never attended synagogue or observed holiday rituals. The impetus to write *Theresienstadt 1941–1945* stemmed from "private reasons," as he "could not endure having the pain of the events leave an abysmal despair amid the yawning emptiness within me."[94]

When later asked if writing it had provided the opportunity for "self-liberation" (*Selbstbefreiung*), Adler responded that a "liberation" (*Befreiung*) had been the result, but that was "small justification for my having survived."[95] Desire to prevent the pain of those events from devolving into despair was the only redemption in confronting the guilt he felt had tinged all. As he admits on the book's final page, "[E]ven he who had not too badly failed the test could not, as an active human being, pass through the camp free of any implication in guilt."[96] The yellow star that sat upon his writing desk throughout his years in London acknowledged this burden.[97]

Lest one doubt the personal pain on which Adler's book is built, one only needs to consider the extended dedication carved as a memorial to his loss and grief in the book's opening pages and quoted in this book's opening chapter. In not even clearly being referred to as his wife, "Geraldine" becomes something more, a metonym for the selflessness and dignity that Adler saw as the only defense against Nazi persecution and the delusional existence that engulfed their prisoners, standing for them, as he hopes his own study will. Underscoring this desire are the last words of the book, set in the same capitals as the dedication:

> ONE MUST BE CAREFUL NOT TO ATTACH TOO MUCH IMPORTANCE TO ONESELF. ALL OF US ARE MORE OR LESS ON THE FRONT LINES AND TEND TOO MUCH TO CONSIDER OURSELVES AS THE CENTRE OF ATTENTION.[98]

No attribution is given, but these are words that Bertha Gross, Bettina's mother, wrote to her children from Theresienstadt.[99] Recorded anonymously, they become representative of the unseen deaths of millions, touching too upon Bettina's private grief. The arc of the book traverses his own catharsis from Gertrud to Bettina, from irrevocable death to a life lived anew, albeit founded upon the past. The dedication's private meaning is not overt, and the concluding epigraph remains obscured, a private touchstone that reinvokes the author's need for selfless "cool" observation in the service of a "higher mission" while continuing "to form the history that forms him."[100] In it, Adler "hopes to abide," the tender acknowledgment of Bertha's presence and loss pointing to the humaneness that will help him do so, and which he aspired to, he the survivor "who can only celebrate his return if he succeeds at being taken into the hearts of his fellow human beings," if only the publishers would let him.[101]

13

The Writer

Ironically, the war provided Adler's first steady means of support in England. In June 1947 he was hired by the British government to lecture to German war prisoners in a camp in the Cornish town of Launceston. Reunited with Bettina after moving into their London apartment in mid-July, a week later he began traveling to Cornwall weekly for the next six months in order to lecture on two general themes: "Perception and Consciousness" and "What Is Art?" The Foreign Office hoped to reintroduce sound social values among the POWs before sending them home, and in discussing "How shall we master consciousness in order to better understand one another?" or arguing for the "Renewal of the human through art," Adler aimed to enable the soldiers to reenter and rebuild a democratic society after twelve years of ideological domination.

"Actually, we talked about a thousand different things," he recalled, "such as whether Hitler was right or not."[1] Like Přemsyl Pitter in Czechoslovakia, Adler engaged the very people who had sought to persecute him, the precept "to love your neighbor as yourself" remaining at the core of his life view. When it came to finding gainful employment, Adler enjoyed little of the same among the circle of postwar exiles and intellectuals in London. He refused suggestions to work in a shop or as a waiter or gardener but was met with a lack of sympathy and outright hostility. Describing what he called a "failure of human kindness," he interpreted friend and foe alike as saying, "When you don't do what we want you to do, then we won't help you at all. Nor will we give you one penny for your scholarly or creative work."[2] What was actually said does not matter; his perceived rejection of his talents and lack of sympathy for his plight set him back on his heels when his stint in Launceston finished in December 1947.

E. M. Forster received him for tea, and a meeting with the historian Arnold Toynbee went well, but Adler had little hope of a university position since he was too old for a junior post and had published too little for a senior one.[3] When applications for positions at the University of Hull and at St. Andrews proved fruitless in the spring of 1948, several urged him to teach German in a boarding school or high school. In spite of a recommendation letter from

Leonard Ashley Willoughby, the leading figure in British German Studies, he could not land such a post. He turned down an offer to return to Germany to help with the British government's efforts to aid displaced survivors and reconstitute its society because Bettina was due to give birth and Adler did not wish "to live or remain in any country that Hitler had ruled over."[4] Nor could Steiner, Canetti, or Baeck help him secure a satisfactory position, despite their fondness and respect for him. He had good administrative experience from his work at the Urania in Prague before the war and at the Jewish museum afterward, but really he wanted to write. With help from the sale of his father's stamps, and what meager savings Bettina managed to save from her job at the button factory, that is what he sat down to do, not knowing what he would do when money ran out.

In the meantime, Adler was granted a son. Jeremy Joshua David Adler was born October 1, 1947, in London.[5] He wanted the boy to have names that could be used in any country, should the child ever wish to emigrate, a gesture that recalls the expulsions Günther and Bettina had endured and projects the potential of future exile, confessing to their tentative stance at the time. As Steiner observed to Canetti in reporting the birth, Jeremy stood for Jeremiah, "our supreme and vital prophet," who predicted and mourned the loss of the Temple in Jerusalem, while Joshua was "our greatest strategist, whose fame was eclipsed by Moses" and David was "the king we all venerate."[6] Symbolizing the loss of the Jewish homeland, the ability to lead the Jews to safety, as well as righteous and effective leadership, the names validate the parents' valuation of memory, action, and art in service to life. Penniless and without foreseeable prospects, it was one of the few things they could control in those precarious days.

October 1 was the birthday of Heinrich Steiner, Franz's father, and the same day that Steiner began work on "Gebet im Garten" ("Prayer in the Garden"), a 252-line lament for the loss of his parents and all who had perished, which he worked on for the next ten days almost without interruption.[7] With Paul Celan's "Death Fugue," it is one of the great poems of the Holocaust, addressing all "errant creatures out at sea" in seeking a forgiveness the speaker knows can never be attained, because

> The prayer of the will does not behoove me,
> For the words themselves turn against myself . . .
> Only at times I turn to my people,
> Partake of their prayer, as one partakes of bread and grief
> Because it is commanded, amid whispering and supplication.
> My prayer amounts to resignation, but this is not enough,
> My prayer is empty of sorrow and therefore not permitted:

For I am full of sorrow that mercy might have mercy,
O have mercy on the errant creatures out at sea,
The errant creatures who land
And on those others, my God, who still did not understand.

This is the lament of a man whose prayer feels futile, whose sorrow feels like a violation marking his guilt in surviving, while "the errant creatures out at sea" remain neither dead nor alive, neither saved nor drowned, but wandering and lost forever. This is why

. . . my praying is not enough,
For I am full of sorrow, and this is not enough:
This sorrow is not for you and me,
Not for the beginning and end,
It is sorrow for only a part,
And what a part:
That mercy might have mercy on those out at sea.

The speaker can never know mercy as long as those at sea remain there. Meanwhile, "One part alone has survived / And has lived to see the hour. / To praise it, / The mouth I made of my wound," so that "Now all the suffering out at sea, / From the play of the will set free, / Shall suffer pain for glory's sake, / Itself turning into glory, / Transforming everything." Lest this sound like redemption, the speaker remains trapped in the garden of his own sorrow as darkness descends. "A deep, a mighty frost has entered my heart," he confesses. "In the dark I stand alone and see nothing anymore. / Woe is thy peace, alas; / Woe is the peace of thy glory. Amen."[8]

As Bettina and Günther, errant creatures who had made it ashore, welcomed their son into the world, Steiner in Oxford was a man bereft of grace in his inability to bring his parents back or to fully mourn their death. He could only ask "a question upon which hinges the very essence of humanity in the twentieth century—ubi sunt? Where are they indeed, the millions who suffered, died, or simply disappeared?"[9] Bettina, however, stood in the same hopeless relation to her lost mother. She, like Steiner, had Günther's account of visiting both their parents in Theresienstadt, but while Bettina knew from her husband of Bertha's journey to Auschwitz, Steiner's parents had disappeared into the abyss of Treblinka in October 1942. And she now had a child, while Steiner's failed romances and precarious health likely meant he would neither marry nor have children, besides his longing for both.[10] For Steiner, the father was no more, nor the mother, nor even the son. Cast ashore while they were left to face their death alone, he had been unable to protect them. All he could do was "make of his wound a mouth" and nothing more. "Amen" ends the "Prayer in the Garden," signifying that "it is so," but for Steiner it amounted to the grim acknowledgment that "so it must be."

Adler could not afford such despair. His son's birth commanded him to say what had happened to the lost and how the living might make a new beginning of their own. This meant sitting at his desk and getting to work, which he did, and his output during his first nine years in London was astounding. By the spring of 1948 he had completed a full draft of *Theresienstadt 1941–1945* and made substantial revisions until it was published in 1955. In 1948 he wrote *Panorama,* his third novel, having begun his second novel *Raoul Feuerstein* in Theresienstadt, the first having been lost. *Panorama* was finished by the fall of 1948, after which he wrote *Die kleinen Gestalten* (*The Small Figures*), a philosophical novella of over eighty pages. In 1949 he wrote a fourth novel, *Die Ansiedlung* (*The Settlement*), over 500 typed pages in manuscript, before writing a 150-page casual study of English society, *Eindrücke eines Ahnungslosen* (*Impressions of an Innocent Abroad*), which he hoped would bring in some money. The years 1950–51 saw the completion of a fifth novel, *Eine Reise* (*The Journey*), and around fifty short stories or "bagatelles," some of which he collected in *Sodoms Untergang* (*The Fall of Sodom*). In 1952, Adler wrote a fifth novel, *Die Prüfung* (*The Test*), and a second draft of *Raoul Feuerstein.* In 1954, while making final revisions to the Theresienstadt book, he turned to *Die unsichtbare Wand* (*The Wall*), completing a first draft in 1956, a year after *Theresienstadt 1941–1945* at last was published to wide acclaim. Altogether, this amounts to six novels with an average length of over 300 pages and a monograph of over 800 pages, including 150 pages of notes and a twenty-page glossary of 650 terms specific to life in the ghetto. Not counting *The Small Figures* or *Impressions of an Innocent Abroad* or the numerous stories and more than 150 poems he produced in these same years, it adds up to about 3,000 published pages of fiction and scholarship (just under 400 a year), all written between 1947 and 1956.

What is most extraordinary is its nature as a *Gesamtkunstwerk.* Adler created a different style for almost every book he wrote while maintaining a unified set of concerns across all of them. *Panorama* is on the surface a *Bildungsroman* about its protagonist, Josef Kramer, a boy born in a city recognizable as Prague just after World War I, who survives the Langenstein concentration camp before emigrating to England. *The Settlement,* however, is a futuristic allegory whose characters discuss Kantian ethics and rationality in an enclosed community much like Theresienstadt where the clocks run backward and the sick are displayed in windows to encourage others to stay healthy. Otherworldly as this sounds, Adler's intent within it was to show that "no matter how bad the society is, . . . it is still possible for people to maintain their moral grounding, the responsibility to do so being a real and practical, rather than an idealistic and utopian aim."[11] In turn, *The Journey* renders the nightmare worlds of Theresienstadt and Auschwitz in a combination of magical realism and stream-of-consciousness narration that never mentions Jews or Nazis or concentration camps but keeps one riveted on the mythic essence of the horrors without falling into graphic sensationalism. *The Test* and *The Small Figures* are shorter novels, but both employ intricate and subtle investigations of the split in human consciousness between rational thought and the mythic imagination. Finally, *The Wall* is Adler's most psychological novel of the group, told entirely from the perspective of Arthur Landau, a survivor of the war and the camps who ends up in a "metropolis" much like postwar London, remaining haunted by the loss of his first wife in the war and thwarted in his attempt to make a new life with his second wife and two children. Add to this that *Theresienstadt 1941–1945* reads in many ways like a novel, drawing readers into the moral conflicts, skewed motivations, and tragic failures of the ghetto's flawed leaders, and one appreciates not only the reach of Adler's art but the many facets of his mind.

H. G. Adler, London, 1955. Credit: The Estate of H. G. Adler 2019, Deutsches Literaturarchiv Marbach.

The will to create such an oeuvre in a short time was indomitable. On first meeting Adler a day after his son's birth, Grete Fischer noted, "I could see that this man only managed to survive what he had suffered by wanting to write, by needing to speak. This was confirmed in the years following, in which he wrote one book after another with vehement swiftness and intensity."[12] Nor did Adler work without a plan, for his was a conscious effort to trace key elements of the onset of the Shoah. Commenting on *Panorama, The Settlement,* and *The Journey* alone, early on he claimed,

> With the three novels I've written so far [he excludes here the draft of *Raoul Feuerstein* begun in Theresienstadt], I have completed a phase in which together I wanted to present the evolution of, the social implications of, and finally my direct experience of the views, events, and problems of recent Central European history, as well as the ethical consequences tied to them.[13]

To complete his fictional account of "the catastrophe," all that was needed was *The Wall,* the novel he considered "my most important and inventive extended prose work," a piercing portrayal of survivor's guilt and postwar hypocrisy amid the search for redemptive love.[14]

There were many days, however, especially between 1947 and 1955, when Günther and Bettina felt themselves on the brink of failure, if not destitution. After Jeremy's birth, Bettina could no longer hold a full-time job, although she took in piecework and painted floral patterns on door handles and chinaware in order to bring in small sums.[15] While postwar government rations were enough for those who had survived the war in England, they were not substantial enough for a camp survivor still needing to build strength and stamina. Adler was always hungry, admitting that "there are days when my very being feels strangled, and then I need what little energy I have to breathe."[16] Yet this did not stop him from working eighteen hours a day at his desk. Between 1947 and 1950, Adler only managed to publish six brief articles in relatively obscure publications, and he only twice recorded for the BBC. Rather than despair entirely, he kept writing, each day rising early and writing letters to friends, colleagues, editors, and publishers before turning to his scholarship and fiction. In the "lair of his apartment, which amid his perpetual homelessness he valued as a safe harbor," he worked to understand his "existence as a witness, as well as to separate what he had witnessed from his existence while working to comprehend what he had experienced and observed in order to diligently render it as a scholar and an artist."[17]

One of his most extended and important correspondences was with Hermann Broch. In May 1948, Veza Canetti wrote to Broch in Princeton to ask if he could help find a US publisher for the Theresienstadt book. Adler had given up on the German market and hoped for a better reception in America.[18] Broch thought it would not be easy to publish such a huge book amid a shaky American market in search of bestsellers, but he recognized it as "an admirable work—objectively in terms of the richness of the material, its theoretical and analytical power and the vivid immediacy of the writing, and subjectively as the achievement of a human being who, in the greatest personal danger, preserved his reason and his keen eye and who was able to absorb and record all these things inwardly."[19] Broch's mother had died in Theresienstadt in December 1942, just six months after being deported from Vienna, which she could not bring herself to leave, regardless of Broch's efforts to get her out. Like Steiner, Broch had chosen exile in 1938, and his eagerness to help with Adler's project was tied to his own sense of loss and guilt, as he had not learned of his mother's death until 1944.[20] Despite a broken hip that kept him hospitalized for ten months, Broch took on the project. He sent the chapters he had read to Hannah Arendt in New York and enlisted Elliot E. Cohen, the editor of *Commentary*, to contact publishers. Realizing that publication might require a subvention for translation and printing costs, he proposed that funds be raised with the help of Arendt, Cohen, Leo Baeck, and even Albert Einstein.[21]

Unfortunately, nothing came of these plans, and Broch wearied of Adler's plight. In July 1949 he complained to Arendt that "one shouldn't concern oneself with other people's concentration camps,"[22] after Adler sent him the manuscripts for *Raoul Feuerstein, The Small Figures,* and *The Settlement*, and three essays on "mechanical materialism" he had hoped to deliver at the University of Cologne that February, an engagement that fell through.[23] Broch admired the rigor of Adler's philosophical and sociological investigation of the underpinnings of Nazi oppression, but he was less enthusiastic about his fiction, observing politely, "[W]e belong to different generations."[24] Finding in *The Settlement* "the image of 'good order' which has a surprising similarity with that of an admittedly 'good concentration camp,'" Broch was troubled by the novel's eschewal of plot for abstract philosophical discussion among its characters, resulting in what he called "an 'allegory without firm allegorical data'" and "an abstraction analogous to that of modern painting."[25]

Coming from a writer he revered, such criticism had to smart. Adler remained confident in his approach and cited Adorno's dictum in his *Philosophy of Modern Music* that "The inhumanity of music must outdo that of the world for the sake of the human" as a way to explain his own effort to "uncover even in the repulsive world the root of the sublime, to convey this to others and to encourage them to seek it out."[26] Adler boldly claims, "I do not exaggerate when I assert that I know of no work of science, philosophy or literature from this century in which, for all the acknowledged despair, so much positive confirmation at least of the ethical autonomy of human beings is demonstrated, as in the case in the 'Settlement.'"[27] To him the novel was meant to serve as "the positive answer to the horrifying questions the Theresienstadt book was compelled to throw up."[28]

Adler first wrote to Broch in the hope of securing a publisher for the Theresienstadt book, but their correspondence developed into something much more for him. The author of *The Sleepwalkers* was someone whom Adler had seen "in my mind's eye in Theresienstadt (alongside the few other contemporaries whom I thought it was important and dignified to think about with the full sympathy of both heart and mind)."[29] Having read Broch's book in 1940 at Canetti's prior urging, he carried its consideration of the "Disintegration of Values" with him into the camps, where he said to himself, "Hermann Broch knew all of this already."[30] The correspondence allowed him to explain Broch's influence on the works that Adler was sending to him and to articulate his core beliefs and intentions when countering Broch's reservations. Unlike the missives sent in the vain hope of an answer in the parable of "The Letter Writers" at the center of *The Wall*, the arrival of Broch's letters from across the ocean every few months buoyed Adler's spirits amid his "great artistic and intellectual loneliness." They reminded him that "it is not only with regard to books and to barbarism that we have returned to the distant past, but also—and this is more pleasing—with regard to human relations, when those who are alone and lonely make contact with each other and preserve precious goods and pass them on to one another."[31]

When at last the correspondence petered out a few months before Broch's death, Adler mourned the loss of a connection that reached back to the prewar past. "[M]y only wealth is untiring industry," Adler told Broch early on, and after lamenting to Franz Kobler in November 1950 that "Broch has given up trying to help," all he could do was turn to the engine of his own industry once again. Work provided him autonomy and volition, but hardest of all was its isolation and loneliness. Adler's letters to Steiner during this period are poignant on this, as he admits, "We [he and Bettina] feel quite alone, and I am, as one calls it, somewhat depressed."[32] Through 1949, Bettina is also described as feeling "okay" or "feeling better" but about to go to the doctor again, and eventually having "gotten over her weariness."[33] Günther had his own health struggles, including three periodontal procedures in six months, and anxiety about how to pay for them. "Each day is pretty much the same," he tells Steiner. "I work from early in the morning until the evening. . . . I see hardly anyone. If I didn't have the radio, I would be entirely cut off from the outside world."[34] Bettina had Jeremy to focus on and care for, but she had forgone both her art and a career. Her days were structured around caring for her son and her husband, who disappeared into his study for most of the day, the two of them reconnecting toward evening to listen to concerts from the BBC. Although Adler assured Steiner that "good cheer still possesses us," he admitted, "I still cannot at all underestimate how much we both (as do you, no doubt) always sense a deep loneliness, which causes us no small amount of anxiety, even though we bear up through it."[35]

Adler's invocation of Adorno in defending *The Settlement* precedes his correspondence with the German philosopher and sociologist, which began in April 1950 and led to a turn in his fortunes. Assigned Adorno's *Philosophy of Modern Music* for review by the BBC, he read it as his correspondence with Broch was beginning to come to an end. In his last letter to Broch he laments, "At the age of forty I have never succeeded in publishing a single line," but he remains convinced that "the question, or rather the challenge, put to human beings is: 'What can you do in a world like this which has acquired such a monstrous and often clown-like, de-ranged countenance, and which, *cum grano salis,* is your world?' "[36]

This question functions like a baton passed from the past to the present, for it soon became the central issue of his respectful but fraught relationship with Adorno and the dilemma at the heart of his post-Holocaust life, art, and thinking. Expressing admiration for his thinking on modern music and his book *The Authoritarian Personality,* Adler's first letter to Adorno cites the same sentence on the need for "inhumanity" in modern music he had quoted four months earlier in a letter to Broch. He concurs with Adorno's denouncement of any artistic naiveté that harkens back to a world before the camps, citing Arnold Schönberg as a "witness to the catastrophe" who had forged an oeuvre in which "the old art had been preserved *and* destroyed." Adler tells Adorno he has been reading *The Authoritarian Personality* while working on a book on Theresienstadt after thirty-two months there before being deported to Auschwitz and two other camps. Adler ends with the central argument of his study: "In all of the camps, so far as I can see, the so-called 'free' society made prisoners wicked, and the Jews had assimilated to Nazi culture in the so-called ghettos, despite their opposition to it."[37]

One would think that, beside praise of his work from a reviewer for the BBC, this last statement would have been provocative enough to inspire a response from someone who also saw the modern bureaucratic state as culpable in the breeding and implantation of fascism. Yet over three months passed before Adorno answered. Only on hearing from the publisher Paul Siebeck that Adler was miffed did Adorno write back, and even then he acknowledged neither Adler's camp experience nor his scholarship. Instead he addresses solely aesthetic concerns, saying that music must not necessarily be "ugly," but rather that there is a tendency to reduce it to broad categories like "hermetic" and "harmonic" rather than valuing the degree to which music manifests an expression of suffering. Adorno goes out of his way to explain to Adler that it is not that art must *necessarily* invoke inhumanity in order to be humane, but that what is sought is the true expression of suffering by whatever means necessary. Adorno doubted that this could be achieved in contemporary culture, yet ironically, in not acknowledging Adler's experience in the camps, he negates at least a form of that expression, implying that Adler had misunderstood his dialectical thinking and reduced it to a binary judgment.

Adler makes clear that he did not consider modern music to be "ugly," nor was he interested in weighing what was "beautiful" against what was "ugly."[38] What mattered to him was whether a work had "structured proportions," and that much of modern music did, even if he conceded that, as Adorno lamented, it failed to perform its former conciliatory function. Stating that all art was symbolic, that it never truly reflected reality in any naturalistic way, Adler writes, "The 'stuff' [of life] is expressed through the medium of one's consciousness, thereby taking on proportions that are expressed through the medium of each individual art form." Why modern art often did not provide consolation, however, was "not something that could be addressed by a theory of art; this is a cultural-historical, sociological, and most of all a religious-sociological (or theological) theme." Where for Adorno the inability of modern art to genuinely console without dissolving into sentimentality or nostalgia was a historical development tied to the corruption of consciousness by capitalism's control over cultural production, for Adler it was a religious question that affected the workings of society and human relations but still could be addressed and altered by the remaking of art through the individual consciousness of the artist.

In their exchange are positions on the historical and the spiritual that each would advance through letters, lectures, and their writings in the years ahead, as well as the kernel of one major debate of postwar intellectual history. For Adorno, modern art was imprisoned by history, whereas Adler saw art as a means to liberate oneself from history through an act of spiritual salvation, as he had pursued by writing poems in Theresienstadt and Langenstein. In fact, as they wrestled with aesthetics in their first letters, Adorno had already written his essay "Kulturkritik und Gesellschaft" ("Cultural Criticism and Society"), although he did not publish it until the following year. In it he famously states that "to write a poem after Auschwitz is barbaric," an edict that has since framed the debate about the struggle between art and history.[39] Adler had no access to Adorno's statement then, but their exchange on the precarious position of the artist amid the menacing realities of history connects with Adorno's dictum.

Adorno responded immediately to Adler's second letter by blithely saying he looked forward to soon having an opportunity to take up their discussion of the aesthetics of harmony and the dialectic it invoked.[40] Given that Adler had also mentioned in his letter the three lectures on mechanical materialism he had hoped to deliver at Cologne in 1949, one would think that Adorno might have invited him to speak at the Institute for Social Research in Frankfurt rather than saying he was interested in reading the one lecture on "The Sociology of the Concentration Camps" and leaving it at that. Adler waited two months to respond, but when he did, he could not resist mouthing back word for word Adorno's excitement "that soon there might be the opportunity to carry on our discussion of the aesthetics of harmony." The absurdity of this as a pressing matter for a Holocaust survivor was likely lost on Adorno, who was deeply consumed with the demands of reestablishing the institute after having returned to Germany from his wartime exile in New York and Los Angeles.[41] Nevertheless, Adler was bold enough to ask in the same letter whether Adorno might arrange a speaking engagement for him in Frankfurt to help finance the trip to Germany that he hoped would help him make the contacts he needed to get published. Worried about overstepping his bounds, Adler concluded, "Forgive me, if I seem too forward, but when things are so bad as to approach despair, one has to grasp at every chance, and that often runs the risk of turning one's needs into a nuisance."[42] He did not know that he was risking utter silence, for Adorno never responded to his request.

Reaching out to Adorno was by no means pointless. Although Adler and he were never close, they kept an eye on one another over the years, eventually meeting face to face in Frankfurt in February 1955.[43] Within days of this Adorno helped to organize a government subvention of 8,500 Deutsche Marks (roughly \$35,000) from the Bundeszentrale für Heimatdienst (the Home Office) to cover printing costs for the Theresienstadt book.[44] That same year he wrote a strong letter of recommendation supporting Adler's application to the Conference on Jewish Material Claims in New York for a research grant for work to gather materials for *Die verheimlichte Wahrheit: Theresienstädter Dokumente* (*The Hidden Truth: Documents from Theresienstadt*), which appeared in 1958.[45] From the start there was a clear difference between their approaches and sensibilities toward the Holocaust. They never clashed directly, but their conflict manifested itself subtly, and over the next decade they seemed to debate one another, consciously or unconsciously, through their work, even when one had no way to know what the other was writing.

Adler's June 1955 letter thanking Adorno for his support of his application to the Conference on Jewish Material Claims poignantly captures their vexed relation. Having been turned down, Adler admits, "This time the blow has hit me especially hard," and then remarks ironically, "How curious, but what little honor it spells for Jewish institutions, that to date my accomplishments, which were deliberately intended to serve Judaism, have been solely sponsored by the Germans."[46] Adler had expected that Jewish organizations would support his work for religious-sociological reasons, rather than the historical guilt behind the German support that Adorno had helped to organize. What is most striking about the letter is that Adler's carbon copy of it is written on the back of recycled pages of typescript from the Theresienstadt book. Throughout the 1950s and

1960s, Adler recycled old manuscripts by using them for copies of letters. In Adler's archive the letter to Adorno appears on the back of one of the manuscript pages of the glossary of 650 Nazi terms particular to Theresienstadt that he developed for his book. The page on which he typed the copy of his letter contains definitions for the fake currency developed in the ghetto (*Ghettokrone*), the Jewish Ghetto Police (*Ghettowache*), the internal leaders in charge of a section of each barrack (*Gruppenältester*), and an entry titled "Haft" (arrest) that explains, "One maintained the fiction that the inmates of the ghetto were not under arrest. One was indeed interned in the 'ghetto', but formally free." Saddest is the entry on the page for "Hamburg," the barracks to which Gertrud had been assigned, underscoring the way in which the document is a palimpsest of real and lived suffering, the struggle to bear witness to it through scholarship, and the loss that lay behind every word that Adler wrote.

Even if Adorno had seen the irony of a letter copied by a survivor on the back of a document defining "ghetto currency" or "ghetto police," the line that ran from Gertrud's residence in "Hamburg" to her death by gas in Auschwitz would have remained unknown. If he had seen such terms, they would have only confirmed his belief in the way that the modern administrative state had come to shape, control, and even define human experience through such codification. Yet what he would have missed was the untold expression of suffering. What "Hamburg" meant to Adler could never be explained to Adorno, a gulf that illustrates their separate positions, Adorno the returned exile who provided crucial help to the camp survivor yet remained strangely mute to his actual experience of suffering, and Adler the survivor who could not help but express dismay at the lack of support from his fellow Jews while copying a letter to a German on a sheet that bore witness to perversions of the German language and culture and the true loss signified by the term "Hamburg."[47]

Rather than disagreeing directly and from entrenched positions, they conducted an unspoken and allusive dialogue over the next decade. Adler caricatures Adorno in *The Wall,* composed at the same time he was writing to Adorno about the possibility of lecturing in Frankfurt.[48] Although in 1956 Adorno eventually invited Adler to deliver the prestigious Loeb Lecture at the University of Frankfurt on "Theresienstadt—die Lehren einer Zwangsgemeinschaft" ("Theresienstadt—The Lessons of a Coerced Community"), initiated that year by Leo Baeck, prior to that Adler received neither a response to his early queries nor an invitation.[49] In *The Wall,* his frustration, and his skepticism about Adorno's views on the Holocaust, shines through his satirical rendering of Professor Kratzenstein, director of the International Society of Sociologists, a stand-in for the institute that Adorno directed. Meeting Kratzenstein at a party of exiled intellectuals in London's "metropolis," Arthur Landau explains that he is writing a sociology of oppressed people. Kratzenstein thinks this a worthy topic, but he is concerned that as a survivor Landau might too easily "get bogged down in ethical matters," a mistake. "[W]hoever was there is rarely right for such a task. Anything subjective is dangerous. . . . Scholarship must present its material in a pure manner. Everything else is almost always a metaphysical joke or nonsense.' "[50] More condescendingly, when Landau musters the courage to see Kratzenstein about funding, he receives little more than a vigorous pat on the back when the Professor exclaims, " 'My goodness, you yourself have been through such an experience. How did you manage it! The fact that you're not bitter and have maintained your love of scholarship, I congratulate you! Just wonderful, I say, wonderful!' "[51] Kratzenstein invites Landau to sit in on the regular meetings of the institute's working group but does not ask him to lecture and he pontificates about how "all suffering . . . was the result of economic conditions." Landau finds that "Kratzenstein's platitudes, propped up with big words, . . . wafted dully about my ears, completely dead, dogmatic declarations that did nothing but elicit the connections between multiple aspects and elucidate them."[52]

Adler's satire is a biting caricature, not an outright attack on Adorno. Kratzenstein is a composite of postwar intellectuals eager to offer theories on the meaning and import of the Holocaust. The Professor's name sounds comic in German, and its combination of "kratzen" ("to scratch") and "stein" ("stone") indicates how Kratzenstein serves as a warped "touchstone" for his generation in much the same way that T. S. Eliot's Prufrock was an epitome of anxiety for the prior generation ("prüfen" in German can mean to probe or poke with a finger, and therefore "touch," and "rock" is of course another word for "stone").[53] Nor was Adler averse to turning his friends into broad types. The character of "So-and-So" in *The Wall* is based on Steiner, who comes off as self-involved in his demands for Landau to help retrieve whatever estate his parents left in Prague and desultory in his efforts to secure contacts for him in London, and as we have seen, the distant and disloyal Otto Bergmann is a stand-in for Canetti. But none of these attacks is launched from personal animosity. Instead, they serve to render the "monstrous and often clown-like, de-ranged countenance" of the postwar world that Adler had pointed out to Broch after quoting none other than Adorno on the need for modern art to use "inhumanity" to "outdo that of the world for the sake of the human."[54]

Adorno composed his own veiled portrait of Adler in the last chapter of *Negative Dialectics*:

> A man whose admirable strength enabled him to survive Auschwitz and other camps said in an outburst against Beckett that if Beckett had been in Auschwitz he would be writing differently, more positively, with the frontline creed of the escapee. The escapee is right in a fashion

> other than he thinks. Beckett, and whoever else remained in control of himself, would have been broken in Auschwitz and probably forced to confess that frontline creed which the escapee clothed in the words "Trying to give men courage"—as if this were up to any structure of the mind; as if the intent to address men, to adjust to them, did not rob them of what is their due even if they believe in the contrary. That is what we have come to in metaphysics.[55]

Jeremy Adler notes that the "escapee" was his father.[56] Adorno likely heard the outburst firsthand when Adler returned to Frankfurt to deliver a private talk at the Institute for Social Research in March 1957. Given the back-and-forth around the title for the talk, underlying tensions surely existed. Adler proposed titling his talk "Film Theresienstadt—Menschliche Verblendung in einer Zwangslage" ("The Theresienstadt Film—Human Delusion amid Coerced Conditions"), but Adorno suggested changing it to "Film Theresienstadt—Ideologien in der Zwangssituation" ("The Theresienstadt Film—Ideologies amid Coerced Circumstances").[57] When Adler protested that he wished to say "nothing at all ideological about the film," Adorno simply took out "The Theresienstadt Film" and titled the lecture "Ideologies amid Coerced Circumstances," which Adler only learned about in a note from Adorno's secretary.[58]

Unsurprisingly, the talk was not well received, as Adler admitted in his thank-you letter to Adorno: "I take away the lesson that, in a scholarly circle which has developed its own scholarly terminology, one cannot, or at least must with caution, introduce a different terminology."[59] The irony is that Adorno sought to frame the terminology from the start. As for Adler's "outburst" on Beckett, a few months later in a letter to the poet and translator Franz Wurm, Adler is dismissive of Beckett's work.[60] In another letter to Wurm in January 1959, he declares, "[N]o one who has been in Auschwitz and who ever since has dealt with Auschwitz and similar matters would bother to read the works of Samuel Beckett. I at least have no interest in doing so. . . . Maybe he would not write such stuff or would take up other subjects if he had spent a single day in Auschwitz."[61] When asked once about Adorno's dictum about poetry being impossible to write after Auschwitz, Adler shot back that it only meant "that Adorno was not in Auschwitz."[62]

Adorno's nameless reference to Adler is a clear challenge to his stance. Altering Adler's outburst to say that if Beckett had been in Auschwitz he would have "been broken" and "forced to confess that frontline creed which the escapee clothed in the words 'Trying to give men courage,'" Adorno undermines the "admirable strength" that allowed the "escapee" to survive. Jeremy Adler finds more troubling implications in Adorno's choice of words in the German.[63] Rather than referring to a "survivor" or "Überlebenden," Adorno chooses "Entronnenen" or "escapee," or more pointedly "the one who got away," both of which strangely position Adorno as a camp commandant or Death itself.[64]

Never referring to the "escapee" as a Jew, Adorno obliterates the attribute for which the victim was persecuted and any possible worth to whatever religious belief might have helped him survive. In its stead Adorno asserts, "Beckett has given us the only fitting reaction to the situation of the concentration camps.... As long as the world is as it is, all pictures of reconciliation, peace, and quiet resemble the picture of death."[65] Adler's own hopeful spirit was for Adorno an impediment to a "truthful" wrestling with Auschwitz.[66] Adorno never names Adler, denying any opportunity to assess both sides. Beckett's approach is deemed "the only fitting reaction," reducing Beckett to a "Holocaust" writer in the skewed way that Kafka is too often read as a prophet of the Shoah. The misfortune is that Adorno and Adler shared more ground than divided them. Both were steeped in musicology, sociology, and philosophy. Both saw the modern bureaucratic state as the nemesis behind the world's ills. Both saw the necessity of art in finding a way to express suffering without negating it by a nostalgic return to traditions or a wallowing in formless expressions of pain. Had they worked more closely together or debated more frequently and openly in public, one wonders what might have resulted. Instead they remain two fighters shadow-boxing in separate rings, the real fight never occurring, no crowd there to see it.

In a posthumously published note written in 1965, Adorno accorded Adler singular praise:

> What most impresses me about Adler is his ability to overcome conditions that would appear to make his work on Theresienstadt impossible. It's hard to imagine that such a gentle and sensible person remained so mindfully present and capable of objectivity amid such an organized hell whose acknowledged aim was the destruction of the self before physical extermination. Such strength should be distinguished entirely from any kind of crude vitality or clumsy urge for self-preservation. Perhaps it even requires a gentleness that, according to shallow opinions, is the first thing to succumb, a sensibility that finds brutality and injustice so intolerable that it feels all the more a sense of responsibility to at least preserve memory, to say the unsayable, and to remain loyal to the victims there, where nothing more can be changed. There is probably also something in Adler of that Jewish-fraternal sense of resistance that leads to the kind of reaction that refuses to accept the inevitable, and out of this refusal comes the capacity not only to escape, but also to bear witness to that which, without the existence of such a sense of resistance, would truly triumph altogether. The constellation of gentleness and resistance is in Adler turned into a moral agent,

> a Kantian "imperative," and therefore he is owed not only the gratitude of those whose story he has told, but also the unadulterated admiration of those who believe they could not, in that respect, have done the same as what he did.[67]

Beyond seemingly left-handed compliments ("that Jewish-fraternal sense of resistance," reference to having "escaped," and whether Adorno *could* not have done the same, or *would* not have), Adorno expresses respect for Adler's work and strength. And yet how different things might have been, had he said this publicly in his lifetime, or in Adler's.

Remarkably, despite their isolation between 1947 and 1955, or perhaps because of it, Günther and Bettina's attention to others remained undiminished. Adler's most pointed admissions of his own struggles are in a series of letters to Steiner, who was gravely ill in an Oxford hospital after suffering a heart attack.[68] Günther wrote twenty-eight letters to his friend between September and November 1949, knowing that, as in "The Letter Writers," he would likely not get a reply. Besides working all day with only a radio to commune with the world, he reports on concert after concert, discussing Vivaldi, Bach, medieval choral music, Baroque composers, Wagner, and Bartok, as if listening on behalf of Steiner, who heard no music for four months other than on the BBC's Light Programme in the hospital common room.[69] After the isolation and bleakness of Theresienstadt and the camps, Adler knew that small gestures or brief messages could remind someone that others were aware, even if they could do little to change one's plight. Whereas Steiner could not reach out to Adler during the war and had in part forsaken the chance before it, Günther's expressions of concern posed as good wishes and advice but were lifelines tossed to a friend in distress. This did not make him a saint or the better man, but it speaks to habits of care that he learned in the camps.

Suse Tieze, the childhood friend who took in Adler on the first night of his return to Prague, also benefited from Bettina and Günther's care. After emigrating to London in January 1949, she lived with the Adlers in cramped quarters until she found work that fall at Lingfield House, a London home for children who had survived the camps.[70] In addition, Bettina now and then baked cakes for Steiner and sent them with Esther Frank, a close friend of his who traveled from London to visit. Between concert reports Günther kept up Steiner's flagging hopes of seeing a selection of Steiner's poems published by Willi Weismann in Munich, even though Weismann had already turned down Adler's *Panorama*. Reporting animatedly on the collected works of Friedrich Schelling, which he borrowed from Steiner, Adler sought to engage his friend's intellect. Although he touched as well on the "narrow province of my own trials and tribulations," he let Steiner know he was thinking of him and counting on his full recovery.[71]

Bettina Adler: Sketch of Franz Baermann Steiner, 1952. Credit: The Estate of Bettina Adler 2019, Deutsches Literaturarchiv Marbach.

From time to time Adler was able to report mild success in securing work. Late November of 1949 saw the broadcast of his talk on "Goethe's *Faust* in Music" for the BBC, and a talk he gave to Club 1943. Founded by the German dramatists Hans José Rehfisch and Alfred H. Unger (Wilhelm's brother), Club 1943 provided a weekly forum of lectures, readings, and concerts in Hampstead that served the exile community as a nonpolitical counterpart to the predominantly left-wing Free German League of Culture. Grete Fischer also helped found it, and through her Adler met eminent émigrés, including the writer Hans Flesch, the former head of the Dresden opera Kurt Wolff, the Goethe biographer Richard Freidenthal, the theater critic Monty Jacobs, the painter Fred Uhlmann, and the novelist Gabriele Tergit.[72] Along with the PEN Center for German-speaking Writers in Exile (which Adler headed from 1973 to 1985) and the Austrian PEN Club in Exile, Club 1943 provided Jewish refugees and intellectuals with an oasis in which to maintain the culture of the world they had left behind and to navigate the one in which they had landed. Roughly half of the ninety thousand refugees who came to England before the war remained there, and London teemed with intellectual life.[73]

Throughout the fall Adler was also excited to work on *Impressions of an Innocent Abroad*, a brief book of observations on English manners and mores that he hoped would be published by his friend Philip Inman, son of Baron Inman, a Labor politician and chair of the BBC. Adler wrote it for the money, but the sweep and accuracy of his observations are striking when one considers how soon he formed them after his arrival in England. The 154-page manuscript also provides insights into Adler's own state of mind while writing it, including the epigraph from the Stoic philosopher Epictetus that Adler plucked from Matthew Arnold's 1879 introduction to Wordsworth's poems:

> As if a man, journeying home, and finding a nice inn on the road, and liking it, were to stay forever at the inn! Man, thou hast forgotten thine object; thy journey was not to this, but *through* this. "But this inn is taken." And how many other inns, too, are taken, and how many fields and meadows! But as places of passage merely. You have an object, which is this: to get home, to do your duty to your family, friends and fellow-countrymen, to attain inward freedom, serenity, happiness, contentment.

As an epigraph to a general discussion of English life, this seems loaded and somber, but Adler makes clear that he is not writing as a tourist or an émigré but as "a fugitive, pure and simple," who had escaped "darkness and uncertainty, terror and destruction" and who found himself grateful to be in a land where "I have found inner peace—and if I may say so—happiness."[74] Adler's real aim was to support his own literary and scholarly writing on the camps that had consumed so many of his "family, friends and fellow countrymen" while hoping to regain and sustain his own "inward freedom, happiness and contentment." No small project, nor does Adler ignore the adjustments he needed to make in getting used to his newfound freedom:

> My English friends must forgive me if even now I experience an inexplicable apprehension when a policeman passes my house. Such fear really is inexplicable if one has not personally suffered during the past years on the continent. For many weeks I could not suppress my wonder at the fact that there still is a country in which order prevails, and only thus is it understandable that I celebrate as my day of liberation that of my arrival in England rather than the day in April 1945 on which I was rescued from the power of Nazi Germany.[75]

Adler does not just remain focused on his own anxiety and past suffering but reminds the British of how much they have to be thankful for as well. Acknowledging the destruction of the war, Adler points out that, compared to what happened on the continent,

> No one in England has been involved in a universal catastrophe in which only moral giants could stand upright. This does not mean that England did not sustain serious losses in human lives and in the destruction and loss of property of all kinds, as well as in the moral sphere. But the nation's substance has not been seriously affected. No one was forced to tell lies, the people could hold their heads high throughout the years. All efforts could be concentrated on the adversary outside without fear of the danger from within. On the mainland, on the other hand, nothing remained for countless men and women but to attempt an inner and personal opposition. This was an inner and personal decision in which each was thrown back on his inner resources.[76]

The line Adler walks is between an analysis of the experience of the war in England and on the continent, and setting the suffering of the Jews above that of the British, a risky strategy in a book for an English audience. Adler surreptitiously uses the occasion to tell his audience what had happened, for even four years after the war, they still did not know what it had been like for him and millions of others. The text is another "place of passage," borrowing Epictetus, for the "journey" of its writing "is not to this, but *through* this" in saying what happened and what it meant for victor and victim alike.

Grete Fischer provided an English translation titled *Comments on the English* for the entire text, and Inman remained a close friend of Adler's, helping him to practice his English when recording for the radio. Yet the project fell through for unknown reasons. Most likely Inman felt the weak British book market could not support it, never mind that anti-German sentiment was still prevalent. Adler's analysis of British life likely was also an impediment, for in his wide-ranging discussion of British newspapers, homes, town and country, neighbors, taste and arts, adventure, he is often critical. Observing that British newspapers are "read by people who, although they value their private lives and their freedom more than anything else, yet desire to resemble each other," or that "English houses are, on average, the worst in Europe," as in his analysis of Theresienstadt, Adler pulls no punches.

Adler's text is not the patriotic celebration of British spirit that Inman or readers might have wanted, but he does make clear his belief in the social structures of English life and governance:

> Those in authority provide the people with the possibility of free development of will and action; they provide democratic rights and personal safety; and they ensure freedom from fear; a freedom which as a guest in this country I value most highly. It may be possible for people to go under and die of hunger, but at least they can do this *as free agents*, untormented by indifference from governmental [bodies] or other

> interference. I am not in the least ironical in dwelling on this bitter fact as of incomparable merit.[77]

Unfortunately, Adler's gratitude, like so many of his other projects at the time, never saw light of day.

Such disappointment began to take its toll, and the family's fortunes reached a nadir in June 1950 when all three contracted mononucleosis.[78] Günther was stricken particularly hard, and the family became so sick that they had to be taken in by Dora Stern, a distant cousin of Bettina's, who also lived in London, the three of them sleeping on mattresses on the floor of her Hampstead home. Stern, in fact, was quite wealthy, but this temporary relief was all she ever provided Bettina or her family, for she disapproved of Bettina's marriage to an impoverished refugee who, in the aunt's eyes, had neglected the health and well-being of his family.[79] Eventually Bettina and three-year-old Jeremy recovered, but Günther continued to suffer from weariness and lack of energy for months. Only an August 1951 vacation, the first for Bettina and Günther, offered by the Wistow Centre for International Friendship and Service in Leicestershire, an ecumenical organization run by Pastor Willi and Lisbeth Baermann to support German refugees, granted them the time and space to recover.[80] There they could walk and rest and escape the heat of the city, as well as think about how Günther could best carry on, "trusting in God, who had miraculously saved me amid all my difficulties, and in the belief that my efforts were important to bringing, beyond shock alone, *hope* to humankind."[81]

Adler's commitment to larger spiritual and cultural goals drew him to volunteer to help Wilhelm Unger found the Library of the German Language in London. Following the British celebration of Goethe's bicentennial with the Goethe Festival of 1949, which helped to restore cultural relations between the British and the Germans, Unger decided to open a library for German literature in London to serve the exile community and encourage cultural exchange between the two countries. Idealistic in essence and scope, it faced an uphill battle for funding and "the not very friendly attitude of the local German representatives and the barely disguised enmity of their unofficial cultural envoys."[82] When it finally was opened by Lord Pakenham in June 1951, most of its holdings had passed through Adler's hands and been catalogued by him. "I see H. G. A.," Unger later wrote, "standing in a large cold room eagerly thumbing through the pages of books that had arrived from a country which one might have turned one's back on forever. A new volume of Goethe or of Hölderlin, a new edition of Kafka or a new book on Adalbert Stiffer? That was the world out of which we came, to which we belonged, and which was now the face of a lost home that we wished to turn to again. . . . Those hours in Adler's home—the muted sound of Schönberg or Anton Webern emanating from the radio—were times of deep self-reflection."[83]

Known as "The Other Germany" among the exile community, the library soon became a haven for all. Its founding required the cooperation of the German publishing industry in the throes of trying to rebuild itself, and Adler's work with Unger led to his first professional break when Unger sent him to the Frankfurt Book Fair in September 1951. Charged with networking with editors and publishers, gathering catalogs, and securing donations of books for the library, Adler was keen to make contacts of his own, meeting Peter Suhrkamp, who in 1933 had rejected Adler's youthful poems, but who now headed Suhrkamp Verlag. Adler spent two months in Germany, traveling to Heidelberg, Stuttgart, Munich, Hamburg, Cologne, and Bonn after his stay in Frankfurt. From there he proudly wrote home to Bettina in late September to say that two of his short stories, "Die Tanzerin Malva" ("The Dancer Malva") and "Eine flüchtige Bekanntschaft" ("A Fleeting Friendship"), had appeared in the important journal *Frankfurter Rundschau*.[84] This was the first publication of his fiction anywhere and shows how important the trip was in making his first inroads among postwar writers and editors in Germany. Unfortunately, Adorno was in America during his Frankfurt visit, denying them a chance to meet.

In Frankfurt, Adler delivered a lecture at the Goethe Haus on Kafka as a religious writer, earning 50 Deutsche Marks. He recorded his essay "Sprachgeist und Sprachverfall" ("The Spirit of Language and Its Decay") for Radio Hessen, for an additional 120 Deutsche Marks.[85] These, with the publication of the two stories, set the pattern he would follow for the next three decades: talks, lectures, and readings given at conferences, universities, bookstores, and Jewish community centers for small honoraria, and essays, discussions, and historical accounts on German radio for larger sums. Often the two strategies fed each other, Adler delivering a talk on a subject he had spoken about on the radio, or using talks and lectures to develop radio essays he would later record. Published essays and excerpts from his scholarly work were also tapped, as Adler made full use of the "trove of experience" that Steiner had encouraged him to mine after he returned to Prague. None of it was easy. It required that he correspond with editors and administrators, continue to generate new topics and ideas, travel regularly to Germany to lecture on and record this material, and use such visits to generate contacts and commissions for essays and lectures he worked on back in London.

Adler embraced the regime of travel and meetings with editors, for it granted him the human contact that he so missed in London. He enjoyed being back on German-speaking soil and returning to the milieu in which he felt most at home: the German language. In the first radio essay he recorded he spoke on the relationship between the deterioration of language and that of the intellect or spirit, which remained a core value, often evident in his critique of Nazi euphemisms such as "special handling" (*Sonderbehandlung*) or "special transport" (*Sondertransport*) to disguise murderous activities behind a scrim of administrative terms. Inspired by the work of Karl Kraus, Adler saw deeply ethical consequences in the misuse of language, such as the Nazis' employment of common verbs such as *betreuen*, which means "to look after or supervise" someone, as code for deportation, imprisonment, and extermination.[86]

Adler's travels introduced him to Germany itself, a country he hardly knew despite having visited his family in Berlin in his university days. Struck by the immense destruction in cities like Cologne, 90 percent of which had been reduced to rubble, he had the chance through repeated journeys back to Germany to witness its rapid rebuilding. By 1955 he could write to Bettina from Frankfurt, "Just five years from now one will no longer see any damage from the war," and he was impressed by the quality of the new construction and the care with which cathedrals and churches were restored to their original splendor.[87] He began to imagine the possibility of visiting Germany with Bettina and Jeremy, no doubt wanting his son to know firsthand the language and culture with which he still so strongly identified. "There are worthwhile people here who are pleasant and in their own way good," he tells Bettina, although quickly reassuring her, "Don't worry, I still admire our England, and I haven't changed any of my views in the least."[88] Writing after a particularly bad meal of kidneys and potato soup in Cologne, he confides, "All well and fine the recovery here, but my life will always be over there—that seems to me the lesson."[89]

The trips to Germany marked a turning point in Adler's life, forging a bridge to a past that in many ways was no longer present, allowing for the formulation of a new future in its stead. But between his journey in 1951 to the Frankfurt Book Fair and his second sojourn in 1955, Adler experienced one last painful break with his childhood: on November 27, 1952, Franz Steiner died of a heart attack in Oxford. He was buried the next day, Adler, Canetti, Suse Tietze, Eric Fried, Hans Eichner, Georg Rapp, and the anthropologist Willy Kühnberg traveling from London to join sixty mourners in snow-covered Wolvergrove Cemetery for the burial.[90] His oldest friend, his closest confidant and companion besides Bettina, and the soul who had most shaped his sensibility as a writer, sociologist, and Jew was gone. The war had denied them many years together, yet because of it they had found the chance to reunite again in England. But only for five years, during which Steiner was so ill that he could no longer travel to do fieldwork, nor muster the energy to complete his many projects. It would be up to Günther to tend to them. His edition of Steiner's poems *Unruhe ohne Uhr* (*Timeless Tumult*) in 1954 was in fact Adler's first postwar book publication. Over the years he wrote articles and essays on his work and a decade later pushed through publication of Steiner's great lyric cycle *Eroberungen* (*Conquests*). In a letter written four months after Steiner's death, he expressed his friend's essence:

> He is one of the most tragic figures I have ever come across, disaster pursued him relentlessly, he was almost always powerless, could almost

> never break free, he suffered endlessly and was steadfast and brave in his pain, but yet unhappiness burned and killed him: he could not grow old. . . . He was a broken man, persecuted and mistreated, and few have suffered more intellectually or physically, to come to terms with themselves, not to despair completely of themselves and the world, to muster their talents over and over again in spite of all obstacles, and to remain true to the end to their own values in the face of such discord. That he was able to achieve this does not simply absolve him of any harsh judgements, but instead underlines his greatness as a human being.[91]

Only a lifelong friend can speak with such frankness and pity. Written in response to a request for a comment on Steiner's life forwarded by Chaim Rabin from Hugo Bergmann (with whom Steiner had lived while studying Arabic at the Hebrew University in Palestine in 1930–1931), the letter runs to thirty-six typed pages and took four days for Adler to write.[92] It pays homage to his dear friend and reads as a final goodbye to the Prague childhood that he had left behind for good.

Franz Baermann Steiner, 1952. Credit: The Estate of H. G. Adler 2019, Deutsches Literaturarchiv Marbach.

None of this could bring Steiner back, nor was there any going back to Prague or the Bohemian Forest they had loved and crisscrossed earlier. "A life without suffering is valueless," Steiner wrote to George Rapp in 1943, for he felt that, given the violence of the war and mass persecution, "there is no other possibility apart from either living in an Eastern-monastic manner by turning all suffering into an illusion, or to live boundlessly in suffering, to allow oneself to be filled with suffering."[93] Steiner did attain a deep level of happiness and fulfillment in the last year of his life when he and the English novelist and philosopher Iris Murdoch fell in love, but he had been haunted by death since the loss of his beloved sister, Suse, to a streptococcal infection in 1932 at age nineteen.[94] Without Steiner, Adler was on his own. Canetti remained a friend, but a cold and unreliable one with whom he quarreled off and on for years. It was with Steiner that he had roamed the streets of Karlín, the forests of Bohemia and southern Europe, and later the labyrinths of Eastern mysticism, Judaism, music, and poetry. Near the end of "Prayer in the Garden" Steiner had written:

All creatures must cross the sea,
For nowhere is mercy found but out at sea,
The mercy of mercy:
These are the errant creatures out at sea,
All those who for the sake of coming home
Suffer the great afflictions and the small.[95]

Read in German by Midia Kraus and in English by Anne Beresford (wife of poet and translator Michael Hamburger) at a memorial sponsored by Club 1943 and the PEN Club of German Writers in Exile on March 3, 1953, the lines would have resonated most for Iris Murdoch, the Canettis, the Hamburgers, Grete Fischer, Erich Fried, and Bettina and Günther Adler, all "creatures at sea" in search of the "mercy of mercy . . . for the sake of coming home."

14

The Scholar

"If lives fall into two halves," writes Adler's son, Jeremy, "he lived his 'life' first. Then the 'work.'"[1] The first copy of *Theresienstadt 1941–1945* arrived on Günther's doorstep in London on November 8, 1955, marking the culmination of the decade-long transition from the "life" to the "work" that began with his return to Prague after the war. Having completed five novels, with a sixth to be finished the following year, over eighty short stories, hundreds of poems, and dozens of essays for print and radio, at forty-five, Adler had made something of his life in more ways than one.

Hans Hennecke, Elias Canetti, H. G. Adler, and Leonora and Wilhelm Unger, London, 1953. Credit: The Estate of H. G. Adler 2019, Deutsches Literaturarchiv Marbach.

The journey had not been easy. It took ten years to research, write, and revise the manuscript, and although he brought a nearly complete draft of the book with him when he left Prague for London, publisher after publisher rejected it. Only with the May 1954 intervention of Fritz Hodeige, one of three editors of the *Civitas Gentium* series of scholarly works in sociology and law published in Tübingen by J. C. B. Mohr (Paul Siebeck), did the book find a champion.[2] Hans Georg Siebeck accepted it for publication before he finished reading the manuscript. Having published such luminaries as Max Weber and Hans Kelsen, Siebeck felt that "we unfortunately live in a time that, on the one hand, wants to forget everything too soon, and on the other, shuts itself off from all that is still readily apparent behind the artificially constructed façade of frivolity and forgetfulness."[3] Adler's book did neither. Nevertheless two impediments had to be overcome, the first being the success of Eugen Kogon's 1946 book *Der SS Staat* (*The Theory and Practice of Hell,* 1954), which sold well in Germany, where the paperback was in its fifth printing.[4] Adler's response to Siebeck's concern was vigorous and thorough. Laying out seven points that distinguished his book from Kogon's, he noted the uniqueness of Theresienstadt and how "it reminded one of a world imagined by Kafka more than any realistic social structure." He argued that "no book, not even one out of Poland," contained as much documentary information or internal accounts. His was a "general social anthropology" of the ghetto, which touched the fields of history, sociology, psychology, philosophy, law, medicine, education, and linguistics. Lastly, Adler argued that his book addressed the SS's entire plan for the extermination of the Jews, that not a single study of Theresienstadt had appeared in German, and that it came with a glossary of some 650 terms and a list of sources that documented the thorough research and verity of the entire work. Nothing like this existed in Kogon's book. Adler maintained that not only was his book the most thorough study to date of Theresienstadt, it spoke to a "different public" than did Kogon's and would find a strong reception among "foreign audiences and the Jewish readership."[5]

Adler's book emphasized that Theresienstadt was unique within the SS system and that it represented the system's central nemesis. He argued that the debasement of human beings who were transformed from subjects into objects by the corrupt administration of power spoke to the undermining of modern societies as a whole rather than just Germany. Lest his study seem merely theoretical, Adler emphasizes its practical import for the Jews, underscoring a distinction between himself and Kogon. Whereas Kogon had aimed to indict the Nazis and the concentration camp system based on his seven-year imprisonment in Buchenwald, Adler bracketed his personal experience to observe the effect of modern bureaucracy run wild on Nazi and Jew alike and how it threatened the postwar world as much as it had eviscerated the history that gave birth to it.

Comparing two brief passages distinguishes the two works. After listing prominent SS officials, including Himmler and Heydrich, Kogon sums up their pursuit of power:

> These men sought only power—power over other men, over institutions, over Germany, over other nations, if possible over the world and the future. All was to go according to their will. Perhaps their pursuit of power was instinctive rather than conscious, under the pretext that it was on behalf of Germany; perhaps they presented a nationalist veneer only to deceive themselves, their environment and the public at large, since naked power for its own sake would probably not yet have been acceptable.[6]

Adler summarizes the same subject:

> Power [in Theresienstadt] reduced life's rationally indescribable richness, the totality of which is history, to the object of an inorganic experiment in which all history was unconsciously negated and driven almost to dissolution. Power itself was conceived of in material terms, and every organic structure was captured using the tools of a technical-administrative apparatus. Thus life, the existence of which cannot be denied, became a "mass to be recorded," a subject for administration that is "deployed" and "supervised" ("betreut"), and for which, in any case, "measures are taken." This certainly reflected the general Occidental crisis of culture, and the demise of Hitler's regime will by no means suffice to overcome this crisis. The consequence of turning every human being into a number denoting an "item" is obvious if life becomes a thing; this has become the almost uncontested practice in the administrations of modern states.[7]

Where Kogon focuses on individual actors pursuing their own ends under the pretext of serving the German cause, Adler gives a more scientific sociological analysis. Adler takes in "all history" and the "general Occidental crisis" while anchoring his conclusions in administrative terms used in both Theresienstadt and the modern bureaucratic state. In fact Siebeck would have struck a nerve when he wrote Adler to accept the book, saying that he hoped "to have the opportunity to supervise [betreuen] the publication" of the book.[8] Adler saw the slow creep of such terms into everyday life as proof that the crisis was by no means over. Similarly, Adler's analysis of Nazi power reaches beyond the war, while Kogon's remains focused on the events and developments of 1933–1945. The difference between them is not quality but factuality and bearing. While

Kogon writes history, Adler uses the historical record to posit a philosophy of history simultaneously addressing fact, motivation, and consequence.

It did not take Siebeck long to appreciate these distinctions and accept the book for publication, but another hurdle was the need to raise a subvention of 8,500 Deutsche Marks to cover printing costs.[9] Adler had told Siebeck that Leo Baeck was "cautiously optimistic" that supporting funds could be raised in America or Switzerland. These hopes never bore fruit, but Adler persevered, and in early February 1955, thirteen years after he and Gertrud were deported to Theresienstadt, Adler traveled to Frankfurt, where he asked for Adorno's support in raising the subvention.[10] By the time Adler returned home a month later, he had a promise for the extraordinary sum of 8,000 Marks from the Bundeszentrale für Heimatdienst in Bonn, and Siebeck could start production immediately.[11] The Bundeszentrale also commissioned him to produce a separate article on "Die Rolle Theresienstadt in der 'Endlösung der Judenfrage,'" which would appear that June in *Aus Politik und Zeitgeschichte*, the weekly magazine of the newspaper *Das Parlament*, whose circulation was thirty-five thousand.[12] The 900 Marks for this assignment, plus the advance of 1,000 Marks he received from Siebeck, was the first substantial money he earned as a writer. It had taken him until the age of forty-five to achieve it.[13]

Adler's return trip to Germany in February 1955 allowed him to personally make his case for war reparations from the German government, something that was neither automatic nor easily accomplished, although it was more effective to apply in person than from abroad. Unlike Jews in Germany, Jews born in Czechoslovakia were not included in the initial reparations offered by Germany. The Czech government was only willing to compensate Czech citizens, and anyone who had declared his or her nationality as German in the 1930 census was considered to have forsaken Czech citizenship. As a stateless person persecuted by the Nazis, Adler was entitled to receive reparations under the 1953 Federal Supplementary Law for the Compensation of Victims of National Socialist Persecution, for "harm to life, body, health and freedom; harm to possessions and assets; harm to career and economic advancement."[14] Due to the difficulty of documenting the possessions he had lost in Prague, and since he had not established a career before deportation, initially he could apply for compensation of loss of liberty and damages to his health, but it took him years to qualify for reparations for damage to his career. As for the loss of assets taken from him and his family in Prague, this remained out of the question. The Communist government of Czechoslovakia refused to take on what it deemed a German problem, nor was it easy to document the losses from outside the country.

Arriving in Cologne on February 7, Adler visited the Bundesministerium, where he received a lump payment of 3,000 Marks toward the 6,300 Marks ($1,600) he was due for his forty-two months of imprisonment.[15] Calculated at the rate of 150 Marks per month for all prisoners, this covered his time as a forced laborer on the railroad and in Theresienstadt, Auschwitz, Niederorschel, and Langenstein.[16] Whether he qualified to receive the additional 3,300 Marks depended on whether the government recognized his work shoveling the airport, on the railroad, and at the book depository of the Prague Jewish Community as imprisonment. Adler argued in person and in German, itself important, as that established him as a member of the "German Volk," meaning that he was a displaced person, not a stateless person, avoiding the 25 percent reduction of reparations to stateless persons who had not settled in Germany.[17]

The next step was to prove and argue for damages to health. Under the law, anyone who could show his earning capacity had been reduced by at least 25 percent was entitled to a monthly pension geared to one of four civil service classes. In October 1953, Konrad Hirsch, a doctor in Swansea, Wales (who helped to proofread the Theresienstadt book), attested that Adler suffered from chronic bronchitis and catarrh and that his earning capacity had been reduced by 33 percent.[18] In July 1956, the German government awarded Adler 4,250 Marks ($1,030) dating back to October 1953 and a pension of 125 Marks ($30) per month going forward. Unfortunately the rate was tied to Adler's current income, a lower rate than Germans who had spent the last decade establishing postwar careers at salaries higher than Adler's sparse earnings as a freelance writer in the early 1950s. Adler was also assigned to the middle-level civil service class, further lowering his pension in relation to other German civil servants. An additional outrage was that, as early as 1951 (two years before the restitution law), the German Parliament passed legislation allowing former members of the Nazi party to rejoin the civil service and have their pensions made whole retroactively.[19]

No amount of money could compensate for the suffering and loss of family and friends by any victims. Some refused to apply for reparations because of the guilt they felt, since millions of others were not alive to do so for themselves. Many others felt stymied when trying to decipher the bureaucratic labyrinth of conditions and classifications. Friends in Germany like Wilhelm Unger and Margrit Baldner helped Adler to press on. The awards he attained were modest, but the promise of a small steady income made a difference, and the initial lump sums created the first cushion against abject poverty that he and Bettina had. The real consequence was the damage that had been done to a career that blossomed with his work for the Urania in the middle 1930s but that had been derailed almost entirely in the twenty years since.

Hence the third category—damage done to career—was the most important but also the most difficult to resolve. This had to do, perversely, with whether victims like himself were seen as having been forced to abandon a career when they were deported, or whether because he had returned to Czechoslovakia right after the war, he had thus forsaken a career in Germany and therefore was entitled to no career compensation. That was the reply he received when he applied for career damages of 10,000 Marks.[20] And yet it was the Germans who had deported him and thousands of others from his homeland, along with millions more from across western and eastern Europe. Adler continued to argue that he was indeed a deportee deserving of capital compensation for damage to his career, and he filed a complaint to this effect in November 1957 but was turned down again the following month. Finally in January 1958 the regional Pension Office for the German state of Rheinland-Pfalz in Düsseldorf awarded him 3,600 Marks, pending the outcome of the decision on whether he was entitled to full compensation as a deportee.

It took until May 1960 to resolve, and the process and outcome affected many more than Adler himself. Seeing his situation as a perfect test case, he sent extensive memoranda to the Bundesministerium, quoting Heydrich's proclamations and internal memos on the deportations, as well as outlining their financing by the Deportation Fund of Bohemia and Moravia, a phony entity created by Eichmann to use wealth stolen from Jewish families and businesses to pay for their own deportation and imprisonment. Adler also made his argument to the United Restitution Organization in Germany and the Central Council of the Jews of Germany. His memoranda to the Bundesministerium were not in vain, for the regulations passed by the state of Rheinland-Pfalz in October 1957 quoted his arguments in several places when finally granting the claim that those deported to Theresienstadt and the East from outside of Germany would indeed be considered victims of German deportation policies and entitled to compensation as deportees in their own right.[21] The revised regulations benefitted Adler and many of the half-million other refugees whose cases were processed by the Düsseldorf office.[22]

Changes in the German laws aimed at speedier processing of claims and fairer decisions on the level of reparations awarded also benefitted Adler, for in May 1960 his status was changed from a middle-level civil class designation to the highest level, nearly doubling his monthly pension. The government paid him a lump sum to cover the difference in arrears back to 1953, and he was awarded an additional 15,000 Marks for damage to his career, bringing the sum to a total of 18,600 Marks ($4,650). By 1960, the upper limit for such damages had been raised to 40,000 Marks, indicating that as a deportee from Czechoslovakia his potential salary was still calculated at less than half of the upper limit, even though his civil class had been pegged at the highest level.

Despite receiving official notice of the death of his parents and Gertrud in 1956, Adler's application for reparations on his father's behalf was denied, as well as any potential reparations for Gertrud or Bettina's mother, as they were determined not to be German citizens at the time of their death. Bettina eventually received a payment of 10,000 Marks ($2,500) for lost earnings in 1962, although it required repeated inquiries to see it through. Only with an additional and special award of 1,500 Marks per month granted him as "artist support" in 1971 did the couple receive a pension comparable to what a middle-class couple would have received when retiring after forty years. A deportee and slave laborer in Theresienstadt and the camps, both the labor he lost and the labor he contributed remained less valued and more invisible than that of citizens of a Germany still interested in protecting its own rather than doing what was just to all who had been harmed by it.

All that Adler could do was find support for the work he knew how to do best. Following news in March 1955 that Bonn would provide the necessary subvention, Siebeck proposed an initial print run of two thousand copies of the Theresienstadt book. This made it possible to price the book at 38 Marks rather than 45, which the publisher hoped would help with sales.[23] Notwithstanding the special attention needed for the book's many tables and indexes during typesetting, production moved along quickly, the biggest hitch being the delay in receiving Leo Baeck's brief foreword praising the book's "scientific rigor" and "an artistic sensibility that is able to understand or intuit the underlying causes." For a time it looked like it would not arrive at all, for the eighty-one-year-old Baeck was seriously injured in an auto accident in London in April 1955. After a June operation, Baeck was strong enough to dictate his foreword from his hospital bed in July, a further sign of the degree to which he stood behind Adler's work and wished to see it known to the world.[24]

Cover of the first edition of *Theresienstadt 1941–1945*. Credit: Author Photo.

Late that fall *Theresienstadt 1941–1945* rolled off the presses to international acclaim, receiving 118 requests for review from thirteen countries.[25] However, the arrival of a first copy at 96 Dalgarno Gardens was accompanied by a trailing irony. Thanking Siebeck for the first copy, Adler laments that the post office had handled the package so badly, "I would never even add this book to my library shelves."[26] The jacket cover had been badly torn, a pity, for Adler had suggested using the official crest of Theresienstadt on it, as he liked how its closed door and stone wall conveyed the sense of the fortress's function as a prison, implying that upon opening the book, the reader was opening the door to the ghetto itself.[27] He requested that a second jacket cover be sent with the other author's copies to follow, but it had to be a disappointment for a book whose research had begun in Theresienstadt as "an act of liberation" to arrive damaged.[28]

The success of *Theresienstadt 1941–1945* would allow Adler to make a "life" out of his "work." As early as the spring of 1955, Adler saw literary and scholarly opportunities in Germany and believed that the publication of his book would help open them up to him. Writing to Bettina in March from Cologne, he observes, "All the writers here are constantly on the road, giving lectures and doing other things in order to make a living. After the T-book is published, I will certainly have to make a return trip, perhaps in November, in order to sit down with Heinz Flügel and see what kinds of lectures might be arranged for me to give."[29] Adding that "one meets a good number of decent people in Germany," Adler could see that there was an intelligent and professional cohort with which to do business, especially among intellectuals who had resisted Hitler's rise and were now eager to rebuild Germany's culture.

Flügel was the editor of the journal *Eckart* and a contributing editor to *Hochland*, both of which were revived after the war after being banned by the Nazis. After publishing Steiner's poems in *Eckart* in 1952, Flügel began publishing Adler's stories, poems, and scholarly articles as early as 1953 and offered him critical advice on how to navigate the postwar literary scene. The fact that the journals were run by Catholic and Protestant intellectuals did not matter, and in some ways helped: their editorial boards were committed to restoring ties between Christians and Jews, despite residual anti-Semitism. The importance of such support was not lost on Adler, and Flügel accepted an essay on "The Sayings of the Fathers" ("Sprüche der Väter"), in which Adler demonstrates that the *Pirkei Avot* is a book "whose sayings for the most part any sensible person could understand without explanation and by which one could know the essence of Judaism."[30] Adler expressed his gratitude by saying, "I very much appreciate what it means for you to dedicate a relatively large amount of space in your journal to Jewish questions and above all Jewish theology. . . . It's really an immensely vital endeavor that *Eckart* has taken on by presenting Judaism from within to educated Germans."[31] Like Adler, Flügel believed in the transformative power of language. He felt compelled to open up and maintain a dialogue with the Jews, visiting Israel in 1959, where his meeting with a Holocaust survivor moved him deeply. "Without the church, apart from the church and against its theology," he wrote in his memoirs, "I had to make my own way to the Jews." Flügel's belief that "Human beings manifest themselves through what they say, and to the degree that their world is transformed into words, thereby responding to the confrontation with nothingness with an answer" would have resonated with Adler.[32] Thus a friendship was formed, spanning Germany's fractured past and in ways that served the civilizing urge of both men.

Bettina also felt a decided change for the better. With seven-year-old Jeremy now in school she was finally able to have some time to her own and responded to Günther's optimism by saying that during the time he had been away she was able to regain a sense of herself for the first time in years:

> I feel again that hovering sense of security felt way back in my childhood and early youth, the hope being that some of the same can return to our life together and not too quickly be lost in everyday concerns.
>
> You married an artist, my dear—after 8 years I still need to concentrate on what needs to be done in order to manage any given day—and even though up until this point nothing catastrophic has occurred, it will nonetheless help to have a bit of money to balance any foolishness or confusion on my part. Still, these years were good for me—one learns to recognize one's limits and know what you can do and what you cannot. Because of that it will go all the better for us moving forward.[33]

Like a breath long held and slowly let out, her letter makes palpable the sacrifices made over the last eight years and the relief in their having finally paid off. The shared sense of their joint project is also why she is at peace and can continue to wait, knowing that there will be further trips abroad for her husband and more weeks and months left to her own, the artist in her having survived and managed through much worse already. On the surface, this might sound like the "little woman" behind the great man, but they both agreed that the "work" meant a "life" for themselves and Jeremy, as well as the chance to restore the "hovering sense of security" of their Prague youth while serving the memory of the many who had disappeared from it. In managing their everyday affairs Bettina may have recognized limits, but as set down in Adler's "Traktat," knowing "what you can do, and what you do" was not just philosophical speculation but a living credo shared between them.

A week later Günther marked a more momentous turn when in a last letter to Bettina from Cologne he reported that, on a whim, he had "bought such a wonderful jacket and pair of pants that I can at last stand before you, Jeremy, and the world. I have had enough of walking around in beggar's rags handed down from the prophet Samuel and about as worn out as the horse the travelling dentist usually rides in on. In the same store I also purchased two particularly splendid shirts and ties, and so I at least have been able to update my wardrobe a bit."[34] Somewhat of a dandy in his Prague days, his whim reveals a renewed sense of himself. Similarly, although he had ceased making entries in his pocket calendar in February 1952 after having asked the question, "What is intellectual work?", later that year Adler bought a calendar for 1956 and began again to record his daily activities. It was as if a new era had dawned. German President Theodor Heuss received him warmly in March, saying that he found the Theresienstadt book to be very powerful.[35] Martin Buber met with him in London that May, followed by Gershom Scholem in August.[36] For the rest of his life Adler set down each day who visited him, where he traveled on the Continent, where he gave a lecture or reading, to whom he wrote letters and from whom he received letters, what exhibition or concert he attended, whether Jeremy, Bettina, or he were ill, and sometimes important anniversaries of key events. Used to keep business matters straight and to make sure he stayed on top of his schedule, the calendar bears witness to someone who felt he now mattered, that he had a place and function in life, work to do and appointments to keep, rather than remaining a destitute and rootless émigré. Günther and Bettina's swearing-in as citizens of the United Kingdom on July 17, 1956, underscored their newfound sense of security and fulfillment.

Luzzi Wolgensinger: H. G. Adler in Zurich, 1957. Credit: Copyright Michael Wolgensinger, with permission from The Estate of H. G. Adler 2019, Deutsches Literaturarchiv Marbach.

The pages of the calendar began to fill, Adler later recalling that "only a chain of miracles allowed us to survive those seven lean years" of 1947–54.[37] Adler made another trip to Germany in July 1955, and lectures, talks, and readings soon materialized. In February 1956, he began a two-month tour of Germany with another stop in Cologne, followed by a week in Hamburg, where he delivered several lectures on Theresienstadt. After that came stops in Lüneberg, Göttingen, Nürnberg, Munich, Tutzing, Tübingen, Frankfurt, Mainz, Bonn, and finally back to Cologne. Some visits involved lectures and talks; others were to establish or maintain contacts. In Frankfurt he met with Adorno again, which led to his delivering the Loeb Lecture the following year, while in Munich he made his first contacts at the Institut für Zeitgeschichte (Institute for Contemporary History), which would play a vital role in his own research and writing. Tübingen meant a visit with Hans Siebeck, and in Cologne he visited the novelist Heinrich Böll, a future Nobel Prize Laureate whom he had met and befriended in London. Because of their shared humanism, literary values, religious faith, and trust in simple decency, they remained close friends until Böll's death in 1985. The fees he collected for doing lectures and talks enabled him to pay for the travel, which in turn allowed him to make further contacts that led to further lectures, readings, and literary assignments. Because he often stayed with friends or in cheap rooming houses, it was a spare and demanding life, not to mention the effort required in writing out lectures and fulfilling assignments once he returned home. But it was a life, and a literary and scholarly one at that, nor was he beholden to anyone for day-to-day employment. At last he had found "intellectual work" of his own.

Tracing every talk and lecture that Adler gave would require a long index of his peripatetic travels and activities. Suffice it to say that between 1955 and 1987, the year before he died, Adler spent two to four months a year in Germany, Austria, and Switzerland during which he gave hundreds of lectures and readings, participated in numerous conferences and symposiums, and kept up contacts with editors, writers, politicians, academics, sociologists, historians, and literary scholars. His pattern was to arrive by train in Cologne, where he would stay with Böll and see Wilhelm Unger, the latter having given up on the German Library in London to become literary editor of the *Kölner Stadt-Anzeiger*, the city's main newspaper. There he recorded radio essays for the *Westdeutscher* Rundfunk (WDR) that were broadcast on German Radio's "Dritte Programme," a prestigious format to which almost every major postwar writer contributed, including Günter Grass, Jean Améry, Böll, Günter Eich, Ingeborg Bachmann, Hans Magnus Enzensberger, and many more. "The radio brought forth a literary genre that had not existed before," observes Hans Jürgen Schultz. "Two-thirds of postwar literature would not exist without it." Beyond the essays and radio plays created for it and the financial support it provided, most important was the audience that tuned in (some sixteen million at its height in 1960) eager for serious, smartly produced, in-depth programming on books, culture, music, and, most vitally, history and current events.[38]

After meeting with August Hoppe and Roland Wiegenstein, producers at the WDR with whom Adler developed ideas for new assignments, he moved on to other venues, mostly to deliver talks on the history and sociology of Theresienstadt and the camps. Many were given at Volkshochschulen (adult education centers) and organizations focused on restoring Jewish-Christian relations. He lectured at universities, gave readings from his poems, stories, and novels at literary venues, participated in panel discussions, and delivered papers at conferences. Terming himself a "freelance scholar," for over thirty years he managed to make a fairly decent, sometimes even good, living at it, although this meant continued displacement through years of travel to Germany and the constant need to perform as "Theresienstadt Adler." And yet by 1962 he observed, "I can live again and am able to look at and handle the events of 1941–1945 like a surgeon—it does not bother me in the least. . . . Anyone who knows of me refers to me (although not in England) as a 'sociologist' and 'contemporary historian,' as well as an 'expert on Jewish questions.' In truth I am only an 'adept devotee,' not a professional, and that suits me just fine. My real profession is writing, as it has always been, but it could be years before others even recognize that."[39]

While such itinerant work might seem more the province of a journeyman writer or journalist, and although he often longed to focus entirely on his true aspiration as a poet, short-story writer, and novelist, Adler's working life had two currents that kept him focused. The first was the responsibility to bear witness to the past and construct a thorough historical record within a larger framework and discussion of its social and political meaning. The success of *Theresienstadt 1941–1945* supplied the *bona fides* for him to lecture and write broadly on this front. Adler, however, was interested not just in recording or explaining the past but also in shaping the future, particularly that of Germany amid efforts to restore a viable democracy that could shield it against a return to the past. This entailed an effort to engage other scholars and intellectuals with his work, and the broader public as well. With each lecture delivered at a conference or continuing education center, and with every radio essay broadcast on Germany's elaborate network of cultural programming, Adler brought the depth of his scholarship to the public at large.

It also mattered that he did so as a survivor and a Jew, although Adler made clear that "I simply wanted to be taken for who I was" and that "above all I did not wish to gain anything from my dismal past."[40] Just as he was grateful to Heinz Flügel for showing the meaning of Judaism "from within" to educated Germans, Adler could do the same for the Shoah, and in ways that did not so much confront the Germans through the raw experience of the witness, but with the contextualizing powers of an intellectual that allowed his audience to face a past, guided by a steady hand, that posed an existential threat to their sense of themselves. Helmut Alt, reporting in the *Frankfurter Rundschau* on Adler's 1956 Loeb Lecture in Frankfurt, wrote, "Whoever wishes to study the extreme limits of human existence, whoever wishes to pose last questions to humankind, Adler makes clear to his audience that one only has to look to Theresienstadt." Nor was the intensity of the encounter any less for survivors. Hearing Adler talk about Judaism with scholarly yet passionate commitment at the "Woche der Brüderlichkeit" ("Week of Brotherhood") in Tutzing in 1956, Gerty Spies not only felt her deepest religious convictions reaffirmed but also had the sense that wherever Adler went he sought out "his fellow survivors in order to hear about their experiences, feel what they felt, and suffer along with them." Delivered with dexterous clarity and resonance, Adler's public readings from his novels and stories offered nuance to the public's engagement with this history, demonstrating further the complexity that could be brought to the subject and a range of approaches necessary to confront what had happened.[41]

The most important material and institutional support he received for his scholarly work on the Shoah was from the Institute for Contemporary History. As early as 1956, Adler visited the institute and met with Helmut Krausnick and Hans Buchheim, two prominent historians and staff members who had been impressed by the Theresienstadt book.[42] Founded in 1949, the institute was dedicated to research on National Socialism and the developments that brought it to power. That it was in Munich, the city in which the Nazi Party was founded, underscored the importance of its mission, as well as the government's financial support for it, although the latter called into question the degree to which its central aim was to prosecute Germany's past or explain it away. The thoroughness of the studies and affidavits produced by its historians led to detailed accounts of the rise to power and workings of the Nazi system, but little was done to cast blame on specific actors or to reveal the degree to which many Nazi officials still held prominent government positions, which might compromise the funding the institute received. Worst of all, in its early years not a word was spent on the victims themselves or what specifically had happened in the camps. Instead there was only a general discussion of what led to Nazism as a general "break" from German history and culture rather than as a direct growth and outcome of a mindset and proclivities decades in the making.

Only in the mid-1950s did it begin to recast its focus and turn to the Holocaust itself, especially after the Rockefeller Foundation awarded the institute a grant of $26,000 in 1956 to fund two years of research on Nazi policies against the Jews. This helped frame a new research initiative to which Adler could potentially contribute as a trained scholar who was also a direct survivor. Nor did it hurt that he had been critical of Jewish leaders in his Theresienstadt book. In the eyes of the institute, "on the grounds of scientific objectivity, the voices of those who had been 'politically persecuted too strongly' had to be kept from dominating."[43] Yet while Adler was happy to advise, initially he was hesitant to participate without a specific project of his own. Buchheim continued to woo him, especially after *Theresienstadt 1941–1945* was awarded the Leo Baeck Prize in 1958. That same year Adler published a second book on Theresienstadt, *Die verheimlichte Wahrheit* (*The Hidden Truth*), a sourcebook of detailed documents from all aspects of life in the ghetto, and the slim volume *Der Kampf gegen die 'Endlösung der Judenfrage'* (*The Struggle Against the 'Final Solution of the Jewish Question'*), which took up a broader discussion of the ideological struggle behind the deportations. Since Buchheim and his colleagues felt that "we ourselves cannot say anything or only insufficiently . . . [and] you certainly would be able to help us further," they were eager to tap Adler's expertise.[44]

That fall the institute extended an invitation for him to write "a work of your choice" on the Holocaust, even though the precise subject and approach of the book remained unclear.[45] In December, Isaac E. Wahler, a Jew who had fled Germany before the war and returned after it as an assistant to Robert Kempner, American deputy chief of counsel for war crimes, contacted Adler about files on the deportation of the Jews kept by the Gestapo in Würzburg, which he had discovered in a barrack in Oberursel/Taunus. Initially they were used in the Nürnberg trials to prosecute Nazi high officials, but Wahler had made photocopies that he brought back to New York. With both his parents having perished in the camps, and impressed by *Theresienstadt 1941–1945*, his hope was that Adler would write a book about the files that would serve as a silent memorial.[46] Recognizing the importance of the files in providing a systematic understanding of the administrative underpinnings of the deportations, Adler suggested to Buchheim that this would make excellent material for "research on the deportation complex precisely from the Gestapo's standpoint" rather than only that of the victims.[47]

Buchheim and Krausnick were at first hesitant, wishing to preserve the institute's commitment to broad historical documentation on the Nazi movement rather than cast aspersions of individual guilt, and to remain "objective" and avoid what its researchers referred to as "emotionalism."[48] Adler, however, assured them that what he intended was a "general overview of the deportations" that would allow him and others "to study the technique of deporting Jews from the 'Old Reich' systematically and in every essential detail," which meant encompassing "the official perspective not only of the Reich Security Main Office but also of the other participating state and regional authorities."[49] In May 1959 the institute offered him an honorarium of 16,000 Marks ($4,000) to be paid in monthly stipends to carry out his research several months each year at its headquarters in Munich while working on a book on the deportations, the hope being that he could complete it in three years.[50] Due to delays in getting hold of the proper documents, the work took longer than expected. In November 1962, the institute agreed to pay a further 20,000 Marks, half then and the other half on the book's completion, then expected to take another three years.[51]

The result was Adler's monumental study, *Der verwaltete Mensch: Studien zur Deportation der Juden aus Deutschland* (*Administered Man: A Study of the Deportation of the Jews from Germany*), eventually published in 1974. Given the institute's growing urge to focus on the Holocaust and Adler's keen interest in the Würzburg files, the project should have served perfectly the needs of both sides—but there were difficulties from the beginning. Government officials hesitated to grant him full access to the Würzburg files, nor did the institute actively help him to attain them. Tired of the recalcitrance of the Bavarian Interior and Justice Ministry, Adler could only observe in exasperation, "I know now that there will not be another Hitler, not even a duodecimo Hitler, but the moral weakness remains, and a Jew who wants to work on Jewish matters in the age of National Socialism cannot expect any help from German government offices, no matter how objectively and carefully he works."[52] He regretted "having obliged myself contractually" and even said that he had been "duped" into taking on the project and used as a political tool rather than a proper researcher.[53] In March 1961, he despaired that, without the cooperation of the authorities in Nürnberg and Würzburg or better archival support from the institute, his efforts would result only in a "miserable patchwork."[54] Even months later, writing to the institute's archivist, the one person who consistently supported him by aiding his research, Adler had to promise outright, "Obviously I can understand the urge of the authorities to shroud personal connections that could be revealed through any permitted scholarly review. But I am exclusively interested in grasping precisely how the process unfolded in itself and to present that as a purely historical-sociological study—the actual persons do not interest me and have no reason to be afraid."[55]

The fact that Adler felt the need to make such an assurance testifies to his awareness of a basic tension within the institute. "In Munich," writes Nicolas Berg, "the interest was in research not on 'guilt' but on 'causes,' not self-enlightenment concerning the 'deepest descent of German history' but knowledge of the structure and course of the Nazi system."[56] Ironically, it was the latter that Adler was most interested in documenting, but as a Jewish victim and scholar he possessed the most dangerous resource of all—memory. The institute, however, wished to approach the Third Reich "from a strictly German perspective" by passing over its extermination policies to shape "a narrative of the seduction and subjugation of the German *Volk*, from the perspective of the regime's fellow travelers."[57] Despite Adler's reassurance that he was more interested in documentation than accusation, his efforts to secure the documents he knew existed were stymied. With bitter sarcasm laced with suspicion, he could only observe, "This Jew may simply be interested in knowledge and not exposing blackguards [*Lumpen*]; he may have even offered a written assurance that he will remain a Jew and should recognize that he is not to get mixed up in any matters involving old Nazis and their patrons. Camp and Gestapo functionaries can perhaps be sacrificed, but for heaven's sake 'honorable' officials have to be spared potential annoyances."[58]

Adler may have consciously chosen to "not live in a country where it might have been likely that the baker from whom I might buy my bread could perhaps have done something awful to Jews in the East," but the fact was that he did have to work with a bureaucracy and civil apparatus still riddled with ex-party members.[59] That he was well aware of it shows up in his frustration at not being able to gain access to documents and in observations he makes in written talks. After his first trip in 1951, he rails against Wilhelm Hoffmann's published account of working at the Hölderlin Archive in Stuttgart during the war and complaining that he could not get his work done because of the bombing: "Whether Germany is destroyed or Stuttgart, the German fulfills his duty, no matter if it's at an SS-posting in a concentration camp or the Hölderlin Archive." By 1956, however, he could say, "The guilt felt towards Jews is so deep that one is almost placed on a pedestal, which almost prevents an unhindered exchange of thought," while it was also clear to him that "people want nothing to do with a return of the Third Reich or anything like it," although he encountered stories of former Nazis still working in "Bonn, in regional offices, at the universities, especially among the student fraternities." By 1970, and after many months spent at the institute over the past twelve years, he confessed to feeling that the moment anyone introduced him and mentioned his camp experience, "a wall was erected between me and the audience," one that "robbed the well-meaning audience of its freedom, as well as mine." His "strongest impression of the post-Nazi era," however, was the unpleasantness of serving as a witness in court against former Nazis and being derided and verbally beaten down by defense attorneys to such an extent that "it felt to me during the trial as if I were taken back to the days before 1945."[60] This makes plain Adler's awareness that guilt lay not only with the head Nazis and those who ran the camps but also with everyday people, civil servants, and petty officials throughout Germany, something confirmed decades later by scholars, but at the time a powder keg no one wished to ignite.[61]

Adler's professional frustration was not helped by the fact that between 1959 and 1962 he underwent several more periodontal procedures and suffered from severe bouts with kidney stones that required hospitalization and surgery. The long stretches of time away from his family were also taxing. During his first extended stay at the institute, he observed to Bettina, "How strange, dear, to be sitting down in Munich and writing you on my own typewriter, making it seem as much like "The Wall" as any letter."[62] A week later he tells her "how much nicer it would be if you were with me or I with you, rather than this forced separation because of work—on one level a separation because of how this endless work takes me so far away from my true calling and from you as well, which is a different kind of separation."[63] Bettina of course missed him, too, but in her letters she spends most of her time comforting him and worrying that not only is the research he is doing tedious, but its subject matter wearing. "Please don't worry about me," he reassures her. "The abyss in which I swim—and I do so quite thoroughly, for I am very diligent—has no effect on me. . . . When I sometimes complain and say I want to be done with this kind of work, it's only because I'd like to have some years free of it and the radio work that has become so necessary in order to pursue purely literary work. But the chances of that are as always pretty slim, which means one must be patient."[64]

The impediments Adler encountered trying to gain full access to the Würzburg files brought home to him Germany's snail-like progress throughout the 1950s in confronting its past. As Berg explains, "this was the time when Gerald Reitlinger's descriptions of genocide and the SS apparatus were being reproached by Hans Buchheim for 'completely lacking understanding and respect for the entire German anti-Nazi resistance movement,' when material from Reitlinger's books made its way into a poem of Paul Celan but not into Germany's historiography, and when Raul Hilberg could find no German publisher for his encyclopedic study *The Destruction of the European Jews*."[65] While efforts had been made to pay reparations to the victims and take responsibility for the atrocities committed by the Nazi leadership, Adler could see firsthand through his research the frequency with which former members of the Gestapo got off almost scot-free. Writing to Bettina from Munich in October 1962, he exclaimed sardonically:

> It's a complete farce, such good men, not a single enemy of the Jews among them, but rather the opposite. They had tried to help, there were witnesses who saw it, even Jewish ones. The Gestapo was against the Nazis. Sure, they had done their duty, but what choice did they have? They were threatened with SS tribunals and with being sent to concentration camps. And they of course had families, and already (in 1948) had been sitting in internment camps, completely innocent while their families suffered in penniless misery. Sure the Jews were gone and would not return, but in 1942 one didn't know that, no one knew that. Then the mild sentences were handed out, a maximum of 14 months in prison (the local main culprit having poisoned himself in 1945), and then upon appeal they were all set free and even received restitution for the detainment they had suffered in all innocence: justice had once again prevailed.[66]

Sarcasm aside, the work wore on him, forcing Adler to constantly confront the past that he had escaped. Two days after mocking the Gestapo's special pleading, he wrote to Bettina about a weekend excursion into the Bavarian countryside that he took with Gertrud Stauder, a longtime friend who, together with the writer and Theresienstadt survivor Gerty Spies, provided much-needed friendship and society outside of the institute. Noting the beauty of the Bavarian countryside, which he found "more rugged and powerful" than the beloved Bohemian Forest of his youth, he mentions with admiration several Rococo and Baroque churches on the journey. In Peißenberg, he notes "the nicely formed mountain" that rises above the town, but when describing the "bulky tower on top," he adds in parentheses "(just like an Auschwitz chimney)."[67] The remark is as astonishing for its casualness as it is revealing of a mind immersed in the bleak reaches of the Holocaust. Bettina, of course, had no firsthand memory of the chimneys at Auschwitz or its ramp. And there were many other ways to describe the tower, most obvious the comparison he could have made to the industrial chimneys dotting the landscape of the London they now called home. But the image speaks to their shared discourse, nor did Bettina make any particular note of it in response. She simply reports how pleased she is to be taking art classes, having taken up drawing again and working with the sculptor Reg Butler at the City and Guilds of London Art School in South Kensington, a welcome respite from worrying about Günther's struggles at the institute, managing and reporting on correspondence arriving at home, and raising Jeremy, who by now was a strapping boy of fourteen.[68]

Arriving back in Munich in June 1963 for two more months of work on the book amid further stalling by the Bavarian Interior and Justice Ministry, Adler confessed to her, "The darkness I feel inside continues, I cannot fend it off, and this time it has set in deep. Yet I'm fighting hard against it, because I love you."[69] His spirits rallied during a quick trip home two weeks later to take care of Bettina after she underwent a hysterectomy, but his contract still called for him to return to Munich. "Since your initial recovery after your operation," he tells her, "I've been feeling much better, although the feelings of isolation still continue, unjustified as well as justified, but don't worry yourself about it."[70] For both the only way out was the way through. Bettina found solace in her art, but Günther was contracted by the institute and his conscience to proceed with the book. The fact that the "darkness" continued to set into him amid a sense of isolation even when among others evinces what would probably be diagnosed as depression spurred on by posttraumatic stress. No doubt the materials of his study and the impediments he faced in getting hold of them helped to augment the symptoms.

Adler finally handed in the first two parts of the book in June 1965, requesting an extension of his contract, although he doubted he would receive one.[71] By then it was becoming clear that the project would far exceed the roughly two hundred pages proposed and would require several more years to complete. Krausnick, who by now was director of the institute, passed it on to his colleague Martin Broszat, who read it over the summer before meeting with Adler at the institute that September. As Adler described it to Bettina, Broszat was "withering" in his criticism, finding the approach to be "unsystematic, inexact, shallow, lacking meticulousness, in short disappointing" while devoting a great deal of time to "correcting" Adler's style.[72] Given Broszat's "downright allergic" reaction to the documentation of Nazi crimes by Jews, Adler could have hardly been surprised had he learned of Broszat's former membership in the Nazi Party, a fact that only came out long after Broszat's death in 1989, a year after his own.[73] Although disappointed, Adler took it as best he could: "I defended myself vigorously and I will continue to do so, but if I don't prevail, it doesn't really bother me. I'm not at all angry and want to keep it from becoming at all personal (as does Broszat)."[74] Adler even felt that, should the institute decline to publish it, he was all the better off, for that would free him to do with it what he wished.[75] It took another year for Krausnick to consider a revised version of the manuscript, but ultimately the institute felt that the book was too fragmentary to publish, even though it was already twice as long as initially planned.[76] Krausnick agreed to allow Adler to continue to work at the institute while providing administrative support but no further financial support. In addition, they were willing to lend the book the "recommendation and support of the institute" in order to help Adler find further financing and a publisher.

For Hans Herzfeld and Ernst Fraenkel, the two external readers to whom Krausnick had sent the manuscript, the main problem with Adler's approach was that the book was not classifiable "either as a documentary or as a research publication."[77] The manuscript was judged to be deeply flawed because of "strongly subjective components" resulting from what the readers saw as the conflict of Adler having been "engaged in scholarship" as "a directly participating contemporary."[78] The grammar of this observation is interesting. In fulfilling the institute's demand for data-driven disengagement, his intent and expertise were valued, but when he was deemed to be an actual witness, he became an object of disregard, no doubt an outgrowth of latent anti-Semitism at the institute. As a "very personally colored product," it manifested a "noticeable disparity between analysis and appraisal of the material" and thus threatened the institute's unwavering emphasis on supposed "objective" research rather than "mythic" memory or mourning.[79] Indeed, at the heart of Institute's trouble with Adler's manuscript is a debate that later developed into the so-called *Historikerstreit* (Historians' Debate) of the late 1980s. Broszat and Saul Friedlander publicly squared off in an extended correspondence on the degree to which supposed "objectivity" fostered by historians such as Broszat and Hans Mommsen only masked a reluctance to grant validity to what were viewed as the "subjective" accounts of Jewish historians. Conducted in private, Adler's dilemma anticipates a matter that later proved to be of national and international importance.[80] At the time the only immediate solution was to release the manuscript for publication by an outside press rather than as an Institute publication.

"And so we parted ways," Adler notes stoically in the introduction to *Administered Man*. He remained on good terms with Krausnick, Buchheim, and Heinz Förster, the organization's administrative head, socialized with each, and used the institute's facilities until 1970 before completing work on the first draft of the entire book in October 1971.[81] With the help of Jacob Robinson of the YIVO Institute for Jewish Research in New York, Adler secured two one-year grants of $1,000 from 1966 to 1968 as further material support, but after that he was on his own until Siebeck paid him an advance of 15,000 Marks ($6,000) upon publication in 1974.[82] Forced to work on the book at his own expense for the last three years of the project, he could not resist quoting Samuel Johnson in his introduction, who said of his own intrepid venture in publishing *A Dictionary of the English Language* that it had been "'written with little assistance of the learned, and without any patronage of the great; not in the soft obscurities of retirement, or under the shelter of academick bowers, but amidst inconvenience and distraction, in sickness and in sorrow.'"[83]

And yet, for all of Adler's travail and disappointment, the reaction of readers to the book's first four hundred pages and the outline for the rest of it was not unreasonable. The project had swelled beyond its initial scope, and the focus of the book changed with time. As Broszat's reaction indicated, Adler's analysis cut close to the bone with its interest in "processes surrounding the act of deportation."[84] Rather than just recording the factual details of the transports, Adler's purview pushed beyond "a documentary or . . . a research publication" in eliciting the "matrix of accountable and unaccountable events" that had set the entire system into motion. This was not so much to lay blame at the feet of specific individuals but to understand the underpinnings of oppression in themselves, much as he had done in his book on Theresienstadt. He sought to address that which

> also concerns states in which injustice not only arises and is also tolerated by the government and even practiced by it, as happens in all countries, but also when such injustice is even expressly intended and is prescribed as a maxim, whereby no means of justice can be obtained against it, and thus people are submitted to cruel practices that subscribe to the conception of an inhumane and discriminatory ideology.[85]

Echoing the perils of the contemporary "administered world" theorized by Adorno and the Frankfurt School, Adler argued that the victims of deportation were in essence "administered people" and that these

> worthless creatures seem to me an extreme example of a thoroughly ignoble state of affairs in which modern man is dehumanized into a "mass," even under the care of the well-meaning tutelage of "public services," thus becoming ever more hopelessly mired within it and miring himself within it even further, ending up hardly capable any longer, indeed hardly even prepared, to free himself from the fiasco of such degrading "massification" and emerge an autonomous creature.[86]

Germany, however, at the time was not ready to see Nazism as any systematic outgrowth of the traditional state; rather, it was considered an aberrant "break" brought on by a barbarous ideology inflicted upon it. This proved even more uncomfortably true among Germany's most prominent historians. Friedrich Meinecke, considered the greatest German historian of the time, felt compelled to write in his 1946 book *The German Catastrophe* that the Third Reich "was not only the greatest misfortune that the German people have suffered, it was also their greatest shame," but in the same work he made no acknowledgment of the existence of the camps or the death of six million Jews.[87] Instead he mourned the influence of a "band of criminals" that led to a rupture in Germany's cultural lineage, while elsewhere arguing that it was the duty of Germany's historians to rescue the "authentic culture" from the tragedy to which it had succumbed, "intermingling everywhere in the preponderant mass of human insufficiency, infirmity, and sin."[88] What was not rescued, however, was the direct experience of the atrocities themselves. Even *Anatomie des SS Staates* (*Anatomy of the SS State*), the standard work produced by Krausnick, Buchheim, Broszat, and Hans-Adolf Jacobsen for the institute in 1965, and which served to inform the judges at the Frankfurt Auschwitz trial that same year, only lays guilt at the feet of an amorphous "Hitler State." There one can find reference to "coercive measures" leading up to the deportations that "were clearly inspired by the thought that the state of emergency provided cover for taking certain violent steps for the 'cleansing of the nation,' which appeared fundamentally necessary according to National Socialist ideology but which could not be taken in peace-time in deference to public opinion at home and abroad," a passage that largely exonerates the German people, points no finger at specific actors, and erases the Jewish victims subject to such "cleansing."[89]

Memory was of course what Adler could supply, but the trick was to find a way that would remain "objectively" historical. Only after the institute rejected the manuscript did he find a solution that combined factual historical research with an archival memory of the deportations. Ironically, what provided the impetus for this breakthrough was the government's own stonewalling. When it became clear that Adler was never going to actually see the handwritten original Gestapo files deposited at the State Archive in Nürnberg under the aegis of the State Attorney of Würzburg, he was forced to turn to other sources. What his research turned up at the Landesamt für Verfassungsschutz (State Office of Central Intelligence) in Munich was a series of files on emigrants, victims of euthanasia, deportees, and others executed or murdered. Most were Jews, but not all, and their stories reached from the Central Reich to concentration camps and ghettos in Riga, Lublin, Auschwitz, and Theresienstadt, as well as to exiles overseas. While the first four parts of *Administered Man* discuss meticulously the rise of Nazism, the formulation of the Final Solution, and the aims, administration, logistics, and financing of the deportations over the course of six hundred pages, Part V simply sets forth the essentials of forty-seven victim files, including quotes from official Gestapo documents and correspondence about their racial status, citizenship, confiscated property, arrest, deportation, or emigration. Detailing such incidents as the impediments faced by Jetti Israel in renewing her German passport in the 1930s, the persecution of Paul Bermann and the seizure of his business and property by the Gestapo after he emigrated to England, the arrest of decorated World War I veteran August Heymann and his deportation to Sachsenhausen and Dachau before his 1942 death in Buchenwald, and the search and seizure of the apartment of the wine merchant Rudolf Leppmann and his wife before their deportation to Theresienstadt, the result is a guided tour through a bureaucratic nightmare bent on turning human beings into objects to be moved, confiscated, or expelled at will. With roughly five pages devoted to each victim, Heinrich Böll pointed out that if the same had been done for the six million who had died, thirty million pages of detailed bureaucratic persecution, theft, and murder would have resulted.[90]

The lessons to be gleaned, however, apply not to just the Jews or the Nazis but rather "to all human beings whose dignity is accosted through the impersonal manner in which files are kept on them by the state and its various organs and governing bodies, not only *because* they are under the control of the state, but also are administered by it."[91] In selecting and quoting from the files, Adler's intent is not so much to show *what* happened, but *how* it did:

> The amount of senselessness and uselessness, whether silly or pedantic, practiced on people and recorded in these files not only provides an insight into the suffering of those afflicted, but also suggests what happened to people in general. Undoubtedly this occurs again everywhere and anywhere a machine comparable to a Nazi state is set up in order to control human beings and is mirrored in official laws, as evident in these proceedings. The start of it is always inhumane and dangerous, but in totalitarian states it is fatal, especially whenever such actions lead to attacks upon, and finally the extermination of, those who are

> unwanted. The central aim of the presentation of the fated stories found in these files is to make this exceedingly clear.[92]

Adler's methodology turns the reader into a kind of participant-observer through immersion in the unfolding process of injustice administered in order that the deadly consequences that follow are imagined fully rather than passively taken in. "In this way," he concludes, "the overwhelming immensity of the events in all their horrid variations arise before the reader without indeed wearing him down through the deadening similarity of the overwhelming horror manifested again by each individual," allowing the "final theoretical part to in fact be anchored in practice and ushered in by examples."[93]

Theory manifests itself from practice in Part VI of *Administered Man*, with a detour through Adler's discussion of the rise of modern administrations reaching back to Kant and Hegel. Quoting as epigraph Kafka's remark to Gustav Janouch that "The chains of tormented human beings are made of foolscap," Adler spends the last two hundred pages of the book laying out what administrative aims *should* entail as well as the danger of what they *can*:

> Any administration becomes dangerous to society the moment it becomes autonomous. . . . Any administration that abuses its power in such manner erects at the same time a counter-world against that of society. Then the administration no longer serves society nor represents it. . . . Eventually the administration seeks to replace or take over society—specifically the ebb and flow of its everyday way of life.[94]

Following on the heels of the sinister administrative practices detailed in Part V, these are not empty words; the direct effect upon a society so governed has already been imagined by the reader.

"Facts" have not sealed "fates." In *Administered Man* the documents not only detail particulars or the culpability of the state, they voice the human beings attached to them who have been released to stand witness against the systems that sought to reduce them to facts in the first place. Their dignity is restored in serving as portents of a future whose "difficult problems, outlined here, [it is still possible to solve] through good will," it being better "to overemphasize (as if this were even possible) the need for people to have protections against the abuse of state power and public administration, rather than those protections, in truth, all too often being reduced or kept barely intact, or at worst entirely ignored."[95]

As he had promised Bettina from its inception, *Administered Man* was indeed Adler's "last comprehensive work on Nazi matters," but in its dedication to the memory of his parents—Emil Alfred Adler and Alice Adler-Fraenkel—its end also harks back to its beginning. The culmination of Emil's deportation to Łódź and Alice's later journey to her death in Maly Trostenets, it brought to a close nearly thirty years of work starting with the first draft of *Theresienstadt 1941–1945* begun in Prague. For him the two books stood like "two columns or signposts erected to commemorate those who died at the hands of this persecution, as well as those who survived it."[96] Adler also made clear that "in no way was it intended as what is all too often clumsily and simply falsely called 'coming to terms with the past' ":

> The past should not be overcome. By this I mean that a person must live in his time, for he cannot help but do so, rather than in times past, nor even in his own past. The commemoration of what is past can nevertheless become a part of his present, such that in a special way it becomes a part of *his* present, or better yet, claims a stake in it, just as he claims a stake in the past within the present in order to make it anew and learn from it.[97]

Adler wrote the Theresienstadt book "in order that I could go on living" and this one "in sickness and in sorrow," but together their two thousand pages fulfilled the covenant he had made with the lost.[98] Now it was time to fulfill that which he held with the living.

15

The Witness

Some lives move in straight lines. Some move in circles, ending where they began as if by clockwork. Others, such as Adler's, are a series of intersecting circles, a journey steered by circumstances and eclectic interests coursing in several directions at once. From the late 1950s onward his life and work were pulled in different directions, sometimes by events so far beyond his control that chronology no longer traces life's vectors as they crisscross and double back, the hands of the clock moving backward and forward at once. Most often at the center lies Theresienstadt and the wider Shoah, which pursued Adler as much as he pursued them.

The "catastrophe" could reappear suddenly. On May 24, 1960, just over a month after he began his first formal work at the Institute for Contemporary History, while visiting Würzburg to research the Gestapo files, Adler saw a headline announcing that Adolf Eichmann had been captured thirteen days earlier by Israeli agents in Buenos Aires and secretly brought to Israel to stand trial for crimes against humanity.[1] This was a bombshell for the world, but for Adler it was news that required immediate action. For some months he had been advising the Attorney General's office in Frankfurt on their effort to bring charges against Hermann Krumey, one of Eichmann's henchmen and the official who ordered the deportation of over 400,000 Hungarian Jews to Auschwitz in 1944. Krumey had been arrested after the war, and again in 1957 and 1960, but he had escaped prosecution and ran a pharmacy in the small town of Korbach. Adler knew that with Eichmann's capture Krumey posed an immediate flight risk, since Eichmann would have known more than anyone the extent of his involvement in the Hungarian operation. Hopping a train to Frankfurt, he urged Judge Hansernst Grabert to issue an arrest warrant. At first Grabert did not understand what Adler meant calling Krumey a "Schreibtischmörder," or "desktop murderer," a term for the Nazi administrators who ordered the death of millions from their desks, and wondered if Adler meant that Krumey had killed himself at his desk. Adler managed to convince the judge of the risk of delay, and Krumey was arrested the next day.[2]

After lunching with Grabert, Adler visited the Attorney General's office to talk with staff about Rolf Günther, namesake Hans Günther, Ernst Möhs, and other members of the "Eichmann Unit" responsible for running Theresienstadt.[3] Two months earlier, Joachim Kügler, an assistant prosecutor at the Frankfurt Auschwitz trials of 1963–1965, had contacted him to ask for help in building the indictment against twenty-four former guards, Gestapo, doctors, and administrators responsible for serial torture and genocide in Auschwitz. Because of his short stay there, Adler could only provide general background material, but he urged Kügler and his office to pursue Krumey, as he thought there was a paper trail to prove his guilt.[4] Once the warrant was issued on May 24, Adler could have called it a day, yet he finished it by visiting Friedrich Krummacher, editor of *Neue Politische Literatur*, to listen to recordings of Hitler, Goebbels, and Himmler as part of his research on the motives behind the deportations.[5] The two men would have been astounded at the news out of Israel.

Adler took a keen interest in the Eichmann affair. At Bettina's suggestion, a week after the announcement of the arrest, he wrote to Franz Wurm in Zurich, who knew Moshe Feldenkrais, the personal trainer of David Ben-Gurion, prime minister of Israel. Adler's hope was to be allowed to interview Eichmann for scholarly reasons or contribute to the prosecution.[6] On June 22, he sent a three-page memorandum to the Israeli Embassy in London, asking that it be forwarded to the Israeli police. He suggested that the arrest was as important for its scholarly as its forensic interests and that he would be glad to make his services available for such research.[7] He attached a list of nineteen topics he wished to ask Eichmann about, from the formation of the Reich Central Office for Jewish Emigration in 1939, to the incorporation of Department IV B 4 and its position in the organization of the SS, to the failed Nisko Plan of 1939–40 for resettling Jews near Lublin, Poland, to the general deportations from Germany beginning in October 1941, to details of the Wannsee Conference and the orders for the Final Solution in 1942, to the establishment of Theresienstadt, to contacts between Eichmann's office and the Reich Foreign Office and Finance Ministry, to the deportations of Jews from Denmark in 1943, and even to the drawing up of the "Heimeinkaufsverträge" (Home Purchase Contracts) used by the Nazis to defraud Jews of their worldly goods in exchange for life-long care in Theresienstadt.[8] He wanted Eichmann to explain nothing less than the bureaucratic infrastructure of the Holocaust, including the motivations, logistics, financing, chain of command, and culpability for it. Adler insisted his questions were driven by scholarship and that he was willing to interview Eichmann on the condition that his answers remain inadmissible in court. The Israeli government, however, intended to seek the same material to display the evil of the Nazi crimes before the world and did not take him up on his proposal.

And yet they were eager for his expertise. In July he met twice with officials at the Israeli embassy in London, including Abraham Selinger, commander of the Israeli police and the head of the Eichmann investigation. On July 11, Selinger asked Adler to write up what he knew about Eichmann's role and responsibility.[9] The result was a forty-one-page affidavit detailing what he knew of Eichmann's hand in the execution of the Final Solution. Adler's research in the Gestapo files in Würzburg and Nürnberg and the materials he supplied to the Attorney General of Frankfurt for the case against Krumey allowed him to detail convincingly Eichmann's knowledge of and role in the deportations.[10] Both *Theresienstadt 1941–1945* and *Die verheimlichte Wahrheit* provided important resources for the prosecution, and as a result of his many years of work on the topic, he not only had amassed an immense trove of photocopied documents but had deep and wide-ranging knowledge of the archives from London to Warsaw to Amsterdam to Prague to Vienna to Jerusalem in which other crucial documents could be found.

After reviewing Adler's affidavit, Selinger's assistant commander, Ephraim Hofstadter, responded on October 5 from Israel to ask for clarification and evidence on twelve points concerning the degree of Eichmann's direct command of the deportation offices in Vienna and Prague, the channels of command, directives regarding the Auschwitz camp, the unrealized plans to construct gas chambers in Theresienstadt, and whether Eichmann's visits to the ghetto were immediately followed by expulsions to Auschwitz.[11] Adler's four-page, single-spaced response is in the Israel State Archives. Its references to passages from his own books, photocopies in archives, suggestions for witnesses who could provide corroborating evidence, and citations of published scholarship are repeatedly annotated by the investigators with checks and exclamation points, all of it providing them with a clear outline of how to proceed, including Adler's suggestion that they consult the second edition of the Theresienstadt book, which would appear in a few weeks.[12]

In November, the Israelis asked him to submit another, shorter affidavit.[13] The difference between the two documents is striking and speaks to a central paradox of the Eichmann trial. In just four pages, versus forty-one, Adler sets out to document his "own awareness during his time in Prague and Theresienstadt of what he knew about the direct and indirect activities of Adolf Eichmann" rather than "what I have learned through long study after the war." He testifies that his intent is to "painstakingly separate my experiences of 20 years ago from my later knowledge." Noting that the "name Eichmann . . . was not familiar to those outside the circle of officials of the Prague Jewish Community" and that he himself did not hear it until summer 1942, Adler says that Eichmann's name appears several times in the "Daily Report" (Tagesbericht) read to prisoners by the Council of Elders on January 19, 1942. Yet given that he did not arrive in Theresienstadt until February of that year, this is a scholarly, historical observation, the very thing Adler claims that he wishes to avoid in the affidavit. The reason he cannot is because, as a "Schreibtischmörder," Eichmann remained more manifest in documents than in person and physically present at the scene of the atrocities. What sat in the bulletproof dock in Jerusalem was a man, albeit an inscrutable, somewhat obtuse, and disturbingly plain one. The challenge, however, was to prove that he was the mastermind behind the Holocaust that the Israelis thought him to be.

Adler's November affidavit concludes with his speculations about whom Eichmann met with in the ghetto (including Leo Baeck and various heads of the Council of Elders) before summarizing his own deportation to Auschwitz and further experience of the camps. "The circle of prisoners who had continual contact with Eichmann in Theresienstadt was very small," he observes. "As far as I can recall, neither my awareness of him nor that of my fellow prisoners increased during the time leading up to the day of my deportation." Not even Eichmann was prepared to deny what he had done, but the question his defense raised concerned what degree he followed orders from above versus what responsibility he had to disobey those orders or suffer the consequences for having implemented them. Adler helped the prosecution construct the paper trail that tied Eichmann to his deeds, as well as his full knowledge of what awaited the Jews on arrival in Auschwitz. However, difficult to reveal was the reasons *why* Eichmann did it and to show that those reasons were tied to his own volition rather than the sadism of those commanding him.

Without direct knowledge of the "monster" and his motives, "monstrosity" had to be inferred from the memos, directives, and bureaucratic euphemisms for deportation and murder left behind. To accomplish that required an act of imagination larger and more complex than the paucity of eyewitness evidence about Eichmann himself. Nor was this a negligible moral or legal dilemma. As would happen later in the Frankfurt Auschwitz trial, the prosecution was forced to outline the bureaucratic organization responsible for the entire system in order to imply what individuals *must have done* without being able to document what they *actually* did.[14] First-person testimony was employed to flesh out the latter, but because the murders were administered from afar by individuals unknown to their victims, such testimony was as horrific and dramatic as it was insufficient legal proof of what the accused had actually done. Although no one doubted the guilt of Eichmann or Krumey, the Holocaust remained more obvious as a crime in its totality than could be documented individually.[15]

When looked at more closely, Adler's forty-one-page affidavit from July supplies a different, subtle combination of factual and personal testimony to evoke the totality of Eichmann's evil. Rather than a dry testament to a series of files and facts, the document reads like a spirited essay out to make an irrefutable case in dramatic fashion. At the start Adler coolly states that his testimony is based only on his own scholarship and references to other files and documents, but he soon announces that he will demonstrate "the extent to which Eichmann, despite doing so 'under orders,' is nevertheless fully answerable for his official actions," which became the central question of the trial.[16] The first of those is the initial deportation of Jews from Germany, Austria, and Czecho-Slovakia in 1941. Adler does not describe it as such, but he well knew that this included the deportation of Emil Adler and his second wife from Prague to Łódź. Quoting the testimony of SS Haupsturmführer Dieter Wisliceny from the Nürnberg trials, Adler uses the captain's words to claim with certainty that these " 'deportations resulted from Eichmann's private initiative' " and that " 'during this time Theresienstadt was also erected as a 'model ghetto,' " foreshadowing his own expulsion and imprisonment too. Not content, however, to rest his case on the testimony of a single witness, Adler writes that he will later prove Eichmann's connection to the "special units" set up for killing Jews after their deportation.

Adler uses the files of the Gestapo in Würzburg, which he was working on in Munich while writing *Administered Man*, to establish Eichmann's personal involvement with the deportations. He cites a letter written January 31, 1942, in which Eichmann demands that "by February 9, 1942" (the day of the arrival of Günther, Gertrud, and her parents in Theresienstadt) all Gestapo offices report the total number of Jews in their districts to Department IV B 4, including all those in lands conquered by the Nazis. "This up-to-date total," states Eichmann, "will be essential to later assignments to transports, especially for the organization of transports for the purposes of evacuation." Central to these "evacuations" was the stripping of all property from the Jews, which Adler contends that Eichmann also oversaw, as well as construction and control of Theresienstadt. Adler establishes Eichmann's ties to two principal components of the Nazi plan, deception and deportation, and explains Eichmann's use of the euphemism of "Sonderbehandlung" ("Special Handling") as code for extermination as early as September 1939. In Theresienstadt, the two roles fused in sinister fashion when in the summer of 1942 some twenty thousand Jews were sent to the "model camp" to "preserve appearances to the outside world," according to an internal Gestapo report quoting Eichmann. Among those arriving was of course Adler's mother, Alice, and she was also one of the first of over ten thousand prisoners that Adler mentions who were transported out of the ghetto to their death in Maly Trostenets in late summer and early fall. Again he makes no mention of such a personal connection, but one cannot help but think how in stating the case as a witness against Eichmann he knew he was stating the case for his parents and himself as well.

After describing the preposterous "beautification" of the ghetto and the deception of inspectors from the Red Cross in 1944, what remains is for Adler to assert that Eichmann's guilt for those who died in Theresienstadt or in the camps "was not at all lessened by the fact that most of the prisoners had never heard of his name." Instead, "Eichmann was entirely empowered to murder, as well as enjoy the alibi needed to cover up his murders, while also recognizing no moral values whatsoever," and Adler concludes, "Though I am not aware of Eichmann personally mistreating Jews, nevertheless his horrible psychological mistreatment of them made him guilty."

This indeed was what the prosecution sought to prove in Jerusalem, but for Adler there was one last point. Noting a 1943 request made to Department IV B 4 for clean uniforms to be sent to 115 louse-infested prisoners in Auschwitz who required "quick" transfer to the Natzweiler concentration camp, Adler infers Eichmann's involvement with their murder on arrival, whereby the Anatomical Institute at the University of Strasbourg was provided with the 115 skeletons for its collection.[17] He segues to a letter written by Krumey, a member of the "Eichmann Unit," which mentions his having written to IV B 4 to say that 88 children from Lidice were "designated for special handling" and that he needed instructions on what to do with them. After mentioning "further correspondence with Rolf Günther of IV B 4 and—if I am not mistaken—also with Eichmann," Adler confirms that all of the children, except for 7 who were determined to be "worth returning to Germany" (as not Jewish), were sent by the Gestapo to Chełmno, "the destination of those 'resettled' from Łódź in spring 1942," where they underwent "special handling." At first glance, describing the murder of the children of Lidice, whose village had been burned to the ground by Hitler as retaliation for the assassination of Heydrich, would seem a fit and moving image with which to end. That wavering phrase—"if I am not mistaken" ("wenn ich nicht irre")—is surprising, however, at the end of a legal document that he had spent 160 hours composing. Why, after such exactitude, connecting so many documents together at such length to make the case against Eichmann and prove the calculation behind the Holocaust, why would Adler risk seeming unreliable or mistaken?

One possible answer rests poignantly in the other key phrase of the passage, the mention of Chełmno, "the destination of those 'resettled' from Łódź in spring 1942." Adler knew that the massacre at Lidice did not happen in the "spring" ("Frühjahr") of 1942, but on June 10, and Eichmann's order that the children be killed in the gas vans of Chełmno was not issued until July 1.[18] Describing Chełmno, correctly, as "the destination of those 'resettled' from Łódź in spring 1942," Adler thus by inference lays at Eichmann's feet not just the death of the Lidice children but that of Emil Adler and Zdenka Pisinger, who were "resettled" from Łódź and killed in Chełmno in the spring of 1942, rather than summer. Purposefully or not, Adler deftly transforms upon the page the "skeletons" garnered by Eichmann from Natzweiler for study in Strasbourg into the lives of his father and stepmother lost to the gas wagons of Chełmno, if not by extension all eighteen of his family members lost to the Shoah.

Eichmann was convicted on December 11, 1961, and sentenced to death four days later. Not all agreed that he should be executed. Numerous people, including many Jews, felt that killing Eichmann meant Israel would be committing the very state-sponsored murder for which he had been convicted, that capital punishment was a violation of Jewish law, and that the killing of one man could not square the murder of six million. Letters and telegrams asking that his sentence be commuted poured in to President Yitzhak Ben-Zvi and Ben-Gurion, as well as a petition drawn up and signed by leading intellectuals and artists in Israel, including Martin Buber, Gershom Scholem, Hugo Bergmann, Leah Goldberg, and Yehuda Bacon. At Buber's suggestion, Bacon wrote to Adler a month before Eichmann's conviction, asking if he would join him in signing a petition against the execution. Adler replied that he, too, was against the death penalty in general and was ready to sign the petition to Ben-Zvi, as any "execution was a concession to murder on the part of the state," a position shared by Buber.[19]

After Eichmann's appeal was rejected by Israel's High Court on the morning of May 29, 1962, Ben-Gurion's government met secretly in the Knesset that afternoon to discuss execution versus clemency. Eleven ministers voted to recommend that the sentence be carried out, with two voting against. A second vote seeking consensus resulted in a unanimous recommendation to the president against clemency.[20] That day Ben-Zvi also received Eichmann's handwritten request to spare his life, arguing again, "I never served in such a high position as required to be involved independently in such decisive responsibilities. Nor did I give any order in my own name, but acted only 'by order of.' "[21] Denying clemency, Ben-Zvi quoted I Samuel 15:33: "As thy sword made women childless, so shall thy mother be childless among women."[22] Two days later, just after midnight, Eichmann was hanged in Ramla Prison and his ashes were scattered at sea beyond Israeli waters.

By no means was the Eichmann case closed, however. Debates about his role in the atrocities, the legality of his capture in Buenos Aires, and the workings of the trial have continued in books and articles by scholars around the world. The most famous is Arendt's *Eichmann in Jerusalem: A Report on the Banality of Evil,* first published in five installments in *The New Yorker,* beginning in February 1963. Part of the fame of Arendt's account lies in the notoriety her articles gained when critics heaped scorn upon her loose and sometimes erroneous handling of facts, as well as her severe criticism of Jewish authorities and the degree to which they facilitated Eichmann's plan rather than resist it. Here it suffices to note that Arendt maintained that "this trial had to take place in the interests of justice and nothing else" but acknowledged that "one of the fundamental problems posed by crimes of this kind . . . [was] that they were, and could only be, committed under a criminal *law* and by a criminal *state,*" thus by an individual criminal rather than a representative "monster."[23] While the prosecution "wanted to present Eichmann to the world as the epitome of both the literal and the symbolic Nazi," Arendt sought to focus on "the person of the defendant, a man of flesh and blood with an individual history, with an always unique set of qualities, peculiarities, behavior patterns, and circumstances."[24]

When the book appeared in translation in Germany in the fall of 1964, Adler felt the need to weigh in on the affair as a public intellectual to whom people turned on such matters. Arendt saw the fleeting references made to *Theresienstadt 1941–1945* in the proceedings as a necessary yet revealing tactic by the prosecution. She argued that if they had relied on it more, their case would have been weakened, "forced to admit that the naming of individuals who were sent to their doom had been, with few exceptions, the job of the Jewish administration."[25] Eichmann and his attorney had read the book to prepare for the trial, but strangely his defense did not develop the argument that the blood of the victims was really on the hands of the Jewish Elders. In an article titled "Was weiß Hannah Arendt von Eichmann und der 'Endlösung'?" ("What Does Hannah Arendt Know About Eichmann and 'The Final Solution'?") published in the *Allgemeine Wochenzeitung der Juden* on November 20, 1964, and broadcast as a half-hour radio program on the Bayerischer Rundfunk ten days later, Adler spends several paragraphs criticizing Arendt's scholarship and her lifting of material from other sources without attribution, notably Raul Hilberg's *The Destruction of the European Jews*.[26] Adler acknowledges that Arendt cites him as the "crown witness for her thesis," but it is on a central tenet that they most differed. Arendt recognized that Eichmann followed orders handed down to him by a corrupt and criminal system, although she held him responsible for lacking the conscience to disobey those orders. Adler, however, states clearly, "No, Eichmann was never part of a government order, but rather the functionary of an institution that was outside the control of the state, more powerful than the state, and which violated the validity of the law."

Accusing Arendt of "resentment against the Zionists," Adler challenges her indictment of the "role of Jewish leaders in the destruction of their own people," insisting that the act of any Jewish functionary

> was *not* his personal action, but rather a function of what had been dictated to him impersonally, and for which he was not responsible. If the utmost was not demanded immediately of the one receiving an order, then he would try to negotiate; that was his way of resisting. He would become ever more difficult until his position weakened. Then in order not to reveal his resistance, he would ease up in the matter at hand, though subjectively he would maintain the same aim as before, as he still hoped to gain certain concessions from his oppressor. Yet whatever was apparently conceded on that day meant nothing the next day, and thus tragedy came to pass, but not because of the cowardice, lack of resistance, sheepish acquiescence and betrayal on the part of the Jewish spokesperson.

Adler agrees there certainly was something "sinister" at work in "the role of the Jews in the implementation of their own catastrophe" and that it demanded "serious discussion," yet he preferred to view the Shoah as a tragic fate set in motion by powers larger than the individuals guilty of the actions they indeed committed. As for Eichmann's "banality," Adler was also emphatically clear: "The cynical, evil, and in no way banal Eichmann earlier appeared as something quite other, but either Frau Arendt does not know it or does not want to know it. . . . [O]nly the bad is to some degree banal, but never evil."

At the time of Eichmann's arrest Adler was already bearing witness to the "catastrophe" in other important, public ways. Four months earlier he had attended the annual meeting of the International Auschwitz Committee (IAC), which that year met in Warsaw. Founded in 1954, the IAC was dedicated to preserving the camp, researching and documenting its history, bringing to light the crimes committed there, campaigning for reparations to its victims, and bringing the SS to justice.[27] It also proved a hotbed of disagreement on whether the committee should focus on what the Jews had suffered or, as its Polish Communist members would have it, what the Germans had done to the Poles.[28] Its founder and leader was Hermann Langbein, a former Communist who in his youth volunteered for the "International Brigade" of the Spanish Civil War, and who had been interred as an "Aryan political" in Auschwitz, where he worked as a secretary for one of the camp doctors. Langbein visited Adler in London in March 1958 to invite him to a meeting of the IAC two months later in Amsterdam. Although Adler "had never had anything to do with official organizations," for this he made an exception and accepted election to its board.[29]

Adler proved a steadfast ally to Langbein throughout his vexed leadership of an organization undermined by Polish Communists who distrusted his having abandoned the Party. Already in 1959, Adler established direct links between the Association of Nazi Camp Survivors in London, an organization he helped found, and the IAC. He was even sharper than Langbein in criticizing the determination of the Conference on Jewish Material Claims Against Germany (the Claims Conference) to negotiate reparations only for Jewish slave laborers from the Krupp corporation, which had built a factory in Auschwitz for the production of gun parts, arguing that "anti-Jewish feelings [would] quite certainly (but very unnecessarily)" result from the deal, "unless your organization can convince the Krupp authorities that it is their solemn duty to compensate *all* former concentration camp inmates (and others) who worked as 'slave labour' for them."[30] Adler was especially attuned to the efforts of Eastern bloc Communists on the committee to undermine Langbein and oust him from the IAC, making it his "personal task" to derail their efforts.[31] Langbein was forced to step down as general secretary in 1961, and Adler resigned too, although they soon joined forces again as leaders of the Comité International des Camps, which continued to work for reparations for all slave laborers.

Although the mid-1950s was a nadir in efforts to bring Nazi criminals to justice, Langbein was at the forefront gathering documentary evidence of their guilt and working with German justice officials to prosecute perpetrators at Auschwitz.[32] By the time Adler joined the IAC, Langbein had made significant strides and could admit to Adler that he planned nothing less than "to commence legal proceedings against the entire organization behind the 'Final Solution.'"[33] By 1959, Fritz Bauer, the attorney general of the West German province of Hesse and later head of the operation that arrested Eichmann, began to prepare what became the Frankfurt Auschwitz trial of 1963–65. As a former secretary to the SS doctor Eduard Wirths, Langbein was an invaluable witness who provided reams of documents to the prosecution through the IAC while tapping Adler's expertise in navigating the resistance of many German officials.[34]

As part of the 1960 conference in Warsaw, a visit was arranged to Auschwitz, where Adler and fellow committee members toured what remained of the camp.[35] The presence of Premier Józef Cyriankiewicz underscored the significance of the occasion, if not the political tensions underlying the debate on how much focus should be on the sufferings of the Jews or the Poles. Adler's presence and support of Langbein helped to shed light on Polish collaboration with the Germans in persecuting and killing Jews, a topic suppressed for decades but later made indelible by Claude Lanzmann in 1985 through his nine-and-a-half-hour film *Shoah*. One may expect to find in letters to Bacon, Wurm, or others some mention of his return to the site where Gertrud and her mother had died, but nowhere does Adler reflect on what it felt like to again walk the ramp at Birkenau or see the ruins of the crematoria. In the manuscript for a talk on his visit, he expresses unease encountering some fifteen thousand visitors the day he was there and that "this monstrous place should become a tourist attraction or destination," but out of discretion for the lives that were lost there, he reveals little of his own loss.[36] This does not mean that he was not moved, but likely that it was a loss borne for so long and so privately, after having spent the last fifteen years immersed in the subject of the camps, few real revelations awaited him at the site itself. Flying back to Warsaw for another meeting of the IAC in June, Adler notes enigmatically in his calendar: "flew over Theresienstadt." What that meant to him a month shy of his fiftieth birthday and thirteen years after he last saw it we cannot know, although years later he wrote, "I don't regret anything that I have lived through. Certainly I regret that there's such a thing as Auschwitz, not to mention many other things. But if it did exist, then I don't regret having been there. What I am today is also thanks to the miserable parts of my life, as well as my own failings and sins."[37]

Adler in his Linden Gardens study, 1960. Credit: The Estate of H. G. Adler 2019, Deutsches Literaturarchiv Marbach.

Adler and Langbein also collaborated on two other projects aimed at bearing witness to as broad a public as possible. One was a collection of documents on Auschwitz comprising the victims' own accounts, reports written by the SS, quotes from the memoir written by Commandant Rudolf Höss published by the Institute for Contemporary History in 1958, everyday accounts given by guards and workers, and selections from the so-called Auschwitz Album, a trove of photos taken by an SS officer that was found in the camp by Lili Jacob after her liberation. The aim was to cover the founding, function, and elaborate organization of the death camp in a narrative that would allow general readers, as Adler put it, "to view the enormity of it all without journalistic or other kinds of gimmicks, or sentimentality, or a refusal to look at the truth getting in the way."[38]

Running over four hundred pages, *Auschwitz: Zeugnisse und Berichte* (*Auschwitz: Testimonies and Reports*) was edited by Adler, Langbein, and Ella Lingens-Reiner and published by the Europäische Verlagsanstalt in 1962. Seventeen years after the end of the war, it was the first major documentary account of Auschwitz in any language and the first time that the experience of the victims was told from "the inside" rather than only from the perspective of the perpetrators. Even for readers familiar with Höss's memoir, the book provided "a completely new and shocking view into the world of the camp" in anticipation of the Auschwitz trial that began the next year, where twelve of its contributors were called as witnesses. Boasting too the first German publication of a timeline for the camp's development and demise, the volume placed the direct personal experience of well-known intellectuals like Primo Levi, Bacon, and Langbein next to unknown everyday victims and perpetrators from many of the twenty-three nations represented in Auschwitz, and remains an extremely useful document now in a sixth, revised edition.[39]

It almost did not come to be. Begun under Langbein's aegis as general secretary of the IAC after Eugen Kogon helped find a publisher, the project was almost scuttled by the turmoil that ousted Langbein as a supposed "renegade" whom the Communist membership did not trust.[40] When the new leadership found out that Adler and Langbein planned to publish it on their own to escape the IAC's wish to focus more on Polish than Jewish victims, the IAC tried to get contributors to withdraw their entries and for the publisher to pull out. Both the publisher and most contributors stood with Adler and Langbein, allowing the volume to maintain an international scope free of partisan politics that avoided any separation between Jewish and Polish versions of the camp. Many of the texts were made available to German readers for the first time, including the first published account by Rudolf Vrba and Alfred Wetzler of their escape from Auschwitz to Slovakia, as well as excerpts from an interview with Eichmann in Argentina by the SS officer Willem Sassen that Langbein brought back with him from the trial in Jerusalem.[41] A succinct, thorough, and engaging overview of the day-to-day horrors of the camp, "not as an outgrowth, but rather as the inevitable consequence of the entire [Nazi] "system," the collection remains, in Katharina Stengel's words, a testament to the "tireless and hard-headed effort to shed light on Nazi persecution undertaken at a time when hardly anyone was interested in this subject."[42]

Closely aligned with this project was Adler and Langbein's script for the radio program *Auschwitz: Topographie eines Vernichtungslagers* ("Auschwitz: Topography of an Extermination Camp"), broadcast by the WDR on October 18, 1961. The import of this event together with the broadcast of the Eichmann trial earlier that year was enormous. Six weeks had passed since the barbed wire of the Berlin Wall bifurcated the country overnight, dividing families and citizens alike, leading the country as a whole to remain tuned in, not knowing what would come next. Germans had spent the last six months reading and listening to daily reports from the trial in Jerusalem as the world contemplated the eerie "normality" of the balding, bespectacled man sitting in a cube on the witness stand, whose only defense was that he had followed orders. Between 8:00 and 11:00 p.m. that autumn night, listeners heard for the first time on German soil the grim history of the atrocities spoken in the words and voices of those who had committed and suffered unspeakable deeds. Many knew about them already, some from family members, others from their own experience. Still others chose to turn away with a shrug or hollow invocations of the country's need to "come to terms with the past" and move on. Hearing it broadcast aloud meant more than publishing the astounding numbers of those killed, or listing the gruesome methods used to kill them. The chilling facts were delivered by human voices, sent out on the airwaves to tell stories that had not yet been told around hearths or kitchen tables, where sons began to ask their fathers what had occurred, wives queried husbands, and neighbors wondered about neighbors, living or dead.

Free of analysis or historical interpretation, the broadcast begins with an excerpt from Höss's testimony at Nürnberg:

> I, Rudolf Franz Ferdinand Höss, submit as sworn testimony the following:
>
> Beginning in 1934, I served continually in the administrations of various concentration camps until when, on May 1, 1940, I was named Commandant of Auschwitz. I estimate that at least 2,500,000 victims were executed and exterminated there through gassing and cremation, while at least another half million died of starvation and sickness. This number represents roughly 70 or 80 per cent of all the people who were shipped to Auschwitz; the rest were used as slaves in the factories of the concentration camps. In the summer of 1944 alone, approximately 400,000 Hungarian Jews were executed.

While the initial effect of hearing these words spoken by a professional actor is like being dropped into the trial at Nürnberg, Adler and Langbein use the format of the radio play to put the listener on trial as well. After a quick interjection by the narrator, who admits, "It's difficult to conceive of such atrocities, even when the camp commandant testifies to them" and that "Even prisoners of Auschwitz could hardly believe them," we hear the taped voice of Otto Wolken, a Viennese doctor and survivor of the camp, who confirms the question in the listener's head:

> It's the question that is always asked and which we asked ourselves: . . . Many think that such murders are not possible in the twentieth century in a civilized world. How did such a thing come about?—To this we must respond by saying: The gassings and exterminations were the secret acts of the Reich. All of the SS who took part were threatened with death if they so much as spoke about them. . . . When I was transported to Auschwitz, I had already spent five years in various German penal and concentration camps. When on the transport I met up with a Pole, who was on his way to be interrogated by a German judge, and who then told me what was going

> on in Auschwitz, I thought to myself: He is lying, he is exaggerating. If that's the way it is, how then is he alive? How is it at all possible that there is anyone . . . who could survive such mass extinction and mass murder? That of course is indeed the accident, the good luck, which somehow saved some of them.

This strikes at the heart of the problem: the plausibility of the events themselves. Wolken's testimony is recorded, as is that by Ella Lingens, a Viennese woman who worked as both a doctor and lawyer, who also talks about how she could not believe what she had heard until she arrived in Auschwitz herself in 1943. What is on trial are not the facts, but comprehension of the facts. Heard through the victims' voices, male and female, the doubts that even they struggled with in the past connect with those of the listener in the present, with the result that victim and citizen stand together faced with an abyss. Nor are Wolken or Lingens identified as Jews. Their stories are delivered in the mellifluous rhythms of their Viennese accents, the sound of chairs creaking and ambient room noise reminding us that they are alive, this is real, their stories have not disappeared, and the onus is on us to work out how to live with them.[43]

Adler and Langbein's radio broadcast could not have occurred at a more opportune time in helping Germans to begin to grapple with what had happened at Auschwitz and how their own countrymen had implemented it. A survey that year by the DIVO Institute for Applied Social Sciences showed 95 percent of German adults followed the Eichmann trial in the press or on the radio or television. By the time of the Frankfurt Auschwitz trial of 1963–65, that dropped to 60 percent, which argues both for a substantial number of people who had become indifferent or resistant to Nazi trials and the degree to which some had reached a saturation point.[44] Part of the reason why had to do with the media's coverage, for reporters tended to fall into clichés about "beasts" and "barbarians" while teetering on the edge of courtroom melodrama, making it difficult for readers and listeners to feel anything in common with the accused.[45] The students and young people who would go on to formulate the "1968 Generation" flocked to the trial, and its reverberations were felt like a shock wave through German society, but a trough of skepticism, ignorance, and denial still existed in the wartime generation and needed alternative means to engage with it.

In the fall of 1961, Adler and Langbein offered something different. In the patchwork of live testimony from survivors such as Wolken, Lingens, and Bacon, combined with the incriminating words of Höss, Heydrich, and Eichmann himself, no moralizing lessons were offered, nor was there a debate about guilt or how to legally prosecute "crimes against humanity." There were only the voices and stories themselves in the crisp accents of the SS, the singsong of German country accents, or the heavy inflection of Czechs, Slovaks, Hungarians, and Poles. Through actors the words of Ruth Klüger, Grete Salus, Rudolf Vrba, and Tadeusz Paczula lived on, as well as those of criminals who had already been hanged. These joined others among the accounts Adler and Langbein anthologized in *Auschwitz: Testimonies and Reports,* published the following year. These were not mere words upon the page nor testimonies submitted as evidence to the trial of a distant "monster." They were the "topography" of the terror that had occurred throughout Germany and Europe, which remained just outside the listener's door, rattling like chains in the memories of survivors and former accomplices alike, and in not a few cases within the walls of their own homes.

Höss opens and closes the broadcast, his last words claiming "full and complete responsibility" for "everything that occurred in the camp," but the cumulative effect is hardly meant to shift the blame onto him alone. The format of the radio essay could not allow for the kind of political or historical analysis needed in the trials to grasp the structure and social meaning of the Holocaust, but it and the trials planted an awareness of the place of Auschwitz in the fabric of German history. Only the broadcast of the American television miniseries *Holocaust* in the 1970s would have as strong an effect on the public consciousness in Germany. Adler and Langbein's broadcast, however, did not exploit melodrama to tell its story, and both Adler and Langbein published substantive scholarly discussions of structural aspects of the Shoah. For now, though, the voices of perpetrator, victim, and survivor alike had been spoken.

Listeners were quick to write to the WDR, which forwarded the response to Adler. "Any honest listener," wrote one, "would have to be deeply affected by the presentation of such atrocities in Auschwitz. It should always be remembered in order that it remains clear how satanic humans can be." A two-page letter from another added, "This shocking report, which bears witness to the past, should now provide the chance for us Germans to take a hard look at ourselves." Not all agreed, however, for some said that dwelling on such matters damaged Germany's reputation. Responding to one such protest, Adler said the broadcast was not meant to "drag the German people through the mud" but rather to point to those "ignoble supporters who themselves had dragged the German people through the mud," ending with a loaded comment by reminding the listener that such a report could only restore Germany's standing in the world, "which is exactly what you yourself want."[46]

Adler's life, however, was not consumed entirely by Theresienstadt and the camps. In 1958, he and the family visited Bernard and Gutza Reder in Florence, the first they had seen one another in twenty-one years, all three "taken in like long-lost siblings."[47] In 1959, he and his family could at last afford to leave the dark, close confines of 96 Dalgarno Gardens for the more pleasant surround of Notting Hill Gate, where they moved into a bright and cheery three-story mews house at 35A Linden Gardens. Formerly a stable, it contained two bedrooms, a study, bath, and large living room, providing enough room to host visitors and friends, such as Ilse Aichinger and her husband, Günter Eich, as well as Ilse's twin sister Helga. Bettina's friend Mary Donovan and her sister Maria came to stay, and the poet and translator Michael Hamburger and his wife, Anne, visited, as well as George and Marianne Steiner, the latter a niece of Kafka who devoted herself to preserving her uncle's manuscripts.[48]

A mix of writers, critics, painters, composers, and émigrés followed the Adlers when in 1964 they moved to an even larger apartment at 47 Wetherby Mansions in Earl's Court Square. Known then as "Kangaroo Valley" because of the large population of Australian immigrants who lived among the smoke-filled bars like the Troubadour, where Bob Dylan made his London debut, the neighborhood also boasted the Poetry Society, which Basil Bunting led as president in the 1970s in support of avant-garde poets like Bob Cobbing, Bill Griffiths, and Eric Mottram, who sought to remake British poetry through the influence of American poets like Robert Creeley, Robert Duncan, and Charles Olson.[49] Diplomats, scholars, writers, and artists of every stripe passed through Adler's study, including the composers Karlheinz Stockhausen and György Ligeti, Kafka's friend and contemporary Johannes Urzidil, and the artist Giséle Celan, the poet's widow. "If this was exile, and it certainly was," recalls Jeremy Adler, "it was an exile buzzing with life." Regardless of such bustle, each morning Günther walked in nearby Brompton Cemetery, as Beatrix Potter once did, coming across the grave of a Mr. Nutkin, the inspiration for her eponymous squirrel, as well as passing the ornate gravestone of the Austrian tenor Richard Tauber. Returning home, he sat down to work at his desk, the yellow star sitting in the aluminum container that had carried his poems from Niederorschel to Langenstein.[50]

Adler's pocket calendar for 1960 notes Jeremy's bar mitzvah in October and before that a month's vacation in the Tyrol in August. Once his first substantial earnings from radio work and reparations materialized, this became an annual event in 1957. Initially, the family stayed in a B&B in the Austrian Alps, but by the mid-1960s, Switzerland became their favorite place for Günther and Jeremy to spend long days hiking and berry-picking, while Bettina relaxed, read, and sketched *en plein air.* Visits from the Eichs, his childhood friend Wolfgang Burghart and family, the young artist Sylvia Finzi, and Yehuda and Josephine Bacon shaped a lively, convivial life amid the restorative powers of nature.

Bettina and Günther with Yehuda Bacon, Austria, 1963. Credit: The Estate of H. G. Adler 2019, Deutsches Literaturarchiv Marbach.

Even amid such sublime surroundings as the Fex Valley or Grindelwald, the artist in Adler remained engaged. "Bought a camera" reads an innocuous, unusual entry in the pocket calendar for July 15, 1960. It hardly seemed important then, but photography came to play a vital role in Adler's life, especially as a tool through which to turn his pastoral hikes and itinerant travels into art. His archive contains some eight thousand photos, a fraction of them casual family photos. Most are travel photos that display an anthropological curiosity similar to Steiner's research on landscapes and marginal communities or are shots of glaciers, rocky and snow-covered peaks, valleys and open vistas, trees and fauna. These are not just snapshots of bucolic wonders but sightings shaped and framed by an artist's eye.

Photography for Adler was as much a philosophical pursuit as an outlet for artistic expression. In *Kontraste und Variationen* (*Contrasts and Variations*), his 1969 book-length essay accompanied by thirty of his own photographs, he states, "What lies behind an image, or perhaps may lie behind it, is like a Platonic idea or a Kantian thing in itself, both of which we do not know as anything other than intellectual abstractions. In contrast to this is the image, which is indeed present to us. To put this another way: our reality consists of the image, is a chain of images, an entire world of images."[51] In framing such images, the photographer

H. G. Adler: *View of Fex Valley through Larches*, 1965. Credit: The Estate of H. G. Adler 2019, Deutsches Literaturarchiv Marbach.

"presents images that are witnesses to ourselves, products of our continual engagement with the world, works shaped by our efforts, which in total are images of ourselves."[52] It follows that "a good image carries the stamp of one's personality," which "is realized through the allure present in 'how I see it,' as well as in the preservation, indeed the affirmation of the personality of a specific person—in this case the photographer—which manifests itself in surface appearances and nowhere else."[53] Adler claims that the camera comes to his aid *as* a writer, for it "imparts the silence to the image that he wishes to evoke in the face of silent or even louder things," a sentiment reaching back to František Drtikol's own "system of silence" employed in his photographs to reveal the "stillness of Being and consciousness." This creates "verbal images" ("Sprachbilder") that "can claim for themselves, practically unchanged over time, their own degree of magnitude."[54]

The Hungarian novelist Péter Nádas experienced this "magnitude" directly when in 2015 he was asked by the Deutsches Literaturarchiv to peruse its vast photographic archive and write an essay to accompany a show of whatever works he selected. Deciding to begin with "A" and make his way through until he found something of interest, Nádas opened up the cartons

H. G. Adler: *Matterhorn*, 1968 Credit: The Estate of H. G. Adler 2019, Deutsches Literaturarchiv Marbach.

containing eight thousand of Adler's photographs and negatives. He knew instantly that he was in the presence of a serious artist. Before turning to fiction, Nádas had worked as a photographer in his youth, so he was no novice. Nádas recalled that the "stamp" of Adler's personality was immediately present, his own intuition telling him that behind the work stood "a person who was not absolutely determined by the things which he believed had determined him, though nevertheless his having had to drift along entirely at the hands of a precarious and random fate had indeed determined the central current of his life."[55]

H. G. Adler: *Ships at Sea*, Ireland, 1984 Credit: The Estate of H. G. Adler 2019, Deutsches Literaturarchiv Marbach.

Addressing the artistry of the photographs themselves, Nádas echoes Adler's ideas about photography, noting how Adler "works like a painter who turns his composition into a surface, a surface formed by the sight of the natural object that is thus abstracted."[56] Nádas also recognized that the photographer must have been a survivor of the camps, as so many of his landscapes contain barriers, whether merely trees, branches, or valleys, between himself and the august, sun-drenched peaks beyond. In addition, Nádas found the images to be "sprung from a loneliness of an unknown nature," one that was not just "a mood and certainly not accidental, but rather one of deep clarity."[57] This in turn is what links Adler's sensibility "to the German Romantics, something that was not even let go of in Auschwitz." The result is that the work poses "the most deeply personal, intimate question about how a person accommodates understanding and feeling at once." The consequence of this is that in both his photography and poetry "we encounter an exceptionally shy, extremely sophisticated metaphysician in an epoch which has of late categorically and with pleasure abandoned the metaphysical once and for all."[58]

As a writer or photographer, for Adler truth lies beneath the surface of reality, and the purpose of art is to extract that truth. Although photography has the added charge of doing this without words, the epiphany that results provides the opportunity to understand or participate in that which cannot be entered on one's own terms. What is sought is "the secret magic of sympathy" by viewer and reader alike, an operation that can lie dormant for years only to occur in the flash of an insight absorbed from a photograph, the momentary appreciation of a character's being and essence, especially when that same character is trapped in a world bent on denying both.[59]

Although Adler admits that one inspiration behind *Contrasts and Variations* was the desire "to arrange a set of photographs that could appear in a book," there are deeper artistic, sociological, and even spiritual aims at work in his photography. As in his literary work and the work of Drtikol, he hoped to speak beyond history to a kind of timeless future resting in the eye of readers or observers who would see what he saw, and thus see it for themselves. On another level, like Steiner's use of the camera to capture the passing daily life of Romany, Ruthenians, and Hassidim, Adler did the same during his many travels, such as on his trips to Israel in 1965 and 1968.

H. G. Adler: *Jerusalem*, 1965 Credit: The Estate of H. G. Adler 2019, Deutsches Literaturarchiv Marbach.

The first involved his giving a talk at the World Congress of Jewish Studies in Jerusalem on "The Jews in National Socialist Camps," while on the second he spoke at the opening of an exhibition of Bernard Reder's works. Seeing Reder's late bronzes for the first time, they made as powerful an impression on him as the sculptor's early stone carvings had made on him and Bettina in Prague. Both trips gave him the opportunity to see the great religious sites he had read about, connecting him with the deepest layers of the religion he had turned to in Auschwitz. Israel's "timeless splendor" impressed him, and the fact that Zionism had not entirely transformed its social and economic structures. In a Jaffa flea market he relished seeing people from Algiers and North Africa, for it meant "the transplantation of European Jews had not completely taken over."[60]

These trips also allowed Adler to visit again with Bacon, Max Brod, Hugo Bergmann, Gutza Reder, Gershom Scholem, Jacob Robinson, and Meir Fraenkel, and friends from his youth he had not seen since before the war. The meeting with Robinson, who had sought Adler's advice when writing *And the Crooked Shall Be Made Straight,* his critique of Arendt's book on the Eichmann trial, led to his speaking on "The Autonomous Jewish Administration in Terezín" at a conference at the YIVO Institute in New York in December 1967.[61] There he stayed with Kurt and Edith Oppens from his graduate school days and saw again Johannes Urzidil, a friend of Kafka's who introduced Adler's reading at the Leo Baeck Institute in Manhattan. Adler also spoke to students at Bronx Community College and to the faculty of the Union Theological Institute.[62] Finally, if nothing else, the trip to New York, a city he found to be as vibrant as the Prague of his youth, meant he could finally close the circle on his initial desire to head to America after the war.

And yet, despite all the success, despite having published four works of scholarship in five years, one of which was awarded the Leo Baeck Prize, and no matter that he had been commissioned to write a major work on the deportations by a preeminent German institute, or that he now managed to make a good living writing and recording radio essays heard throughout Germany, or that he was asked to lecture on Jewish culture and history, the implications of the Holocaust, or even life in England at centers of continuing education, conferences, and symposia—still there was something missing. By age fifty, Adler was a respected and engaged public intellectual, a highly regarded resource for scholar and jurist alike. But he was not, at least in the broader public's mind, known as a literary artist.

Exactly why that is so remains the nagging question of Adler's career. No single reason rises above all others, and several factors contributed to the difficulty in finding good publishers, the poor sales that resulted, and the critical neglect that hung like a veil over his achievement, obscuring it until twenty years after his death. Years before publishing his first book, Adler felt the problem lay at the heart of the German book market, which lacked three key elements necessary to support his work: "money, literary sophistication, and the courage to take risks."[63] Also, because of his scholarship and the need to lecture and write for the radio to make a living, he had become known as "Theresienstadt Adler." Beyond spending two to four months a year in Germany, Adler also lived in London and remained outside the social circles of most German writers, nor did he have any standing within or regular access to the university system. It is easy to see why he remained on the outside looking in as postwar German letters were shaped by luminaries such as Günter Grass, Ingeborg Bachmann, Paul Celan, and his friend Heinrich Böll. All were members of Gruppe 47 (Group 47), the annual gathering of writers and intellectuals founded in 1947 by Hans Werner Richter that greatly influenced the development and support of young German writers. Adler never attended their meetings and remained suspicious of their agenda, his requests to be invited to read having been turned down, even though he was friends with several of its members. For him, the effort to battle reactionary forces in politics and publishing tended to set up another set of rules brokered to serve the participants' own careers.[64] So when he did manage to engage with the wider public, it most often was as "Theresienstadt Adler," cementing his identity as a scholar-survivor rather than supporting his nascent career as a fiction writer.

What was not a factor, however, was any lack of effort. Adler approached every major publisher in Germany he could think of, but with praise and respect for the novels came polite refusals, the 1953 response of a Kiepenheuer & Witsch editor being typical. Turning down *Eine Reise* for financial reasons, she apologized, since "your work has found a sophisticated, poetic form which should be made available to German literature, and especially to the German public."[65] At the beginning of the 1950s, Adler could be philosophical in thinking, "There are two responses a publisher can have to an unknown author: either he falls in love with his work or he thinks he has a bestseller on his hands."[66] Yet over time, both rejection and long delays by publishers in returning manuscripts led to the exasperation he revealed to Sigfried Unseld in 1956 when remarking, "Any other writer in my situation, especially as a Theresienstadt and Auschwitz survivor, would have long since lost his sense of humor, and instead would be bitter and say: All these reassurances of 'reparations' and any other catch phrases are nothing but lies and hot air as soon as you step beyond kitsch and sentimentality and enter the realm of art."[67]

Turned down again and again throughout the 1950s, in a 1960 letter to Franz Wurm he laments,

> It could be that I am—perhaps mostly for the literati themselves—not able to be embraced as a contemporary, since my works present something that does not at all appear traditional, and therefore cannot be

> accepted or rejected as such, but also is not something that is timely, and certainly not fashionable (or misunderstood as passably fashionable), which makes it difficult to support them. Thus I appear neither modern nor unmodern, but rather objectionable, suspect, a nuisance that they cannot actually get rid of, no matter how much they may want to, that being the reason—without being able to cite any supposed or actual flaws—they defile my texts and thus me.[68]

Adler's feeling of being "defiled" ("schändet") might seem extreme, but at fifty, and after a decade of failing to bring his novels to the printed page, his frustration bordered upon bitterness, if not hopelessness. Even when others spoke of or admired his "success in Germany and everywhere else," he was quick to caution that it was folly to overestimate it, since "the right time for my literary works will not come so soon."[69] Yet amid adversity, all he could do was continue to write and experiment with new styles while bearing witness in fiction and poetry to what he had lived and known.

16

The Maker

In spite of continued struggles to find publishers for his works, Adler's fortunes turned. After the 1960 appearance of *Die Juden in Deutschland* (*The Jews of Germany*), tracing the history of Jews in Germany from the Enlightenment to the Holocaust, over the next nine years Adler published six books of fiction—two novels and four collections of short stories—as well as *Contrasts and Variations*. Only with the 1964 publication of *Die Erfahrung der Ohnmacht: Beiträge zur Soziologie unserer Zeit* (*The Experience of Powerlessness: Contributions Towards a Sociology of Our Time*) did Adler return to scholarship, although his subject there was modern society more than the Holocaust itself. It would take him until 1974 to complete his next, and last, great study of the camps, *Administered Man*. In the fifteen years he spent researching and writing it, his aim was to secure his spot on the literary stage with Böll, Heimito von Doderer, and Canetti, his far more successful friends.

The greatest obstacle in Adler's way was a state of mind that stemmed from a philosophical debate in the 1950s and his first encounter with Adorno and other postwar intellectuals. Writing in 1958 about the reaction he received when reading his literary work before an audience of one hundred at a meeting of the "Grünwalder Kreis" in Cologne, Adler notes the animosity that greeted certain writers at the time, no matter the strength of their work:[1]

> It was a great moral success, though in part there was also some pretty strong opposition. This was especially true above all for a group of seemingly gifted young writers, whose impeccable political sentiments no one could doubt, and who admire my Theresienstadt book and me. Yet they have succumbed to a literary dogma that could be called something like "The Fear of Clichés," and they have no idea how it applies to me. Because they discover condemnable "clichés" in my language and cannot recommend that any of it be published, but instead the opposite, they even go so far as to vehemently reject any possibility

> of publication. Such rejection will not hinder my success, but it could delay it and make it difficult to achieve. I wish I had enough time here to be more precise about the nature of their argument, besides noting their lack of appreciation for complexity, for tragedy, for humor, satire and subtle irony, but above all for religious conviction.[2]

The zeal to eradicate reactionary politics and Nazi holdovers in government was well-meaning, but when such sentiments became rules about what literature could or could not do, they risked becoming almost as oppressive as those whom they opposed.

No "rule" had more influence on the limits of the German literary imagination than Adorno's dictum that "to write a poem after Auschwitz is barbaric." Adler believed instead in the need to use *all* means of confronting "the catastrophe." Amid widespread acceptance of Adorno's stance, Adler could not go his own way without encountering skepticism of any "poetic" style that smacked of bourgeois traditionalism or an aesthetics that others felt distanced the reader from "what happened," or risked fostering the decadence and escapism that had failed to mitigate the Nazi threat in the first place.

Resistance to artful, nuanced accounts of the Holocaust manifested itself in many forms. Publishers seeking to reach the general audience preferred historical realism that tapped the life-and-death "drama" of survival in the camps, leading to the success of works like Erich Maria Remarque's *Der Funke Leben* (*The Spark of Life*) in 1952 and Bruno Apitz's 1958 novel *Nackt unter Wölfen* (*Naked Among Wolves*). Even in England a publisher suggested to Adler that he should rework *The Journey* into something more like Norman Mailer's *The Naked and the Dead*.[3] In Germany, however, feelings ran especially high, and Adler's literary work received a prickly reception from the "Grünwalder Kreis." There was also a critical prejudice against any kind of aestheticism, especially when it involved an artistic depiction of the camps by anyone who experienced them firsthand. Günter Grass could mythologize the petty willfulness and stupidity of the Nazi followers through Oskar Matzerath and his tin drum, but as Ernestine Schlant observes, postwar German literature and culture maintained "a lack of interest in and concern for Jews as equally entitled others and acting subjects of their own history and present."[4]

When it came to Adler's *The Journey*, a more rare response of outright hostility emerged, in some ways outing prejudices buried below the polite rejection offered by many others. "As long as I live, this book will not be published in Germany," Peter Suhrkamp is said to have stated to his staff at Suhrkamp Verlag on reading the manuscript.[5] Siegfried Unseld and fellow editor Friedrich Podszus, however, remained very interested in the manuscript, and Unseld worked to place it with another publisher. But Suhrkamp was right: he died in 1959 and *The Journey* did not appear until 1962 from Bibliotheca Christiana, a small Christian publisher in Bonn headed by Knut Erichson.[6]

Suhrkamp himself was no stranger to the misery of the camps. In 1936 he took over the S. Fischer Verlag publishing house when its Jewish founders were stripped of ownership, and although the Nazis forced him to change the name to Suhrkamp Verlag in 1942, he maintained the firm's high standards. He spent six months at the end of the war in the Sachsenhausen concentration camp for having failed to denounce a suspected informant. While no rationale for his denunciation of *The Journey* has survived, the novel had a powerful effect on him. If he objected to its transformation of the camp experience into a "ballade" whose "lyrical irony" in his view made a mockery of the horrors, his reaction suggests that an experimental and inventive approach still held power to move and engage the reader on an emotional level. If his objection was that Adler's "tale" struck too close to his own misery in Sachsenhausen, then the imaginative had powerfully invoked the real, giving the lie to the belief that only realism could do justice to the suffering.

Adler would not have been shocked at Suhrkamp's condemnation, for he had lambasted what he felt was the publisher's conservative artistic stance as early as 1952. In a four-page summary of Suhrkamp's published views on "What I Expect from a Modern Novel," Adler abjures them, "even if only among my own unpublished papers." Bemoaning demands that a novel have three central characters seated in a particular social milieu covering no more than three days if set in a particular moment or seven years if encompassing an era, that it resolve its plot through an unusual occurrence, that its language mirror everyday speech, that its rhythm cohere to that of modern life, and that it remain fictional despite any use of realism, Adler concludes that Suhrkamp has "no idea about the compositional possibilities of a work of art" and is nothing less than a "low-brow, befuddled nutcase." Adler knew that his own novels, especially *The Journey*, would not pass muster with any of these demands and contrasts his own artistic values in declaring, "It would make more sense to say that all of a novel's layers [Schichten] (that's a better word than 'levels' ['Ebenen']) must be so present that its composition—the only thing it advances—manifests itself as true." He concludes, "The modern novel must not depict the modern, or it can select parts of the modern where one does not recognize the rhythm of modern life, or where it is suspect or even denied that such a rhythm even exists, or where this rhythm is even spurned in favor of something else that is posed against it."[7]

It's a wonder Adler chose to submit *The Journey* to Suhrkamp Verlag at all. That he did attests to the limited number of quality publishers in Germany at the time. Unseld finally rejected *The Journey* in 1958, after holding on to the manuscript at Suhrkamp for three years. Adler observed to his friend, the photographer Luzzi Wolgensinger:

> While the official publishing industry certainly can be blamed for many of the failures that have occurred, this does not explain it all. The nature of the texts themselves is an important reason. [It's obvious] how they [the editors] are blind to anything that is pioneering, and whenever that is not the case—as happens in many, especially longer works—the publishers, editors, critics, newspaper people, etc., feel threatened or wounded, which in turn means there is no incentive to print such works. One can only battle against it, which I do continuously and constantly, meaning that I am probably much more hands-on than most of the flock of literati rushing about, and more than most serious writers usually are.[8]

Writers often project their struggles onto the editors who have rejected them, but in fact Adler was either seen as too traditional, and out of touch with the times, or too modernist, and unconvincing or even decadent. Less obvious was that his work was also thoroughly authoritative, decidedly unique, and deeply entwined with the German language itself, an attribute that supersedes the others. Of all the novelists who wrote about the Shoah, there are only four Jewish survivors who had direct experience of the camps and who wrote in German: Edgar Hilsenrath, whose novel *Nacht* (*Night*) was published in 1964; Jurek Becker, whose *Jakob der Lügner* (*Jacob the Liar*) came out in 1969; and Fred Wander, whose autobiographical novel *Der siebente Brunnen* (*The Seventh Well*) appeared in 1970.[9] Adler is the fourth, and with the appearance of *Eine Reise* in 1962, he was the first Jew writing in German to publish a novel about his ordeal.[10]

Seen another way, Adler was neither too traditional nor too modernist but literally unlike any other writer of his time. There were no Jewish survivors writing novels in German, much less with the subtlety and irony with which he wielded the language. Nor were there any novelists who had first published seminal scholarship on the Holocaust, even if Adler said that the Theresienstadt book should be read "like a Kafka novel with reversed signification," nightmares become reality.[11] Given his love of wordplay, his extensive efforts to document and call out Nazi euphemisms, and his ability to immerse the reader in the "wordscape" of guards, officers, bystanders, and victims, Suhrkamp's reaction to *The Journey* is less surprising. What Peter Suhrkamp read was not merely a novel but a sonic playback of his own horrific experience in Sachsenhausen. What he heard in the opening pages were the voices of the camp layered one upon another and the booming voice of the survivor:

> No one asked you, it was decided already, you were rounded up and not one kind word was spoken. Many of you tried to make sense out of what was going on, so you yourselves had to inquire. Yet no one was there who could answer you. "Is this how it's going to be? For a little while . . . a day . . . years and years . . .? We want to get on with our lives." But all was quiet, only fear spoke, and that you could not hear. Old people could not accept what was going on. Their complaining was unnerving, such that around those left untouched by such suffering a cold and hideous wall was erected, the wall of pitilessness.[12]

Suhrkamp would surely have appreciated Adler's wordplay in the German. English cannot capture the "you" as second-person plural informal, which identifies the speaking voice as the pejorative and insulting tone of the officers condemning the victims, or the victims' collective and desperate reflections. Both the oppressor and the victim are heard in the voice of the unnamed survivor-narrator positioned to relay the "tale" ("Erzählung") to follow.[13]

Subtle wordplay is not the stuff of historical realism, which employs a faux documentary mode to convince us of depictions that confirm rather than challenge our own expectations. *The Journey* slips in and out of the voices of the oppressor, victim, and survivor, often switching from one to the other without notice or transition. The novel's use of montage is amplified as it unfolds and the victims are rendered as phantasmic bricks marching, or as bird heads on crutches, or as wheels churning through mud, or when the Lustigs' daughter Zerlina is turned into a rabbit killed in a crematorium, or a local reporter is placed on top of a column commemorating victims of the plague, while the current victims marching by beg him to take their picture and record that they are there and exist.

All is not a dream, however, for the Lustigs are also shown suffering the real deprivation of Ruhenthal (ironically, "Peaceful Valley"). There seventy-five-year-old Leopold Lustig works on the garbage detail, which Leo Baeck did in Theresienstadt, hauling rubbish to the outskirts where "[t]he sinister is buried . . . without anyone noticing," as are the victims in the ghetto, "the town of visible ghosts."[14] We see Leopold die in the infirmary, after which his wife, Caroline, her sister Ida, and his daughter, Zerlina, leave for a nightmare realm meant to signify Auschwitz. Only his son, Paul later awakens from a dream of being in a grave before passing through the ruined town of Unkenburg, where he lives for a time in an abandoned military barracks. Eventually he leaves for home, having "vanquished at last" the rubbish and ruinous existence he has survived.[15]

The other survivor of *The Journey*'s transformative nightmare is the reader, who either has not gone through the experience, and thus cannot know it entirely, or who did—as Suhrkamp did—and cannot entirely forget it or might be unwilling to confront it, because of what he survived, or what others did not. Yet only a survivor who knew the visceral language of suffering itself, as well as possessing the ability to contextualize it in German, could maneuver the reader through the text this way. This effort to render "l'univers concentrationnaire" as an intertwined array of actors, intentions, experiences, and perceptions in tension with one another at best, or in conflict at worst, keeps Adler's narrative and voice ever shifting throughout *The Journey*.

With the publication of *Unser Georg und andere Geschichten* (*Our George and Other Stories*) in 1961, and *The Journey* the following year, Adler finally broke through the wall of rejection he had long encountered, but sales and wide acclaim did not follow. Even the praise of critics, many of whom as friends or colleagues were eager to champion his work, was not sufficient, as reviewers could not decide if his work was traditional or modern.

In the *Frankfurter Hefte*, Roland Wiegenstein wrote, "Adler is a learned man who knows a great deal, yet his prose never for a moment betrays what it owes to such learning. But what is most striking to me is the rigor with which artistic means hardly seen anymore are employed here and used as an instrument to capture the experience of our times."[16] Ruth Bowert, reviewing the book on the Norddeutscher Rundfunk, noted that the stories embodied contemporary subject matter while remaining "timeless and placeless" in their use of satire to "expose the myopia of human behavior."[17] Franz Wurm, on the Schweizer Rundfunk, emphasized Adler's sly use of humor, which "feigns a pleasantness that stands in such stark contrast to what the stories are actually about that it risks the stories taking on a reality completely their own."[18] Several saw connections to Kafka's use of the absurd, to the biting satire of Karl Kraus, and to the fabulism of the Prague German writers Gustav Meyrink (*The Golem*), Leo Perutz, and Alfred Kubin. What is hardly mentioned in the reviews, however, is just what "contemporary subject matter" is at the heart of Adler's stories. Wiegenstein writes, "Whoever is sensitive to subtle reverberations will soon sense that these parables cannot be separated from the horrors that cloud the horizon of this century," but the stories almost entirely avoid historical material, nor would one, at first glance, think them to be written by a Holocaust survivor.[19]

No doubt this is on purpose, for Adler's generally fabulist approach eschews psychological realism or intricate plot in order to force readers to make the connection to contemporary events on their own. "Ein dunkler Tag" ("A Dark Day") opens by announcing, "One day the sun did not rise above the entire republic and darkness reigned," which sounds like a Grimm tale yet is spoken from the twentieth century. What follows, however, is not a descent into modern horrors but a bemused account of the people's panic and their government's ineptitude, none of it mattering when the sun does rise the next day and the narrator sardonically observes, "after a few weeks everything was back to normal throughout the land."[20] In another story a cloven, literal scapegoat named Hans (again, a name Adler disowned for himself) crosses the desert after being expelled from a town, only to find refuge in another town when his skills as a dressmaker are valued, although the yearly ritual of expelling a scapegoat continues in his hometown. As in "A Dark Day," things return to normal and the absurd becomes quotidian, which seems all the more absurd. The irony is that the world goes on regardless of a present reality imbued with suffering.[21]

Adler's stories do not remain completely free of the darkness that lies beneath them, and at the center of the book is "Erinnerungen an ein vergangenes Jahrhundert" ("Memories of a Previous Century"). More a journalistic account than a fictional tale of character and plot, the tone powers the story's gallows humor in reassuring the reader that "what was especially loved was killing people hygienically, thereby causing no one to get their hands dirty," or that after such catastrophe, "Therefore it's no wonder that all the arts and sciences blossomed like never before or after, since no one could ever be satisfied with merely superficial advances, which we ourselves know all too well today."[22] Such archness is what allows Adler to deftly render the volume's titular tale of Georg, an aged and worn-out twenty-two-year-old skeleton mourned by the art students who are forced to replace him while remaining grateful for his presence as "a guardian spirit" in their future works, death literally at the heart of art, as it resides below the surface of Adler's stories.

At the time, Christoph Schwerin concluded in the *Streit-Zeit-Schrift*, "Adler is indeed not a popular writer, and his little book will not speak to the snobs who in all their progressiveness are too good for it. No literary prize would do anything to help the situation and no publishing house will make money from his books. Most likely few people in his time will recognize his stature. He is, in secret, a master of German literature, and there is no denying that."[23] It is understandable that the slim volume of ninety-four pages remained what even its maker saw as no more than the "visiting card of an unknown author."[24]

The Journey was reviewed more widely and prominently, and yet its strongest supporters also left the book in a kind of no man's land between prewar and postwar worlds. Heinrich Böll noted curiously in *Der Tagesspiegel*, "It is a very German book, a very German journey, and yet no accident that the word 'German' never appears once in Adler's tale." Böll does not explain why it is particularly "German," nor does he reflect on the influence of fabulist Czech writers like Meyrink and Kubin in Adler's use of myth and fable to render experience rather than remaining in the historical vocabulary of Nazis, Germans, and Jews. Instead, Böll writes, "His book is called a tale, and it describes a catastrophe that involves the loss of a home, a journey, and a great deal about rubbish, and through these three—home, journey, rubbish—the tale probes deep into the present."[25] Heimito von Doderer claimed a more "universal grasp" for the novel as a "prose ballade," emphasizing its aesthetics rather than its historical engagement. "A ballade makes no accusation, nor does it forgive anything," he writes. "It crystalizes its form, freeing its author, freeing its reader, its subject set free and unburdened, . . . not in the least encumbered by its own weightiness. An entire mountain of horror is turned into song."[26]

The Journey is cast either as a moving historical engagement speaking to the contemporary world or a timeless expression of universal truth on the high plane of art. Elias Canetti, whose praise of the manuscript in a 1952 letter to Adler that was used in the publisher's catalog, planted the seed for each when he wrote:

> I find *The Journey* to be a masterpiece. It is written in an especially beautiful, clear prose, free of resentment or bitterness, the expression of an essential catharsis to which only you or those who suffered a similar fate can lay claim. I believe that your experience, which many others experienced as well, has received here a complete poetic transformation unachieved by anyone else until now. The terrible things that happened to people are depicted here in such a way that they are suspended and delicate and tolerable, as if they could not lay a hand on the essence of humankind. I have to say that you have restored *hope* to modern literature again. One can only say that this book will receive the recognition that it deserves, for it will become the classic work of this kind of "journey," of every kind of displacement and desolation, no matter whom it happens to.[27]

High praise, but given Canetti and Doderer's emphasis on the novel's "suspended" and "delicate" voice free of "resentment and bitterness" and all "accusation," critics and readers wishing to remain socially engaged may have felt trepidatious.

Nor did Canetti's prediction that it would become "the classic work of this kind of 'journey' " always remind reviewers of the specific "catastrophe" that inspired it. Because its publisher primarily brought out Christian texts, many of the reviews appeared in Christian journals, tending to transform Paul Lustig's survival into a story of triumphant resurrection rather than conscious endurance, while almost all neglected that it had anything to do with what the Jews had suffered.[28] Rare was the reviewer who, like Roland Wiegenstein, openly acknowledged, "The reader can hardly continue reading without clapping shut the book and crying out, tossing aside this fable and its truth, the truth of Theresienstadt."[29] Only for the few able to tackle the moral and imaginative dilemma that Adler posed in his fiction did he remain a "Geheimtipp" ("insider's tip") combining a prewar modernism with a sense of *engágement* that remained perennial rather than fashionable, imaginative rather than overtly political.

H. G. Adler: *Heinrich Böll*, 1962. Credit: The Estate of H. G. Adler 2019, Deutsches Literaturarchiv Marbach.

What Adler found in Knut Erichson and Bibliotheca Christiana was a publisher who believed in his work and was committed to bringing it out in the most distinctive form possible. *The Journey* did not sell out of its initial print run of three thousand copies, but Erichson published two further collections of Adler's stories: *Der Fürst des Segens* (*The Prince of Blessings*) in 1964, and *Sodoms Untergang* (*The Fall of Sodom*) in 1965. All three books were impeccably designed by the renowned typographer Hermann Zapf and printed on high-quality paper, with elegant bindings and slip covers featuring prominent quotes by Canetti and Doderer.[30] *Eine Reise* was particularly striking in its red cloth binding with the title embossed in gold on the spine, announcing that this was a novel of high artistic merit whose publication should be seen as a notable event. Unlike Suhrkamp, Erichson recognized the book's consequence, telling Adler in a letter accompanying the first copies he sent to him in London:

> As Germans we are so burdened with what happened and what you have depicted in this book that we hardly know what to say. I personally decided to bring out the book as a memorial to all of the friends of my father who were persecuted like you were, and whose fate has never

> allowed me a moment's peace. Even if *Eine Reise* has no "success," I am its publisher, and as the one responsible for the business side of our firm I am convinced that this book must be published.[31]

Knowing the role she had played, Erichson wrote also to Bettina on the same day. "I have already written to your husband that the publication of this work means more to us than just 'bringing out a new book.' Even if the book should meet with no commercial success, I would have brought it out as a memorial to the friends of my father, above all Professor Moral, who in 1938, after we had hidden him for days in my parents' house, took his own life."[32] No doubt thinking of those she had lost herself, Bettina summed up what the moment meant to her and Günther:

> We have known for some time that only a man who knows the importance of remembrance and loyalty could bring out the book. What you have written has moved me very deeply. The public success that you say you are not concerned about may perhaps come sooner than we think. In any case I am hoping for it for you as much as I do for my husband, who has borne long enough his responsibility to the dear dead amid the tragic abyss of the past. More than anything I hope that this will make for a close relationship, perhaps even a friendship, in which the weight of time is countered by a sense of gratification. What for you may feel as having taken too long is for us the conclusion of an already much too long and perhaps much too courageously borne past. I know my husband's work and future lie bright and immediate before him. You cannot imagine the joy it all brings to him, imparts to him, and how it helps him carry on.[33]

Despite Bettina's hopes, after selling over a thousand copies in the first year of publication, sales of *The Journey* dropped off, although the strong start led the publisher to take on *The Prince of Blessings* and then to bring out a second collection of "bagatelles," *The Fall of Sodom*, in 1965.

The Prince of Blessings collected the parables, observations, and allegories composed "in the face of reality" between 1938 and 1945, and *The Fall of Sodom* gathered forty-seven "bagatelles," supposed "trifles" of no matter, although like Beethoven's brief pieces they are deceptively complex, serious works that also employ sardonic wit to confront reality, and their brevity involves a conscious effort to see the whole through the fragmentary.[34] "Der Vorhang" ("The Curtain") opens the collection, musing in just over a single page how, although the curtain

Bettina Adler: *Self-Portrait*, 1967. Credit: The Estate of Bettina Adler 2019, Deutsches Literaturarchiv Marbach.

has fallen, "the tragedy is over and the unfortunate resolution has irrevocably come to pass, though in fact nothing has occurred which can explain the tragedy or make sense of how it came about."[35] The curtain falling in a theater of course implies a larger history. "Geänderte Verhältnisse" ("Changed Relations"), which Adler reprints from his debut collection, *Unser Georg*, strikes a similarly bemused posture on how well "the public institutions and services of the country function and move right along" as people "joyfully go about their business just as they used to," or until "the wheel of history supplies yet another fate whereby relations will be changed yet again, though hopefully not irrevocably."[36]

As in "Das Bündel" ("The Bundle"), which mysteriously appears on a street corner, causing Hans Poltermann and his neighbors to wonder about and fear its contents, each brief story or parable contains a vestige of a horrific or tragic past that remains present but invisible. Adler subtly but fearlessly confronts the reader with fragments of a world whose sense of itself rests as much on its troubled past as on its own unwillingness to confront it amid the concomitant absurdity of the present. "Can't you see that everything is a pre-arranged farce?" yells a wife to her husband in the title story, as their modern Sodom really is burning and the police commissioner who told them to flee was right when at the story's end the woman is turned to salt after looking back at the burning city in utter fascination.[37] The implication is that Sodom's "fall" rests not with the fire itself but with the willful blindness of its citizens. As the narrator of "Memories of a Past Century," also reprinted from *Unser Georg*, states, "Humankind just follows fruitful progress and has nothing to give our miserable world but a feeling of being horrified or to look on with a sympathetic smile."[38] The irony is that this is said with no sense of irony at all. Meanwhile, Max Brod was reminded of Kafka and felt that Adler's bagatelles "probed deep into the darkness that haunts human beings," and Hilde Spiel praised Adler's ability to "abstract, reduce, distill reality, while at the same time revealing to us the substrata of life" in both collections, although neither sold well.[39]

Decreasing sales made Adler nervous, for he knew Erichson did not have the resources to fully back *The Journey* and that the publishing house could not keep him. Adler asked Erichson's help in landing a larger, more prominent publisher, thinking that if his reputation grew, Bibliotheca Christiana too would benefit. Walter Verlag, the Swiss publisher known for publishing cutting-edge writers like Ernst Jandl, Alfred Andersch, Alexander Kluge, and Alfred Döblin, seemed a possibility, and Erichson tried to help. Adler's hopes were dashed, however, when Otto F. Walter, son of the founder and the person behind the firm's avant-garde reputation, resigned in December 1966.[40] Writing to Erichson in March 1967, Adler looked back with despair:

> As a result of things falling through at Walter, my twenty-one-year search for a publisher who can afford to and *wants* to bring out my works has come to nothing. . . . [There is] no one who has the good will or even the power to publish books by me, to see that they are noticed by the media and the press, to get them into the bookstores, or otherwise promote my fiction and other writing. It's really a pretty precarious situation when one is closing in on 60 while leading an uncertain, fleeting existence and yet still senses within oneself the strength and desire for creative work. . . . Hence, in short, you still have me hanging like a weight around your neck, and we will have to both hope for a miracle.[41]

Three months later Grete Fischer convinced Joseph Rast, the new executive director of Walter Verlag, to take on Adler.[42] At the end of their annual hiking vacation in the Swiss Alps, he and Bettina stopped in Basel to meet Rast, who said that he would publish *Panorama* the following year.[43] Miraculously, but with the steadfast support of Bettina, Grete Fischer, and Knut Erichson, Adler had gained a late second chance.

The first of the six novels Adler wrote in the decade following the war, *Panorama* was the second to appear in his lifetime. Except for *Hausordnung* (*House Rules*), a satirical work completed in 1967 and published just before his death in 1988, *Panorama* would be his last, as *The Wall* did not appear until the following year, Adler having died not knowing that it would. *Panorama* brought his first literary distinction when it was awarded the Charles Veillon Prize, Switzerland's most prestigious literary prize, in May 1969. Max Wehrli praised the novel for forgoing "any kind of sensational means, nor does it pursue any kind of fashionable, avant-garde experimentation. The writer belongs to an older generation; his book is an attempt at mastering the past through writing." No doubt this last phrase would have irked Adler, as he rejected all notions of mastering the past (*Vergangenheitsbewältigung*). Wehrli invokes tension between the traditional and the new and wonders whether "the fictional novel and the historical document are indeed irreconcilable." Yet he casts aside doubts:

> Adler's novel reflects deep artistry. Through the precise proportionality of its parts, through the varied implementation of recurring motifs, through the hidden rhythms of the intricately composed text, darkness and evil are brought into a new order of language that lifts the spirit. Perhaps it is also the distinction of such a work that the reader remains caught in the tension between the stuff of life and art, thereby making clear that there is writing that is something more than just writing. Indeed, it is perhaps the paradoxical nature of the novel's form to bring out this tension again and again, to maintain a way forward and through all the words and images to invoke the entirety of man's moral, social, and religious existence and help him to embrace it once again.[44]

Bridging the "stuff of life and art" as well as achieving "a new order of language" that addresses the "entirety of man's moral, social, religious existence," Adler ironically fulfills the criteria of Suhrkamp that he had derided, but in a less formulaic manner, and through the compositional integrity of what he valued in a work of art.

Adler's valuation was not simply an aesthetic choice. In "Einladung zu meinem *Panorama*" ("Invitation to My *Panorama*"), published in Walter Verlag's catalog when *Panorama* appeared, Adler outlines his view of that novel's artistry.[45] He writes of the "Panorama-Situation of Humankind" ("Panorama-Situation des Menschen"), likening it to the technical forerunner of cinema that displayed wonders of the world to the viewer as passing photographs viewed in a wooden cabinet, whereby "each stands on his own, and yet at the same time in a way—even as an observer—is connected to the outer world." Via this symbol, Adler sees the novel as a "new kind of attempt . . . at the coming-of-age-novel, but with unexhausted means that also allow it to be done in a new way," as his protagonist is not "developed from the outside" but instead "illustrated from within."

In addition to this inner life, *Panorama* covers thirty years of history in ten "scenes," from Josef Kramer's childhood in Prague during World War I, to time spent with a foster family in the countryside, the experience of a repressive boarding school, involvement with a mystical circle as a university student, forced labor on a railroad, and ultimately the horrors of Langenstein, the same camp that Adler survived. Nevertheless, as Adler explains, while the novel is "generated within the stadia of its time, it is also just as much set above its time, as if describing no history at all." Ultimately, he argues, this lends it "the character of a rhapsody, an epic work of art, and not just a novel composed of novelistic events." Adler writes, "This particular claim is supported by the nature of the [novel's] linguistic form." *Panorama* uses what he calls a "structured syntax, one repeated deliberately with constantly fresh intonations throughout the entire work, while at the same time introducing surprising motifs in broad strokes and in particulars, there being—perhaps its chief linguistic distinction—a hidden rhythmical form to the entire text which has its own and (I think) unique cadence."

Responding to an early draft, Canetti worried that the novel's subject matter was too "immense" and that Adler had perhaps adhered too relentlessly to his formal approach, but nevertheless he felt it an "impressive achievement," adding:

> So much within it moved me in the deepest way. The knack for capturing each setting's atmosphere is as striking as the feel for the spiritual essence of each different niveau. The autobiographical nature of the book is unmistakable, but it is structured in such a way that numerous distinct worlds are clearly juxtaposed against one another. The originality of the technique that you have employed in this work does not always make it easy to fully appreciate the richness of its subject matter, and yet it is a *conscious* formal approach that is consistent throughout.

Arriving in a letter in 1952, such praise heartened Adler, but no doubt Canetti's recognition of the conscious artistry he had achieved after having survived "experiences and human losses of the most terrible type" would have meant the most.[46]

In a 1974 letter to Theodor Sapper, Adler underscores the novel's musical aesthetic in describing it as "ten 'musical movements,' each of which . . . approximates the structure of the classical sonata."[47] Adler writes that the fifth chapter, in which Josef Kramer reflects on the resonance of Johannes Tvrdil's gong, ends " 'on the dominant.'" Josef contemplates the sense of the note's finality as he realizes that

> his memory will die with him, no one recalling it, both the true and the false teachings meaningless, for Josef is meaningless, Herr Koppelter is meaningless, Thomas as well, even Johannes is meaningless, soon it will not be memory but rather just the sound of the gong reverberating among the shadows, spreading throughout the world from the tower room like wafts of smoke, as Johannes opens the window during the night and plays much louder until it is no longer just chamber music but now a blaring temple music, though this music has the quality of being heard by only a few, even though its incredible sound vibrates over all, spreading out in unearthly, trembling waves and pressing to the furthest reaches of space, and now tumbling into and setting this room aglow as an almost unbearably strong voice calls, "And so one must penetrate to the truth, to the one and only, which is God himself."[48]

The passage renders in fiction the formative time in Adler's youth when he and Steiner visited Drtikol's mystical circle and speaks to elements of Adler's later artistry as a novelist. There is a direct link between Josef's writing, his thoughts, and music in the shift from writing in his journal, to his memory of the day's events, and finally to music. Josef feels his writing to be "a vain game of fragile words, . . . he wanting to just sleep and wake up and sleep again," yet he knows that in sleep, "as soon as one image freezes for a moment it is ripped away, . . . memory's riches remaining dubious, even when one memorializes them in a journal, for soon they seem strange, strange, and unattainable."[49] Images replaced by other images invoke the central motif of the panorama, while the striking of the gong echoes the bell that sounds each time a new picture appears in the panorama that Josef visits at the beginning of the novel. Later the garish striking of a steel rail outside the barracks in Auschwitz recreates violently the gong heard here, while the sounding of a bell in each chapter (except for the return of young Josef's hiking group, the Wanderers, to the natural sounds of the forest) indicates divisions of time marked by sound, whether a passing tram car, a doorbell, a chime to invoke the mystical, or a church bell.[50] The unfolding of clause after clause in the sentence quoted above functions as a "Textdichtung" that Adler ascribed to Schönberg's compositional style. These elements are "correlative links and correspondences" that make up the book's musical score, which Adler described to Sapper as a "ten-movement suite, which could be better understood as a 'partita,' " each scene referring at least once to the "basic 'panoramic' situation (or what is made manifest): the sight of things that cannot be grasped."[51]

Adler in Grindelwald, 1978. Credit: Manfred Sundermann.

This pursuit of the ungraspable echoes Schönberg's similar commitment. As epigraph to his 1976 essay "Arnold Schönberg: Eine Botschaft an die Nachwelt" ("Arnold Schönberg: A Message to the After-World"), Adler quotes the composer's credo: "So long as I hold stock in my thoughts and dreams, I will never be able to believe anything other than that ideas must be thought and expressed, even when they will not be understood, even when they are not capable of being understood."[52] Inside the panorama, failure to grasp what is seen is caused by the impediment of the glass pane between the viewer and the image. But a perceptual and a cognitive aphasia occur as well, for Josef cannot see or understand "the universe," although the music of the gong reverberates through his body. Yet who sees "the universe" of the text when linking the motifs of the panorama, sleeping, waking, and the bells that sound across chapters is the reader.

The warp and woof of the sentences may mimic Josef's wandering consciousness as he descends into sleep, but their performance as "Textdichtung" supplies a cadence that carries us from chapter to chapter. Josef may be depicted "from the inside out," but it is *we* who see him that way. Adler's musical structure allows us to connect the micro and the macro into a vision of reality that comes *from* Josef and is *of* him but is also structurally *beyond* him as a musical score and novel that only we can hear and read.[53]

Adler said of *Panorama* that it was "steeped in autobiography," but to him it was the music of its rendering that mattered most.[54] Having said to himself in Theresienstadt that, if he survived, he would render his experience "in both scholarly and artistic fashion," it is often cited as the rationale for the program that Adler set for himself.[55] In fact, he was committed to transcending mere reportage or the indulgence of memoir to the same degree in both projects.[56] Even depicting the nadir of Josef's life as a prisoner in Langenstein, Adler turns visceral suffering into a formal litany of what "the lost" must suffer through while clinging to the residual humanity of their own hope and fear:

> Nothing else is here, no nails on the walls, no stools, no table, no bench, nothing, nothing at all, no beds, no straw mattresses, nothing but the bodies of the lost, clothed in rags of many colors, a few blankets scattered about, under which are bodies, as well as caps, ragged pieces of cloth without shape, a couple of tin bowls, some spoons, perhaps some other possessions, layer upon layer thickly packed together, living fear manifest within dried-up and evaporated bodies consumed by hatred and despair, though most of all fear, which will not die, even when they are whipped, as a sneer transforms itself into sleeplessness, and hope arises amid the decay, though perhaps hope cannot eradicate decay, but instead struggles against fear.[57]

Such a passage strikes one as both a scene endured firsthand and also the report of how that author looked upon such misery with the eye of an artist composing a picture. One remains outside the bounds of memoir, transported to where the "real" is reduced through the myth to its elements—suffering, hope, and fear—suspended by the mindful cadence of a single sentence.

For Adler, the integrity of a work of art was not a mere matter of taste or aesthetics but a moral issue. A 1961 exchange of letters with Hans Reichmann, president of the Association of Jewish Refugees in Great Britain, reveals Adler's conviction that only the artistic elevation of experience through the novel could serve his purpose. Reichmann recalls hearing him tell about walking through Goslar, just west of Halberstadt, dressed in prison garb after his release from the dreadful Langenstein concentration camp in April 1945. Hearing Beethoven played on a piano in an apartment, Adler rang the doorbell and was greeted by two elderly ladies horrified by his appearance. He quietly told them they had nothing to fear, that he had been attracted to the music, especially since it had been years since he had heard any. He asked if he could come in to listen, and amazingly they invited him in and played more, after which he began to tell them the story of his imprisonment.[58]

Reichmann asked Adler to write this story for *AJR Information*, the Association's newsletter, but he politely declined, noting that he had used the anecdote in his as-yet-unpublished novel *Eine Reise*. He then makes the claim, which he would repeat, that he sought to render his experience of the war in scholarship and art, "far away from mere depiction, and particularly far away from reporterly or journalistic renderings, which may have their purpose, but are not for me."[59] Adler rarely passed on a proffered assignment, his bread and butter, and he published several articles in *AJR Information*, so the venue would have been familiar. Yet carefully shaping his experience in scholarship and art for him meant to step beyond memoir, not just a choice of one kind of approach, but against another.

Adler, however, also had strong views on the use of acute suffering and despair in fictional renderings, for he was highly critical, even deeply offended, by what he saw as the misappropriation and misunderstanding of the details of the camps in novels and plays that he felt could not have been written by anyone who had survived them. His most intensely felt *bête-noire* was the work of Samuel Beckett. Even Franz Wurm, perhaps his most trusted literary confidant, and a friend of Beckett, could not convince Adler of his stature as a modern artist. "I don't worry at all about Mr. Beckett," Adler told Wurm in 1957, although Beckett's work had already secured international fame. "If he were to gradually cease writing, or even do so soon, it would be no great loss to literature. The questions he poses, which he exaggerates greatly, appear to me ones that you just do not see printed anymore in legitimate works in which quite the opposite has occurred in various ways for years and years."[60] Two years later, with Beckett's stock rising higher, Adler confided to their mutual friend Luzzi Wolgensinger:

> His success and my lack of success thus far are of a piece. You see, people are fed up with the good, although paradoxically there is an utter lack of the good, and so one takes up with Beckett, who indeed writes well, but writes of nothing good. I'm afraid people are too enamored of themselves, and thus are inclined to read about their own dirt, but I don't wish to read anything about my own dirt. I am arrogant enough to say that I don't even need to read about it, nor do I want to. What I write can, among other things, be understood as a complete vanquishing of Beckett's standpoint, but not very many wish to vanquish him, and

> therefore I am not published. I think producing a good, though most importantly, a truthful book about Auschwitz or Hiroshima is far more useful than reading all of Beckett's collected writings. If one wants to tackle such "stuff" artistically, which except for Schönberg in his "Survivor in Auschwitz" has for sure happened but rarely, then the facts must be transcended within the depiction. When that does not happen, whether out of failure or on purpose, or where, as with Beckett, one does not even try, I find all such efforts to be wasted. Even when painted or written with mastery, dreck is dreck, I am at liberty to toss it away.[61]

Such a stance is surprising from the man whom Böll praised in his Frankfurt Lectures for his ability "to describe something as harmless as garbage collection [in *The Journey*] in order to reveal the truly sinister" and somewhat suspect if it stems only from Adler's disappointment at his own lack of success compounded with his jealousy of Beckett's fame.[62] But it would be a mistake to dismiss it as the outcroppings of envy. In Adler's rejection of Beckett lies a deeper point about the aim of his own work that many critics failed to appreciate.

"I really have no desire for sweetcakes, Wiener schnitzel, or similar treats from literature," Adler wrote, "but I do want something more or different than such an unsuccessful portrayal of ultimate human degradation if I do not receive at the same time even a breath of metaphysics," an aspiration that he shares with Stifter and Kafka, both of whom point toward the transcendent, albeit in different manners and to different ends. Setting aside Adler's reading of Beckett, or the false standard he asserts, namely that "he would not write such stuff, or at least would go about it differently, if he had spent but a single day in Auschwitz," what emerges is Adler's deep-seated engagement with literature and art as a spiritual, if not Jewish, act of faith. Countering what he saw as Beckett's narrow focus on degradation and despair with Schönberg's "Survival in Auschwitz" makes clear that Adler's objection to Beckett is not a rejection of modernity or new forms of expression, but with the ends for which those means are employed.

Adler's 1976 essay makes clear his deep admiration of Schönberg's unique and modern approach to music, as well as the integrity of his unrelenting pursuit of artistic truth, rather than settling for mere technique or empty mastery. But the most important quality he valued in Schönberg was that the composer's "unswaying commitment to teaching was—one might say (at least I may say)—the central gift of his Jewish heritage, namely the value of teaching as the highest of all arts."[63] One may not expect teaching to be the preeminent quality of a great modern master, but Schönberg's teaching of Alban Berg and Anton Webern in Vienna, and John Cage, Lou Harrison, and Leon Kirchner in the United States, and others, had a profound influence on twentieth-century music.[64] Adler, however, means not simply classroom teaching but the need for one's art to speak to educate those who come after.

This moral project is evinced by the subtitle of the Schönberg essay, "Eine Botschaft an die Nachwelt," an echo of the subtitle of the first essay Adler wrote six months after the camps, "Nach der Befreiung: Ein Wort an die Mitwelt" ("After the Liberation: A Word to the Everyday World"). There Adler describes how people broken in spirit, who had had their human dignity stripped away from them, soon died, and that a trained eye could see their end approaching. Adler, however, does not just recall the suffering he survived, but hopes, as early as December 1945, that "the best of us will find a way together to serve humanity." What is important to Adler is "not what we have suffered, but what we have experienced, and how that must be heard and understood."[65] His Schönberg essay thirty years later might seem to take up a different subject, but at the center of both lies a commitment to sharing with the world what had happened, for the sake of *that* world and for the victims themselves.

In this lies the pledge "to serve humanity" rather than what Jeremy Adler calls the "fallacy of negativism" often found in postwar critical theorists such as Adorno, since "Adler's work seeks to argue the opposite position, ultimately grounded in his Jewish faith, that a system of beliefs, ethical values and the basic political concepts of human rights and democracy do make sense" and remain viable in the post-Holocaust world.[66] For Adler, Beckett and others focused too much on "what we have suffered," whereas in his own work he sought "to maintain the ability to convey to my listeners and readers transcendental meaning through what I express."[67] Noting elsewhere how to read two of his "parables," he advises, "these pieces should be understood as a type of Midrash (because as I say, before something is understood within them something is grasped through them, which is part of the intention behind each)."[68] Similarly, confirming Franz Kobler's sense that the impetus behind his fiction is analogous to Hamlet's struggle "to be," Adler observes, "This was granted to me in part in the bad years and therefore led to a tortuous formulation in which the messianic stance almost of its own accord revealed its Jewish influence."[69] We see a humanistic, methodological, and spiritual enterprise at work, one tied to the suffering endured in the camps, but also to a greater urge to prevail, not merely to survive.

"Beckett offers up the exact opposite of what I wish and hope for, and which I seek artistically," he told Wurm in 1976. "Again and again he takes people down to a place of utter worthlessness and leads us to an impasse from which I hope to lead us out."[70] Adler's pursuit of a higher understanding and a reaffirmation of the good had to do with where he had been, and it was deeply tied to the history of the Jews, not just contemporary reality. "We Jews have it so hard," he acknowledged to Kobler, "and our general misery is thus so great because we are always driven to extremes, always to the limits of what can be endured, at which point we are almost destroyed yet remain still standing, albeit wounded and shattered, but still there and nevertheless strong."[71] Ironically, what he hoped to gain was a renewal and revivification of the German classicism of Lessing, Schiller, and Goethe, which Adorno and colleagues argued had gone up in smoke in the crematoria of Auschwitz.

Adler's struggle to establish himself as a fiction writer demanded endurance, for despite positive reviews and the Charles Veillon Prize, *Panorama* fared no better with readers than *The Journey* or his three volumes of short stories. After the publication of *Ereignisse* (*Occurrences*), a 1969 volume of new stories and some selected from his three previous books of short fiction, by 1973 Adler was again without a publisher. With sales declining, he had long braced for this possibility. In the first six months of 1965, *The Journey* sold only seventy-one copies, while *The Prince of Blessings* sold twenty-six.[72] By that same year, in comparison, three thousand copies of *Theresienstadt 1941–1945* and one thousand copies of *The Hidden Truth* had been printed and continued to sell, and *The Jews of Germany* had appeared in a second edition of five thousand copies, making Adler a relative "bestseller" as a scholar while his far more inventive novels and stories were neglected.[73]

After thoroughly revising *Panorama* in 1968, Adler seemed to sense a dead end, even as he hoped for a late turnaround. "I feel now like an empty sack," he admitted to Wurm, "for everything that I have written is now with the publisher, to whom I have said that with this book he has a real chance if only he does the right kind of publicity, and above all without scrimping on it. Unfortunately I am afraid that those in charge are not that interested in me and most of all not in working with me, and that's too bad, for I am a real person and not just a *rebus litterarum*."[74] Walter Verlag mounted a better and stronger publicity campaign than had Bibliotheca Christiana but with similar results. The reviewer for the *Neuer Zürcher Zeitung* hailed *Panorama* as a "difficult, esoteric, highly sophisticated masterpiece," but Hans Kricheldorff felt that the "deliberate artlessness of the language, its almost relentless parataxis, . . . hardly allowed any chance for an epic feel."[75] Where one critic could see the artistic strategy at work to be almost too esoteric for the general reader, another found it to fall short of what he expected in a historical epic. Waltraut Schmitz-Bunne, writing in *Hochland*, could see a way between the two in how reviewers appeared to need the "modern bag of tricks" including "deliberate alienation, intentional banality, elaborate absurdity as an anti-symbol, in addition to following the edict that literature must be socially engaged or it is not literature at all." What should happen, he argued, was that "the reader realizes that life in fact is like a panorama—a curious, somewhat mysterious succession of images that indeed do not follow the rules of art."[76] Otto Beer in *Der Tagesspiegel* appreciated that "no matter how much [*Panorama*] may be deeply determined by autobiography, it is nonetheless the leitmotif of an entire generation," but when he reviewed *Occurrences* a year later he found the prose to be "severe, puritanical" in presenting a "*conditio humana* from the middle of our century in a grotesque form carried out *ad absurdum*."[77] Adler in other words was free to be artful but not too artful, or historical but not too historical, and certainly not grotesque in rendering the pathos and agony of his journey. Peter Bautz, writing for the *Stuttgarter Zeitung*, took perhaps the most condescending approach, concluding, "Critics also err in presuming certain standards from an author who himself was a prisoner in Auschwitz, as if the most terrible kind of reality could be rendered in the most artful manner."[78]

As with "The Letter Writers" in *The Wall*, Adler's "messages" would have to wait to be received by a future he could only dream of and at times despaired might never come.

17

The Man

When the first copy of *Administered Man* reached him in London in February 1974, Adler could not help noticing that Siebeck had mailed it to him on February 8, the thirty-second anniversary of his deportation to Theresienstadt, which he had entered in his thirty-second year.[1] Soon to turn sixty-four, Adler had lived a life of severe ruptures, and yet the book he held in his hands was, like all the others he published, a source of healing balm. Since it had taken fifteen years to research, write, and publish, one might expect its author to slow down and think of retirement, as his pension would soon begin. Yet for Adler retirement meant retrieval, and from the mid-1970s on, much of his focus was on polishing unpublished works like *The Settlement* and the "Traktat," as well as scores of poems and stories. He felt renewed, writing new fiction and poetry in his Earl's Court study overlooking the quiet, tree-lined street below.

By 1970, Adler had published just thirteen of the twenty-three books that appeared in his lifetime, meaning that the appearance of nearly half his work still lay ahead.[2] While the 1950s centered on writing and publishing his Theresienstadt work and the 1960s were dominated by his fiction, the last fifteen years of his life saw the publication of *Administered Man* and seven volumes of poetry, the first since *Meer und Gebirge*, in 1931, his first book. He also published a novel, a book of essays, and *Vorschule einer Experimentaltheologie: Betrachtungen über Wirklichkeit und Sein* (*Toward an Experimental Theology: Observations on Reality and Being*), the culmination of the "Traktat" he had begun in his long letter to Bettina from Milan in 1938. Only *Administered Man* and the essays in the 1976 volume *Die Freiheit des Menschen* (*The Freedom of Man*) were published by Hans Siebeck of J.C.B. Mohr. The rest appeared from small presses like Europäische Ideen, the short-lived Albert Knauss Verlag, or avant-garde ones like Bob Cobbing's Writers Forum at the Poetry Society and Jeremy Adler's Alphabox Press. This milieu replicated the aesthetic camaraderie fostered by his friendship with the experimental Austrian poets Ernst Jandl and Frederike Mayröcker, and

Helmut Heißenbüttel of the Stuttgart School. Weeks before his sixtieth birthday, Adler admitted in an interview that "there was hardly any time left for success to come about," yet with typical defiance he declared, "I no longer am looking for any help from a publisher."[3] Although he did continue to publish his scholarly works and made a small breakthrough with his poetry, for the most part he was forced to write for the drawer, quipping to Jürgen Serke, "I am somewhat famous for not being known."[4]

Regardless of such lack of recognition, Adler set about unifying the strands of his writing into a coherent whole. His archive contains no less than nine folios of poetry organized according to distinct periods in his creative output, each poem clearly marked with the dates on which it was written and revised, with titles for each grouping, totaling just over one thousand pages when published as *Andere Wege* (*Different Ways*) in 2010. Add to this two collections of published and unpublished essays arranged around themes of Judaism, politics, the Holocaust, and literature, which he intended to be read in unison, as well as two titled collections of stories, whose drafts and revisions he also dated, and one realizes that Adler was not just writing for the drawer but for a "present future" powerfully immediate to him. Never nostalgic, he longed to use every bit of the past, readying it for the future.

This concern is abundant in his works, sometimes literally. His uncollected short story "Gestern und Heute" ("Yesterday and Today") is the first-person meditation of a man who discovers that he lives "always in the past," especially among those consumed by the rush of the present. This is not a problem, for he finds it easier "to live with the guilt which I maintain like a legacy, hence a very rich and multifaceted guilt, so beautifully outdated and full of familiar pain, while it is difficult for the others rushing along to even grasp their guilt." The man may not "belong to the vanguard," but he does possess "his own tranquility and the fable of his own forsaken loneliness." When it comes to the possibility of someone "bestowing a word that could bring about grace" for the others, however, the man of the past taps the neglect he has suffered by declaring defiantly, "Not me, certainly not me," forcing those in the present to fend for themselves. "Neue Elemente" ("New Elements") likewise takes up the burden of the past as a "cause for worry, a pointless cause for worry, but all the more consuming, all the more hopeless, a risky venture without place or grace." And yet too often politicians and intellectuals are content to harken to the past as if they really knew "the pain, the misdeeds, the unredeemed promise" evident in "the tormented eyes paired with the horrors, endless war, persecution, and the spilling of innocent blood." Better indeed, the tale sardonically offers, for the present to take the "smooth road to the future in all its hurry, blowing on the full-throttled horn of perpetuity with the winds of stupidity."[5]

Adler's narratives, resembling lyrical essays on the moral and spiritual bankruptcy of the postwar world more than stories with character and plot, are more than the disguised complaints of someone passed over by the present. Their compressed intensity stakes out a mode between the biting piquancy of the aphorism and the moral resonance of the parable. Often only a few pages, as are the "bagatelles" of *The Fall of Sodom*, their brevity belies their power to tap deep veins of alienation and groupthink. In three short unpublished pieces completed in 1985, Adler sums up this malaise when he observes in "So hat es geheissen" ("That's What It Was Called"), "[W]e turn around within the confines of our own imprisonment and learn while standing on our own feet how comfortable it is to kneel before the final end. In the face of it, every countermand is countermanded. With complete calculation everything is made to seem like a dream. We hang on, but in turn are held down and feel ourselves part of a middling existence." Added to this is the sense of time winding down, as in "Zuneigung und Richtung" ("Inclination and Direction"), where "many people are inclined, or are forced to feel inclined to act together, marching one next to the other, . . . even though an urgent sense of time lost has already set in, making it hard to do anything or change anything in the end." More weary than bleak, both bemused and skeptical, socially engaged yet lyrical, the voice that speaks these tales as warning knows it will likely remain unheard. As in "Verloschene Eile" ("Extinguished Urgency"), it can only counsel, "Devote yourself to your sense of dismay, but do not yield to it until your end reveals it to be true or untrue, and your offended hopes fall away from your unfurrowed brow."

Adler's late poems also betray his sense of life winding down amid the woes of a past still present before his impending future. "Eine ewige Zeit" ("An Eternal Time"), also from 1985, addresses this personal theme in its opening lines: "Little disturbs you, and so you walk on / Traversing the emptiness / Of an ungraspable youth, the untimely graves / Of your own childhood!"[6] As a poet, however, the "past" meant more to Adler than his own childhood, and Jürgen Serke notes, "Adler's poetry is a return of speech to a world that is speechless. It is a return to a language immersed in the German tradition."[7] As he described it, "In the lyric poetry I write one must pay special attention to its *spoken* qualities (versus its logic), because the thematic content that can be presented elsewhere, meaning in other forms (i.e., aphorisms, narratives, and news reportage), has for me nothing to do with pure poetry."[8] Instead, "Stärke der Vergangenheit" ("The Strength of the Past") is what he wishes to tap as his "breath forms its thanks / Just before leaving, a salutary / Sense of silent astonishment worshipping unheard / Traces of the path, the long road there." Embracing the tradition of Klopstock, Goethe, Hölderlin, and Rilke, Adler remade it in his own guise, allowing him to

"Courageously / leave the past," since "You know, that you belong to it, / That you are linked to it," even while moving ahead on what he describes in the last line of his last collected poem as "The slow / faithful journey home quickly subsumed by memory."[9]

Despite the general neglect of the wider public, there were many writers, scholars, and friends in his later years who recognized his achievement as well as working to support and promote his work. Founded in Cologne in the early 1970s, the Society of Friends of H. G. Adler was organized by Pastor Willehad P. Eckert, Wilhelm Unger, and Eberhard Bethge, the student and biographer of Dietrich Bonhoeffer, to fund new publications, sell remaindered copies of earlier books, and provide income. Sales were limited, but in honor of Adler's sixty-fifth birthday, in 1975 the society produced *Buch der Freunde* (*The Book of Friends*), edited by Eckert and Unger. This gathered remembrances, contributions, introductions, and summations by, among others, Böll, Canetti, Heimito von Doderer, Theodor Heuss, Johannes Urzidil, Grete Fischer, Ingeborg Drewitz, Hermann Broch, and Walter Jens. It was followed ten years later by *Zu Hause im Exil: Zu Werk und Person H. G. Adlers* (*At Home in Exile: On the Work and Character of H. G. Adler*), edited by Heinrich Hubmann and Alfred O. Lanz, with analysis of his writing and scholarship by J. P. Stern, Peter Staengle, Rüdiger Goerner, Joachim Hackethal, Yehuda Bacon, and Bethge, as well as several of the earlier contributors. With a doctoral dissertation on *Panorama* that Lanz published in 1984, critical and scholarly attention began to swell. By the late 1990s and early 2000s, with the help of the poet and publisher Michael Krüger and Henning Ritter, an editor at the *Frankfurter Allgemeine Zeitung*, and others, Jeremy Adler's efforts led to new editions of *Eine Reise* and *Panorama*, followed by translations into English, French, Spanish, Italian, and Hebrew, and an edition in Czech of selected works in several volumes. Conferences and symposia on Adler's life and work were held in Prague, Marbach, Vienna, Paris, Toronto, Vancouver, London, and Berlin. A major exhibition curated by Marcel Atze at the Deutsches Literaturarchiv, Marbach am Neckar, helped to draw wider attention in traveling to Prague, Vienna, and Berlin. Retrospectives were published in major German, Swiss, and British newspapers upon Adler's centennial in 2010 and a volume devoted to him in the *Text + Kritik* series. The man himself, however, would not live to see it. All he could do was try to organize the *Gesamtkunstwerk* he had envisioned. With wounded resignation he noted, "I think I can say justifiably that I am the most neglected German writer of talent," although he quickly added, "But one day my books will have their hour."[10]

Awarding of the Buber-Rosenzweig Medal, Berlin, 1974. Credit: The Estate of H. G. Adler 2019, Deutsches Literaturarchiv Marbach.

Adler expected that *Administered Man* would not be understood until "two or three hundred years hence," even though the book culminated thirty years spent researching and writing on the Shoah.[11] Heinrich Böll, writing in *Der Speigel*, praised it as a comprehensive "lexicon of the deportations" that should be excerpted in textbooks, but few other reviews followed. Honors, however, did follow, beginning with the Buber-Rosenzweig Medal in 1974, the Bundesverdienstkreuz (Medal of Service to the Nation) awarded by Chancellor Helmut Schmidt in 1975, and the honorary title of Professor bestowed by the president of Austria in 1977, which meant Bettina would receive a small pension upon Adler's death. He became a corresponding member of the Bavarian Academy of Sciences and Humanities and, in 1980, an honorary member of the Pedagogical Academy of Berlin. On his seventy-fifth birthday in 1985 the Austrian Institute of London celebrated his contributions to the arts and sciences, and the London-based German scholar J. P. Stern commended his writing as "an act of preservation—the essence of all writing—aimed at the future."[12] A special issue of the journal *Europäische Ideen* appeared that year with poems and testimonies by Böll, Ernst Jandl, Friederike Mayröcker, Walter Jens, and Helmut Heißenbüttel, among others, also in honor of his birthday. The writer and his work were valued and celebrated, and although he felt himself "somewhat of a terra incognita in the field of German literature," Adler appreciated that his struggles to gain publication had forced him "to be even more truthful, and the truth is always feared."[13] Whereas after the Shoah he had abjured public celebration while privately noting important anniversaries of deportations and deaths, in later years he became more reconciled with the past, his and Bettina's home becoming a place where Jeremy and his wife, Eva, and their friends provided a link between past and future.

Adler had occasion for his own backward look when, six years after receiving the Charles Veillon Prize for *Panorama*, he received the Buber-Rosenzweig Medal at a reception attended by over eight hundred people at the Hochschule für Musik in Berlin on March 3, 1974. Awarded first in 1968 by the German Coordinating Council of Societies for Christian-Jewish Cooperation to those judged to have actively contributed to Christian-Jewish relations, recipients have included Eugen Kogon, Friedrich Dürrenmatt, Yehudi Menuhin, Isaac Bashevis Singer, Richard von Weizsäcker, Daniel Barenboim, and Daniel Liebeskind. The ceremony marks the start of the Woche der Brüderlichkeit (Week of Brotherhood), which since 1952 has involved lectures and panels that address ways to improve social relations throughout Germany and the world, especially between Christians and Jews.

The theme for 1974 was "Der geplante Mensch" ("The Planned Person"), a chilling echo of Adler's own title for the 1,100-page opus he had just published on the systematic treatment of human beings. Rabbi Peter Levinsohn and Pastor Martin Stöhr cited Adler's "service in bringing to light the history of the Jews during the years of Hitler's rule" as well as his "contributions to the dialogue between Christians and Jews."[14] In the *laudatio* that followed, however, Bethge noted that Adler's achievement lay not just in his scholarly work but also in his literary art and its ability to "startle and engage us, as it were, whenever the words of a man truly touch us and, shaken, we are confronted by them, . . . we are changed: transfixed and enchanted and consoled." Bethge cited Adler's "relentless drive to cleanse language of anything fashionable, oppressive, or mendacious," which Bethge said had existed long before "the occupation of Prague imposed his life's theme upon him."[15]

Accepting the medal, Adler recalled his roots, but in a different way. Citing Bernard Reder's advice to him in his youth that it was important to know when it was appropriate to take as well to give, he acknowledged that it meant a great deal to be presented the award in Berlin, where his mother had been born and her parents were buried. Adler recalled visiting the city as a child, and in 1933, when "the man who shall remain unnamed" came to power. He was also reminded of the friendship between Moses Mendelssohn and Lessing, part of "the chain of give and take . . . amid the rarely, partially realized symbiosis of the German and Jewish spirit." Adler extended that chain to include the nineteenth-century Jewish scholar Leopold Zunz, the foster son of Samuel Meyer Ehrenberg, whose own family Adler described as a "typical example of many gifted families composed of Jews from different backgrounds, as well as convinced converts, such as the Protestant theologian Hans Ehrenberg, a cousin of Franz Rosenzweig." Adler turned to Rosenzweig's "tireless effort in service to great Jewish thinkers" in his last years, which Leo Baeck had told him about, and invoked Baeck's tenet: "People are not measured in masses, but as persons."

Adler's final link in the chain was back to Prague, recalling Martin Buber's last visit there in January 1937. Buber had warned the youth of Prague not to succumb to what he had perceived as their collective prejudice against prior generations.[16] He was speaking to the same post–World War I generation who, through the Wandervogel, Communist groups, and rising nationalism, were committed to correcting the catastrophe they felt their parents had handed them, a sentiment not altogether alien to Adler's own worldview as an adolescent. However, speaking in 1974 amid the bombings, kidnappings, and murders of the Baader-Meinhof Group, as well as the disgruntled 1968 generation who saw their parents as nothing less than corrupt, Adler quoted Buber's concern that such a prejudice against the past "would no longer allow the living stream of tradition to find any means of access to the soul." Adler, meanwhile, could only ask, "Why must it be so and where indeed are we headed?" As an answer, he warned via Buber: "Next to prejudice against the spirit is the prejudice against the *truth*."[17]

Unspooling a chain of family, mentors, and influences that included Reder, his mother, nineteenth-century Jewish intellectuals, twentieth-century Jews and converts who were later led back to Judaism, and finally Baeck's and Buber's call for valuing persons and truth, Adler traced his own religious and spiritual journey through the thinkers, artists, and writers who influenced him. He had grown up as a baptized, secular Jew who belonged to the "Jews in the first third of the twentieth century, who through almost subtle spiritual denial and Christian conversion ended up returning to a Judaism newly thought through and able to keep an open mind to Christianity."[18] This was a far cry from the younger man skeptical of Christianity and its attitude toward the Jews. Such an evolution, moreover, led from his Protestant mother through the Jewish intellectuals who had meant the most to him, weaving the many threads of his life and intellect together. Adler may have indeed been awarded the Buber-Rosenzweig Medal for his fifteen years of work on *Administered Man*, but in accepting it he marked the coalescence of his whole religious, cultural, and intellectual identity.

Yet Adler would not rest on his laurels, nor could he afford to. With the dramatic scaling back of German radio programming in the late 1960s, his main source of income dwindled considerably. He continued to travel to Germany,

Austria, and Switzerland to lecture and read, but the trips were shorter and the opportunities fewer. Review and essay work for magazines continued, but such assignments were few and low-paying. Fortunately, his German reparations increased with the cost of living, and when he turned sixty-five, Adler received a British pension as well as a small pension from various radio stations in Germany. Although the sum awarded by the German government for reparations was thereby reduced, with the help of a one-time payment of 5,000 Deutsche Marks arranged in 1976 by Helmut Kohl, then head of the Christian Democrats and the future chancellor, followed by yearly awards from Germany's "Kunstlerhilfe" ("Artist Assistance") fund, he and Bettina remained comfortable in their later years.[19]

Bettina and Günther Adler, Grindelwald, 1978. Credit: Manfred Sundermann.

The years, however, had taken their toll. By the late 1970s, a number of health problems forced him to adjust his workload and slow down. Adler had suffered from chronic bronchitis since the camps, and he had kidney stones in the late 1950s and early 1960s as well as bouts with dental surgery, but until then he had remained generally healthy and able to hike and walk briskly. An attack of arrhythmia in 1968, however, was the precursor of heart ailments that led to the heart attack he suffered in Munich in late 1979, where he was hospitalized for over two months before returning home in early 1980. Another heart attack followed in May 1981, and eventually congestive heart failure set in, leading to extended hospital stays.[20] And yet, just over a year before Adler died he read his poems at London's Germanic Institute, and a year before that, weakened and fragile, he did an hour's television interview for the ZDF.

The realms that engaged Adler most deeply near the end of his life were the same as those of his youth: nature, art, poetry, and religion. *Meer und Gebirge* (*Sea and Mountains*), the title of his earliest volume, reflects the bond with nature found in his photographs, but *Fenster* (*Windows*), his first book as a mature poet, published in 1974, also speaks to a view of life captured through the artist's lens, recalling Josef Kramer's effort to focus fragments of the world presented to him through the ever-changing images of the panorama. *Theresienstadt Picture Book,* Adler's sardonic title for his cycle of poems capturing the ghetto's horrors with expressionistic intensity, also conceives of reality as an unfolding set of linked images. His 1979 volume of poems, *Blicke* (*Glances* or *Vistas*), confirms a view of life as a string of moments punctuated by "glances" that open up deep "vistas" of understanding. One need only think of the "trained eye" Adler invokes in his 1945 essay "Nach der Befreiung" ("After the Liberation"), recognizing a fellow prisoner doomed to death imminently, to appreciate the "glance" as a prevailing aesthetic metaphor. As his preferred yet discarded title for *The Prince of Blessings* made clear that his collection of early stories stood *Gegenüber der Wirklichkeit* or *In the Face of Reality,* Adler as a photographer, poet, and writer interpreted reality on his own terms rather than being defined, controlled, or persecuted by those who sought to define his reality for him.

The "glance," however, had to add up to and be tied to a "vision." Born of the real and immediate conditions of life filtered through the transformative power of art, the engagement that lies at the heart of Adler's life project is spiritual, be it on the level of philosophy, belief in the power of myth, or his evolving commitment to Judaism and belief in himself as a Jew. This comes into focus in the publication of his penultimate book. Without a major project to work on after the publication of *Administered Man* in 1974, Adler returned to his "Traktat" of 1938, some forty years after its inception, to see whether he could defend his thinking on the relationship between Being and reality, the central topic of his life.

Adler at opening of Holocaust art, Manchester, UK, 1980. Credit: The Estate of H. G. Adler 2019, Deutsches Literaturarchiv Marbach.

"My idea is that Being is larger than reality," Adler states in an extended conversation in English with Derek Bolton beginning January 5, 1981, in which he tests his ideas for the book that was later published in 1987.[21] Adler's central intent and core belief was shaped as early as his forest wanderings with Steiner, his reading of the *Bhagavad Gita* and *Upanishads*, his participation in František Drtikol's mystical circle, and his close reading of Eric Unger's philosophy. "At 27, I had the vision that we should aim for the ungraspable . . . There are two ways in this fabric[,] social and personal. In the former I keep my eye on the best and the worst done by men, in the latter I aim at the ungraspable." At first this may seem innocuous, but when we recall that at twenty-seven Adler was only a year away from traveling to Milan in the hopes of escaping the looming cloud of Nazism (as well as composing his first "Traktat" in his letter to Bettina), the consequences seem much larger. Whether this is the life philosophy shaped by the circumstances unfolding before him, or if it was the philosophy he brought to whatever circumstances that he encountered, that "eye" trained on "the best and worst done by men" was what helped him survive Theresienstadt and the camps, while the reach for the "ungraspable" is reflected in the poems and stories written there, as well as the scholarship aimed coolly at parsing such horrors as an act of "self-liberation."

Nor are these the thoughts of a misty-eyed optimist. Adler makes clear that he considers himself a "hopeless pessimist," since as far as he can see, "Man is always in flight from himself" and the history of humankind is "nothing but the history of the battle for nourishment, sexual contentment, survival and assertion, property, a story of trials for completeness." All of these attempts fail, but "together they replace our main battle," which is to pursue "the deepest level of consciousness" in order to know our true selves. This ceases to be merely a question of epistemology in its consequences for politics. According to Adler, "The state oppresses man because it fears nothing more than that he become aware of his own humanity," with the result that "*present man is almost never himself*" (his emphasis). This gives rise to the state's power over him, forcing the "freedom of will" to be "constantly under the pressure of limitation by the freedom of power." As a result, he argues, "Whatever is done of superior ethical value does not succeed by means of politics but despite it, and in the best case, against politics, against its reality, and almost a miracle, against the arrogance of its power, in conspicuous loathing of politics."

After asking "What now?," Adler explains, "We recognize already that this question cannot have any longer a mystical, political, or scientific character, but rather only a theological one." His theology, however, remains in the end social and political, and applicable to the present:

> We live in a period of political outgrowth; politics has usurped everything that can be meaningful in social communities in view of their reality: it allows no more than even the slightest trace of free movement, it pesters man with a penetration that excludes everything else, it suffocates his own thought and feeling, after it has cut his own action at the roots, it humiliates him beyond humanity and puts him in peace and war even lower than a machine, but at the same time ties him to the machine, and values him as no one.

This is the struggle amid the "community of grace and guilt" that is humankind. And yet on the other end of such political pessimism there lies a theological, if not a deeply Jewish, hope. "One cannot redeem oneself if one is unable to redeem the world," Adler laments, but within this lies the hope for "a *new* approach which we seek, beyond our feeling and reasoning, something which in reality can bring ourselves above ourselves, and hence nearer perfection." In this the aim is clear, namely "to prepare humanity for the threshold of achieving a new step of consciousness which will pass beyond rational man." Only then will the ultimate be possible: "the perfection, the totality of all totalities, redemption, salvation, the 'Messiah,' . . . that reality beyond which no other being exists, . . . a 'kingdom of this world,' beyond which there is no real kingdom, nor was there, nor is realizable, and never was." In the meantime, the task remains clear: "*know yourself, and know what you can do, and what you do*" (his emphasis).

In 1983 Adler noted, "The book would not exist if I had not been young when I began it, and it would not exist if I had not lived to be old." Shamanistic, transcendent, savvy, realistic, pessimistic, hopeful, and despairing, its contents record not so much a philosophy as a deeply rooted sensibility, a creed of how to walk through life, and to what purpose. That he had lived to return to it would seem miraculous enough. However, as he exhorts in the title of his 1937 poem "Immer das Unerreichbare im Sinn" ("Always Keep the Unreachable in Mind"), which he quotes at the end of the *Experimental Theology*, Adler's project remained paradoxical, unfinished, and constantly striving, if only in the belief that "that which can indeed be reached / will also be achieved."[22]

Many a life has been crushed by its ambition, many another by heady success. Despite numerous disappointments, Adler navigated a course that freed him of both. He could not avoid being "Theresienstadt Adler," but he turned that burden into a livelihood as an independent scholar and radio essayist, as well as serving those lost to the catastrophe, those who survived and were wounded by it, and the generation that followed. Literary fame eluded him, but still he produced a substantial body of novels, stories, and poems, innovative work ahead of its time and devoid of fashionable tropes or market sensibilities. Running through it all was the poetry.

Once Adler completed the "Traktat" on October 14, 1984, the fortieth anniversary of his arrival in Auschwitz, duly noted in his pocket calendar, there was a decided downturn. The book would not see print until 1987, but it was as if his life's work was complete. When Jürgen Serke visited in July 1986 to interview him for what became the first profile of his life and work, Serke found a man who, walking among the neglected graves of Brompton Cemetery near Earl's Court Square, illustrated Ilse Aichinger's description of him as "someone who had walked through darkness and yet was still standing." That Adler's work had been largely neglected was, for Serke, "a scandal which lay at the door of Germany's publishers," and yet despite it and the many losses he had suffered, despite "the separations of his childhood . . ., the isolation, the need for solitude in order to survive . . ., the confines of his fate, the monadic nature of his existence," he remained convinced of his own credo, "Hatred is no method by which to live."[23]

By the end of the summer of 1987, even walking had become difficult for Adler, weakened by congestive heart failure. After a month's visit to a Swiss chalet they had rented for years in Grindelwald, Günther and Bettina returned to London only to see his condition take a turn for the worse. Entries in his pocket calendar ceased, the last marking the October 24 death and November 1 cremation of Jirka Steiner, husband of Kafka's niece Marianne. Both were close friends, with whom they spoke Czech, and Marianne's work with Kafka's papers put her in regular correspondence with Malcolm Pasley, Max Brod, and Klaus Wiegenbach, writers and scholars whom Adler knew personally. Jirka's death closed a circle that stretched from his Prague childhood, where he sat on the same school bench as Kafka's nephew Felix Hermann, to the literary and scholarly career he had forged with Bettina over the last forty years in London.[24]

"When he completed the proofs of the *Vorschule*, he began to lose hold on life itself," his son Jeremy recalls. "He seemed to rise to a different sphere, as if talking in tongues, and made predictions—such as the collapse of Communism—some time before it became apparent."[25] In his more cogent moments he received friends at home and dictated notes to Jeremy, some of which echoed the *Experimental Theology*. "The limitations of the intellect and the possibilities of intuition," said one. "Recognize what you do or can do," admonished another. Other notations were more poetic, and Jeremy and Günther worked on a translation of "Immer inmitten" ("Ever in the Midst"), the poem that Viktor Ullmann had set to music in Theresienstadt. Its first stanza reads:

Ever in the midst, ever in the midst
I stepped through all areas of wonder,
Far from home but near the spring:
What has the soul not suffered?
Now wandering in the moss,
Now the thorn tearing it
Ever in the midst, ever in the midst.

Forced to move into a nursing home in the summer of 1988, when it became too difficult for Bettina to take care of him, Adler sometimes hallucinated about the camps and being chased by guards within them. Bettina would sleep in a bed next to him, at times alleviating his fears, or feeding him and caring for him as best she could while a candle burned on the nightstand. After a life of doing everything he could to survive, it seemed that what he could not easily do was die. But in the end he died alone. On the evening of August 21, 1988, when a nurse came in to check, she found him. Bettina, Jeremy, and his wife Eva arrived a few hours later to see him looking years younger and at peace.

Hugo Gryn, the popular rabbi of the West London Synagogue, himself a survivor of Auschwitz and a radio broadcaster at the BBC, performed the funeral two days later. In his eulogy Gryn referred to Günther as one of the thirty-six Tzadikim Nistarim, the mystical just men upon whose righteousness the existence of the world depends. Friends came from the Continent and across England to praise his spirit, work, and life. Jeremy delivered his own eulogy, reporting that his father told him on his deathbed of how he longed to know the Talmud, "above and below, outside and in." He was also reminded of the legendary scholars in Babylon, who like his father and the Jewish refugees in England, wrote in exile. For Jeremy, Rabbi Akiba, the "Chief of the Sages" in the Talmud, framed Günther's central accomplishment when he advised: "In a place where there are no men—do your best to be a man."

At the grave the son recited the Kaddish before being overcome with tears. Bettina then invited the attendees back to their apartment in Earl's Court Square. As if a reminder of Adler's birth in Habsburg Prague, a representative from the Austrian Cultural Institute read a statement of sympathy. Jeremy read his father's poem "Zeitlos" ("Timeless"), its final lines asking, "Do the paths / Divide? Does one still stand timeless on the earth?" before concluding:

> The answer rises up and arches high
> And hidden, at last piercing only
> Its very roots. Whoever depends on it must
> Not be afraid, to him all will be revealed
> In the shadowed prayer of enchantment
> Realized in a glance. The path leads on,
> Ah, leads on indeed; ahead the strangeness beckons.[26]

Crowded into the study, Bettina's brother and sister represented in body the exile that had brought them all to England, while figures like Helge Michie, twin sister of Ilse Aichinger, echoed the rich intellectual life Günther and Bettina had forged there. Carlo Caratsch, his doctor friend in Zurich, joined the coterie of postwar youth—the architect Manfred Sundermann, the painter Sylvia Finzi, the Wittgenstein scholar Derek Bolton, and the literary scholar Katrin Kohl—he had so patiently mentored, as well as Mary Donovan, Maria Gross's pupil as a social worker and a familiar family presence. The immediacy of Jewish burial prevented Yehuda Bacon from attending, as well as the sculptor Günther Oellers, Elias Canetti, and Ilse Aichinger, while Greta Fischer, Günter Eich, Heimito von Doderer, Heinrich Böll, and others had predeceased him. Time itself had stripped Adler of many of his friends, while life's circumstances separated him from his childhood, native land, and past. Even his expectation of burial in Brompton Cemetery did not come to be, as no grave was available, so the Edgwarebury Lane Cemetery was where he was interred. An exile in life, so too in death.

Bettina Adler lived another three years before dying of lung cancer in 1992. She took comfort in visiting the local synagogue, something she had not done when Günther was alive, but which somehow helped her to feel close to her husband. She continued to draw and paint, and after years of entertaining guests in the house, she took in a series of young women as boarders for companionship, among them Lucy Isman, who worked at the BBC, and Ariel Friedlander, daughter of the biographer of Leo Baeck. When cancer was diagnosed, she faced it calmly, informed friends and family, and even started reading Plato. As she had done for her brother and sister, as well as for Günther and all who entered their home, she managed her life and affairs until a week before her death, taking leave of six of her family and friends gathered at her bedside.[27]

Hans Günther Adler died on the twentieth anniversary of the 1968 Warsaw Pact invasion of Czechoslovakia. Thousands of people in Prague took to the streets to demand the human rights they would achieve with the Velvet Revolution a year later in 1989. Elsewhere the stirrings of peaceful protest that would bring down the Berlin Wall were under way. Adler did not live to see this, nor the publication a month later of his novel *House Rules,* whose narrator tries to glean meaning from the regulations imposed on apartment dwellers with maddening, if not laughable, stricture. "The path that leads from *Eine Reise,*" writes John White, "to *Hausordnung* is a clear one and it is paved with a demonic administrative efficiency."[28] The counterforce against that demonic vector, however, is life itself, long habituated to patient survival and the simple rewards of its own affirmation.

In an obituary read at the Berlin Free University on February 10, 1989, forty-seven years after Adler's arrival in Theresienstadt, the Hölderlin scholar Alfred Kelletat recalled being in Prague on February 8, 1942:

> As we walked down the street early that Sunday morning . . ., we saw here and there small groups of sad, anxious people carrying their belongings in suitcases, knapsacks, or carts. Though the scene puzzled us, we also knew right away that they were Jews forced to leave the city. We felt uneasy and ashamed, and inquired with colleagues who said they heard people had taken their lives in order to escape this expulsion. We did not know where this dark "journey" led. But there it was. We saw it with our own eyes, we felt it in our hearts, but our mouths did not cry out, and we did not lift a hand against such wrong. We told ourselves we were not the guilty, . . . and yet we indeed became the guilty. And I cannot help but think: I might well have witnessed Adler on his way to Theresienstadt on February 8, 1942.

Kelletat met Adler shortly after the end of the war, but the possibility of having been present at his deportation haunted him. He, like many, summed up Adler as "a man, whom the bitterest of experience had not forced into hate, but which had taught him the good, and whose unassuming courage allowed him to stare at the Gorgon without being turned to stone, and who in a world of lies told the truth."[29]

Asked to sum up himself, Adler replied as a participant-observer:

> He is incredibly curious to meet new people and enjoys it when they prove interesting, and he loves nature very much, the mountains very much. He takes great joy from good (or at least what he calls good) music. He loves art, he loves writing, and he is interested in his religion and the religion of other peoples. Many other things interest him as well, which also can be seen very much in his book, *Administered Man*, for he is especially interested in the administration of power. He attempted in *Administered Man* to show . . . that it's not just a question of separating powers, but that power *as* power must without question be separated from any administration. This Adler considered his greatest scholarly achievement.[30]

And just as Adler asked, "What is intellectual work?," one can also ask, "What then is a life?" To ask this is to try to touch upon the mystery of any existence, but to ask it of H. G. Adler is to ask it of a man caught up in the arc of history that continues to shape the most probing and disturbing questions of what it means to be a human being. To pretend to have the real answer is to risk a hubris greater than the question itself. In Chapter 4, Number 3 of *Pirkei Avot* we are told: "Despise no man and consider nothing impossible, for there is no man who does not have his hour and there is no thing that does not have its place."[31] That Adler was too often denied the same in life was his tragedy; that he sought to live by it while in all ways living *immer inmitten* was his triumph.

NOTES

Chapter 1

1. *T*, 59.
2. Adler refers to this in numerous letters, almost always stating that the lecture took place on the anniversary of Kafka's birth. In a letter to Hartmut Binder on December 5, 1966, Adler describes it in detail and says that he gave the lecture "on or about" July 3, 1943, although the precise date cannot be known.
3. Letter to Emil Utitz, August 4, 1943, *DLA*.
4. *T*, 129.
5. Ibid., 128.
6. Adler, "Der Untergang von Franz Kafkas Schwestern," unpublished note, *DLA*.
7. Franz Kafka, *The Trial*, trans. Breon Mitchell (New York: Schocken, 1998), 158–159.
8. Jürgen Serke links the passage to Adler's Holocaust experience in "Weniger geborgen als für immer versteckt: Der tote H. G. Adler und die lebendige Katastrophe des Exils," in *Jüdischer Almanach 1994 des Leo Baeck Instituts* (Frankfurt: Jüdischer Verlag, 1994), 92.
9. *T*, v.
10. *ZV*, 68
11. Fritz Groothues, radio interview with Adler, marked "broadcast in Berlin, Fall 1985," *DLA*.
12. *LB*, November 23, 1945.

Chapter 2

1. Adler, "Zu Hause im Exil," in *WV*, 19.
2. Adler, "Nachruf bei Lebzeiten," in *WV*, 8.
3. See Peter Filkins, "Memory's Witness—Witnessing Memory," in *Witnessing, Memory, Poetics: H. G. Adler & W.G. Sebald*, ed. Helen Finch and Lynn L. Wolff (Rochester: Camden House, 2014), 42.
4. "Nachruf bei Lebzeiten," in *WV*, 8.
5. Scott Spector, *Prague Territories: National Conflict and Cultural Innovation in Franz Kafka's Fin de Siècle* (Berkeley: U of California P, 2000), 15.
6. Details and quotes by Adler about his family history are generally from Adler's letter to Wilhelm Unger of May 10, 1950 (*LWU*). Twenty-one single-spaced, typewritten pages, it is the most thorough account we have of Adler's ancestry, childhood, and life up until age forty. Unger was then an editor at the BBC, for which Adler wrote several freelance reviews. Unger helped found the German Library in London, a library of contemporary German literature meant to serve refugees. Unger, who left Germany right before the war, returned as theater critic for the *Kölner Stadt-Anzeiger* and worked as an editor for the *Westdeutscher Rundfunk* and the *Allgemeine Wochenzeitung der Juden in Deutschland*, all of which Adler wrote for. With

Heinrich Böll and Paul Schallück, Unger founded the Kölnische Gesellschaft für christliche-jüdische Zusammenarbeit and the Bibliothek Germania Judaica. He remained one of Adler's closest friends from 1950 onward.

7. The first description appears in "Zu Hause im Exil," in *WV*, 20, the second in *LWU*.
8. Manfred Sundermann, who befriended Adler in London in the mid-1970s, confirmed this in a letter on October 30, 2014. Adler told Sundermann that he worried someday it would become known that he had been baptized, which might be seen to undermine his legitimacy as a Jew and his writing on Judaism. A record of Adler's baptism on November 26, 1922, exists in the Czech National Archives.
9. Alice Adler, *LHGA*, December 16, 1925, and January 16, 1926. Emil Adler, *LHGA*, October 31, 1922.
10. Adler, "Zu Hause im Exil," in *WV*, 19.
11. Nancy M. Wingfield, *Flag Wars and Stone Saints: How the Bohemian Lands Became Czech* (Cambridge, MA: Harvard UP, 2007), 5.
12. See Theodor Herzl, "Die Juden Prags zwischen den Nationen," *Das jüdische Prag*, ed. Robert Weltsch (Berlin: Jüdischer Verlag, 1978), 7. Quoted in Wilma Iggers, *The Jews of Bohemia and Moravia* (Detroit: Wayne State UP, 1992), 232.
13. H. G. Adler, "Letter from H. G. Adler to Chaim Rabin," in *From Prague Poet to Oxford Anthropologist: Franz Baermann Steiner Celebrated*, ed. Jeremy Adler, Richard Fardon, and Carol Tully (Munich: Iudicium, 2003), 202.
14. Derek Sayer, *The Coasts of Bohemia: A Czech History*, trans. Alena Sayer (Princeton: Princeton UP, 1998), 145. The most notorious of these trials was that of Leopold Hilsner, who was convicted in 1899 of the "ritual murder" of a nineteen-year-old Czech girl, Anežka Hrůzová, in a forest outside of Polná in southeastern Bohemia. Tomáš Masaryk vehemently attacked the death sentence handed down, and eventually Hilsner was pardoned by Emperor Charles I of Austria in 1918.
15. Quoted in Klaus Wagenbach, *Kafka's Prague, A Travel Reader*, trans. Shaun Whiteside (Woodstock, NY: Overlook Press, 1996), 70.
16. Adler, "Gedenken an Prag," *DLA*, 11.
17. See Spector, *Prague Territories*, 12, 15.
18. Sayer, *Coasts of Bohemia*, 115–116.
19. Joseph Rothschild, *East Central Europe Between the Two Wars* (Seattle: U of Washington P, 1974), 134–135.
20. Alfred Otto Lanz, "'Zu Hause im Exil': Biographische Skizze über H. G. Adler," in *ZE*, 141.
21. Johannes Urzidil, *Prager Triptychon* (Munich: Albert Langen–Georg Müller, 1960), 13.
22. Mathias Schreiber, "'Zwanzig Jahre keinen Verlag gefunden': Interview mit H. G. Adler," *Kölner Stadt-Anzeiger* (May 28, 1969): Feuilliton, 8.
23. Adler, "Zu Hause im Exil," in *WV*, 20.
24. Quoted in *S*, 332.
25. *P*, 9.
26. "Sonderinterview von Alfred Joachim Fischer mit H. G. Adler," in *ZE*, 196.
27. I am indebted to Lawrence Langer for noting the connection to the "Beast of Bergen-Belsen" in conversation. Adler revised *Panorama* before it was published in 1968, by which time he would have known the name's notoriety.
28. *P*, 51.
29. "Sonderinterview von Alfred Joachim Fischer mit H.G. Adler," in *ZE*, 192.
30. "'Es gäbe viel Merkwürdiges zu berichten': Interview with Hans Christoph Knebusch," in *WV*, 32. Adler also speaks of this time in *LWU*.
31. *LWU*.
32. "Erinnerungen an Leo Baeck, den deutschen Widerstand und die Konzentrationslager. Gespräch mit Herrn Dr. H. G. Adler," *Deutschland-Berichte* 21, no. 3 (March 1985): 42.
33. "Zu Hause im Exil," in *WV*, 20–21.
34. Wolfgang Burghart, *LHGA*, October 5, 1947, *DLA*.
35. Adler, "Nach der Befreiung," in *NB*, 43.
36. Adalbert Stifter, *Indian Summer*, trans. Wendell Frye (New York: Peter Lang, 1985), 14.
37. Ibid., 267, 327.

38. Ibid., 467.
39. Interview with Hans Christoph Knebusch, in *WV*, 33.
40. "'Da gäbe noch viel mehr zu berichten'": Interview with Friedrich Danielis," *Das Pult* 14, no. 63 (1982): 48.
41. Quoted in Sayer, *Coasts of Bohemia*, 157.
42. Quoted in Livia Rothkirchen, *The Jews of Bohemia and Moravia: Facing the Holocaust* (Lincoln: U of Nebraska P and Jerusalem: Yad Vashem, 2005), 26.
43. Václav Beneš, "Czechoslovak Democracy and Its Problems, 1918-1920," in *A History of the Czechoslovak Republic, 1918–1948*, ed. Victor S. Mamatey and Radomír Luža (Princeton: Princeton UP, 1973), 41. Starting in 1921, Czechoslovak citizens could define themselves in the state census by identifying with their mother tongue (versus the Habsburg identification by "language of daily use"), be it Czechoslovak, German, Ruthenian, Magyar, Polish, or Other, while Jews could identify their nationality through religion (half of whom did). In the 1930 census (the only other one done in the First Republic), the restriction to identification by mother tongue was tightened further, whereby a nationality other than the mother tongue could only be chosen if the person spoke it in neither his family nor household, though Jews could still identify by religion. See Jeremy King, *Budweisers to Czechs: A Local History of Bohemian Politics 1848–1948* (Princeton: Princeton UP, 2005), 164–168.
44. Spector, *Prague Territories*, 92. See also Angelo Maria Ripellino, *Magic Prague*, trans. Michael Henry Heim (Los Angeles: U of California P, 1994), 20.
45. Sayer, *Coasts of Bohemia*, 157–158.
46. Ripellino, *Magic Prague*, 20.
47. Zdeněk Kirchner, "Situation of Czech Photography," in *Czech Modernism: 1900–1945*, ed. Jaroslav Anděl et al. (Museum of Fine Arts, Houston. Boston: Bulfinch Press, 1989), 115.
48. Johannes Urzidil, *The Living Contribution of Jewish Prague to Modern German Literature*, trans. Michael Lebeck (New York: Leo Baeck Institute, 1968), 8.
49. Adler, "Gedenken an Prag," *DLA*, 3.
50. Spector, *Prague Territories*, 94–98.
51. Thomas Ort, *Art and Life in Modernist Prague: Karel Capek and His Generation, 1911–1938* (New York: Palgrave MacMillan, 2013), 2.
52. Spector, *Prague Territories*, 40.
53. Ort, *Art and Life in Modernist Prague*, 42–46. See also Carl Schorske, *Fin-de-Siècle Vienna: Politics and Culture* (New York: Vintage, 1981), xvii–xxx.
54. Ort, *Art and Life in Modernist Prague*, 49.
55. Josef Čapek, letter to his future wife, April 8, 1913, quoted in Anděl et al., *Czech Modernism*, 25.
56. Egon Erwin Kisch, "Germans and Czechs," in *Egon Erwin Kisch, The Raging Reporter: A Bio-Anthology*, ed. and trans. Harold B. Segel (West Lafayette: Purdue U, 1997), 95. See also Hillel J. Kieval, *The Making of Czech Jewry* (New York: Oxford UP, 1988), 13.
57. *LWU*.
58. Franz Kafka, *Dearest Father*, trans. Hannah and Richard Stokes (Richmond, UK: Oneworld Classics, 2008), 20.
59. Ibid., 32.
60. Quoted in Spector, *Prague Territories*, 142. For discussion of Bergmann's role see Spector, *Prague Territories*, 135–142. Also see Kieval, *Making of Czech Jewry*, 99–103.
61. Martin Buber, "Judaism and the Jews," in *On Judaism*, ed. Nahum N. Glatzer (New York: Schocken, 1967), 21.
62. Kieval, *Making of Czech Jewry*, 132.
63. Ibid., 180.
64. Ibid., 189.
65. Ibid., 193. Emil Adler's decision to have himself and his son baptized as Protestants in 1922 could reflect his urge to align himself with the Czech independence movement and Masaryk, both of whom identified as Protestant, versus choosing Catholicism, the religion of the Habsburgs. I am indebted to Thomas Ort for this insight.
66. Adler, "Zu Hause im Exil," in *WV*, 21.

Chapter 3

1. H. G. Adler, "Der freideutsche Jugendtag 1913," in *FM*, 188. Also see Christian Niemeyer, *Der dunklen Seiten der Jugendbewegung: Vom Wandervogel zur Hitlerjugend* (Tübingen: Francke Verlag, 2013).
2. Unless otherwise noted, information on the Jugendbewegung is taken from Peter D. Stachura, *The German Youth Movement 1900–1945* (New York: St. Martins, 1981), and Walter Z. Laqueur, *Young Germany: A History of the German Youth Movement* (New Brunswick, NJ: Transaction Books, 1984).
3. Adler, "Der freideutsche Jugendtag 1913," in *FM*, 172.
4. H. G. Adler, "Letter from H. G. Adler to Chaim Rabin," in *From Prague Poet to Oxford Anthropologist: Franz Baermann Steiner Celebrated*, ed. Jeremy Adler, Richard Fardon, and Carol Tully (Munich: Iudicium, 2003), 204.
5. Such lackings were felt by many and were summed up by Peter Suhrkamp in his 1932 essay "Sons Without Fathers and Teachers: The Condition of Bourgeois Youth," where he writes, "Youth finds in the youth group the education it seeks and the ideals it needs, even in the form of shallow slogans. Above all, young people find in the youth group a sense of human order. . . . The influence of comrades in communities of young people is greater in every way than that of parents and teachers, even when these are much loved." Quoted in Thomas A. Kohut, *A German Generation: An Experiential History of the Twentieth Century* (New Haven: Yale UP, 2012), 75.
6. Peter Demetz believes that these values, more than anything else, enabled Adler to survive Theresienstadt and the subsequent camps. Author interview, March 28, 2012.
7. Quoted in Barbara Shambolis, "Werner Heisenberg," in *Jugendbewegt greprägt: Essays zu autobiographischen Texten von Werner Heissenberg, Robert Jungk und vielen anderen*, ed. Barabara Shambolis (Göttingen: V & R Unipress, 2013), 375n. Known as the Prunner Gelöbnis (The Prunn Pledge), it was formulated at a meeting of the Pfadfinder near Prunn Castle in Bavaria in 1919.
8. Adler, "Der freideutsche Jugendtag 1913," in *FM*, 176.
9. The distinction between Gemeinschaft and Gesellschaft was coined by Ferdinand Tönnies in the late nineteenth century. See Strachura, *The German Youth Movement 1900–1945*, 17.
10. *P*, 144.
11. Alfred Otto Lanz, " 'Zu Hause im Exil': Biographische Skizze über H. G. Adler," in *ZE*, 142.
12. Kohut observes that such discussions "allowed participants to feel sophisticated as members of an intellectual elite standing outside and above bourgeois society, but because these discussions did not lead to action, they were risk free" (*A German Generation*, 65). Adler's mother expressed concern that Vogel was older in a letter to Günther on November 21, 1924. Such friendships between adolescents and young men, superseding parental relations, represented a further attraction of the movement.
13. Laqueur, *Young Germany*, 41.
14. Adler, "Der freideutsche Jugendtag 1913," in *FM*, 166.
15. See Stachura, *The German Youth Movement 1900–1945*, 32–34, for details on this gathering and its consequences.
16. Adler, "Der freideutsche Jugendtag 1913," in *FM*, 158, and Stachura, *The German Youth Movement 1900–1945*, 63.
17. Stachura, *The German Youth Movement 1900–1945*, 60. Rüdiger Ahrens notes that the Weiße Ritter never were granted an official troop designation. See Shambolis, *Jugendbewegt geprägt*, 463.
18. Laqueur, *Young Germany*, 138.
19. Ibid., 139.
20. Adler, "Der freideutsche Jugendtag 1913," i1.
21. *P*, 171–172.
22. Ibid., 143.
23. Ibid., 173. Kohut confirms how organized challenges helped mediate the anxiety of possible failure, whereby the "individual did not need to achieve greatness on his or her own; greatness was achieved with and through others" (*A German Generation*, 67).

24. Laqueur, *Young Germany*, 143.
25. Adler, "Die freideutsche Jugendtag 1913," 180.
26. Rudolf Mehnert quoted by Adler, "Der freideutsche Jugendtag 1913," 175.
27. Quoted in Adler, "Der freideutsche Jugendtag 1913," 176.
28. Adler, "Der freideutsche Jugendtag 1913," 180. See also Kohut, *A German Generation*, 75–76.
29. For more on the "Freien Gruppe Prag," see *OB*, 13. Unless otherwise noted, information on Steiner and his friendship with Adler is from Adler's letter to Chaim Rabin of March 17, 1953, published in English translation in J. Adler, Fardon, and Tully, eds., *From Prague Poet to Oxford Anthropologist*, 199–239. The letter appears in the original German in book form as H. G. Adler, *Über Franz Baermann Steiner: "Brief an Chaim Rabin,"* ed. Jeremy Adler and Carol Tully (Göttingen: Wallstein, 2006).
30. Jeremy Adler and Richard Fardon, "An Oriental in the West: The Life of Franz Baermann Steiner," in *Taboo, Truth, and Religion: Selected Writings of Franz Baermann Steiner, Vol. 1* (New York: Bergahn Books, 1999), 34–37. This biographical essay also provides a detailed overview of Steiner and Adler's childhood and friendship. See also Ulrich van Loyen, *Franz Baermann Steiner: Exile und Verwandlung, zur Biografie eines deutschen Dichters und jüdischen Ethnologen* (Bielefeld: Aisthesis Verlag), 2011.
31. Interview with Hans Christoph Knebusch, in *WV*, 36.
32. J. Adler and Fardon, "An Oriental in the West," 30–32.
33. Ibid., 40.
34. Adler, *LG*, September 22, 1939.
35. Paul Kornfeld quoted in J. Adler and Fardon, "An Oriental in the West," 22.
36. J. Adler and Fardon, "An Oriental in the West," 80.
37. Ibid., 81.
38. Scott Spector, *Prague Territories: National Conflict and Cultural Innovation in Franz Kafka's Fin de Siècle* (Berkeley: U of California P, 2000), 14.
39. Ibid., 18–19.
40. Adler, affidavit for Hans Oplatka, October 1979, *DLA*.
41. "Letter from H. G. Adler to Chaim Rabin," in J. Adler, Fardon, and Tully, eds., *From Prague Poet to Oxford Anthropologist*, 216.
42. Richard H. Davis, *The Bhagavad Gita: A Biography* (Princeton: Princeton UP, 2015), 20–21.
43. *LWU*.
44. Ibid.
45. Ibid.
46. *P*, 179.
47. Ibid., 182.
48. Vladimir Birgus, *The Photographer František Drtikol* (Prague: Kant, 2000), 5–63. See also Anna Fárová, *František Drtikol: Art-Deco Photographer* (Munich: Schirmer Art Books, 1993), 9–77.
49. Vladimir Birgus, *František Drtikol: Modernist Nudes* (San Francisco: Robert Koch Gallery, 1997), 2.
50. Vladimir Birgus, *Fotograf František Drtikol* (Prague: Prostor, 1994), 193.
51. Josef Moucha, *František Drtikol*, trans. Derek and Marzia Paton (Prague: Torst, 2007), 22.
52. Ibid., 5.
53. Stanislav Doležal, Anna Fárová, and Petr Nedoma, *František Drtikol: Fotograf, Mailř, Mystik* (Prague: Vydala Galeire Rudolfinum, 1998), 76.
54. Birgus, *Fotograf František Drtikol*, 195.
55. Fárová, *František Drtikol*, 69 and 72, respectively.
56. Ibid., 26.
57. Although Mombert's poetry is little read today, he was a contemporary of Stephan George and Christian Morgenstern, poets who also displayed Romantic attributes traceable to Nietzsche. Alban Berg set Mombert's verse to music, and his work was included by Franz Marc and Wassily Kandinsky in the *Blauer Reiter* anthology of 1913. Martin Buber also dedicated his *Ekstatische Konfessionen* of 1908 to Mombert. See Raymond Furness, *Zarathustra's Children: A Study of a Lost Generation of German Writers* (Rochester: Camden House, 2000), 52, 55.

58. Manfred Bosch, "Schalom Ben-Chorin und H. G. Adler als Debütanten im Radolfzeller Heim-Verlag," *Hegau: Zeitschrift für Geschichte, Volksbunde und Naturgeschichte des Gebietes zwischen Rhein, Donau und Bodensee*, 6 (2004): 288–289.
59. Günther Adler, *Meer und Gebirge* (Radolfzell am Bodensee: Heim-Verlag Adolf Dreßler, 1931), 15 and 18, respectively.
60. Ibid., 27.
61. Adler, "Der Dichter Alfred Mombert," *Hochland* 58, no. 1 (October 1965): 85.
62. Ibid., 86.
63. *AW*, 142–143.
64. Jethro Bithell, *Modern German Literature 1880–1938* (London: Methuen, 1939), 464.
65. Furness, *Zarathustra's Children*, 59.
66. "Letter from H. G. Adler to Chaim Rabin," in J. Adler, Fardon, and Tully, eds., *From Prague Poet to Oxford Anthropologist*, 207.
67. *LHGA*, December 16, 1933.

Chapter 4

1. Angelo Maria Ripellino, *Magic Prague*, trans. Michael Henry Heim (Los Angeles: U of California P, 1994), 113.
2. Ibid., 6.
3. Jana Claverie and Alena Kubova, *Prague* (Paris: Vilo Publishing, 2002), 43.
4. Quoted in Vladimir Birgus, *The Photographer František Drtikol* (Prague: Kant, 2000), 14
5. Thomas Ort, *Art and Life in Modernist Prague: Karel Capek and His Generation, 1911–1938* (New York: Palgrave MacMillan, 2013), 51.
6. Birgus, *The Photographer František Drtikol*, 30.
7. František Šmejkal, "From Lyrical Metaphors to Symbols of Fate: Czech Surrealism of the 1930s," in *Czech Modernism: 1900–1945*, ed. Jaroslav Anděl et al. (Museum of Fine Arts, Houston. Boston: Bulfinch Press, 1989), 66.
8. Claverie and Kubova, *Prague*, 10.
9. Ibid., 85.
10. Quoted in Ort, *Art and Life in Modernist Prague*, 37.
11. Quoted in Jaroslav Anděl, "In Search of Redemption," in *Czech Modernism: 1900–1945*, ed. Jaroslav Anděl et al. (Museum of Fine Arts, Houston. Boston: Bulfinch Press, 1989), 18.
12. Ort, *Art and Life in Modernist Prague*,17.
13. Ibid., 49.
14. Ibid., 51–52.
15. Ibid., 138.
16. Anděl, "In Search of Redemption," 27.
17. Ort, *Art and Life in Modernist Prague*, 137.
18. Quoted in Alison de Lima Greene, "Czech Modernism 1900–1920," in *Czech Modernism: 1900–1945*, ed. Jaroslav Anděl et al. (Museum of Fine Arts, Houston. Boston: Bulfinch Press, 1989), 52.
19. *DPS*, 21–22.
20. Alice Adler to Günther Adler, March 23, 1929.
21. Wolfgang Burghart, *LHGA* , October 5, 1947.
22. Albrecht Schneider, "Music and Gestures: A Historical Introduction and Survey of Earlier Research," in *Musical Gestures: Sound, Movement, and Meaning*, ed. Rolfe Inge Godøy and Marc Leman (New York: Routledge, 2010), 88. See also Karl Dèzes, "In memoriam Gustav Becking," in *Gustav Becking zum Gedächtnis* (Tutzing: Hans Schneider Verlag, 1975), 343–345.
23. Nigel Nettheim and Gustav Becking, "How Musical Rhythm Reveals Human Attitudes: Gustav Becking's Theory," *International Review of the Aesthetics and Sociology of Music*, 27, no. 2 (December 1996): 101–122 (accessed online December 28, 2017).
24. Jeremy Adler in conversation, January 8, 2015.
25. Kurt and Edith Oppens settled in New York, where he worked as a piano tuner and she taught piano at a school founded by the exiled writer and musician Hermann Grab. Beginning in

1951, the couple was involved with the Aspen Music Festival each summer for forty years. Kurt Oppens wrote numerous articles and reviews on music, publishing frequently in prominent journals such as *Opernwelt* and *Merkur*. Their daughter Ursula became an internationally acclaimed pianist.

26. Gustav Becking, *LHGA*, October 11, 1936.
27. H. G. Adler, letter to Peter Brömse, December 21, 1961.
28. Torsten Fuchs, "Gustav W. Becking (1894–1945) Musikwissenschaftftler," in *Prager Professoren 1938–1945: Zwischen Wissenschaft und Politik*, ed. Monika Glettler and Alena Míšková (Essen: Klartext Verlag, 2001), 234. Background on Herbert Cysarz can also be found in Peter Becher's article on Cysarz in the same volume, 277–297. See also Dèzes, "In memoriam Gustav Becking," 351.
29. Quoted in *S*, 333.
30. Manfred Voigts, "Adlers Beziehung zu Erich Unger," paper presented at Prague conference on Adler's centennial in 2010. See also Esther J. Ehrman, "Introduction," in "Erich Unger's 'The Natural Order of Miracles': I. The Pentateuch and the Vitalistic Myth," trans. Esther J. Ehrman, *Journal of Jewish Thought and Philosophy* 11, no. 2 (2002): 136.
31. Gershom Scholem, *Walter Benjamin: The Story of a Friendship*, trans. Harry Zohn (New York: New York Review of Books, 2001), 117–120. For a discussion of Unger, Goldberg, Benjamin, Scholem, and their ideas on Jewish mysticism see Gary Smith, "'Die Zauberjuden': Walter Benjamin, Gershom Scholem, and Other German-Jewish Esoterics between the World Wars," *Journal of Jewish Thought and Philosophy* 4 (1995): 227–243.
32. Ehrman, "Introduction," 136.
33. Erich Unger, *The Imagination of Reason* (London: Routledge & Keegan Paul, 1952), 109.
34. Adler, "Erinnerung an den Philosophen Erich Unger," *Eckart: Blätter für evangelische Geisteskultur* 29 (1960): 183.
35. Ibid., 185.
36. Ibid., 183.
37. Ibid., 183–184.
38. Alfred Joachim Fischer, "Begegnungen mit H. G. Adler," in *ZE*, 160.
39. "'Es gäbe viel Merkwürdiges zu berichten': Interview with Hans Christoph Knebusch," in *WV*, 35.
40. I am indebted to Jeremy Adler for information on the Gross salon.
41. Interview with Hans Christoph Knebusch, in *WV*, 36.
42. Robert N. Proctor, *Racial Hygiene: Medicine Under the Nazis* (Cambridge, MA: Harvard UP, 1988), 169–170.
43. Wilhelm Unger, "Das andere Deutschland," in *BF*, 14.
44. The story is lost, but Adler describes it in *LWU*.
45. Today these addresses are Křižikova 76 and Šaldova 7.
46. Derek Sayer, *The Coasts of Bohemia: A Czech History*, trans. Alena Sayer (Princeton: Princeton UP, 1998), 170, 221.
47. Nancy M. Wingfield, *Flag Wars and Stone Saints: How the Bohemian Lands Became Czech* (Cambridge, MA: Harvard UP, 2007), 11.
48. Peter Demetz, *Prague in Black and Gold* (New York: Hill and Wang, 1997), 331.
49. See Sayer, *Coasts of Bohemia*, 163–165.
50. Wingfield, *Flag Wars*, 11.
51. Ibid., 246.
52. Ibid., 243, 251.
53. Demetz, *Prague in Black and Gold*, 356.
54. Peter Demetz, *Prague in Danger* (New York: Farrar, Straus and Giroux, 2008), 33.
55. Demetz, *Prague in Black and Gold*, 356. See also H. G. Adler, *DPS*, 33–35.
56. For a discussion of the essay and its history see Katrin Kohl, "'Zur Bestimmung der Lyrik': H. G. Adlers Poetik zwischen den Zeiten," *Text + Kritik* 163, no. 7 (2004): 60–70.
57. Ort, *Art and Life in Modernist Prague*, 5. The anecdote on Mann's arrival comes from Jeremy Adler.
58. The quote appears in *LFW*, June 10, 1966. For discussion of the relationship between Adler, Canetti, and Steiner see *BB* and *OB*.

59. *P*, 265.
60. Ibid., 295.
61. Ibid., 268.
62. Ibid., 305.
63. Ibid., 307.
64. See Livia Rothkirchen, *The Jews of Bohemia and Moravia: Facing the Holocaust* (Lincoln: U of Nebraska P and Jerusalem: Yad Vashem, 2005), 86–92, and Václav L. Beneš, "Czechoslovak Democracy and Its Problems, 1918–1920," in *A History of the Czechoslovak Republic, 1918–1948*, ed. Victor S. Mamatey and Radomír Luža (Princeton, NJ: Princeton UP, 1973), 39–51.
65. Rothkirchen, *Jews of Bohemia*, 37.
66. Quoted in Jeremy King, *Budweisers to Czechs: A Local History of Bohemian Politics 1848–1948* (Princeton: Princeton UP, 2005), 168.
67. See Ibid., 169–170, for discussion of eroding relations between Czechs and Germans in the 1930s.
68. Ibid., 172.
69. Demetz, *Prague in Danger*, 30.
70. See Rothkirchen, *Jews of Bohemia*, 52–54, for the Beneš quote and details of the refugee situation.
71. See Ibid., 52.
72. See Ibid., 54–55.
73. This and quotes that follow, *LWU*.
74. *DPS*, 15. For the Brod quote see *OB*, 20. Adler describes Prague as a "beautiful stony corpse" in *Panorama*.
75. Chad Bryant, *Prague in Black: Nazi Rule and Czech Nationalism* (Cambridge, MA: Harvard UP, 2007), 23.
76. Quoted in King, *Budweisers to Czechs*, 173
77. Quoted in Sayer, *Coasts of Bohemia*, 22.
78. For details on the takeover of Czechoslovakia see Bryant, *Prague in Black*, 25–26.
79. *AW*, 130.
80. Demetz, *Prague in Danger*, 18.
81. Elias Canetti, *The Play of the Eyes*, trans. Ralph Manheim (New York: Farrar, Straus, Giroux, 1986), 317–318.
82. Adler, "Zu Hause im Exil," in *WV*, 22.

Chapter 5

1. Quoted in *OB*, 59.
2. *AW*, 99.
3. *LFBS*, July 14, 1938, *ZV*, 43.
4. Chad Bryant, *Prague in Black: Nazi Rule and Czech Nationalism* (Cambridge, MA: Harvard UP, 2007), 107.
5. *LFBS*, July 14, 1938, in *ZV*, 46.
6. *LFBS*, September 5, 1938, in *ZV*, 50–51.
7. *LFBS*, December 28, 1936, in *ZV*, 32.
8. *LFBS*, September 5, 1938, in *ZV*, 47.
9. Jaroslav Preiss (1870–1946) was general director of the influential Živnostenská Bank of Czecho-Slovakia; Rudolf Beran (1887–1954) was prime minister of Czecho-Slovakia from December 1938 to April 1939; Jozef Tiso (1887–1947) was president of the fascist Republic of Slovakia from 1939 to 1945. See *ZV*, 296.
10. *LFBS*, October 8, 1938, in *ZV*, 53, 55. Adler refers to the epic battle of the White Mountain, November 8, 1620, at Bílá Hora, near Prague. Bohemian soldiers were defeated by forces loyal to the Habsburg Empire, resulting in Habsburg control of Czech lands for three hundred years.
11. *LWB*.
12. *LFBS*, October 8, 1938, in *ZV*, 55.
13. *LFBS*, May 20, 1938, in *ZV*, 41.
14. *FS*, 9–10.

15. "Unser Herzog," in *FS*, 47.
16. "Der Bescheid," in *FS*, 53, and "Feindfreund," in *FS*, 72.
17. "Gerechtigkeit," in *FS*, 44–45.
18. *LFBS*, December 28, 1936, in *ZV*, 32.
19. *LFBS*, October 8, 1938, in *ZV*, 36.
20. *LFBS*, March 5, 1939, in *ZV*, 39.
21. *LFBS*, March 5, 1939, in *ZV*, 60.
22. Quoted in Tully's introduction, in *ZV*, 10.
23. *ZV*, 62.
24. *ZV*, 64.
25. Livia Rothkirchen, *The Jews of Bohemia and Moravia: Facing the Holocaust* (Lincoln: U of Nebraska P and Jerusalem: Yad Vashem, 2005), 100.
26. Ibid., 107.
27. Bryant, *Prague in Black*, 50–51.
28. Franz Baermann Steiner, letter to Rudolf Hartung, July 4, 1947, quoted in *OB*, 59.
29. *BB*, 52.
30. *LFBS*, April 24, 1939, in *ZV*, 63.
31. *W*, 412.
32. *LWB*.
33. *LG*, September 14, 1939.
34. *LG*, August 30, 1939.
35. H. G. Adler, undated *LG*, although written in September 1939.
36. This last description appears in a letter by Prof. Derek Bolton of the Institute of Psychiatry, King's College London, to the German Research and Support Fund as part of an unsuccessful 1986 application for underwriting to help cover publication costs. Bolton worked with Adler in the 1980s to revise the manuscript for his *Vorschule für eine Experimentaltheologie.* While in his letter Bolton does not explain the exact nature of "intuition," Adler confirmed to a friend that it was similar to looking at a chessboard and knowing there was an almost infinite number of possible moves, but that any experienced player "intuits" the array of moves most sensible or likely, and chooses among those while considering the potential moves of an opponent, which can never be known absolutely. This was the kind of situational thinking free of dogmatic preconceptions that Adler espoused. Bolton states its aim is "the possibility of a radically new development in human consciousness" through "the essential role of activity in knowledge, and the rejection of Reason as the absolute measure of reality." Bolton's letter is in Adler's archive. The chessboard analogy stems from my February 18, 2015, interview with the painter Friedrich Danielis, who shared it in a conversation with Adler, who approved of the analogy. With his wife, the cellist Susan Salm, Danielis knew and stayed with Adler in London from the 1970s onward. An extensive conversation about the *Experimentaltheologie* was conducted with Adler by Bolton on January 5, 1981, also in the Adler archive. The manuscript for it also includes Bolton's English translation of the 1941 version of Adler's "Traktat," which is 197 pages in manuscript. It informs the outline of Adler's ideas here, as does my interview with Bolton on March 26, 2014.
37. Gertrud Klepetar, *LHGA*, September 4, 1939, and January 27, 1940.
38. Ibid., January 17, 1940.
39. Ibid., January 18, 1940.
40. Ibid., January 27, 1940.
41. Ibid., January 18, 1940.
42. *LG*, October 2, 1939, and *LHGA*, December 31, 1940.
43. *LG*, November 9, 1939.
44. Gertrud Klepetar, *LHGA*, November 1, 1939.
45. Ibid., October 16, 1939.
46. Gertrud Klepetar, letters to Prof. Heyde, *DLA*.
47. Gertrud Klepetar, *LHGA*, November 2, 1939.
48. *LG*, November 7, 1939.
49. Gertrud Klepetar, *LHGA*, November 20, 1940.
50. *LG*, November 20, 1939.

51. Ibid., October 11, 1939.
52. Ibid., September 23, 1939.
53. Ibid., September 14, 1939.
54. Ibid., September 27, 1939.
55. Ibid., October 18, 1939.
56. Ibid., October 20, 1939.
57. Ibid., October 20, 1939.
58. Ibid., November 14, 1939.
59. Rothkirchen, *Jews of Bohemia*, 110.
60. *J*, 24.
61. See Peter Filkins, "Memory's Witness—Witnessing Memory," in *Witnessing, Memory, Poetics: H. G. Adler & W.G. Sebald*. ed. Helen Finch and Lynn L. Wolff (Rochester: Camden House, 2014), 42–46.
62. Rothkirchen, *Jews of Bohemia*, 105.
63. Ibid., 108.
64. Bryant, *Prague in Black*, 6.
65. Ibid., 64.
66. Rothkirchen, *Jews of Bohemia*, 113.
67. Bryant, *Prague in Black*, 59–65.
68. *LWB*.
69. Pepa Kress, *LHGA*, June 8, 1950.
70. *LWB*.

Chapter 6

1. In a community weekly of March 1940, Jaroslav Polák-Rokycana saw the Hebrew clock as symbolic of the need to return to Eretz Israel, although that had become impossible by then. See Livia Rothkirchen, *The Jews of Bohemia and Moravia: Facing the Holocaust* (Lincoln: U of Nebraska P and Jerusalem: Yad Vashem, 2005), 119.
2. See *T*, 3–21, for details on Jewish persecution in the Protectorate.
3. Ibid., 7.
4. Chad Bryant, *Prague in Black: Nazi Rule and Czech Nationalism* (Cambridge, MA: Harvard UP, 2007), 83.
5. For a summary of the imposed restrictions see *T*, 6–12.
6. "'Es gäbe viel Merkwürdiges zu berichten': Interview with Hans Christoph Knebusch," in *WV*, 39.
7. Bryant, *Prague in Black*, 84–89.
8. Ibid., 89.
9. Vojtech Mastny, *The Czechs Under Nazi Rule: The Failure of National Resistance, 1939–1942* (New York: Columbia UP, 1971), 165.
10. Ibid., 160.
11. George F. Kennan, *From Prague After Munich: Diplomatic Papers 1938–1940* (Princeton: Princeton UP, 1968), 117–118.
12. Adler, "Schilderung des Verfolgungsvorganges," *DLA*.
13. Quoted in *OB*, 63.
14. *LG*, October 21, 1941. Adler says he is not sure if it was 1933 or 1934. Information on the declared religion and ethnicity of the family members comes from the Prague National Archives.
15. *T*, 6.
16. Ibid., 11.
17. Bryant, *Prague in Black*, 131.
18. Ibid., 135.
19. Quoted in Ibid., 146. For an account of the consequences of victories in the East for Nazi policy on the Jews, see Christopher R. Browning, *The Origins of the Final Solution: The Evolution of Nazi Jewish Policy, September 1939–March 1942* (Lincoln: U of Nebraska P, 2004), 309–330.

20. *T*, 19.
21. Bryant, *Prague in Black*, 146–147. For a more detailed account of Heydrich's hold over the Protectorate see Robert Gerwarth, *Hitler's Hangman: The Life of Heydrich* (New Haven: Yale UP, 2011), 218–277.
22. Bryant, *Prague in Black*, 147. The wide range is because many of those killed were Polish Jews murdered in secret by special "Einsatzgruppen" deployed by the SS, for which there were no registration lists or deportations.
23. Ibid., 147–148.
24. *LWB*.
25. *LG*, August 20, 1941.
26. Ibid., August 25, 1941.
27. Ibid., October 10, 1941.
28. *LWB*.
29. Ibid.
30. *LG*, October 20, 1941.
31. *LWB*.
32. Ottla Beihof, *LHGA*, October 15, 1941.
33. *LG*, October 22, 1941.
34. *LHGA*, September 6, 1941.
35. Ibid., October 7, 1941.
36. Ibid., October 20, 1941.
37. *T*, 12.
38. The idea for this occurred after Himmler was nauseated by a mass shooting and worried about the psychological "hardship" suffered by the executioners. He asked Arthur Nebe, head of Einsatzgruppe B, for a more "humane" method, and Nebe recalled having returned home drunk and falling asleep in his garage with the engine running, thus leading to the construction of the special vans. See Patrick Montague, *Chełmno and the Holocaust: The History of Hitler's First Death Camp* (Chapel Hill: U of North Carolina P, 2011), 199–200.
39. *LHGA*, November 26, 1941.
40. *LG*, November 27, 1941.
41. Magda Veselská, "'The Museum of an Extinct Race'—Fact vs. Legend: A Contribution to the Topic of the So-called Jewish Councils in Central Europe," *Judaica Bohemiae* 2 (2016): 41–85. For photos of the museum during the war, see her book *Archa pamêti: Cesta pražského židovského muzea pohnutým 20. Stoletím* (Prague: Academia, Židovské muzeum v Praze, 2012), 264–265. See also Jan Björn Potthast, *Das jüdische Zentralmuseum der SS in Prag: Gegenforschung und Völkermord im Nationalsozialismus* (Frankfurt: Campus Verlag, 2002), 411–463.
42. *LWB*, October 17, 1947. See also Jeremy Adler, "A Note on Kafka's Library," *German Life and Letters* 46 (1993): 176–178.
43. See Veselská, *Archa pamêti*, 265.
44. *LWB*.
45. *J*, 27.
46. *T*, 55.
47. Ibid., 31.
48. Ibid., 55–58.
49. Ibid., 59.
50. Ibid., 60.
51. Christopher R. Browning stressed the importance of Adler's preparation as a trained scholar in a paper delivered at a roundtable on "H. G. Adler's Shoah Trilogy" at the Modern Language Association conference in Vancouver, January 8, 2015.

Chapter 7

1. See Wolfgang Benz, *Theresienstadt: Eine Geschichte von Täuschung und Vernichtung* (Munich: C.H. Beck, 2013), 7–13.

2. For the establishment and plans for Theresienstadt, see Chapter 2 of *T*. For the minutes from the October 10, 1941 meeting see *T*, 642–645.
3. *T*, 16
4. For the tally on children see Nora Levin, Foreword to *The Terezín Diary of Gonda Redlich* (Lexington: UP of Kentucky, 1992), vii.
5. *T*, 45. For details on deportations to and from Theresienstadt, see Chapter 3 of *T*. The numbers of deaths, deportations, and survivors vary slightly in different studies, but they generally align with one another. Unless otherwise noted, I cite the statistics Adler gives in his own study.
6. Viktor Kuperman, Sergei Makarov, and Elena Makarova, *University Over the Abyss* (Jerusalem: Verba, 2004). The list of lecturers can be found at http://www.makarovainit.com/list.htm (accessed April 13, 2018).
7. http://www.ghetto-theresienstadt.info/pages/g/ghettobuecherei.htm (accessed January 4, 2018). See also Benz, *Theresienstadt*, 107.
8. *T*, 107. For details on the unique economic and cultural "reforms" introduced in Theresienstadt, see *T*, 103–107.
9. *T*, 103. For details on the conditions in Theresienstadt between 1941 and 1945, see Chapters 4–7 of *T*.
10. A gas chamber was planned for the Small Fortress toward the end of the war but was never built.
11. See http://www.yivoencyclopedia.org/article.aspx/Terezin (accessed January 3, 2018).
12. Peter Demetz, *Prague in Black and Gold* (New York: Hill and Wang, 1997), 246.
13. Livia Rothkirchen, *The Jews of Bohemia and Moravia: Facing the Holocaust* (Lincoln: U of Nebraska P and Jerusalem: Yad Vashem, 2005), 144, 148.
14. Robert Gerwarth, *Hitler's Hangman: The Life of Heydrich* (New Haven: Yale UP, 2011), 204.
15. *T*, 20.
16. Mark Roseman, *The Wannsee Conference and the Final Solution* (New York: Metropolitan Books, 2002), 81–82.
17. Christopher R. Browning, *The Origins of the Final Solution: The Evolution of Nazi Jewish Policy, September 1939–March 1942* (Lincoln: U of Nebraska P, 2004), 317.
18. Wolfgang Benz, "Theresienstadt in der Geschichte der deutschen Juden," in *Theresienstadt in der Endlösung der Judenfrage*, ed. Miroslav Kárný, Vojtěch Blodig, and Margita Kárná (Prague: Panorama, 1992), 70.
19. "Geschichte des Ghettos Theresienstadt 1941–1943," quoted in Rothkirchen, *Jews of Bohemia*, 240.
20. Zdenek Lederer, *Ghetto Theresienstadt* (New York: Howard Fertig, 1983), 49.
21. *LB*, November 23, 1945.
22. *LG*, September 22, 1942.
23. *LWU*. For a chronicle of Adler's work assignments and activities see PFS, 94–95.
24. "'Es gäbe viel Merkwürdiges zu berichten': Interview with Hans Christoph Knebusch," in *WV*, 45.
25. *LG*, September 22, 1942.
26. Adler, "Warum habe ich mein Buch *Theresienstadt 1941–1945* geschrieben," in *WV*, 112.
27. Adler, *LFBS*, August 11, 1946, in *ZV*, 126; *LFW*, August 28, 1953; and *LFK*, September 19, 1961. Mandl remained friends with Adler, becoming a writer, musician, and historian of music composed and performed in Theresienstadt.
28. Adler, *LFW*, February 12, 1961.
29. *LFBS*, September 11, 1945, in *ZV*, 85.
30. *AW*, 158
31. See Ruth Vogel-Klein, "Bilder der Shoah in Gedichten von H. G. Adler und Franz Baermann Steiner," in *Literatur und Anthropologie: H. G. Adler, Elias Canetti und Franz Baermann Steiner in London*, ed. Jeremy Adler and Gesa Dane (Göttingen: Wallstein, 2014), 65.
32. Jürgen Matthäus, "Operation Barbarossa and the Onset of the Holocaust, June–December 1941," in Browning, *Origins of the Final Solution*, 249.
33. Ian Kershaw, *Popular Opinion and Political Dissent in the Third Reich: Bavaria 1933–1945*, 2nd edition (London: Oxford, 2002), 277. Quoted in Browning, *Origins of the Final Solution*, 389.
34. Vogel-Klein, "Bilder der Shoah in Gedichten von H. G. Adler und Franz Baermann Steiner," 64.

35. Katrin Kohl, "Die Lyrik von H. G. Adler," in *AW*, 1034.
36. *AW*, 160–161.
37. *LG*, March 24, 1942.
38. Interview with Hans Christoph Knebusch, in *WV*, 44.
39. See http://www.holocaustresearchproject.org/ghettos/piaski.html (accessed January 3, 2018).
40. For a summary of the evolution of the euthanasia, see Browning, *Origins of the Final Solution*, 184–193.
41. *LB*, April 2, 1946.
42. Philipp Manes, *As If It Were Life: A WWII Diary From the Theresienstadt Ghetto* (New York: Palgrave MacMillan, 2009), 70.
43. *T*, 89.
44. Ibid., 222, 204, respectively.
45. Manes, *As If It Were Life*, 112.
46. *T*, 27 and 107, respectively.
47. For a detailed account of Hitler's reprisals and the destruction of the village of Lidice, see http://www.holocaustresearchproject.org/nazioccupation/lidice.html (accessed January 3, 2018).
48. *T*, 121–122.
49. The first quote is from a radio interview recorded with Adler by Simon Brough for BBC Radio 4 in 1986 but never used; *DLA*. The second is from Adler, "Rund um die Todesrampe (Fragment, Prag Herbst 1945)," *DLA*.
50. *T*, 122.
51. Ibid., 124.

Chapter 8

1. Albert H. Friedlander, *Leo Baeck, Teacher of Theresienstadt* (Woodstock, NY: Overlook, 1991), 42.
2. Leonard Baker, *Days of Sorrow and Pain: Leo Baeck and the Berlin Jews* (New York: Oxford UP, 1978), 152, 176, 286, 305.
3. "Survival: An Address at the Concentration Camp (Academic Address given on June 15, 1944, at the Community House, Theresienstadt)," *The Synagogue Review: Journal of the Reform Synagogues of Great Britain* (November 1962): 1. Quoted in Friedlander, *Leo Baeck*, 215.
4. "Mystery and Commandment," *Judaism and Christianity: Essays by Leo Baeck*, trans. Walter Kaufmann (New York: Meridian, 1961), 171.
5. Baker, *Days of Sorrow and Pain*, 152.
6. Friedlander, *Leo Baeck*, 260.
7. Leo Baeck, "Individuum Ineffabile," *Eranos-Jahrbuch* XV (1948): 410. Quoted in Friedlander, *Leo Baeck*, 253.
8. *LB*, December 23, 1945.
9. Baker, *Days of Sorrow and Pain*, 40.
10. Adler, "Die Freiheit des Judentums (Erste Folge)," *Die Pforte* 5, no. 47 (March 1953): 129.
11. Baker, *Days of Sorrow and Pain*, 44, 52, 60–61, 304. In Theresienstadt, Baeck became convinced of the need for a homeland in Palestine. Adler also came to see the need for Israel to exist, although neither man thought Zionism a cure-all for restoring Jewish faith.
12. Adler, "Die Freiheit des Judentums (Erste Folge)," 123–124.
13. Adler, "Judentum in Politik und Theologie von Heute," unpublished manuscript dated February 1946, *DLA*.
14. Adler, "Religion des Gedenkens und Orthodoxie des Herzens," in *OH*, 160.
15. Adler, "Leo Baeck in Theresienstadt," *AJR Information* (December 1956): 7.
16. Adler, "Rechenschaft in dunkler Zeit — Leo Baeck und Sein Werk," in *OH*, 169.
17. Quoted in Adler, "Jüdische Existenz," *Eckart* 24 (1954/55): 338.
18. Adler, "Das unbekannte Judentum," *Tribune: Zeitschift zum Verständnis des Judentums* 1 (1962): 232.
19. Adler, "Judentum in Politik und Theologie von Heute."

20. Adler, "Jüdische Existenz," 339.
21. Adler, "Gibt es etwas typisch jüdisches?", *DLA*.
22. Fritz Groothues, radio interview with Adler, marked "Broadcast in Berlin, Fall 1985," *DLA*.
23. *FS*, 116–119.
24. Adler, "Die Umwerter aller Werte/Nietzsche und die Folgen," in *FM*, 117.
25. *FM*, 120.
26. Ibid., 121.
27. Quoted by Adler in Ibid., 134.
28. Quoted by Adler in Ibid., 140
29. *T*, 205.
30. Chapter 5 of *T* provides a detailed summary of these months.
31. *T*, 112.
32. Undated letter, definitely written before April 1, 1942. The fact of Adler having access to an electric light is noted by Adler in a 1986 oral history recorded by Konrad Wood for the Imperial War Museum, the tape for which is in the *DLA*.
33. See Jeremy Adler, "Afterword," in *T*, 808.
34. *LFBS*, August 30, 1945, in *ZV*, 83. Drafts of his translation, *DLA*.
35. Adler, *Raoul Feuerstein, DLA*, 2, 17, 19, 167, 168, 171, 177, 178.
36. Adler, letter to Philipp Manes, June 16, 1943, *DLA*. See also Viktor Kuperman, Sergei Makarov, and Elena Makarova, *University Over the Abyss* (Jerusalem: Verba, 2004), 90.
37. Letter to Emil Utitz, August 4, 1943.
38. *PFS*, 96n.
39. *AW*, 8, 1069–1070. The note to the poem in *AW* points out that Goethe used that title for the poem he placed at the beginning of his collected works of 1787 and his collected poems of 1827.
40. Adler, "Dichtung aus Theresienstadt," in *NB*, 85.
41. *AW*, 184.
42. Ibid., 195.
43. Ibid., 198–199.
44. Adler, "Dichtung in der Gefangenschaft als inneres Exil," in *OH*, 102.
45. *AW*, 228–229.
46. See *BB*, 76, where Jeremy Adler points out the link between his father's intricate forms and the poetry of the German Baroque forged by poets like Andreas Gryphius and Johann Christian Günther amid the historic ravages of another catastrophic epoch, the Thirty Years War.
47. *BB*, 78.
48. Rüdiger Görner, "Überleben—Überwinden?: Eine Betrachtung zum Werk H. G. Adlers," in *Salzburger Jahrbuch Für Philosophie* XXXV (1990): 86.
49. *T*, 582.
50. Robin Freeman, "Excursus: 'Nedej zahynouti nam ni budoucim, satý václave': Klein, Ullmann, and Others in Terezín," *Tempo* 60, no. 236 (April 2006): 40–41.
51. "Dichtung in der Gefangenschaft als inneres Exil," in *OH*, 102.
52. A poster in Adler's archive advertises an event at the Urania he hosted on December 5, 1935, "Seven Composers in Search of a Publisher." Ullmann performed his "5 Variations and Double Fugue upon a small piano piece by Schönberg," op. 19, no. 4. The other composers were Hans Winterberg, Wilhelm Maria Wesely, Karl Maria Pisarowitz, Walter Süsskind, Kurt Seidl, and Frederike Schwartz. Ullmann's first extant song cycle, "Six Songs to the Verse of Albert Steffen," op. 17, was performed at the Urania on May 13, 1937, with the American singer Harriet Henders as soloist. See http://www.ullmann-lieder.com/en/a-composer-of-songs/ (accessed January 4, 2018). Ullman's renowned "Second String Quartet" was also performed by the Klein Quartet at the Urania that same year. See Ingo Schultz, "Wege und Irrwege der Ullmann-Forschung," *Viktor Ullmann: Die Referate des Symposions anlässlich 50. Todestags 14.-16. Oktober 1994 in Dornach und ergänzende Studien*, ed. Hans-Günter Klein (Hamburg: Bockel Verlag, 1996), 35.
53. Adler, letters to Joža Karas, June 16, 1973, and to Jitka Ludvová, September 24, 1978, *DLA*. See also Ingo Schultz, ed., *Viktor Ullmann: 26 Kritiken über musikalische Veranstaltungen in Theresienstadt* (Hamburg: Bockel Verlag, 1993), 12.

54. See Livia Rothkirchen, *The Jews of Bohemia and Moravia: Facing the Holocaust* (Lincoln: U of Nebraska P and Jerusalem: Yad Vashem, 2005), 275, for a history of the opera's composition and rediscovery. Jeremy Adler says that after a patron expressed interest in mounting a performance in Prague with Karel Berman, the original Kaiser in the rehearsals in Theresienstadt, Jeremy consulted his friend the musicologist Julie Halitsky. She introduced Jeremy to her fiancé, the conductor Kerry Woodward, who met with H. G. Adler about the possibility of transcribing the rehearsal copy of the score. Unfortunately, a crackdown in Czech politics scuttled this plan, but with Adler's permission Woodward arranged for the performance in Amsterdam with himself as conductor. Adler never sold or profited from the manuscript, and he placed it for safekeeping in the Archiv Goetheana in Dornach, Switzerland, in 1987. It is now housed in the Paul Sacher Stiftung in Basel.
55. Schultz, "Wege und Irrwege der Ullmann-Forschung," 31. Ullmann was supposed to set two other Adler poems to complete the cantata but did not do so. The two poems were "Abschied" (later "Abscheid des Verurteilten" or "Departure of the Damned," *AW*, 241) and "Es ist Zeit" ("It is Time," *AW*, 218). The original text for these can be found in the notes to the published score of "Immer inmitten" in Viktor Ullmann, *Sämtliche Lieder*, Edition Schott (2005), ED 8199. I am indebted to Laurence Wallach for pointing this out.
56. Although dated September 4, 1943, no record survives of the cycle having been performed in Theresienstadt.
57. *AW*, 1093.
58. Ibid., 252, 254.
59. Ibid., 236.
60. *T*, 594. See also Rothkirchen, *Jews of Bohemia*, 276.
61. *T*, 123, 144–145.
62. Ibid., 126–129.
63. *J*, 128.
64. *T*, 129–131.
65. Ibid., 147.
66. Quoted in Rothkirchen, *Jews of Bohemia*, 259.
67. *T*, 599.
68. *J*, 81.

Chapter 9

1. Zdenek Lederer, *Ghetto Theresienstadt* (New York: Howard Fertig, 1983), 251.
2. Adler, "Rund um die Todesrampe," *DLA*.
3. Leonard Baker, *Days of Sorrow and Pain: Leo Baeck and the Berlin Jews* (New York: Oxford UP, 1978), 311. Baeck was criticized by Hannah Arendt and Paul Tillich, among others, for keeping silent about the gas chambers. Adler also felt "the general ignorance of the probable fate of all who were deported from Theresienstadt to the East led most of those in the camp into a thoughtlessness and self-deception that often bordered on an alteration of consciousness." See *T*, 128.
4. Unless noted, details of arrival, selection, and the workings of the gas chambers and crematoria can be found in Franciszek Piper's chapter on "Gas Chambers and Crematoria" in *Anatomy of the Auschwitz Death Camp*, ed. Yisrael Gutman and Michael Berenbaum (Bloomington: Indiana UP, 1994), 157–182.
5. Miklos Nyiszli, "Sonderkommando," *AZB*, 85. For the mention of Adler's camp number, see *LB*, December 19, 1945. That Adler was stamped with a Buchenwald number and not permanently tattooed indicates that he was likely designated to be sent to a smaller labor camp upon entrance into Birkenau.
6. Lederer, *Ghetto Theresienstadt*, 251.
7. Quoted in Piper, "Gas Chambers and Crematoria," 170.
8. Nyiszli, *AZB*, 87.
9. *Panorama*, 373.
10. Ruth Franklin underscores the rare fictional view Adler grants his reader of the shower room. See her article "The Long View," *The New Yorker*, January 31, 2011, p. 75.

11. Testimony of Yehuda Bacon, Trial of Adolf Eichmann, Session 68, at http://www.nizkor.org/hweb/people/e/eichmann-adolf/transcripts/Sessions/Session-068-05.html (accessed August 28, 2018). Also see Yehuda Bacon, "Mit der Neugier von Kindern," in *AZB*, 151–153. For the name of the "Aryan" kapo, see Danuta Czech, "The Auschwitz Prisoner Administration," in *Anatomy of the Auschwitz Death Camp*, ed. Yisrael Gutman and Michael Berenbaum (Bloomington: Indiana UP, 1994), 374.
12. Piper, "Gas Chambers and Crematoria," 174.
13. Irena Strzelecka, "Women," in *Anatomy of the Auschwitz Death Camp*, ed. Yisrael Gutman and Michael Berenbaum (Bloomington: Indiana UP, 1994), 410.
14. Hermann Langbein, *People in Auschwitz*, trans. Harry Zohn (Chapel Hill: U of North Carolina P, 2004), 84.
15. Denuta Czech, *The Auschwitz Chronicle 1939–1945* (New York: Holt, 1990), 296.
16. Shmuel Krakowski, "The Satellite Camps," in *Anatomy of the Auschwitz Death Camp*, ed. Yisrael Gutman and Michael Berenbaum (Bloomington: Indiana UP, 1994), 52.
17. For details on the Quarantine Camp see Otto Wolken, "Chronik des Quarantänelagers Birkenau," in *AZB*, 139–150.
18. *P*, 356–358.
19. Sofia Pantouvaki, "Typology and Symbolism in Prisoners' Concentration Camp Clothing During World War II," ΕΝΔΥΜΑΤΟΛΟΓΙΚΑ 4 (2012): 80–86.
20. *S*, 342.
21. Czech, *Auschwitz Chronicle*, 295. See also Yisrael Gutman, "Auschwitz—An Overview," in *Anatomy of the Auschwitz Death Camp*, ed. Yisrael Gutman and Michael Berenbaum (Bloomington: Indiana UP, 1994), 17.
22. Robert-Jan van Pelt, "A Site in Search of a Mission," in *Anatomy of the Auschwitz Death Camp*, ed. Yisrael Gutman and Michael Berenbaum (Bloomington: Indiana UP, 1994), 123.
23. Czech, *Auschwitz Chronicle*, 564, 731.
24. Hermann Langbein, *People in Auschwitz*, trans. Harry Zohn (Chapel Hill: U of North Carolina P, 2004), 48.
25. *LWU*.
26. Ibid.
27. *P*, 370.
28. Ibid., 371. Chapter 3.1 of the *Sayings of the Fathers* reads, "Mark well three things, and thou wilt not fall into the clutches of sin. Know whence thou art come, whither thou art going, and before whom thou art destined to give an account and reckoning." *The Living Talmud*, ed. and trans. Judah Goldin (Chicago: U of Chicago P, 1958), 118.
29. Adler, "Religion des Gedenkens und Orthodoxie des Herzens," in *OH*, 159.
30. *The Living Talmud*, 141 and 69, respectively.
31. The Buber quote appears in "Religion des Gedenken und Orthodoxie des Herzens," in *OH*, 158–159. Adler's ideas on exodus, wandering, and return appear in his essays, "Gibt es etwas typisch jüdisches?", *DLA*, and "Jüdische Existenz," *Eckart* 24 (1954/55): 339.
32. *LWU*. See also *PFS*, 102.
33. Shamai Davidson, "Human Reciprocity Among the Prisoners in Jewish Concentration Camps," 6, at http://www.yadvashem.org/odot_pdf/Microsoft%20Word%20-%203554.pdf (accessed January 6, 2018).
34. David Rousset, *The Other Kingdom*, trans. Ramon Guthrie (New York: Reynal & Hitchcock, 1947), 41. On stable pairings and value systems see Leo Eitinger, "Auschwitz—A Psychological Perspective," in *Anatomy of the Auschwitz Death Camp*, ed. Yisrael Gutman and Michael Berenbaum (Bloomington: Indiana UP, 1994), 475–476.
35. Marc Buggeln, *Slave Labor in Nazi Concentration Camps* (Oxford: Oxford UP, 2014), 44–45.
36. Harry Stein, "Buchenwald-Stammlager," in *Der Ort des Terrors: Geschichte der nationalsoziallistischen Konzentrationslager, Vol. 3—Sachsenhausen, Buchenwald*, ed. Wolfgang Benz and Barbara Distel (Munich: C.H. Beck, 2006), 330.
37. Ibid.
38. Wolfgang Grosse, *Aus dem Umkreis der Kamine: Überlebende eines KZ-Außenkommandos berichten* (Duderstadt: Mecke, 2009), 56.
39. Buggeln, *Slave Labor in Nazi Concentration Camps*, 40.

40. Ibid., 50.
41. Grosse, *Aus dem Umkreis der Kamine,* 56–57. Other details of the camp's founding, function, and organization stem from Grosse's entry on "Niederorschel" in *Der Ort des Terrors: Geschichte der nationalsoziallistischen Konzentrationslager,* vol. 3, *Sachsenhausen, Buchenwald,* ed. Wolfgang Benz and Barbara Distel (Munich: C. H. Beck, 2006), 534–537.
42. Grosse, *Aus dem Umkreis der Kamine,* 69.
43. See the account of Leopold Fischer quoted in ibid., 34. See also Simcha Bunem Unsdorfer, *The Yellow Star* (New York: Thomas Yoseloff, 1961), 118f.
44. For the percentage of nations and young people, see Grosse, *Aus dem Umkreis der Kamine,* 55.
45. For an account of the entire journey see Unsdorfer, *The Yellow Star,* 117–124.
46. See Ivan Ivanji's account in Grosse, *Aus dem Umkreis der Kamine,* 67.
47. Grosse, *Aus dem Umkreis der Kamine,* 89, 92.
48. Nikolaus Wachsmann, *KL: A History of the Nazi Concentration Camps* (New York: FSG, 2015), 468–469. See also Grosse, *Aus dem Umkreis der Kamine,* 77.
49. See Jeremy Adler, "The One Who Got Away," *Times Literary Supplement* (October 4, 1996): 18. Such an act of defiance through dignity was quite irrational and risked execution. While no absolute date and locale is recorded for this event, Niederorschel would seem the most likely place, given the commandant's intolerance for trivial violations followed by sudden beatings, as well as the fact that the commandant of Niederorschel is the only official Adler mentions having had a problem with. Otto Wolken reports a similar incident involving a prisoner named Dr. Günther Braun, a professor of dermatology at Rostock University, in the Quarantine Camp of Birkenau at about the same time Adler was housed there. Braun was slapped by the SS man, then severely beaten and kicked by the Kapo standing by, but the dignity of his request might well have inspired Adler to stand up to Masorsky a few weeks later in Niederorschel. See Otto Wolken, "Chronik des Quarantänelagers Birkenau," in *AZB,* 144.
50. Wachsmann, *KL,* 452–454.
51. Grosse, *Aus dem Umkreis der Kamine,* 62–67.
52. Ibid., 67, 107.
53. Transport Records, Auschwitz-Birkenau State Museum. See also ibid., 196.
54. Unsdorfer, *The Yellow Star,* 147.
55. Ibid., 148.
56. See Grosse, *Aus dem Umkreis der Kamine,* 67. He quotes Ivanji as working in the weaving mill. Given Adler's later correspondence with Drössler and his lifelong friendship with Ivanji, most likely he worked alongside both in the weaving mill. Adler is listed as a skilled cutter in a December 1944 work report, further supporting the likelihood of his working alongside Drössler. Grosse agreed with this conjecture when I interviewed him in Niederorschel on May 26, 2016.
57. Jeremy Adler, "H. G. Adler: Letters to Johannes Drössler," in *Der Mnemosyne Träume: Festschrift zum 80. Geburtstag von Joseph P. Strelka,* ed. Ilona Slawinski et al. (Marburg: Francke, 2007), 16.
58. J. Adler, "The One Who Got Away," 18.
59. J. Adler, "H. G. Adler: Letters to Johannes Drössler," 11.
60. *AW,* 255.
61. Ibid., 258.
62. For Schiff's work assignment and theft of paper see Unsdorfer, *The Yellow Star,* 147, 169.
63. Grosse, *Aus dem Umkreis der Kamine,* 100.
64. Wolfgang Grosse, "Niederorschel," in *Der Ort des Terrors: Geschichte der nationalsoziallistischen Konzentrationslager, Vol. 3—Sachsenhausen, Buchenwald,* ed. Wolfgang Benz and Barbara Distel (Munich: C.H. Beck, 2006), 536.
65. Grosse, *Aus dem Umkreis der Kamine,* 128.
66. Unless otherwise noted, details of the founding, organization, mortality rate, and function of Langenstein-Zwieberge are from Denise Wesenberg's "Langenstein-Zwieberge" in *Der Ort des Terrors: Geschichte der nationalsoziallistischen Konzentrationslager, Vol. 3—Sachsenhausen, Buchenwald,* ed. Wolfgang Benz and Barbara Distel (Munich: C.H. Beck, 2006), 487–491.
67. André Sellier, *A History of the Dora Camp,* trans. Stephen Wright and Susan Taponier (Chicago: Ivan R. Dee, 2003), 227.

68. See the account of Mierwaldis Berzins-Birze in *Die Kraft im Unglück: Erinnerungen an Langenstein-Zwieberge—Außenlager des KZ Buchenwald*, ed. Ellen Fauser (Langenstein: Stiftung Gedenkstätten Sachsen-Anhalt, n.d.), 36. I am indebted to Frau Fauser for an extensive tour of the camp arranged by Manfred Sundermann, and to Jeremy Adler for pointing out the connection to Goethe and Klopstock.
69. *S*, 336.
70. For Adler's account see *LWU*. Adler depicts the same incident in *P*, 391–392.
71. For further corroboration of the officer's discovery of the poems, see also J. Adler, "The One Who Got Away," 18.
72. Adler, letter to Kurt Kotouč, August 10, 1945. Kotouč was also imprisoned in Niederorschel and after the war returned to his native Czechoslovakia. Ivan Ivanji also confirmed this in a June 20, 2011, author interview.
73. *AW*, 265.
74. Account of Victor Oden in Fauser, *Die Kraft im Unglück*, 66.
75. Account of Paul Le Goupil in Fauser, *Die Kraft im Unglück*, 72. See also account of Ivan Ivanji in Grosse, *Aus dem Umkreis der Kamine*, 197.
76. Sellier, *A History of the Dora Camp*, 228.
77. Account of Edmund Wojnowski in Fauser, *Die Kraft im Unglück*, 74.
78. The Czech's name appears in a letter from Charles Odic to Adler, November 28, 1946. My thanks to Isabel Filkins for translating the French of Odic's letters to Adler.
79. For details of Adler and Ivanji's liberation see Grosse, *Aus dem Umkreis der Kamine*, 197.
80. Adler, "Schilderung des Verfolgungsvorganges," *DLA*.
81. *S*, 336.
82. *LB*, November 23, 1945.
83. *LWU*.
84. Ibid.
85. H. G. Adler, letter to Johannes Drössler, August 2, 1947, in J. Adler, "H. G. Adler: Letters to Johannes Drössler," 15.

Chapter 10

1. *LFBS*, June 22, 1945, in *ZV*, 68.
2. See *ZV*, 321. Steiner did not finally leave until 1938, but he credited Burghart's advice as having saved his life.
3. *LFBS*, July 9, 1945, in *ZV*, 69–70.
4. *LFBS*, July 30, 1945, in *ZV*, 70–72.
5. *LHGA*, August 7, 1945, in *ZV*, 73.
6. Adler, *LB*, January 11, 1946.
7. Bettina's first letter to him was written in English. He begins his by saying she can continue to write in English, or even French, but he needs German to adequately say what he wishes to write to her. After receiving this letter, Bettina writes to him in German as well.
8. Sven Kramer observes, "There is a performative aspect to the negotiation and establishment of a shared narration of their postwar lives," and that what was at stake held the potential to actually change their lives. Sven Kramer, "Shaping Survival Through Writing: H. G. Adler's Correspondence with Bettina Gross, 1945–1947," in *H. G. Adler—Life, Literature, and Legacy*, ed. Julia Creet, Sara R. Horowitz, and Amira Bojadzija-Dan (Evanston, IL: Northwestern UP, 2016), 70.
9. *LHGA*, October 21, 1945.
10. *LB*, November 20, 1945.
11. Ibid., November 23, 1945.
12. *LHGA*, November 28, 1945.
13. Ibid., November 30, 1945.
14. *LHGA*, December 1, 1945.
15. Ibid., December 4, 1945.
16. *LB*, December 5, 1945.
17. Second *LB*, December 5, 1945.

18. *LB*, December 7, 1945.
19. Kramer, "Shaping Survival Through Writing," 78.
20. *AW*, 298.
21. *W*, 329.

Chapter 11

1. Fritz Groothues, radio interview with Adler, marked "Broadcast in Berlin, Fall 1985," *DLA*.
2. Adler, *LFBS*, August 30, 1945, in *ZV*, 79.
3. According to Jeremy Adler, his friend and doctor Wolfgang Burghart estimated that he had lost ten years of life expectancy as a result of the camps.
4. Information on Bettina's childhood is in a brief memoir written by Emanuel Gross, *DLA*. Jeremy Adler supplied information about her time in Wales in a letter to the author, January 4, 2016.
5. *LFBS*, October 3, 1945, in *ZV*, 87.
6. Pavel Kohn, *Schlösser der Hoffnung: Die geretteten Kinder des Přemsyl Pitter erinnern sich* (Munich: Langen Müller, 2001), 22–23. See also Olga Fierz, *Kinderschicksale in den Wirren der Nachkriegszeit: Eine Rettungsaktion für jüdische und deutsche Kinder 1945–1947 in der Tschechoslowakei* (Fürth im Wald: Vitales, 2000), 175.
7. Fierz, *Kinderschicksale in den Wirren der Nachkriegszeit*, 176.
8. Kohn, *Schlösser der Hoffnung*, 87.
9. Fierz, *Kinderschicksale in den Wirren der Nachkriegszeit*, 45.
10. Kohn, *Schlösser der Hoffnung*, 127.
11. Ibid., 124–125.
12. Author interview with Yehuda Bacon, April 16, 2014.
13. Jeremy Adler notes that if his father had possessed the means, he would have adopted Bacon.
14. Fierz, *Kinderschicksale in den Wirren der Nachkriegszeit*, 148.
15. Kohn, *Schlösser der Hoffnung*, 24.
16. Ibid., 25.
17. Steiner, *LHGA*, August 19, 1945, in *ZV*, 77. Throughout the fall of 1945, Steiner continued to ask Adler's help in reestablishing his Czechoslovak citizenship after having identified as Jewish in the 1930 census.
18. Adler, *LFBS*, January 22, 1947, in *ZV*, 136. Sattler's occupation is mentioned by Ernst Wiechert in a letter to Bettina Gross, September 2, 1946, *DLA*.
19. Adler, *LFBS*, November 20, 1945, in *ZV*, 101.
20. Jan Björn Potthast, *Das jüdische Zentralmuseum der SS in Prag: Gegenforschung und Völkermord im Nationalsozialismus* (Frankfurt: Campus Verlag, 2002), 268. Adler also describes these figures in *The Wall*.
21. For a discussion of Adler and Shek's collection of materials, see *T*, 704. Adler also wrote a summation of the state of the museum's collection in 1946, "Theresienstadt im Prager Jüdischen Museum," *DLA*.
22. For a discussion of the transition from Shek's project to Adler's work at the museum see Magda Veselská, "Early Documentation of the Shoah in the Czech Lands: The Documentation Project and the Prague Jewish Museum (1945–1947)," *Judaica Bohemiae* 1 (2017): 47–87.
23. Second *LB*, December 5, 1945.
24. *W*, 385.
25. Adler, *LB*, January 14, 1947.
26. Derek Sayer, *The Coasts of Bohemia: A Czech History*, trans. Alena Sayer (Princeton: Princeton UP, 1998), 240.
27. Ibid., 242–243.
28. *LFBS*, January 30, 1946, in *ZV*, 112.
29. Police Registry, Czech National Archives.
30. *LFBS*, November 8, 1945, in *ZV*, 93.
31. *LFBS*, August 30, 1945, in *ZV*, 81.
32. First *LB*, December 5, 1945.
33. *LB*, December 11, 1945.

34. Ibid., December 9, 1945.
35. Ibid., December 11, 1945.
36. *NB*, 47.
37. Sven Kramer, "Shaping Survival Through Writing: H. G. Adler's Correspondence with Bettina Gross, 1945–1947," in *H. G. Adler—Life, Literature, and Legacy*, ed. Julia Creet, Sara R. Horowitz, and Amira Bojadzija-Dan (Evanston, IL: Northwestern UP, 2016), 81.
38. *LB*, December 13, 1945.
39. Ibid., December 19, 1945.
40. See Peter Longereich, *The Unwritten Order: Hitler's Role in the Final Solution* (Stroud: The History Press, 2001), 31–34, and Michael Stolleis, *Nahes Unrecht, fernes Recht: Zur Juristischen Zeitgeschichte im 20. Jahrhundert* (Göttingen: Wallstein, 2014), 48–61.
41. See Kramer, "Shaping Survival Through Writing," 74–76.
42. *LB*, December 19, 1945.
43. Ibid., December 23, 1945.
44. *LHGA*, January 2, 1946.
45. Ibid., December 15, 1945.
46. Ibid., December 15, 1945.
47. *LB*, December 17, 1945.
48. *LHGA*, January 11, 1946.
49. Ibid., December 30, 1945.
50. *LB*, December 30, 1945.
51. Ibid., January 6, 1946.
52. *LHGA*, January 11, 1946.
53. *LB*, January 6, 1946.
54. *LYB*, August 31, 1947.
55. Ibid., September 15, 1947.
56. Ibid., December 15, 1947.
57. Ibid., July 29, 1953, and March 25, 1953, respectively.
58. Ibid., July 29, 1953, and Friedrich Danielis, "'Es gäbe es noch viel mehr zu berichten . . .': Interview mit H. G. Adler," *Das Pult* 14, no. 63 (1982): 47.
59. *LB*, January 6, 1946.
60. Ibid., February 12, 1946.
61. Ibid., May 6, 1946.
62. Ibid., March 4, 1946.
63. *LHGA*, December 12, 1945.
64. Ibid., December 26, 1945.
65. Ibid., January 12, 1946.
66. *LB*, January 6, 1946.
67. Ibid., June 6, 1946.
68. Adler, "Der Besuch," *DLA*.
69. *AW*, 302.
70. *LHGA*, September 14, 1946.
71. Ibid., September 4, 1946.
72. *LB*, September 23, 1946.
73. *LHGA*, September 15, 1946.
74. *LB*, September 23, 1946.
75. *LHGA*, September 23, 1946.
76. Ibid., September 25, 1946.
77. *LB*, September 24, 1946.
78. *LHGA*, September 15, 1946.
79. Ibid., September 26, 1946.
80. Ibid., September 15, 1946.
81. Ibid., September 15, 1946.
82. *LB*, September 24, 1946.
83. *LHGA*, September 25, 1946.
84. Ibid., September 26, 1946.

85. *LB*, September 26, 1946.
86. Ibid., December 9, 1946.
87. Jewish Community of Prague, *LHGA*, October 1, 1946, *DLA*.
88. *LFBS*, December 21, 1946, in *ZV*, 129. Jeremy Adler notes that, at Bettina's urging, Alfred Wiener wrote a letter in support of Adler's visa application.
89. *LB*, December 9, 1946.
90. Ibid., January 19, 1947.
91. Ibid., February 4, 1947.
92. Ibid., February 3, 1947.

Chapter 12

1. Bettina Adler, account dated July 14, 1989, *DLA*.
2. *BB*, 56.
3. Ibid., 57. See also *OB*, 44.
4. *BB*, 40.
5. *S*, 327.
6. *BB*, 47.
7. Elias Canetti, *The Play of the Eyes*, trans. Ralph Mannheim (New York: Farrar, Straus, Giroux, 2005), 318. Also see *BB*, 45.
8. *OB*, 119.
9. *BB*, 41, and *OB*, 105.
10. *BB*, 46–49.
11. Jeremy Adler, "'Mensch oder Masse?' H. G. Adler, Elias Canetti and the Crowd," in *Literatur und Anthropologie*, ed. Jeremy Adler and Gesa Dane (Göttingen: Wallstein, 2014), 195, 191, respectively. See also *T*, 565.
12. Letter from Jeremy Adler, February 8, 2016.
13. Eiluned and Peter Lewis, *The Land of Wales*, 2nd edition (London: B.T. Batsford, 1945), 58. See also Maxwell Fraser, *West of Offa's Dyke: South Wales* (London: Robert Hale, 1958), 96–97.
14. Lewis, *Land of Wales*, 60.
15. *LFBS*, December 21, 1946, in *ZV*, 130. Tully notes that, because of his Czech citizenship, Steiner could not serve as the official witness, although he took on that role at the ceremony.
16. *W*, 558.
17. For an overview of the group and a selection from Fried's anthology, see Jeremy Adler, "An Unknown Group of Exile Poets in London," *Literatur und Kultur des Exils in Grossbritannien*, ed. Siglinde Bolbecher et al., *Zwischenwelt* IV (1995): 163–192. See also *OB*, 87–98.
18. The reason the anthology was not published was a lack of funds, although Fried had published a selection of his own poems and one of Steiner's two years earlier.
19. *AW*, 291. Jeremy Adler's essay on the group includes this poem, but I have translated the version found in *AW*, it being slightly different than that used in Fried's anthology. For Fried's letter to Claasen see *OB*, 94.
20. Franz Baermann Steiner, *Am stürzenden Pfad: Gesammelte Gedichte*, ed. Jeremy Adler (Göttingen: Wallstein Verlag, 2000), 257.
21. *W*, 615.
22. J. Adler, "An Unknown Group of Exile Poets in London," 174.
23. Steiner, letter to Rudolf Hartung, July 4, 1948, quoted in *OB*, 94.
24. *W*, 93.
25. Ibid., 97.
26. Ibid., 182.
27. Ibid., 451.
28. Grete Fischer, *Dienstboten, Brecht und Andere* (Olten and Freiburg im Breisgau: Walter Verlag, 1966), 336.
29. Anthony Grenville, *Jewish Refugees from Germany and Austria in Britain 1933–1970: Their Image in AJR Information* (London: Vallentine Mitchell, 2010), 126.
30. Email from Jeremy Adler, January 7, 2016.

31. Ibid.
32. In a letter to Steiner on January 23, 1949, Adler provides a window onto such neglect. He does not expect to receive help from Ernst Kaiser, a friend of Steiner's in London who had translated some of Steiner's poems. "At your suggestion I called him up, and he began to talk at length, though mostly about how little time he had. He said he would certainly call me back, and that I could drop off the manuscript [of his novel *Panorama*] before leaving [for Cologne], but nothing ever happened, although it would have cost him nothing to follow through." See *ZV*, 161.
33. Louise London, *Whitehall and the Jews* (Cambridge, UK: Cambridge UP, 2001), 11. Of these 90,000, some 80,000 were Jewish refugees, while another 50,000 to 60,000 Jewish refugees fled Communist regimes in the late 1940s and 1950s. See Angela Davis, "Belonging and 'Unbelonging': Jewish Refugee and Survivor Women in 1950s Britain," *Women's History Review*, 26, no. 1 (2017).
34. Letter to Ernst Wiechert, May 1, 1946.
35. Letter to Ernst Wiechert, late March 1947.
36. Manuscript for BBC Deutsche Sendung review of *Der Totenwald*, broadcast May 20, 1947, *DLA*.
37. *LYB*, May 29, 1947.
38. See *OB*, 91. Grete Fischer, whom Adler met in October 1947, and who had left Prague for England in 1934, four years earlier than Fried, would seem to have also been in a position to help Adler, for she had placed ten scripts with the German Service between August 1940 and March 1942. However, she often failed to provide the kind of propaganda demanded by her editors and had trouble navigating the political and cultural demands of wartime England. See Jennifer Taylor, "Grete Fischer: 'Outside Writer' for the BBC," in *'Stimme der Wahrheit': German-language Broadcasting by the BBC*, ed. Charmian Brinson and Richard Dove, *The Yearbook of the Research Centre for German and Austrian Exile Studies 5* (Amsterdam: Rodopi, 2003), 43–55.
39. *LB*, March 8, 1947.
40. Ibid., March 11, 1947.
41. Ibid., March 5, 1947.
42. Ibid., April 21, 1947.
43. Interview with Jeremy Adler, May 16, 2016, while visiting all three of Adler's London residences. That the Adlers also were not welcomed by the Jewish residents of the neighborhood was not unusual, as tensions prevailed between Anglo-Jews and more assimilated and secular Jews arriving from the continent. See Anthony Grenville, "Religion," in *Changing Countries: The Experience and Achievement of German-speaking Exiles from Hitler in Britain from 1933 to Today*, ed. Marian Malet and Anthony Grenville (London: Libris, 2002), 179.
44. Stefan Howell and Irene Wells, "Everyday Life in Prewar and Wartime Britain," in *Changing Countries: The Experience and Achievement of German-speaking Exiles from Hitler in Britain from 1933 to Today*, ed. Marian Malet and Anthony Grenville (London: Libris, 2002), 103–104. Figures on Adler's finances come from his statement to the National Health Service on March 7, 1950, *DLA*.
45. Interview with Jeremy Adler, May 16, 2016.
46. Adler, statements to National Insurance, March 7, 1950, and June 1, 1955, *DLA*. In a November 3, 1951, letter to Bettina, Adler mentions how much a loan from Canetti has helped. The notation of a loan of £200 appears in the 1950 statement to the National Insurance, preceding the 1951 mention of Canetti's loan, but it is likely the same loan, for Adler mentions no other loan. Given Canetti's financial struggles, the loan likely came from his lover Marie-Louise von Motesiczky, whose family was wealthy. Steiner gave £25 to Adler outright and would hear nothing of it being paid back. See Steiner, *LHGA*, August 18, 1950, in *ZV*, 250.
47. "Erinnerungen an Leo Baeck, den deutschen Widerstand und die Konzentrationslager. Gespräch mit Herrn Dr. H. G. Adler," in *Deutschland Berichte* 21, no. 3 (March 1985): 43. Adler recalls Baeck depositing $300 in his account in *LFK*, March 21, 1954.
48. *LB*, February 25 and March 5, 1947. See letter from Albert Hyamson, February 27, 1947, inviting him to speak at the synagogue. See also *T*, 625 and H. G. Adler, "Die Geschichte des Prager Jüdischen Museums," in *Monatshefte* 103/2 (Summer 2011): 161.

49. http://www.wienerlibrary.co.uk/Our-History (accessed January 10, 2018). Ilse Wolff, chief librarian from 1947 to 1966, recalled the strong community at the Wiener Library and in neighboring Manchester Square, where celebrations broke out with the announcement of the founding of Israel in 1948. See Marietta Bearman and Erna Woodgate, "Postwar: The Challenge of Settling Down," in *Changing Countries: The Experience and Achievement of German-speaking Exiles from Hitler in Britain from 1933 to Today*, ed. Marian Malet and Anthony Grenville (London: Libris, 2002), 223.
50. Adler, "Concentration Camps to be Investigated by Social Science," *The Wiener Library Bulletin* 1, no. 3/4 (March–May 1947): 15.
51. Lawrence L. Langer, *Versions of Survival: The Holocaust and the Human Spirit* (Albany: SUNY Press, 1982), 4–5.
52. Saul Friedlander, *Memory, History, and the Extermination of the Jews of Europe* (Bloomington: Indiana UP, 1993), viii. For an analysis of Friedlander's method see Hayden White, "Historical Discourse and Literary Theory: On Saul Friedlander's Years of Extermination," in *Den Holocaust erzählen? Historiographie zwischen eissenschaftlicher Empirie und narrativer Kreativität*, ed. Norbert Frei and Wulf Kansteiner (Göttingen: Wallstein, 2013).
53. Fischer, *Dienstboten, Brecht und Andere*, 336–337.
54. See Christopher R. Browning, *The Origins of the Final Solution: The Evolution of Nazi Jewish Policy, September 1939–March 1942* (Lincoln: U of Nebraska P, 2004), 299–300 and 431–433.
55. *T*, 95.
56. For discussion of the relationship between Adler's use of objective fact and subjective response, see Peter Filkins, "Both Sides of the Wall: Theresienstadt in H. G. Adler's Scholarship and Fiction," in *Literatur und Anthropologie: H. G. Adler, Elias Canetti und Franz Barman Steiner in London* (Göttingen: Waldstein, 2014), 82–96, specifically 83–84.
57. Peter Staengle, "H. G. Adler," in *Kritisches Lexikon zur Deutschsprachigen Gegenwartsliteratur*. 44. Nachlieferung (Munich: Text + Kritik, 1993), 7.
58. Filkins, "Both Sides of the Wall," 88–91. See also Jeremy Adler, "Afterword," *T*, 805.
59. *T*, 126.
60. Ibid., 128.
61. Hayden White observes a similar effect, noting how in Saul Friedlander's *The Years of Extermination* "the text is replete with different literary, rhetorical, or discursive genres . . . which at once punctuate the narration and impede narrativization and, at the same time, create a level of figurative meaning alongside of and modulating the facts given in the chronological record." See Hayden White, "Historical Truth, Estrangement, and Disbelief," conference paper uploaded to https://www.academia.edu/9052840/Friedlander_Estrangement_and_Disbelief (accessed January 10, 2018).
62. *T*, 128–129.
63. Ibid., 129.
64. Miroslav Kárný, Vojtěch Blodig, and Margita Kárná, eds., *Theresienstadt in der "Endlösung der Judenfrage"* (Prague: Panorama, 1992), 26–27; Ruth Bondy, conference proceeding, quoted in *PFS*, 162; Livia Rothkirchen, "The Zionist Character of the 'Self-Government' of Terezin (Theresienstadt): A Study in Historiography," in *Yad Vashem Studies* XI (1976): 56–90; Wolfgang Benz, *Theresienstadt: Eine Geschichte von Täuschung und Vernichtung* (Munich: C.H. Beck, 2013), 8, 227. The letter from Adler-Rudel and the letters to and from Franz Wurm are quoted in *OB*, 140.
65. *T*, xvii.
66. Ibid., 16.
67. Ibid., 63.
68. Ibid., 75.
69. Ibid., 97.
70. Ibid., 98.
71. Ibid., xvii.
72. Ibid., 568
73. Ibid., 594, and letter to Gershom Scholem, October 2, 1963, *DLA*.
74. Ibid., 594.
75. Ibid., 181.

76. Ibid., 204.
77. H. G. Adler, "Gedanken zu einer Soziologie des Konzentrationslagers," in *WV*, 142.
78. *T*, 560.
79. Ibid., 558.
80. Ibid., 562.
81. Ibid., 565.
82. Ibid., 561.
83. Jeremy Adler quotes Hermann Levin Goldschmidt's description of the book as a prophetic "accusation," while he sees it as "pronouncing a Biblical warning." See "Afterword," in *T*, 807.
84. *T*, 567.
85. Ibid., 568–569.
86. Ibid., 569.
87. Ibid., 570.
88. Jeremy Adler observes that in even coining the term "Zwangsgemeinschaft," "The author accepts neither the vocabulary of the Nazis nor the traditional concepts of social science. He wants to rethink modernity." See "Afterword," in *T*, 804.
89. *T*, 570
90. *LFK*, September 22, 1955.
91. *T*, xx–xxi.
92. "Sonderinterview von Alfred Joachim Fischer mit H. G. Adler," in *ZE*, 194–195.
93. *T*, xxi.
94. Adler, "Warum habe ich mein Buch *Theresienstadt 1941–1945* geschrieben?" in *WV*, 111.
95. " 'Es gäbe viel Merkwürdiges zu berichten': Interview with Hans Christoph Knebusch," in *WV*, 45.
96. *T*, 601.
97. *S*, 342.
98. *T*, 601.
99. J. Adler, "Afterword," in *T*, 808.
100. *T*, 601.
101. Rüdiger Görner, "Überleben—Überwinden?: Eine Betrachtung zum Werk H. G. Adlers," in *Salzburger Jahrbuch Für Philosophie* XXXV (1990): 82.

Chapter 13

1. Adler's notes on his lectures to German POWs and his "Kurzer Lebensbericht" of December 1952, *DLA*. See also " 'Es gäbe viel Merkwürdiges zu berichten': Interview with Hans Christoph Knebusch," in *WV*, 58.
2. Adler, "Kurzer Lebensbericht," *DLA*.
3. Letter from Jeremy Adler, April 2, 2016.
4. *S*, 338.
5. Adler announced the name to Steiner in an October 2, 1947, letter as "Jeremias Joshua David Adler," his usage of the German version of "Jeremy" harkening to a world now lost to him. See Tully, in *ZV*, 148.
6. Letter to Elias Canetti, October 23, 1947, quoted in Ulrich van Loyen, *Franz Baermann Steiner: Exil und Verwandlung* (Bielefeld: Aisthesis Verlag, 2011), 438. Otto Dov Kulka first pointed out the significance of the names when I interviewed him on March 17, 2014, in Jerusalem. Jeremy Adler confirmed this in an email to the author on December 29, 2015.
7. Steiner, *LHGA*, October 10, 1947, in *ZV*, 149.
8. The German original of the poem is from a special issue of *Modern Poetry in Translation*, ed. Michael Hamburger, No. 2, New Series (Autumn 1992): 74–86. I have slightly emended Hamburger's translation.
9. Carol Tully, "Franz Baermann Steiner and Spain: 'The Prayer in the Garden' and Manrique's 'Coplas a la muerte de su padre,' " in *From Prague Poet to Oxford Anthropologist: Franz Baermann Steiner Celebrated*, ed. Jeremy Adler, Richard Fardon, and Carol Tully (Munich: Iudicium, 2003), 148–149.

10. On Steiner's relations with women and longing for a family, see "Letter from H. G. Adler to Chaim Rabin," in *From Prague Poet to Oxford Anthropologist: Franz Baermann Steiner Celebrated*, ed. Jeremy Adler, Richard Fardon, and Carol Tully (Munich: Iudicium, 2003), 236.
11. Adler, "Die ethische Grundideee der *Ansiedlung*, ausgelegt nach dem Text," manuscript, *DLA*.
12. Grete Fischer, *Dienstboten, Brecht und Andere* (Olten and Freiburg im Breisgau: Walter Verlag, 1966), 335–336.
13. Adler, letter to Hans Hennecke, November 24, 1951.
14. Adler, letter to Stephan Zapletal, July 23, 1970.
15. Jeremy Adler, letter to the author, April 2, 2016.
16. *LFW*, June 4, 1953, quoted in *OB*, 137.
17. Adler, "Nachruf bei Lebzeiten," in *WV*, 11.
18. Atze cites the letter from Veza Canetti, no doubt written on her husband's behalf. See *OB*, 131. For Adler's hope for publication in the United States, see "Zu Hause im Exil" in *WV*, 22.
19. Hermann Broch, *LHGA*, September 10, 1948, in *HBHGA*, 147.
20. *HBHGA*, Letter 4, 188n1.
21. *HBHGA*, 149, and 189n1.
22. Quoted in John J. White and Ronald Speir's introduction, in *HBHGA*, 138.
23. *LWU*.
24. Hermann Broch, *LHGA*, December 9, 1949, in *HBHGA*, 162.
25. Ibid., 163–164.
26. Adler, letter to Hermann Broch, December 16, 1949, in *HBHGA*, 166, 168.
27. Ibid., 166.
28. Ibid., 168.
29. Adler, letter to Hermann Broch, September 24, 1948, in *HBHGA*, 148.
30. Adler, letter to Dr. Bloch, n.d., *HBHGA*, 153. For Canetti's suggestions see *OB*, 132.
31. Adler, letter to Hermann Broch, July 4, 1949, in *HBHGA*, 160.
32. *LFBS*, December 12, 1948, in *ZV*, 160.
33. *LFBS*, January 23, December 12, and December 20, 1949, in *ZV*, 161, 205, 211.
34. *LFBS*, October 6, 1949, in *ZV*, 180–181.
35. *LFBS*, December 20, 1949, in *ZV*, 211.
36. Letter to Hermann Broch, July 7, 1950, in *HBHGA*, 183 and 181, respectively. White and Speirs employ "de-ranged" to render the odd hyphenation of "ver-rückt" in the German. See 199n7.
37. *LTWA*, April 4, 1950. For discussion of Adler and Adorno's correspondence, see Jeremy Adler, "'Die Macht des Guten im Rachen des Bösen,'" *Merkur*, 54, no. 6 (June 2000): 475–486, and *BB*, 98–101.
38. Adorno uses "ugly" or "hässlich" in responding to Adler having quoted his call for the need to use "inhumanity" ("Unmenschlichkeit") in modern art, but Adler does not use "hässlich" in his first letter.
39. Theodor W. Adorno, *Gesammelte Schriften*, vol. 10, ed. Rolf Tiedemann et al. (Frankfurt: Suhrkamp, 1997), 30.
40. *LHGA*, July 26, 1950.
41. Jeremy Adler, "Good against Evil?: H. G. Adler, T.W. Adorno and the Representation of the Holocaust," in *Studies in Social and Political Thought 2: Social Theory After the Holocaust*, ed. Robert Fine and Charles Turner (Liverpool: Liverpool UP, 2000), 91.
42. *LTWA*, September 28, 1950.
43. Adler, *LB*, February 28, 1955.
44. White and Speirs' introduction, *HBHGA*, 142.
45. *LTWA*, April 21, 1955. Adorno confirms sending a strong recommendation in his response on April 25, 1955.
46. *LTWA*, June 13, 1955.
47. Adorno was the son of a secular Jewish father and a Catholic mother. He later converted to Protestantism.
48. Jeremy Adler discusses this caricature in *BB*, 102–107.
49. http://www.jta.org/1956/06/11/archive/frankfurt-university-introduces-lectures-on-jewish-history (accessed January 12, 2018).

50. *W*, 97.
51. Ibid., 333
52. Ibid., 336.
53. I am indebted to Robert Bell of Williams College on the possible etymology of Prufrock's name.
54. Adler's caricature of Adorno could hardly have stung, for Adorno never read it. *The Wall* was drafted initially in 1956, and Adler was writing it when the two first met face to face, but it was not published until 1989, a year after Adler's death and twenty years after Adorno's.
55. T.W. Adorno, *Negative Dialectics*, trans. E.B. Ashton (New York: Seabury, 1973), 367–368.
56. Jeremy Adler, "The One Who Got Away," *Times Literary Supplement* (October 4, 1996): 19, and *BB*, 104ff.
57. *LTWA*, October 29, 1956, and Adorno, *LHGA*, October 31, 1956.
58. E. Richter, *LHGA*, November 8, 1956.
59. *LTWA*, April 4, 1957.
60. A cousin of Bettina's who escaped Prague on a Kindertransport in 1939 and who in 1949 moved to Zurich, Wurm became friends with Paul Celan and Beckett and remained Adler's closest literary correspondent after Steiner's death.
61. *LFW*, January 26, 1959. Jeremy Adler also confirmed in a March 13, 2016, email that H. G. Adler frequently made the same remark in private. An occasion for this would have been when Adler took his son to see *Waiting for Godot* in London in 1965, but in fact Jeremy recalls his father liking the production of Beckett's play at the Royal Court Theater.
62. Armin Halstenberg, "'Ich bin ein denkender Dichter,'" interview with H. G. Adler in *Kölner Stadt-Anzeiger: Bunte Blätter* (March 16–17, 1974): 2.
63. *BB*, 103–107.
64. J. Adler, "Die Macht des Guten im Rachen des Bösen," 484–485.
65. Adorno, *Negative Dialectics*, 380–381.
66. *BB*, 105.
67. Theodor W. Adorno, *Gesammelte Schriften*, vol. 20, ed. Rolf Tiedemann et al. (Frankfurt: Suhrkamp, 1997), 495.
68. See Tully, in *ZV*, 170–201.
69. Steiner, *LHGA*, November 28 and December 23, 1949, in *ZV*, 202 and 212.
70. *LFBS*, September 14, 1949, in *ZV*, 174.
71. *LFBS*, November 12, 1949, in *ZV*, 194.
72. Anthony Grenville, "Club 1943," in *AJR Journal* 11, no. 12 (2011), 1–2.
73. For an overview of intellectual life among refugees see Anthony Grenville, *Jewish Refugees from Germany and Austria in Britain 1933–1970: Their Image in AJR Information* (London: Vallentine Mitchell, 2010), 161–186.
74. Adler, *Comments on the English*, trans. Grete Fischer, *DLA*, 1–2. I have corrected obvious misspellings in Fischer's manuscript.
75. Ibid., 3.
76. Ibid., 4–5.
77. Ibid., 64.
78. Adler, *LFBS*, July 4, 1950, in *ZV*, 243. Jeremy Adler recalls the specific illness and their lying on mattresses on the floor at the home of Bettina's cousin.
79. Email from Jeremy Adler to the author, January 6, 2016.
80. Adler, *LFBS*, August 27, 1951, in *ZV*, 268.
81. Adler, "Kurzer Lebensbericht," *DLA*.
82. Ibid.
83. Wilhelm Unger, "Das andere Deutschland," in *BF*, 16–17.
84. *LB*, September 26, 1951.
85. Adler, *LFBS*, August 27, 1951, in *ZV*, 271, and *LB*, September 29, 1951.
86. For a discussion of Adler's thoughts on language see Lynn L. Wolff, "'Die Grenzen des Sagbaren': Toward a Political Philology in H. G. Adler's Reflections on Language," in *H. G. Adler—Life, Literature, and Legacy*, ed. Julia Creet, Sara R. Horowitz, and Amira Bojadzija-Dan (Evanston, IL: Northwestern UP, 2016), 273–301.
87. *LB*, February 9, 1955.
88. Ibid., February 24, 1955.

89. Ibid., February 9, 1955.
90. Adler, letter to Esther Frank, November 29, 1952. See also Ulrich van Loyen, *Franz Baermann Steiner: Exile und Verwandlung, zur Biografie eines deutschen Dichters und jüdischen Ethnologen* (Bielefeld: Aisthesis Verlag), 614.
91. Adler, "Letter to Chaim Rabin," in *From Prague Poet to Oxford Anthropologist: Franz Baermann Steiner Celebrated*, ed. Jeremy Adler, Richard Fardon, and Carol Tully (Munich: Iudicium, 2003), 225.
92. Adler, *Über Franz Baermann Steiner: "Brief an Chaim Rabin,"* ed. Jeremy Adler and Carol Tully (Göttingen: Wallstein, 2006), 67.
93. Franz Baermann Steiner, "Letter to George Rapp, October 29, 1943," in *Orientpolitik, Value, and Civilization: Franz Baermann Steiner: Selected Writings, Vol. II*, ed. Jeremy Adler and Richard Fardon (Oxford: Bergahn, 1999), 116–117.
94. Canetti speculated that Steiner died from joy when Murdoch proposed marriage, causing his heart to "burst smilingly," although it is generally agreed that after seeing Murdoch the night before, he died while on the phone to someone the next day. See Peter Conradi, *Iris Murdoch: A Life* (New York: Norton, 2001), 350, and in J. Adler and Fardon, eds., *Franz Baermann Steiner*, 10.
95. Hamburger, *Modern Poetry in Translation*, 86, my translation. Details of the memorial are noted in Adler, *Brief an Chaim Rabin*, 73.

Chapter 14

1. Jeremy Adler, "The One Who Got Away," *Times Literary Supplement* (October 4, 1996): 18.
2. *LHS*, May 25, 1954.
3. *LHGA*, June 30, 1954.
4. Siebeck, *LHGA*, June 8, 1954.
5. *LHS*, June 10, 1954. The points Adler outlines to Siebeck can also be found in Jeremy Adler's Afterword in *T*, 816–817.
6. Eugen Kogon, *The Theory and Practice of Hell*, trans. Heinz Norden (New York: Octagon, 1976), 268.
7. *T*, 562.
8. Siebeck, *LHGA*, June 30, 1954. Years later Adler took up the use of "betreuen" as a euphemism for "deportation and extermination" developed by Eichmann's office in Prague in his essay "Die Sprache der Gewalt und ihre Wörter," in *Abhandlungen aus der Pädigogischen Hochschule Berlin*, ed. Alfred Kelletat (Berlin: Colloquium, 1980), 179–217, here 201–203. Werner and Manfred Sundermann, who knew and lived with the Adlers in London in the 1970s, also confirm that its usage in everyday exchanges with any kind of administrative entity particularly upset him.
9. Siebeck, *LHGA*, June 30, 1954.
10. *LHS*, January 25, 1955.
11. Ibid., March 5, 1955.
12. Ibid., March 11, 1955.
13. For the honorarium for the article, see Adler, *LHS*, June 27, 1955. The advance for the entire book is proposed by Adler in *LHS*, March 5, 1955, and appears in the final contract dated July 19, 1955.
14. Ariel Colonomos and Andrea Armstrong, "German Reparations to the Jews After World War II: A Turning Point in the History of Reparations," in *The Handbook of Reparations*, ed. Pablo de Greif (Oxford: Oxford UP, 2008), 403.
15. *LB*, February 7, 1955. The value of Deutsche Marks is calculated in dollars based on the exchange rate at the time. Adjusted for inflation, $1,000 in 1955 would be around $8,800 in 2016. Adler's entire compensation for loss of liberty during forty months of imprisonment was roughly $13,500 in today's dollars.

    Wilhelm Unger had visited the Bundesministerium in autumn 1954 to plead Adler's case, and Adler knew by that November he would receive 5,550 Marks. See Margrit Baldner, *LHGA*, November 15, 1954. For the standard rate paid per month to prisoners, see Marilyn Henry, *Confronting the Perpetrators: A History of the Claims Conference* (London: Vallentine

Mitchell, 2007), 37. Unless otherwise noted, all figures for Adler's reparations are from documents and correspondence found in the file "Entschädigungsfragen" ("Questions of Reparations"), *DLA*.

16. Christian Pross, *Paying for the Past: The Struggle over Reparations for Surviving Victims of the Nazi Terror*, trans. Belinda Cooper (Baltimore: Johns Hopkins UP, 1998), 51.
17. Adler, letter to Margrit Baldner, December 3, 1954. It was not until a 1956 revision of the law that German-speaking citizens of other countries were recognized as displaced rather than stateless persons.
18. Konrad Hirsch, *LHGA*, October 30, 1953.
19. Pross, *Paying for the Past*, 21.
20. The highest amount available for damage to career at the time was 25,000 Marks. In applying for 10,000, Adler no doubt felt restrained by his middle-level civil class designation. See Ibid., 50.
21. Hans Reichmann, *LHGA*, April 15, 1958.
22. Pross, *Paying for the Past*, 80. See also Henry, *Confronting the Perpetrators*, 47.
23. Siebeck, *LHGA*, June 30, 1954.
24. Adler, *LHS*, April 20, 1955, and June 7, 1955. See also *T*, xi.
25. *LFW*, December 7, 1955.
26. *LHS*, November 8, 1955.
27. Ibid., July 13, 1955.
28. "'Es gäbe viel Merkwürdiges zu berichten': Interview with Hans Christoph Knebusch," in *WV*, 45.
29. *LB*, March 5, 1955.
30. "Die Sprüche der Väter," *Eckart* 26 (1957), 132.
31. Letter to Heinz Flügel, December 25, 1954.
32. Information on and quotes from Heinz Flügel appear in his Wikipedia entry at https://de.wikipedia.org/wiki/Heinz_Fl%C3%BCgel (accessed November 15, 2017).
33. *LHGA*, March 6, 1955.
34. *LB*, March 13, 1955.
35. Theodor Heuss, *Tagebuchbriefe 1955–1963* (Tübingen: Wünderlich, 1970), 161.
36. Dora Segall, *LHGA*, May 11, 1956, and August 13, 1956.
37. Letter to Kurt Oppens, June 25, 1962.
38. Peter Marchal, *Kultur- und Programmgeschichte des öffentlich-rechtlichen Hörfunks in der Bundesrepublik Deutschland: Ein Handbuch, vol. I, Grundlegung und Vorgeschichte* (Munich: Kopaed, 2004), 371, 396.
39. Letter to Kurt Oppens, July 12, 1962.
40. "Meine Erfahrungen mit Deutschland," undated manuscript (ca. 1970), *DLA*.
41. Helmut Alt, "Das 'KZ' in soziologischer Sicht: Vorlesung über Theresienstadt an der Frankfurter Universität," *Frankfurter Rundschau*, July 27, 1956, Feuilleton. Gerty Spies, manuscript for "Bericht für Evangelische Akademie Tutzing," March 22, 1956, *DLA*. Often audience members were so engaged by Adler's talks that they would introduce themselves and share their own stories afterward, in some cases leading to subsequent contact, correspondence, even friendship. Such was the case with Manfred Sundermann in Paderborn, Germany, whose father had fought in the war, as well as future friends Carlo Caratsch, Fred Kurer, and Gian Nogler in Zurich, all of whom relayed in interviews memorable first meetings with Adler at his lectures and readings.
42. Chapter 4 of Nicolas Berg's *The Holocaust and the West German Historians* provides a useful overview of the founding and mission of the Institut für Zeitgeschichte and a discussion of Adler's role within it. Unless otherwise noted, all details are taken from the American edition of the book, trans. Joel Golb (Madison: U of Wisconsin P, 2015).
43. Berg, *The Holocaust and the West German Historians*, 144.
44. Hans Buchheim, *LHGA*, August 21, 1959. Also cited in ibid., 165.
45. *VM*, xvii. Also cited in Berg, *The Holocaust and the West German Historians*, 165.
46. *VM*, xviii–xix.
47. Letter to Hans Buchheim, December 6, 1958. Also cited in Berg, *The Holocaust and the West German Historians*, 166.

48. Lucy S. Dawidowicz, *The Holocaust and the Historians* (Cambridge, MA: Harvard UP, 1981), 63.
49. Letter to Hans Buchheim, March 5, 1959. Also cited in Berg, *The Holocaust and the West German Historians*, 167.
50. Hans Buchheim, *LHGA*, May 11, 1959.
51. Adler notes this additional honorarium in *LB*, November 30, 1962. This sum was to cover eight months of work, at least four of which needed to be spent at the institute. Adler was not contracted to spend more time at the institute because he did not wish to be away from home more than two months at a time, and he needed time away from the project to produce more work for the radio and to fulfill other literary assignments.
52. Letter to Hans Buchheim, February 27, 1961.
53. Letters to Hans Buchheim, February 27, 1961, and January 27, 1961, respectively. Also cited in Berg, *The Holocaust and the West German Historians*, 167.
54. Letter to Heinz Förster, March 10, 1961. Also cited in Berg, *The Holocaust and the West German Historians*, 167.
55. Letter to Anton Hoch, December 18, 1961.
56. Berg, *The Holocaust and the West German Historians*, 145.
57. Ibid., 175.
58. Letter to Hans Buchheim, February 27, 1961. Also quoted in Ibid., 168.
59. Friedrich Danielis, " 'Es gäbe es noch viel mehr zu berichten . . .': Interview mit H. G. Adler," *Das Pult* 14, no. 63 (1982): 47.
60. H. G. Adler. "Notiz über den Deutschen Charakter," dated February 21, 1952; "Eindrücke von einer Deutschlandreise," dated April 16, 1956; "Meine Erfahrungen mit Deutschland," n.d. but clearly after 1969, all *DLA*.
61. The best-known works that discuss the culpability of everyday Germans are Christopher R. Browning's *Ordinary Men: Reserve Police Battalion 101 and the Final Solution in Poland* (New York: HarperCollins, 1992) and Daniel Jonah Goldhagen's *Hitler's Willing Executioners: Ordinary Germans and the Holocaust* (New York: Knopf, 1996).
62. *LB*, March 23, 1960.
63. Ibid., March 29, 1960.
64. Ibid., April 12, 1960.
65. Berg, *The Holocaust and the West German Historians*, 194.
66. *LB*, October 27, 1962. Indeed the vast majority of SS and the Gestapo were never convicted of any crimes or brought to trial. See U.S. Holocaust Memorial Museum, "SS: Decline, Disintegration, and Trials," Holocaust Encyclopedia: https://www.ushmm.org/wlc/en/article.php?ModuleId=10007404 (accessed November 19, 2017).
67. *LB*, October 29, 1962.
68. Bettina Adler, *LHGA*, November 2, 1962. In this period Bettina and Günther begin to number their letters again, as they did with their early correspondence between Prague and South Wales, the need for keeping business matters and news straight demanding a more orderly system in carrying out their shared project.
69. *LB*, June 8, 1963.
70. Ibid., July 4, 1963.
71. Ibid., June 6, 1965.
72. Ibid., September 22, 1965.
73. Berg, *The Holocaust and the West German Historians*, 193, 14, and 229. Helmut Krausnick was also later revealed to be a former Party member, as were other German historians of the time.
74. *LB*, September 22, 1965.
75. Ibid., September 24, 1965.
76. Ibid., November 15, 1966.
77. Berg, *The Holocaust and the West German Historians*, 169.
78. *VM*, 2–3. Quoted as well in ibid.
79. Berg, *The Holocaust and the West German Historians*, 169, 229.
80. For the Broszat/Friedlander correspondence see *Reworking the Past: Hitler, the Holocaust, and the Historians' Debate*, ed. Peter Baldwin (Boston: Beacon, 1990).

81. The entry for October 7, 1971, in Adler's pocket calendar notes the book's completion. The calendar records numerous social outings with Krausnick, Buchheim, and Förster.
82. Jacob Robinson, *LHGA*, May 16, 1966. The advance against royalties paid by Siebeck for *Der verwaltete Mensch* is also listed in Adler's contract for the book.
83. *VM*, xx.
84. Ibid., xix.
85. Ibid., xxix.
86. Ibid., xxx.
87. Friedrich Meinecke, *The German Catastrophe: Reflections and Recollections* (Boston: Beacon Press, 1950), 86, quoted in Lucy S. Dawidowicz, *The Holocaust and the Historians* (Cambridge, MA: Harvard UP, 1981), 43. For the observation on Meinecke's lack of acknowledgment of the Holocaust, see Dawidowicz, *The Holocaust and the Historians*, 58–59.
88. Friedrich Meinecke, "Irrwege in unserer Geschichte?," *Der Monat* 2 (1949): 5. Quoted in Berg, *The Holocaust and the West German Historians*, 36.
89. Martin Broszat, "The Concentration Camps 1933–45," trans. Marian Jackson, in Helmut Krausnick, Hans Buchheim, Martin Broszat, and Hans-Adolf Jacobsen, *Anatomy of the SS State* (New York: Walker, 1968), 469.
90. Heinrich Böll, "Die 32,80 RM des Jakob Strauss: Zu H. G. Adlers Buch *Der verwaltete Mensch*," in *BF*, 66.
91. *VM*, 648.
92. Ibid., 649.
93. Ibid., 650.
94. Ibid., 987.
95. Ibid., 989.
96. *LB*, April 30, 1960.
97. *VM*, xxiv.
98. Ibid., xvii, xviii.

Chapter 15

1. Adler, *LB*, May 26, 1960.
2. Ibid. Krumey remained incarcerated until he was convicted in 1965, but his sentence was only five years and he was released on time served. After an appeal by the prosecution, Krumey was retried in 1968–1969 and sentenced to life without parole. Adler supplied written testimony and documents that were used in both trials. See the Holocaust Research Project at http://www.holocaustresearchproject.org/holoprelude/eichmen.html (accessed November 22, 2017). Adler's archive contains numerous documents and news articles on the Krumey trial.
3. Adler, *LB*, May 26, 1960.
4. Ibid., March 23, 1960.
5. Ibid., May 26, 1960.
6. *LFW*, May 30, 1960. Curiously this letter turned up in the Israeli State Archives, Jerusalem, in a file containing correspondence and other documents submitted to the Israeli police.
7. Adler, *LYB*, March 28, 1961. Adler says it was Zeev Shek, former Israeli ambassador to London, then ambassador to Paris, who suggested he send it to the London embassy.
8. Adler's memorandum is in the Israeli State Archives in Jerusalem.
9. Adler notes the dates for the two meetings, July 11 and 22, 1960, in his pocket calendar. He confirms meeting with Selinger in London in *LFW*, September 6, 1960.
10. The affidavit is dated July 16–21, 1960. Adler claimed to have spent 160 hours working on it in *LYB*, September 4, 1960, and in *LFW*, September 6, 1960. Equaling roughly three to four weeks of full-time labor, this is either a calculation of time spent researching and drafting the document, before completing and signing it, or further work he put into it between July and September. The first would argue that he had been asked to supply sworn testimony by Israeli officials before he met with Selinger in London. Most likely Zeev Shek would have been behind such a request, initiating it in June while urging Adler to send his nineteen-point memorandum to the Israeli Embassy in London. That November, Adler sent a second

edition of his Theresienstadt study to Shek, asking him to send it to Israel, where it was read by the trial judge, prosecution, defense, and presumably Eichmann himself. A copy of the affidavit is in the *DLA*.

11. Ephraim Hofstadter, *LHGA*, October 5, 1960, Israel State Archives, Jerusalem.
12. Adler, letter to Ephraim Hofstadter, October 11, 1960, Israel State Archives, Jerusalem.
13. John (Dr. Hans G.) Adler, "Eidesstattliche Erklärung," November 28, 1960, Israel State Archives, Jerusalem. Adler used the forename "John" on official documents after he moved to the United Kingdom, but never in person or in letters.
14. Devin O. Pendas, *The Frankfurt Auschwitz Trial, 1963–1965: Genocide, History, and the Limits of the Law* (New York: Cambridge UP, 2006), 115.
15. Ibid., 298.
16. John (Dr. Hans G.) Adler, "Eidesstattliches Gutachten," July 21, 1960, *DLA*.
17. At his trial Eichmann claimed that he did not recall authorizing the transfer of the 115 Jews to Natzweiler, whose commandant was Josef Kramer, later commandant of Birkenau. Eichmann's claim that he did not direct the operation has been shown to be largely true, as it was Himmler who granted permission for it from above. See Deborah Lipstadt, *The Eichmann Trial* (New York: Schocken, 2011), 108, and the entry for medical experiments conducted by the SS Ahnenerbe Society on prisoners in Auschwitz at http://auschwitz.org/en/history/medical-experiments/august-hirt (accessed December 2, 2016).
18. Branik Ceslav and Carmelo Lisciotto, "The Massacre at Lidice," http://www.holocaustresearchproject.org/nazioccupation/lidice.html (accessed November 22, 2017).
19. Adler, *LYB*, November 12, 1961. The petition, however, was kept private and remained in Israel, meaning that Adler never got the chance to sign it. Instead, Buber suggested that those outside Israel should write Ben-Zvi directly. See Yehuda Bacon, *LHGA*, May 6, 1962, quoted in *OB*, 148. For views of intellectuals opposed to Eichmann's execution, see Erica Weiss, "Finding 'Neo-Israelite' Justice for Adolf Eichmann," *Hebraic Political Studies* 4, no. 2 (Spring 2009): 169–188.
20. Yechiam Weitz, "'We Have to Carry Out the Sentence,'" *Haaretz* (July 27, 2007). See also Weiss, "Finding 'Neo-Israelite' Justice for Adolf Eichmann."
21. Unsigned article, "Eichmann Begged Israel to Spare His Life, New Papers Reveal," *The Times of Israel* (January 27, 2016).
22. Weitz, "'We Have to Carry Out the Sentence.'"
23. Hannah Arendt, *Eichmann in Jerusalem: A Report on the Banality of Evil* (New York: Penguin, 1994), 286 and 262, respectively.
24. Lipstadt, *The Eichmann Trial*, 130, and Arendt, *Eichmann in Jerusalem*, 285, respectively.
25. Arendt, *Eichmann in Jerusalem*, 120.
26. Adler, "Was weiß Hannah Arendt von Eichmann und der 'Endlösung'"?, *Allgemeine Wochenzeitung der Juden* 19, no. 34 (November 20, 1964): 8. The manuscript for the radio broadcast is also in the *DLA*.
27. Katharina Stengel, "Einleitung zur Neuausgabe," *Auschwitz: Zeugnisse und Berichte*, 6th edition, ed. H. G. Adler, Hermann Langbein, and Ella Lingens-Reiner (Frankfurt: CEP—Europäische Verlagsanstalt, 2014), iii.
28. For discussion of tensions between Jewish and non-Jewish victims, see Katharina Stengel, *Hermann Langbein: Ein Auschwitz-Überlebender in den erinnerungspolitischen Konflikten der Nachkriegszeit* (Frankfurt: Campus Verlag, 2012), 276–279.
29. *LHL*, June 15, 1959, quoted in Stengel, "Einleitung zur Neuausgabe," vii.
30. Letter on behalf of Association of Nazi Camp Survivors to Ernst Katzenstein of the Claims Conference, February 6, 1960, quoted in Stengel, *Hermann Langbein*, 260. The Association of Nazi Camp Survivors in London consisted of a small group of émigrés who met monthly, most often at Adler's apartment. Its mission was to heighten awareness of the financial plight of survivors, as well as to found a safe house for homeless survivors. That project never saw fruition, but Adler made sure the organization contributed to the broader discussion on reparations, memorials, and prosecutions. An article in the *Willisden Citizen* on May 25, 1962, *DLA*, covers the founding of the Association.
31. Stengel, *Hermann Langbein*, 309.
32. Ibid., 160.

33. *LHGA*, March 26, 1959, quoted in ibid., 370.
34. For the lead-up to the trial see Stengel, *Hermann Langbein*, 417–442.
35. Adler's pocket calendar records that he flew to Warsaw on January 21, 1960, and visited Auschwitz and stayed in Krakow on the 24th before returning to London on the 26th. The entry on the 24th notes the presence of Premier Cyriankiewicz.
36. "Polen/Inoffiziele Eindrücke," manuscript dated February 5, 1960, *DLA*.
37. " 'Es gäbe viel Merkwürdiges zu berichten': Interview with Hans Christoph Knebusch," in *WV*, 39.
38. Adler, *LFW*, October 7, 1962, quoted in Stengel, "Einleitung zur Neuausgabe," xxv.
39. Stengel, "Einleitung zur Neuausgabe," xix–xxii.
40. Ibid., xiv.
41. Ibid., xx–xxi.
42. Adler, Introduction to *Auschwitz: Zeugnisse und Berichte*, ed. H. G. Adler, Hermann Langbein, and Ella Lingens-Reiner (Frankfurt: Europäische Verlagsanstalt, 1962), 5. Also Stengel's introduction to the sixth edition, "Einleitung zur Neuausgabe," xxv.
43. Typescript of the broadcast, *DLA*. It was rebroadcast in its entirety by the WDR on January 27, 2015, the sixtieth anniversary of the liberation of Auschwitz. The complete program can be heard and the manuscript downloaded at http://www1.wdr.de/radio/wdr5/auschwitz142.html (accessed January 14, 2018). It is available on three CDs under the same title, H. G. Adler and Hermann Langbein, *Auschwitz: Topographie eines Vernichtungslagers, Überlebende Berichten* (produced by Der Audio Verlag, Cologne, 2015).
44. Pendas, *The Frankfurt Auschwitz Trial*, 252–258.
45. Ibid., 263.
46. Listener letters to Adler sent on by August Hoppe at the WDR, *DLA*.
47. Adler, letter to Heinz Flügel, September 14, 1958.
48. Mauro Nervi, "Marianne Steiner Dead," *The Kafka Project*, http://www.kafka.org/index.php?aid=272 (accessed December 1, 2017).
49. Richard Caddel and Peter Quartermain, "Introduction: A Fair Field Full of Folk," *Other: British and Irish Poetry since 1970* (Middletown, CT: Wesleyan UP, 1999), xxiv–xxv. Both Günther and Jeremy Adler read at the Poetry Society as part of Cobbing's Sound Poetry Festival held several times in the 1970s.
50. Jeremy Adler, "The One Who Got Away," *Times Literary Supplement* (October 4, 1996): 18.
51. *KV*, 10
52. Ibid., 12.
53. Ibid., 16–17.
54. Ibid., 24–25. For the Drtikol quote see Anna Fárová and Manfred Heiting, *František Drtikol: Art-Deco Photographer*, trans. Paul Kremel (Munich: Schirmer Books, 1993), 63.
55. Péter Nádas, *Düsteres Idyll: Trost der deutschen Romantik. Marbacher Magazin* 149 (Marbach: Deutsche Schillergeschaft, 2015), 5.
56. Ibid., 28.
57. Ibid., 46.
58. Ibid., 20–21.
59. *KV*, 19.
60. Adler, "Der Flohmarkt von Jaffa," *DLA*.
61. Max Weinrich, *LHGA*, January 16, 1967. The manuscript for the talk is in the *DLA*.
62. Adler, *LFW*, December 20, 1967.
63. Adler, letter to Hans Hennecke, November 23, 1953.
64. Adler's disdain for Gruppe 47 is evident in his archive on a copy of Joachim Kaiser's article in the *Frankfurter Rundschau* on the group's twentieth anniversary meeting. Adler supplies his own handwritten title: "Das schöne Nazideutsch der 'Gruppe 47' " ("The lovely Nazi German of 'Group 47' "). That the "irresistible and domineering" Grass was mockingly referred to as the prevailing "dictator," or that F.C. Delius is described as having read a text titled "Butzbach, Butzbach über alles" would have resonated with him as a decadent throwback to Nazi terminology and demagoguery.
65. Cited in Ruth Vogel-Klein, "The Reception of H. G. Adler's *Eine Reise [The Journey]* in the Federal Republic of Germany," from a paper delivered at "A Modernist in Exile: The

International Reception of H. G. Adler," a conference at the University of London, May 19–20, 2016.

66. Letter to Joachim Schondorff, December 12, 1952.
67. Letter to Sigfried Unseld, October 20, 1956. Also quoted in Ruth Vogel-Klein's 2016 conference paper in London. Elsewhere Vogel-Klein notes that it took Unseld another two years to return the manuscript. Since Adler had only a few typed copies available for submission, this meant further delays in placing the book. See her article, "'Keine Anklage'?: H. G. Adlers Roman 'Eine Reise' (1951/1962), Publikation und Rezeption," in *Die ersten Stimmen: Deutschsprachige Texte zur Shoah 1945–1963*, ed. Ruth Vogel-Klein (Würzburg: Könighausen & Neumann, 2010), 91.
68. *LFW*, September 18, 1960.
69. *LLW*, February 2, 1959.

Chapter 16

1. The "Grünwalder Kreis" was founded in Munich in 1956 by Hans Werner Richter as a "democratic fire brigade" committed to rooting out right-wing extremism and anti-Communism in postwar West Germany. Besides Munich, it had chapters in Berlin, Frankfurt, Hamburg, Stuttgart, and Cologne, and members included Alfred Andersch, Paul Schallück, Siegfried Lenz, Ernst Nolte, Martin Walser, and again Böll. See Johannes Heesch, "Der Grünwalder Kreis," in *Demokratische politische Identität: Deutschland, Polen und Frankreich im Vergleich*, ed. Gesine Schwan, Jerzy Holzer, Marie-Claire Lavabre, and Birgit Schwelling (Wiesbaden: Verlag für Sozialwissenschaften, 2006), 35–69.
2. *LFK*, March 5, 1958.
3. See Jeremy Adler, "Afterword," in *J*, 288. For discussion of resistance to Adler's novels by editors, critics, and the public, see Sara R. Horowitz, "Recovered Gems: Neglect and Recovery of Holocaust Fiction," in *H. G. Adler: Life, Literature, Legacy*, ed. Julia Creet, Sara R. Horowitz, and Amira Bojadzija-Dan (Evanston, IL: Northwestern UP, 2016). More on resistance to *The Journey* can be found in Ruth Vogel-Klein, "'Keine Anklage'?: H. G. Adlers Roman 'Eine Reise' (1951/1962), Publikation und Rezeption," in *Die ersten Stimmen: Deutschsprachige Texte zur Shoah 1945–1963*, ed. Ruth Vogel-Klein (Würzburg: Könighausen & Neumann, 2010).
4. Ernestine Schlant, *The Language of Silence: West German Literature and the Holocuast* (New York: Routledge, 1999), 239.
5. Jeremy Adler, "Afterword," *in J*, 288. There is no record of this remark by Suhrkamp or by Adler in a letter or interview, but Jeremy Adler heard the story often from his father, and both Hocheneder and Atze quote it. Ruth Vogel-Klein offers a convincing argument about Carl Zuckmayer's recollection of Suhrkamp's refusal to ever talk about his own arrest, ill treatment by the Nazis, and illness in Sachsenshausen. Suhrkamp said, "Accounts of such brutality . . . do nothing to deter anything, but instead awaken man's underlying urge for brutality . . . and thereby evil spirits are stirred up and invoked anew." See Vogel-Klein, "'Keine Anklage'?", 91.
6. Ruth Vogel-Klein, "The Reception of H. G. Adler's *Eine Reise [The Journey]* in the Federal Republic of Germany," from a paper delivered at "A Modernist in Exile: The International Reception of H. G. Adler," a conference at the University of London, May 19–20, 2016.
7. Adler, "Romanwünsche eines Verlegers," *DLA*. Suhrkamp's article appeared in the August 15, 1952, issue of the *Frankfurter Börsenblatt*.
8. *LLW*, February 2, 1959.
9. Hilsenrath (b. 1926) was interred in the Ukraine ghetto of Czernowitz, Becker (1937–1997) was imprisoned as a boy in Sachsenhausen, and Fred Wander (1917–2006) survived both Auschwitz and Buchenwald.
10. Astonishing as that sounds, one has to only consider the statistics. In 1933 there were roughly half a million Jews in Germany, half of whom emigrated before the war. Of the remaining quarter-million, most died in the Shoah. From the few thousand who managed to survive, how many novelists would likely emerge? Given the millions more Polish, Hungarian, Ukrainian, Czech, and Romanian victims, it is no surprise that we have dozens more books from each of those languages, especially if we include the most prevalent narrative form to emerge from the Holocaust, the memoir.

11. *LWB.*
12. *J*, 7. For a discussion of the difficulties of translating this passage, see Peter Filkins, "Stimme und Stimmung," *Monatshefte* 103, no. 2 (Summer 2011): 249–256.
13. For a discussion of Adler's careful use of singular and plural pronouns to mediate the relation between oppressor, victim, and reader, see Peter Filkins, "Memory's Witness—Witnessing Memory" in *Witnessing, Memory, Poetics: H. G. Adler & W.G. Sebald*, ed. Helen Finch and Lynn L. Wolff (Rochester, NY: Camden House, 2014), 42–46.
14. *J*, 65 and 67.
15. Ibid., 284.
16. Roland Wiegenstein, "Auf den ersten Blick," *Frankfurter Hefte* 17, no. 10 (October 1961): 717.
17. Transcript of Ruth Bowert's radio review, NDR, Hamburg, October 18, 1962, *DLA*.
18. Transcript of Franz Wurm's broadcast, "Was haben Sie neulich gelesen?" Schweizer Rundfunk, Zürich, December 2, 1962, *DLA*.
19. Wiegenstein, "Auf den ersten Blick."
20. Adler, *Unser Georg und andere Geschichten* (Vienna: Bergland Verlag, 1961), 5, 17.
21. Franz Wurm emphasizes the return to normality, while Bowert notes how for the citizens and leaders of "A Dark Day," "once the crisis has subsided, all one needs to do is to let things return to the way they used to be, if the situation allows."
22. *UG*, 49 and 50.
23. Christoph Schwerin, untitled review, *Streit-Zeit-Schrift* (March 1963), 60.
24. Adler, *LKE*, February 14, 1962.
25. Heinrich Böll, "Wir Deutsche: ein fahrendes Volk," in *Der Tagesspiegel* (September 22, 1963): 37. The German word for rubbish is "Abfall"; both Böll and Adler are well aware that it is also the biblical word used for man's downfall from paradise.
26. Heimito von Doderer, review of *Eine Reise*, in *Forum* (January 1964), reprinted in a prospectus by Bibliotheca Christiana, *DLA*.
27. Elias Canetti, "Jenseits von Groll und Bitterkeit," in BF, 73. For Canetti's influence on the book's reception, see Vogel-Klein, "'Keine Anklage'?," 97.
28. See Vogel-Klein, "'Keine Anklage'?," 94–105, for a discussion of the book's initial reviews, the Christian themes evinced in them, and the absence of reference to the Jews or the Holocaust.
29. Roland Wiegenstein, "Eine Reise," in *Neue Rundschau* 4, 1963, reprinted in a prospectus by Bibliotheca Christiana, *DLA*.
30. Zapf was the designer of, among other typefaces, Palatino (with which he set Adler's books) and Optima, two of the most predominantly used to this day, including on the Vietnam War Memorial and the 9/11 Memorial in New York. See Bruce Weber, "Hermann Zapf, 96, Dies; Designer Whose Letters Are Found Everywhere," *New York Times* (June 10, 2015): A24.
31. *LHGA*, November 23, 1962.
32. Knut Erichson, *LB*, November 23, 1962.
33. Bettina Adler, *LKE*, November 28, 1962.
34. For discussion of Adler's employment of parables and bagatelles, see Rüdiger Görner, "Zwischen Freiheit und Fremdbestimmung: Überlegungen zu H. G. Adlers ontologischer Panoramatik," *Monatshefte* 103, no. 2 (Summer 2011): 179.
35. *SU*, 10–11.
36. Ibid., 20–23.
37. Ibid., 145.
38. Ibid., 104.
39. Hilda Spiel, "Im Kern der Dinge: Zu zwei Prosabänden H. G. Adler," *Frankfurter Allgemeine Zeitung* (February 5, 1966): Feuillton. Brod's comments are extracted from a letter of his to Adler in "Kritiken und Stellungnahmen zu H. G. Adler und seinen Werken," which served as copy for promotional materials drawn together for Bibliotheca Christiana, *DLA*.
40. For background on Otto F. Walter see http://www.literapedia-bern.ch/Walter,_Otto_F (accessed November 30, 2017). On his departure from the firm see *Der Spiegel*, January 16, 1967, at http://www.spiegel.de/spiegel/print/d-45441082.html (accessed November 30, 2017).
41. *LKE*, March 13, 1967.
42. Knut Erichson, *LHGA*, June 15, 1967.

43. Adler, *LKE*, September 16, 1967.
44. Max Wehrli, "Laudatio," Lausanne, May 17, 1969, *DLA*.
45. Adler, "Einladung zu meinem *Panorama*: H. G. Adler über seinen neuen Roman," *Literarium* 16 (Olten/Freiburg im Breisgau: Walter Verlag, 1968), 3, *DLA*.
46. Elias Canetti, "Jenseits von Groll und Bitterkeit," in *BF*, 72–73.
47. Letter to Theodor Sapper, January 21, 1974, *DLA*.
48. *P*, 218–219.
49. Ibid., 218.
50. Thomas Krämer sees the absence of bells rung or struck in the novel's more pastoral settings as symbolic of "an organic organization of time, which is orientated toward the natural unfolding of the day and the vital needs of the community," versus the frantic pace of city life or the menacing control imposed on Josef in school or in the concentration camp. See his *Die Poetik des Gedenkens: Zu den autobiographischen Romanen H. G. Adler* (Würzburg: Könighausen & Neumann, 2012), 118–120.
51. Letter to Theodor Sapper, January 21, 1974, *DLA*.
52. Adler, "Arnold Schönberg: Eine Botschaft an die Nachwelt," *Literatur und Kritik* 103 (1976): 129.
53. Rüdiger Görner notes that "In the panoramic approach to the camp experience and its documentation, history and events are splayed out; all facets remain relevant to each other and the camp itself becomes, as Adler says, entwined with the history of a realm, and simultaneously through it with world history as well." See Görner, "Zwischen Freiheit und Fremdbestimmung," 179.
54. "Sonderinterview von Alfred Joachim Fischer mit H. G. Adler," in *ZE*, 192.
55. "'Es gäbe viel Merkwürdiges zu berichten': Interview with Hans Christoph Knebusch," in *WV*, 45.
56. Thomas Krämer sees Adler's novels as an effort to step beyond the early efforts of witness literature and argues that they should be read as Adler's "expression of a conscious effort to forge an identity," although he observes of *Panorama* that "the rhythmical, lyrical language which distinguishes the novel as a whole" coheres with "Adler's apt acknowledgment that his novels should be understood as poetry." See his *Die poetik des gedenkens*, 90 and 158.
57. *P*, 353.
58. Hans Reichmann, *LHGA*, August 18, 1961.
59. Letter to Hans Reichmann, September 10, 1961.
60. *LFW*, December 28, 1957.
61. *LLW*, February 2, 1959.
62. Heinrich Böll, *Frankfurter Vorlesungen* (Munich: DTV, 1968), 73.
63. H. G. Adler, "Arnold Schönberg: Eine Botschaft an die Nachwelt," *Literatur und Kritik* 103 (1976): 139.
64. http://www.classiccat.net/schonberg_a/biography.php (accessed November 30, 2017).
65. Adler, "Nach der Befreiung," in *NB*, 46–47.
66. Jeremy Adler, "Good against Evil?: H. G. Adler, T.W. Adorno and the Representation of the Holocaust," in *Studies in Social and Political Thought 2: Social Theory After the Holocaust*, ed. Robert Fine and Charles Turner (Liverpool: Liverpool UP, 2000), 73.
67. H. G. Adler, "Literarische Selbsteinsicht," an unpublished essay submitted but not used as publicity material by Walter Verlag for *Panorama, DLA*.
68. Adler, *LLW*, February 2, 1959.
69. *LFK*, October 22, 1964.
70. *LFW*, April 14, 1976.
71. *LFK*, October 22, 1964.
72. *LFW*, October 29, 1965.
73. The figures for the first two books appear in *LFW*, March 23, 1965, while the figure for the third book mentioned appears in *LFK*, June 25, 1961.
74. *LFW*, April 18, 1968.
75. Unsigned review, "Panorama," *Neue Zürcher Zeitung* (November 21, 1969): 85, and Hans Kricheldorff, "H. G. Adler: Panorama," *Neue Deutsche Hefte* 1 (1969): n.p.
76. Waltraut Schmitz-Bunse, "Panorama," *Hochland* 62 (1970): 181.

77. Otto F. Beer, "Alle meine Lager," *Der Tagesspiegel* 25, no. 7281 (August 24, 1969): 41, and *Verrückte Zeit, verrückte Geschichten, Der Tagesspiegel* 26, no. 7485 (April 26, 1970): 59, respectively.
78. Peter Bautz, "Großer Lebensbilderbogen: H. G. Adler's Roman *Panorama*," *Stuttgarter Zeitung* 25, no. 157 (July 12, 1969): 52.

Chapter 17

1. *LHS*, February 12, 1974.
2. Since his death in 1988, an additional eight volumes have appeared: two novels, *Hausordnung* (*House Rules*) and *Die unsichtbare Wand* (*The Wall*); his collected poems; two volumes of essays; a volume of stories; his *Brief an Chaim Rabin*; and his chapbook-length essay on Prague writers, all of which were ready for publication in his lifetime had he found a publisher willing to publish them.
3. Mathias Schreiber, " 'Zwanzig Jahre keinen Verlag gefunden': Interview with H. G. Adler," *Kölner Stadt-Anzeiger* (May 28, 1969): Feuilliton, 8.
4. Jürgen Serke, "Weniger geborgen als für immer versteckt: Der Tote H. G. Adler und die lebendige Katastrophe des Exils," in *Jüdische Almanac 1994 des Leo Baeck Instituts* (Frankfurt: Jüdischer Verlag im Suhrkamp Verlag, 1993), 93.
5. First drafted in 1963, "Gestern und Heute" was published in *Literatur und Kritik* in May 1974: 196–199, and published again by the same journal, with "Neue Elemente" (first drafted in 1967) in September/October 1990: 359–364. They have also recently been collected in H. G. Adler, *Schuldig und Unschuldig: Gesammelte Erzählungen, Band 4*, ed. Franz Hocheneder (Vienna: Löcker Verlag, 2016).
6. Quoted in *S*, 332. The poem, however, does not appear in *AW*.
7. *S*, 339.
8. Adler, letter to Alfred O. Lanz, January 14, 1976.
9. *AW*, 996, 1014, 1018.
10. Armin Halstenberg, " 'Ich bin ein denkender Dichter,' " interview with H. G. Adler, *Kölner Stadt-Anzeiger: Bunte Blätter* (March 16–17, 1974): 2.
11. "Sonderinterview von Alfred Joachim Fischer mit H. G. Adler" in *ZE*, 196.
12. J.P. Stern, "Zum 75. Geburtstag H. G. Adlers," in *ZE*, 148.
13. "Sonderinterview von Alfred Joachim Fischer mit H. G. Adler," in *ZE*, 197.
14. *Deutschland-Berichte* 10, no. 4 (April, 4, 1974): 20.
15. Eberhard Bethge, "Dichter und Deuter in unserer Zeit: Laudatio auf H. G. Adler zur Verleihung der Buber-Rosenzweig-Medaile am 3. März 74 in Berlin," in *ZE*, 185.
16. See Maurice S. Friedman, *Martin Buber's Life and Work* (Detroit: Wayne State UP, 1988), 171.
17. H. G. Adler, "Dankansprache für die Verleihung der Buber-Rosenzweig-Medaile," *DLA*.
18. Ibid.
19. Details of such funds, *DLA*.
20. Adler pocket calendar, November 1979 and May 1981, *DLA*.
21. The transcription of their conversation is in the *DLA*.
22. *AW*, 152.
23. *S*, 327, 338, 342. The quote from Aichinger is from a poem she wrote for Adler's seventy-fifth birthday. It appears in full in *Europäische Ideen* 60, ed. Andreas W. Mytze (1985): 1.
24. *S*, 332.
25. This quote and other details of Adler's final days come from an email from Jeremy Adler to the author, December 6, 2017. Adler's archive contains the notes dictated to Jeremy and other medical accounts of his death.
26. *AW*, 1006.
27. I am indebted to Jeremy Adler, Manfred Sundermann, and Derek Bolton for details of Adler's death, funeral, and the reception, as well as Bettina's passing.

28. John J. White, "H. G. Adler," manuscript for a talk delivered by White at the invitation of W. G. Sebald at the University of East Anglia in May 1992, *DLA*. Sebald refers at length to Adler's Theresienstadt book for the penultimate scene of his 2001 novel, *Austerlitz*.
29. Alfred Kelletat, "Nachruf auf H. G. Adler (1910–1988)," *DLA*.
30. "Sonderinterview von Alfred Joachim Fischer mit H. G. Adler," in *ZE*, 201.
31. *The Living Talmud*, ed. and trans. Judah Goldin (Chicago: U of Chicago P, 1957), 157.

SELECTED BIBLIOGRAPHY

Chronology of Major Works by H. G. Adler

Theresienstadt: Das Antlitz einer Zwangsgemeinschaft. Tübingen: Mohr, 1955. Second edition was published in 1960. The second edition of 1960 was reprinted, with an afterword by Jeremy Adler, in 2015 by Wallstein in Göttingen. Translated from English by Belinda Cooper. Edited by Amy Loewenhaar-Blauweiss, and Jeremy Adler. *Theresienstadt, 1941–1945: The Face of a Coerced Community.* New York: Cambridge University Press, 2017.

Der Kampf gegen die "Endlösung der Judenfrage." Bonn: Bundeszentrale für Heimatdienst, 1958.

Die verheimlichte Wahrheit: Theresienstädter Dokumente. Tübingen: Mohr, 1958.

Die Juden in Deutschland: Von der Aufklärung bis zum Nationalsozialismus. Munich: Kösel, 1960.

Unser Georg und andere Geschichten. Wien: Bergland Verlag, 1961.

Eine Reise: Erzählung. Bonn: Bibliotheca Christina, 1962. English translation: Peter Filkins. *The Journey.* New York: Random House, 2008.

Auschwitz: Zeugnisse und Berichte. Edited by H. G. Adler, Hermann Langbein, and Ella Lingens-Reiner. Frankfurt am Main: Europäische Verlagsanstalt, 1962.

Der Fürst des Segens: Parabeln, Betrachtungen, Gleichnisse. Bonn: Bibliotheca Christiana, 1964.

Die Erfahrung der Ohnmacht: Beiträge zur Soziologie unserer Zeit. Frankfurt am Main: Europäische Verlagsanstalt, 1964.

Sodoms Untergang: Bagatellen. Bonn: Bibliotheca Christiana, 1965.

Panorama: Roman in zehn Bildern. Olten and Freiburg: Walter, 1968. English translation: Peter Filkins. *Panorama.* New York: Random House, 2011.

Ereignisse: Kleine Erzählungen und Novellen. Olten und Freiburg im Breisgau: Walter, 1969.

Kontraste und Variationen. Würzburg: Echter, 1969.

Der verwaltete Mensch: Studien zur Deportation der Juden aus Deutschland. Tübingen: Mohr, 1974.

Die Freiheit des Menschen Aufsätze zur Soziologie und Geschichte. Tübingen: J.C.B. Mohr (P. Siebeck), 1976.

Vorschule für eine Experimentaltheologie: Betrachtungen über Wirklichkeit und Sein. Stuttgart: Steiner, 1987.

Hausordnung: Wortlaut und Auslegung. Wien: Wiener Journal, 1988.

Die unsichtbare Wand. Vienna and Darmstadt: Zsolnay, 1989. English translation: Peter Filkins. *The Wall.* New York: Random House, 2014.

Der Wahrheit verpflichtet: Interviews, Gedichte, Essays. Edited by Jeremy Adler. Gerlingen: Bleicher, 1998.

Über Franz Baermann Steiner: Brief an Chaim Rabin. Edited by Jeremy Adler and Carol Tully. Göttingen: Wallstein, 2006.

Andere Wege: Gesammelte Gedichte. Edited by Franz Hocheneder, Katrin Kohl, and Jeremy Adler. Klagenfurt: Drava, 2010.

Die Dichtung der Prager Schule: zum 100. Geburtstag von H. G. Adler. Wuppertal: Arco, 2010.

Nach der Befreiung: Ausgewählte Essays zur Geschichte und Soziologie. Edited by Peter Filkins with Jeremy Adler. Paderborn: Konstanz University Press, 2013.

Orthodoxie des Herzens: Ausgewählte Essays zur Literaur, Judentum und Politik. Edited by Peter Filkins with Jeremy Adler. Paderborn: Konstanz University Press, 2014.

Schuldig und Unschuldig: Gesammelte Erzählungen, Band 4. Wien: Löcker, 2016.

Critical Resources on H. G. Adler's Work

Adler, Jeremy. "Afterword." In *The Journey*, 285–292. New York: Random House, 2008.

———. "Afterword." In *Theresienstadt 1941–1945: The Face of a Coerced Community*, 803–828. New York: Cambridge University Press, 2017.

———. *Das bittere Brot: H. G. Adler, Elias Canetti und Franz Baermann Steiner im Londoner Exil*. Göttingen: Wallstein, 2015.

———. "Der Wahrheit Verpflichtet." In *Der Wahrheit Verpflichtet*, 205–304. Gerlingen: Bleicher, 1998.

———. " 'Die Welt als Panorama.' Afterword to *Panorama*, by H. G. Adler." In *Panorama* by H. G. Adler, 609–626. Vienna: Zsolnay, 2010.

———. "Erich Fried, F. B. Steiner and an Unknown Group of Exile Poets in London." In *Literatur und Kultur des Exils in Großbritannien*, edited by Siglinde Bolbecher, 163–192. Zwischenwelt, IV. Vienna: Theoder Kramer Gesellschaft und Verlag für Gesellschaftskritik, 1995.

———. "February 8, 1942. H. G. Adler is Deported to Theresienstadt." In *Yale Companion to Jewish Writing and Thought in German Culture, 1096–1996*, edited by Sander L. Gilman and Jack Zipes, 599–605. New Haven: Yale University Press, 1997.

———. " 'Good Against Evil? H. G. Adler, T.W. Adorno and the Representation of the Holocaust." In *Social Theory After the Holocaust*, 71–100, edited by Robert Fine and James Turner. Liverpool: Liverpool University Press, 2000.

———. "H. G. Adler: A Prague Writer in London." In *Keine Klage über England? Deutsche und Österreichische Exilerfahrungen in Großbritannien 1933–1945*, 13–31, edited by Charmian Brinson. Munich: Iudicium, 1998.

———. " 'Mensch Oder Masse?': H. G. Adler, Elias Canetti and the Crowd." *Literatur und Anthropologie: H. G. Adler, Elias Canetti und Franz Baermann Steiner in London*, 176–196. Göttingen: Wallstein, 2104.

———. "The One Who Got Away: H. G. Adler and Theodor Adorno: Two Approaches to Culture after Auschwitz." *Times Literary Supplement*, October 4, 1996, 18–19.

Arnold, Hans Ludwig, ed. *H. G. Adler—Text + Kritik 163*. Munich: Boorberg, 2004.

Atze, Marcel, *"Ortlose Botschaft": der Freundeskreis H. G. Adler, Elias Canetti und Franz Baermann Steiner im englischen Exil. Marbacher Magazin 84*. Marbach am Neckar: Deutsche Schillergesellschaft, 1998.

———. " 'Was hast du ihm gesagt, dem Mörder?': H. G. Adler." *Auschwitz Prozeß 4Ks 2/63*, 648–655, edited by Irmtaud Wojak. Frankfurt: Fritz Bauer Institut, 2004.

Berghahn, Klaus L., and Rüdiger Görner, eds. *Monatshefte. Special Issue: H. G. Adler—Dichter Gelehrter Zeuge* 103/2 (Summer 2011).

Böll, Heinrich. *Frankfurter Vorlesungen*. München: Deutscher Taschenbuch-Verlag, 1968.

Creet, Julia, Sara R. Horowitz, and Amira Bojadzija-Dan, eds. *H. G. Adler: Life, Literature, Legacy*. Evanston, IL: Northwestern University Press, 2016.

Dane, Gesa, and Jeremy Adler, eds. *Literatur und Anthropologie H. G. Adler, Elias Canetti und Franz Baermann Steiner in London*. Göttingen: Wallstein, 2014.

Demetz, Peter. "Afterword." In *Panorama*, 441–450. New York: Random House, 2011.

———. "H. G. Adler," in *After the Fires: Recent Writing in the Germanies, Austria, and Switzerland*. San Diego: Harcourt Brace Jovanovich, 1992.

Eckert, Willehad P., and Wilhelm Unger, eds. *Buch der Freunde: H. G. Adler: Stimmen über den Dichter und Gelehrten mit unveröffentlichter Lyrik : zum 65. Geburtstag am 2. Juli 1975*. Köln: Wienand, 1975.

Finch, Helen, and Lynn L Wolff, eds. *Witnessing, Memory, Poetics: H. G. Adler and W.G. Sebald*. Rochester, NY: Camden House, 2014.

Görner, Rüdiger. "Ins Innere des Wortes." *Literatur und Kritik* 237/238 (October 1989): 298–304.

———. "Überleben—Überwinden?: Eine Betrachtung zum Werk H. G. Adlers." *Salzburger Jahrbuch Für Philosophie* 35 (1990): 75–88.

Hocheneder, Franz. "H. G. Adler—Werk und Nachlass: Eine bio-bibliographische Studie." Diss., University of Vienna, 1997.

———. *H. G. Adler (1910–1988): Privatgelehrter und freier Schriftsteller: Eine Monographie*. Wien: Böhlau, 2009.

———. "Special Bibliography: The Works of H. G. Adler (1910–1988)." *Comparative Criticism* 21 (1999): 293–310.

Hubmann, Heinrich, and Alfred O Lanz, eds. *Zu Hause im Exil: Zu Werk und Person H. G. Adlers*. Wiesbaden: Steiner, 1987.

Kohl, Katrin. "Die Lyrik von H. G. Adler." In *Andere Wege: Gesammelte Gedichte*, 1033–1054. Klagenfurt: Drava, 2010.

Kolářová, Eva. "H. G. Adler." In *Das Theresienstadt-Bild in Werken der Häftlinge 1941–1945*. Ústí nad Labem: Albis International, 1998.

Kramer, Sven. "Belated Exile in H. G. Adler's Novel *Die Unsichtbare Wand*." In *Exile and Otherness: New Approaches to the Experience of the Nazi Refugees*, 227–248, edited by Alexander Stephan. Bern: Lang, 2005

———. "Die Politik der Erinnerung in H. G. Adlers Roman 'Die Unsichtbare Wand.'" *Sprache im technischen Zeitalter* 198 (2011): 220–227.

Krämer, Thomas. *Die Poetik des Gedenkens: Zu den autobiographischen Romanen H. G. Adlers*. Würzburg: Könighausen & Neumann, 2012.

Lanz, Alfred Otto. *"Panorama" von H. G. Adler, ein 'moderner Roman': "Panorama" als Minusverfahren des Entwicklungsromans und Negation der Möglichkeit rationaler Welterkenntnis*. Bern: Lang, 1984.

Nádas, Péter, ed. *Düsteres Idyll: Trost der deutschen Romantik. Marbacher Magazin 149*. Marbach: Deutsche Schillergesellschaft, 2015.

Serke, Jürgen. "Der versteinerte Jüngling, der ein weiser Mann wurde." *Böhmische Dörfer: Wanderungen durch eine verlassene literarische Landschaft*, 327–343. Vienna: Zsolnay, 1987.

———. "'Die Toten, die uns hinterlassen hatten . . .': H. G. Adler und das Gedenken als die Pflicht zum Beginn." Afterword to *Die unsichtbare Wand* by H. G. Adler, 781–794. Vienna: Zsolnay, 1989.

———. "Weniger geborgen als für immer versteckt: Der Tote H. G. Adler und die lebendige Katastrophe des Exils." *Jüdische Almanach 1994 des Leo Baecks Institut*, 82–102. Frankfurt: Jüdischer Verlag im Suhrkamp Verlag, 1993.

Speirs, Ronald, and John J. White. "Hermann Broch and H. G. Adler: The Correspondence of Two Writers in Exile." *Comparative Criticism* 21 (1999): 131–199.

Staengle, Peter. "H. G. Adler." *Kritisches Lexikon Zur Deutschsprachigen Gegenwartsliteratur*. 44. Nachlieferung, 1–15. Munich: Text + Kritik, April 1, 1993.

Tully, Carol, ed. *Zeugen der Vergangenheit: H. G. Adler, Franz Baermann Steiner: Briefwechsel 1936–1952*. München: Iudicium, 2011.

Vogel-Klein, Ruth, ed. *Die ersten Stimmen: Deutschsprachige Texte zur Shoah 1945–1963*. Würzburg: Königshausen & Neumann, 2010.

———. "Eine fremde Welt: H. G. Adler, *Eine Reise*." *Germanica* (2008): 13–28.

———. "H. G. Adler: Zeugenschaft als Engagement." *Monatshefte* 103, no. 2 (2011): 185–212.

Voigts, Manfred. "H. G. Adler und Erich Unger: Versuch Eines Zugangs zur 'Vorschule Für Eine Experimentaltheologie.'" *Brücken: Germanistisches Jahrbuch Tschechien-Slowakei* 19, no. 1 (2011): 253–271.

Zimmermann, Hans Dieter. "Vom Internat zum Lager: H. G. Adlers 'Panorama' Des 20. Jahhunderts." *Sprache im technischen Zeitalter* 49, no. 198 (2011): 213–219.

General Sources

Adler, Jeremy, Richard Fardon, and Carol Tully, eds. *From Prague Poet to Oxford Anthropologist: Franz Baermann Steiner Celebrated.* München: Iudicium, 2003.

Anděl, Jaroslav, et al. *Czech Modernism: 1900–1945.* Houston: Museum of Fine Arts, 1990.

Arendt, Hannah. *Eichmann in Jerusalem: A Report on the Banality of Evil.* New York: Penguin, 1994.

Baeck, Leo. *Judaism and Christianity.* Translated by Walter Kaufmann. New York: Atheneum, 1981.

Baker, Leonard. *Days of Sorrow and Pain: Leo Baeck and the Berlin Jews.* New York: Oxford University Press, 1980.

Benz, Wolfgang. *Der Ort des Terrors: Geschichte der nationalsozialistischen Konzentrationslager 3.* München: Beck, 2006.

———. *Theresienstadt: Eine Geschichte von Täuschung und Vernichtung.* München: Beck, 2013.

Berg, Nicholas. *The Holocaust and the West German Historians: Historical Interpretation and Autobiographical Memory.* Madison: University of Wisconsin Press, 2015.

Berghahn, Marion. *Continental Britons: German-Jewish Refugees from Nazi Germany.* New York: Berghahn Books, 2007.

———. "Women Emigrés in England." In *Between Sorrow and Strength: Women Refugees of the Nazi Period,* edited by Sibylle Quack, 69–80. New York: Cambridge University Press, 1995.

Birgus, Vladimír, Ivana Kočí, Jiří Bareš, and František Ferdinand Drtikol. *The Photographer František Drtikol.* Prague: Kant, 2000.

Brinson, Charmian, and Richard Dove, eds. *"Stimme der Wahrheit": German-language Broadcasting by the BBC.* Amsterdam: Rodopi, 2003.

Brinson, Charmian, and Marian Malet, eds. *Exile in and from Czechoslovakia During the 1930s and 1940s.* Amsterdam: Rodopi, 2009.

Browning, Christopher R. *The Origins of the Final Solution: The Evolution of Nazi Jewish Policy, September 1939–March 1942.* Lincoln: University of Nebraska Press, 2007.

Bryant, Chad. *Prague in Black: Nazi Rule and Czech Nationalism.* Cambridge, MA: Harvard University Press, 2009.

Buber, Martin. *On Judaism.* Translated by Nahum Glatzer. New York: Schocken Books, 1995.

Buggeln, Marc. *Slave Labor in Nazi Concentration Camps.* Oxford: Oxford University Press, 2014.

Claverie, Jana , and Alena Kubova. *Prague.* Paris: Vilo, 2002.

Czech, Danuta. *Auschwitz Chronicle, 1939–1945.* New York: H. Holt, 1990.

Dawidowicz, Lucy S. *The Holocaust and the Historians.* Cambridge, MA: Harvard University Press, 1981.

Demetz, Peter. *Prague in Black and Gold: Scenes from the Life of a European City.* New York: Hill and Wang, 1997.

———. *Prague in Danger: The Years of German Occupation, 1939–45: Memories and History, Terror and Resistance, Theater and Jazz, Film and Poetry, Politics and War.* New York: Farrar, Straus and Giroux, 2008.

Ehrman, Esther J. "Erich Unger's 'The Natural Order of Miracles': I. The Pentateuch and the Vitalistic Myth." *Journal of Jewish Thought and Philosophy* 11, no. 2 (2002): 135–152.

Ehrmann, František, and Rada židovských náboženských obcí (Czechoslovakia). *Terezín.* Prague: Council of Jewish Communities in the Czech Lands, 1965.

Eisert, Christian, Ulrich Prinz, and Sommerakademie J. S. Bach, eds. *Viktor Ullmann: Beiträge, Programme, Dokumente, Materialien: Veranstaltungen in der Sommerakademie Johann Sebastian Bach Stuttgart 1998.* Stuttgart: Internationale Bachakademie; Bärenreiter, 1998.

Fárová, Anna, and Manfred Heiting. *František Drtikol: Art-Deco Photographer.* Translated by Paul Kremel. München: Schirmer Art Books, 1993.

Fauser, Ellen, ed. *Die Kraft im Unglück: Erinnerungen an Langenstein-Zwieberge—Außenlager des KZ Buchenwald.* Langenstein: Stiftung Gedenkstätten Sachsen Anhalt, n.d.

Fierz, Olga. *Kinderschicksale in den Wirren der Nachkriegszeit: Eine Rettungsaktion für jüdische und deutsche Kinder 1945–1947 in der Tschechoslowakei*. Fürth im Wald: Vitales, 2000.

Fischer, Grete. *Dienstboten, Brecht und andere Zeitgenossen in Prag, Berlin, London*. Olten u. Freiburg: Walter, 1966.

Friedlander, Albert H. *Leo Baeck, Teacher of Theresienstadt*. Woodstock, NY: Overlook Press, 1991.

Furness, Raymond. *Zarathustra's Children: A Study of a Lost Generation of German Writers*. Rochester, NY: Camden House, 2000.

Gerwarth, Robert. *Hitler's Hangman: The Life and Death of Reinhard Heydrich*. New Haven: Yale University Press, 2011.

Grenville, Anthony. *Jewish Refugees from Germany and Austria in Britain, 1933–1970: Their Image in AJR Information*. London: Mitchell, 2010.

———. "Listening to Refugee Voices: The Association of Jewish Refugees Information and Research on the Refugees from Hitler to Britain." In *Refugees from the Third Reich to Britain*, edited by Anthony Grenville, 199–211. The Yearbook of the Research Centre for German and Austrian Exile Studies 4. Amsterdam: Rodopi, 2002.

Grosse, Wolfgang. *Aus dem Umkreis der Kamine: Überlebende eines KZ-Aussenkommandos berichten*. Duderstadt: Mecke, 2009.

Gutman, Israel, and Michael Berenbaum, eds. *Anatomy of the Auschwitz Death Camp*. Bloomington: Indiana University Press, 1994.

Henry, Marilyn. *Confronting the Perpetrators: A History of the Claims Conference*. London: Vallentine Mitchell, 2007.

Herbst, Ludolf, and Constantin Goschler. *Wiedergutmachung in der Bundesrepublik Deutschland*. München: Oldenbourg, 1989.

Iggers, Wilma. *The Jews of Bohemia and Moravia: A Historical Reader*. Detroit: Wayne State University Press, 1992.

———. *Women of Prague: Ethnic Diversity and Social Change from the Eighteenth Century to the Present*. New York: Berghahn Books, 1995.

Kárný, Miroslav. *Theresienstadt in der "Endlösung der Judenfrage."* Prague: Panorama, 1992.

Kieval, Hillel J. *The Making of Czech Jewry: National Conflict and Jewish Society in Bohemia 1870–1918*. New York: Oxford University Press, 1988.

King, Jeremy. *Budweisers into Czechs and Germans: A Local History of Bohemian Politics, 1848–1948*. Princeton: Princeton University Press, 2002.

Klein, Hans-Günter, ed. *Viktor Ullmann: Die Referate des Symposiums anlässlich 50. Todestags 14–16 Oktober 1994 in Dornbach und ergänzende Studien*. Hamburg: Bockel, 1996.

Kogon, Eugen. *The Theory and Practice of Hell: The German Concentration Camps and the System Behind Them*. New York: Octagon Books, 1976.

Kohn, Pavel. *Mein Leben gehört nicht mir: Über Persönlichkeit und Werk des Humanisten Přemysl Pitter*. Furth im Wald: Vitalis, 2000.

———. *Schlösser der Hoffnung: Die geretteten Kinder des Přemsyl Pitter erinnern sich*. München: Langen Müller, 2001.

Kohut, Thomas A. *A German Generation: An Experiential History of the Twentieth Century*. New Haven: Yale University Press, 2013.

Krausnick, Helmut, et al. *Anatomy of the SS State*. Translated by Richard Barry, Marian Jackson, and Dorothy Long. New York: Walker, 1968.

Kuperman, Victor, Sergei Makarov, and Elena Makarova. *University over the Abyss: The Story Behind 489 Lecturers and 2309 Lectures in KZ Theresienstadt 1942–1944*. Jerusalem: Verba, 2000.

Langbein, Hermann. *People in Auschwitz*. Chapel Hill: University of North Carolina Press, 2004.

Laqueur, Walter, and Mazal Holocaust Collection. *Young Germany: A History of the German Youth Movement*. New Brunswick, NJ: Transaction Books, 1984.

Lederer, Zdenek. *Ghetto Theresienstadt*. New York: Fertig, 1983.

Levi, Primo. *If This Is a Man*. New York: Orion Press, 1959.

Levi, Primo, and Raymond Rosenthal. *The Drowned and the Saved*. New York: Summit Books, 1988.

Lipstadt, Deborah E. *The Eichmann Trial*. New York: Nextbook/Schocken, 2011.

Malet, Marian, and Anthony Grenville, eds. *Changing Countries: The Experience and Achievement of German-Speaking Exiles from Hitler in Britain, from 1933 to Today*. London: Libris, 2002.

Mamatey, V.S., and Radomír Luža, eds. *A History of the Czechoslovak Republic, 1918–1948*. Princeton: Princeton University Press, 1973.

Manes, Philipp. *As If It Were Life: A WWII Diary from the Theresienstadt Ghetto*. Translated by Ben Barkow, Klaus Leist, and Janet Foster. New York: Palgrave Macmillan, 2009.

Marchal, Peter. *Kultur- und Programmgeschichte des öffentlich-rechtlichen Hörfunks in der Bundesrepublik Deutschland: Ein Handbuch. 1*. München: Kopaed, 2004.

Mastny, Vojtech. *The Czechs Under Nazi Rule: The Failure of National Resistance, 1939–1942*. New York: Columbia University Press, 1971.

Mendelsohn, Ezra. *The Jews of East Central Europe Between the World Wars*. Bloomington: Indiana University Press, 1983.

Montague, Patrick. *Chelmno and the Holocaust A History of Hitler's First Death Camp*. Chapel Hill: University of North Carolina Press, 2011.

Moucha, Josef, Derek B. Paton, and Marzia Paton. *František Drtikol*. Prague: Torst, 2007.

Ort, Thomas. *Art and Life in Modernist Prague: Karel Čapek and His Generation, 1911–1938*. New York: Palgrave Macmillian, 2016.

Pendas, David O. *The Frankfurt Auschwitz Trial, 1963–1965: Genocide, History, and the Limits of the Law*. New York: Cambridge University Press, 2006.

Potthast, Jan Björn. *Das jüdische Zentralmuseum der SS in Prag: Gegnerforschung und Völkermord im Nationalsozialismus*. Frankfurt: Campus, 2002.

Pross, Christian. *Paying for the Past: The Struggle over Reparations for Surviving Victims of the Nazi Terror*. Translated by Belinda Cooper. Baltimore: Johns Hopkins University Press, 1998.

Redlich, Egon. *The Terezín Diary of Gonda Redlich*. Translated by Laurence Kutler. Lexington: University Press of Kentucky, 1999.

Reulecke, Jürgen. *"Ich möchte einer werden so wie die . . .": Männerbünde im 20. Jahrhundert*. Frankfurt: Campus, 2001.

Ripellino, Angelo Maria. *Magic Prague*. Translated by Michael Henry Heim. Berkeley: University of California Press, 1994.

Roseman, Mark. *The Wannsee Conference and the Final Solution*. New York: Metropolitan, 2002.

Rothkirchen, Livia. *The Jews of Bohemia and Moravia Facing the Holocaust*. Lincoln: University of Nebraska Press and Jerusalem: Yad Vashem, 2005.

Rothschild, Joseph. *East Central Europe Between the Two World Wars*. Seattle: University of Washington Press, 1974.

Rousset, David. *The Other Kingdom*. New York: Fertig, 1982.

Safrian, Hans. *Die Eichmann-Männer*. Wien: Europaverlag, 1992.

Sayer, Derek. *Prague, Capital of the Twentieth Century: A Surrealist History*. Princeton: Princeton University Press, 2015.

———. *The Coasts of Bohemia: A Czech History*. Princeton: Princeton University Press, 1998.

Schlant, Ernestine. *The Language of Silence: West German Literature and the Holocaust*. New York: Routledge, 1999.

Shambolis, Barbara, ed. *Jugendbewegt geprägt: Essays zu autobiographischen Texten von Werner Heissenberg, Robert Jungk und vielen anderen*. Göttingen: V & R Unipress, 2013.

Smith, Gary. "'Die Zauberjuden': Walter Benjamin, Gershom Scholem, and Other German-Jewish Esoterics between the World Wars." *Journal of Jewish Thought and Philosophy* 4, no. 2 (1995): 227–243.

Spector, Scott. *Prague Territories: National Conflict and Cultural Innovation in Franz Kafka's Fin de Siècle*. Berkeley: University of California Press, 2002.

Stachura, Peter D. *The German Youth Movement, 1900–1945: An Interpretative and Documentary History*. New York: St. Martin's Press, 1981.

Starke, Käthe. *Der Führer schenkt den Juden eine Stadt: Bilder, Impressionen, Reportagen, Dokumente*. Hamburg: Christians, 1978.

Steiner, Franz Baermann. *Orientpolitik, Value, and Civilisation*, edited by Jeremy Adler and Richard Fardon. New York: Berghahn, 1999.

———. *Taboo, Truth, and Religion*, edited by Jeremy Adler and Richard Fardon. New York: Berghahn Books, 1999.

Stengel, Katharina. *Hermann Langbein: ein Auschwitz-Überlebender in den erinnerungspolitischen Konflikten der Nachkriegszeit.* Frankfurt: Campus, 2012.

Ullmann, Viktor, and Ingo Schultz. *Viktor Ullmann: 26 Kritiken über musikalische Veranstaltungen in Theresienstadt.* Hamburg: Bockel, 1993.

Unger, Erich. *The Imagination of Reason; Two Philosophical Essays.* London: Routledge & K. Paul, 1952.

Unsdorfer, Simcha Bunem. *The Yellow Star.* New York: Yoseloff, 1961.

Urzidil, Johannes. *Prager Triptychon.* München: A. Langen, G. Müller, 1960.

———. *The Living Contribution of Jewish Prague to Modern German Literature.* New York: Leo Baeck Institute, 1968.

Utitz, Emil. *Psychologie des Lebens im Konzentrationslager Theresienstadt.* Wien: A. Sexl, 1948.

Venezia, Shlomo, Béatrice Prasquier, Simone Veil, Marcello Pezzetti, Umberto Gentiloni, Jean Mouttapa, Andrew Brown, and US Holocaust Memorial Museum. *Inside the Gas Chambers: Eight Months in the Sonderkommando of Auschwitz.* Cambridge: Polity Press, 2015.

Veselská, Magda. "Early Documentation of the Shoah in the Czech Lands: The Documentation Project and the Prague Jewish Museum (1945–1947)." *Judaica Bohemiae* 1 (2017): 47–87.

———. " 'The Museum of the Extinct Race'—Fact vs. Legend: A Contribution to the Topic of the So-Called Jewish Councils in Central Europe." *Judaica Bohemiae* 2 (2016): 41–85.

Wachsmann, Nikolaus. *KL: A History of the Nazi Concentration Camps.* New York: Farrar, Straus and Giroux, 2015.

Wagenbach, Klaus. *Kafka's Prague, A Travel Reader.* Translated by Shaun Whiteside. Woodstock, NY: Overlook, 1996.

Wingfield, Nancy M. *Flag Wars and Stone Saints: How the Bohemian Lands Became Czech.* Cambridge, MA: Harvard University Press, 2007.

Zahra, Tara. *The Lost Children: Reconstructing Europe's Families after World War II.* Cambridge, MA: Harvard University Press, 2011.

INDEX

Page numbers in *italics* refer to images.